THE PRIMETIMER
GUIDE TO
STREAMING TV

The Primetimer Guide to Streaming TV

Aaron Barnhart, Editor

Managing Editors
Mark Blankenship
Jed Rosenzweig
Brianna E. Westervelt

Senior Contributors
Sarah D. Bunting
Andy Dehnart
Jon Hein
Joe Reid
Claire Spellberg Lustig
Norman Weiss

Foreword by Tim Brooks

Hollywood

Für Diane

The Primetimer Guide to Streaming TV

Copyright 2022 Primetimer Ventures LLC

First edition, 2022

Primetimer Ventures LLC
1812 W Burbank Blvd # 7225
Burbank, CA 91506-1315

www.primetimer.com

Distributed to the trade by Pathway Book Service

ISBN 978-1-946248-11-4 (paper)

Printed in the USA

2 4 6 8 10 9 7 5 3 1

Table of Contents

Foreword by Tim Brooks

Television programming has evolved greatly in its 70-plus years of wide availability in the United States, and so has the documentation of that programming. "What's on?" has been a question viewers have been asking from the start, even in the 1940s when they might have had only one or two channels available, and those were on only a few hours per day.

Now it seems like we have — what? — more TV programs than stars in the sky or grains of sand on the beach. Perhaps it is time for a curated guide, a compilation of what is best and where it can be found in this complicated era of streaming TV.

Oddly enough, our grandparents had the same problem, in a somewhat different way. For them television shows were an addition to the hundreds of network radio shows they were already familiar with; how could they find out what was on the new medium and where to find it?

To serve this need *TV Guide* was launched as a local magazine in New York in 1948. It merged with similar magazines in other markets to become national in 1953, and by the 1960s it was the most widely circulated publication in the country, with 19 million subscribers. It dealt only with current TV, which was appropriate for the time since so few shows were rerun (most early shows were broadcast live and not rerun at all; later filmed shows were rerun only selectively, usually by local stations late at night).

In the mid-1970s when Earle Marsh and I approached publishers about a compendium of all TV shows, both past and present, we were met with a wall of rejection. "No one cares about old TV," we were told, and for current ones just look at the listings. But viewers did care about "old TV," the shows they remembered, as well as current favorites. That became blindingly clear when NBC aired the first major "clip show," its fiftieth anniversary special in 1976 with hundreds of clips from older TV shows. It was an enormous ratings hit and CBS and ABC quickly followed with their own anniversary shows, plus assorted retrospective specials.

When our *Complete Directory to Prime Time Network TV Shows* finally came out in 1979 it was an immediate best seller. The *Complete Directory* went through nine updated editions from 1979 to 2007, documenting in a convenient format the flood of new and older shows that were now becoming available on cable TV as well as on videotape and later DVDs (remember them?). The latest edition, in 2007, was 1,832 pages long!

But what was a flood of programming has now become a tsunami, with the advent of streaming services like Netflix and Hulu (and many others) and their vast array of shows both new and old. It is time for someone to give us a guide to the best of this huge new wave of programming and Aaron Barnhart is the ideal person to do that. A friend of the *Complete Directory* for many years, he has been writing knowledgeably about television's evolution for three decades. With *The Primetimer Guide to Streaming TV* he provides a roadmap to this newest source of programming that is spreading rapidly across the country.

Welcome to the newest chapter in the evolution of television, with this handy guide to the best of what it offers.

Tim Brooks, a former television executive, is a noted historian of radio, television and the recording industry. He is the co-author (with Earle Marsh) of The Complete Directory to Prime Time Network and Cable TV Shows.

Editor's Note

I thank Tim Brooks for his kind words in the Foreword, but I must set the record straight: This isn't my book. At least, it's not *entirely* my book. *The Primetimer Guide to Streaming TV* would not have happened without the contributions of many others whose names are listed below and on the following pages.

In 2018, as I was returning to the world of professional TV watching, my friend Tim Goodman — then the chief television critic for *The Hollywood Reporter* — wrote a series of columns arguing for a different approach to our line of work. The endless stream of content was stressing out viewers, Tim observed, and in this environment critics should be acting more as *curators,* imposing order on chaos, hand-selecting things to watch based on what was worthwhile and appropriate for various tastes and time constraints. So let me begin with a tip of the hat to Tim for his advocacy of an idea that has informed my work at Primetimer and is at the heart of this ambitious guide you are reading now.

A number of friends read drafts of this book and gave valuable feedback: Sue Trowbridge, Carol Powers, Gavin Fritton, Erin Clermont, Susan Cox and Dave Hokansen have my grateful thanks. Howard Mortman, Katherine Pongracz, Michael Schneider and Jason Snell were generous with insights. My weekly radio interrogations from Chip Franklin kept me on my toes.

Support, both financial and emotional, is essential to any successful book project. I must thank two people above all for their support of *The Primetimer Guide to Streaming TV*. The first is my partner in this venture, Jed Rosenzweig, the publisher of Primetimer, who brought me out of retirement and made writing about television fun again. Had it not been for Jed's constant encouragement, I never would have attempted to surf this 100–foot wave.

Attempting a project of this magnitude is one thing, finishing it is another. And there is simply no way I would have been able to complete this project without Diane Eickhoff, my wife and companion in all things intellectual, emotional and spiritual. She helped me through my transition back to the world of criticism and she lived with this book for its entire gestation. Diane likes to say that she could wake me from a deep slumber and within moments get me talking about almost any subject (knowledgeably or not). Yet when it comes to describing my love for her and the debt that I owe her, words fail me. I have dedicated this book to Diane.

Aaron Barnhart
January 2022

Acknowledgments

Behind this book is a large database of television shows and movies that managing editors Mark Blankenship, Brianna Westervelt, Jed Rosenzweig and I built from scratch. The editing skills of these three were essential to getting this guide done, and the finished product is immeasurably better because of them.

I am indebted to these Primetimer editors and contributors whose analysis and reviews were the basis for many of the entries in Part II: Tara Ariano, Sarah D. Bunting, Andy Dehnart, Jon Hein, Joe Reid, Claire Spellberg Lustig, Mike Attebery, Alex Welch, Andy Hunsaker, Chris Billig, Chris Feil, Emma Fraser, Jade Budowski, Josh Zyber, Jessica Liese, Kelly Kessler, Kevin O'Keeffe, LaToya Ferguson, Lauren Garafano, Naomi Elias, Omar Gallaga, Stephen Hladik, Thomas J. West III and the incomparable Norman Weiss. In addition, Carol Powers and Una Morera made valuable contributions to this guide as it was being compiled.

The line between television critics and critically-minded viewers has been blurring since I began writing as a fan in the early 1990s. So it was important to me that *The Primetimer Guide* include the voices of viewers who appreciate good TV, recognize mediocre TV and love discussing the difference. Part II, therefore, also includes insights from the following contributors to our Primetimer Forums (forums.primetimer.com). Their comments appear in the text wherever you see the balloons (🗨).

Mariah Abell, Marie Acosta, Matt Adams, Alicia Arnold, Turner Arrington, Karin Aultman, Charlotte Bednar, Erik Bhatnagar, BKing, D. Buchanan, Christina Burns, Dr. Karlisa Callwood, Johnna Childs, Joanna Cornish, Elizabeth Crossno, Brett Davies, Jennifer Dohan, Susan Evans, Pat Freedman, Margo G., Michele Gallagher, Carol Gibbs, Laura Meredith Gibson, Diana Hancock, Jason Harbaugh, Bob Heer;

Marny Heit, Patricia Hurd, Dana Hurleigh, iRarelyWatchTV36, Tanya Izzo, Ed J., Scott Josephson, justmehere, Brenna Kingsbury, Jayne Kleissler, Miriam Kushel, Amy M, Cody M., Marylee, Jennifer Mathews, Cynthia McLendon, Angus McLeod, Julianne Messer, MissLucas, Judith Morse, Erin O'Hara-Meyers, Susan E. Myers, Shannon O'Donnell, Elena Omard, Melinda Ott, Maria Papadopoulos, Candace Allen Poe, Sara Power;

Marcie Q., Timothy Q., Corinne R, Barb Roman, Jodi Ross, Audra Rouse, Steven Samiljan, scrb, Donna Shrout, Jeremy Smith, Michelle Smith, Tara Sproles, Melinda Stevenson, Brendan Stewart, Alison Stuart,

Joy Thomas, Mike Tripicco, Tinita Wheaton, Whimsy, Nichole White, Debra Whitmore, Larry Williams, Lisa Winston Wilentz, D.C. Wilson, Jo Woerner, Ed Wohlford, Leslie Wooten and Cynthia Z.

Primetimer community manager Michelle "Silverstormm" St John and the moderators of the Primetimer Forums have kept track of a mind-boggling number of shows over the years, all while helping to keep the conversations enlightened and civil. My thanks to Michelle and our current moderators, listed here under the screen names by which they are known to the forums community:

AgentRXS, aquarian1, Athena, bettername2come, Black Knight, CheshireCat, CountryGirl, Cranberry, deaja, Door County Cherry, dubbel zout, EmilSkoda, Emma Snyder, festivus, halgia, helenamonster, jenrising, jewel21, JTMacc99, kariyaki, Khaleesi, Lady Calypso, nodorothyparker, OtterMommy, Pallas, paulvdb, peachmangosteen, PrincessPurrsALot, ProfCrash, raven, Sakura12, saoirse, Scarlett45, scarynikki12, secnarf, sempervivum, shantown, starri, statsgirl, Superclam, tessaray, TexasGal, The Crazed Spruce, theatremouse, thewhiteowl, txhorns79, WendyCR72 and Whimsy.

— AB

Part I

–

The Cord
Has Been Cut

A History of Streaming TV

Early days to YouTube (1990s-2006)

Using the Internet to transmit video to the public is as old an idea as the Internet itself. For most of that time, however, consumer bandwidth speeds were so slow that even video downloads were excruciating, to say nothing of on-demand streaming. Nonetheless, as the World Wide Web sputtered to life in the 1990s, fueled by anemic 56K modems, several well-funded ventures attempted to stream alternative TV channels on the web.

The best-known of these was Pseudo, fronted by a tech entrepreneur named Josh Harris who had all kinds of ideas, such as equipping his apartment with dozens of cameras and offering a 24/7 web stream of everything (yes, everything) that he and his girlfriend did there. The content of these early streaming channels was terrible, as was the viewing experience. After the dot-com stock bubble popped in 2000, interest in streaming video waned.

It revived in 2005, thanks to the wider availability of broadband and the arrival of YouTube, which quickly became the leading hub for user-generated video content. Television networks made some of their content available online, but users had to go to the individual networks' websites, and the experience was less than satisfactory. YouTube, though, was easy to use with a powerful search engine (Google acquired it in 2006), and soon millions of users had discovered that it was a great place to watch pirated versions of TV shows, both current and classic.

Hulu and Netflix (2007-2014)

The networks were eager to avoid repeating the missteps of the music industry during the heyday of Napster. Disney made shows like *Lost* and *Desperate Housewives* available on iTunes in 2005, but that was for downloading only. In 2007 a group of investors led by NBC launched Hulu, a centralized site for viewing network TV shows. Disney signed on as a partner in 2009 and eventually gained a majority stake in Hulu. CBS went its own way with CBS All Access, now Paramount+.

Meanwhile, Big Tech was also wading into the video stream. Executives at the DVD rental service Netflix developed an interface so that customers could watch TV shows and movies on demand instead of waiting for discs to arrive in the mail. Netflix's project had originally begun on the hardware side with a dedicated streaming player. When the company decided to focus on building an app, the executive in charge of the hardware effort left Netflix and started Roku. In 2009 Apple released an open video standard for its revolutionary iPhone, allowing at least the possibility of streaming TV shows on wired and wi-fi networks. In time cellular bandwidth caught up with home network speeds. The streaming revolution was ready to be televised.

By 2010 Netflix was streaming more video than it was shipping on DVD. Demand for the convenient new service grew rapidly, as Netflix went from 12 million subscribers in 2009 to 24 million in 2011 to 54 million in 2014. Hulu, its closest competitor, grew from 1 million to 6 million subscribers during this time.

Research uncovered a noticeable "Netflix effect" for series like *Breaking Bad*, which doubled its audience on the AMC cable channel after previous seasons began streaming. But this begged the question: Why have cable at all? Streaming offered a seemingly endless buffet of video. And if a network show was popular, wouldn't it wind up on streaming eventually? These were questions that viewers fed up with high cable and satellite bills increasingly asked. By 2014 nearly 10 million U.S. households had cut the cord, with subscribers to streaming channels being the group most likely to cancel their cable service.

Though Netflix kept pouring money into content acquisitions, its executives realized that the studios behind *Friends, The Office* and other hit shows would eventually claw those properties back and put them on their own competitive streaming platforms. Survival for Netflix, in the long term, meant developing a catalog of its own hit shows and movies.

Netflix did not approach this strategy timidly, outbidding prestige channels AMC and HBO for the right to produce a political thriller, *House of Cards*. It was the first of many prestige series to make their appearance as "Netflix Originals." A revival of *Arrested Development* followed, and in 2014 Netflix won its first Emmy for best comedy series with *Orange Is the New Black*. The streaming giant also signed Adam Sandler, Marvel Studios and LucasFilm to movie deals and produced broad-appeal sitcoms like *Fuller House, Grace and Frankie* and *The Ranch*.

Peak TV (2015-2019)

At the studios that produced TV shows, streaming dollars were an accelerant thrown on an already overheated system. By 2015 there were nearly 400 original scripted series on television, up from 211 scripted series in 2010. No one even tried to count the number of unscripted shows. One network executive borrowed a term from the oil industry and it quickly caught on in Hollywood: *Peak TV,* a term suggestive of over-production, a supply of television that could not possibly have enough demand to meet it.

But that prediction proved premature. Netflix grew its content budget by one-third every year starting in 2015, expanded to 190 countries and set its sights on becoming a producer of content without historical precedent. By 2018 the company was spending, and making, more money on television than any network — it out-grossed the entire domestic movie box office that year. Among the brand names signed to Netflix development deals were Spike Lee, Ryan Murphy, Shonda Rhimes, Barack and Michelle Obama, David Letterman, Kenya Barris and Chelsea Handler. The joke was that you weren't a Hollywood insider unless you had a deal with Netflix.

Meanwhile consumers were continuing to cord-cut, in addition to the growing number of millennials who were "cord-nevers." Amazon and Google brought out their own inexpensive streaming players to compete with Roku. HBO made its HBO GO streaming service available for the first time to non-cable subscribers. In 2017 Hulu and Google rolled out bundles of cable and broadcast channels delivered over the Internet. The humble TV antenna, once nearly extinct in urban America, began reappearing in millions of windows and rooftops.

In time the traditional networks began responding to Netflix like the existential threat that it was. Disney bought Fox, took majority control of Hulu and launched Disney+. WarnerMedia combined content from all of its cable channels and film studios to launch HBO Max. Viacom and CBS, which split up in 2006, got back together to launch Paramount+. Reality TV's big tent Discovery Networks launched Discovery+.

Big Tech was busy during this period as well. Amazon beefed up its spending on Prime Video and, more importantly, promoted it more aggressively to the millions of Amazon Prime members who weren't watching Prime Video even though it was free to them. Apple launched Apple TV+ in 2019 with a small library of prestige programs like *The Morning Show*. Netflix signed up its 200 millionth subscriber and became the biggest producer of TV content in dozens of countries.

Lockdown and critical mass (2020-2021)

Along with stationary bikes and home delivery, the business of Streaming TV flourished during the COVID-19 lockdown. In the second quarter of 2020 alone, Netflix added 26 million subscribers worldwide — and all of them, it seems, were at home watching *Tiger King*. Hulu soared from 28.5 million U.S. subscriptions to 36.6 million during the pandemic.

What to put before this captive audience proved a challenge as time passed and studio sets remained shuttered by the virus. Netflix had stockpiled months of content and could gleefully boast of having "new movies every week." Peacock loaded up on live soccer telecasts from England and scored the streaming rights to *Yellowstone*, cable's biggest show. Disney moved the theatrical releases for *Hamilton* and Pixar's *Soul* to Disney+. WarnerMedia announced that every theatrical release from its Warner Bros film division in 2020 would simultaneously drop on HBO Max.

Magnolia Network, a cable channel featuring HGTV superstars Chip and Joanna Gaines, was supposed to launch in summer 2020, but the pandemic took a sledgehammer to that plan. Instead, Magnolia content was launched on Discovery+, the new streaming platform from HGTV's owner. "The cart and the horse have definitely been reversed," Chip Gaines admitted.

Indeed, with the arrival of Disney+, HBO Max, Peacock, Paramount+ and Discovery+ it could fairly be said that streaming was the one carting cable around. Including Apple TV+, there were now nine well-financed general entertainment streaming channels and dozens more boutique streamers putting tens of thousands of original, network and legacy shows and films at users' fingertips.

With the profusion of streaming platforms, the demand for fresh content grew to unprecedented levels. According to FX Content Research, a total of 559 scripted shows were produced for domestic cable, broadcast and streaming in 2021, in addition to thousands of news, reality and nonfiction shows. After a decade of dizzying growth there was little indication that the market had reached Peak TV.

Such variety and volume was liberating and — like everything else in the pandemic year — exhausting as well. "I just finished Game of Thrones and now I'm left with nothing to watch. I have HBO Max, Hulu, Netflix, Amazon Prime," wrote one overwhelmed viewer on Facebook. Media outlets that recommended several "bingeable" shows every week were being implored by binged-out readers to suggest shows that could be watched in an hour or less.

In some ways old television habits hadn't changed. Short on time and open to suggestions (even from algorithms), viewers sought out water-cooler shows. Top-10 lists published by Netflix, Nielsen and Reelgood confirmed this: Only a few titles out of the scores of new releases every month generated any sort of buzz. Back at the streaming platforms, researchers were slicing and dicing the audience using data from billions of streams, figuring out with unprecedented speed and accuracy whether a show was clicking with its intended audience.

And here was another Netflix effect at work: The streaming giant often dropped all new episodes of a show at once, allowing it to come up with a verdict on the entire season within a matter of days. When *The Irregulars* dropped on Netflix in 2021, one reviewer described it as Sherlock Holmes meets *Stranger Things* meets *Bridgerton*. It seemed tailor-made — or rather, algorithm-made — for a large portion of the Netflix audience. Sure enough, *The Irregulars* shot to the top of Netflix's list of Top 10 most-watched titles. Within days, however, data showed a steep decline in interest as viewers worked their way through the episodes. *The Irregulars* was cancelled shortly thereafter.

When vaccines arrived and people began venturing out to restaurants and movie theaters, industry forecasters predicted that cash-strapped consumers would drop their streaming subscriptions. Instead, they held onto streaming and continued cutting the cord. One year after the lockdown began, just 58 percent of U.S. households had traditional cable or satellite, down from 88 percent nine years earlier. For the first time, more Americans reported watching Streaming TV than traditional Pay TV in their homes.

The lockdown also saw the comeback for a viewing behavior that had fallen out of fashion in an on-demand world — channel-surfing. Platforms like PlutoTV, Tubi and Peacock offered stacks of "live" channels, which were actually just 24/7 loops of themed programming, arranged in a familiar cable-style grid that viewers could mindlessly click through. Instead of choosing something off the menu, viewers could now select a "Play Something" button on Netflix, and the algorithm would serve up a show based on their viewing history.

Streaming TV now and beyond (2022–)

The rush to Streaming TV has exceeded industry expectations. In the most extreme case, Disney revised its initial forecast of 40 million Disney+ subscribers by 2024 to *240 million* subscribers. "I think by the end of the decade, everyone is going to be watching TV via streaming," said Anthony Wood, the man who left Netflix to create Roku.

Powered by torrents of revenue, the streamers' programming budgets continue to expand, especially as Hollywood hurries to scale up and meet the challenge of Netflix and Amazon. Disney will spend $33 billion companywide, with most of that spent on content for Disney+, Hulu and its streaming sports asset ESPN+. WarnerMedia has plans to merge with Discovery, while ViacomCBS and NBCUniversal are spending billions in an existential push to establish their brands on streaming platforms.

Meanwhile, Big Tech continues to expand in the streaming space. Netflix will spend $20 billion in 2022. Amazon will spend $12 billion on Prime Video and IMDb TV, its lean-back streamer. And then there's Apple, which has billions of dollars already invested in Apple TV+, with production budgets that rival those of Netflix and Amazon and a CEO, Tim Cook, who was plainly thrilled by the 2021 Emmy Awards triumph for the Apple TV+ comedy *Ted Lasso*. Surely the world's largest corporation aspires to more than streaming's best-funded boutique platform.

Streaming TV seems poised for even more growth, but as always the viewers will determine if that happens. In particular, the industry must deal with two long-term challenges that their customers are facing. One challenge is *economic*: keeping monthly fees competitive, since customers can easily drop services that aren't good value. The other challenge is *efficient*: helping viewers find the shows they want to watch without so much frustration. As part of the solution to both problems, we introduce *The Primetimer Guide to Streaming TV.*

The Primetimer Guide
to Cutting the Cord

Not too long ago, your local cable company was one of the biggest cash cows in town. And no wonder: If you weren't being aggressively upsold a Cinemax subscription you didn't want, you were discovering new charges on your monthly bill. (Our favorite: paying rent on a cable modem you could find on eBay for $20.) Some of us tried to save money by attaching satellite dishes to the outside of our homes, only to discover that satellite TV had technical limitations and even worse customer service than cable (how is that even possible?). Such were the aggravations we put up with in order to conveniently watch our favorite programs, live sports and news.

Today there's an alternative. You can cut the cord — sever the umbilical link to the cable or satellite company you use now — enjoy a crazy amount of high-quality entertainment and, in most cases, pay a lot less than you currently shell out for a Pay TV subscription. It's all possible thanks to the Streaming TV revolution described in the previous chapter. Streaming today is more than Netflix and Hulu: It's also Disney+, HBO Max, Peacock and other new streaming platforms that together have vastly expanded the universe of on-demand video content. Tens of millions of cable and satellite customers have cut the cord and gone all-in with Streaming TV.

All of the major television and film studios have launched streaming platforms, offering their content directly to consumers without a cable or satellite middleman. (See "Your Favorite Network Shows Are Probably on Streaming," page 10.) All you need in order to access this video extravaganza is a reasonably-priced Internet connection and some lightweight gear that you can install yourself without waiting at home between 10 a.m. and 2 p.m. This guide will show you how.

By making the move to Streaming TV, you can watch the on-demand shows in this guide. Unlike cable or satellite, streaming platforms were built from the ground up to give you what you want to watch, when you want and *where* you want to watch it — on big screens, medium-sized screens or on that phone you carry around. With the monthly fee for a typical streaming platform costing less than what you used to pay for Cinemax (even with that sweet deal), you could save hundreds of dollars a year on home entertainment.

Your Favorite Network Shows Are Probably on Streaming

From 2019 to 2021, the parent companies of the studios that produce most broadcast and cable network programming launched their own streaming platforms. As a result, most network shows are now being repurposed to streaming.

When deciding if you need to hang onto your cable or satellite subscription, the following chart may be helpful.

Company	Broadcast & cable channels it owns		Streamer(s)
Comcast (NBCUniversal)	NBC Syfy USA Bravo E!	Oxygen Universal Kids Golf Channel CNBC MSNBC	Peacock
AT&T (WarnerMedia)*	HBO CNN TNT TBS The CW	Cartoon Network Adult Swim Turner Classic Movies TruTV	HBO Max CNN+
ViacomCBS	CBS Showtime Nickelodeon Nick at Nite MTV Comedy Central CMT Logo	Paramount Network Pop TV Smithsonian Chan. TV Land VH1 BET Flix	Paramount+
The Walt Disney Company	ABC ESPN FX Disney Channel Nat'l Geographic	A&E History Lifetime LMN	Hulu Disney+ ESPN+
Discovery Networks*	Discovery TLC Food Network HGTV Animal Planet Travel	Oprah Winfrey Net Science Channel Magnolia Network Motor Trend American Heroes Dest. America	Discovery+

* AT&T has announced a deal to spin off WarnerMedia assets and merge them with Discovery assets, pending governmental approval.

So if today is the perfect day to cut the cord, why haven't you done it yet? Hey, we get it: The hassle is real. Cable and satellite companies make it exceedingly hard to quit them, and the mere thought of replacing our home TV setup is enough to give many of us a headache. If it's not broken, we reason, why fix it? But the old way *is* broken. Consumers have been clamoring for greater control over their viewing choices and Streaming TV has delivered. They wanted better things to watch, too, and the streaming platforms have substantially upped the game in that regard as well.

This short guide will walk you step by step through the one-time process of replacing your cable or satellite provider with a Streaming TV setup. We've included some common scenarios which may be helpful. If you've already cut the cord, you might still want to read through this section, as the information has been updated for 2022.

STEP 1: YOUR LIST

You will find cord-cutting a satisfying experience if you do it with as little compromise as possible. Even if you choose one of the more expensive streaming options listed here, you'll very likely save money compared with your current setup and more importantly, you'll be happy.

To ensure a smooth transition, it's good to make a list. Write down all the shows you currently watch, any shows on your wishlist (based on recommendations from *The Primetimer Guide*, friends and family) and any cable channels you like to watch live.

Now look up your favorite shows and find out if and where they stream. One way is simply to look them up in Part II of this guide. Or you can type the show's title into a search engine like **Reelgood, JustWatch** or **Watchworthy**, which link to the libraries of dozens of streaming platforms. If a show is streaming on multiple platforms, compare to see which episodes are available on each.

Why Shows Don't Stream

You may come across some shows that aren't streaming. Here are the most common types:

► **Syndicated shows like *Jeopardy!*:** Syndication was created to provide revenue for local TV stations, and streaming would undermine that income stream. Some syndicated talent may jump to streaming, like Judy Sheindlin did in 2021 when she shut down production on her long-running *Judge Judy* show and launched a nearly identical one, *Judy Justice*, on IMDb TV. But don't bet on *Jeopardy!* moving to streaming any time soon. The solution is either to put up an antenna or subscribe to a Cable TV Replacement service that includes local TV stations.

▶ **Cable news:** CNN, Fox and MSNBC have streaming platforms either announced or launched, but with separate programming that doesn't duplicate what's on their cable channels. If you want to keep

---

Those TV Channels You've Never Heard Of

Classic Movies Channel. Jersey Shore. Docurama. TheGrio. Cheddar News. FailArmy. WeatherNation. Grit. This Old House. If you start seeing strange new channels like these, you've likely bought a new Smart TV or plugged in a TV antenna and done a channel scan.

A slew of new free, ad-supported TV channels have come online in recent years. They fall into two categories:

▶ **Broadcast TV channels.** With the switch to digital broadcasting in the 1990s, local TV stations were able to split their signals into multiple channels. In addition to the flagship station — usually a high-definition network affiliate — most TV signals have several standard-definition subchannels, typically classic TV and film channels (MeTV, Antenna TV, Cozi TV, Movies!), niche channels (Comet for sci-fi, Grit for westerns, Bounce for Black programming, Dabl for lifestyle), religious programming, news and weather.

▶ **Streaming TV channels.** More recently, thousands of free streaming channels have been launched around the world. Though many can be watched on standalone apps, many Smart TVs now include tiers of streaming channels (sometimes called Internet TV channels) so users can channel-surf them in the same loop as their regular TV stations. Many free streaming channels are extensions of existing media brands (ABC News Live, USA Today, Bob Ross, Court TV). A growing number are "lean-back" channels that offer 24/7 loops of programming from popular TV brands (Stories by AMC, Hallmark Movies & More, TV Land Sitcoms).

These free channels add a lot of variety and are a nice complement to your premium streaming services. Be advised, though, that the commercial breaks on some of these channels might drive you bananas.

---

watching your favorite CNN, MSNBC or Fox News hosts, you'll need a Cable TV Replacement service. If you just want news on demand, see "Flash! You Don't Need to Pay for 24/7 News," page 14.

► **C-SPAN:** The only Cable TV Replacement service that carries C-SPAN is DirecTV Stream. If you want your government fix and don't plan to get DirecTV Stream, you'll have to watch the live feeds on the c-span.org website or with the C-SPAN Now smartphone app, which you can screencast to your TV.

► **Sporting events:** Most major live sporting events are carried on broadcast TV and ESPN. You'll need an antenna or Cable TV Replacement service for the TV stations. Like the cable news channels, ESPN offers a separate streaming app that doesn't duplicate what's on the live cable channel (ESPN+ doesn't even carry the flagship *SportsCenter* show). For ESPN, ESPN 2 and regional sports channels, you'll need a Cable TV Replacement service.

► **Rentals:** Some older shows that you enjoy watching on cable may not be available for streaming because the rights holder can't or won't make a streaming deal. The only way to watch these shows online is to rent or purchase them.

STEP 2: HARDWARE

When cord-cutting, the goal is to improve the viewing experience while also saving money. Many people, though, will use this occasion to *spend* money, maybe on a new 4K TV and a nice soundbar. By no means do you have to do this. As long as your TV has an HDMI port for connecting a streaming player, you're good to go. Most people reading this already have a Roku, Chromecast, Fire TV or Apple TV connected to their TV for watching Netflix and renting videos.

On the other hand, with the money you save by switching to streaming, you can afford a new 65-inch Smart TV, and everything will certainly look better on that, won't it? With that in mind, let's review your hardware options:

► **Smart TV.** If you've had a Roku box or Chromecast dongle plugged into your TV for a few years, it probably needs an upgrade. The wi-fi antenna and processor speed are much better in the newer models. Then again, you could ditch the plug-in box altogether and get a Smart TV with the streaming player built in. You can even get one that runs on the latest Roku, Google or Fire TV operating system.

Flash! You Don't Need To Pay for 24/7 News

CNN, MSNBC and Fox News pull in some of Cable TV's largest audiences and are hugely profitable for cable and satellite operators. That explains why these channels have not migrated to streaming. Instead, their corporate owners have chosen to launch separate branded streaming platforms (**Fox Nation, NBC News Now** and **CNN+**). Cord-cutters can get the original cable news channels only if they shell out $35 or more per month for a Cable TV Replacement service.

Let's say, though, that you're looking for actual news reporting and breaking-news coverage, as opposed to a bunch of celebrity anchors and pundits offering their narratives and spin. Great news! There's a growing market for 24-hour TV news and it's all happening away from cable. The channels listed below are all backed by major news organizations and have global reach. Best of all, they're free to watch.

Newsy is the first 24-hour news channel available on broadcast TV. Aimed at people who like their news straight, without political slant, it's owned by E.W. Scripps, a major broadcast TV chain with deep roots in newspaper publishing. In 2021 Scripps made Newsy a live-around-the-clock broadcast service, available on local TV as a subchannel in more than 130 markets.

On the streaming side, the news divisions of ABC, CBS and NBC have had streaming platforms for years but have only recently started making significant investments in them. **ABC News Live** created a signature one-hour nightly newscast in 2020, anchored by Linsey Davis. **NBC News Now** followed suit with a nightly newscast anchored by Tom Llamas. **CBSN**, launched in 2014, announced a major overhaul in early 2022, including a competing one-hour newscast and originals hosted by Norah O'Donnell, Gayle King and other network talent. All three streamers continue to add live news coverage throughout the day.

Sky News, launched in 1989 and owned by Comcast, is a respected British news service that carries a great deal of U.S. reporting, plus international headlines and weather (and almost no ads).

Al Jazeera English, based in Doha, Qatar, launched in 2006 to expand the audience of the popular Arabic-language news channel. The anchor desk moves through the day, from Doha to London to Washington, D.C. AJE is the most seasoned of a crop of English-language global news services including **France 24**, Germany's **DW** and Russia's **RT.**

To ease you through your cable-news withdrawal, the audio feeds of **CNN, MSNBC** and **Fox News** are available through **TuneIn.**

▶ **Internet:** Now that you'll be streaming all the time, do you need more Internet bandwidth? Maybe, maybe not. Streaming video is very efficient: A theater-quality 4K picture needs bandwidth of 18mbps (megabits per second) per stream, and HD requires only 8mbps. Even with multiple users streaming in your household at once, commonly-available Internet speeds of 50mbps to 100mbps should suffice. If you notice the picture downscaling from high-definition to standard, or the image freezing and pixels dropping out, try the next-higher tier of Internet speed and see if that helps.

▶ **TV antenna**: Why would you want to revert to a technology that your grandparents used? Well, assuming you've done Step 1 and determined that you don't need to watch live cable channels, then an antenna can give you dozens of local TV channels without monthly fees. (Yes, we said *dozens*: See "Those TV Channels You've Never Heard Of," page 12.) Today's antennas are unobtrusive and simple to install. An antenna will pass along TV signals even when your Internet fails.

▶ **Antenna DVR.** If you want to record shows off the antenna, then you'll need to get an Antenna DVR. These are smaller than the older types of DVRs and usually don't need to be in the same room as the TV, so long as they're connected to the home network. Some are more technically imposing than others, and some charge monthly fees for the listings data that makes a DVR smart. The **Fire TV Recast** from Amazon and **TiVo Edge for Antenna** are both easy to use and offer models with lifetime listings data (no monthly fees).

STEP 3: STREAMING PLATFORMS

All streaming services and platforms are accessed through apps that you install on your streaming player or Smart TV, just like you install apps on your smartphone. You'll choose your apps based on the information you gathered in Step 1.

Streaming apps fall into one of three categories:

▶ **Cable TV Replacements:** Services like YouTubeTV and Sling offer a familiar basic cable viewing experience with a Cloud DVR for saving programs. In many cases you can add local TV stations to the bundle. Cable TV Replacement services cost $25 to $65 a month, depending on how many channels are in the bundle.

► **Premium Streaming Platforms:** These are the brands you know: Netflix, Prime Video, HBO Max, Disney+, etc. Most of the shows that you wrote down in Step 1 are streaming on these platforms.

► **Free Streaming Platforms:** These are streamers that cost nothing but a few minutes of your time every hour for commercial breaks. PlutoTV, IMDb TV, Tubi and many others are owned by the same large companies that own cable and TV networks and premium streaming platforms. Their libraries are vast and often overlap those of the premium streamers.

For more, see "A Reference to Popular Streaming Services," beginning on page 19.

COMMON CORD-CUTTING SCENARIOS

Now let's see some ways you might put together a Streaming TV setup that works for you. These scenarios cover only your monthly spending on TV, plus upfront costs. They assume that you already have high-speed Internet or are planning to get it. Also, we've set the cost of Prime Video at zero because most U.S. households already have an Amazon Prime membership; if yours doesn't, add $9 a month for Prime Video. You can also install Free Streaming apps for even more variety.

The budget-minded smorgasbord

Netflix (standard plan)	$ 15.50
Peacock Premium	$ 5
Showtime-Paramount+ bundle*	$ 12.50
Hulu, ad-supported*	$ 5.83
Prime Video (included w/Amazon Prime)	$ 0
Total monthly streaming fees …	$ 38.83
Upfront cost: TV antenna + DVR …	$250
* based on annual rate	

A TV antenna takes the place of a cable or satellite subscription in this thrifty scenario that still gives cord-cutters a wide variety of choices. It will appeal to viewers whose favorite shows are available on streaming and can live without basic cable.

Assuming you currently spend $85 a month on Pay TV (which was the median amount for U.S. cable subscribers in 2021), you'd be saving $46 a month in this scenario. At that rate you'd cover the cost of the new hardware and save hundreds more in Year 1 alone.

Simple and elegant

HBO Max	$ 15
Prime Video (w/Amazon Prime)	$ 0
YouTubeTV	$ 65
Total monthly streaming fees …	$ 80

This antenna-free scenario will appeal to cord-cutters who like the basic cable experience and want to keep it simple. YouTubeTV offers more than 100 cable channels, your local TV stations and a Cloud DVR from one central interface.

Variety and flexibility

Netflix (basic plan)	$ 10
Sling Orange	$ 35
Paramount+ Essential*	$ 4.17
Hulu with ads*	$ 5.83
HBO Max with ads*	$ 8.33
Peacock Premium*	$ 4.17
Prime Video (w/Amazon Prime)	$ 0
Total monthly streaming fees …	$ 67.50
Upfront cost: TV antenna-AirTV bundle …	$ 99

* based on annual rate

This combines an antenna with a value-priced Cable TV Replacement service and some value-priced premium streamers, offering a wide variety of entertainment without breaking the bank. Many premium streamers offer ad-supported versions at a lower cost. Having both an Antenna DVR and Cloud DVR offers the flexibility of saving local and cable shows in addition to searching for on-demand programs. Sling Orange offers a decent-sized package of basic cable channels including CNN and ESPN, which can be bundled with an antenna and Sling's AirTV Antenna DVR at a special price.

A Reference to Popular Streaming Services

CABLE TV REPLACEMENTS

These services offer cable channels without the wire and, if you like, can also provide local TV stations without the antenna. They come with Cloud DVRs for effortless saving of shows. And they offer multiple simultaneous streams on your TV, computer and mobile devices. For users who find they can't get all the live sports, news and entertainment they want from streaming platforms only, these services are worth the extra expense.

Prices and channel lineups may have changed since *The Primetimer Guide* went to press. A comparison site like **Suppose.tv** pulls the latest lineup and pricing data from all the top streaming services, matches it to the channels you select from its menu, then shows you the most competitive offers from the services that best match your preferences.

YouTube TV

Best-in-class YouTubeTV is renowned for its ease of use, unlimited DVR and deep menu of channels. YouTubeTV's user experience is outstanding; you might even say it's addictive. You'll find yourself stumbling upon channels you forgot existed, like MTV Classic, and you'll be impressed by the powerful DVR.

Pricing: At $64.99/month, you get all the broadcast stations in your market (including PBS) and more of the top cable channels than any of the other all-in-ones. If you want more than three streams at once, that will cost $10/month extra, but you also get 4K and offline viewing with that.

Hulu with Live TV

If Hulu, Disney+ and ESPN+ are all on your wishlist, this is the Live TV service for you. Hulu shook things up in late 2021 by adding its popular subscription streamers Disney+ and ESPN+ to all Hulu + Live TV plans. This is great news for people who were planning to grab those services anyway. Though reviewers find Hulu's Live TV interface dated compared with YouTubeTV's interface, Disney+ and ESPN+ run on separate apps with more user-friendly interfaces.

Pricing: $69.99/month for the ad-supported Hulu, 80+ popular Cable TV channels, 50 hours of Cloud DVR and the Disney+ and ESPN+ services. To watch Hulu without ads costs $75.99/month. (For more about Hulu, see page 25.)

DirecTV Stream

Watch sports channels you can't stream anywhere else — for a price. In 2019, after the new owners of several regional sports networks raised their rates, other all-in-one streamers dropped them. But not AT&T, the parent company of DirecTV. A laggard in the all-in-one streaming competition, AT&T saw this as a chance to stand out, and agreed to the pricey terms. If your market is home to one of the MLB, NBA or NHL teams whose local broadcast rights are exclusive to Bally Sports, YES or AT&T SportsNet, you'll need DirecTV Stream to stream those games, and the added costs will be passed on to you.

The biggest strike against DirecTV Stream is that its majority owner is AT&T, the cable and satellite giant, and its pawprints are all over this supposedly next-generation product. Besides the unnecessary set-top box for $5/month (no thanks), reviewers have complained of a poor user experience, lack of Google Chromecast support and, maybe the worst sin, getting calls from DirecTV reps trying to upsell them to the dish.

Pricing: You'll need the Choice option, which starts at $90/month and includes a full lineup of entertainment channels plus any in-market regional sports networks. Out-of-market networks will cost more: According to Suppose.tv, a Chicago-based fan of St. Louis Cardinals baseball will shell out nearly $150/month for a Choice package that offers regional network coverage of the Cubs' archrival. (Switching loyalties to the White Sox would be cheaper.)

Fubo

Popular among sports fans for its global and American sports channel choices. With its shelves stocked with live and on-demand sports programming, Fubo has become the choice of more than 1 million subscribers, 96 percent of whom watch sports. It doesn't have the regional networks that DirecTV Stream has a lock on and it doesn't carry any of the Turner networks, including TBS and TNT — which is a problem if you like watching NBA games or the MLB playoffs. (In late 2021 Fubo's

CEO hinted that the company was trying to get the Turner networks back, so check the site.) And though you'll be able to get your local TV stations with Fubo, it had the smallest bundle of entertainment channels of any of the four Cable TV Replacement services we compared.

Pricing: $64.99/month for the Starter plan with 250 hours of Cloud DVR, $69.99/month for Pro (more streams and 1,000 hours of DVR storage), $79.99/month for Elite (more channels). There's a separate Latino bundle with 33 Spanish-language channels and Cloud DVR for $32.99/month.

VALUE-PRICED CABLE TV REPLACEMENTS

If you plan to get local TV via antenna but still want some basic cable channels, these services give you skinny bundles at a value price.

Sling

Two substantial but smaller-sized bundles of cable networks for $35/month, plus Cloud DVR. Sling Blue and Sling Orange have a lot of overlap, but only Orange has channels owned by Disney, including ESPN. Some Smart TVs have Sling integration, which means Sling (cable) and antenna channels appear side-by-side when you're channel-surfing, just like old times.

Philo

An even more stripped-down lineup than Sling's, but at just $25/month it may be just what you need. Paramount Network, AMC, and the full suit of Discovery and MTV networks (including Comedy Central and VH1) are here. Unlimited Cloud DVR is included.

Frndly

Very skinny bundles of family-friendly networks, including Hallmark and History, come in plans ranging from $6.99/month to $10.99/month. Some tiers offer Cloud DVR.

Fanatiz

If it's only *deportes* you want, this niche streamer offers a soccer-heavy package *en Español,* with replays on demand, for $7.99/month.

Premium Streaming Platforms: The "Big 9"

As Netflix has taught us, Streaming TV can hold its own with broadcast and cable when it comes to producing blockbuster programs and movies. These are the cream-of-the-crop streaming services. They spend billions per year on original content and win the lion's share of prestigious television awards.

Flush with cash, the largest streamers are racing to stockpile as much quality content as their budgets will allow. The next step, inevitably, is consolidation. Already Discovery and WarnerMedia have announced plans to merge, and more M&A activity is predicted in the near future. That will either wind up making the "Big 9" even bigger, as they gobble up smaller streamers, or reducing the ranks of this league of giants, perhaps to the Big 7 or even fewer.

Four streaming platforms are backed by traditional ad-supported networks: HBO Max, Peacock, Hulu and Paramount+. These four will sell you a value-priced version of their platform if you agree to watch "limited" commercial interruptions (note the quote marks). Except for Peacock Premium, the ad-supported versions give you access to all the content of the regular platform. Think of them as paid trial versions — if you enjoy what you get with an ad-supported streaming platform, it might be worth it for you to upgrade to the ad-free version.

Netflix

The go-to streamer if you want the most-watched TV shows. Netflix continues to dominate in market share and, just as important, mindshare: It's the No. 1 destination for viewers the moment they turn on the TV. (If they even need to do that. Many TV remotes now have a button that will power on the set and go straight to Netflix.) In 2020, 80% of the most-watched series in the U.S. were on Netflix.

Pricing: All Netflix tiers are ad-free. For $10/month you get a sharp, reliable standard-definition (480p) picture on one screen at a time. Upgrade to high-definition and 2 screens at a time for $15.49/month or 4K/UHD quality and other extras for $20/month.

Originals of note: *Squid Game, Bridgerton, The Crown, Tiger King, The Queen's Gambit, Never Have I Ever, Bridgerton, Stranger Things, The Lost Daughter, Nailed It!, Queer Eye, You, Cobra Kai, Bird Box* and many more

Size matters. With more than 200 million subscribers worldwide, Netflix generates a stupendous amount of cash flow. That allows it to produce thousands of hours of original programming; Netflix's annual content budget may exceed $20 billion in 2023.

"But they don't have *The Office* anymore!" In early days Netflix grew its audience by streaming established hits like *The Office* and *Friends*. Many of those shows and movies have since been clawed back by their studios so they could launch streaming services to compete with Netflix. Occasionally Netflix will pay top dollar to hang onto a TV show's rights, as it did with *Seinfeld* in 2021. Thanks to its enormous catalog of Netflix originals, however, the streamer is less reliant on other people's shows.

The global advantage. Netflix is in 190 countries and is savvy about leveraging hit shows in one country to viewers in others. Witness such international phenomena as *Squid Game, Babylon Berlin* and the *Narcos* franchise. Perhaps you've noticed an Israeli thriller like *Possessions* or one of several dubbed shows from Eastern Europe in your Netflix feed. If you don't mind reading subtitles or listening to dubbed voices (some viewers turn on both options), you can make some satisfying cross-cultural finds.

HBO Max

HBO and more add up to an excellent value in premium TV. For the price of a regular HBO subscription, you get a lot more with HBO Max. Stream all the movies and acclaimed shows you expect from HBO anytime, plus titles from other WarnerMedia companies like TNT, TBS, Adult Swim, Cartoon Network and Warner's TV division. This gives HBO Max's library impressive depth, and since WarnerMedia has been in the hitmaking business for more than 30 years, the overall quality is high.

Pricing: $15/month ($150/year) gets you HBO Max with no ads, plus offline downloads and 4K video. There's also a budget plan: $10/month ($100/year) for HD-quality video that's ad-supported (no downloads). Either way, you can install and the app and simultaneously stream on up to 5 devices.

Originals of note: *Hacks, Station Eleven, The Flight Attendant, And Just Like That..., Gossip Girl*; then there's the HBO library with newer shows like *Mare of Easttown, Succession, Betty* and *100 Foot Wave* joining such legacy titles as *The Sopranos, The Wire, Six Feet Under, Oz, Game of Thrones, Sex and the City, Enlightened, The Leftovers* and long-running factual series *Real Time With Bill Maher, Real Sports With Bryant Gumbel* and *Hard Knocks*.

The best ad-supported service: Maybe it's the relatively high $10 monthly fee, but HBO Max's ad-supported tier gets high marks from viewers for having fewer and shorter commercial interruptions than other ad-supported premium tiers.

Prime Video

Deep collection of originals and acquired content plus NFL games.
The typical Amazon household doesn't renew its Prime subscription for
the TV shows. Until recently the majority of Prime members didn't even
look at Prime Video. But Amazon has been changing that. Its budget for
spending on content is almost as large as Netflix's and WarnerMedia's.
And while Prime Video content doesn't innovate on the scale of HBO
or Netflix programming (at least not yet), its depth and variety are
still impressive. Recently Amazon inked a 10-year deal with the NFL,
making Prime Video the exclusive home of NFL *Thursday Night Football*;
previously it had shared the rights with Fox.

Pricing: This streaming channel is part of the Amazon Prime subscription
($119/year), which includes free expedited shipping on select Amazon
purchases, streaming music, photo storage and more. Prime Video
is also available by itself for $9/month. Install on unlimited devices;
3 simultaneous streams max.

Originals of note: *Bosch, The Marvelous Mrs. Maisel, Small Axe, The
Tick, Transparent, The Underground Railroad, All Or Nothing, Being the
Ricardos, Clarkson's Farm, Invincible, LuLaRich, The Wheel of Time, One
Night in Miami, The Wilds, The Boys, Hanna, Jack Ryan, Homecoming*

It's a streamer … and a hub for *other* streamers. Amazon, like Apple,
combines its branded streaming service with a broader video platform.
Prime Video subscribers have the option of adding other premium
services directly to their account, including Paramount+, Discovery+,
Starz, AMC+, Epix, BritBox and more. If your digital life revolves around
Amazon products — you have a Fire Stick and Echo smart speakers,
and are talking to Alexa all day long — then managing all your streams
through Prime Video may be helpful. Just know that this interface exists
primarily for *Amazon's* benefit, so it can promote movie rentals and
content from its fledgling ad-supported service IMDb TV (see below)
more easily to users.

Disney+

**Five big family entertainment brands add up to one massive streaming
launch.** Over the years The Walt Disney Company has acquired some of
the best-known family brands in show business: Marvel, Pixar, LucasFilm
and National Geographic. These four definitely put the "plus" in Disney+.
When combined with the assets of Disney (including its recent purchase
of select Fox Entertainment assets like *The Simpsons*), and offered at a
nearly irresistible promotional price, it's no wonder Disney+ started flying
into homes. The service picked up 100 million subscribers in little over a

year after launching in 2019 and is now the third-largest streamer in the U.S., behind Netflix and Prime Video.

Pricing: $8/month or $80/year. There's also a "Disney bundle" that packages Disney+ with Hulu and ESPN+ for $15/month ($20/month for the no-ads version of Hulu; annual rate not available). Maximum 7 profiles, 10 devices and 4 simultaneous streams.

Originals of note: *The Mandalorian, WandaVision, Hamilton, Soul, Encore!, High School Musical: The Musical – The Series, Star Wars: The Clone Wars, Doogie Kameāloha, M.D., The Right Stuff, The Beatles: Get Back, The Falcon and the Winter Soldier, The Book of Boba Fett*

There's plenty to binge, provided you're patient. Like HBO Max, Disney is thinking old-school when it comes to rolling out new shows and new seasons of returning shows. To keep the buzz going as long as possible, Disney+ typically posts three episodes of a new season in Week 1, with one new episode per week after that. So if you prefer watching all the episodes in a season, you'll have to wait until all of them have dropped (and avoid the spoilers).

Hulu

Streaming's oldest player is a three-headed monster. Launched in 2008, Hulu began as a DVR replacement and 15 years later, that's still a primary virtue for many of its 40 million subscribers. But it is also building an impressive library of originals of note and is the streaming home of FX. And if that weren't enough, Hulu is also a leading Cable TV Replacement service. While wearing all these hats might cause confusion among consumers trying to decide whether they need Hulu or not, Disney has made that choice easier by adding Hulu to its popular Disney+ bundle.

Pricing: The ad-supported Hulu plan is $7/month or $70/year; ad-free is $13/month (no annual plan). Or get it with the Disney+ bundle; see the Disney+ listing above. Live TV plans start at $65/month with 50 hours of Cloud DVR.

Originals of note: *Only Murders in the Building, Dopesick, The Handmaid's Tale, Letterkenny, The Great, Mrs. America, Normal People, Shrill, Ramy, PEN15, The Act, Solar Opposites, Little Fires Everywhere, Harlots, Summer of Soul, How I Met Your Father*

FX is Hulu's secret weapon: One of cable TV's prestige brands of the past two decades, FX brought viewers *The Shield, Nip/Tuck, Damages, Fargo, Dave, American Horror Story, Archer, It's Always Sunny in Philadelphia* and much more. FX was acquired in 2019 by Disney, which has made it a featured brand on Hulu. Many FX shows now debut on Hulu before appearing on FX on cable.

Paramount+

A well-rounded streamer that needs some fine tuning — and a big hit. CBS and Viacom were separate companies until re-merging in 2019, so they didn't get their streaming service launched until March 2021. It's definitely a work in progress. There are thousands of reasons to get Paramount+, as the combined ViacomCBS catalog includes shows from CBS and CBS All Access, live NFL games and *Inside the NFL*, Paramount movies, 20 years of reality from MTV, live *Big Brother* feeds, kids shows from Nickelodeon, comedy specials and *South Park* from Comedy Central and more. But the first year of Paramount+ was missing the buzz-making show that Disney+, Apple TV+ and Peacock all enjoyed in their first two years. Worse, Viacom sold the rights to *Yellowstone* to NBCUniversal before the merger with CBS, meaning that a rival platform was streaming cable's No. 1 show instead of Paramount+.

Pricing: Paramount+ is just $5/month with ads, or $50/year, which seems like a bargain, but read the caveat below. If you're a fan of Paramount+ shows you'll almost certainly be upgrading to Premium, which promises "no ads, except live TV and a few shows" — or as the rest of the world calls it, "some ads" — for $100/year (or $10/month).

Originals of note: *Star Trek: Discovery, Star Trek: Picard, Star Trek: Lower Decks; The Good Fight, Evil, The Challenge, 1883;* soccer from Serie A (Italy), Brazil and the UEFA Champions League.

Paramount, plus commercials — *lots* of commercials: You'd think that paying $5/month for the Paramount+ Essentials plan would spare you from being bombarded by commercials, but you'd be wrong. We agree with the *Tom's Guide* reviewer who, when comparing the ad breaks on various streamers, declared Paramount+ "the worst of the bunch." What's especially galling is that a company that also owns lean-back streamer PlutoTV (covered later in this section) charges admission to Paramount+ viewers for the same user experience.

Peacock

Live sports, network sitcoms and reality plus some great originals make Peacock a solid addition to your streaming menu. Blending the best of live and on-demand TV at a value price (with ads), Peacock seems like a no-brainer. Its deep catalog includes *The Office, SNL, Law & Order, This Is Us,* films from Universal Pictures and Focus Features, *Sunday Night Football*, sports talk and much more. Its early Peacock originals generally debuted well.

Pricing starts at free: You don't get the live sports or most Peacock originals with the free version of the channel, but you do get most of the back catalog, which compares well with other lean-back streamers like

PlutoTV and Tubi. The full Peacock experience is $4.99/month with ads or $9.99/month "without ads," though "a small amount of programming will still contain ads." So it's not "without ads." That said, films on Peacock tend to have a long pre-roll of ads, allowing the feature to stream commercial-free. Just like at the movies!

Originals of note: *Girls5eva, One of Us Is Lying, The Amber Ruffin Show, We Are Lady Parts, Saved by the Bell, Departure, Rutherford Falls*

Discovery+

Reality's biggest bundle of shows may not make it through 2022. One of the last of the major holdings of cable channels to jump into the stream was Discovery Networks, with the launch of Discovery+ at the beginning of 2021. Discovery operates not only its flagship Discovery channel but TLC, Food Network, HGTV, Animal Planet, Travel, Oprah Winfrey Network, Science Channel, Magnolia Network, Motor Trend, American Heroes and Destination America. For its streaming channel Discovery also leased popular reality shows from A&E, Lifetime and History. An estimated 20 million households subscribe to Discovery+

Not long after Discovery+ launched, Discovery Networks and WarnerMedia announced a merger, driven by both companies' desire to be more competitive in the streaming space. While that would suggest that Discovery+ programs would be folded into WarnerMedia's streaming channel HBO Max — adding value to one of the most expensive streamers on the market — nothing had been decided as of press time.

Pricing: $4.99/month or $6.99/month ad-free.

Originals of note: *Design Star, Fixer Upper;* shows from Discovery Networks streaming on Discovery+ include *BattleBots, Deadliest Catch, Blue Planet, Naked And Afraid, The Last Alaskans, Amy Schumer Learns to Cook*

Apple TV+

Unique among streaming platforms, Apple TV+ is built almost entirely on originals, one of which is *Ted Lasso*. At first glance it seems audacious to ask customers to pay $5/month for access to a library of fewer than 200 titles. Apple is betting that users will make this their third or fourth streaming subscription. So far that doesn't appear to be happening — Apple has yet to release figures but reportedly it has fewer than 20 million streaming subscribers, making Apple TV+ the smallest of the Big 9 — although that's not stopping it from investing heavily in programs. It spent $10 million to acquire *Boys State*, which was then a record for a documentary film, and the budget for *The Morning Show* was on the order of *Game of Thrones*. So far its batting average is stellar: *Ted Lasso* swept the Emmy Awards in its rookie season, and there are many more recommended Apple TV+ shows in Part II of this guide than one would expect from a streamer that has produced so few originals.

Pricing: $4.99/month, no ads; free for 90 days if you buy a qualifying Apple device.

Originals of note: *Ted Lasso, The Morning Show, Defending Jacob, Schmigadoon!, Central Park, Dickinson, Home Before Dark, For All Mankind, Little America, Visible: Out on Television, Mythic Quest, Hear the Sound, 1971: The Year Music Changed Everything, Servant*

Other Premium Services of Note

Niche streamers bring TV programs into your home that formerly were only available via DVD rentals or not at all. There are more than 200 streaming video-on-demand platforms serving a wide variety of niches, and your streaming player should have apps for all of them; optionally you can get some of these as add-ons to Prime Video, Apple TV or Hulu. Most offer 7-day free trials so you can decide if they're right for you.

PBS Passport

A great way to support public TV and unlock all the content you missed. For a $60 annual pledge to your local PBS station, you get access to more than 2,500 titles in the PBS vault, including the occasional full-season drop of episodes before they air on TV. Rediscover the shows you haven't seen in years, like *NOVA* and *Great Performances*, go down a Ken Burns rabbit hole or watch that curious revival of *Firing Line* with the host who sounds nothing like William F. Buckley Jr.

Epix, Starz and Showtime

Better known as movie channels, these ad-free premium services are also quietly turning out prestige TV shows. Sprinkled throughout Part II of this guide are recommendations for shows from these three premium cable channels-turned-streamers: *Get Shorty, Blindspotting, Perpetual Grace LTD, P-Valley, Billions, Shameless* among others. In the past viewers who've heard good buzz about these shows have waited until they migrated to Netflix or Prime Video. But that may not be an option in the future. The growth of the streaming market is encouraging the corporate owners of these brands to invest more deeply in their streaming channels. In other words, if you like what Epix, Starz and Showtime are offering, don't wait — get them. Monthly fees range from $5.99 for Epix to $99/year for Showtime (as of press time Showtime is also offered in a bundle with Paramount+ for $11.99/month).

AMC+ (Acorn TV, Sundance, IFC, Shudder, ALLBLK)

Boutique streamers will scratch that niche. There are streaming channels for lovers of Bollywood films, Nordic noir, Canadian reality shows, global sports, Japanese anime, yoga, on and on and on. You can explore these boutique streamers through the channel store of your streaming player. For the purposes of this guide, we've included channels from AMC Networks, the best-known brand in niche streaming.

Though AMC is better known as the studio behind *Mad Men, Breaking Bad* and *The Walking Dead,* it has also cultivated a suite of boutique streaming channels including Acorn TV (British), Sundance Now (global), IFC Films Unlimited (indie films), Shudder (suspense) and ALLBLK (from the founder of BET). The flagship AMC+ streamer is loaded with content from the AMC channel and select programs from AMC's other streamers. These ad-free channels range from $4.99/month to $8.99/month.

BritBox

There's a lot more to UK television than sitcoms and murder mysteries. And you'll get the full spectrum on BritBox, without ads. A 50/50 venture of Britain's BBC and ITV broadcasters, BritBox offers chat shows, gardening shows, news and factual programming, Slow TV (e.g., two hours of video shot from a train) and, yes, all the Britcoms and detective shows you can eat. $6.99 a month, $69.99 per year.

Curiosity Stream

From the creator of the Discovery channel, this streamer is a fantastic value if you enjoy documentaries. Thousands of hours of factual programs are developed every year, a fact no one knows better than John Hendricks, who built Discovery on the curation of documentary TV in the 1980s and '90s. For a ridiculous $2.99/month or $19.99/year (or less, as the annual rate is often discounted) you can tap into a huge number of high-quality docs on science, history, math, travel and other topics from leading broadcasters and studios around the world.

AD-SUPPORTED (FREE) STREAMING CHANNELS

This fast-growing sector of Streaming TV offers a trove of entertainment at a very attractive price: *free.* It's done following a formula that has worked since the dawn of television: These platforms acquire libraries of low-cost titles, then make their money inserting commercial breaks (usually with blunt force) into the streams.

While there are scores of platforms in the ad-supported streaming space, these are the five we're keeping our eyes on. They're backed by some of the biggest brands in entertainment and tech and they are all investing in original programming, not just renting other people's libraries.

PlutoTV

Watch ViacomCBS shows and movies in either lean-back or on-demand mode. Using a familiar channel guide interface, PlutoTV offers dozens of channels covering every genre: movies, reality, comedy, drama, sports, news, music, lifestyle. While many of these channels are available elsewhere online, they are presented conveniently side by side with popular branded channels from ViacomCBS, which also operates Paramount+.

Signing into PlutoTV is optional; you're free to watch anonymously. In fact, everything about PlutoTV is designed to evoke the days when you could just flip on the set, grab the clicker, lean back and surf aimlessly. Many Smart TV models now include select PlutoTV channels alongside local broadcast stations, enhancing the "lean-back" experience.

Typical fare: Branded channels include Paramount Movie Channel, PlutoTV Documentaries, Showtime Selects, CSI, Teen Mom OG, Star Trek, The Price Is Right, BET on PlutoTV, Jersey Shore and Survivor.

Tubi

Fox's answer to PlutoTV draws from a wide variety of content providers, including Fox. Tubi amassed an impressive and eclectic library of titles from hundreds of content providers to become one of the biggest streaming channels before Fox bought it in 2020. The more than 30,000 titles in Tubi's collection at any given time may be more hit-and-miss than PlutoTV's, but it feels more global and multicultural. Tubi's interface is similar to a conventional streaming service, with endless thumbnails. You can do some live viewing here but it's really set up as an on-demand collection.

Typical fare: Content partners include A&E, Lifetime, LOL! Network and Fox Sports. Tubi has vast curated collections including British TV, Bollywood Dreams, Black Cinema, Drafthouse Films, K-Drama, Only Free on Tubi, Spaghetti Westerns, Zombies. And like IMDb TV, Tubi has started to stream original content, much of it produced by Fox, including adult animation, documentaries, thrillers, horror, sci-fi and romance.

IMDb TV

Amazon is pouring resources into its free streaming service, making it a solid alternative to PlutoTV. IMDb TV is named for one of the web's oldest websites, the Internet Movie Database, which Amazon acquired in 1998. Amazon has begun to position IMDb TV as an ad-supported streamer distinct from its premium channel, Prime Video. More intriguingly, it is investing heavily in originals for IMDb TV, including a multi-series deal with *Law & Order* creator Dick Wolf. Much of the MGM-Lionsgate library of movies and reality, which Amazon acquired in 2021, will likely be streamed on IMDb TV.

Typical fare: Originals include *Judy Justice*, *Alex Rider* (acquired from Prime Video), and *Leverage: Redemption*. IMDb TV will also get first dibs on Universal films after they stream on Peacock.

The Roku Channel

So that's where all those Quibi shows went. Though known mostly for its streaming player and popular Smart TVs, Roku has used its hardware advantage to quietly put its Roku Channel on 50+ million home screens. Many more have the app on their non-Roku devices because it's free, easy to use and even serves up some exclusive content.

In 2021 Roku acquired many of the shows produced for Quibi, the short-form streamer that spectacularly burned through $1.7 billion before collapsing. Rebranded Roku Originals, they're going to get a lot more eyeballs on them than they ever did on Quibi.

Typical fare: iHeartRadio audio and video streams, content from *other* ad-supported streamers like PlutoTV and Reelz, and Quibi series including the *Reno 911!* revival, British spoof *Mapleworth Murders* and *Chrissy's Court* with judge Chrissy Teigen (average Quibi episode length: 7 minutes).

Facebook Watch

Yes, Facebook has a streaming video channel — and it's produced some notable TV shows. Launched in 2017, Facebook Watch is a hub for watching video on the world's biggest English-language social media platform. Watch contains both user-generated video (the kind you find yourself stopping on as you scroll your page) and Facebook Watch Originals, including a few good enough to be included in Part II of this book. Since its launch in 2017, Facebook has reportedly poured billions of dollars into original programming, which of course is nothing to Facebook.

Typical fare: *Will Smith's Bucket List, Sorry for Your Loss, Red Table Talk, Humans of New York: The Series, Cardi Tries*

Hoopla and Kanopy

Got a library card? Then you can unlock thousands of hours of video content and a whole lot more, absolutely free, thanks to two complementary services offered by public library systems nationwide. Participating libraries load their patrons' Hoopla and Kanopy accounts with credits, allowing them to download a certain number of videos per month. (The credits aren't free — the library pays for every download — so support your local library!)

- ► **Hoopla** is a massive virtual warehouse whose shelves are overflowing with movies, TV shows, audiobooks, eBooks, even comics. Hoopla is jam-packed with British mysteries and Britcoms, including hard-to-find titles.

- ► **Kanopy** is a well-curated collection of world cinema, not unlike the arthouse video store that every city used to have. Kanopy is the only streamer with legendary PBS filmmaker Frederick Wiseman's entire body of work, and a fair amount of The Criterion Collection is also there.

Part II

-

1,000+ Shows, Movies and Specials Recommended by Primetimer

Key to Terms in This Section

(AD) means the show has Audio Description (see page 34).

From our forums: See the Acknowledgements on page *xi*.

Original means the show was produced exclusively for that streaming platform.

S3E2 is shorthand for Season 3, Episode 2.

TV-MA, TV-14, TV-PG, etc. are industry-generated content ratings, explained at **tvguidelines.org**.

🏆 Organizations That Honor TV Shows

AFI: American Film Institute, a public-private foundation created by President Johnson in 1965, honors 10 outstanding films and 10 outstanding TV shows annually.

BAFTA: British Academy of Film and Television Arts. The BAFTA Awards are the UK's Oscars and Emmys rolled into one.

Critics Choice: The Critics Choice Association is an organization of 500 working press in broadcast, print and online entertainment. The Critics Choice Awards are televised in January.

Emmys: Industry awards handed out in comedy, reality and drama by The Television Academy and in documentary by the National Academy of Television Arts & Sciences.

Peabody Awards: This panel of critics and scholars hands out what have been called the Pulitzer Prizes of broadcasting.

SAG: The Screen Actors Guild is the actors' union. Its awards are especially coveted as they are honors from one's peers.

TCA: Television Critics Association is made up of working press covering the entertainment industry. It hands out awards every summer in a private, non-televised ceremony.

3rd Rock from the Sun
TV-PG, 1996–2001
Peacock, Hoopla, PlutoTV, IMDb TV,
6 seasons, 139 episodes
Classic sitcom created by Bonnie and Terry Turner, with John Lithgow, Kristen Johnston, French Stewart, Joseph Gordon-Levitt, Jane Curtin, Simbi Kali, Elmarie Wendel and Wayne Knight.

Space-age farce about aliens studying and mimicking the ways of humans tapped a bottomless font of hilarity, thanks to John Lithgow and company.

Four aliens infiltrate Ohio using their superior intellect, yet never quite grasp the important cultural subtleties of Earthlings. Posing as the Solomon family, they're led by a bombastic, self-assured brainiac named Dick (Lithgow), who aspires to nothing higher than teaching at a backwater college. Lithgow brilliantly oversold every *3rd Rock* scene he was in, and along with his co-stars (including Curtin and Knight as the human love interests) formed a stellar comic ensemble.

▸▸ The show finished strong in Season 6,

including a finale where Elvis Costello (for no reason) pops in to sing "Fly Me to the Moon."

🏆 Emmys for best comedy series (2 wins), Lithgow for best actor in a comedy (6 wins) and Johnston for supporting actress (3 wins)

8-Bit Christmas
PG, 2021
HBO Max original, 1 hr 37 mins (AD)
Movie (family comedy) with Winslow Fegley, Neil Patrick Harris, Steve Zahn and June Diane Raphael.

In the late '80s, a kid goes on an epic quest to acquire a Nintendo Entertainment System for Christmas. From its sly humor to its warm heart to its understanding of how wanting a particular toy can shape your entire holiday season, this film works as a contemporary analogue to *A Christmas Story*.

9-1-1
TV-14, 2018–present
Hulu, 5 seasons, 78 episodes (AD)
Medical drama created by Brad Falchuk, with Angela Bassett, Peter Krause, Oliver Stark, Aisha Hinds, Kenneth Choi, Rockmond Dunbar, Corinne Massiah, Marcanthonee Reis, Jennifer Love Hewitt and Ryan Guzman.

From the creators of *Glee* and *American Horror Story* comes an addictive adrenaline-rush procedural about first responders starring Angela Bassett. Some viewers were reminded of early *ER*, with its formula of crazy emergency calls and soap opera storylines. What it didn't remind viewers of: those first responder shows with *Chicago* in their titles. Bassett, playing a LAPD sergeant married to a LAFD captain (Krause), brought genuine star power to what is too often cookie-cutter, formula-driven TV.

💬 **From our forums:** "I did not realize this

Audio Description Is the Best Thing Hiding on Your TV

Audio Description is an optional feature that allows users to hear the visual details of a program described to them by a narrator. These descriptions are usually inserted unobtrusively during gaps in the program's dialogue. Developed in the 1980s at WGBH in Boston as Descriptive Video Service, AD has been around a long time, but broadcasters and cable networks, with the exception of Turner Classic Movies, did not embrace the technology. That has changed in the Streaming TV era. According to the Audio Description Project of the American Council of the Blind, which maintains a useful resource at **adp.acb.org**, 6,884 described titles were available across Streaming TV platforms in the U.S. as of January 2022.

Though primarily aimed at blind and visually disabled users, AD has grown in popularity, thanks to non-disabled viewers who enjoy the added information, especially with complicated shows featuring busloads of characters and shifting timelines. Millennials who like monitoring more than one screen at a time find that descriptions (as well as captions) help them follow along.

was a Ryan Murphy show. No wonder all the gore." "Pretty fun if extremely preposterous. As long as this talented cast keeps bringing it, this show will continue to work for me."

🏆 Critics Choice Award for best action series

9-1-1: Lone Star

TV-14, 2020–present
Hulu, 3 seasons, 42 episodes (AD)
Medical drama created by Brad Falchuk, with Rob Lowe, Ronen Rubinstein, Sierra Aylina McClain, Jim Parrack, Natacha Karam, Brian Michael Smith, Rafael L. Silva, Julian Works, Brianna Baker and Gina Torres.

Rob Lowe leads this Austin-based spinoff that replicates the pacing and operatics of *9-1-1* but is more woke. Though the action is about calls to 911, it's the other 9/11 — as in, the terrorist attacks — that figures in firefighter Owen Strand's (Lowe) storyline. After rebuilding his firehouse in NYC post-9/11, Strand accepts a similar task in Austin after a firehouse there is tragically destroyed. There he assembles a progressive-as-hell workforce and they get to work answering the bonkers 911 calls that pour in night and day. Somewhere in there he finds time to flirt with an EMS played by Tyler, who's obsessed with finding her missing sister. Don't stop to think too hard about any of this, just go with it.

11.22.63

TV-MA, 2016
Hulu original, 8 episodes
Limited series (historical drama) with James Franco, Sarah Gadon, George MacKay, Chris Cooper, Cherry Jones, Daniel Webber, Kevin J. O'Connor and Lucy Fry.

James Franco plays an English teacher who travels back in time to stop the Kennedy assassination in this affecting adaptation of Stephen King's novel. Aided by strong performances from Cooper as Franco's friend and Fry as Lee Harvey Oswald's wife, this series's appeal comes from its ability to surprise us, whether with a joke about cell phone service in the 1960s or the attachment Franco's character feels for the alternate life he's created in the past. That said, if you tuned in expecting a new take on JFK conspiracy theories, or a fresh take on the spy thriller, you won't be disappointed either.

13 Reasons Why

TV-MA, 2017–2020
Netflix original, 4 seasons, 49 episodes (AD)
Teen drama with Dylan Minnette, Christian Navarro, Alisha Boe, Brandon Flynn, Justin Prentice, Ross Butler, Devin Druid, Amy Hargreaves and Miles Heizer.

Dark, controversial series about a teen who kills herself and leaves 13 audio cassettes behind. Rape culture, school shootings and bullying were among the issues confronted head-on in this massive hit for Netflix. Each tape and episode focused on a different character who affected the departed Hannah (Katherine Langford). It was a great storytelling device but made Liberty High seem like the most violent and horrible school in America. Who needs dystopia?

💬 **From our forums:** "The show reminded me of both *Pretty Little Liars* and *Veronica Mars.*"

▶▶ Don't overlook the companion documentary, *13 Reasons Why: Beyond the Reasons,* in the program's Extras tab, featuring discussion of teen suicide with professionals.

13TH

TV-MA, 2016
Netflix original, 1 hr 40 mins (AD)

Movie (documentary) directed by Ava DuVernay, with Angela Davis, Newt Gingrich, Van Jones, Cory Booker and Bryan Stevenson.

Essential documentary explains how a historic constitutional amendment was tragically abused. As anyone who watched the Daniel Day-Lewis film knows, passage of the 13th Amendment abolishing slavery was Abraham Lincoln's crowning achievement. Less well known is how the amendment was weaponized against the very people it liberated. DuVernay's incisive, Oscar-nominated doc is a fact-based journey from the Civil War to Jim Crow to what's been called "the new Jim Crow" — mass incarceration for profit. She interviews both liberal and conservative critics of the system.

▸▸ Pairs well with *Crime + Punishment*

🏆 3 Critics Choice awards, including best doc feature and director (DuVernay), Oscar nominee for best documentary

16 And Recovering
TV-14, 2020–present
Paramount+, 4 episodes
Docuseries directed by Steve Liss.

Students battling addiction to alcohol and opioids attend a special high school where they can be themselves and get better. One of the best reality shows to come out of the MTV factory in years, *16 And Recovering* follows students and faculty at Northshore Recovery High School in Beverly, Mass., which gave director Liss tremendous access. This community of addicts based on mutual respect is not only a terrific educational environment but makes for exceptional television. Each episode focuses on a few students and ends with title cards describing what happened to them since filming concluded. The vulnerability of everyone sharing their stories on camera allows viewers an honest look at addiction, one that runs counter to the usual stereotypes.

24
TV-14, 2001–2010
Hulu, IMDb TV, 8 seasons, 195 episodes
Action thriller with Kiefer Sutherland, Mary Lynn Rajskub, Carlos Bernard, Dennis Haysbert and Elisha Cuthbert.

One of the best thrillers ever made for television, *24* made Kiefer Sutherland's Jack Bauer an enduring action hero. Part of the early wave of innovative dramas that included *The Sopranos* and *CSI*, *24* took two overdone TV genres — the family drama and the political thriller — and crashed them together, creating something new and exciting. Every season took place in "real time," with 24 episodes (12 in Season 9) covering a single adrenaline-filled day that had Jack Bauer fighting bad guys, defusing bombs and in the end, saving America.

▸▸ Season 5, the year *24* won an Emmy for best drama, is a highlight. It begins with a shocking assassination and ends with Bauer taking on Charles Logan (Gregory Itzin), maybe the most diabolical person that a Hollywood screenwriter could imagine winning the presidency in 2006.

🏆 TCA Award for program of the year

30 Rock
TV-14, 2006–2013
Peacock, Netflix, 7 seasons,
138 episodes (AD)
Workplace comedy created by Tina Fey, with Tina Fey, Alec Baldwin, Jane Krakowski, Tracy Morgan, Jack McBrayer, Scott Adsit and Judah Friedlander.

Tina Fey's pioneering comedy brought the rapid-fire pace of a cartoon to a workplace sitcom filled with appealingly quirky characters. Set at a sketch comedy program not unlike *SNL*, where Fey was head writer, *30 Rock* was single-camera at a time when most sitcoms were still filmed in front of audiences. It's beloved for Liz Lemon's (Fey) banter with her overconfident corporate boss Jack Donaghy (Baldwin), strong supporting characters like Kenneth the page (McBrayer), and an endless supply of TV-insider jokes that will have you googling such things as "MILF Island" and "Queen of Jordan."

▸▸ Four episodes, pulled from streaming platforms in 2020, showed characters played by Jon Hamm and Jane Krakowski in blackface (S3E2, S5E4, S4E10, S6E19).

🏆 Emmy for best comedy series (3 wins)

72 Hours
TV-14, 2013
IMDb TV, 9 episodes
Reality competition with R. Brandon Johnson.

It's *The Amazing Race* but with actual character development and the interesting dynamic of strangers working together. Three teams of three strangers have 72 hours to navigate spectacular terrain, and the first to reach a briefcase wins $100,000. Though not as innovative or spectacularly shot, it is better-paced and more absorbing than other *Amazing Race* wannabes.

76 Days
PG-13, 2020
Paramount+, 1 hr 33 mins
Movie (documentary) directed by Weixi Chin and Hao Wu.

Medical workers and patients grapple with the unknown during the first wave of the COVID-19 outbreak in Wuhan, China. Regardless of what theory you accept about the origins of the novel coronavirus, clearly Wuhan factored in some way — which is what makes this unflinching and intimate film about the outbreak there of COVID-19 such a valuable document of that time before the world knew it had a pandemic on its hands.

🏆 Peabody Award

100 Foot Wave
TV-14, 2021
HBO Max, 7 episodes (AD)
Docuseries with Garrett McNamara, Nicole McNamara, Andrew Cotton and Laird Hamilton.

A surfing legend goes looking for the most terrifying ride he can find off the coast of Portugal. In 2010 Garrett McNamara, whose derring-do and ingenuity allowed him to take on enormous waves no surfer had attempted before, moved to the seaside town of Nazaré, Portugal. He was seeking the largest and, it need hardly be said, deadliest wave ever. This docuseries introduces you to a cast of entertaining and compelling characters in a maritime quest of Melvillean proportions.

The 100
TV-14, 2014–2020
Netflix, 7 seasons, 100 episodes
Sci-fi drama with Eliza Taylor, Marie Avgeropoulos, Bob Morley, Lindsey Morgan, Richard Harmon, Paige Turco, Henry Ian Cusick, Christopher Larkin, Jarod Joseph and Isaiah Washington.

Decades after nuclear war forces the remnants of humanity to live in a spaceship circling the planet, 100 juvenile delinquents are sent back to Earth to see if it's habitable again. Based on the YA novels by Kass Morgan, this show developed for the CW network feels a lot like *Lost* with teenage protagonists. Though fans loved to complain about plot holes and uneven scripts, the show's appealing young cast and willingness to go to unexpected places kept them tuning in for 7 seasons.

🗨 **From our forums:** "I still can't believe how much I enjoy this show despite how much nitpicking is available, though it's

For shows sorted by streaming platform, see page 381.

probably the nitpicking that makes it so enjoyable."

1883
TV-MA, 2021–present
Paramount+ original, 10 episodes (AD)
Historical drama created by Taylor Sheridan, with Sam Elliott, Tim McGraw, Faith Hill, Isabel May, LaMonica Garrett, Marc Rissmann, Eric Nelsen, James Landry Hébert and Billy Bob Thornton.

Well-cast prequel to the blockbuster series *Yellowstone* explores how the Dutton family came to Montana and built their empire. From the pen of *Yellowstone* creator Sheridan comes this fine addition to the Dutton mythology. Everything you like about the original is here: senseless violence, brutal ethical choices, cinema-quality visuals and a certain tender-heartedness beneath the savagery. Dutton is played by music superstar McGraw in his biggest role to date, alongside real-life wife Hill. It won't take long for fans to see bits of John Dutton's personality in the ancestor. The Duttons daughter Elsa (May) adds a level of danger that only a teenage girl can. But the two-episode origin story that opens *1883* is carried by Elliott, who sets the strong emotional tone that's as crucial to Sheridan's stories as unfettered aggression and endless ambition.

1922
TV-MA, 2017
Netflix original, 1 hr 42 mins (AD)
Movie (horror) with Thomas Jane, Molly Parker, Dylan Schmid, Neal McDonough and Brian d'Arcy James.

A farmer wants to kill his wife and convinces his son to help, but there are unintended consequences. Rock-solid adaptation of a Stephen King novella with excellent performances.

1971: The Year That Music Changed Everything
TV-MA, 2021
Apple TV+ original, 8 episodes (AD)
Docuseries created by Asif Kapadia, with Elton John, Graham Nash, Ringo Starr, Linda Ronstadt, Chrissie Hynde and Mick Jagger.

Intelligent docuseries assesses how popular musicians helped Americans pivot after the devastating aftermath of the 1960s. Marvin Gaye, Aretha Franklin, David Bowie, Bob Marley, Joni Mitchell, Lou Reed, the Staple Singers and The Who are just some of the artists who mark 1971 as a very special year. Their personal transformations, in turn, changed America. You'll see how in this masterwork that interweaves archival video with a host of reminiscences and a score that won't quit.

The A Word
TV-MA, 2016–present
Prime Video, 3 seasons, 18 episodes
Drama with Max Vento, Lee Ingleby, Christopher Eccleston, Molly Wright, Pooky Quesnel, Morven Christie, Leon Harrop, Greg McHugh, Vinette Robinson and Matt Greenwood.

A British family's life is upended after their youngest member is diagnosed with autism. Created by Peter Bowker, a former teacher who worked with children with learning disabilities, *The A Word* has been praised for its authenticity as it examines the effects of an autism diagnosis on a multigenerational, less-than-perfect family.

💬 **From our forums:** "As the mother of a son on the spectrum I love the way the issue is handled. I can identify with so much of the roller coaster life." "The characters did a lot of changing in 6 episodes."

▶▶ The spinoff *Ralph and Katie* was commissioned by the BBC in 2020.

A.P. Bio

TV-14, 2018–2021
Peacock original, 4 seasons,
42 episodes (AD)
Comedy with Glenn Howerton, Patton Oswalt, Paula Pell, Lyric Lewis, Mary Sohn, Jean Villepique, Eddie Leavy, Jacob Houston, Aparna Brielle and Nick Peine.

Glenn Howerton plays a failed professor now teaching high school in this sitcom where the humiliations of teenagerdom and teaching converge. After Jack Griffin (Howerton) loses his dream job at Harvard, he sulks back to Toledo to live in his dead mother's house and teach A.P. biology at the local high school, where he's confronted by awkward students and an absurdly inept principal (Oswalt). Teen angst meets *Community* in this comedy that is sharp and cynical but rarely mean.

🐟 **From our forums:** "Jack is an awful person but there's something funny about the whole setup. They're giving the kids good one-liners, too."

▶▶ The show's first 2 seasons aired on NBC before making the move to Peacock for its third and fourth seasons.

Abacus: Small Enough to Jail

Not Rated, 2017
PBS Passport, Hoopla, Kanopy,
1 hr 28 mins
Movie (documentary) directed by Steve James.

Jaw-dropping doc dramatically recounts the federal government's sole criminal case after the financial meltdown of 2008 — and it was against a small bank run by Chinese immigrants. Sensing an open-and-shut case, Manhattan district prosecutor Cy Vance went after the country's 2,531st largest bank for mortgage fraud. Boy, did he mess with the wrong people. James (*Hoop Dreams*) masterfully weaves historical details about the mortgage crisis into this gripping legal drama about the bank's costly 5-year legal battle, all but overlooked by the media in the nation's media capital.

🏆 Critics Choice Award for best political documentary

Abbott Elementary

TV-PG, 2022
Hulu, 13 episodes (AD)
Sitcom created by Quinta Brunson, with Quinta Brunson, Tyler James Williams, Janelle James, Lisa Ann Walter, Chris Perfetti and Sheryl Lee Ralph.

Network TV's next great mockumentary series is set at an inner-city school where an idealistic teacher is learning the hardest lesson of all — survival. Brunson not only plays the "I love teaching!" lead Mrs. Teagues, she created *Abbott Elementary*, which doubles as a not-always-lighthearted indictment of an underfunded public education system. That medicine goes down a lot easier thanks to mile-a-minute comedy, easily identifiable characters like the woke white teacher and the grizzled veteran educator, and storytelling built off real-life stories of teachers, for whom juggling kids, bureaucrats and parents is all in a day's work.

Acapulco

TV-14, 2021–present
Apple TV+ original, 10 episodes (AD)
Comedy with Enrique Arrizon, Fernando Carsa, Damián Alcázar, Camila Perez, Vanessa Bauche, Raphael Alejandro, Chord Overstreet and Eugenio Derbez.

In 1984, a young go-getter working at a luxury resort in Mexico slowly moves up in the world. Arrizon shines at the center of this loopy, loving comedy, bouncing between his family, his co-workers, and the stream of resort guests. It's a refreshing lark filled with beautiful vacation scenery to boot.

Accused: Guilty or Innocent
TV-14, 2020–present
Discovery+, Hulu, 7 episodes
True crime directed by Matt Kennedy.

Unusual docuseries tells stories of crime from the perspective of the accused. Each episode follows a defense team as it prepares to go to court to exonerate their client, who stands accused of a crime ranging from aggravated assault to vehicular manslaughter to attempted murder. Crime scenes are reinvestigated and courtroom tactics are frankly discussed (like whether the client should testify and needs "toughening up" for what's coming). It's very effective, sometimes even shocking.

▶▶ Pairs well with *I Am A Killer*

The Act
TV-MA, 2019
Hulu original, 8 episodes (AD)
Limited series (drama) with Patricia Arquette, Joey King, AnnaSophia Robb, Chloë Sevigny, Calum Worthy and Denitra Isler.

Patricia Arquette is creepily effective as a manipulative mom who forces her child to feign mental illness in this dramatization of a true-crime case. She plays Dee Dee Blanchard, who forced her young child Gypsy Rose to feign a debilitating illness. Later, Gypsy (played as an adult by Joey King) gets her revenge. This series brings humanity to both mother and daughter that true-crime accounts largely leave out.

🗨 **From our forums:** "I was hoping to find another limited series to get into after watching *Dirty John*, and voilà! Joey and Patricia are both very good in this."

🏆 Emmy for best supporting actress in a limited series (Arquette)

Adventure Time
TV-PG, 2010–2018
Hulu, HBO Max, 10 seasons, 279 episodes

Animated comedy with John DiMaggio, Jeremy Shada, Tom Kenny and Hynden Walch.

Landmark cartoon follows a boy named Finn and his adopted brother Jake (who's also a dog with magical powers) in weird, wonderful escapades. One of those kid shows that's really for grownups, *Adventure Time* cleverly imparts corny ideals like cooperation and kindness through silly, surreal escapades.

▶▶ Spawned four new hour-long HBO Max specials in 2020, collectively titled *Adventure Time: Distant Lands*, with a second spinoff (*Adventure Time: Fionna and Cake*) announced by HBO Max in 2021.

🏆 Emmy Awards for best short-form animated program and individual achievement in animation

After Life
TV-MA, 2019–2022
Netflix original, 3 seasons,
18 episodes (AD)
Dark comedy created by Ricky Gervais, with Ricky Gervais, Tom Basden, Tony Way, David Bradley, Ashley Jensen, Penelope Wilton, Diane Morgan, Kerry Godliman, Paul Kaye and Mandeep Dhillon.

Ricky Gervais stars in this deep, dark yet remarkably nuanced and tender examination of death and the hereafter. Tony (Gervais) has just lost his wife to cancer. His father has dementia and keeps asking where Lisa is. To cope, Tony watches the video diaries that Lisa left behind and drinks heavily. Doesn't sound like laugh-a-minute Ricky from *Extras* or *The Office*, does it? But as he plods through his dark period, Tony finds ways to get on, making new friends and having small, touching revelations about loss and grieving.

🗨 **From our forums:** "It covered the full range of emotions and though so much was tragically sad, it was also funny and I actually laughed out loud."

▶▶ Will there be a fourth season? Gervais previously ruled it out, but ahead of the show's third season (which Netflix announced as the last), he suggested he might be willing to return.

Agents of Chaos

TV-MA, 2020
HBO Max, 3 hrs 56 mins (AD)
Movie (documentary) directed by Alex Gibney, with Andrew Weissman, Andrew McCabe, John Brennan, Carter Page and Felix Sater.

Alex Gibney's fast-paced and slickly produced rewind of the 2016 presidential campaign advances a paranoid scenario that Russian agents helped elect Donald Trump. Gibney, in his familiar triple role as narrator, interviewer and director, has assembled an impressive array of talking heads, archival video and theories about what role, if any, Russia played in Trump's election. The case to be made is murky and convoluted at best, as Gibney himself admits, and subsequent revelations about the Democratic Party's promotion of the Russia-Trump connection cast further doubt on the scheme. If nothing else, this is an entertaining if overlong look into the army of cyber-ops troublemakers working for Vladimir Putin and his cronies.

Alex Rider

TV-14, 2020–present
IMDB TV original, 2 seasons, 16 episodes
Action drama with Otto Farrant, Vicky McClure, Ace Bhatti, Stephen Dillane, Ronke Adekoluejo, Brenock O'Connor, Nyasha Hatendi, Haluk Bilginer, Thomas Levin and Ana Ularu.

A teenager recruited to be a British secret agent makes for an appealing take on the spy genre. Based on Anthony Horowitz's young adult novels, this is —

like so much good YA fare — something completely relatable and enjoyable to adult viewers. The show puts Alex (Farrant) and his multicultural group of friends into realistic and quite modern situations while reminding us from time to time that they are, after all, teenagers.

🗨 **From our forums:** "I'm enjoying this despite always figuring things out early on."

Ali Wong: Baby Cobra

TV-MA, 2016
Netflix original, 1 hr
Comedy special with Ali Wong.

Wong broke into the mainstream with this killer set that she filmed while 7 months pregnant. This unrepentant TMI monologue from Wong, then known mostly as a writer on *Fresh Off the Boat*, earned her comparisons to Louis C.K. and Aziz Ansari that later proved unfortunate — but they weren't wrong. Wong's contrariness and willingness to go there are qualities we both value and vilify in our comedians.

Alias

TV-14, 2001–2006
Prime Video, 5 seasons, 105 episodes
Action drama created by J.J. Abrams, with Jennifer Garner, Ron Rifkin, Victor Garber, Carl Lumbly, Kevin Weisman, Michael Vartan, Greg Grunberg, Merrin Dungey and Bradley Cooper.

In the series that made her a star, Jennifer Garner plays Sidney Bristow, who's recruited out of college to spy for a shadowy syndicate. Created by J.J. Abrams before he made *Lost* and *Fringe*, the series already shows his confidence in a signature high-octane style. Garner underwent intense physical and mental training for the role and it showed from the pilot episode, where she pulled off a daring caper disguised in a vibrant red wig.

For shows sorted by streaming platform, see page 381.

🗨 **From our forums:** "Just went through all of it. Did it have its ups and downs? Sure. Show me a long-term series that doesn't. The family dynamic was and still is one of the most compelling on television."

🏆 SAG Award for best actress in a drama (Garner)

Alias Grace
TV-MA, 2017
Netflix original, 6 episodes (AD)
Limited series (historical drama) created by Mary Harron and Sarah Polley, with Sarah Gadon, Anna Paquin, Edward Holcroft, Zachary Levi, Rebecca Liddiard, Kerr Logan, David Cronenberg and Paul Gross.

Enjoyably chilling adaptation of Margaret Atwood's historical novel, based on a brutal frontier murder in 1840s Canada. Did Grace Marks (Gadon) kill her former employers, or was she just in the wrong place when they died? Was she insane? Could mid-19th-century hypnotism make her "knowable" to the men who would decide her fate? As a limited series, Atwood's scrupulously researched story offers a suspenseful retelling but no easy answers. And it underscores, as the author does in *The Handmaid's Tale* and other works, how much sway men have always had over the lives of women.

🗨 **From our forums:** "It's a glorious book. And I'm thrilled with the adaptation and especially Sarah Gadon. A Canadian story done in a way that stands up next to any American or British prestige TV."

The Alienist
TV-MA, 2018–2020
HBO Max, 2 seasons, 18 episodes (AD)
Crime drama with Daniel Brühl, Luke Evans, Dakota Fanning, Douglas Smith, Robert Wisdom, Matthew Shear, Ted Levine and Martin McCreadie.

Caleb Carr's blockbuster novels about 19th-century detectives become a well-acted period police procedural. This visually striking, often gory series brings to life the early history of profiling against the backdrop of seedy New York in the 1800s. *The Alienist* creates a fascinating tension between depraved criminals and investigators who are just learning to understand them.

🗨 **From our forums:** "I'm glad I stuck around after the premiere which I confess to not loving."

All American
TV-14, 2018–present
Netflix, 4 seasons, 71 episodes (AD)
Drama with Daniel Ezra, Taye Diggs, Samantha Logan, Michael Evans Behling, Bre-Z, Greta Onieogou, Cody Christian, Karimah Westbrook and Monet Mazur.

Taye Diggs and Daniel Ezra light up the screen in this richly drawn teen drama inspired by the life of NFL player Spencer Paysinger. Spencer (Ezra) is a football star at Crenshaw High School in inner-city L.A. when he's recruited by Billy Baker (Diggs), a coach at Beverly Hills High. The Black hopeful arriving at the lily-white school is a familiar premise, yet the storylines aren't so predictable and the stakes are satisfyingly high. All of the main characters are appealing, including Coop (Bre-Z), Spencer's out lesbian friend at Crenshaw, who's left to fend for herself with him gone.

🗨 **From our forums:** "As someone who is not at all into football but loved *Friday Night Lights*, I'm in!" "I thought it was solid, though you can see the tropes coming a mile away. I was pleasantly surprised at the number of hot guys present. Or maybe I shouldn't have been, since it's a CW show."

▶▶ S3E17 served as a backdoor pilot for the spinoff series *All American: Homecoming*.

All Creatures Great and Small
TV-PG, 2020–present
PBS Passport, 2 seasons,
14 episodes (AD)
Historical drama with Nicholas Ralph, Anna Madeley, Samuel West, Rachel Shenton, Callum Woodhouse, Imogen Clawson and Matthew Lewis.

Remake of the 1978 PBS series about an English country vet updates James Herriot's story but remains sweet and humane. In 1937 England, after young Herriot (Ralph) is hired on in a small Yorkshire town by an eccentric veterinarian, he has numerous memorable encounters with his animal patients and human neighbors. Based on Herriot's fictionalized account of his years in practice, this version is considered edgier than the original (which aired 1978–1990). Yet everyone here is still more charming and kind-hearted than most people on TV these days, making this show a soothing liniment in a world of pain.

▶▶ Two Christmas specials have also been produced.

All or Nothing: Manchester City
TV-PG, 2018
Prime Video original, 8 episodes (AD)
Docuseries with Ben Kingsley, Pep Guardiola, Mikel Arteta, Vincent Kompany, Raheem Sterling, Sergio Agüero and Kevin De Bruyne.

Go behind the scenes with the greatest coach in the world's biggest sport as his club relentlessly pursues another title. For *Ted Lasso* fans who might be interested in seeing how an actual English football coach operates, you can't do better than Pep Guardiola. The master motivator has made Manchester City a perennial Premier League champion and this series, filmed during City's remarkable 2017–18 season, shows how.

▶▶ A spinoff of the *All or Nothing* anthology series produced by NFL Films that focuses on the *other* kind of football.

Allen v. Farrow
TV-MA, 2021
HBO Max, 5 episodes (AD)
Docuseries created by Kirby Dick, Amy Ziering and Amy Herdy, with Dylan Farrow, Ronan Farrow, Mia Farrow, Soon-Yi Previn, Carly Simon, Gloria Steinem and Fletcher Previn.

Get uncomfortably close to Woody Allen, Mia Farrow and her children during the time that Allen is said to have molested Dylan Farrow. Like recent projects on the predations of R. Kelly and Jeffrey Epstein, this docuseries allows the public to hear, for the first time, the in-depth testimony of a survivor who has lived most of her life at the center of a story she couldn't control. Though well-made and affecting, *Allen v. Farrow* has been criticized for being a heavily skewed brief for Allen's accusers.

Ally McBeal
TV-PG, 1997–2002
Hulu, 5 seasons, 112 episodes
Comedy-drama created by David E. Kelley, with Calista Flockhart, Greg Germann, Jane Krakowski, Vonda Shepard, Peter MacNicol, Lisa Nicole Carson, Portia de Rossi, Lucy Liu and Courtney Thorne-Smith.

A sensation when it debuted in 1997, David E. Kelley's sexy lawyer show makes for a deeply fascinating rewatch. Strong ratings — and a national uproar — greeted this show starring Flockhart as a female lawyer who was falling apart over a man and practiced law in very short miniskirts. Perhaps *Ally McBeal* killed feminism, or at least pressed pause on it. But the show also gave us a dancing baby, launched the TV careers of Krakowski, de Rossi and Liu, brought musical performances back to TV and helped network comedy break free of the stale sitcom format.

🏆 Emmy for best comedy series, SAG Award for best comedy ensemble

Alpha House

TV-MA, 2013–2014
Prime Video original, 2 seasons, 21 episodes
Satirical comedy created by Garry Trudeau, with John Goodman, Clark Johnson, Matt Malloy and Mark Consuelos.

Long-forgotten political comedy from "Doonesbury" creator Garry Trudeau falls somewhere between the madcap satire of *Veep* and the chilling realism of *House of Cards*. Inspired by a group of real-life U.S. senators who shared a D.C. crash pad, *Alpha House* follows four Republican senators and their respective staffs as the rise of the Tea Party puts their political futures in jeopardy. And despite the late-Obama-years topicality of the jokes, episodes of *Alpha House* do well in rewatch. In one Season 2 scene, a senator played by Janel Moloney pulls out a gun inside the Capitol, forcing a lockdown of the building. Jokes like that cut closer to the bone today.

▶▶ Chuck Schumer, Elizabeth Warren and John McCain are just a few of the politicians and media types who make winking cameos in the show.

Altered Carbon

TV-MA, 2018–2020
Netflix original, 2 seasons, 18 episodes (AD)
Sci-fi drama with Joel Kinnaman, Anthony Mackie, Renée Elise Goldsberry, James Purefoy, Martha Higareda, Chris Conner, Ato Essandoh, Trieu Tran, Simone Missick and Dina Shihabi.

Stylish alt-future allegory imagines that the rich can avoid death by having their thoughts and memories transferred to another body. Based on the cyberpunk novel by Richard T. Morgan and reportedly more expensive to make than *Game of Thrones*, *Altered Carbon* revolves around Tak Kovacs, a 24th-century political prisoner who's given his freedom in order to solve a murder. Along the way the viewer is expected to figure out the rules that govern this world that are both strange (transferable memories) and familiar (social inequality).

💬 **From our forums:** "Weird series. I enjoyed it, but it took a few episodes to find its footing. This might have been one of the few Netflix shows where it wouldn't have hurt to have 12 or 13 episodes per season."

▶▶ The role of Tak was played by Kinnaman in Season 1 and Mackie in Season 2 (which was set 30 years later).

Always Be My Maybe

PG-13, 2019
Netflix original, 1 hr 41 mins (AD)
Movie (romantic comedy) with Ali Wong, Randall Park, James Saito, Michelle Buteau, Daniel Dae Kim and Keanu Reeves.

Randall Park and Ali Wong play childhood friends who reconnect and discover they *might* have feelings for each other. This romcom got stellar reviews — always a good sign that it's safe for viewing by a wider audience. The chemistry between the two leads is undeniable and there's lots of wry social commentary baked inside the romantic story.

The Amber Ruffin Show

TV-14, 2020–present
Peacock original, 30 mins
Sketch comedy with Amber Ruffin and Tarik Davis.

Her critically acclaimed comedy show is the first late-night hit of the streaming-TV era. Launched in the heart of the pandemic, this budget effort from a writer on *Late Night With Seth Meyers* quickly found an audience with its lively host and sharp takes on race and politics. Ruffin's banter with Davis is like listening to two old friends who are on the same comic wavelength. Comedy bits are sophisticated amalgams of pop-culture critique and slapstick and often include Ruffin's various forays into song, which are all the more endearing because she's not the most tuneful performer and couldn't care less.

Amend: The Fight for America

TV-MA, 2021
Netflix original, 6 episodes (AD)
Docuseries directed by Ava DuVernay, with Will Smith, Bryan Stevenson, Larry Wilmore, Samira Wiley, Mahershala Ali, Bobby Cannavale, Laverne Cox, Graham Greene, Randall Park and Lena Waithe.

Will Smith hosts this vital and entertaining civics lesson that explains the origins of the 14th Amendment to the U.S. Constitution and why it's more important — and contested — than ever. Watch this after Netflix's *13TH*, DuVernay's film explaining how the amendment ending slavery in the U.S. led to mass incarceration. *Amend* focuses on the so-called citizenship amendment, and shows how influential it is today, impacting court cases on many hot-button issues including gay marriage and voting rights. The use of celebrities dramatically reciting the words of Frederick Douglass and other defenders of freedom is a nice touch.

America to Me

TV-14, 2018
Starz original, 10 episodes
Docuseries directed by Steve James, Bing Liu, Rebecca Parrish and Kevin Shaw.

A moving and at times troubling look into life at a public high school where Black and white students have very different experiences. Located less than a mile from the West Side of Chicago, Oak Park-River Forest High School has a diverse student body that makes it a natural place to study, up-close, the differences between how White and Black kids treat each other, and how they're treated by staff and teachers. Everyone here speaks with remarkable honesty about the challenges that face them. The vulnerability in *America to Me* is unflinching and admirable, and it comes from everyone from school security guards to parents, teachers to administrators. Narrated by producer-director Steve James, who also directed the classic *Hoop Dreams*.

America's Got Talent

TV-PG, 2006–present
Peacock, Hulu, 16 seasons, 409 episodes
Reality competition created by Simon Cowell, Jason Raff and Ken Warwick, with Simon Cowell, Howie Mandel, Heidi Klum, Terry Crews and Sofia Vergara.

Years of tweaking with the format, host and judges has produced the ultimate short-attention-span show. Though known as summer fare, *AGT* is actually one of the most-watched network shows any time of the year. Viewers who long ago tuned it out may be pleasantly surprised to see what it's become: an uplifting, slickly-produced showcase of genuine talent, not just delusional amateurs who need a truth bomb dropped on them by Simon Cowell. *AGT* is as summer as oldies radio and weak beer, with ventriloquists to boot.

America's Next Top Model

TV-PG, 2003–2018
Hulu, Prime Video, Netflix, 24 seasons, 318 episodes

For shows sorted by streaming platform, see page 381.

Reality competition with Tyra Banks, J. Alexander, Jay Manuel, Nigel Barker, Twiggy, Janice Dickinson and André Leon Talley.

A staple of early competition shows from the '00s, *Top Model* was noted for almost constant drama on- and off-camera and for glamorizing ideals of beauty and desirability that have since fallen out of fashion. Supermodel Tyra Banks dreamed up this contest, an *American Idol* of modeling where the winner of each cycle got a contract and a head start in a notoriously fickle industry. Perhaps reflecting that volatility, the show churned through judges (17 of them in 23 cycles, many of them fired by Banks).

▶▶ Start with Season 2, when *Top Model* began to gather buzz with some sharply defined hopefuls and a nude photo shoot (edited for network TV, of course).

The American Barbecue Showdown

TV-G, 2020–present
Netflix original, 8 episodes (AD)

Reality competition with Melissa Cookston, Kevin Bludso, Rutledge Wood and Lyric Lewis.

Hyper-focused cooking competition where contestants grill chicken, smoke brisket and pull pork is a fitting, all-American response to *The Great British Baking Show*. Stocked with the usual eccentric contestants (like one who declares himself a "grill-billy"), this is a serious show about a surprisingly tricky culinary art that rewards patience. A standout is judge Melissa Cookston, a trailblazing BBQ pitmaster who drawls out withering lines but isn't nasty so much as tough; her expertise adds heft to challenges.

▶▶ The series was renewed for a second season in late 2021.

American Crime

TV-14, 2016
Hulu, 10 episodes

Drama anthology series created by John Ridley, with Felicity Huffman, Regina King, Timothy Hutton, Richard Cabral, Elvis Nolasco, Lili Taylor, Benito Martinez, Brent Anderson, Connor Jessup and Shane Jacobsen.

Not to be confused with *American Crime Story*, this unjustly overlooked anthology series from John Ridley explored hot-button topics through patient, nuanced season-long arcs. Utilizing a fine company of actors in different storylines each season, Ridley took on racism, the criminal justice system, immigration and other issues — and yet it never felt like an issues-driven show. Though Season 1, with its *Crash*-like mix of race and crime, was less compelling, the show really shined in its last 2 seasons on ABC (which, to its credit, kept the low-rated show going that long).

▶▶ Season 2 featured King in an extraordinary story about gender, privilege and assault at a private school. Season 3, set among migrant workers in the South, examined the hidden costs of our low-price economy.

🏆 Emmy for best actress in a limited series (King)

American Crime Story

TV-MA, 2016–present
Netflix, 10 episodes

Limited series (drama) created by Ryan Murphy, with Sarah Paulson, Courtney B. Vance, Sterling K. Brown, Cuba Gooding Jr., David Schwimmer, John Travolta, Nathan Lane, Ricky Martin, Darren Criss and Edgar Ramírez.

This true-crime anthology from Ryan Murphy launched with two dynamite seasons on the O.J. Simpson case and the Gianni Versace murder. Productions like this used to be called docudramas, but that doesn't do justice to the quality of the *American Crime Story* series, which have attracted top talent and won television's most coveted prizes.

▶▶ *Season 1:* The enduring appeal of the O.J. Simpson case intersected so many of the country's obsessions — sports, sex, gossip, race, wealth, true-crime. Tracking the case from the night of the crime through the trial's media-cultural aftermath, *ACS* completely reframes the Simpson story, casting L.A. County prosecutor Marcia Clark (Paulson), often portrayed as a media villain, as a doomed, chain-smoking hero.

▶▶ *Season 2:* The script is flipped in this retelling of the 1997 crime spree that ended in the murder of Versace by Andrew Cunanan (Criss). Employing a *Rashomon*-like format, in which each episode starts just before the events in the previous episode, *ACS* reframes the high-profile killing, not as a lurid gay-on-gay crime but as a shattering portrait on the toxicity of American homophobia. This season is a big, loud, sometimes campy TV extravaganza with something to say.

▶▶ *ACS: Impeachment*, which relived the trial of President Bill Clinton, was not as well received as the first 2 seasons.

🏆 Emmy for best limited series (2 wins)

American Experience: The Voice of Freedom
TV-G, 2021
PBS Passport, 1 hr 40 mins
Movie (documentary) with Marian Anderson and Renée Elise Goldsberry.

Powerful reevaluation of Marian Anderson — the Black singer known for her 1939 concert on the steps of the Lincoln Memorial — puts her career in the overall context of systemic racism. Rob Rapley's superb documentary amplifies the imposing cultural barriers that Anderson nimbly scaled as she became a world-class Black contralto

and early warrior in the battle for civil rights. Scholars, musicians and historians illuminate what it must have felt like to be an invisible Black woman demanding to be seen and heard. The words of Anderson herself, taken from her memoir and spoken by *Hamilton* star Goldsberry, will cut you to the quick.

American Factory
PG-13, 2019
Netflix original, 1 hr 50 mins (AD)
Movie (documentary) directed by Steven Bognar and Julia Reichert, with Cao Dewang.

Vital documentary about the Chinese takeover of an American auto plant won an Academy Award for the Obamas. For their first Netflix project, Barack and Michelle Obama signed onto *American Factory*, about a shuttered windshield factory in Ohio that is bought and reopened by a Chinese billionaire. Just like that, thousands of former workers have jobs again, though not exactly at their old union wages and with new bosses from China, who can sing the corporate anthem by heart. As the two cultures inevitably clash, *American Factory* is empathetic and fair-minded toward everyone without being heavy-handed or humorless.

🏆 Oscar for best documentary feature

American Gods
TV-MA, 2017–2021
Starz original, 3 seasons, 26 episodes
Fantasy drama created by Bryan Fuller, with Ricky Whittle, Ian McShane, Emily Browning, Yetide Badaki, Bruce Langley, Omid Abtahi, Crispin Glover, Demore Barnes, Gillian Anderson and Pablo Schreiber.

Gillian Anderson and Ian McShane headline this well-received adaptation of the Neil Gaiman novel about mythological gods dwelling among us. In this inventive adaptation from

Fuller (*Pushing Daisies*), an ex-con named Shadow Moon (Whittle) becomes bodyguard to an ancient god and is pulled into the conflict between the O.G. deities and their newer rivals, who roam the earth in modern disguises. As you'd expect from a Gaiman tale, there's a lot to chew on here — but McShane, as he did on *Deadwood*, makes it go down easier, bringing humor and guile to his role as a Norse god. Anderson is well-cast as a new god, Media, who first appears as a character inserted into an episode of *I Love Lucy*. Media would be delighted if all the old gods perished.

American Horror Story
TV-MA, 2012–2013
Prime Video, Netflix, Hulu, 10 seasons, 113 episodes (AD)
Anthology series (horror) created by Ryan Murphy and Brad Falchuk, with Sarah Paulson, Jessica Lange, Chloë Sevigny, Zachary Quinto, James Cromwell, Lily Rabe, Emma Roberts and Frances Conroy.

Ryan Murphy and Brad Falchuk developed this over-the-top tribute to the horror genre where anything could happen at any time. After a bumpy first season, the *AHS* anthology found its voice in Season 2, using outsized performances from its stars to balance its reliance on horror tropes and occasional runaway-train feel.

▸▸ *Season 3: Coven*. A school for witches in New Orleans is the setting for this season of *AHS*, with power struggles inside the coven that are complicated by an ageless voodoo priestess and a plantation mistress who has recently emerged from her grave. High-concept camp at its best, this installment of Ryan Murphy's anthology series is also its most female-centric. There are kicky performances from a murderers' row of

actresses including Lange, Bassett, Bates, Conroy and LuPone.

🏆 Emmys for supporting actor (Cromwell), best actress (Lange) and supporting actress (Bates) in a miniseries or movie

American Idol
TV-PG, 2002–present
Hulu, 20 seasons, 659 episodes
Reality competition with Ryan Seacrest, Lionel Richie, Katy Perry and Luke Bryan.

One of the earliest competition shows, its meteoric success destroyed the idols that music and TV industry executives had built to their ideas of success. It was one of the great debates of the new millennium: Why couldn't people get enough of *American Idol*? Was it the opportunity for anyone to show up at an audition and be discovered? Was it the audience voting? Was it Simon Cowell? It was all that, plus the talent, plus the novel notion that consumers, rather than industry people, should choose their stars. The live broadcasts produced, at the show's white-hot peak, some truly electric hours of television, and the competition has launched more than 300 singing and acting careers.

▸▸ Rights issues have sadly kept the show's first 15 seasons off streaming.
🏆 9 Emmys

American Murder: The Family Next Door
TV-MA, 2020
Netflix original, 1 hr 22 mins (AD)
Movie (true crime) directed by Jenny Popplewell.

Harrowing account of the 2018 murder of Shannan Watts and her two daughters goes beyond the genre to explore the dual identities we keep online and IRL. Director Popplewell shepherds the film with a careful hand, as she and editor

Simon Barker work with "found footage," using home movies, text messages and social media posts, eschewing formulaic talking-head interviews. The result is a narrative that's more intimate but also harder to watch as Shannan's marriage unravels and her murder approaches.

▶▶ In November 2020, Netflix said *American Murder: The Family Next Door* had been viewed by 52 million households in its first-month, making it the service's most-viewed documentary to date.

American Pickers

TV-PG, 2010–present
Hulu, Prime Video, 22 seasons,
332 episodes (AD)
Reality show with Mike Wolfe, Danielle Colby-Cushman and Frank Fritz.

This long-running reality staple is the followup that PBS never thought of: following antique hunters as they roam the backroads of America looking for undiscovered treasures in shops, barns, garages and homes. Forget about the cattle call at the convention center. In *American Pickers* heartland-based treasure hunters Wolfe and Fritz go to people's homes, hoping to find priceless objects collecting dust in their cupboards. These charming hosts enjoy nothing more than visiting with everyday folks, and it's not just the excitement when a bit of hidden history is uncovered, but the enthusiasm of the pickers as they rifle through their clients' stashes, that make this show great comfort viewing.

An American Pickle

PG-13, 2020
HBO Max original, 1 hr 28 mins (AD)
Movie (comedy) with Seth Rogen and Sarah Snook.

An immigrant worker in a pickle factory is preserved in brine for 100 years and wakes up in contemporary Brooklyn. Rogen takes on dual roles in this amusing

historical parody with aplomb, playing both Herschel and his great-grandson Ben.

American Splendor

TV-MA, 2003
HBO Max, 1 hr 41 mins
Movie (documentary) directed by Shari Springer Berman and Robert Pulcini, with Paul Giamatti, Hope Davis, Harvey Pekar, Joyce Brabner, Molly Shannon, James Urbaniak, Judah Friedlander and Donal Logue.

Crusty alt-comic personality Harvey Pekar got the Paul Giamatti treatment in this clever triple-decker film. Best known for his slice-of-life comic series *American Splendor*, his friendship with cartoonist R. Crumb and his kabuki-style appearances on *Late Night With David Letterman* in the '80s, Pekar appears in this superb film that is one part documentary (he's interviewed along with Brabner, his no-nonsense wife), one part docudrama (Giamatti as Harvey and Davis as Joyce) and one part cartoon (several of Pekar's stories are animated).

▶▶ The directors were nominated for an Oscar for best adapted screenplay.

American Vandal

TV-MA, 2017–2018
Netflix original, 2 seasons,
16 episodes (AD)
Satirical comedy with Tyler Alvarez, Griffin Gluck, Jimmy Tatro, Travis Tope, Melvin Gregg, Lou Wilson, Taylor Dearden and Jessica Juarez.

Teenagers steal the show in this intelligent, snarky, trope-packed sendup of the true-crime TV genre. In this razor-sharp satire, a pair of California high school students set out to solve relatively low-stakes mysteries. In the first season, the question is who spray-painted phalluses on cars in their school parking lot. The resulting notoriety gets the filmmakers invited to investigate a "turd burglar" at a Catholic school in Season 2. *American Vandal* doubles as a brilliant satire of high schoolers in all their self-seriousness and naiveté.

🎣 **From our forums:** "I love that just like *Serial* and *Making a Murderer,* we don't actually find out every single thing about the case."

🏆 Peabody Award

The Americans
TV-MA, 2013–2018
Prime Video, 6 seasons, 75 episodes
Drama with Keri Russell, Matthew Rhys, Holly Taylor, Keidrich Sellati, Noah Emmerich, Costa Ronin, Lev Gorn, Richard Thomas, Alison Wright and Margo Martindale.

Sleek alt-history showcased Keri Russell and Matthew Rhys as Russian spies who embed in America as ordinary suburbanites during the Reagan years. This is one of those shows that fans confess to rewatching multiple times, and why not? *The Americans* featured all the spy-games tropes — wigs, gunfights, extramarital sex — but the explosive moments typically featured words and not weapons. As Philip and Elizabeth Jennings, Rhys and Russell portrayed the ebb and flow of a regular marriage that also happened to involve some less-than-conventional intimate moments. And espionage. Joe Weisberg and Joel Fields were given the freedom to create the show they wanted and to end it on their terms.

🏆 TCA Award for outstanding drama series (3 wins); Emmy for lead actor in a drama (Rhys)

Amy Schumer Learns to Cook
TV-PG, 2020
Discovery+, 2 seasons, 8 episodes
Celebreality show with Amy Schumer and Chris Fischer.

If you're going to remember only one remote-shot TV show from the pandemic, make it this one. Shot in her home without a crew, this Emmy-nominated Food Network show co-starred the comic, hubby Chris Fischer and nanny/camera operator Jane. Of course, Schumer didn't *need* to learn to cook, since Fischer is a chef and James Beard Award–winning cookbook author. But that only underscored why this was the perfect "why not?" show of the quarantine and a hoot to boot.

Amy Schumer: Growing
TV-MA, 2019
Netflix original, 1 hr
Comedy special directed by Amy Schumer, with Amy Schumer.

The star of *Inside Amy Schumer* has a lot to say about being pregnant. Some viewers may wonder, "Wait, another Netflix comedy special about being pregnant — didn't Ali Wong do 2 of those?" Those viewers would be men. Carrying a baby does seem to be an almost endless source of raunchy humor and Schumer, you might say, delivers.

⏩ Her 2015 special *Amy Schumer: Live at the Apollo* is a fine substitute if you have HBO Max.

Amy Schumer: Live at the Apollo
TV-MA, 2016
HBO Max, 1 hour
Comedy special directed by Chris Rock, with Amy Schumer.

With a sweet smile and lots of daggers, Schumer eviscerates double standards about sex, sexuality and pleasure. The historic Apollo Theater isn't the most obvious place for a white lady who's had issues with racial humor to put on a show. But Schumer, under the direction of Chris Rock, delivers a solid set of R-rated jokes about bikini waxes and other subjects that will delight the ladies and might make the men uncomfortable.

And Just Like That...

TV-MA, 2021–present
HBO Max original, 10 episodes (AD)
Comedy-drama created by Darren Star, with Sarah Jessica Parker, Cynthia Nixon, Kristin Davis, Chris Noth, Sara Ramirez, Nicole Ari Parker, Karen Pittman, Cathy Ang, Alexa Swinton and Niall Cunningham.

This return to the world that *Sex And The City* built finds the tone shifting to something more dramatic than its predecessor. Samantha's gone, but the returning characters have deepened, and they're joined by people who were sorely missing from the original — including people of color and non-binary characters. That gives the show satisfying dimensions and there are enough narrative risks to keep fans engaged, even when they're frustrated that it's not the *Sex And the City* they remember.

🗨 **From our forums:** "Add me to the list of people who are hate-watching this show."

Angels in America

TV-MA, 2003
HBO Max, 6 episodes
Limited series (drama) created by Tony Kushner, with Meryl Streep, Al Pacino, Emma Thompson, Justin Kirk, Mary-Louise Parker, Patrick Wilson, Jeffrey Wright, Ben Shenkman and James Cromwell.

Emma Thompson, Meryl Streep, Al Pacino and Jeffrey Wright dazzled in this adaptation of the acclaimed play about AIDS in 1980s New York City. Prior Walter (Kirk), a gay man with AIDS in the 1980s, is informed by a wild and occasionally lusty angel (Thompson) that he will become a prophet in the age of a plague. That's the premise for this poetic, political and moving limited series featuring Streep, Pacino and others in multiple roles. Based on Kushner's Pulitzer-winning screenplay, which had been produced for the stage long before 9/11, *Angels in America* expands to epic dimensions over its runtime, reflecting the apocalyptic sensibility of a nation in 2003 — and today as well.

🏆 11 Emmy Awards, including best miniseries

Angie Tribeca

TV-14, 2016–2018
Hulu, 4 seasons, 40 episodes
Satirical comedy created by Steve Carell and Nancy Carell, with Rashida Jones, Jere Burns, Andree Vermeulen, Deon Cole, Hayes MacArthur, Kiersey Clemons, Bobby Cannavale and Matthew Glave.

Steve and Nancy Carell created this gloriously dumb spoof of police procedurals. Obviously the Carells loved the Leslie Nielsen *Police Squad!* show and more celebrated *Naked Gun* movie franchise, because *Angie Tribeca* — starring Rashida Jones as a detective in the RHCU (Really Heinous Crimes Unit) — is stuffed with the elements that made those old spoofs so great. The show is littered with sight gags, running gags, puns and double entendres ("This is *my* bust!") and it bubbles with fun-loving energy among all involved.

Anne with an E

TV-PG, 2017–2020
Netflix original, 3 seasons, 27 episodes (AD)
Family drama created by Moira Walley-Beckett, with Amybeth McNulty, Geraldine James, R.H. Thomson, Dalila Bela, Lucas Jade Zumann and Helen Johns.

Though grimmer than the *Anne of Green Gables* millions of girls grew up with, this adaptation is well suited to our times — and Anne is still adorable. L.M.

Montgomery's heroine Anne Shirley is still a precocious, loquacious redheaded orphan, but in this engaging remake from a *Breaking Bad* writer, Anne is also prone to dark thoughts and anxiety about her future. These traits, frankly, make her more appealing to viewers of both sexes (and a truer reflection of the troubled author who created her).

Archer

TV-MA, 2009–present
Hulu, 12 seasons, 126 episodes (AD)
Animated comedy with H. Jon Benjamin, Judy Greer, Amber Nash, Chris Parnell, Aisha Tyler, Jessica Walter, Lucky Yates and Adam Reed.

Tireless sendup of the spy genre is always changing things up, making each new season a distinct delight. At its heart *Archer* is a workplace comedy, set at the occasionally effective ISIS spy agency, which would get a lot more done if everyone there wasn't at each other's throats constantly. Only *Veep* can rival *Archer* in the volume and quality of its putdowns and no show can match it for risk-taking. Reed and his writing team have been fearless about resetting the show, as with its epic Season 5 tribute to *Miami Vice* or the dreamscape years when Archer was in a coma (Seasons 8–9).

🏆 Emmys for outstanding animated program and individual achievement in animation

Are You Being Served?

TV-PG, 1972–1985
BritBox, 10 seasons, 69 episodes
British comedy with Mollie Sugden, John Inman, Frank Thornton, Wendy Richard, Nicholas Smith, Trevor Bannister, Arthur English and Harold Bennett.

Of all the classic Britcoms, this one — set at venerable but fading London department store — has had the most staying power. With its heavily reliance on stereotypes, double entendres, risqué visual gags and slapstick, *Are You Being Served?* is an undeniably overstuffed slice of 1970s lowbrow humor. Characters like the flamboyant Mr. Humphries (Inman), or Mrs. Slocombe's (Sugden) many references to her cat as "my pussy" would be *verboten* today. *Fawlty Towers* it is not, yet few British sitcoms of its era offered such a biting (and enduring) critique of the country's class system.

Are You The One?

TV-14, 2014–2019
Paramount+, Hulu, Netflix, 8 seasons, 88 episodes
Reality competition.

The fascinating Season 8 of this hookup show was devoted to bisexual, trans and non-binary young people looking for love while sorting out their own sexuality. MTV promoted it as "the first sexually fluid reality dating competition show in the United States," and it delivered, with cast members that were easy to root for, reflecting the full spectrum of human sexuality.

▶▶ A spinoff series, *Are You the One? Second Chances*, aired in 2017 and was filmed in Melbourne, Australia.

Arrested Development

TV-14, 2003–2019
Hulu, Netflix, 5 seasons, 84 episodes (AD)
Sitcom created by Mitchell Hurwitz, with Jason Bateman, Portia de Rossi, Will Arnett, Michael Cera, Alia Shawkat, Tony Hale, David Cross, Jeffrey Tambor, Jessica Walter and Ron Howard.

Jason Bateman led a dream team of comedic actors in this beloved comedy about an over-the-hill real estate dynasty. Especially during its first 3 seasons when it was a network sitcom, *Arrested Development* packed a lot into 20 minutes of episode: madcap farce, quick-witted banter, cutaway gags, satire (especially of soap-opera excesses), rope-tight storylines and all those memorable characters.

▶▶ Hulu only streams the shows made for Fox (Seasons 1–3). Netflix, which paid for Seasons 4–5, has all episodes available to stream.

🏆 Emmy for best comedy series; TCA Award for outstanding comedy (2 wins)

Arrow
TV-14, 2012–2020
Netflix, 8 seasons, 170 episodes
Superhero drama created by Greg Berlanti, with Stephen Amell, David Ramsey, Emily Bett Rickards, Katie Cassidy, Paul Blackthorne, Willa Holland, Colton Haynes, Rick Gonzalez, Echo Kellum and John Barrowman.

DC comic about a billionaire playboy who becomes a bow-and-arrow wielding crimefighter becomes a long-running series. Amell has charisma to burn in the lead role, but the show gives ample attention to the large cast of supporting characters who work with Green Arrow in his fight for justice. Flashbacks (and eventually flash forwards) give the series an epic scope, and its top-notch fight scenes are well-choreographed fun.

Ash vs. Evil Dead
TV-MA, 2015–2018
Starz original, 3 seasons, 30 episodes (AD)
Comedy-horror series created by Sam Raimi, with Bruce Campbell, Lucy Lawless, Ray Santiago and Dana DeLorenzo.

Bruce Campbell returns as Ash Williams, who has to give up his mundane existence working at a convenience store to once again fight off an army of the undead. This series, built on the *Evil Dead* film trilogy, finds Campbell in classic form, tossing off

sarcastic *bon mots* while finding ever-more-creative ways to kill zombies.

🗨 **From our forums:** "They've already done a better job establishing the newer characters than a lot of shows on TV. The pace was consistent and there weren't any dull moments."

Asian Americans
TV-14, 2020
PBS Passport, 5 episodes
Docuseries with Daniel Dae Kim, Tamlyn Tomita and Sandra Oh.

Exceptional, eye-opening historical and contemporary look at the group that experienced the largest increase in racially motivated attacks of any group in the past decade. Not a feel-good docuseries, there's a definite tone of anger at how Asian-Americans have been treated over 150 years, as is amply documented here. A timely and important program.

🏆 Peabody Award

Astronomy Club
TV-MA, 2019
Netflix original, 6 episodes (AD)
Sketch comedy created by Kenya Barris, with Jonathan Braylock, Shawntane Monroe Bowen, Caroline Martin, Jerah Milligan, Monique Moses, Keisha Zollar, James III and Ray Cordova.

Binge this blend of social satire and pure silliness, then ask yourself why Netflix stopped at one season. With roots in an all-Black comedy troupe at New York City's UCB Theater, *Astronomy Club* has a quasi-familial vibe, as seen in the *Real World*–esque house where the eight-person cast meets to bounce ideas off each other. This alone is worth watching, but the sketches that emerge from these sessions invariably hit their marks.

At Home with Amy Sedaris
TV-14, 2017–2020
HBO Max, 3 seasons, 30 episodes
Sketch comedy created by Amy Sedaris and Paul Dinello, with Amy Sedaris, Cole Escola, Ana Fabrega, Heather Lawless and David Pasquesi.

A manic sendup of homemaking shows is a great vehicle for Sedaris to show off her chaotic energy. *At Home With Amy Sedaris* will only incidentally teach the viewer a few tips and tricks for gracious living. More likely you'll hear something like, "My advice to any woman out there who is unsure about whether or not they're ready to raise a child — I say *have one* and try it out for a day! You'll figure it out real quick."

🐟 **From our forums:** "Irreverent and quirky, with gags that sneak up on you. I'm generally not one to LOL but this show manages it."

Atlanta
TV-MA, 2016–present
Hulu, 3 seasons, 31 episodes
Comedy created by Donald Glover, with Donald Glover, Brian Tyree Henry, Zazie Beetz and LaKeith Stanfield.

Glover stars, writes and directs this comic drama about being young, Black, ambitious and poor in America. In the titular Georgia city, Earn (Glover) tries to do right by his girlfriend and help his cousin become a rap superstar, but no matter what he does, the results are surreal. Strange and brilliant, *Atlanta* is a *tour de force* for Glover — a comedy that revels in the hijinks of nuanced and appealing characters, but which can deftly swerve into horror, satire, action-movie violence and statements about Black life that are some of the most incisive on TV. It's frankly amazing that one series, from basically one man, can do so many things and do them so well.

🐟 **From our forums:** "When I started watching this show, I never would have guessed that Earn would be the third most interesting character. It's impressive how many themes they cover given they only have 20 minutes an episode."

🏆 Peabody Award, Emmy and TCA awards for best comedy series

Atypical
TV-MA, 2017–2021
Netflix original, 4 seasons, 38 episodes (AD)
Comedy-drama with Keir Gilchrist, Jennifer Jason Leigh, Brigette Lundy-Paine, Michael Rapaport, Nik Dodani, Jenna Boyd, Graham Rogers, Fivel Stewart and Amy Okuda.

Well-above-average dramedy about a teenager on the spectrum who seeks a more independent life. It feels like you're watching a real family deal with actual issues on *Atypical* — not just Sam (Gilchrist) wanting more autonomy but his mom (Jason-Leigh) wanting to remember what life was like before kids and his doting sister Casey (Lundy-Paine) struggling with gender identity.

🐟 **From our forums:** "This is the most charming and likable I've ever found Michael Rapaport. Hearing him say how he just wanted to have one thing in common with his son . . . it hit me."

Away
TV-14, 2020
Netflix original, 10 episodes (AD)
Drama with Hilary Swank, Josh Charles, Vivian Wu, Mark Ivanir, Ray Panthaki, Ato Essandoh and Talitha Eliana Bateman.

Underappreciated space drama stars Hilary Swank as a female astronaut who leaves her family behind to go to Mars. Think going into space is challenging? Try managing family crises via interplanetary FaceTime calls and a dysfunctional crew and once-per-episode crises that threaten to blow them all to bits. Definitely a job for a double Oscar winner, and Swank is up to the task. Back on Earth, her faithful hubby (Charles) and understandably devastated daughter (Bateman) add resonance to this intriguing series from Jason Katims (*Friday Night Lights*).

Awkwafina Is Nora from Queens

TV-MA, 2020–present
HBO Max, 2 seasons, 20 episodes

Comedy created by Awkwafina, with Awkwafina, Lori Tan Chinn, BD Wong, Bowen Yang and Jennifer Esposito.

The rapper-actress stars as a fictionalized version of herself, growing up in Queens and trying to live a more exciting life. Nora struggles with everything from getting a job to getting a check cashed, lending the comedy a relatable edge. And she's got a foul-mouthed grandmother (Chinn) who steals every scene she's in.

▶▶ Pairs well with *Broad City*

Baby God

TV-MA, 2020
HBO Max, 1 hr 18 mins (AD)

Movie (documentary) directed by Hannah Olson, with Quincy Fortier.

A Las Vegas fertility doctor inseminated hundreds of patients using his own sperm without their consent … and that's only the start of this fascinating, horrifying documentary. There is so much to unpack in the story of Dr. Quincy Fortier — his skeevy gynecological practice, the allegations of sexual assault, the ethics of DNA registries, even the social history of childbearing — that this needed to be a docuseries instead of an 80-minute film.

▶▶ Pairs well with *Love Fraud*

The Baby-Sitters Club

TV-PG, 2020–present
Netflix original, 2 seasons, 18 episodes (AD)

Family comedy with Sophie Grace, Momona Tamada, Shay Rudolph, Malia Baker, Xochitl Gomez, Alicia Silverstone, Marc Evan Jackson and Mark Feuerstein.

The characters in a beloved 1990s YA novel series have found their way to 2020 and they couldn't be a better fit. Ann M. Martin captivated a generation with her books about a group of middle-school friends who weren't solving mysteries or facing down a fascist regime, but simply running a business to provide their community with top-notch babysitting. Netflix's adaptation has a confidence that doesn't announce itself as an edgy reimagination, but instead harnesses the books' most enduring appeal: their relatably humane and forthright characters.

🏆 Emmy for best young performer in a children's show (Grace)

Babylon Berlin

TV-MA, 2017–present
Netflix, 3 seasons, 28 episodes

Historical drama with Volker Bruch, Liv Lisa Fries, Leonie Benesch, Lars Eidinger, Misel Maticevic, Fritzi Haberlandt, Jens Harzer, Karl Markovics, Jördis Triebel and Christian Friedel.

Lavish period drama brings to life Weimar Germany, where messy democracy rules the day and anything-goes libertinism fuels the night. The most expensive German TV production ever, this sprawling, escapist crime-noir extravaganza is based on the detective novels of Volker Kutscher. *Babylon Berlin* shows a city grappling with immense social problems, yet bursting with a creative spirit that Hitler won't be able to crush.

▶▶ Available to watch in its original

German with English subtitles or dubbed in English.

The Babysitter
TV-MA, 2017
Netflix original, 1 hr 25 mins (AD)
Movie (horror) with Samara Weaving, Robbie Amell, Bella Thorne, Judah Lewis, Hana Mae Lee, Ken Marino and Leslie Bibb.

A boy has a crush on his babysitter until he discovers she's in a satanic cult that holds meetings in his family's living room. Action director McG gives this movie a fun, smart-alecky edge and Samara Weaving shows the genre chops she honed a few years later in *Ready Or Not*.

The Bachelor/Bachelorette
TV-14, 2002–present
Hulu, HBO Max, Discovery+, 44 seasons, 469 episodes (AD)
Reality competition created by Mike Fleiss, with Chris Harrison, Jesse Palmer, Tayshia Adams and Kaitlyn Bristowe.

The twin dating competitions are arguably the most phenomenal of all prime-time reality phenomena — fascinations as well as abominations well-suited to our age of social media sharing and outrage. Dating shows have been on TV since 1965. An old MTV series called *Next* had one person "date" a bus full of other singles, one at a time, pulling the ripcord when each date became unbearable. What was novel about *The Bachelor* and *Bachelorette* was that they took a simple daytime-TV concept and married it to high-gloss prime-time production values. And unlike almost all the partnerships formed on these shows, the marriage held. Charges of storyline manipulation behind the scenes are commonplace and to be expected; stakes are high for ABC and little is left to chance. Many viewers admit to hate-watching these shows, savoring the breakups of couples who are packaged on-air as soulmates. But ABC has savvily managed its failures and controversies, working them into the fibers of the franchise. With *Bachelor* and *Bachelorette* series now airing year-round, there's little reason to think America will be breaking up with its most lurid reality hit anytime soon.

▶▶ As this book went to press, no one streamer could lay claim to the entire *The Bachelor* franchise. Current seasons and select earlier seasons can be streamed on Hulu, while other seasons are available to stream on HBO Max. Further complicating matters, Warner Bros signed a deal in 2021 to license several *other* seasons to Discovery+.

▶▶ Season 13 of *The Bachelor* (featuring Jason Mesnick, a castoff from Season 4 of *The Bachelorette*), which ended in a love triangle too zany to be scripted, earned the show its highest-ever ratings and one of the more whiplash-inducing outcomes in *Bachelor-Bachelorette* annals. *The Bachelorette*'s Season 1 is worth a watch for the performance by Trista Rehn, who has since become a legend of the format.

▶▶ Host Chris Harrison departed in 2021 after unsuccessfully fending off charges of racial insensitivity. Former contestants took his place: Jesse Palmer hosted *Bachelor* and Tayshia Adams and Kaitlyn Bristowe co-hosted *The Bachelorette*.

▶▶ For a lightly-fictionalized look at how shows like *The Bachelor* get made, *UnREAL* (see page 303) is worth a watch.

Back
TV-MA, 2017–present
AMC+, 2 seasons, 12 episodes
Dark comedy created by Simon Blackwell, with David Mitchell, Robert Webb, Penny Downie, Jessica Gunning, Louise Brealey, Oliver Maltman, Geoffrey McGivern and Olivia Poulet.

Gloriously decadent adult comedy about foster brothers who struggle for control over the family pub after Dad dies. This has a premise that takes some setting up, but with two accomplished comic actors as the dueling brothers (Mitchell and Webb, *Peep Show*) and the uniformly smart writing of Blackwell (*Veep*), who balances blunt humor with subtle emotion, it's a show worth sticking with.

▶▶ A third season was expected sometime in 2022.

Back to Life
TV-MA, 2019–present
Showtime original, 2 seasons, 12 episodes

Comedy-drama created by Daisy Haggard, with Daisy Haggard, Geraldine James, Richard Durden, Adeel Akhtar, Jo Martin, Jamie Michie, Christine Bottomley and Liam Williams.

Daisy Haggard (*Episodes, Breeders*) co-wrote and shines in the starring role as a woman who returns to her insular hometown after 18 years in prison. Not everyone in the seaside village of Hythe is pleased to see Miri (Haggard) back after she pays her debt to society. A mixture of realism and absurdism, quotidian struggles, silly banter and the emotional toll that comes from being the town pariah, *Back to Life* navigates its tonal shifts with help from a diverse and interesting cast. Miri's slow-growing romance with Billy (Akhtar) is highly enjoyable, while her fallout with old friend Mandy (Bottomley) adds poignancy.

🐾 **From our forums:** "While it took me a couple of episodes to warm to it, I became quite fond of it. But I'm a sucker for dark comedy."

▶▶ Pairs well with *Fleabag*

Bad Education
TV-MA, 2019
HBO Max, 1 hr 48 mins

Movie (dark comedy) with Hugh Jackman, Allison Janney, Ray Romano, Annaleigh Ashford, Rafael Casal, Alex Wolff, Hari Dhillon, Geraldine Viswanathan, Welker White and Stephanie Kurtzuba.

Hugh Jackman and Allison Janney headline this based-on-true-events film about a beloved school superintendent who bilks his district out of millions. Jackman is convincing as Frank Tassone, a Long Island administrator whose embezzlement scheme was exposed mere weeks after his private school was ranked one of America's finest. Janney, if anything, outdoes Jackman in her role as Tassone's assistant superintendent.

🏆 Emmy for outstanding TV movie

Bad Trip
TV-MA, 2021
Netflix original, 1 hr 26 mins (AD)

Movie (comedy) directed by Kitao Sakurai, with Eric André, Lil Rel Howery, Michaela Conlin and Tiffany Haddish.

Forget every trope you know about hidden-camera prankster movies, because Eric André reinvents the form in *Bad Trip*. Framed as a road-trip movie, this is an accessible introduction to the young comedian, an anarchist with a Robin Williams–like sense of humor. André and director Kitao Sakurai know that it's possible to make people laugh without being mean. In the end credits we see the film's "victims" responding to the news that they've just been captured on camera — mostly they're overjoyed.

Baghdad Central
TV-14, 2020
Hulu, 6 episodes

Historical drama with Waleed Zuaiter, July Namir, Youssef Kerkour, Bertie Carvel, Clara Khoury, Corey Stoll, Maisa Abd Elhadi, Leem Lubany and Thaer Al-Shayei.

The twist in this military-political thriller — set shortly after the invasion of Iraq in 2003 — is that the lead is a former Baathist inspector during Saddam Hussein's regime whose daughter has disappeared. Based on Elliott Colla's book of the same name, *Baghdad Central* is told from the perspective of those whose country was occupied, so it doesn't feel like a rehash of every other drama set in this region. Zuaiter is magnetic as ex-Iraqi policeman Muhsin al-Khafaji in this production from the UK's Channel 4.

Band of Brothers
TV-MA, 2001
HBO Max, 10 episodes
Limited series (historical drama) created by Steven Spielberg and Tom Hanks, with Damian Lewis, Scott Grimes, Ron Livingston, Shane Taylor, Donnie Wahlberg, Peter Youngblood Hills and Matthew Leitch.

Still the best modern dramatization of the bonds that men form under the duress of war. Based on Stephen Ambrose's nonfiction bestseller, this WWII saga follows the Easy Company in the U.S. Army's Airborne Division as they travel together from basic training to the fall of Japan. This blue-chip HBO adaptation is among Spielberg's and Hanks's best work anywhere. And Lewis as unit commander Dick Winters — in the role that introduced him to American audiences — is a revelation.

🏆 Peabody Award, Emmy and TCA awards for best miniseries

Baptiste
TV-MA, 2020–2021
PBS Passport, 2 seasons, 14 episodes
Drama with Tchéky Karyo, Anastasia Hille, Michel Biel, Barbara Sarafian, Tom Hollander, Boris Van Severen, Fiona Shaw, Dorka Gryllus and Ace Bhatti.

Pure catnip for fans of mysteries and crime dramas, this spinoff of *The Missing* marks the return of Tchéky Karyo as detective Julien Baptiste. Retired and recovered from the brain tumor that dogged him through 2 series of *The Missing* (see page 209), Baptiste doesn't even want to take on the case of a missing girl caught up in a sex-trafficking ring. But a colleague insists and points him to the girl's "uncle" (Hollander). From there comes a chase, a grisly find and a deception — and by then both Baptiste and you the viewer are deep into this unfolding story, a crime drama both familiar and artfully executed.

💬 **From our forums:** "I like that Baptiste acknowledges he is not what he used to be. He is a reminder that some of us are older but still have value."

Barb and Star Go to Vista Del Mar
PG-13, 2021
Hulu, 1 hr 47 mins (AD)
Movie (comedy) with Kristen Wiig, Annie Mumolo, Jamie Dornan, Damon Wayans Jr., Ian Gomez, Wendi McLendon-Covey and Vanessa Bayer.

Two gal pals try to shake up their lives by going on vacation to a Florida resort hotel, only to get embroiled in a villain's nefarious plot to destroy everyone who lives there. While Wiig and Mumolo are their typically hilarious selves, Dornan's often-musical performance is the highlight of the film.

Baroness Von Sketch Show
TV-14, 2016–2021
AMC+, 5 seasons, 46 episodes
Sketch comedy with Carolyn Taylor, Meredith MacNeill, Aurora Browne and Jennifer Whalen.

Another fine under-the-radar Canadian comedy in the tradition of *Schitt's Creek*. This very funny quartet of 40-something women have long deserved greater attention south of the border. Sketches range from the silly (the woman whose hair grows to mammoth proportions thanks to dry shampoo) to highly gender-specific (camping tips when you're on your period) to sharply social (how companies anesthetize workers against labor organizing).

Barry

TV-MA, 2018–present
HBO Max, 3 seasons, 24 episodes (AD)
Dark comedy created by Bill Hader and Alec Berg, with Bill Hader, Henry Winkler, Sarah Goldberg, Anthony Carrigan, Stephen Root, Paula Newsome, Glenn Fleshler, D'Arcy Carden, Kirby Howell-Baptiste and Darrell Britt-Gibson.

Bill Hader showed us something when he played a hit man whose life changes when he walks into an acting class. We've seen this premise before, most memorably with Tony's nephew Christopher in *The Sopranos*, but *Barry* takes the concept to new heights. With the great Henry Winkler as his coach and Hader as a terrible — but highly motivated — newbie stage actor, this show makes full use of its comic potential. And yet this is also a drama about consequences and why society should be run by morally inclined people rather than antiheroes.

🏆 Emmy awards for Hader as best actor and Winkler as supporting actor in a comedy series, Peabody Award

Baseball

TV-PG, 1994–2010
PBS Passport, 11 episodes
Docuseries directed by Ken Burns, with Daniel Okrent, George F. Will, Doris Kearns Goodwin, Gerald Early, Buck O'Neil, Bob Costas, John Thorn, Studs Terkel and George Plimpton.

Widely regarded as Ken Burns's best work after his masterpiece on the Civil War. Like most Burns projects, *Baseball* is as much a social history as a history of America's pastime. Its 9 parts, or "innings," in 1994 touched on matters of race that was both clear-eyed and generous, thanks to the inimitable voice of Negro Leagues great Buck O'Neil, one of Burns's go-to talking heads. The 2010 continuation, or "extra inning," covered MLB's steroids scandal.

Baskets

TV-MA, 2016–2019
Hulu, 4 seasons, 40 episodes
Dark comedy created by Louis C.K., Zach Galifianakis and Jonathan Krisel, with Zach Galifianakis, Louie Anderson and Martha Kelly.

Zach Galifianakis plays Chip, an unsuccessful clown who returns home to star in the family rodeo, and his twin brother Dale. The standout in this surreal comedy, however, isn't Chip or Dale. It's their mom Christine, played by Louie Anderson, who won an Emmy for this role. Not only is Anderson a revelation in drag, but as Mrs. Baskets — owner of Bakersfield's own Baskets Family Rodeo — her very presence explains why those two boys turned out the way they did.

💬 **From our forums:** "I love the delicate humor of this show, it's realistic and quirky."

BattleBots

TV-14, 2015–present
Discovery+, 5 seasons, 65 episodes
Reality competition.

Classic death-match competition between scary robots is better than ever. Originally airing on Comedy Central in the early '00s, *BattleBots* offered new evidence of the axiom that David Letterman and a steamroller had long ago proven: Watching objects get violently destroyed is ridiculously entertaining. This revival is from the original creators of *BattleBots*, and now that it's on

Discovery+ there's a bit less comedy and a bit more science. But it's still built around the stories of these little remote-controlled hellions and their mad creators, and who will outlast the field in a season-long tournament.

Battlestar Galactica (2004)
TV-14, 2004–2009
Peacock, 4 seasons, 74 episodes
Sci-fi drama created by Ronald D. Moore and Glen A. Larson, with Edward James Olmos, Mary McDonnell, Jamie Bamber, James Callis, Tricia Helfer, Grace Park, Katee Sackhoff, Michael Hogan, Aaron Douglas and Tahmoh Penikett.

A trailblazing example of how you turn an OK show into one that is dynamic, relevant — a classic, even. Anyone can take a well-done series like *MacGyver* or *The Equalizer* and "reimagine" it, but what Ronald D. Moore did with 1970s mediocrity *Battlestar Galactica* was breathtaking. Moore combined sexiness, special effects and good storytelling into believable drama in outer space that didn't feel overly preachy and put entertainment first. Small wonder there's now a *reboot* of the remake in the works!
🏆 2 Peabody Awards and multiple technical Emmys

Batwoman
TV-14, 2019–present
HBO Max, 3 seasons, 56 episodes
Superhero drama with Javicia Leslie, Ruby Rose, Camrus Johnson, Rachel Skarsten, Meagan Tandy, Nicole Kang, Dougray Scott and Rachel Maddow.

Fully woke reboot features the first Black actor to play the crusading hero, starting with Season 2. Ruby Rose exited the title role after Season 1 of *Batwoman*, so producers brought in Leslie as Ryan Wilder, a Black, gay ex–homeless person, ex–felon who is also the cousin of Bruce Wayne. The transfer wasn't smooth —

Rose's character wasn't written out of the show until later in Season 2 and viewers complained the storylines were needlessly convoluted — but *Batwoman* won praise for taking on hot-button topics without forgetting it's a kick-ass action series.
🗨 **From our forums:** "Season 2 really struggled in how it started, having to introduce a whole new Batwoman, but I think they ended things pretty well."

Beanie Mania
PG, 2021
HBO Max original, 1 hr
Movie (documentary).

Beanie Babies — the unlikeliest craze since tulip mania — is entertainingly relived by the housewives at the eye of the storm. In 1996, a secretive toymaker began sending out dozens of varieties of animal-shaped beanbags to mom-and-pop stores. Led by a group of suburban moms who took to the doe-eyed cuties, a speculative frenzy blew up that would sweep the nation and drive the prices for some Beanie Babies as high as $20,000 or more. *Beanie Mania* is one of those docs made by Brits that makes you wonder if they understand Americans better than we do, putting the mob scenes, rampant speculation and ridiculous media hype into perfect context.
▶▶ Pairs well with *LuLaRich*

The Beast Must Die
TV-14, 2021–present
AMC+, BritBox, 5 episodes
Anthology series (thriller) with Cush Jumbo, Jared Harris, Billy Howle, Douggie McMeekin, Maeve Dermody and Mia Tomlinson.

Better-than-average British prestige detective series stars Cush Jumbo as a mother out for revenge against the man she believes killed her son in a hit-and-run. Jumbo's intense performance is the standout in a fine ensemble in this latest adaptation of the 1938 novel by Cecil Day-Lewis (Daniel's father). Harris, as the obnoxious patriarch she's pursuing, and Howle, as a detective investigating the incident, are no slouches either. At just 5 episodes, this series doesn't flag at all.

▶▶ Unrelated to the 1974 horror-whodunit of the same title

The Beatles: Get Back
TV-14, 2021
Disney+ original, 3 episodes (AD)
Docuseries directed by Peter Jackson, with John Lennon, Paul McCartney, George Harrison, Ringo Starr, Billy Preston, Yoko Ono and George Martin.

Director Peter Jackson's awe-inspiring compilation of previously unseen footage gets us intimate with the Beatles as they make the album *Let It Be*. Even to those of us who've read the in-depth histories and watched earlier Beatles docs, this series is a revelation. By unearthing all of this "lost" material (originally shot for the 1970 film *Let It Be*) Jackson has deepened our understanding of who the Beatles were at the end of their glorious run — and he upends conventional wisdom about how their final songs were made.

▶▶ The secret sauce to this film is machine learning. When the Beatles didn't want to be overheard, they played their instruments; AI was able to mute those sounds to reconstruct hours of candid conversation.

▶▶ Pairs well with *Summer of Soul*

Becker
TV-PG, 1998–2004
PlutoTV, 6 seasons, 129 episodes
Comedy with Ted Danson, Hattie Winston, Shawnee Smith, Alex Désert, Terry Farrell and Saverio Guerra.

Ted Danson, in the first of several great post-*Cheers* roles, played a grumpy doc at a clinic in the South Bronx. You never heard much about *Becker* during its run on CBS. To be sure, it was overshadowed by a far superior show, *Everybody Loves Raymond*. Still, as '90s sitcoms go it's got more solid laughs in it than, say, *Friends* or *The Nanny*. Becker is surrounded by equally jaded foils in Margaret (Winston), the overworked clinic nurse; Jake (Désert), the blind newsstand owner; and Reggie (Farrell), the sweet-and-sour proprietor of Becker's usual coffee shop.

Becoming Cousteau
PG-13, 2021
Disney+, 1 hr 34 mins (AD)
Movie (documentary) directed by Liz Garbus.

Jacques Cousteau's career as an oceanographer was more remarkable, and his personal life more complicated, than his millions of fans from TV knew. Using wonderful on-board footage from Cousteau's pathfinding ship *Calypso*, as well as video clips from his hundreds of hours of film and TV programs, we get an intoxicating reminder of how Cousteau's underwater filmmaking altered our view of the ocean. Then, without diminishing his prior achievements, director Garbus shows how Cousteau evolved to become an early activist in the fight to halt climate change.

The Bee Gees: How Can You Mend a Broken Heart
TV-MA, 2020
HBO Max, 1 hr 51 mins (AD)
Movie (documentary) directed by Frank Marshall, with Barry Gibb, Maurice Gibb and Robin Gibb.

Fabulous retrospective look at the brother act who created some of the most iconic songs of the '60s, '70s and '80s. Mind-blowing is not too strong a description for the cumulative effect of this film, which briskly and incisively reviews 40 years of cultural change to

For shows sorted by streaming platform, see page 381. **61**

explain why the Gibbs might be the greatest performing family in pop music history or at least, as one critic describes them here, pop's greatest chameleons. Writing one chart-topping song after another, their studio breakthroughs (many of which are detailed here) changed the course of commercial music. Through all the adversity, from internal feuds to the anti-disco movement, the Bee Gees showed remarkable resilience and creativity, and this stimulating film takes the full measure.

Behind the Candelabra
TV-MA, 2013
HBO Max, 1 hr 58 mins
Movie (drama) directed by Steven Soderbergh, with Michael Douglas, Matt Damon, Rob Lowe, Scott Bakula, Dan Aykroyd, Debbie Reynolds, Mike O'Malley, Cheyenne Jackson and Paul Reiser.

Michael Douglas is Liberace and Matt Damon is the boy toy he adopts — do we really need to say more? Based on the autobiographical novel by Liberace's 1970s assistant and lover Scott Thorson, this Soderbergh-directed film eschews the campy, gossipy treatment viewers might have been expecting. Douglas and Thorson are riveting as two lonely men who hook up in the most emotionally needy sense of the word. Fine supporting work abounds, including Lowe as a creepy plastic surgeon who will resculpt Scott's visage into something more pleasing to the master.
🏆 Emmy and TCA awards for best movie or miniseries

Behind the Mask
TV-14, 2013–2015
Hulu original, 2 seasons, 20 episodes
Docuseries created by Josh Greenbaum.
Team mascots are revealed in this highly entertaining docuseries. Josh Greenbaum

follows four different mascots, from high school to the pros, performing for crowds large and small. Along with insight into their unusual jobs, we learn that these four costume wearers are not your typical camera-hungry reality show stars. One is an awkward teenager who comes alive when he's in costume.

Being the Ricardos
R, 2021
Prime Video original, 2 hrs 11 mins
Historical drama directed by Aaron Sorkin, with Nicole Kidman, Javier Bardem, J.K. Simmons, Nina Arianda, Tony Hale, Alia Shawkat and Jake Lacy.
Writer-director Aaron Sorkin is in his element — television — in this knowing, laugh-out-loud and timely movie based on one chaotic week at America's most popular show in 1951, *I Love Lucy*. Sorkin's rapid-fire speechifying is on full display here, but the bigger feat is how he convincingly shows both the genius of Lucille Ball and Desi Arnaz — Hollywood's original power couple — and their humanity. Kidman magically disappears into the persona of this remarkable woman. Bardem is equally compelling as Arnaz, whose mastery over the network and the show's sponsors is sorely needed during a week when they are vexed by a political scandal involving Lucy and a tabloid story involving Desi. Simmons, as Jim Frawley (aka Fred Mertz), leads a formidable supporting cast.

Belushi
TV-MA, 2020
Showtime original, 1 hr 48 mins
Movie (documentary) directed by R.J. Cutler, with Judy Belushi Pisano, Dan Aykroyd, Harold Ramis, John Landis, Penny Marshall, Carrie Fisher, Ivan Reitman and Jim Belushi.

Previously unheard audio interviews with John Belushi's friends and colleagues give depth to this recounting of his life, career and early demise. Belushi's reign was bright and brief and this film is adulatory toward his talent and vitality, yet also frank about his internal demons and the abusive behavior that led to his death at the age of 33 (something that fans of a certain age still find sad and infuriating). Made with years-old audio tapes with cooperation from his widow, *Belushi* is part of the wave of audio-driven films that lets us hear from those who knew the subject best, some of whom (like Ramis and Fisher) have since passed.

Bessie

TV-MA, 2015
HBO Max, 1 hr 55 mins
Movie (drama) directed by Dee Rees, with Queen Latifah, Mo'Nique, Michael K. Williams, Khandi Alexander, Tika Sumpter, Oliver Platt, Bryan Greenberg and Charles S. Dutton.

Queen Latifah brings to life Bessie Smith, a pivotal figure in the rise of the blues. Yet another reminder of what makes Queen Latifah such an enduring figure in entertainment — she can reach deep down for emotions that tie viewer to actor to historical figure, and she can credibly recreate what it must have been like to hear Smith on stage, channeling her drama-filled life into performance and defining an era in music.

🏆 Emmy for best TV movie, SAG Award for best actress in a movie or miniseries

Best Leftovers Ever!

TV-G, 2020–present
Netflix original, 8 episodes (AD)
Reality competition with Jackie Tohn, David So and Rosemary Shrager.

A calmer, more assured version of *Nailed It!* benefits from its realistic approach to food and charming panel of judges. From the producers of *Nailed It!*, this competition has contestants whipping up dishes incorporating ingredients that actually do look like they've been sitting in a fridge for a few days. Tohn both hosts and judges alongside So and Shrager, with lots of playfulness in their interactions and solid tips for what to do with that box of Chinese takeout. The contestants, who are competing for a $10,000 "casharole," are actually decent cooks, and this raises the quality of the show beyond the failure comedy of *Nailed It!*.

Betas

TV-MA, 2013–2014
Prime Video original, 11 episodes
Comedy with Joe Dinicol, Karan Soni, Jon Daly, Charlie Saxton, Maya Erskine, Ed Begley Jr. and Madeline Zima.

Raunchy millennial comedy follows a group of tech wannabes trying to make a fortune with their online dating app. Yes, it sounds a lot like *Silicon Valley*, which debuted a year after this did. But give *Betas* its due: The four coders at the heart of the show are better-developed than the core players of *Silicon Valley*, the setups are amusing, the writing solid (though the sexual chatter already feels dated) and at just 11 episodes, it's easy to binge.

Better Call Saul

TV-MA, 2015–present
Netflix, 6 seasons, 63 episodes (AD)
Drama created by Vince Gilligan and Peter Gould, with Bob Odenkirk, Rhea Seehorn, Jonathan Banks, Michael McKean, Giancarlo Esposito, Michael Mando and Patrick Fabian.

Bob Odenkirk kills it as low-rent lawyer Jimmy McGill, who evolves (if that is the right word) into *Breaking Bad*'s flashy but morally compromised Saul Goodman. With his absurdly confident style and carefree approach to unethical lawyering, Saul quickly became a fan favorite on *Breaking Bad.* This prequel, introduces us to new characters like Jimmy's brother Chuck (McKean) and explores the backstories of *Breaking Bad* characters like Mike (Banks). Though we see more of Jimmy/Saul's darker side than in the original, this show is no less entertaining or well-crafted.

🗨 **From our forums:** "*Breaking Bad* was a multi-year exploration of the cost of pride: how people get so obsessed with protecting the image they have of themselves in their head that they destroy what they tell themselves they love most. *Better Call Saul* is an exploration of the price of remorse: how the attempt to erase what can't be erased, the past, in all the chronic pain the past can summon, only leads to more pain."

▶▶ The show's 13–episode concluding Season 6 is set to air as 2 half-seasons beginning in 2022.

🏆 Peabody Award, TCA Award for outstanding drama series

Better Things
TV-MA, 2016–2022
Hulu, 5 seasons, 52 episodes
Comedy created by Pamela Adlon and Louis C.K., with Pamela Adlon, Mikey Madison, Hannah Riley, Olivia Edward and Celia Imrie.

Pamela Adlon co-created and stars in this groundbreaking show about a single mom with three daughters and a lot of issues. The point of view of Sam Fox (Adlon) is one of the most unique on TV. The show is a character study on a divorced working mom and her three daughters (not to mention her aging mother) told in poignant snapshots. It's hard to pinpoint a single reason for this, but *Better Things* has emerged as one of the most quietly revolutionary shows of the past decade.

🏆 Peabody Award, Critics Choice Award as "most exciting new show"

Betty
TV-MA, 2020–2021
HBO Max, 2 seasons, 12 episodes
Comedy-drama with Dede Lovelace, Kabrina Adams, Nina Moran, Ajani Russell, Rachelle Vinberg, Alexander Cooper and Katerina Tannenbaum.

An all-girls skateboarding collective in NYC crashes the sport's aggressively male subculture in this fast-moving show. Based on Crystal Moselle's 2018 film *Skate Kitchen*, the show stands apart even from most HBO fare thanks to its bare-bones storytelling and the natural skate skills of the actors, most of whom appeared in the film. *Betty* offers an exhilarating peek at the nooks and crannies of the city that are familiar to members of its skating subculture. Almost documentary-like in feel, *Betty* is a celebration of youth, friendship and equality.

Between Two Ferns with Zach Galifianakis
TV-14, 2008–2018
Prime Video, 23 episodes
Comedy talk show with Zach Galifianakis.

Ebulliently cringe talk-show lampoon features Galifianakis asking insane questions of his A-list guests and interrupting them for bizarre product placements. Because so many famous guests have agreed to do this thing (Hillary Clinton, Barack Obama, Brad Pitt, Justin Bieber, etc.), it's both thrilling and nerve-wracking to see what inappropriate thing Galifianakis is going to do next. And that's before they see the final cut, whacked down to 8 minutes and festooned with error-ridden graphics. The energy never sags between the ferns, and the guests usually come off as good sports who understand the lunacy of the PR machine they help feed.

▶▶ Succeeded by *Between Two Ferns: The*

Movie
🏆 Emmy for best shortform live entertainment program (2 wins)

Beverly Hills 90210
TV-PG, 1990–2000
Paramount+, Hulu, 10 seasons, 292 episodes
Teen drama created by Darren Star, with Jason Priestley, Shannen Doherty, Luke Perry, Jennie Garth, Tori Spelling, Ian Ziering, Gabrielle Carteris, Brian Austin Green, Carol Potter and James Eckhouse.
Before *Sex And the City*, Darren Star reinvented teen TV when he and producer Aaron Spelling brought this soapy treatment of upper-crust high school to millions of young viewers on Fox. For Rupert Murdoch's brash upstart TV network, nothing said "we don't care what your parents watch" like *90210*. (They were probably watching *Fresh Prince of Bel Air*, which also debuted in the fall of 1990.) The long-running saga about friendships and romantic entanglements among a close-knit group of Beverly Hills teens, *90210* became comfort TV for a generation of viewers. And it made megawatt celebs out of its stars, although Doherty's off-camera antics led to her firing after Season 4. The show ran for 10 seasons, long enough for everyone to graduate high school, matriculate college and enter adult life.
▶▶ Spinoff *Melrose Place* was also a big hit for Fox in 1992, and both shows earned reboots on The CW in the late '00s. Much of the show's original cast reunited for the six-episode Fox series, *BH90210*, in 2019.

The Big Bang Theory
TV-PG, 2007–2019
HBO Max, Paramount+, 12 seasons, 279 episodes (AD)
Sitcom created by Chuck Lorre and Bill Prady, with Jim Parsons, Johnny Galecki, Kaley Cuoco, Simon Helberg, Kunal Nayyar, Melissa Rauch and Mayim Bialik.
One of TV's all-time great ensembles kept *The Big Bang Theory* true to itself, yet the show remained fresh and entertaining season after season. Four brilliant young men, omnivorous in popular culture as well as science, have one trait in common: They don't know the first thing about women. From that simple premise came 12 seasons of laughs that went well beyond the show's nerdy origins. Though the star of the show was Parsons, who won four straight Emmys for playing Sheldon, the whole was cast and improved with Bialik's Amy and Rauch's Bernadette, whose additions enabled other characters to find new dimensions.

Big Brother
TV-MA, 2000–present
Paramount+, 23 seasons, 820 episodes
Reality competition with Julie Chen Moonves.
It is formulaic, occasionally awesome, other times kinda garbage, but always addicting and one of the most successful American reality franchises ever, with no end in sight. Summer wouldn't be summer without this long-running reality series set inside a house with dozens of spy cameras and a cash prize for the one who manages to outlast the others. And with live 24/7 video feeds on Paramount+, in addition to 3 weekly episodes on CBS, there are plenty of opportunities to get sucked into the *Big Brother* Borg.
▶▶ Three editions of the winter spinoff series *Celebrity Big Brother* have been produced, in 2018, 2019 and 2022.

Big Little Lies
TV-MA, 2017–2019
HBO Max, 2 seasons, 14 episodes (AD)
Drama created by David E. Kelley, with Reese Witherspoon, Nicole Kidman, Shailene Woodley, Zoë Kravitz, Adam

Scott, Laura Dern, James Tupper, Alexander Skarsgård, Jeffrey Nordling and Iain Armitage.

Reese Witherspoon and Nicole Kidman light it up in this high-gloss whodunit that spawned a raft of imitators. Why was this adaptation of Liane Moriarty's novel such a breakout hit, inspiring all those lookalikes (*Little Fires Everywhere*, *The Undoing*)? Maybe it was the vicarious joy viewers felt seeing rich, privileged white people coming undone. The first season's timing, in the early months of the Trump White House, could have been a factor. Maybe it was the pleasure of seeing two powerhouse actresses and a raft of great characters all sparring with each other. Most likely it's because David E. Kelley churned out some of the best scripts of his long career, blending comedy and drama in a way that sizzled and got the most out of his top-notch cast.

🐾 **From our forums:** "I want to delete this show from my memory and watch it all over again from the beginning."

🏆 Emmy and TCA awards for best limited series

Big Love
TV-MA, 2006–2011
HBO Max, 5 seasons, 53 episodes (AD)
Drama with Bill Paxton, Jeanne Tripplehorn, Chloë Sevigny, Ginnifer Goodwin, Amanda Seyfried, Douglas Smith, Grace Zabriskie, Matt Ross, Mary Kay Place and Melora Walters.

The show that made polyamory respectable, HBO's Mormon-themed drama also took faith and (yes) fidelity seriously. The highest compliment that can be paid to this series about Barb and Bill (Tripplehorn and Paxton) and the marriage they expanded to include Margene (Goodwin) and young Nicki (Sevigny) is that it wound up being so relatable. When Bill and one of his wives had issues, they weren't specific to LDS

or polygamist life — they were just issues. Bill's domineering dad Frank (Bruce Dern) was the best of the large supporting cast.

🐾 **From our forums:** "I actually like Bill. I think he's a conflicted man, but honestly tries to do the right thing by his faith. I didn't appreciate Barb so much, but on second viewings of the show I'm appreciating her a lot more. She works hard at avoiding the manipulation that's inherent to women in polygamy."

Big Mouth
TV-MA, 2017–present
Netflix original, 5 seasons, 51 episodes (AD)
Animated comedy created by Nick Kroll, Andy Goldberg, Jennifer Flackett and Mark Levin, with Nick Kroll, John Mulaney, Jessi Klein, Jason Mantzoukas, Fred Armisen, Maya Rudolph, Jordan Peele, Jenny Slate, Andrew Rannells and Richard Kind.

Middle school and all its embarrassing trials — puberty, crushes, masturbation, periods, depression, divorce — are taken to mortifying heights by this raucous animated comedy featuring a large voice cast of comedians. In addition to the kids themselves, their *bête noires* are also turned into cartoon creatures with names like Depression Kitty, Anxiety Mosquitos, Shame Wizard and Hormone Monstress (Rudolph, in a role that won her an Emmy for best cartoon voice-over).

🐾 **From our forums:** "Hilarious, raunchy, bonkers and poignant all at the same time. It totally captured the middle school/puberty experience."

▸▸ In 2019, Netflix announced plans for a spinoff, *Human Resources*, which is expected to bow sometime in 2022.

Big Shot
TV-PG, 2021–present
Disney+ original, 10 episodes (AD)

Family comedy-drama created by Brad Garrett, David E. Kelley and Dean Lorey, with John Stamos, Jessalyn Gilsig, Richard Robichaux, Yvette Nicole Brown, Sophia Mitri Schloss, Nell Verlaque, Tiana Le, Monique A. Green, Tisha Custodio and Cricket Wampler.

John Stamos plays a disgraced college basketball coach whose only opportunity to stay in the game is at a private girls school. America's favorite uncle learns lessons from his young charges in this feel-good series that's all Disney. The surprise is it's from producer David E. Kelley, who's been churning out harder-edged stuff lately (*Big Little Lies*, *The Undoing*). But Kelley creates a world that is poignant and female-driven, with notes of an old after-school special.

🐾 **From our forums:** "My son and I just watched the first 2 episodes. I love Stamos, so it's a treat for me, and anything we can watch together and agree on is good in my book."

▶▶ Disney+ renewed the series for a second season, set to go into production in 2022.

Big Sky
TV-14, 2020–present
Hulu, 2 seasons, 32 episodes (AD)
Drama created by David E. Kelley, with Katheryn Winnick, Kylie Bunbury, Ryan Phillippe, Brian Geraghty, Dedee Pfeiffer, Jesse James Keitel, Valerie Mahaffey, John Carroll Lynch, Patrick Gallagher and Natalie Alyn Lind.

Better-than-average network thriller features two female private detectives taking on a kidnapping ring in Montana. Based on the novels by C.J. Box, this David E. Kelley drama for ABC at first seemed to be echoing familiar women-in-danger tropes. But unusual twists soon pushed viewers along spooky new back highways and the show's power tandem of Cassie (Bunbury) and Jenny (Winnick)

gelled on-screen. A narrative reboot at S1E10 helped as well.

🐾 **From our forums:** "It is just so weird and crazy, but I kind of love it."

Big Time Adolescence
R, 2019
Hulu original, 1 hr 31 mins (AD)
Movie (comedy) with Pete Davidson, Griffin Gluck, Jon Cryer, Emily Arlook, Thomas Barbusca and Machine Gun Kelly.

A high school student comes of age under the dubious tutelage of the 20-something burnout who used to date his sister. This movie is funny, but it also lands some serious emotional punches as it shows these two friends growing and changing.

Billions
TV-MA, 2016–present
Showtime original, 6 seasons, 72 episodes
Drama with Paul Giamatti, Damian Lewis, Maggie Siff, Dave Costabile, Condola Rashad, Daniel K. Isaac, Kelly AuCoin, Jeffrey DeMunn, Asia Kate Dillion and Malin Akerman.

It's an unrealistic, cartoonish portrait of misdeeds on Wall Street, but it's got Damian Lewis facing off against Paul Giamatti — what more do you want? U.S. Attorney Chuck Rhoades (Giamatti) might come from money, but he loathes people who use their wealth to live above the law. That's why he's gunning for Bobby Axelrod (Lewis), a hedge fund manager who skirts all kinds of legal and ethical standards to make himself richer — and is close to Chuck's wife Wendy (Siff). Besides the endless scheming and head-butting between the two leads, *Billions* offers some funny and even touching moments as well as great views of Manhattan.

Some shows may have moved; see page 183.

Billy on the Street
TV-14, 2011–2017
HBO Max, 5 seasons, 54 episodes
Comedy, Reality show with Billy Eichner.

This genre-defying reality/comedy/ game show, set on the streets of New York, is a whirling dervish that captures everything we love about its frenetic host and its host city. Eichner (*Difficult People, Impeachment: American Crime Story*) was still a struggling comic when he partnered with Funny or Die to create this roving, rapid-fire quiz show that sees him confronting unsuspecting pedestrians with pop culture questions. Get the answer right, you get a dollar. Get it wrong, you get an insult. Either way, he's on to his next contestant in a matter of seconds.

▸▸ Beginning with Season 2, a different guest star runs down the street with Eichner each week (Anna Kendrick, Tina Fey, Sarah Jessica Parker, Seth Rogen).

Bird Box
R, 2018
Netflix original, 2 hrs 4 mins (AD)
Movie (thriller) with Sandra Bullock, John Malkovich, Sarah Paulson and Jacki Weaver.

Sandra Bullock riveted millions as a mom trying to save her children from a mysterious suicidal force. This dystopian thriller set the benchmark for streaming blockbusters. For a while there, it seemed like everyone was talking about it.

The Black Church
TV-14, 2021
PBS Passport, 3 hrs 40 mins
Movie (documentary) directed by Shayla Harris and Stacey L. Holman, with Henry Louis Gates Jr., Cornel West, Oprah Winfrey, Chinisha Scott, Michael Eric Dyson, John Legend, Al Sharpton, T.D. Jakes and Raphael G. Warnock.

Henry Louis Gates takes us on a lively tour of American history as seen through the lens of the Black churches that were spiritual, political and cultural homes for himself and millions of others. Though Gates always tries to bring an informal, personal touch to his PBS programs, *The Black Church* feels especially so. He is at home in the Black church and enjoys an easy intimacy with the church musicians and pastors he spends time with on camera. The songs are well-chosen and the stories lend warmth to what is a remarkable history of African-American religion.

A Black Lady Sketch Show
TV-MA, 2019–present
HBO Max, 2 seasons, 12 episodes (AD)
Sketch comedy created by Robin Thede, with Robin Thede, Gabrielle Dennis, Ashley Nicole Black, Quinta Brunson, Laci Mosley and Skye Townsend.

Robin Thede's humor explores the lives of Black women with gags on everything from church to parenting to office culture. Promoted as "the first sketch comedy series to be written by, directed by and starring Black women," the Emmy-nominated series benefits from Thede's off-camera friendships with many of the other members of her ensemble. Their camaraderie and the sketches that present ever-changing views of what it means to be a Black lady, give this show an original voice.

🗨 **From our forums:** "This show continues to kill it with the guest stars."

🏆 TCA Award for outstanding sketch/ variety series

Black Love
TV-14, 2017–present
Hulu, 4 seasons, 25 episodes
Docuseries created by Codie Elaine Oliver and Tommy Oliver.

Famous and not-so-famous Black couples offer fascinating windows into what makes their relationships work. The Olivers, who do the interviewing but stay off-camera, aim for a minimalist feel — no narrator, very little music and people's first names only (though yes, "Viola" is Viola Davis). The couples start with how they met and go from there, talking in anecdotes. Embarrassment and annoyance between the two will creep in occasionally, but the couples are still together, examples of resilience and the complexity and messiness of love.

Black Mirror

TV-MA, 2011–present
Netflix original, 5 seasons,
22 episodes (AD)
Anthology series (dystopian drama) created by Charlie Brooker.

The stories in this acclaimed futuristic drama explore our fixation with technology and how it has the potential to undermine society as we know it. "The Twilight Zone with gadgets," as one critic put it, is one way to look at this series that's now regarded as among the best of the decade. Set in the near-future, most episodes take the idea of bettering humanity through science and technology and push it to often dystopian ends. Brooker, the show's creator and writer, has been cited for his bold and imaginative writing.

▶▶ Beloved episodes include "San Junipero" (S3E4), where two women fall in love thanks to a simulated reality machine that also casts a long shadow over their relationship; "USS Callister" (S4E1), with Jesse Plemons as a socially awkward nerd who escapes into a simulated, *Star Trek*–style world; and *Bandersnatch*, a choose-your-own-ending movie about a choose-your-own-adventure game.

🏆 Peabody Award, Emmys for outstanding TV movie (2 wins) and writing (2 wins)

Black Monday

TV-MA, 2019–present
Showtime original, 3 seasons,
30 episodes
Comedy created by David Caspe and Jordan Cahan, with Don Cheadle, Andrew Rannells, Paul Scheer, Regina Hall, Casey Wilson, Yassir Lester, Ken Marino and Horatio Sanz.

Farcical period piece lampoons financial titans behaving badly in the Reagan era. One year before the 1987 stock market crash known as "Black Monday," Mo Monroe (Cheadle), who runs a low-level investment firm with his partner Dawn Darcy (Hall), sets in motion a chain of events that he thinks will score his firm a top-notch client. While the bad-boy antics of other shows and movies about Wall Street are present, the sharply written, perfectly delivered comedy more than makes up for it.

🗨 **From our forums:** "Thirty minutes of ridiculous, nostalgia-laced escapism is just what I needed."

Black Sails

TV-MA, 2014–2017
Starz original, 4 seasons, 38 episodes
Fantasy drama with Toby Stephens, Luke Arnold, Hannah New, Jessica Parker Kennedy, Toby Schmitz, Tom Hopper, Clara Paget, Zach McGowan and Hakeem Kae-Kazim.

The lives of pirates as thrillingly portrayed by a rogue's gallery of non-American actors. Think you're not interested in a swashbuckling action series? You might want to arrrr-reconsider! Along with sword fights and lusty nights ashore, we see the intricacies of the pirates' daily lives. Their complex web of alliances, betrayals and love affairs make for yarns that may well take you captive.

🏆 3 Emmys

Black Summer
TV-MA, 2019–present
Netflix original, 2 seasons,
16 episodes (AD)
Horror series with Jaime King, Justin Chu Cary, Christine Lee, Zoe Marlett and Kelsey Flower.

Fast-paced and loaded with political and cultural references, this isn't your everyday zombie apocalypse show. A group of strangers bands together in a desperate attempt to survive. Sounds familiar, but *Black Summer* is nothing like *The Walking Dead.* ("No long, fraught discussions," Stephen King tweeted approvingly. "No endless flashbacks.") And, in a not-so-veiled reference to the American refugee crisis, the survivors are forced to evade their so-called military protectors.

🗨 **From our forums:** "The zombies are fast so they are actually scary. You can't just stroll along to get away from them. Also, we learn enough about people to make them interesting without having them, in an apocalypse, speechify for hours."

Black-ish
TV-14, 2014–2022
Hulu, 8 seasons, 165 episodes (AD)
Sitcom created by Kenya Barris, with Anthony Anderson, Tracee Ellis Ross, Marcus Scribner, Yara Shahidi, Miles Brown, Marsai Martin, Jenifer Lewis, Deon Cole and Laurence Fishburne.

Sitcom about a Black family living in an affluent and white neighborhood is both edgy and familiar and never not funny. Able to touch on serious matters and say out loud what its viewers are thinking, *Black-ish* well reflected the age in which it appeared. Yet it also bears the marks of classic TV comedy, with its sharply

defined characters and tight, efficient writing.

🗨 **From our forums:** "The plots themselves are familiar but the dialogue and quips really elevate the show. Jokes are fast and furious. Visual gags, like the one about all the 'white savior' movies, are clever and spot on."

▶▶ Pairs well with *The Conners*

🏆 Peabody Award

The Blacklist
TV-14, 2013–present
Netflix, 9 seasons, 182 episodes
Drama with James Spader, Megan Boone, Diego Klattenhoff, Harry Lennix, Hisham Tawfiq, Amir Arison, Mozhan Marnò and Ryan Eggold.

James Spader is the rakish FBI informant Red Reddington in this pulpy procedural renowned for its delicious guest turns. Pivoting from *Boston Legal* to this long-running NBC hit, Spader is on-brand as a high-profile criminal who comes in from the cold bearing a "blacklist" of dangerous criminals and an offer to help rein them in. Red makes an enigmatic demand to be paired with rookie FBI profiler Liz Keen (Boone), setting in motion a dense, fascinating mythology involving the two crimefighters. When combined with the criminal-of-the-week element and guest appearances from Red's many associates, enemies, lovers and friends, the result is a network show unlike any other.

▶▶ It's best to watch *The Blacklist* from the beginning, or at the very least avoid jumping in at Season 9, which is set 2 years in the future after a turning point.
▶▶ The most recent season's episodes are on Peacock, but all the rest are on Netflix, which shelled out a then-record $2 million per episode in 2014 to stream *The Blacklist.*
▶▶ For suggestions of related shows, see "If You Liked *The Blacklist,*" page 371.

Bless the Harts

TV-14, 2019–2021
Hulu, 2 seasons, 34 episodes
Animated comedy created by Emily
Spivey, with Kristen Wiig, Maya Rudolph,
Jillian Bell, Ike Barinholtz, Kumail
Nanjiani, Fortune Feimster, Jeremy
Rowley, Drew Tarver and Emily Spivey.

**Like *King of the Hill* but with women,
this short-lived series celebrated a family
rich "in friends, family and laughter."**
Set in a sleepy Carolina town, this cartoon
revolves around the gentle misadventures
of broke single mom Jenny (Wiig), her
wacky mother (Rudolph) and teenage
daughter (Bell) and her likable boyfriend
Wayne (Barinholtz). Created for Fox and
slated on its testosterone-heavy Sunday
animation lineup, *Bless the Harts* never
found its audience, but anyone who loved
Hank and Peggy Hill will enjoy spending
time with the Harts.

Blindspotting

TV-MA, 2021–present
Starz original, 8 episodes (AD)
Comedy-drama created by Daveed
Diggs and Rafael Casal, with Jasmine
Cephas Jones, Helen Hunt, Jaylen Barron,
Atticus Woodward, Benjamin Earl Turner,
Candace Nicholas-Lippman and Rafael
Casal.

**Charming and occasionally surreal
spinoff to the 2018 film.** Ashley (Jones)
is a single mom in Oakland coping with
the absence of her partner, who has been
sent to jail. Using humor and rapid-
fire dialogue, *Blindspotting* probes the
complexities of multicultural urban life
without preachiness. As Ashley, Jones
gives the show a sympathetic central
character, while Hunt is terrific as the free-
spirited mother of Ashley's imprisoned
partner.

🐾 **From our forums:** "The weirdest thing
to get used to were the little musical
moments. If you can guarantee the movers

will dance while they pack up my boxes, I
will definitely hire them!"

Bling Empire

TV-MA, 2021–present
Netflix original, 8 episodes (AD)
Reality show with Anna Shay, Kevin
Kreider, Kelly Mi Li, Kim Lee, Kane Lim,
Christine Chiu and Gabriel Chiu.

**Formulaic, authentic, utterly addictive
series tags along with a close-knit group
of extremely wealthy Asian-Americans.**
This show from the producer of *Keeping
Up with the Kardashians* is basically
"Keeping Up with the Crazy Rich Asians."
Its authenticity is admirable: The cast
isn't pretend-rich; they include the son
of a real estate developer, high-end
cosmetic surgeons and the daughter of
a defense contractor. Both serious and
comedic, *Bling Empire* balances genuinely
surprising revelations and drama with
a lot of playful fun between people who
are actual friends, not random moneyed
millennials assembled by producers into a
group of "friends."

Blood Brother

PG, 2013
Tubi, Kanopy, 1 hr 32 mins
Movie (documentary) directed by Steve
Hoover, with Rocky Braat and Steve
Hoover.

**An aimless young American finds his
purpose in life in caring for HIV/AIDS
kids in India.** Rocky Braat admits early
on in *Blood Brother* that he has intimacy
issues, but as we learn from Steve Hoover's
intense, emotional documentary, that
independent spirit allowed Rocky to
leave his career and possessions behind
and move to India to care for HIV/
AIDS–infected children. This is less of a
social-issues film than a meditation on
caregiving, how it can bring happiness
both to the one receiving care and the one
giving it.

🏆 Sundance Film Festival's Grand Jury Prize

Bloodlands
TV-14, 2021–present
Acorn TV, 4 episodes
Crime drama with James Nesbitt, Lorcan Cranitch, Charlene McKenna, Lisa Dwan, Lola Petticrew, Chris Walley and Ian McElhinney.

This grim but unpredictable thriller wraps Northern Ireland's troubled history and a detective's own past around a kidnapping case. Actor-turned-writer Chris Brandon created this atmospheric drama that was produced by *Line of Duty* creator Jed Mercurio. With a solid performance from Nesbitt as Tom Brannick, this show packs a lot of nuance, mood and historical resonance into its first four episodes.

Bloodline
TV-MA, 2015–2017
Netflix original, 3 seasons, 33 episodes (AD)
Drama with Kyle Chandler, Ben Mendelsohn, Sissy Spacek, Linda Cardellini, Norbert Leo Butz, Jacinda Barrett, Chloë Sevigny, Katie Finneran, John Leguizamo and Owen Teague.

Ben Mendelsohn won an Emmy for his role in this thriller about a family being torn apart by secrets. When Danny Rayburn (Mendelsohn) returns to his family's oceanfront hotel in Florida, no one seems very happy to see him. The show sets about explaining why, moving slowly into dark waters in this well-timed thriller that surfaces a shocking twist with the power of a shark bite. Chandler and Spacek are also standouts.

📡 **From our forums:** "Season 1 was so good. Season 2 was starting to border on implausible. The first episode of Season 3 was truly awful. There are no redeeming characters anymore and I've lost interest in all of them."

Blown Away
TV-PG, 2019–present
Netflix original, 3 seasons, 24 episodes (AD)
Reality competition directed by Mike Bickerton, with Nick Uhas.

A glassblowing competition proves to be crackerjack entertainment. Another entry in the "nice people playing nice" competition shows (we have a list of those; see page), these tightly paced half-hour episodes pull you in with their charm and keep you watching as they immerse you in the highly particular craft of turning sand into art.

📡 **From our forums:** "The competition was more like *Face Off* or *Forged in Fire* than *Project Runway*." "I would love to see it expand to an hour so that more techniques and skills could be explained." ▶▶ The show's four-episode holiday-themed third season appears on Netflix under the title *Blown Away: Christmas*.

Blue Planet
TV-G, 2001
Discovery+, 8 episodes
Docuseries with David Attenborough.

Even after 2 decades it remains a marvel of cinematography, revealing just a few of the marine marvels that had previously escaped human notice. *Blue Planet* was as much a quantum leap in nature filmmaking as Jacques Cousteau's TV specials were in the previous generation. Loaded with innovative underwater shots, the series showcased Attenborough's unmatched narration and his signature globetrotting approach to telling the story of the oceans that cover most of the planet. The program's most glaring defect, in hindsight, was its failure to reckon with the impact of climate change, something Attenborough would atone for in *Blue Planet II*.

🏆 2 Emmys

Blue Planet II
TV-G, 2017–2018
Discovery+, 8 episodes
Docuseries with David Attenborough.

Sir David takes us on a breathtaking look at the world's oceans, with a focus on the impact of Earth's rising temperature on marine life. Come for the stunning 4K footage, stay for Attenborough's peerless ability to tell you the story behind what you're looking at. Like any good nature series, there are plenty of dramatic encounters to keeps one's attention from flagging. But Sir David never wanders far from the series's major throughline — the devastating impact of climate change on the marine world.

🏆 Emmy for Attenborough's outstanding narration

Bo Burnham: Inside
TV-MA, 2021
Netflix original, 1 hr 27 mins (AD)
Comedy special directed by Bo Burnham, with Bo Burnham.

Not your usual comedy special, Burnham (*Promising Young Woman*) wrote and performed this solo special while in lockdown during the pandemic. A talented comic singer, Burnham uses music and humor to explore the otherwise depressing topic of being completely cut off from the lifeblood of your career: human interaction. This scripted collection of jokes, songs and monologues at times feels like an intimate (almost *too* intimate) documentary about the COVID era.

Boardwalk Empire
TV-MA, 2010–2014
HBO Max, 5 seasons, 57 episodes (AD)

Drama created by Terence Winter, with Steve Buscemi, Michael Shannon, Kelly Macdonald, Shea Whigham, Stephen Graham, Vincent Piazza, Michael K. Williams, Paul Sparks, Gretchen Mol and Michael Stuhlbarg.

Prestige drama from a writer on *The Sopranos*, set in the free-flowing world of Prohibition-era Atlantic City. Like so many gangster dramas, this one has an operatic quality as it depicts the sprawling network of bootleggers, thugs, prostitutes and G-men who are swimming in a sea of illegal booze. Buscemi's solid as kingpin Nucky Thompson, but the show arguably belongs to supporting player like Pitt, Mol and Shannon, who descend into moral quagmires as they try to survive.

🏆 20 Emmys

Bob (Hearts) Abishola
TV-PG, 2019–present
Paramount+, 3 seasons, 58 episodes (AD)
Sitcom created by Chuck Lorre and Gina Yashere, with Billy Gardell, Folake Olowofoyeku, Christine Ebersole, Gina Yashere, Matt Jones, Maribeth Monroe, Shola Adewusi, Barry Shabaka Henley and Vernee Watson.

Slow-build romance between an African national and a regular guy from Detroit is loaded with laughs and touching moments. Bob (Gardell) is a compression-sock manufacturer in Detroit. Recovering from a heart attack, he falls for his Nigerian nurse, Abishola (Olowofoyeku). The cultural exchange is lively, thanks to British comedian Yashere, who developed the show with Lorre and plays Abishola's friend Kemi. Ebersole is a pistol as Bob's mom.

The Bob Newhart Show
TV-PG, 1972–1978
Hulu, 6 seasons, 142 episodes
Classic sitcom created by Lorenzo Music, with Bob Newhart, Suzanne Pleshette,

Bill Daily, Marcia Wallace, Peter Bonerz and Jack Riley.

Of all the Bobs played by Bob Newhart on network TV over the decades, it was the first — Chicago psychologist Bob Hartley — who's been the most enduring. Hi, Bob! Playing a shrink in the 1970s was not only the socially relevant move but wound up the perfect fit for Newhart's passive-aggressive humor in this winning sitcom from Mary Tyler Moore's studio. His practice should not be studied by aspiring therapists, but students of comedy will find the Newhart show holds up as a model of writing economy. It also had TV's best small ensemble before *Frasier*: at the office, perpetual patient Mr. Carlin (Riley), secretary Carol (Wallace) and Jerry the dentist (Bonerz); at home, neighbor Howard (Daily) and Bob's cool-headed wife Emily (Pleshette), who got the best lines on the show.

▶▶ Where did the Thanksgiving episode start? Right here, with "Over the River and Through the Woods" (S4E11), good for a historical watch if not many laughs. If you want those, start with "Death Be My Destiny" (S5E19) and watch to the end of this strong-finishing series.

Bob's Burgers
TV-PG, 2011–present
Paramount+, Prime Video, Hulu,
12 seasons, 239 episodes (AD)
Animated comedy with H. Jon Benjamin, Dan Mintz, Eugene Mirman, John Roberts, Kristen Schaal, Larry Murphy and David Herman.

Deadpan comedy about a burger-joint proprietor and his family who live in the apartment upstairs has become as much a part of the popular culture as *The Simpsons*. Patriarch and title character Bob (Benjamin), perpetually enthusiastic wife Linda (Roberts), hyper-weird son Gene (Mirman) and hard-nosed, bunny-eared daughter Louise (Schaal) all have

strong comic personalities, though ones we've seen on other prime-time cartoons. But we've never seen anyone like the show's breakout character, Tina Belcher (Mintz). The eldest of Bob and Linda's children, Tina's flat affect, tendency toward panic, roiling teenage emotions and hormones have made her an avatar for the awkward teenage girl inside us all.

▶▶ Benjamin is the namesake voice of both *Bob's Burgers* and *Archer*.

🏆 2 Emmys for best animated program

Bobby Kennedy for President
TV-MA, 2018
Netflix original, 4 episodes (AD)
Docuseries directed by Dawn Porter, with Peter Edelman, Paul Schrade, William Arnone and Harry Belafonte.

Striking archival footage, some never before seen, offers a fresh look at RFK's ascent from his brother's enforcer to a singular voice in the American conversation. Why did Robert F. Kennedy's last-minute campaign for president in 1968 capture the imagination of America? Why was his assassination while on that campaign so deeply felt? Director Dawn Porter's film, with its eye for detail and personality, explains the Kennedy phenomenon and the cultural forces that made it — and what was lost when he died.

BoJack Horseman
TV-MA, 2014–2020
Netflix original, 6 seasons,
77 episodes (AD)
Animated comedy created by Raphael Bob-Waksberg, with Will Arnett, Amy Sedaris, Alison Brie, Aaron Paul and Paul F. Tompkins.

Alternately hilarious and sad, this complex Hollywood satire about a former animal star is already regarded as a cartoon classic. BoJack (Arnett), a horse with very human traits, was once a big star. Now, washed up and drinking too much in his Hollywood Hills home, he's trying to make a comeback with the help of his ghostwriter Diane (Brie). Other regulars include permanent house guest Todd (Paul) and BoJack's former sitcom rival, a lovable Lab named Mr. Peanutbutter (Tompkins). The show's most famous episodes have centered on BoJack's alcoholism, depression and anger; dementia, rape and suicide have anchored other stories. To explore such a challenging emotional spectrum, designer Lisa Hanawalt has pushed animation to its limits. The writers keep loyal viewers engaged with strong characters and fantastic visual gags.

🗨 **From our forums:** "I had to take a breather from marathoning it because things got kinda heavy."

🏆 Critics Choice Award for best animated series (4 wins)

Bonding
TV-MA, 2019–2021
Netflix original, 2 seasons,
15 episodes (AD)
Comedy-drama with Zoe Levin, Brendan Scannell, Micah Stock, Theo Stockman and Matthew Wilkas.
Lighthearted sitcom follows two former high school friends who decide to go into business as BDSM sex workers. Tiff (Levin), aka "Mistress May," and her assistant Pete (Scannell) form a solid bond while performing bondage in this nimble, sex-positive relationship comedy.

Bones
TV-14, 2005–2017
Hulu, Prime Video, 12 seasons,
245 episodes (AD)
Drama with Emily Deschanel, David Boreanaz, Michaela Conlin, T.J. Thyne, Tamara Taylor and John Francis Daley.
Sparks fly between a forensic anthropologist and an FBI agent who frequently butt heads as they try to solve murders in this breezy crime procedural. Agent Seeley Booth (Boreanaz) and Dr. "Bones" Brennan (Deschanel) are the Sam and Diane of crime TV: The series made it for 9 seasons largely powered by their mental sparring and romantic tension. The supporting characters helped form an unlikely community that made *Bones* stand out from the procedural pack.

The Book of Boba Fett
TV-14, 2021–present
Disney+ original, 1 seasons, 7 episodes
Drama created by Jon Favreau, with Temuera Morrison , Ming-Na Wen, Jennifer Beals, David Pasquesi and Matt Berry.
This spinoff of *The Mandalorian* follows the classic *Star Wars* bounty hunter as he tries to take control of the territory once run by Jabba the Hutt. Critics have been sharply divided on this show, which is among the more narratively ambitious entries in the *Star Wars* universe. There's a lot of character building, beginning with the show's namesake, a popular character dating back to the 1970s finally getting his own backstory and fresh adventures set in the aftermath of the original *Star Wars* story.

Borat Subsequent Moviefilm
R, 2020
Prime Video original, 1 hr 35 mins (AD)
Movie (comedy) with Sacha Baron Cohen and Maria Bakalova.
The notorious Kazakhstani returns to America for a series of largely improvised and ridiculously uncomfortable scenes with everyday folks and celebrity politicians. As Borat's daughter, Bakalova was a surprise Oscar nominee for best supporting actress and just like the first movie, the screenplay was Oscar–nominated as well.

Bored to Death

TV-MA, 2009–2011
HBO Max, 3 seasons, 24 episodes (AD)
Comedy created by Jonathan Ames, with Jason Schwartzman, Zach Galifianakis, Ted Danson, Heather Burns and John Hodgman.

Brilliant if largely forgotten, this comedy miracle teamed Jason Schwartzman, Ted Danson and Zach Galifianakis in a detective farce set in the NYC literary scene. Overshadowed at HBO by *Curb Your Enthusiasm*, this one never got the love it deserved. Novelist Jonathan Ames created a fictional version of himself (Schwartzman) as a struggling writer who begins moonlighting as a private investigator in Brooklyn. His friend Ray (Galifianakis) and editor (Danson) soon get pulled into his capers. Tonally audacious, *Bored to Death* blended farce with more tender moments.

Born into Brothels

R, 2004
Tubi, Hoopla, 1 hr 25 mins
Movie (documentary) directed by Zana Briski and Ross Kauffman.

Insightful and even inspiring film follows children whose mothers are prostitutes in Calcutta's red-light district. While making a film about Indian sex workers, the directors found it hard to get access to the women — but their children were all around. So, ingeniously, they began teaching them photography and got the kids to take cameras into places where the directors couldn't. Though highly acclaimed for its intimate view of the children's lives, the film has sparked years of debate over the directors' methods and for what critics said was an overly harsh depiction of the children's mothers.

🏆 Oscar for best documentary feature

Bosch

TV-MA, 2014–2021
Prime Video original, 7 seasons, 68 episodes (AD)
Crime drama with Titus Welliver, Jamie Hector, Amy Aquino, Lance Reddick, Madison Lintz, Troy Evans, DaJuan Johnson, Gregory Scott Cummins and Scott Klace.

The grilled-cheese sandwich of streaming procedurals, *Bosch* spreads prestige TV elements over an ordinary cop show with satisfying results. Everyone underestimates detective Hieronymus "Harry" Bosch (Welliver), including many TV critics. So it's worth noting that the person who adapted Michael Connelly's novels for the screen, Eric Overmyer, worked on both *Law & Order* and *The Wire*. With a balanced blend of procedural plots and season-long arcs, solid writing and inspired, age-appropriate casting choices (lots of '90s greats show up here), this is a nice-and-easy show to sink your teeth into.

💬 **From our forums:** "The pace sped up near the end of the fourth episode. It took a while to introduce the characters, plot, look/feel of L.A., etc." "I'm sure the vets from *The Wire* made me notice this, but it had a lighter touch of politics and the city."

⏩ *Bosch: Legacy*, a spinoff series starring Welliver, is set to bow on Amazon's IMDb TV in 2022.

Boss Level

TV-MA, 2020
Hulu original, 1 hr 34 mins (AD)
Movie (action) with Mel Gibson, Naomi Watts, Michelle Yeoh and Frank Grillo.

A special forces agent has to escape a time loop that keeps resulting in his murder. Grillo's performance as the agent is especially strong and it gives human stakes to this high-concept story.

Boston Legal

TV-14, 2004–2008

Hulu, IMDb TV, 5 seasons, 101 episodes

Drama created by David E. Kelley, with William Shatner, James Spader, Candice Bergen, Rene Auberjonois, Mark Valley and Julie Bowen.

The interplay between James Spader and William Shatner may never again be matched in lawyer shows. Toward the end of *The Practice*'s eight-season run, the show decided that Spader would take over as the show's lead lawyer, and that worked out so well that this spinoff was born. It worked because Kelley took the heavy dramatics of *The Practice* and turned it into absurd semi-comedy. *Boston Legal* lasted 100 episodes, won 2 Emmys for Spader and one for Denny Crane — uh, William Shatner.

🏆 Peabody Award

A Boy Called Christmas

PG, 2021

Netflix original, 1 hr 46 mins (AD)

Movie (family comedy) directed by Gil Kenan, with Henry Lawfull, Maggie Smith, Jim Broadbent, Michiel Huisman, Kristen Wiig, Stephen Merchant, Toby Jones and Sally Hawkins.

Star-studded cast tells a beautifully animated origin story of Santa Claus, with lots of callouts for the grownups in the audience. In a faraway land, a king (Broadbent) dispatches his subjects to go on quests in search of magic and hope. That's the Christmas story that an old auntie (Smith) tells her young hearers in this charming production from director Kenan (*Monster House*) and screenwriter Ol Parker (*Best Exotic Marigold Hotel*), who clearly took inspiration from *The Princess Bride*.

▶▶ Pairs well with *Klaus*

Boys State

PG-13, 2020

Apple TV+ original, 1 hr 49 mins (AD)

Movie (documentary) directed by Amanda McBaine and Jesse Moss.

A raucous and entertaining exercise in civil society offers sobering insights into how the political game is played today. Every year across the country the American Legion sponsors Boys State (and Girls State) as an exercise in "citizenship development" involving thousands of high schoolers, some of whom — Bill Clinton and Joe Biden, among others — go on to make politics a career. Filmed at the 2018 Texas Boys State in Austin, this spellbinding doc captures the propulsive energy of the weeklong, seat-of-the-pants initiation into campaigning and how Boys State has become a mirror of the divisive politics that grown-ups play for keeps.

The Boys

TV-MA, 2019–present

Prime Video original, 2 seasons, 16 episodes (AD)

Superhero drama created by Eric Kripke, with Karl Urban, Jack Quaid, Antony Starr, Erin Moriarty, Dominique McElligott, Jessie T. Usher, Laz Alonso, Chace Crawford, Tomer Capon and Karen Fukuhara.

Superheroes turn out to be horrible people working for a mega-corporation bent on world domination ... unless The Boys can stop them. The Seven are more than superheroes, they're rock stars — selfish, entitled rock stars working for privately held Vought, which would like to outsource them to the military for megabucks. This would all be a leaden and cynical satire of DC Comics superheroes (and comic-book narratives generally) if not for the lively adaptation of the Garth Ennis books by Seth Rogen and Evan

For shows sorted by streaming platform, see page 381.

Goldberg, who worked similar wonders with *Preacher*.

💬 **From our forums:** "I was repulsed by all the gore, some of which required that I look away. Otherwise, I was hooked." "The PR side of the Seven is actually quite amusing — prearranged 'team ups,' vetted crimes, supporting narratives, all geared towards getting positive publicity and better exposure. Capitalist superheroism by appointment."

▸▸ A third season is expected in mid–2022.

Breaking Bad
TV-MA, 2008–2013
Netflix, 5 seasons, 62 episodes (AD)
Drama created by Vince Gilligan, with Bryan Cranston, Aaron Paul, Anna Gunn, Betsy Brandt, RJ Mitte, Dean Norris, Bob Odenkirk, Giancarlo Esposito, Jonathan Banks and Steven Michael Quezada.
Bryan Cranston created one of TV's most indelible characters in Walter White, a milquetoast chemistry teacher who evolves into a ruthless drug kingpin. You might say this touchstone of contemporary prestige TV has the right chemistry. There's the sitcom star who's more than ready for his close-up, the supporting cast that can match his intensity and also go darkly comedic, the storyline as hair-raising and addictive as any that has been dreamed up for television — and all of this in the remarkably evocative backdrop of Albuquerque, which the producers chose for the tax credits.

▸▸ *Breaking Bad* creator Vince Gilligan reunited with Aaron Paul and a number of other familiar faces in 2019 for the Netflix original *El Camino: A Breaking Bad Movie*, which continues Jesse Pinkman's story after the events of the series.

🏆 2 Peabody Awards, Emmy for best drama series (2 wins), lead actor in a drama (Cranston, 4 wins) and supporting actor (Paul, 3 wins)

Breeders
TV-MA, 2020–present
Hulu, 2 seasons, 20 episodes
British comedy with Martin Freeman, Daisy Haggard, Alun Armstrong, Joanna Bacon, George Wakeman, Jayda Eyles, Stella Gonet and Michael McKean.
British couple with young children alternate between the joys of parenting and the despair of having to parent. Paul (Freeman) and Ally (Haggard) have two young ones with a third on the way. If that's not enough to stress out a working couple, Ally's dad (McKean) has just shown up. *Breeders* joins a growing club of edgy parenting sitcoms, but unlike *Workin' Moms* and *The Letdown*, this is more about how child-raising impacts a marriage. In one episode, Paul and Ally are secretly thrilled that Sprout, the family gerbil, has finally died — but explaining loss to their children and dealing with the unexpected effects of grief throws the family off-kilter.

▸▸ A third season is set to air in 2022.

Bridgerton
TV-MA, 2020–present
Netflix original, 2 seasons, 16 episodes (AD)
Historical drama with Phoebe Dynevor, Regé-Jean Page, Jonathan Bailey, Adjoa Andoh, Ruth Gemmell, Nicola Coughlan, Polly Walker, Claudia Jessie, Julie Andrews and Golda Rosheuvel.
Perhaps you think Netflix's most-watched show of 2020 is not for you; the Lady begs to differ. Superproducer Shonda Rhimes takes on Regency England in this lavish, sexy costume drama with a modern vibe. Lady Violet Bridgerton (Gemmell), a widow, is raising eight children in 19th-century London, including Daphne (Dynevor), whose

search for a suitor becomes the talk of the town thanks to the anonymous scandal sheet penned by "Lady Whistledown" (voiced by Julie Andrews). Based on Julia Quinn's *Bridgerton* novels, this is Austen-era English society with all the sense and sensibility you'd expect, but with a *Gossip Girl* sheen and actors and actresses of color in the cast. That includes the dashing Simon (Page), a fan favorite whose courtship of Daphne was the central storyline of Season 1.

From our forums: "I liked most of the characters even though the lead couple left me cold." "Enjoyed it more than I thought I would. The Season 1 finale pulled everything together perfectly."

▶▶ Before Season 2 had even premiered, the streamer renewed *Bridgerton* for Seasons 3 and 4.

▶▶ For suggestions of related shows, see "If You Liked *Bridgerton*," page 371.

Broad City
TV-14, 2014–2019
Hulu, 5 seasons, 50 episodes
Comedy with Abbi Jacobson, Ilana Glazer, Hannibal Buress, Arturo Castro, John Gemberling, Paul W. Downs and Chris Gethard.

Two funny New York women enjoy their adventures together more than being with men, doing drugs or holding bizarre jobs. A smarter, grosser *2 Broke Girls*, this is the kind of broad (so to speak) comedy that in the past was reserved for male duos. Laugh-out-loud physical comedy pairs well with goofy banter and the general grubby weirdness of these ladies' lives. As it evolves, the show also becomes observant of how money (or lack thereof) can seriously hobble urban dwellers' lives, while still checking the LMAO box.

Broadchurch
TV-MA, 2013–2017
Netflix, 3 seasons, 24 episodes
Crime drama with David Tennant, Olivia Colman, Jodie Whittaker, Andrew Buchan, Carolyn Pickles, Arthur Darvill, Charlotte Beaumont and Adam Wilson.

David Tennant and Olivia Colman are paired up as detectives who are haunted by the death of an 11-year-old boy. Set in a quiet seaside town full of secrets, *Broadchurch* eschews the familiar course of many crime shows for something more emotional, character-driven and even beautiful. Colman, whom everyone recognizes now as middle-aged Queen Elizabeth from *The Crown*, forms one of TV's all-time great detective duos with Tennant. And not that you watch shows like *Broadchurch* for the scenery, but that's brilliant, too.

🏆 Peabody Award, BAFTA TV Award for best drama

Brockmire
TV-MA, 2017–2020
Hulu, 4 seasons, 32 episodes
Comedy with Hank Azaria, Amanda Peet, Tyrel Jackson Williams and Hemky Madera.

Hank Azaria hit an inside-the-park home run in this role as sportscaster Jim Brockmire, whose career imploded and is now calling minor-league baseball games in Pennsylvania. Small-ball foibles, absurd storylines and crackling dialogue are enough to commend 3 short seasons of *Brockmire*, but Peet also delivers an all-star performance as the ballclub's owner. It's a credit to both her and Azaria that their characters are so dysfunctional yet compelling and even sympathetic.

From our forums: "Having covered minor league baseball for 30 years, I love the line it is managing to straddle between completely awesomely ridiculous and completely awesomely accurate!"

Brooklyn Nine-Nine
TV-14, 2013–2021
Peacock, Hulu, 8 seasons,
153 episodes (AD)
Sitcom created by Michael Schur and
Daniel J. Goor, with Andy Samberg,
Andre Braugher, Melissa Fumero, Terry
Crews, Stephanie Beatriz, Joe Lo Truglio,
Chelsea Peretti, Dirk Blocker and Joel
McKinnon Miller.

**Think of it as *Barney Miller* on Adderall,
only funnier.** With its precinct room full
of cut-ups who often seemed to take more
pleasure in office shenanigans than their
cases, the 99th bore more than a passing
resemblance to the fictional 12th Precinct
of *Barney Miller*. Led by their deadpan,
openly gay commander Holt (Braugher)
and star detective Peralta (Samberg),
the *B99* gang were depicted as more
progressive, effective and community-
focused than the real-life NYPD seen in
the news. The show's long run — it was
canceled by Fox after Season 5, only to be
picked up by NBC — allowed *B99* to serve
fans with recurring storylines, like an
oddly elusive bandit who keeps escaping
the cops' clutches and the unfortunate
Halloween costume choices of Peralta's
partner Boyle (Lo Truglio).

▸▸ Season 8, filmed during the pandemic
and after the police murder of George
Floyd, incorporated both news events
while trying to keep the show a comedy.
Critics were divided on whether it
succeeded.

Buffy the Vampire Slayer
TV-14, 1996–2003
Hulu, Prime Video, 7 seasons,
145 episodes
Fantasy drama created by Joss Whedon,
with Sarah Michelle Gellar, Nicholas
Brendon, Alyson Hannigan, Anthony
Head, James Marsters, Emma Caulfield
Ford, Michelle Trachtenberg, Charisma
Carpenter, David Boreanaz and Seth
Green.

**This Gen X blend of romance, mystery
and the undead marked an important
cultural shift in TV storytelling.** Unlike
the traditional damsel in distress, Buffy
Summers (Gellar) doesn't fear vampires;
thanks to her physical and mental powers
she can dispatch them like so many
hapless stormtroopers. Though Buffy takes
her mysteriously granted powers seriously,
she just wants to be a normal student and
hang with her friends at Sunnyvale High.
It was a brilliant setup for years of young-
adult entertainment leading to hundreds
of novels, comic books, fan fiction
creations and a spinoff series, *Angel*.

▸▸ Season 6 was the show's high-water
mark, including the beloved musical
episode, "Once More With Feeling," which
even drew audiences to movie theaters for
sing-alongs.

▸▸ Creator Joss Whedon was disciplined
by his studio in late 2020 after reports
surfaced that multiple female stars of *Buffy*
had complained about Whedon's behavior
on the set.

Bunheads
TV-PG, 2012–2013
Hulu, 18 episodes
Comedy-drama created by Amy
Sherman-Palladino, with Sutton Foster,
Kelly Bishop, Kaitlyn Jenkins, Julia
Goldani Telles, Bailey De Young and
Emma Dumont.

**Sutton Foster plays a Vegas showgirl-
turned-small town dance instructor,
leading a cast of aspiring young dancers
in this too-short-lived series.** ABC
Family (now Freeform) gave up too soon
on *Bunheads*, a promising effort from
Gilmore Girls creator Amy Sherman-
Palladino starring Foster, a Tony winner
who oozes talent on stage. The show
probably took too long to develop —
Foster's character didn't even officially get
her dance gig until well into the season —
but when it worked, it was extraordinary.

Gilmore Girls fans will spot many familiar faces.

🗨 **From our forums:** "After several viewings I have concluded that I like Foster's take on the witty, tall, self-deprecating brunette much more than Lauren Graham's."

Burn Notice
TV-PG, 2007–2013
Hulu, Prime Video, 7 seasons,
111 episodes
Crime drama with Jeffrey Donovan, Bruce Campbell, Gabrielle Anwar and Sharon Gless.

Maybe the best from USA Network's stable of light, fun procedurals from the '00s. In the superb pilot episode, spy Michael Western (Donovan) receives his "burn notice" that he's exiled from the intelligence agency that employs him — while he's on assignment. After a bare-knuckle escape, he winds up in south Florida, mulling his fate and keeping on his toes by helping one hapless schlub after another out of danger, with help from Sam (fan favorite Campbell) and Fiona (Anwar). The formula of action, spy intrigue and amusing family drama goes down as easy as a mojito.

Burning Love
TV-14, 2012–2013
PlutoTV, 3 seasons, 42 episodes
Satirical comedy with Michael Ian Black, Ken Marino, Ryan Hansen, Abigail Spencer, Beth Dover, June Diane Raphael, Janet Varney, Joe Lo Truglio, Rob Huebel and Kumail Nanjiani.

Everything you want from a *Bachelor-Bachelorette* parody — plus a giant panda outfit. The eminently mockable *Bachelor* franchise is the target of this series. The first season finds firefighter Mark Orlando (Marino) trying to "ignite the flames of love!" in a cast of aspirants played by the likes of Spencer, Dover,

Kristen Bell and whoever that is inside the panda suit. In Season 2, former contestant Julie (Raphael) returns to choose among a harem including Brody, Nanjiani and Hansen. Season 3 reunites contestants from the previous 2 seasons to compete for a cash prize of … $900.

Calibre
TV-MA, 2018
Netflix original, 1 hr 41 mins (AD)
Movie (thriller) with Jack Lowden, Martin McCann, Tony Curran, Ian Pirie and Kate Bracken.

Two friends on a hunting trip try to cover up a horrifying accident, but the residents of a nearby town suspect them anyway. This is a remarkably tense film with satisfying twists and excellent lead performances.

Californication
TV-MA, 2007–2014
Showtime original, 7 seasons,
84 episodes
Comedy-drama with David Duchovny, Natascha McElhone, Evan Handler, Pamela Adlon, Madeleine Martin, Stephen Tobolowsky and Madeline Zima.

David Duchovny followed *The X-Files* with this underappreciated cable series, playing an alcoholic novelist whose writer's block stems from his inability to resist L.A.'s hedonistic side. For most of its history Showtime has played second-fiddle to HBO and for good reason. But *Californication* was a rare creative success, at least for its first 2 seasons, thanks largely to its charming, unapologetically compromised lead. Filled with dark humor and premium-cable-channel sex, the show revels in Hank's many sordid escapades, yet nods occasionally toward deeper themes about purpose and interconnectedness.

For shows sorted by streaming platform, see page 381.

Call the Midwife
TV-PG, 2012–present
Netflix, PBS Passport, 11 seasons,
96 episodes (AD)
Historical drama created by Heidi
Thomas, with Vanessa Redgrave, Laura
Main, Jenny Agutter, Stephen McGann,
Judy Parfitt, Helen George, Cliff Parisi,
Linda Bassett, Max Macmillan and
Victoria Yeates.

**Long-running period piece explores
the professional and personal lives of
a group of midwives working in the
East End of London in the 1950s and
'60s.** Anyone who savors the emotional
sweep and period specificity of a series
like *Downton Abbey* will be quickly
pulled into the world of these midwives.
With medical procedures depicted with
remarkable frankness and offset by the
generous nature of these servants, this is
a rich and ultimately uplifting portrait of
the communities that women create.

▸▸ Like so many beloved series from
across the pond, *Call the Midwife* has aired
an annual Christmas special each year
since its 2012 debut.

▸▸ Pairs well with *All Creatures Great and
Small*

The Capture
TV-MA, 2019–present
Peacock, 6 episodes (AD)
British drama with Holliday Grainger,
Callum Turner, Ron Perlman, Ben Miles,
Laura Haddock, Ginny Holder, Cavan
Clerkin, Peter Singh, Barry Ward and Lia
Williams.

**Intelligent, up-to-date thriller will
heighten your paranoia about deepfake
video technology.** After being acquitted of
a war crime, British soldier Shaun Emery
(Turner) is accused of killing his attorney,
but detective Rachel Carey (Grainger)
begins to suspect Shaun is being framed
as part of an elaborate conspiracy.
Grainger is effective as both a gritty cop

and a person confronted with deepfake
and other tech-savvy espionage she does
not understand. Rachel's confusion and
disorientation is utterly relatable, making
The Capture not just a compelling thriller
but a warning about the bizarre new
reality upon us.

▸▸ A second season was commissioned by
the BBC in 2020.

Capturing the Friedmans
Not Rated, 2003
HBO Max, 1 hr 47 mins
Movie (documentary) directed by
Andrew Jarecki.

**Director Andrew Jarecki revisits a
screaming-headlines case of sexual
molestation from the 1980s and finds a
huge injustice was done.** Father and son
Arnold and Jesse Friedman were charged
with molesting neighborhood kids in
the basement of their Long Island house.
While the media had a field day, the five-
person Friedman family disintegrated.
Jesse's brother David captured it all on
camera and let Jarecki use the riveting
video in his film. Through interviews with
alleged victims and his own research,
Jarecki exonerates one of the accused.
This Oscar-nominated film is crusading
documentary filmmaking of a high order.

🏆 Sundance Film Festival Grand Jury
Prize

Cardi Tries
Not Rated, 2020–present
Facebook Watch original, 2 seasons,
17 episodes
Celebreality show created by Jesse
Collins, with Cardi B.

**The hip-hop superstar delights as she
tries something new in each episode.**
Over these 15-minute episodes, Cardi B
tries ballet (taught by the one and only
Debbie Allen), ranching, stunt driving and
more. She isn't exactly great at any of these
new pastimes, but that's what makes it

so much fun. Who doesn't want to watch Cardi B read *Everyone Poops* to a nursery school classroom?

The Casketeers

TV-14, 2018–present
Netflix original, 4 seasons,
32 episodes (AD)
Docuseries directed by Susan Leonard, with Francis Tipene and Kaiora Tipene.

Unexpectedly uplifting docuseries goes inside a Maori-run mortuary business in Auckland, New Zealand. Francis Tipene is the jovial, fastidious, opinionated co-owner of Tipene Funerals, serving Auckland's sizable Maori and Tonga (Polynesian) populations. Kaiora, his partner in business and life, is just as particular about the bottom line as Francis is about casket lining. Humor, local culture and lump-in-throat moments seamlessly blend together. Francis says he's in the business of "uplifting" souls that have shed their mortal bodies and helping usher them to a plane where life continues. Uplift is what *Casketeers* does for its audience as well.

▶▶ At press time, Season 3 and 4 had yet to land on Netflix.

Castle Rock

TV-MA, 2018–2019
Hulu original, 2 seasons,
20 episodes (AD)
Horror series with Bill Skarsgård, André Holland, Lizzy Caplan, Melanie Lynskey, Paul Sparks, Barkhad Abdi, Jane Levy, Yusra Warsama, Sissy Spacek and Elsie Fisher.

Well-known Stephen King characters and a couple of newbies are deployed in macabre stories set in the fictional town of Castle Rock, Maine. These are satisfying sci-fi and horror stories about families trying to love each other through difficult situations. As a woman literally stalked by regret, Spacek's performance

in Season 1 is a highlight of her long career (which began, of course, with *Carrie*). King fans will also love Easter eggs like the Shawshank Prison that most of the first season revolves around and a young Annie Wilkes from *Misery* as a key character in Season 2.

🐾 **From our forums:** "I love that the characters aren't stupid for the sake of making the story last longer. I enjoy that it's driven by realistic drama with a hint of supernatural. And the acting … beyond."

Castlevania

TV-MA, 2017–2021
Netflix original, 4 seasons,
32 episodes (AD)
Animated drama created by Warren Ellis, with Richard Armitage, James Callis, Alejandra Reynoso, Theo James, Adetokumboh M'Cormack, Jaime Murray, Graham McTavish, Emily Swallow, Jessica Brown Findlay and Yasmine Al Massri.

Nifty — and very adult — adaptation of the classic Konami/Nintendo video game that gets more expansive with each season. The premise is familiar to anyone acquainted with the Castlevania world: A monster hunter is trying to stop Vlad Dracula, who has declared he will kill everyone in their town as revenge for the murder of his wife. As beautifully illustrated as a high-quality comic book, this adaptation is more violent and crass than the game, but in some ways loftier, too. As the episodes and bodies pile up, prolific comic-book writer Warren Ellis steers the story into more cosmically grand territory, making this a battle between forces of reason and those of religion.

🐾 **From our forums:** "Such a great show and what a perfect ending to the story. Season 4 was beautiful to look at and tied up all S3 plot points."

Some shows may have moved; see page 183.

Casual

TV-MA, 2015–2018
Hulu original, 4 seasons, 44 episodes
Comedy-drama created by Jason
Reitman and Zander Lehmann, with
Michaela Watkins, Tommy Dewey, Tara
Lynne Barr, Nyasha Hatendi and Julie
Berman.

**Tonally deft comedy follows a single
mom who moves in with her brother
after a divorce and tries not to drive him
crazy.** A unicorn among adult-sibling
shows, *Casual* finds a space between
funny and mean and poignant — but not
cheesy. The mother-daughter duo (played
by Watkins and Barr) are the highlight;
their relationship feels entirely believable,
which isn't surprising in a series produced
by Reitman, who was also behind *Juno*.

Catastrophe

TV-MA, 2015–2019
Prime Video original, 4 seasons,
24 episodes (AD)
Comedy created by Sharon Horgan and
Rob Delaney, with Sharon Horgan, Rob
Delaney, Mark Bonnar, Ashley Jensen,
Daniel Lapaine and Jonathan Forbes.

**An middle-aged couple decides to stay
together after their one-night stand
unexpectedly results in a baby in this
fearless, warts-and-all comedy.** Before
she created *Divorce* for HBO, Horgan
put herself on the American map with
this comedy that refuses to sugarcoat
its characters' problems or deny their
capacity for love and joy. The result is both
funny and quite moving as Horgan and
Delany dive headlong into performances
that are ugly, zany and subtle by turns.

Central Park

TV-PG, 2020–present
Apple TV+ original, 2 seasons,
18 episodes (AD)
Animated comedy created by Josh Gad,
Loren Bouchard and Nora Smith, with

Tituss Burgess, Daveed Diggs, Josh Gad,
Kathryn Hahn, Leslie Odom Jr., Stanley
Tucci and Kristen Bell.

**Ambitious cartoon from the creator
of *Bob's Burgers* has a song in its heart.**
When a wealthy heiress named Bitsy
(voiced by Tucci) decides to buy up
New York's Central Park and turn it
into condos and shopping plazas, the
Tillerman family — who actually live
in the park — snap into action. And on
occasion, they break into a Broadway-style
musical number or two. The cast is loaded
in this sincere, heartwarming tale with
some catchy show tunes.

▶▶ The biracial character of Molly
Tillerman was voiced in Season 1 by
Kristen Bell, who's white. After George
Floyd's murder, Bell stepped down and
Emmy Raver-Lampman was hired to voice
Molly.

The Central Park Five

Not Rated, 2012
PBS Passport, Hoopla, Kanopy,
1 hr 59 mins
Movie (documentary) directed by Ken
Burns, David McMahon and Sarah Burns.

**The exposé that revived interest in a
1980s travesty of justice and led to the
miniseries *When They See Us*.** With
crime on the rise in America's cities again,
a fresh watch of this explosive docuseries
might be in order. The rape of a jogger in
New York's Central Park in 1989 led to five
Black and Latino teens being convicted,
first in the media and then in court,
for a crime they didn't commit. Burns,
McMahon and Burns tell the story from
the perspective of the exonerated men, all
of whom served between 6 and 13 years
in prison.

🏆 Peabody Award

The Chair

TV-MA, 2021–present
Netflix original, 6 episodes (AD)

Comedy-drama created by Amanda Peet and Annie Julia Wyman, with Sandra Oh, Jay Duplass, Bob Balaban, Nana Mensah, Everly Carganilla, David Morse, Holland Taylor and Ron Crawford.

At a New England university, a woman of color (Sandra Oh) takes over an English department full of sleepy profs and woke students. Anyone familiar with the state of liberal-arts schools knows that it's ripe for satire, and *The Chair* — co-written by Peet and a Harvard doctoral student — does not disappoint. Professor Kim (Oh) inherits an overwhelmingly old, white, male faculty; kids hyper-vigilant about any breach of political correctness; young, hip profs who favor tweeting over term papers; and postmodernism permeating everything but the locker room. Throw in a love interest and some sparkling physical comedy and you have a sendup of campus life way more interesting than a Chaucer lecture.

Challenger: The Final Flight
TV-14, 2020
Netflix original, 4 episodes (AD)
Docuseries directed by Daniel Junge and Steven Leckart.

This top-notch docuseries captures the day the space program lost its innocence. It's the unforgettable day that America somehow forgot. On January 28, 1986, the space shuttle *Challenger* exploded shortly after liftoff, prompting an immediate investigation that dominated the nightly news for weeks. NASA had always warned Americans of the dangers of space flight, but it had never warned about agency incompetence or bureaucratic timidity — and as this fast-paced account amply documents, those were the two things that ultimately brought down the *Challenger*. Many key players in the space shuttle project speak candidly here about their role in the disaster. And yet the voices you can't forget are those of the spouses, the children and the friends for whom the tragedy still has the power to overwhelm.

Charm City Kings
R, 2020
HBO Max original, 2 hrs 5 mins (AD)
Movie (drama) with Jahi Di'Allo Winston, Meek Mill, Teyonah Parris and William Catlett.

Against his mother's wishes, a 14 year-old kid in Baltimore is committed to being part of a group of motorbike riders who call themselves The Midnight Clique. This is a meaty coming-of-age story with an astonishing lead performance from Winston.

Charmed (2018)
TV-14, 2018–present
Netflix, 4 seasons, 72 episodes
Fantasy drama created by Amy Rardin, Jessica O'Toole and Jennie Snyder Urman, with Melonie Diaz, Madeleine Mantock, Sarah Jeffery, Rupert Evans and Jordan Donica.

In this reboot of the 1998 WB series, three sisters discover that they're the world's most powerful good witches and are destined to protect the world from evil. Those of us who remember *Charmed*'s original incarnation (all the Shannen Doherty drama!) may wonder if it had enough heft to undergo a queer-positive reimagining with Latina actors. It certainly does. And it's a nice reminder that the old WB network shows like *Buffy*, *Angel* and *Charmed* defined a type of campy-scary entertainment that audiences still crave today.

🗨 **From our forums:** "What I love about this reboot is that the Elders are just older witches with far too much responsibility heaped on them, who have had to fight back against puritanism, demon hordes, etc. It makes them human. It gives them nuance."

For shows sorted by streaming platform, see page 381.

Chasing Coral
TV-PG, 2017
Netflix, 1 hr 33 mins (AD)
Movie (documentary) directed by Jeff Orlowski.

Coral reefs around the world are turning a ghastly shade of pale, and as this spectacular underwater doc explains, that's a very bad thing. Though one of many topics covered by Sir David Attenborough in his nature films, the bleaching of the world's coral reefs deserves its own 90-minute treatment because it's an utterly devastating development. Reefs support a critical mass of marine life, and their eradication through climate change has huge implications for life above and below water. This film shows how it happens with heartbreakingly gorgeous time lapse–photography.

Chasing the Thunder
TV-PG, 2018
Discovery+, 1 hr 36 mins
Movie (documentary) directed by Mark Benjamin and Marc Levin.

The longest ocean chase in history pits a notorious poaching ship against environmentalists determined to hunt it down. From the creators of *Brick City* comes this feature-length recut from their unjustly overlooked *Ocean Warriors* series, involving the adventurous activists of Sea Shepherd. Two of their vessels spent 110 days trying to track down the *Thunder*, well-known for making money off blast fishing, which literally blows up all marine life. Taking place on the lawless high seas, it's a chase that may never be replicated again and it's captured with all the suspense and action of a crime doc.

Cheat
Not Rated, 2019
Hoopla, 4 episodes

Limited series (thriller) directed by Louise Hooper, with Katherine Kelly, Molly Windsor, Tom Goodman-Hill, Lorraine Ashbourne, Peter Firth and Parker Sawyers.

Perfectly paced psychological thriller centers on two brainy women trying to get in each other's head — and a man getting murdered in the process. This co-production of Britain's ITV and Sundance combines cable-TV seduction and murder with an indie-film vibe. Windsor plays a university lecturer and Kelly a pupil she accuses of plagiarism. As the feud between the two women escalates, their tangled web of career and personal connections raises the stakes so viciously that either one of them is capable of committing a heinous act.

Cheer
TV-MA, 2020–present
Netflix original, 2 seasons,
15 episodes (AD)
Docuseries directed by Greg Whiteley, Arielle Kilker and Chelsea Yarnell.

It's 2 compelling Netflix shows in one: a feel-good look inside the world of college cheerleading in Season 1 and a stomach-turning drama centered on a *Cheer* star who was booked on sex-related charges while Season 2 was filming. Cheerleaders are nature's drama factories, so it's surprising that Netflix's cameras didn't find their way to Corsicana, Texas, and the unlikely cheerleading powerhouse at Navarro College until recently. Under its demanding coach Monica Aldama, young men and women pull off eye-popping choreographed cheers, suffer horrendous injuries, go out and do it all over again. Given the seriousness of the charges against cheerleader Jerry Harris, though, we recommend starting with "Jerry" (S2E5), which recounts his behavior toward others that led to his arrest — and, just as disturbing, the failure of anyone in power to deal responsibly with credible charges leveled against Harris. Then go back and watch from the beginning; it's still a great show, if now unintentionally cringe-inducing.

🏆 3 Emmys including best unstructured reality program

Cheers

TV-PG, 1982–1993
Paramount+, Peacock, Hulu, 11 seasons, 270 episodes

Sitcom created by Glen Charles, Les Charles and James Burrows, with Ted Danson, Rhea Perlman, John Ratzenberger, George Wendt, Kelsey Grammer, Woody Harrelson, Kirstie Alley, Shelley Long, Bebe Neuwirth and Nicholas Colasanto.

After Norman Lear and *M*A*S*H* but before *Seinfeld* and *Friends*, the Boston bar where everyone knows your name was TV's favorite gathering place. The seminal hangout show of the 1980s, *Cheers* set a new standard for multi-camera sitcoms, with character development and a massive, talented ensemble. Though Danson's Sam Malone was ostensibly the lead, everyone worked so well together that the cast *en masse* often seemed like the real star. Remarkably, the quality kept improving even as more new characters joined.

▶▶ It took until halfway through *Cheers*'s run for the show to discover its best recurring gag: "Bar Wars," a battle of the pranks with sworn enemy Gary's Olde Towne Tavern. Dreamed up by writers David Isaacs and Ken Levine, "Bar Wars" featured some highly creative pranks (one involved 50 sheep) and the competition brought out the best and worst in the Cheers gang. With one exception, the 7 episodes ended in humiliating defeat to Gary (S6E23, S7E10, S8E21, S9E2, S10E7, S10E23, S11E19).

🏆 Emmy for best comedy series (4 wins), TCA Heritage Award

The Chef Show

TV-14, 2019–present
Netflix original, 2 seasons, 25 episodes (AD)

Docuseries directed by Jon Favreau, with Jon Favreau and Roy Choi.

Writer-director Jon Favreau is joined by chef Roy Choi, who worked on his film *Chef*, and famous guests as they chat and cook in a show as cozy as a warm kitchen. Favreau knows how to cook but he's eager to step up his game and it's clear he loves being able to observe Choi in his element. It's the chill, pleasant rapport between grasshopper and master that makes the show so appealing. Be sure to have the subtitles on — they both talk under their breath — and grab those recipes because you can make them, too.

Chef's Table

TV-MA, 2015–present
Netflix original, 6 seasons, 30 episodes (AD)

Docuseries created by David Gelb.

This show gets back to basics, introducing us to great cooks and their passion for their work and art. Not since Julia Child was on PBS has there been such a talky show about food. Six chefs narrate stories of their lives and anecdotes from their careers as chefs, what drives them and how they got to where they are. Their words are accompanied by lush visuals and an inspired soundtrack. Combined, it shows the beauty and profundity of even the smallest of moments connected with food.

Chernobyl

TV-MA, 2019
HBO Max, 5 episodes (AD)

Some shows may have moved; see page 183.

Limited series (historical drama) created by Craig Mazin, with Jared Harris, Stellan Skarsgård, Emily Watson, Paul Ritter and Jessie Buckley.

This unflinching dramatization of the 1986 nuclear disaster in present-day Ukraine generated critical buzz for months. *Chernobyl* plays out like a tightly edited horror movie — except it really happened. And it's led by yet another beautifully tragic role for Harris, here as the Soviet nuclear physicist Valery Legasov, whose job it is to document the worst reactor failure in history even as the regime is downplaying the results. He is the moral thread of this powerful series, overruling his sense of patriotic duty with the imperative to tell the world how the unthinkable happened.

▸▸ Pairs well with *When the Levees Broke*

🐿 **From our forums:** "The sets and locations wonderfully captured the 1980s Soviet look, where you could feel the whole environment was just kind of in oppressive decline."

🏆 Peabody Award, Emmy and TCA awards for best limited series

Chewing Gum
TV-MA, 2015–2017
HBO Max, 2 seasons, 12 episodes
British comedy created by Michaela Coel, with Michaela Coel, Danielle Walters, Robert Lonsdale, Shola Adewusi, Susan Wokoma, Maggie Steed and Kadiff Kirwan.

In her first TV series, Michaela Coel lights it up as an ultra-religious virgin who decides it's time to have sex and learn about the world. Goofier and less devastating than Coel's followup series *I May Destroy You*, this adaptation of her play *Chewing Gum Dreams* shows a similar commitment to creating structurally audacious TV entertainment. Besides the teasing of sexual mores, we watch characters stop behaving in the

ways they were taught to behave and evolve in fascinating ways on screen.

🐿 **From our forums:** "It's like a cross between *Broad City* and *Shameless*." "If Tichina Arnold and Lucille Ball had a baby, it would be Michaela Coel."

🏆 BAFTA for female performance in a comedy

The Chi
TV-MA, 2018–present
Showtime original, 4 seasons, 40 episodes
Drama created by Lena Waithe, with Alex R. Hibbert, Jacob Latimore, Yolonda Ross, Michael Epps, Jason Mitchell, Hannaha Hall, Curtiss Cook, Shamon Brown Jr., Luke James and Genesis Denise Hale.

On Chicago's South Side, teens and adults strive for a better life while looking danger and occasionally death in the eye. Part coming-of-age, part social-issues drama, *The Chi* has been praised for offering a realistic view of Chicago not seen in those NBC first-responder dramas, though in other ways it is a conventional sprawling Showtime soap.

🐿 **From our forums:** "I binge-watched the (first) 3 seasons and the reduction in quality of each season is jarring. This show has a way of just dropping story lines."

▸▸ After multiple allegations of sexual harassment against Mitchell, his character Brandon was written out in Season 3.

Chicago Fire
TV-14, 2012–present
Peacock, 10 seasons, 207 episodes (AD)
Drama created by Michael Brandt and Derek Haas, with Jesse Spencer, Taylor Kinney, Christian Stolte, Monica Raymund, Kara Killmer, Yuri Sardarov, David Eigenberg, Joe Minoso and Jeff Hephner.

This solid, old-school show about the personal and professional lives of first

responders in the Windy City is well integrated with the other *Chicago* dramas. From the producer that brought you *Law & Order*, the city that brought you *Backdraft* and the network that brought you the crossover episode comes *Chicago Fire*. Viewers wanting more of an adrenaline rush should watch *9-1-1*, but the characters on this series have developed well over the years. Ingeniously, they and their counterparts from *Chicago Fire* spinoffs *Chicago Med* and *Chicago P.D.* all frequent the same fictional bar; one regular on *Fire* even changed careers and wound up on *Chicago P.D.*

▶▶ *Chicago P.D.* is the cop procedural, which means it's right in the wheelhouse of executive producer Dick Wolf (*L&O*). In addition to well-paced crime stories, *P.D.* features strong female characters and a shady commander that viewers like to dislike.

▶▶ *Chicago Med* hardly reinvents the medical show wheel, but it hits all the right beats and features *Law & Order* alumna Merkerson as a nurse-turned-administrator.

Childrens Hospital
TV-MA, 2008–2016
Hulu, 7 seasons, 87 episodes
Satirical comedy created by David Wain, Rob Corddry and Jonathan Stern, with Ken Marino, Rob Huebel, Rob Corddry, Malin Åkerman, Lake Bell, Erinn Hayes, Megan Mullally, Henry Winkler, Michael Cera and Zandy Hartig.

Often-hysterical sendup of medical dramas offers bite-sized parodies of a well-worn genre. It's one of those shows where you'd love to be sitting in the writers' room when they were thinking up these characters: "A Patch Adams doctor who wears a clown outfit, but he scares everyone because he looks like Gacy." "A female medical chief on crutches like Weaver on *ER*, and everyone's sexually

attracted to her." "A Meredith Grey type whose thoughts we can hear out loud … and they're really stupid." Set in São Paulo, Brazil, this spoof utilized a who's who of the alt-comedy scene and inspired a raft of spinoffs including *NTSF:SD:SUV* (cop shows), *Newsreaders* (current-affairs TV) and *Medical Police* (too complicated to explain here — see separate listing).
🏆 4 Emmys

Chilling Adventures of Sabrina
TV-14, 2018–2020
Netflix original, 4 seasons, 36 episodes (AD)
Fantasy drama created by Roberto Aguirre-Sacasa, with Kiernan Shipka, Ross Lynch, Lucy Davis, Miranda Otto, Chance Perdomo, Michelle Gomez, Jaz Sinclair, Tati Gabrielle, Adeline Rudolph and Richard Coyle.

Fun, noirish spin on the classic comic fancies the Teenage Witch battling the evil forces that threaten her family and her town while just living her life. The role seems tailor-made for Shipka, who as Sally Draper in the later seasons of *Mad Men* explored much of this same coming-of-age territory. Negotiating with her peers and grownups around Greendale, she shows us both her worldlywise smarts and her tender innocence.

Cinema Toast
TV-MA, 2021–present
Showtime original, 10 episodes
Comedy-drama anthology series created by Jeff Baena.

Trippy, absurdist and at times poignant, this experimental series uses archival film to create unexpected new stories. Trapped at home, writer-director Jeff Baena brainstormed pairing old films with new dialogue — resulting in mashups that a lot of film-school grads probably wished *they'd* thought up during the pandemic. In one, Nick Offerman and Megan Mullally dub their voices into an old Jimmy Stewart film, transforming it into an episode of *Grace and Frankie*.

The Circle

TV-MA, 2020–present
Netflix original, 3 seasons,
38 episodes (AD)
Reality competition with Michelle Buteau.

Viewers can't believe how easily they got hooked on a show where dating prospects *send texts to each other*. What makes this show — basically *Big Brother* meets Instagram — so damn compelling? Eight strangers enter a building and live in separate dwellings, never meeting but only interacting via text messages and profile pics. Contestants are free to pass themselves off as someone else, but saying *The Circle* is a show about catfishing doesn't get at its appeal. It's a deeply interesting social experiment, one that anyone who has kindled a relationship entirely on social media will instantly relate to.

▶▶ Netflix has renewed *The Circle* through Season 5.

▶▶ For suggestions of related shows, see "If You Liked *The Circle*," page 372.

The Circus

TV-14, 2016–present
Showtime original, 6 seasons,
102 episodes
Docuseries with John Heilemann, Mark McKinnon, Alex Wagner, Mark Halperin and Jennifer Palmieri.

Produced in real time, this weekly political docuseries feels more substantial than anything on the news, thanks to the reporters' deep access and experience. Showtime took a page from HBO's long-running *Hard Knocks* franchise and applied it to politics beginning with the 2016 presidential election, with reporting from veteran journalists and MSNBC tandem Heilemann and Halperin. (The latter exited in 2018 after several women accused him of sexual harassment earlier in his career.) Along with a team of seasoned political operatives, the correspondents cover the week's biggest political stories, often embedding themselves with newsmakers in the eye of the storm.

City on a Hill

TV-MA, 2019–present
Showtime original, 2 seasons,
18 episodes (AD)
Crime drama with Kevin Bacon, Aldis Hodge, Lauren E. Banks, Amanda Clayton, Jill Hennessy and Mark O'Brien.

Fictionalized account of the "Boston Miracle" that cleaned up city corruption in the 1990s, stars Kevin Bacon as a corrupt-yet-redeemable FBI agent who helps take down a family of crooks. This mashup of Ben Affleck and Matt Damon's earlier crime films (e.g., *The Town*), with help from Chuck MacLean's dramatized depiction of the Boston Miracle, sits like *The Wire* does at the intersection of crime and politics. Season 1 follows an odd alliance of cops and prosecutors who work together to catch an elusive band of violent carjackers.

City So Real

TV-14, 2020
Hulu, 5 episodes
Docuseries directed by Steve James.

In 2019 Chicago chose a new mayor — and after watching this tough but well-done series you may wonder who would want the job. As he did in *Hoop Dreams* (see page 160) and his *30 for 30* film on Allen Iverson, director Steve James confidently guides us into moments that are necessary but painful to see. And it's clear that as Lori Lightfoot campaigns for mayor, Chicago is a town in pain. But it's also a very alive city with an incredible mix of neighborhoods and nationalities, and this five-parter will make even non-residents appreciate it better. Besides, Chicago's struggles are ones all American communities face to some degree or another.

The Civil War
TV-14, 1990
PBS Passport, 9 episodes
Docuseries directed by Ken Burns, with Sam Waterston, Julie Harris, Jason Robards, Morgan Freeman, Garrison Keillor, David McCullough, Arthur Miller and Shelby Foote.

Nothing has approached Burns's magnum opus as a chronicle of the suffering, romance and moral necessity of America's greatest conflict. Its tropes have been imitated and mocked over the years. Despite a colossal running length, it is far from a comprehensive history of the Civil War (the western theater, for example, scarcely exists here). Foote is colorful talking head, but his Southern-sympathetic takes have not aged well. No matter — this is a timeless visual narrative and a cultural moment. Burns revitalized public interest in the Civil War and helped steer us to a reckoning with its root cause.

🏆 Peabody Award

Clarice
TV-14, 2021
Paramount+, 13 episodes
Crime drama with Rebecca Breeds, Michael Cudlitz, Lucca De Oliveira, Nick Sandow, Devyn A. Tyler, Kal Penn and Jayne Atkinson.

What happens when you take Hannibal Lecter out of the world that he built? You get a pretty good cop show, that's what. One year after the events in *Silence of the Lambs*, Agent Starling — the character immortalized by Jodie Foster in the movie — is tasked with hunting down

serial killers again. Despite the limitations of a network procedural, *Clarice* works because Breeds doesn't try to reinvent Jodie Foster's performance in the film.

▶▶ Low ratings led CBS to cancel the show after one season in June 2021, and although a relocation to Paramount+ was initially in play, stalled contract negotiations left the show in limbo.

Clarkson's Farm
TV-PG, 2021–present
Prime Video original, 8 episodes (AD)
Celebreality show with Jeremy Clarkson, Gerald Cooper, Kaleb Cooper, Kevin Harrison, Ellen Helliwell, Lisa Hogan and Charlie Ireland.

Longtime *Top Gear UK* host bought a farm in 2008; now he's running it. The 1,000-acre Curdle Hill Farm in Oxfordshire was bought by the automotive host in 2008, but Clarkson only began managing operations in 2019. The show has become quite the phenomenon in the UK thanks to its favorable image of the farming life. Though Clarkson and his girlfriend Lisa are clearly learning on the job, he's surrounded by able (and quirky) farmhands who know their way around a field of grain and a meadow of sheep.

Class Action Park
TV-MA, 2020
HBO Max original, 1 hr 30 mins (AD)
Movie (documentary) directed by Seth Porges and Chris Charles Scott, with John Hodgman, Chris Gethard, Alison Becker and Jason Scott.

The story of New Jersey's infamously treacherous water park is both tragic and transporting. During its 1980s heyday, Action Park was dogged by horror stories about injuries and deaths on their rides. And as this film vividly documents, the rumors were completely true. The best thing about *Class Action Park* is the tone of the interviews. Almost everyone, from park employees to guests and next of kin, speaks about the rides with a mixture of awe, regret and the kind of hysterical gallows humor of someone who just sprinted past a graveyard at midnight.

Clifford the Big Red Dog
PG, 2021
Paramount+, 1 hr 36 mins (AD)
Movie (family comedy) with Darby Camp, Jack Whitehall, John Cleese and Tony Hale.

Parents (if not critics) loved the adaptation of the children's book about the plus-sized pooch and the girl who loves him. Despite looking like he's been green-screened into every shot, the 10-foot-high crimson Lab is lovable, and that's what saves this live action animated cartoon shot in New York City. Cleese completists will enjoy his appearance as a dog rescue genie.

Cobra Kai
TV-14, 2018–present
Netflix original, 4 seasons, 40 episodes (AD)
Comedy-drama with William Zabka, Ralph Macchio, Courtney Henggeler, Mary Mouser, Tanner Buchanan, Xolo Maridueña and Martin Kove.

The two leads of *The Karate Kid* are grown up now, but they're still rivals in this delightful revisit to a 1980s classic. As adults, Daniel Larusso (Macchio) and Johnny Lawrence (Zabka) are still in conflict. But their characters are more multi-dimensional than in the movie and it's not so easy to decide who to root for here. *Cobra Kai* shows deep affection for the film and its sequels and shares its lighthearted tone, suggesting it was created by Karate Kid fans. New teens on the block play out the current drama, but the *senseis* are the touchstones of this sweet, funny and entertaining return to SoCal karate.

From our forums: "The show is at its core about two middle-aged men who just cannot let go of who they were at 17."

Cocaine Cowboys: The Kings of Miami
TV-MA, 2021
Netflix original, 6 episodes (AD)
Limited series (crime drama) directed by Billy Corben, with Willy Falcon, Sal Magluta, Jim DeFede and Marilyn Monachea.

This wild docuseries from director Billy Corben tells the jaw-dropping story of the Miami drug traffickers whose prosecution was even crazier than the illegal operation they ran. Corben, whose passion for Miami drug culture was revealed in his 2006 film *Cocaine Cowboys*, packs a ton of material into this twisty, turning series about Willy Falcon and Sal Magluta, two high school dropouts and world-class speedboaters who were eventually busted for running a massive drug operation. But their notoriety began then, as they embroiled their attorneys, families, friends, state and federal governments in trials, retrials, hung juries, fugitive pursuits, jury-tampering rackets and more. This is a stylish piece of work, with two central antiheroes, dozens of other central figures in the story participating and, not least, a great soundtrack.

CODA
PG-13, 2021
Apple TV+ original, 1 hr 51 mins (AD)
Movie (drama) with Emilia Jones, Marlee Matlin, Troy Kotsur, Daniel Durant and John Fiore.

A hearing girl wants to go to school to be a singer, even though it will mean leaving her Deaf parents and brother to fend for themselves as they run a small fishing business. *CODA* is a beautiful, life-affirming film that made multiple best-of-the-year lists.

🏆 Sundance Film Festival's Grand Jury Prize

▶▶ Pairs well with *Hear And Now*

Colin in Black & White
TV-14, 2021
Netflix original, 6 episodes (AD)

Limited series (drama) created by Ava DuVernay and Colin Kaepernick, with Jaden Michael, Nick Offerman, Mary-Louise Parker and Colin Kaepernick.

Nicely closing a circle that began with his historic kneel-down, Colin Kaepernick narrates this dramatized memoir showing how his childhood shaped his football career and worldview. It's about as subtle as a quarterback sack, but arguably that is what makes *Colin in Black & White* work. This scripted recreation of events of Colin's life as a biracial child, with solid performances from Offerman, Parker and Michael, adds emotional heft to Kaepernick's narration (which feels more like the stuff of documentary).

The Comeback
TV-MA, 2005–2014
HBO Max, 2 seasons, 21 episodes

Comedy created by Lisa Kudrow and Michael Patrick King, with Lisa Kudrow, Lance Barber, Robert Michael Morris, Laura Silverman, Damian Young and Malin Akerman.

Lisa Kudrow's daring turn as a washed-up sitcom star may have been the most impressive by a *Friends* cast member after *Friends*. In 2 seasons separated by almost 10 years, this mockumentary followed Valerie Cherish (Kudrow), an actress who's desperate to regain the fame she enjoyed as a B-list sitcom star and who eventually finds herself on a prestige drama. It's perhaps the *ne plus ultra* of cringe comedy, putting

its heroine in one humiliating situation after another as she tries to remain relevant or at least recognizable. Yet it also allowed moments of disarming humanity to emerge at the most opportune of times.

▶▶ Don't be surprised if *The Comeback* makes another comeback; Kudrow and co-creator King are considering Season 3.

Comedians in Cars Getting Coffee
TV-14, 2012–2019
Netflix, 11 seasons, 84 episodes (AD)

Talk show created by Jerry Seinfeld, with Jerry Seinfeld.

Jerry Seinfeld struck comedy gold yet again with spirited conversations between himself and a funny guest in cars and diners. With a different classic car, comedian and diner in every episode, there's little predictable about *Comedians in Cars* except that Jerry will laugh a lot — and so will you. Featuring superstars like Eddie Murphy and Tina Fey as well as up-and-comers like pre-*Daily Show* Trevor Noah and *SNL*'s Melissa Villaseñor, *Comedians in Cars* has redefined the great American talk show.

▶▶ Production hasn't officially ended but in 2021 Seinfeld said he was moving on: "I think I'm going to put that volume on the shelf."

▶▶ Pairs well with *Between Two Ferns with Zach Galifianakis*

The Comedy Store
TV-MA, 2020
Showtime original, 5 hrs

Docuseries with Jim Carrey, Jay Leno, David Letterman, Whitney Cummings, Bill Burr, Neal Brennan, Howie Mandel, Tim Allen, Anthony Jeselnik and Bert Kreischer.

This docuseries traces the history of one of America's most influential comedy clubs, as told by the legends who worked there. From David Letterman and Jay Leno through Nikki Glaser and, um, Louis

C.K., Mitzi Shore's club changed American entertainment and this five-parter covers the waterfront. Though it's not exactly reflective about how it fast-tracked problematic comics like Louis C.K. or Andrew Dice Clay, it does unearth some interesting stories like the rise and fall of Freddie Prinze and the forgotten standup career of Michael Keaton.

The Comey Rule
TV-MA, 2020
Showtime original, 3 hrs 30 mins (AD)
Limited series (historical drama) with Jeff Daniels, Brendan Gleeson, Holly Hunter, Michael Kelly, Michael Hyatt, Scoot McNairy, Jennifer Ehle, Jonathan Banks, Brian d'Arcy James and T.R. Knight.

Lightly fictionalized adaptation of the former FBI director's memoir recounts his infamous dealings with Donald Trump. From James Comey's ascent to FBI director to the Hillary Clinton email scandal, Donald Trump's test of Comey's loyalty over dinner, Comey's firing and Capitol Hill testimony, *The Comey Rule* is a solid, if scripted, flash history that doesn't really favor Comey (who comes off as an unlikable prig) and offers a dramatic take on those events for those with the stomach to relive them. It will appeal to viewers who prefer docudramas to documentaries and would rather watch actors (especially a seasoned veteran of docudramas like Daniels) than talking heads.

Community
TV-14, 2009–2015
Netflix, Hulu, Prime Video, 6 seasons, 110 episodes (AD)
Sitcom with Joel McHale, Gillian Jacobs, Danny Pudi, Alison Brie, Ken Jeong, Yvette Nicole Brown, Jim Rash, Donald Glover and Chevy Chase.

Formally daring sitcom that's ostensibly about a community college study group is, in hindsight, a show about the nature of comedy itself. This series was self-referential from the beginning, but as it progressed it got even more invested in commenting on popular storytelling styles, even as it was employing them. This is occasionally exhausting, but the ideas are on the whole amusing and the cast finds a way to help us care about the characters. *Community* is the show that put Glover on the map before he went on to create *Atlanta*.

Comrade Detective
TV-MA, 2017
Prime Video original, 6 episodes (AD)
Satirical comedy with Channing Tatum, Florin Piersic Jr., Joseph Gordon-Levitt, Jenny Slate, Olivia Nita, Jason Mantzoukas, Florin Galan, John DiMaggio, Corneliu Ulici and Chloë Sevigny.

Weirdly subversive miniseries parodied '80s buddy-cop films, Communist propaganda and 21st-century anti-Americanism. *Comrade Detective*, the greatest Romanian TV show that never was, supposedly was produced in the late '80s by the Communist regime to reinforce anti-Western views among viewers in that Soviet bloc country. Marrying a truckload of Hollywood action movie tropes to over-the-top violence and cartoon clichés about capitalism and Communism, it's enjoyable simply as genre satire. But it also gives a good ribbing to anti-Western propaganda and the failed social experiment that — at the time this series was supposedly made — was on its last legs.

The Confession Tapes
TV-MA, 2017–2019
Netflix original, 2 seasons, 11 episodes (AD)
Limited series (true crime) created by Kelly Loudenberg.

Each episode examines videotaped confessions that were used to convict people of crimes and raises troubling questions about how they were procured. Polygraph tests and voice analysis used to be considered unimpeachable evidence in court, but are now of dubious worth. Soon we may be adding to that list videotaped confessions, for reasons this series makes damningly clear. Many confessions are extracted after hours of interrogation without an attorney present, as detectives use threats, flattery and trickery in their rush to close the case. Director Loudenberg has chosen sympathetic subjects and compelling experts who help pick apart the allegedly airtight cases against them.

▶▶ Pairs well with *When They See Us*

Confirmation
TV-14, 2016
HBO Max, 1 hr 50 mins
Movie (drama) with Kerry Washington, Wendell Pierce, Greg Kinnear, Jeffrey Wright, Eric Stonestreet, Bill Irwin, Grace Gummer, Dylan Baker, Alison Wright and Malcolm Gets.

Kerry Washington is Anita Hill in this A-list dramatization of the 1991 Supreme Court nomination hearings for Clarence Thomas. Surprisingly, the heavy in this well-done HBO docudrama isn't Thomas or his defenders — it's Joe Biden (Kinnear), the senator from Delaware who is infuriatingly weak in his defense of Hill and her culture-shaking revelation that Thomas spent years sexually harassing her.

The Conners
TV-PG, 2018–present
Hulu, 4 seasons, 71 episodes (AD)
Sitcom with John Goodman, Laurie Metcalf, Sara Gilbert, Alicia Goranson, Michael Fishman, Emma Kenney, Ames McNamara, Jayden Rey, Jay R. Ferguson and Katey Sagal.

A handful of sitcoms have survived the departure of their leads, but none did it as well as *The Conners*, which is arguably better without Roseanne Barr. The 2018 revival of *Roseanne* was a bona fide hit and a triumph for its pro-Trump star. Then Barr posted volatile tweets and just like that, she and her name were gone from the show. Fortunately, the writing and acting talent remains: Goodman, Metcalf and especially Gilbert, whose Darlene character should've been the center of the reboot in the first place.

🗨 **From our forums:** "People continue to make some bad choices or struggle with addiction, money is always an issue, family members annoy each other. It's real life, but funnier."

Continent 7: Antarctica
TV-PG, 2016
Disney+ original, 6 episodes
Docuseries directed by J.J. Kelley, with Chris Browning.

Antarctica's first reality show will flip your idea of it upside down. National Geographic, of course, is behind the first docuseries to be filmed in Antarctica, and this will bust your *March of the Penguins*–formed preconceptions of it being nothing but barren tundra. This series excels at presenting the continent and its human inhabitants in a way that makes it seem both enchanting and forbidding. Exceedingly beautiful imagery includes a hypnotic, must-see effect, as the screen rotates 180 degrees three times, like an iceberg flipping over and revealing what's attached to its underside. *Continent 7* also profiles some of the people who actually live and work in Antarctica — a surprisingly large number — all of them dedicated to worthy scientific missions.

▶▶ Pairs well with *The Last Alaskans*

Conversations with a Killer: The Ted Bundy Tapes
TV-MA, 2019
Netflix original, 4 episodes (AD)
True crime directed by Joe Berlinger.

For those who never get tired of going down this rabbit hole, a new angle on a defining story in American crime. Ted Bundy is a lot of people's "first" — the first serial killer whose story was widely shared with the public and the first case that got many people of a certain age interested in the true-crime genre. They'll appreciate hearing some voices that have been left out in most Bundy coverage: namely, the women who were affected by him. That includes his victims, the millions of women terrified by his killing spree, the policewoman who started connecting some of Bundy's crimes early on and Bundy's fiancé, who has understandably kept a low profile in the decades since his conviction.

Corporate
TV-MA, 2018–2020
Paramount+, 3 seasons, 26 episodes
Comedy with Matt Ingebretson, Jake Weisman, Adam Lustick, Anne Dudek, Aparna Nancherla and Lance Reddick.

Two junior execs grapple with their soul-sucking work at a corporation that makes everything from snack foods to weapons of mass destruction. One critic called this "*The Office* as scripted by radical pranksters," although *Corporate* has a sweeter quality than that description might suggest. Beyond the two leads, there are interesting storylines for other employees at the megacorp, giving the show greater depth while extending its critique of corporate America beyond the executive suite.

💬 **From our forums:** "A lot of this resonated with me the way *Office Space* did when I had a soul-sucking corporate job in the early 2000s. It's satirical without being too ridiculous."

Cougar Town
TV-14, 2009–2015
Hulu, Prime Video, 6 seasons, 102 episodes
Sitcom with Courteney Cox, Christa Miller, Busy Philipps, Dan Byrd, Josh Hopkins, Ian Gomez, Brian Van Holt and Bob Clendenin.

Writer-producer Bill Lawrence (*Ted Lasso*) cooked up a delightfully loony show about the lives of 40-something women. The best of the post-*Friends* series on network TV, *Cougar Town* teamed Cox with the versatile Miller and reintroduced audiences to the talented Philipps. Storylines were along the lines of what an audience that has aged 10 years since *Friends* might expect: parent-child bonds, post-divorce relationships, adult friendships and wine. Oh, so much wine.

💬 **From our forums:** "I absolutely loved the first 2 seasons of this show. I still like the heartfelt moments and am invested enough in this show that I care about the characters and want to watch every week."

Counterpart
TV-MA, 2017–2019
Starz original, 2 seasons, 20 episodes (AD)
Sci-fi drama with J.K. Simmons, Olivia Williams, Harry Lloyd, Nazanin Boniadi, John Funk, Sara Serraiocco and Nicholas Pinnock.

J.K. Simmons in a tantalizing dual role centered on a Cold War between parallel universes. Simmons plays both Howard Silk — a milquetoast office worker in Berlin — and his *bête noire*, a ruthless secret agent in a galaxy far, far away. Over the course of this action-filled series, Howard realizes he's a crucial cog in the struggle between the two worlds and that he's on a collision course with his counterpart.

🗨 **From our forums:** "Reminded me very much of old cold war movies like *The Spy Who Came In From The Cold*." "I enjoyed the atmosphere of this show but had some trouble following the plot."

Country Music
TV-PG, 2019
PBS Passport, 8 episodes
Docuseries directed by Ken Burns, with Peter Coyote, Marty Stuart, Rosanne Cash, Brenda Lee, Dolly Parton and Hank Williams Jr.

Ken Burns's eye-opening look into country's multiracial roots and its multitudinous cultural impact has a fantastic soundtrack and a cast of hundreds. It's 8 parts and 16 hours long, but there's not a false note or a dull stretch in this beautifully crafted account of country music's origins and evolution. Unlike his other films, Burns avoids scholarly talking heads and mostly lets the musicians tell the story. Many country artists are amateur historians and folklorists including Merle Haggard, singer-songwriter Marty Stuart and Rhiannon Giddens. You will never have a more complete or enjoyable course in music appreciation. *Country Music* is also full of surprising provocations about race, class and gender, but Burns knows better than to let these get in the way of appreciating this very American music form and the people and forces that created it.

Couples Therapy
TV-MA, 2019–present
Showtime original, 2 seasons, 19 episodes
Reality show with Orna Guralnik.

The best TV therapy show, hands down. Each season Dr. Guralnik works with three couples seeking to mend their relationships. Episodes are filmed in an office with cameras behind two-way glass, so sessions unfold naturally. There aren't quick cuts or talking head interviews interrupting the flow and shaping the narrative. It's not salacious or grubby. Instead, it effectively hooks viewers with real people's honesty and vulnerability, making us root for them to get their trains back on track. And it shows how hard that work is to do.

Crashing (British series)
TV-MA, 2016
Netflix original, 6 episodes
Limited series (British comedy) created by Phoebe Waller-Bridge, with Phoebe Waller-Bridge, Jonathan Bailey, Julie Dray, Louise Ford, Damien Molony, Adrian Scarborough and Amit Shah.

A group of 20-somethings in London share a run-down decommissioned hospital they agree to watch over in exchange for cheap rent. Not to be confused with the HBO Pete Holmes comedy of the same name, this quick, enjoyable binge shows Waller-Bridge (its creator and star) exploring the themes she would develop further in her next comedy, *Fleabag*.

Crazy Delicious
TV-PG, 2020–present
Netflix original, 6 episodes (AD)
Reality competition with Jayde Adams, Heston Blumenthal, Niklas Ekstedt and Carla Hall.

Taking culinary competition to the next level, contestants are tasked with making the wonderfully bizarre from the ingredients featured in the edible Garden-of-Eden set. British celebrity chef Heston Blumenthal is renowned for experimental cooking and pairing unexpected items, which he encourages others to do in *Crazy Delicious*. The mandate is always that the food must not only taste good but be imaginative or strange. One cook's "wacky ingredients

For shows sorted by streaming platform, see page 381.

on a pizza crust" entry is deemed not as inventive as the rival who created a volcano of "rocks" (black pizza dough) with "lava" (red sauce).

Crazy Ex-Girlfriend
TV-14, 2015–2019
Netflix, 4 seasons, 62 episodes
Musical comedy with Rachel Bloom, Vincent Rodriguez III, Santino Fontana, Donna Lynne Champlin, Pete Gardner, Vella Lovell, Gabrielle Ruiz and Scott Michael Foster.

Rachel Bloom's groundbreaking series made musical numbers hip again. Taking risks from the beginning, *Crazy Ex-Girlfriend* started with a lead character struggling with mental health issues and built a world around her with fine supporting characters and vibrant original musical numbers. ("Anti-Depressants Are So Not A Big Deal" was nominated for an Emmy.) Though it ran on a low-rated network, its influence can be seen all across prestige TV today.

🗫 **From our forums:** "I'm really pleased with how *CEG* has progressed. They could have played her rock bottom for farce or for drama, but they played it honestly and accomplished elements of both."

🏆 Emmys for original music and choreography

Crazy, Not Insane
TV-MA, 2020
HBO Max, 1 hr 59 mins (AD)
Movie (true crime) directed by Alex Gibney, with Dorothy Otnow Lewis.

The findings of a forensic psychiatrist who has dedicated her career to the study of murderers and their motives. Master docmaker Gibney (*Going Clear*) profiles Dr. Dorothy Lewis and her work, which is based not on *how* a killer went about their work but *why*. The unsettling and at times nauseating film (especially when serial murderers'

horrific childhoods are explored) includes tasteful animated reenactments of Lewis's jailhouse sessions and readings (by Laura Dern) of her case notes.

Crime + Punishment
TV-MA, 2018
Hulu original, 1 hr 52 mins
Movie (documentary) directed by Stephen T. Maing, with Edwin Raymond, Sandy Gonzales, Rukia Lumumba and Manuel Gomez.

Damning investigation into abusive policing at the NYPD has lessons for every city and town in America. "New York is Ferguson on steroids," says one police officer in this film that connects the dots between aggressive policing in NYC and the NYPD's informal policy of shaking down citizens for money. Using hidden microphones and inside informants, director Maing paints a depressing picture of a city that relies on fines and bail bonds from its police to shore up its budget deficits. Maing also introduces us to several inspiring cops who wouldn't stay silent and have some practical advice for how to heal the rift between law enforcement and the communities they serve.

The Crime of the Century
TV-MA, 2021
HBO Max, 3 hrs 50 mins (AD)
Limited series (true crime) created by Alex Gibney, with Patrick Radden Keefe.

Oscar winner Alex Gibney delivers his usual trenchant exploration of the corporate, political and healthcare system failures that created America's opioid crisis. Gibney (*Taxi to the Dark Side*) argues that, like most disasters, the opioid crisis was no accident. Starting with Purdue Pharma's aggressive marketing of OxyContin, Gibney details the infuriating chain of reinforcing events — enabling legislation, medical professionals' indifference and above all, unquenchable greed — ends with the explosion of deaths related to an even more powerful opioid, fentanyl.

Crime Scene

TV-MA, 2021
Netflix original, 2 seasons,
7 episodes (AD)
True crime directed by Joe Berlinger.

A new take on the true-crime genre is this compelling "wheredunnit" from a veteran documentary filmmaker. In 2013 someone was found in the water-supply tank atop the Cecil, a Hollywood hotel linked to so many macabre events that it served as inspiration for *American Horror Story*'s "Hotel" season. Director Joe Berlinger challenges us to consider the role of place in crimes.

▶▶ For Season 2, "Times Square" (3 episodes), *Crime Scene* explains how the so-called Torso Killer was able to prey all too easily on sex workers in the seedy hellhole that was Times Square in the 1970s.

Crip Camp: A Disability Revolution

TV-MA, 2020
Netflix original, 1 hr 46 mins (AD)
Movie (documentary) directed by Nicole Newnham and James Lebrecht.

Learn from this rollicking account how a 1970s summer camp launched a movement. From executive producers Barack and Michelle Obama, *Crip Camp* places the fight for the civil rights of the disabled in America at a summer camp for disabled teens. Over several decades we follow the campers' personal lives and how that life-affirming camp led to their participation in the movement to end the discriminatory treatment of people like them.

🏆 Peabody Award

The Crown

TV-MA, 2016–present
Netflix original, 4 seasons,
40 episodes (AD)
Historical drama created by Peter Morgan, with Claire Foy, Olivia Colman, Matt Smith, Tobias Menzies, Vanessa Kirby, Helena Bonham Carter, Josh O'Connor, Emma Corrin, John Lithgow and Gillian Anderson.

Eight decades of British royal history, from Elizabeth II's childhood as queen-in-waiting to the present, as reimagined by the incomparable Peter Morgan and a prestige cast. Morgan, who wrote *The Queen* and other dishy historical dramas (*Frost/Nixon, Longford*), outdoes himself in this sweeping saga about the House of Windsor that starts with the public record and splashes gobs of freewheeling speculation and colorful dialogue upon it. Using a new set of actors every other season, *The Crown* follows the journeys of Elizabeth, Philip and their "issue" (i.e., children) as they grapple with family dynamics, prime ministers and an increasingly fickle public. Americans have gone wild for *The Crown* and heaped dozens of honors on it, but British voters have been more reserved, with just 4 BAFTA technical awards and one acting (Kirby, for her sublime turn as young Princess Margaret).

▶▶ Season 5 is set for release in November 2022.

▶▶ The royals are played by different actors as the series marches through time. Foy portrays Queen Elizabeth II in the first 2 seasons, while Colman portrays the queen in Seasons 3–4. Smith plays Prince Philip in the first 2 seasons, Menzies plays him in Seasons 3–4 and so forth.

▶▶ For suggestions of related shows, see "If You Liked *The Crown*," page 372.

Cruel Summer

TV-14, 2021–present
Hulu, 10 episodes
Teen drama with Olivia Holt, Chiara Aurelia, Froy Gutierrez, Harley Quinn Smith, Michael Landes, Andrea Anders, Ben Cain, Blake Lee and Allius Barnes.

Hooky cable hit follows two teen girls and the crime that ties them together. Using the three-timelines approach of *This Is Us* copied by many shows, *Cruel Summer* jumps between 1993, 1994 and 1995 to unravel the mystery of a girl who's gone missing and the rival who's accused of playing a part in her disappearance. A deliciously twisty story and two leads you couldn't turn away from made this cable channel Freeform's biggest hit.

📡 **From our forums:** "That was a great finale. I admit that I was shocked by that last reveal."

CSI: Vegas

TV-14, 2021–present
Paramount+, 10 episodes
Crime drama with Paula Newsome, Matt Lauria, Mandeep Dhillon, Mel Rodriguez, Jorja Fox and William Petersen.

This revival is solid fan service for those who loved the original *CSI*, but there will be a different look in Season 2. *CSI's* layered storytelling and cinematic tracking shots made it the first great procedural of the era that ushered in high-definition TVs and DVRs. It disappeared just before streaming took off, but in 2021 it returned with four cast members from the original *CSI* (only Marg Helgenberger was missing). The *CSI: Vegas* pilot pulls you right back in with its familiar video funnel effect, moody sets and stylized killings. Petersen and Fox only agreed to be in this starter season, so don't expect them to carry the show going forward.

📡 **From our forums:** "I hope Grissom and Sara come back for Season 2 but I'll watch it even if they don't. Vegas gives a much more interesting pool of possible crimes than Miami ever did."

Curb Your Enthusiasm

TV-MA, 2000–present
HBO Max, 11 seasons, 110 episodes (AD)
Comedy created by Larry David, with Larry David, Jeff Garlin, Cheryl Hines, Susie Essman, Richard Lewis and J.B. Smoove.

After co-creating *Seinfeld*, Larry David took to HBO and cast himself at the center of TV's defining cringe comedy. David has called the character on his show (also Larry David) the man he'd like to be: someone with no regard for the social contract and its many subclauses. Simply put, "TV Larry" is a despicable human being who has, over the years, killed a swan and tried to hide the body, posed as an incest survivor, dated a woman in a wheelchair for benefits like good parking and line-cutting … yet we keep coming back for more, because part of us relates to whatever Larry is going through. The brilliance of *Curb* is its uncanny ability to find the humor in these terrible situations. The show's theme song has become a favorite in memes featuring deadpan humor.

▶▶ We have no favorite episodes of *Curb Your Enthusiasm*: They are all terrible and they are all delectable.

🏆 2 Emmys

Cut Throat City

R, 2020
Netflix, Hoopla, 2 hrs 3 mins
Movie (action) directed by RZA, with Terrence Howard, Ethan Hawke, Wesley Snipes, Shameik Moore, Demetrius Shipp Jr., T.I. and Kat Graham.

Hip-hop superstar RZA directs this story about four friends who reluctantly agree to pull off a heist in post-Katrina New Orleans. Smart, substantive and violently nerve-jangling, this urban drama gives us a quartet of likable young men who encounter all kinds of impressively drawn Big Easy characters as they plan their crime of desperation.

Da 5 Bloods

R, 2020
Netflix original, 2 hrs 34 mins (AD)
Movie (drama) directed by Spike Lee, with Delroy Lindo, Jonathan Majors, Clarke Peters, Norm Lewis, Isiah Whitlock Jr. and Chadwick Boseman.

A Spike Lee career highlight, this direct-to-Netflix action feature follows Vietnam vets as they return there to dig up a treasure they buried during the war. The name Spike Lee should disabuse the reader from thinking this is just another war flick. Though Lee expertly captures the hell of combat, *Da 5 Bloods* is chiefly a character study of men firmly planted in the Black experience in America. Led by Lindo, whose PTSD has driven him to the MAGA side of town, each of the four men on the quest for gold is really seeking something more — to make sense of the wounds and losses they endured in combat. The plot twists will be familiar to Lee fans, as are the director's many paeans to classic films from the genre. But the takeaway is one that Lee and co-writer Kevin Willmott tried less effectively in *BlacKKKlansman* but deliver with an emotional wallop here: They remind us that the past is the present and that we reap what we sow.

Dallas Cowboys Cheerleaders: Making the Team

TV-PG, 2006–present
Paramount+, 16 seasons, 140 episodes
Reality competition with Kelli McGonagill Finglass and Judy Trammell.

Possibly the most amazing long-running reality show you've never heard of, let alone watched. Primetimer readers have long been obsessed with this series

from cable's CMT, and with good reason: It's one of the best-known and best-run talent competitions on Earth. Hundreds of women each year try out for the iconic NFL team's cheer squad, in auditions run by two former Cowboys cheerleaders. With such a huge pool of ambition, real-world stakes and a surprisingly grueling process, how can you not have drama?

Damages

TV-MA, 2007–2012
Hulu, Starz, 5 seasons, 59 episodes
Drama with Glenn Close, Rose Byrne, Tate Donovan, Zachary Booth, Ted Danson, William Hurt, Marcia Gay Harden, Lily Tomlin and Martin Short.

Glenn Close and Rose Byrne chewed every bit of scenery in an unpredictable legal thriller that's rarely been matched. Close brought *gravitas* and Emmy glory to the FX cable channel in 2007 with her portrayal of Patty Hewes, a cutthroat high-powered New York City lawyer with plenty of blood on her hands and a killer pair of sunglasses. *Damages* began like so many legal whodunits but about half an hour into the first episode, it took off around the corner and viewers spent the rest of that season chasing its shadow. Joining Close were a slew of big names, but the greatest casting triumph was Byrne, a relative unknown given the daunting task of facing off against Close. Wide-eyed Ellen Parsons proved the perfect foil to Patty. Using a two-timeline narrative structure was novel back then and it added intrigue rather than confusion to the superb production.

Daria

TV-14, 1997–2001
Paramount+, 5 seasons, 65 episodes
Animated comedy with Tracy Grandstaff, Wendy Hoopes and Julian Rebolledo.

The *Beavis And Butt-Head* spinoff was nothing like the original (or anything

else on TV at the time). Sixteen-year-old Daria Morgendorffer was a friend of the two dorks before she moved away and disconnected entirely from that show. *Daria* had its own animation style and sensibility and in its title character (Grandstaff) it possessed a voice unique to television. Daria was an old soul who suffered so many fools around her, including her high-powered, well-meaning but inept parents; dipsy sister Quinn; and most everyone at school except for her equally catty friend Jane Lane. In time Daria evolved, and the young woman who went off to college 2 seasons later was different from the cynical girl at the show's outset.

▶▶ The Daria universe is set for a reboot. Tracee Ellis Ross is attached to *Jodie*, a new series focused on Jodie Lanson, a recurring character in the original series.

Dark
TV-MA, 2017–2020
Netflix original, 3 seasons,
26 episodes (AD)
Thriller with Louis Hofmann, Karoline Eichhorn, Lisa Vicari, Maja Schöne, Jördis Triebel, Andreas Pietschmann, Stephan Kampwirth, Paul Lux, Christian Hutcherson and Oliver Masucci.

German-language thriller has the most complex, time-bending narrative you may ever see. You think *Lost* messed with your head when it came to time travel? This German–language thriller drew a crowd in the U.S. for its intricate storytelling where everything means something.

🗨 **From our forums:** "If you really hate time travel and sci-fi, this may not be for you, but I would give it a chance because it is so well done. It also focuses on family issues and the problems that individual characters are dealing with. Before watching the last couple of episodes, my husband and I made a list of main

characters and family relationships to try and reduce the confusion."

▶▶ Available in its original German with subtitles or dubbed.

The Dark Crystal: Age of Resistance
TV-PG, 2019
Netflix original, 10 episodes
Fantasy drama with Nathalie Emmanuel, Anya Taylor-Joy, Taron Egerton, Mark Hamill, Caitriona Balfe, Jason Isaacs, Simon Pegg, Keegan-Michael Key and Harris Dickinson.

Prequel to Jim Henson's 1982 cult classic reacquaints us with the terrifying magic that made the original film so fascinating and scary. Though this series has a glossier new package, it's still remarkably true to its bizarre roots. And even though the Dark Crystal universe is still inhabited entirely by puppets, it's going to scare the crap out of you and your kids just like it did to audiences 40 years ago.

🗨 **From our forums:** "Newer CGI technology makes for a smoother, more nuanced presentation. I'm not going to rip into it nor overanalyze performances. I just enjoyed it for what it is."

🏆 Emmy for outstanding children's program (the show was canceled days later)

Dash & Lily
TV-14, 2020
Netflix original, 8 episodes (AD)
Romantic comedy with Austin Abrams, Midori Francis, Troy Iwata, James Saito and Dante Brown.

Super-cute Christmassy adaptation of the YA novel follows two teens who get to know each other through a notebook they take turns leaving around NYC. In this pursuit romcom, teen opposites Dash (Abrams) and Lily (Francis) don't actually meet up until late in the season. Instead, they leave messages for each other in the notebook that they leave in telegenic parts throughout the city, including the legendary Strand bookstore. It's an intriguing if improbable setup and the execution is holiday-perfect, as cozy as a knitted blanket. From Rachel Cohn and David Levithan, who also gave us the Nick and Nora novels.

From our forums: "Straight-up adorable and I'm very glad the episodes are so short." "I also loved the bookstore where so much of the plot was centered — look at those beautiful books!"

Dating Around

TV-MA, 2019–present
Netflix original, 2 seasons,
12 episodes (AD)
Reality show.

A simple but remarkably effective gimmick whisks the viewer through 5 first dates, demonstrating what a blur it is for all involved. Here's the gimmick: The dater stays the same, but the person sitting across the table keeps changing. Without a narrator explaining every single moment to the viewer, different dates seamlessly move in and out of the frame. The result is a slightly disorienting stream of drinks and breezy banter. And isn't that how most first dates go? Half of the appeal of this understated and brilliantly edited reality series is that it doesn't treat its audience like morons.

Dave

TV-MA, 2020–present
Hulu, 2 seasons, 20 episodes (AD)
Comedy with Dave Burd, Andrew Santino, Gata, Taylor Misiak, Christine Ko, Travis Bennett, Gina Hecht and David Paymer.

White YouTube rapping sensation gets his own sitcom — and it's much funnier than it sounds. Aptly described as *Curb Your Enthusiasm* meets *Atlanta*, it stars the comedian known in real life to millions as rapper Lil Dicky. Like Larry David, Burd creates an exaggerated version of himself (more selfish, clueless and self-destructive). Like Donald Glover, he's not afraid to hit the minor chords, with storylines involving his hype man's bipolar disorder and his own white privilege in a Black-dominated industry. As for viewers who think a rap show isn't for them, Dave's videos are hugely entertaining and, like any good musical number, they cleverly move the story along.

Dave Chappelle: Sticks & Stones

TV-MA, 2019
Netflix original, 1 hr 5 mins
Comedy special with Dave Chappelle.

Almost as controversial as his 2021 special *The Closer* but with better material. No one currently embodies Jerry Seinfeld's description of comedy as a toxic and self-correcting universe better than Chappelle. *Sticks & Stones* is wall–to–wall with topics that would make most comics flinch: suicide, Michael Jackson, mass shootings, trans people and, yes, cancel culture. A rewatch of this acclaimed Atlanta-based special suggests that in 2019 Chappelle thought of his critics as just another foil for his no-holds-barred act. They're more than that, as *The Closer* proved, but that doesn't diminish the achievement of *Sticks & Stones*, a showcase of a comic provocateur at his peak.

🏆 3 Emmys including best variety special

David Byrne's American Utopia

TV-14, 2020
HBO Max, 1 hr 45 mins (AD)
Musical special directed by Spike Lee, with David Byrne.

Spike Lee directs a concert film of David Byrne's exhilarating stage show inspired by his 2018 album of the same name. Along with capturing great performances of Byrne's newer songs and several of his Talking Heads classics, this film communicates the exuberance of a show he's been honing for years. His interplay with a large group of on-stage musicians — all wearing the same gray suits — is joyous and cathartic. Their energy is intriguingly balanced by the avant-garde choreography. This is boundary-pushing performance art that also succeeds at improving your mood.

▸▸ Pairs well with *Stop Making Sense*

🏆 2 Emmys

David Makes Man

TV-MA, 2019–present
HBO Max, 2 seasons, 20 episodes
Drama created by Tarell Alvin McCraney, with Akili McDowell, Nathaniel Logan McIntyre, Phylicia Rashād, Alana Arenas, Ade Chike Torbert, Travis Coles, Cayden K. Williams and Isaiah Johnson.

Character-driven coming-of-age drama revolves around a 14-year-old Black boy in Miami who dreams of a better life. David (McDowell) lives in the projects with his hard-working single mother Gloria (Arenas) and neighbors who watch out for him. At his magnet school, dedicated teachers like Dr. Woods-Trap (Rashād) clearly want him to succeed. But will he? This is the question at the heart of *David Makes Man*, from the Oscar-winning writer of *Moonlight*. Tonally the show is jumpy, from gritty authenticity to dreamy escapism with hints of *DeGrassi* and *The Wire*. What keeps you watching, though, is the character drama of a young man at an inflection point, developing before your eyes.

💬 **From our forums:** "I was really impressed with the actress who plays Gloria throughout the entire season. Her performance made me break down in tears several times."

🏆 Peabody Award

Dawson's Creek

TV-14, 1998–2003
Hulu, Netflix, 6 seasons, 128 episodes
Teen drama created by Kevin Williamson, with James Van Der Beek, Katie Holmes, Michelle Williams, Joshua Jackson, Meredith Monroe, Chad Michael Murray, Kerr Smith and Busy Philipps.

They didn't speak like any Gen–Yers we knew, but Dawson Leery and his highly articulate high school mates set the tone for a new breed of teen soaps. Kevin Williamson's semi-autobiographical coming–of–age series put the fledgling WB network on the map. It explored every possible configuration of couples among its four main characters with a wry self-awareness rarely seen on network TV, making stars of its talented young cast in the process.

▸▸ Licensing fees stripped Paula Cole's "I Don't Want to Wait" from the opening credits on home video and streaming for years, so there was much rejoicing in late 2021 when Netflix paid to restore the show's iconic theme song.

Dead Pixels

TV-14, 2019–present
CW Seed, 2 seasons, 12 episodes
Fantasy comedy with Alexa Davies, Will Merrick, Charlotte Ritchie, Sargon Yelda and David Mumeni.

Well-observed Britcom follows a handful of quirky young people obsessed with an online role-playing fantasy game. Three friends are so into playing *Kingdom Scrolls* online that they duck out of real-world social engagements to immerse themselves in the medieval world of trolls and wizards and feudal politics. It's not really the game that *Dead Pixels* is interested in (though *World of Warcraft* fans will appreciate the in-jokes). Rather, it's the players' interactions and their outsized frustrations as they navigate the tedium of a massive online game, where most of their points are gotten by shooting livestock.

▶▶ Pairs well with *Detectorists*

Dead Set
TV-MA, 2008
Netflix, 5 episodes
Limited series (comedy-horror) created by Charlie Brooker, with Riz Ahmed, Jaime Winstone, Adam Deacon, Warren Brown, Andy Nyman, Beth Cordingly, Kathleen McDermott, Kevin Eldon, Raj Ghatak and Chizzy Akudolu.

As they're living in their sequestered house, the cast of a British season of *Big Brother* fail to realize a zombie apocalypse is happening outside. *Black Mirror* creator Charlie Brooker does much more than stage some fabulously gory horror hijinks — he also offers a trenchant take on insipid, amoral reality-TV culture.

▶▶ Netflix Brazil produced a remake of *Dead Set* in 2020 called *Reality Z*, with English audio and subtitles.

Dead to Me
TV-MA, 2019–present
Netflix original, 2 seasons, 20 episodes (AD)
Dark comedy created by Liz Feldman, with Christina Applegate, Linda Cardellini, James Marsden, Sam McCarthy, Luke Roessler, Max Jenkins and Diana Maria Riva.

Christina Applegate and Linda Cardellini bond convincingly in this hard-to-categorize show about two women in a grief support group. *Dead to Me* is a very funny buddy comedy with loss and grief at its center. These women should by no rights be friends, since Judy (Cardellini) is the hit-and-run driver who killed Jen's husband Steve (Marsden, seen here often in flashbacks). Instead of playing this for laughs or melodrama, the show explores the emotional aspects that

make both women sympathetic, even as ugly details of their lives spill out.

🗨 **From our forums:** "On paper, you shouldn't be rooting for their friendship so hard … but there is such a deep connection between them you can't see them not being in each other's orbits. Christina Applegate and Linda Cardellini just make the whole thing work."

▶▶ A third (and final) season planned for 2021 was delayed by COVID and later, Applegate's multiple sclerosis diagnosis.

Deadliest Catch
TV-PG, 2005–present
Discovery+, 17 seasons, 283 episodes
Reality show with Mike Rowe (narrator), Phil Harris, Sig Hansen, Johnathan Hillstrand, Andy Hillstrand, Keith Colburn, Jake Anderson, "Wild" Bill Wichrowski and Steve "Harley" Davidson.

Crab fisherman is one of the most dangerous jobs in the world, and you'll understand why as you watch these men navigating the Bering Sea during fishing season. This long-running series follows the crews of several fishing vessels during crab season. Some of the best reality shows are just edited versions of a reality that would exist even if cameras weren't there. *Deadliest Catch* remains the best example of this, though it wouldn't be possible without the bravery and craftsmanship of both the fisherman and the people who film the show, who stand on the freezing deck of a crab boat for hours at a time. While it can get repetitious, with crab pots being thrown overboard and pulled in over and over again, the show works because it shows the harsh reality of a tough job that most every one of us has, at one time or another, depended upon for our repast.

🏆 Emmy for best unstructured reality show (3 wins)

Deadwater Fell
TV-14, 2020
AMC+, Acorn TV, 4 episodes
Limited series (crime drama) with David
Tennant, Cush Jumbo, Matthew McNulty,
Anna Madeley, Lorn Macdonald and
Maureen Beattie.

**Another gritty British crime drama
with David Tennant, this time as the
sole survivor of a suspicious house
fire.** The star of *Broadchurch* returns in
another twisty whodunit. After his family
perishes in the blaze, it's discovered that
everyone had been drugged. The facade of
happiness is shattered when it's revealed
that the seemingly perfect family was far
different than the image they projected.
Everyone has something to hide in this
small Scottish town. Besides Tennant,
Deadwater Fell is also a vehicle for the
sublime talents of Jumbo, as a neighbor
through whose eyes we see much of the
drama unfold.

Deadwood
TV-MA, 2004–2006
HBO Max, 3 seasons, 36 episodes
Historical drama with Ian McShane,
Timothy Olyphant, Molly Parker, Brad
Dourif, W. Earl Brown, John Hawkes,
Paula Malcomson, Dayton Callie, Leon
Rippy and William Sanderson.

**Ian McShane and Timothy Olyphant
both had career-defining roles as rivals
in the wildest of Wild West towns.** David
Milch, whose talents were wasted on
network television, went to HBO with his
idea for a Western that would make Sam
Peckinpah seem like a wuss. Set in the
real-life boom town of Deadwood, S.D.,
in the 1870s, Milch's aim with *Deadwood*
was to show civilization emerging from
the crude and cruel near-anarchy of the
American frontier. The show's relentless
profanity is more than shtick; it's a symbol
of chaos in the untamed West. The whole
cast is great but especially Olyphant as

the part-time sheriff Seth Bullock and
Ian McShane as saloon/whore-keeper Al
Swearengen, whose menacing eyes and
killer lines helped him eat up every scene
he was in.

▸▸ In 2019, after years of delays, HBO
aired *Deadwood: The Movie* (HBO Max),
continuing the storylines of the series.

🏆 8 Emmys, TCA Heritage Award

Deaf U
TV-MA, 2020–present
Netflix original, 8 episodes (AD)
Docuseries with Rodney Burford,
Cheyenna Clearbrook, Tessa Lewis, Alexa
Paulay-Simmons, Renate Rose, Daequan
Taylor, Dalton Taylor and Cameron
Symansky.

**Illuminating real-life drama follows 7
students at Gallaudet University, the
nation's only all-Deaf school of higher
learning.** *Deaf U* centers on hard-of-
hearing and Deaf people without being
about that, focusing instead on the drama
of their world: cliques and prejudices,
romance and accusations, trauma and
aspiration. The cast quickly develop into
well-rounded characters capable of often
painful honesty and self-evaluation.
Their interactions feel natural, perhaps
because they all know each other. The
short episodes are sufficient for *Deaf U*
to unpack ideas that are rare for a reality
TV show to tackle so forthrightly, like sex
and sexuality, abuse, depression, abortion,
religion and code-switching.

🏆 Critics Choice Award for best
unstructured docuseries

Dear White People
TV-MA, 2017–2021
Netflix original, 4 seasons,
40 episodes (AD)
Comedy-drama created by Justin
Simien, with Logan Browning, DeRon
Horton, Marque Richardson, Ashley
Blaine Featherson, Giancarlo Esposito,

Antoinette Robertson, Brandon P. Bell and John Patrick Amedori.

Set on an elite college campus where racial tensions have come to a boil, this series uses a talented (and unheralded) ensemble to bring uncomfortable topics to the screen. Simien's adaptation of his 2014 film by the same name didn't catch on until George Floyd was murdered — and the audience soared 600 percent. Signing on in the first year of the Trump administration, it anticipated the anxieties and anger Black people would feel, making *Dear White People* one of the most canny shows in the political moment. But it's also a brilliant relationship drama stacked with fresh, attractive, largely Black talent in satisfying character arcs.

🎙 **From our forums:** "This show is excellent at showing that there is no such thing as 'all Black people.' We are getting to see that there is a difference of opinions, philosophies, life history, experiences, expectations and perspectives among Black people. While Black people have always known this, it has not been prevalent in media depictions."

Defending Jacob

TV-MA, 2020
Apple TV+ original, 8 episodes (AD)
Limited series (crime drama) with Chris Evans, Michelle Dockery, Jaeden Martell, J.K. Simmons, Cherry Jones, Pablo Schreiber, Betty Gabriel and Sakina Jaffrey.

Emotional adaptation of the bestselling novel revolves around a teenager accused of murder and his parents, including a local prosecutor, who will do anything to clear his name. William Landay's legal thriller was optioned as a movie years ago, but this was worth the wait. As a supersized movie (aka limited series), *Defending Jacob* has one unexpected twist after another. The family's slow disintegration as the case

drags on is reminiscent of *Ordinary People*.

🎙 **From our forums:** "Easily watchable. It kept me hooked, kept me surprised, it didn't try to jerk me around like so many shows do these days or jump around in the timeline or try to be overly arty or clever. That said, I'm not sure they stuck the landing."

Degrassi: The Next Generation

TV-PG, 2002–2015
HBO Max, IMDb TV, Tubi, PlutoTV,
14 seasons, 385 episodes
Teen drama with Miriam McDonald, Aubrey Drake Graham, Christina Schmidt, Melissa McIntyre, Sarah Barrable-Tishauer, Cassie Steele, Stefan Brogren, Jake Goldsbie, Shane Kippel and Ryan Cooley.

Few shows have done so much with so little as this low-budget Canadian teen soap which stood out for its willingness to take on tough topics. Starting with 1979's *The Kids of Degrassi Street*, young viewers have flocked to this franchise about middle and high school students. From sex and teen pregnancy to mental disorders, drug abuse and death, the Degrassi kids have faced it all, courting controversy with parents and self-appointed TV watchdogs. But the kids kept coming, through 5 spinoffs (and one on the way from HBO Max). Of these, *Degrassi: The Next Generation* was the longest running and best known. It launched the careers of Drake in Seasons 1-7 and Nina Dobrev in Seasons 6-9 of the series, later just called *Degrassi*.

🏆 Peabody Award

DeMarcus Family Rules

TV-14, 2020–present
Netflix original, 6 episodes (AD)
Celebreality show with Jay DeMarcus and Allison DeMarcus.

A nice throwback to the early days of celebrity couple reality shows, featuring Rascal Flatts bassist Jay DeMarcus and his beauty-queen wife Allison. Since the early 2000s, when Nick Lachey and Jessica Simpson made *Newlyweds*, celeb-couple shows have become dominated by couples who are famous only for appearing on other reality shows: *Rob & Chyna*, *Very Cavallari*, *Miz and Mrs.*, etc. This series — about the fabulous life of a country music superstar, his triple-crown pageant-winning wife and the two precocious children they're raising in Nashville — feels ever so slightly more real.

Departure
TV-14, 2019–present
Peacock original, 2 seasons,
12 episodes (AD)
Drama with Archie Panjabi, Kris Holden-Ried, Tamara Duarte, Rebecca Liddiard, Mark Rendall and Christopher Plummer.

Archie Panjabi and Christopher Plummer lead this remarkably taut thriller about … transportation accidents. When a passenger jet mysteriously crashes, UK aviation official Howard (Plummer) and investigator Kendra (Panjabi) soon suspect foul play. And it's off to the races as they probe a mess of potential motives and suspects. Season 2 deals with a suspicious train crash in Michigan. At just 6 episodes per season, each one is a great light binge.

▶▶ *Will & Grace* alum Eric McCormack joins the cast for the show's third season, due sometime in 2022.

Derry Girls
TV-MA, 2018–present
Netflix, 2 seasons, 12 episodes (AD)
British comedy with Saoirse-Monica Jackson, Louisa Harland, Nicola Coughlan, Jamie-Lee O'Donnell, Dylan Llewellyn, Tara Lynne O'Neill, Kathy Kiera Clarke, Tommy Tiernan, Ian McElhinney and Siobhan McSweeney.

Biting, raunchy comedy about working-class Catholic schoolkids in 1990s Northern Ireland offers a fresh take on the nostalgic high school sitcom. Derry, located near the border with Ireland, is the setting for Lisa McGee's show set in the waning years of the Irish "troubles." *Derry Girls* has elements you'd expect — comically strict nuns, mean teens, biting sarcasm — but the situations are uproarious, the burns are wonderfully sick and the region's fraught history so distinct that the combination is a comedy unlike any other.

🗩 **From our forums:** "Hilarious, surprising and somehow mean and sweet at the same time."

▶▶ The brogues are so thick that even some Irish viewers have complained that dialogue is hard to follow, so turn on the subtitles *and* the Audio Description.

Design Star: Next Gen
TV-G, 2021–present
Discovery+ original, 6 episodes
Reality competition with Allison Holker.

This spinoff is better than the original because it's purely about design and wastes no time on manufactured reality drama. *Design Star* was HGTV's all-time most successful franchise, though less successful at minting future design stars. Contestants in this reboot have a clear sense of what they wanted to do, and the judges fairly and competently assess their work. Thanks to the pandemic, every designer worked in isolation, so the focus stayed on design rather than gratuitous sniping between team members. Boo to the producer who thought it would be great TV to have the eliminated contestant return to their studio … to find the door locked.

🗩 **From our forums:** "I don't like it as much as the UK's *Interior Design Masters*

     For a key to terms used in this section, see page 33.

(Netflix), but it is nice to see people showcase their talent. I like that they are stressing the importance of social media, which most creators will admit is a must today."

Detectorists
TV-PG, 2014–2017
Acorn TV, IMDb TV, 3 seasons, 19 episodes
British comedy created by Mackenzie Crook, with Mackenzie Crook, Toby Jones, Rachael Stirling, Gerard Horan, Pearce Quigley and Divian Ladwa.

This comedy classic explores the lives of men who are singularly devoted to their hobbies and the women who love them despite that. It starts out as just another quirky British comedy, with best friends Andy (Crook) and Lance (Jones) spending their free time digging for bits of metal and attending meetings of the (very small) Danebury Metal Detecting Club. Over the course of 18 episodes, though, the show digs deeper. In particular Andy's relationship with Becky (Stirling) is pushed to the brink by his obsession, forcing them to say and do things that are surprisingly reflective and heartfelt.

🐦 **From our forums:** "What a tremendous little show! I'm so sorry that it's over."

Detroiters
TV-MA, 2017–2018
Paramount+, 2 seasons, 20 episodes
Comedy with Sam Richardson and Tim Robinson.

Sam Richardson and Tim Robinson are touchingly great as best friends and likable idiots who make local TV ads while dreaming of greatness Come for the slapstick comedy and crazy farce, stay for the relationship between two sweet, laid-back dudes whose ridiculousness knows no bounds.

🐦 **From our forums:** "I'm a fan of It's Always Sunny in Philadelphia and there

are notable similarities in tone and style, although this show isn't as crude and the main characters are more screwups than awful people."

The Deuce
TV-MA, 2017–2019
HBO Max, 3 seasons, 25 episodes (AD)
Historical drama created by David Simon and George Pelecanos, with Maggie Gyllenhaal, James Franco, Lawrence Gilliard Jr., Margarita Levieva, Emily Meade, Daniel Sauli, Chris Bauer, Chris Coy, Michael Rispoli and David Krumholtz.

The creator of The Wire digs deep into another gritty subculture, exploring how porn and prostitution shaped Times Square in the 1970s and '80s. Surprisingly fun and energetic despite its depressing backdrop and misogynistic theme, The Deuce creates a world around Gyllenhaal's superb rendering of Eileen (Candy) Merrell, a hooker who becomes a mogul in the adult film industry.

🐦 **From our forums:** "I worked in Times Square in those years and I have to tell you it really rings true. You would run into people in the life in the coffee shops and bars all the time."

Deutschland 83/Deutschland 86/ Deutschland 89
TV-MA, 2015–2020
Hulu, 3 seasons, 26 episodes
Historical drama created by Anna Winger and Jörg Winger, with Jonas Nay, Maria Schrader, Florence Kasumba, Sylvester Groth, Fritzi Haberlandt, Ludwig Trepte and Alexander Beyer.

Likable spy thriller follows an East German double agent operating behind enemy lines in West Germany. Set in different years of the Communist decline (hence the title changes), this German-language series draws much of its charm from the disorientation Rauch feels as he carries out his mission in free, prosperous West Germany, only a few miles from his home in the shabby, statist East.

🎙 **From our forums:** "Thank you, Hulu, for introducing me to this show now that *The Americans* is over!"

▸▸ In German with English subtitles.

🏆 Peabody Award

Devil's Playground
Not Rated, 2002
Roku Channel, 1 hr 17 mins
Movie (documentary) directed by Lucy Walker.

Amish teenagers leave their communities and party hearty during a rite of passage known as *rumspringa*. The idea, according to director Walker, is that this will be the Amish child's one and only time to be rebellious before returning to the fold and a life of sobriety. Indeed, only about 15 percent of teens who undertake *rumspringa* leave their communities. This sophisticated doc shows how their elders have rigged the system, all but ensuring that their offspring will eventually come home.

▸▸ Walker, who's British, brings an outsider's view to many of her American films, like 2021's *Bring Your Own Brigade* (Paramount+), which explores how the deadly outbreak of wildfires in the West can't be blamed entirely on climate change.

Devs
TV-MA, 2020
Hulu, 8 episodes
Sci-fi drama created by Alex Garland, with Sonoya Mizuno, Nick Offerman, Jin Ha, Cailee Spaeny, Stephen McKinley Henderson and Alison Pill.

Nick Offerman leads a strong cast that brings our worst fears about Big Tech to life. In this near-future tech thriller, writer-director Alex Garland (*Annihilation*) argues that human behavior is predictable and quantum intelligence will suss out everything we do before we actually do it. Naturally, a secretive tech company will figure this out first — and why not have that company run by a shaggy genius played by Offerman? Take that irresistible premise and tuck it inside a well-constructed conspiracy hunt and you have *Devs,* which was better than its one-and-done cancellation might suggest.

Dexter
TV-MA, 2006–2013
Showtime original, 8 seasons, 96 episodes
Crime drama with Michael C. Hall, Jennifer Carpenter, David Zayas, James Remar, C.S. Lee, Luna Lauren Velez, Desmond Harrington, Julie Benz and John Lithgow.

This sun- and blood-drenched adaptation of the novels about crime-solving sociopath Dexter Morgan bent TV's storytelling trajectory in ways we only realized years later. Michael C. Hall was fresh off his triumph on *Six Feet Under* when he took on the Dexter role — quite a pivot from a sensitive and religious gay man to a sadistic killer with a peculiar bloodlust for murdering other criminals who have managed to elude justice. But both were oddly upright in their own ways. In a pleasing sendup of America's *CSI* fervor at the time, Dexter gains his leads by working as a forensic analyst for the very institution tasked with investigating his crimes — the Miami Metro Police Department.

▸▸ Season 4 is the one to watch, as Dexter squares off with Lithgow's notorious Trinity Killer in a cat-and-mouse game that doesn't end the way anyone expected.

🏆 SAG Award for best actor in a drama (Hall)

Dexter: New Blood

TV-MA, 2021

Showtime original, 10 episodes

Limited series (crime drama) with Michael C. Hall, Jack Alcott, Julia Jones, Johnny Sequoyah, Alano Miller, Jennifer Carpenter, Clancy Brown and John Lithgow.

Picking up 10 years after the events of the original series, Dexter Morgan is living a quiet life in upstate New York, where he's dating the chief of police and suppressing his vigilante tendencies. And how long do you think *that* will last? In the time it takes to say, "Well, there goes a cartoon psychopath that maybe Dexter will be tempted to dispatch" … done! Michael C. Hall's return to the *Dexter* universe, along with original showrunner Clyde Phillips and costar Jennifer Carpenter as Deb (still dead but talking to him as a *Six Feet Under*-style ghost), is the kind of fan-service template that we can expect to be used in similar show revivals in the future. For *Dexter* fans that hate-watched the show after Season 4, *New Blood* will offer satisfying if frosty closure.

Dick Johnson Is Dead

PG-13, 2020

Netflix original, 1 hr 29 mins (AD)

Movie (documentary) directed by Kirsten Johnson, with Dick Johnson, Michael Hilow, Ana Hoffman and Kirsten Johnson.

A man with dementia gamely goes along with various death scenarios (mostly violent) cooked up by his daughter, the director of this wildly imaginative documentary. Kirsten Johnson has been capturing real life her whole career, but contemplating the loss of her father leads her to dream up this series of overly dramatic concepts which she then films, using her dad as a participant (including his own funeral, with friends and family

in attendance). Though done with a light touch, Johnson never lets you forget the stakes involved. A beautiful film.

🏆 Special Jury Award, Sundance Film Festival; 3 Critics Choice Awards; Oscar nomination for best documentary

Dickinson

TV-14, 2019–2021

Apple TV+ original, 3 seasons, 30 episodes (AD)

Comedy-drama with Hailee Steinfeld, Adrian Enscoe, Anna Baryshnikov, Jane Krakowski, Toby Huss, Ella Hunt, Chinaza Uche and Gus Birney.

Young-adult period piece fancifully imagines how poet Emily Dickinson spent her teenage years — like getting high with Wiz Khalifa. Part of a wave of factually fast-and-loose historical shows like *The Great* and *Miracle Workers*, *Dickinson* uses the life of the iconic 19th-century poet to comment on the personal and political issues of our time. It does this through an emotionally wrought performance by Steinfeld as young Emily and a rocking soundtrack. Just remember, when you watch John Mulaney portray Henry David Thoreau as an insufferable egomaniac: This isn't a history lesson.

🏆 Peabody Award

Dirty John: The Betty Broderick Story

TV-14, 2020

Netflix, 8 episodes (AD)

Anthology series (drama) with Amanda Peet, Christian Slater, Rachel Keller and Missi Pyle.

One of the most lurid and well-known true-crime cases in recent memory gets a powerful refresh thanks to Amanda Peet's portrayal of the scorned Betty. In the second series inspired by Christopher Goffard's "Dirty John" podcast, Peet makes us feel like we're watching someone responding to systematic abuse by being driven to the breaking point. Slater is also notable as Betty's coolly manipulative ex.

Dirty Money

TV-14, 2018–present
Netflix original, 2 seasons,
12 episodes (AD)
Docuseries.

If American Greed and Frontline had a child that was allowed to use curse words, it would be Dirty Money. An all-star lineup of directors produced episodes for this Netflix deep dive into the many ways corporate America jettisons common decency in pursuit of shareholder returns. Oscar-winner Alex Gibney, who's an executive producer on the series, takes on Volkswagen's emissions scandal; HBO doc standout Erin Lee Carr drills down on Big Pharma price-gouging; Jesse Moss (Con Man) exposes predatory payday-lending practices; and Fisher Stevens's exploration of all the ways that Donald Trump is a modern-day P.T. Barnum will stick with you for a long time.

Disenchantment

TV-14, 2018–present
Netflix original, 2 seasons,
40 episodes (AD)
Animated comedy created by Matt Groening, with Abbi Jacobson, Eric André, Nat Faxon, John DiMaggio, David Herman and Maurice LaMarche.

Matt Groening's gift to Netflix is this fractured fairy tale about an alcoholic princess, an edgier medieval Futurama that gets better as it rambles along. In the fantastical kingdom of Dreamland, Princess Bean (Jacobson) embarks on adventures with her elf sidekick Elfo (Faxon) while being shadowed by her literal personal demon, Luci (André). Clearly someone was taking notes off Bojack Horseman, because Disenchantment exposes with emotional honesty the problems of its characters'

lives. And it lets them mature in a way Bart and Homer never will, so that we wind up actually caring about these 2-D figures.

Dispatches from Elsewhere

TV-14, 2020
AMC+, 10 episodes
Drama created by Jason Segel, with Jason Segel, André 3000, Eve Lindley, Richard E. Grant and Sally Field.

After they all respond to the same flyer, a group of ordinary Philadelphians stumble into a game that reveals a mystery hiding just beneath the surface of their daily lives. This idiosyncratic, enjoyably weird series bears all the hallmarks of an auteur and indeed, Segel (How I Met Your Mother) both created and stars in this show, full of structural surprises and philosophical yearning. As he brings together four lonely characters desperate to connect, Segel unexpectedly gave viewers the perfect, feel-good story for the year of lockdown.

Divorce

TV-MA, 2016–2019
HBO Max, 3 seasons, 25 episodes
Comedy-drama created by Sharon Horgan, with Sarah Jessica Parker, Thomas Haden Church, Molly Shannon, Talia Balsam, Sterling Jerins, Charlie Kilgore and Tracy Letts.

Sarah Jessica Parker and Thomas Haden Church are wounded people who clash in this biting comedy about the dissolution of a 17-year marriage. From Sharon Horgan, the Irish actress and comedian who starred in Catastrophe, comes this series about the drawn-out ending of a worn-out marriage. Often bleak except when interrupted by uproarious putdowns, Divorce initially drove many viewers away with its tone, though it lightened up a bit in Season 2. As with Parker's last HBO show, it's the cast that keeps you coming back, with Church as her comically brooding husband and Shannon and Letts as their friends, also in a rocky marriage.

Doctor Thorne

TV-G, 2016
Prime Video original, 4 episodes
Limited series (historical drama)
created by Julian Fellowes, with Harry Richardson, Tom Hollander, Stefanie Martini, Rebecca Front, Richard McCabe and Alison Brie.

From *Downton Abbey* creator Julian Fellowes, this period piece about a penniless young woman who ingratiates herself into high society has a charming, tongue-in-cheek insouciance of its own. Fellowes's adaptation of the Anthony Trollope novel by the same name stars Brie as the brash American ingenue who grows up among the turbulent passions of her benefactors. Featuring a British cast almost genetically suited for the droll goings-on, *Doctor Thorne* is an easy watch at under 3 hours.

Doctor Who

TV-PG, 1963–present
BritBox, HBO Max, 12 seasons, 160 episodes
Sci-fi drama with David Tennant, Matt Smith, Peter Capaldi, Jodie Whittaker, Jenna Coleman, Nicholas Briggs, Karen Gillan, Billie Piper and Paul Kasey.

James Bond has nothing on the Doctor, the most versatile and appealing character in British entertainment history. Appearing a mere 11 years after Queen Elizabeth's coronation, this extraterrestrial time-traveler has been played by 13 actors including, most recently, a woman, and by the time you read this a 14th Doctor will likely have been cast. Though scholarly essays have been written about the show's place in British culture and pop history, the secret

to its success is that it was so simple, anyone could jump in and start watching it with no prior knowledge about the show. The world can always use someone like The Doctor, a clever, well-spoken *deus ex machina* who pops out of its humble blue police callbox (aka Tardis) at random, defeats the Daleks or some other enemy of humankind, then disappears. Revived after a 26-year hiatus, *Doctor Who* continues to win over fans and critics; someday The Doctor will be even more iconic than the Queen.

🏆 Peabody Award, BAFTA Award for best drama

Documentary Now!

TV-14, 2015–present
Netflix, 3 seasons, 21 episodes
Comedy created by Fred Armisen, Bill Hader and Seth Meyers, with Bill Hader, Fred Armisen, Helen Mirren, Owen Wilson, Connie Chung, Michael Keaton and Natasha Lyonne.

You don't have to love docs to enjoy this high-concept anthology series that spoofs a popular documentary film or format in each episode. These short parodies can stand on their own as mockumentaries. But having Helen Mirren introduce each film does add a level of class, and if you recognize the classic doc being spoofed, it only adds to the enjoyment.

▶▶ Beloved episodes among film nerds include "Co-Op" (S3E3), which lampoons the 1970 D.A. Pennebaker doc filmed during the making of the cast album for Stephen Sondheim's *Company*; and "Waiting for the Artist" (S3E4), starring Cate Blanchett in an insightful sendup of performance artist Marina Abramović.

The Dog House: UK

TV-G, 2020–present
HBO Max, 2 seasons, 17 episodes (AD)

Docuseries with Perry Fitzpatrick and Andrew Buchan.

Remarkably intimate and revealing look inside the adoption process at a British dog shelter. If real life is already supplying more uncertainty and terror than you ever wanted, perhaps you'd like to visit a bucolic meadow where gentle handlers prepare sweet pups to find their forever homes? We watch prospective adopters arrive, describe their lives and the sort of dog they want and we realize how sensitive shelter staff must be in proposing just the right match for them. We follow dog and prospective human to the "leafy meeting pen," where staffers watch on a closed-circuit feed to see how well they did. Most satisfyingly, we check in "some time later …" to see how our dog and human pairs are getting on.

Dolemite Is My Name
R, 2019
Netflix original, 1 hr 58 mins (AD)
Movie (comedy) with Eddie Murphy, Keegan-Michael Key, Mike Epps, Craig Robinson, Tituss Burgess and Wesley Snipes.

Eddie Murphy's acclaimed passion project explains how Rudy Ray Moore became a Blaxploitation icon. Murphy plays Moore, whose legend traces to his character Dolemite, a comedian and pimp who just happens to know prostitutes trained in kung fu. Hands down it's the best Eddie Murphy performance in decades and makes it easy to remember why he — and not just the subject of this film — is legendary.

Dollface
TV-MA, 2019–present
Hulu original, 2 seasons, 20 episodes (AD)
Comedy with Kat Dennings, Brenda Song, Shay Mitchell, Esther Povitsky, Beth Grant and Malin Akerman.

Slightly trippy comedy about a woman seeking to restore her long-neglected female friendships after getting dumped. Aided by a strong supporting ensemble, *Dollface* is notable for its use of magical realism (e.g., a cat talks to us while driving a bus full of women going through breakups). Akerman makes a memorable appearance as Jules's boss, a Gwyneth Paltrow–esque lifestyle mogul. At the time Hulu picked up *Dollface* for Season 2, it was the streamer's "best performing new binge series."

🗨 **From our forums:** "Some of the fantasy sequences seemed pretty pointless, but I ended up liking the show a lot. The chemistry between the ladies was really solid throughout."

Dolly Parton's Christmas on the Square
TV-PG, 2020
Netflix original, 1 hr 38 mins (AD)
Movie (family comedy) directed by Debbie Allen, with Christine Baranski, Dolly Parton, Jenifer Lewis, Josh Segarra, Jeanine Mason and Treat Williams.

A rich woman plans to sell the small town she owns and ruin the residents' lives — and then an angel arrives. Like Dolly Parton herself, this movie is campily aware of its own ridiculousness and that makes it even more fun to watch.

🏆 2 Emmys including best TV movie

Dolly Parton's Heartstrings
TV-14, 2019
Netflix original, 8 episodes (AD)
Anthology series (music-dramatic) with Dolly Parton, Delta Burke, Julianne Hough, Melissa Leo, Colin O'Donoghue, Kathleen Turner and Ginnifer Goodwin.

Each episode is like a TV movie based on a different Dolly song. The idea behind *Heartstrings* is that country music tells memorable stories about people. The 8 Parton classics featured here include

"Jolene," presented here as a modern-day suburban love triangle; and "These Old Bones," about an old woman from Parton's childhood. Be warned, she doesn't appear in all episodes, which is a shame because everything in life could use more Dolly.

Don't F**k With Cats: Hunting an Internet Killer

TV-MA, 2019
Netflix original, 3 episodes (AD)
Limited series (true crime) directed by Mark Lewis, with Deanna Thompson and John Green.

They always say that psycho killers start by torturing animals; this guy did it online, setting off a global manhunt. When an anonymous poster uploads a snuff film of kittens, a group of Canadian Internet sleuths make it their mission to find him. This 3-parter doesn't have the most coherent storyline and there are some who argue it never should've been made, since publicizing the deeds and name of the killer (now behind bars) only feeds his ego. But this docuseries's WTF factor and riveting, wait-there's-more narrative style made it a natural for Netflix — and one of its biggest hits of 2019.

🔊 **From our forums:** "This was both fascinating and very difficult to watch. It's hard to recommend because as an avid animal lover, I was so distressed by the videos."

🏆 Emmy for best writing, nonfiction

Don't Look Up

R, 2021
Netflix original, 2 hrs 18 mins (AD)
Sci-fi comedy directed by Adam McKay, with Leonardo DiCaprio, Jennifer Lawrence, Meryl Streep, Cate Blanchett, Jonah Hill, Mark Rylance, Tyler Perry, Timothée Chalamet, Ron Perlman and Ariana Grande.

Packed with A-list actors, this satire follows a pair of astronomers who try to convince the world to care that a comet is hurtling toward Earth. Director McKay is better known for prestige films like *The Big Short* and *Vice*, so it's understandable that critics went in expecting *Dr. Strangelove*-level absurdism and were annoyed to get *It's a Mad, Mad, Mad, Mad World* instead. Some critics liked the film — and what's not to like, with President Streep taking scientific advice from PhD student Lawrence and her advisor, Dr. DiCaprio? — declaring it to be an allegory for today's debauched media-political ecosystem, noting that you could easily substitute "COVID" or "climate" whenever you heard the word "comet." But that might be overthinking this film, one of Netflix's most over-the-top (and popular) releases of 2021.

Doogie Howser, M.D.

TV-PG, 1989–1993
Hulu, 4 seasons, 97 episodes
Family comedy created by Steven Bochco and David E. Kelley, with Neil Patrick Harris, Max Casella, Belinda Montgomery, Lawrence Pressman, Kathryn Layng, James Sikking and Markus Redmond.

Sweet, likable and unlikely collaboration between three future TV heavyweights. This light drama about a medical prodigy who went into practice while his pals were still in high school teamed up a young writer named David E. Kelley, his boss on *L.A. Law*, Steven Bochco and rising star Neil Patrick Harris. Though the title became a punchline (because Doogie *is* a funny name), the ratings show it was also a series people were invested in, and it remains a standout from a more innocent bygone era of TV.

🔊 **From our forums:** "The episode (S4E1) on the 1992 L.A riot is fantastic."

🏆 3 Emmys

Some shows may have moved; see page 183.

Doogie Kamealoha, M.D.
TV-PG, 2021–present
Disney+ original, 10 episodes (AD)

Family comedy created by Kourtney Kang, with Peyton Elizabeth Lee, Emma Meisel, Matthew Sato, Jason Scott Lee, Kathleen Rose Perkins, Mapuana Makia, Jeffrey Bowyer-Chapman and Wes Tian.

Inventive reimagining of *Doogie Howser* with a teenage girl practicing medicine in sunny Hawaii. If your standard response to a TV show's reboot is, "Who asked for this?" prepare to be pleasantly surprised. Peyton Lee is winning as a girl prodigy whose choice of a medical career earns her the nickname "Doogie," while Jason Scott Lee is wonderful as her supportive father. Though *Doogie Howser* fans will notice many references to the original, nostalgia isn't the reason to watch this show.

▶▶ Show creator Kang was a producer on *How I Met Your Mother* which starred Doogie Howser himself, Neil Patrick Harris.

Doom Patrol
TV-MA, 2019–present
HBO Max original, 3 seasons, 34 episodes (AD)

Fantasy comedy with April Bowlby, Diane Guerrero, Matt Bomer, Brendan Fraser, Timothy Dalton, Joivan Wade, Riley Shanahan, Matthew Zuk and Alan Tudyk.

Well-received adaptation of the DC Comics title follows outcasts who earn their superpowers through traumatic events and now fight for a world that rejects them. After a series of uninspired movies, the DC universe seems to have found its sweet spot on HBO Max with dark dramas that have strong emotional cores. Great writing and a fundamental strangeness help keep *Doom Patrol* watchable hour after hour.

▶▶ And keep watching, as this ragtag band of remade humans go on even more fascinating adventures in Seasons 2 and 3.

Dopesick
TV-MA, 2021
Hulu original, 8 episodes (AD)

Limited series (drama) created by Danny Strong, with Michael Keaton, Rosario Dawson, Peter Sarsgaard, Michael Stuhlbarg, Will Poulter, Kaitlyn Dever, Jack McDorman, Phillipa Soo and Mare Winningham.

Michael Keaton plays a doctor whose community is decimated by OxyContin in this adaptation of the *New York Times* bestseller about the opioid crisis. If you prefer to get your history from docudramas, *Dopesick* doesn't scrimp on details about the OxyContin epidemic and the Sackler family's role in it, but it is twice as long as the docuseries *Crime of the Century*, thanks to numerous subplots that often have little to do with the opioid epidemic. Keaton, a kindly family physician in Coal Country, is recruited by a relentless sales rep for Purdue Pharma, who assures him that OxyContin is the "safe" opioid. This claim, which will be debunked by others — notably an FBI field agent (Sarsgaard) and DEA officer (Dawson), who eventually go after Purdue — will result in Sam being overwhelmed by addicts, not to mention guilt at his own role in this disaster.

Downton Abbey
TV-PG, 2011–2016
PBS Passport, BritBox, Prime Video, Netflix, Peacock, 6 seasons, 52 episodes (AD)

Historical drama created by Julian Fellowes, with Hugh Bonneville, Michelle Dockery, Maggie Smith, Laura Carmichael, Joanne Froggatt, Brendan Coyle, Robert James-Collier, Jim Carter, Phyllis Logan and Elizabeth McGovern.

In early 20th-century England, the Crawley family and their servants endure everything from the onset of world war and the upheaval of British society to secret romances and untidy kitchens. Memorable characters, fulsome storylines and writing that always shines and occasionally dazzles (or leads to outbursts of laughter) endeared this British-American production to millions on both sides of the pond.

▶▶ The series has spawned 2 theatrical feature films to date: 2019's *Downton Abbey* and 2022's *Downton Abbey: A New Era*.

🏆 3 SAG Awards for best drama, 2 Emmys for Maggie Smith

Dr. Death
TV-MA, 2021
Peacock original, 8 episodes (AD)
Limited series (crime drama) with Joshua Jackson, Christian Slater, Alec Baldwin, Dominic Burgess, Grace Gummer, AnnaSophia Robb and Kelsey Grammer.

Joshua Jackson plays Christopher Duntsch, an inept neurosurgeon who mutilated several of his patients and eventually murdered two of them. Based on the true-crime podcast, *Dr. Death* certainly succeeds as the tale of a monstrous villain, but leavens the horror by frequently foregrounding the doctors and DAs who brought Duntsch down. Baldwin and Slater, who play two of those crusading doctors, have enough chemistry to warrant their own spinoff.

The Drowning
TV-14, 2021
AMC+, Acorn TV, 4 episodes
Limited series (thriller) created by Francesca Brill and Luke Watson, with Jill Halfpenny, Cody Molko, Rupert Penry-Jones, Deborah Findlay, Dara Devaney and Deirdre Mullins.

Years after a woman is told her boy has drowned, she thinks she sees him in a crowd and is determined to bond with him again. In this taut mystery, Jodie (Halfpenny) stops at nothing to prove that the teenager she's spotted on the street is the grown-up version of her 4-year-old, whose disappearance (*not* drowning, as the police claimed) she's never gotten over. Implausible or not, Halfpenny gets us completely invested in Jodie's quest.

The Duchess
TV-MA, 2020
Netflix original, 6 episodes (AD)
Comedy-drama created by Katherine Ryan, with Katherine Ryan, Rory Keenan, Katy Byrne, Steen Raskopoulos and Michelle de Swarte.

Britcom about an unapologetic single mom trying to have another kid is raunchy and occasionally heartwarming. Based on the Canadian comic's standup set, this mom-behaving-badly series touches on, and occasionally stampedes through, topics like bullying, horrible exes and every parent's desire to spend a few uncomplicated years with their offspring — in this case her young daughter Olive (Byrne) — before they turn on you.

💬 **From our forums:** "Three minutes in and you will know if Katherine's sharp-tongued antihero is for you. As the series progresses, it shows another side of itself, one that's full of heart and warmth. *The Duchess* manages to avoid falling into the trap of similar shows, portraying single parenthood as something tragic and messy. Katherine may not be perfect but we never see her looking anything less than glamorous, confident and fiercely independent."

Duck Dynasty
TV-PG, 2012–2017
Tubi, PlutoTV, 11 seasons, 130 episodes

Reality show with Si Robertson, Jase Robertson, Willie Robertson, Phil Robertson, Korie Robertson and Kay Robertson.

The Robertsons, a conservative Evangelical family, originally made their living selling products to duck hunters, but thanks to this reality show they've become their own pop-culture brand. At its peak, this was the most popular nonfiction show on cable, thanks to the antics of Willie Robertson, the hirsute head of the family's Duck Commander business who runs it with his wife Korie; Si Robertson, a master craftsman of duck reeds; the family matriarch Kay, full of down-home wisdom; and many other characters. If you've ever known a Southern family with funny, eccentric people in it, you'll probably relate to the antics. You might even forgive the Robertson family member who once told *GQ* he thought homosexuality was a sin. For better or worse, *Duck Dynasty* may be TV's most entertaining emblem of the red state/blue state divide.

Dynasties
TV-PG, 2018
Discovery+, PlutoTV, 6 episodes
Docuseries with Sir David Attenborough.

Embedding with just one group of animals per episode, this is a nice change of pace from Attenborough's usual "now this!" approach. The filmmakers, for instance, spent more than a year filming the same family of big cats, following their movements and tracking their life events. Though that meant being exposed to some heartbreaking things, Attenborough doesn't oversell when he calls these "the most intimate and intense stories of their kind ever told."

Dynasty (2017)
TV-14, 2017–present
Netflix, 5 seasons, 108 episodes (AD)

Drama with Elizabeth Gillies, Rafael de la Fuente, Robert Christopher Riley, Sam Adegoke, Grant Show and Alan Dale.

The remake of the 1980s hit has the DNA of the original but is smartly updated to our own age of excess. As obscure as the original *Dynasty* was world-beating, this reboot of the Carrington family saga comes from two producers with solid soapy credentials: Josh Schwartz and Stephanie Savage (*The O.C.*, *Nancy Drew*). It's dumb, it's fun, it goes down easy and it delivers consequences to fictional billionaires for their evil schemes that the real ones will probably never see.

💬 **From our forums:** "The writing on the show feels kind of like a runaway train to me . . . it isn't thought through in some respects, while it is very carefully mapped out in others. I give them credit though, jaws do drop and cleverly."

Eagleheart
TV-14, 2011–2014
HBO Max, 3 seasons, 34 episodes
Satirical comedy created by Andrew Weinberg, Michael Koman and Jason Woliner, with Chris Elliott, Jack Wallace, Maria Thayer, Brett Gelman, Michael Gladis and Pete Gardner.

Alt-comedy legend Chris Elliott plays marshal Chris Monsanto in this spot-on *Walker, Texas Ranger* spoof. Conan O'Brien's Conaco produced this from an idea by former *Conan* writer Michael Koman, who went on to co-create *Nathan For You*. It's kind of amazing to see Elliott coming full circle with a concept he first introduced 30 years earlier, when he regularly popped up on David Letterman's late-night show as various cop-show characters (The Conspiracy Guy, The Fugitive Guy, etc.).

Easy (2016)
TV-MA, 2016–2019
Netflix original, 3 seasons,
25 episodes (AD)
Anthology series (comedy) created by
Joe Swanberg, with Michael Chernus,
Jane Adams, Elizabeth Reaser, Jacqueline
Toboni, Zazie Beetz, Aya Cash, Kiersey
Clemons and Dave Franco.

A strong indie sensibility elevates these single-episode stories about everyday Chicagoans in love and sex. Mumblecore film giant Swanberg continues that genre's commitment to conversations and sex scenes that seem real and unmediated. The narrative beats in these brief tales are organic and subtle, reminding us that small, everyday interactions can have lasting effects. The cast members, many of them from the indie circuit, know how to make this material crackle.

▶▶ Pairs well with *Modern Love*

The Eddy
TV-MA, 2020
Netflix original, 8 episodes
Limited series (drama) with André
Holland, Joanna Kulig, Amandla
Stenberg, Leila Bekhti, Randy Kerber,
Ludovic Louis, Lada Obradovic, Jowee
Omicil and Adil Dehbi.

Rich ensemble drama is centered on a struggling jazz club and the rundown Paris neighborhood where it's located. Though ostensibly centered on a troubled American expat named Elliot Udo (Holland), *The Eddy* is about the rhythms of life in a community with a *'Round Midnight* vibe. Elliot and his fellow artists — many played by musicians with no previous acting experience — perform original songs scored by pop legend Glen Ballard to demonstrate that making music is a great way to tell the world how you feel. Created by *His Dark Materials* writer Jack Thorne, with episodes directed by Damian Chazelle (*La La Land*), this

is a satisfying approach to expansive storytelling.

Elementary
TV-14, 2012–2019
Paramount+, Hulu, 7 seasons,
154 episodes
Crime drama with Jonny Lee Miller, Lucy
Liu, Aidan Quinn and Jon Michael Hill.

Lucy Liu plays a platonic Watson to Jonny Lee Miller's Sherlock Holmes in this utterly satisfying slice of network comfort fare. Updating a classic work for a contemporary audience while staying true to the canon isn't easy. Sherlock is still abrasive and caustic, he doesn't suffer fools and he hasn't softened just because his best friend is a woman. However, his drug addiction has chipped away at his know-it-all armor, revealing a vulnerable core. Meanwhile, *Joan* Watson (Liu) has been a steadfast support. She's an investigator and his equal in most respects. *Elementary*'s strength is in its nuanced portrayal of a partnership that extends far beyond the crimes they solve.

Ellen Degeneres: Here and Now
TV-PG, 2003
HBO Max, 1 hr
Comedy special with Ellen DeGeneres.

Filmed before her talk show started but after her sitcom was canceled, this now-classic special gave us a taste of what was coming from Ellen. After 18 years of watching her bite-sized monologues on daytime TV, it's satisfying to go back and watch DeGeneres effortlessly hold forth at the peak of her standup career. She delivers an hour of solid material at a steady but relentless pace, keeping NYC's Beacon Theater in stitches with observations about microwave ovens, hands-free phones, germophobia and her new status as a gay icon.

Emily in Paris
TV-MA, 2020–present
Netflix original, 2 seasons,
20 episodes (AD)
Romantic comedy created by Darren
Star, with Lily Collins, Philippine Leroy-
Beaulieu, Ashley Park, Lucas Bravo,
Samuel Arnold, Bruno Gouery and
Camille Razat.

**From the creator of *Sex and the City*
and *Younger* comes this story of an
American millennial in Paris.** What if
your job suddenly sent you to the world's
most glamorous city? If you were a young,
confident woman, you might create an
Instagram account called @EmilyInParis.
That's the setup for this confection about
an ambitious American who is clueless in
some ways but intuits, correctly, that Paris
is her oyster.

🗨 **From our forums:** "*Emily In Paris* is the
most unrealistic show I've ever watched.
And I love every second of it. I see that it
was produced by MTV and it definitely
gave me *Hills* vibes."

Encore!
TV-PG, 2019–present
Disney+ original, 12 episodes (AD)
Musical with Kristen Bell.

**Kristen Bell hosts this heartwarming
series that brings onetime high school
musical comrades back together for
one more big show.** Gimmicky, yes,
but the show is a kind-hearted treasure.
These people aren't here for reality-TV
fame. They're genuinely invested in
something that might seem a little silly
on the surface. *Encore!* pairs these people
with professionals — choreographers,
music directors — to fine-tune their craft.
The goal isn't to make them Broadway-
ready but to really bear down and make
something special.

▸▸ Pairs well with *The Great British
Baking Show*

The End of the F***ing World
TV-MA, 2017–2019
Netflix original, 2 seasons,
16 episodes (AD)
Dark comedy with Jessica Barden and
Alex Lawther.

**Maybe the unlikeliest teen romance
ever, James — who is pretty sure he's a
psychopath — plans to kill Alyssa but
instead bonds with her on a road trip.**
Unlikable? Yes. Problem children? To put
it mildly. Yet these two engaging leads
navigate their relationship so deftly, you
wind up wanting them to succeed.

🗨 **From our forums:** "Isn't it funny how
a story that started out with this kid very
flatly telling us he kills cats had us rooting
for him by the end? I think part of why it
works is it knows we've seen these stories
a million times before and plays off of that
with a wink. A good soundtrack doesn't
hurt either."

🏆 Peabody Award, BAFTA TV Award
for best drama series

The English Game
TV-14, 2020
Netflix original, 6 episodes (AD)
Limited series (British drama) created by
Julian Fellowes, Oliver Cotton and Tony
Charles, with Edward Holcroft, Kevin
Guthrie, Charlotte Hope, Niamh Walsh,
Craig Parkinson, James Harkness, Ben
Batt, Henry Lloyd-Hughes, Gerard Kearns
and Kerrie Hayes.

**The 1879 contest for soccer's biggest
prize is the backdrop for this drama
of class struggle from the creator of
Downton Abbey.** It's early days for the
beautiful game — football for some,
soccer for others — and the Old Etonians,
an upper-class London team, have a
firm grip on the burgeoning league
and England's prestigious FA (Football
Association) Cup. But a working-class
team in a northern England mill town is
set on changing that.

📣 **From our forums:** "It's kind of the perfect show for us — the history of his favorite sport for him and a period drama for me. It isn't the most exciting show, which is why we're watching an episode a week instead of 1–2 episodes a night."

Enlightened
TV-MA, 2011–2013
HBO Max, 2 seasons, 18 episodes
Comedy-drama created by Laura Dern and Mike White, with Laura Dern, Diane Ladd, Luke Wilson, Mike White, Sarah Burns and Timm Sharp.

Laura Dern's portrayal of a woman who goes on a holistic wellness retreat after a nervous breakdown at work has only grown in stature since it first aired. In its simplest terms, *Enlightened* was about improvement, both of self and the world around us and what it takes to make either possible (spoiler: don't hold your breath). It featured moments of high-wire comedy and moments of disarming grace, which Dern handled with skill and humor. Though critics loved it, HBO was disappointed in the show's ratings and canceled it far too soon.

▶▶ Dern's real-life mother, Diane Ladd, had a supporting role in the outstanding episode "Consider Helen" (S1E9), in which an overlooked, hectoring old mother is reconsidered.

Enola Holmes
PG-13, 2020
Netflix original, 2 hrs 3 mins (AD)
Movie (action) with Millie Bobby Brown, Henry Cavill, Sam Claflin and Helena Bonham Carter.

Stranger Things **star adds to the enjoyment of this family-friendly film about Sherlock Holmes's little sister.** Even better, the mystery she solves is juicy enough to satisfy Sherlock fans.

Episodes
TV-MA, 2011–2017
Showtime original, 5 seasons, 41 episodes
Comedy with Matt LeBlanc, Stephen Mangan, Tamsin Greig, John Pankow, Kathleen Rose Perkins and Mircea Monroe.

Matt LeBlanc is outstanding as a cartoon version of himself — one that's nothing like Joey. By far the best post-*Friends* outing for LeBlanc was this sitcom that followed two struggling husband-and-wife screenwriters (Mangan and Greig) who get saddled with creating a show around LeBlanc over their objections. Over the course of 5 seasons, the trio bond and squabble and experience success and failure. All the while LeBlanc is amusing as a smooth-talking bro with the attention span of a squirrel.

The Equalizer (2021)
TV-14, 2021–present
Paramount+, 2 seasons, 20 episodes (AD)
Crime drama with Queen Latifah, Tory Kittles, Adam Goldberg, Lorraine Toussaint, Chris Noth, Liza Lapira and Laya DeLeon Hayes.

Queen Latifah seriously upgrades this remake of the 1980s vigilante drama. Edward Woodward's *Equalizer* was one of the gems from the golden age of private investigators, but give Latifah her due — she's got incredible range and makes this gender-swapped reboot fun to watch. The pilot alone requires her to pose as a public defender and a billionaire's driver, and to speed away from danger on a getaway motorcycle. Her band of roguish smarties are perfectly cast individually and all this overcomes the formulaic procedural casing this show is squeezed into.

Escape at Dannemora
TV-MA, 2018
Showtime original, 8 episodes

For shows sorted by streaming platform, see page 381.

Limited series (crime drama) directed by Ben Stiller, with Benicio Del Toro, Paul Dano, Patricia Arquette, Bonnie Hunt, Eric Lange, David Morse and Jeremy Bobb.

Patricia Arquette is sensational as the female guard who helped two convicts flee a New York prison in a story based on true events. Almost as disturbing as her role on *The Act* is Arquette's portrayal of Tilly Mitchell, the guard whose sexual and emotional entanglements with the prisoners lead to her moral collapse. Equally impressive is Ben Stiller's turn as a dramatic director, especially in Episode 5 as he extracts tension from every fraught second of the prison break.

🏆 SAG and TCA awards for best actress in a limited series (Arquette)

Euphoria
TV-MA, 2019–present
HBO Max, 2 seasons, 16 episodes (AD)

Teen drama with Zendaya, Hunter Schafer, Jacob Elordi, Maude Apatow, Alexa Demie, Barbie Ferreira, Sydney Sweeney, Angus Cloud, Eric Dane and Storm Reid.

A group of high school students navigate sex, drugs, love, friendship and identity with a variety of intense results. *Euphoria* is graphic in every sense of the word, but those who don't mind seeing teen characters in fraught situations may enjoy this wild coming-of-age series. In the central role of Rue, Zendaya gives a bravura performance (she even sings).

📢 **From our forums:** "I'm in awe of Zendaya. Full stop. I think she's amazing." "I thought the show did a good job of showing that abortion, while necessary and protected, can also be hard."

🏆 Best actress Emmy for a drama series for Zendaya

Eurovision Song Contest: The Story of Fire Saga
PG-13, 2020
Netflix original, 2 hrs 3 mins (AD)

Movie (musical comedy) with Will Ferrell, Rachel McAdams, Dan Stevens and Pierce Brosnan.

Will Ferrell kills it as one half of an Icelandic duo who get an unexpected chance to represent their country in the Eurovision Song Contest. As overly confident underachiever Lars Erickssong, who lives with his father Erick (Brosnan) in a remote fishing village, Ferrell deftly navigates a host of improbable movie-comedy events with partner Sigrid (McAdams) to advance to the televised finals of "the singing Olympics" in Scotland. Great scenery and loud music accent what is Ferrell's unlikeliest film.

▶▶ The song "Husavik" was nominated for an Oscar — a first for a song with Icelandic lyrics.

Everything Sucks!
TV-14, 2018
Netflix original, 10 episodes (AD)

Limited series (comedy) with Jahi Di'Allo Winston, Peyton Kennedy, Patch Darragh, Claudine Mboligikpelani Nako, Quinn Liebling, Elijah Stevenson, Rio Mangini and Sydney Sweeney.

At a high school in Boring, Oregon, in 1996, teen misfits from the AV club try their best to survive adolescence. Come for the '90s nostalgia — which covers everything from Zima to the Verve Pipe — stay for the well-written teen characters whose hangups are mirrored by their parents' problems. As the young protagonists, Winston and Kennedy's performances give oomph to some recognizable high school tropes.

Everything's Gonna Be Okay
TV-14, 2020–2021
Hulu, 2 seasons, 20 episodes

Comedy created by Josh Thomas, with Josh Thomas, Kayla Cromer, Adam Faison, Maeve Press, Maria Bamford and Richard Kind.

Josh Thomas (*Please Like Me*) created and stars in this unconventional family dramedy that takes on autism, grieving and puberty with an off-kilter perspective. The premise you've seen before — a family is left orphaned, leaving a young adult in charge of his kid sibs — but the execution is very different. Nicholas (Thomas) is gay and he's in care of two half-sisters, one of whom, Matilda (Cromer), is on the spectrum. Add a male love interest in Alex (Faison) and you have drama.

🐾 **From our forums:** "I loved it, partly because it reminded me of *Please Like Me* but also because I loved Matilda and Genevieve."

Evil

TV-14, 2019–present
Paramount+ original, 2 seasons,
26 episodes (AD)
Crime drama created by Michelle King and Robert King, with Katja Herbers, Mike Colter, Aasif Mandvi, Michael Emerson and Christine Lahti.

Creepily good network procedural got even better when it moved to streaming. CBS didn't quite know what to do with this spooky-silly series about church investigators probing supernatural claims — sort of a Catholic *X-Files*. For Season 2, though, *Evil* moved to Paramount+ where the show's producers, Robert and Michelle King, already had *The Good Fight*. There the show has become more irreverent and leaned into what it does best — knocking out a case every week with a shrug, a wink and a splash of holy water.

🐾 **From our forums:** "There isn't anything else on TV like this and it hits my creepy sweet spot. There are genuinely scary moments and some things are just the right kind of unsettling, not slasher horror which I hate. Plus, weird humor."

The Expanse

TV-14, 2015–2022
Prime Video original, 6 seasons,
62 episodes (AD)
Sci-fi drama with Wes Chatham, Dominique Tipper, Steven Strait, Shohreh Aghdashloo, Cas Anvar, Frankie Adams, Cara Gee and Shawn Doyle.

Ambitious space opera got better after it was rescued by Amazon (reportedly at the behest of Jeff Bezos). Based on the book series by pseudonymous James S.A. Corey, this multi-layered series is filled with political intrigue, rich character development and the occasional thrilling space battle. Alas, for 3 seasons on cable's SyFy it also showed the signs of a low-budget production. Canceled at a critical point in the narrative, the show found a new home at Amazon Prime — and a bigger budget.

🐾 **From our forums:** "They've seriously changed the direction of the entire narrative of the show more than once, without giving anyone whiplash. At the start we had a mystery about a missing girl. Then it turned into a political thriller about the manufacturing of a secret bioweapon, then it turned into a larger scale political thriller about corruption and warmongering. The only ongoing storyline is that of humanity looking for reasons to divide itself."

▶▶ Accompanying Season 6 is a series of webisodes titled *The Expanse: One Ship*. The episodes are available in the show's X-Ray bonus content section on Prime Video.

Exterminate All the Brutes

TV-MA, 2021
HBO Max, 4 episodes (AD)
Docuseries directed by Raoul Peck, with Josh Hartnett.

From the director of *I Am Not Your Negro*, **comes a self-important, heavy-handed, messy, radical take on white history that's impossible to stop watching.** It's not exactly woke history to point out the parallels between European colonialism and the settlement of the American West. But you wouldn't know it from listening to gravelly voiced Raoul Peck, director and narrator of this four-hour treatise. Peck presents this historical backgrounder on the roots of white supremacy as though he's Moses bringing tablets of truth to the unwashed HBO masses. And yet the result, while less of a documentary than an extremely intense (and long) educational film, is compelling, thanks to Peck's creative and ironic use of archival images and reenactments, which feature Hartnett in a variety of roles — always, though, as a colonizer.

F Is For Family
TV-MA, 2015–present
Netflix original, 4 seasons,
36 episodes (AD)
Animated comedy created by Bill Burr and Michael Price, with Bill Burr, Laura Dern, Justin Long, Debi Derryberry, Sam Rockwell and Haley Reinhart.

Comedian Bill Burr created this dark yet warm-hearted animated series about an Irish-American family in the 1970s. Loosely based on Burr's upbringing in suburban Pennsylvania, this abrasive but foul-mouthed cartoon ultimately pays tribute to a family that sticks together through thick, thin and every '70s fad. Dern is wonderfully, surprisingly nuanced as the mom, communicating vulnerability and saltiness in equal measure.

The Fades
TV-14, 2011
Hulu, HBO Max, Prime Video, Hoopla,
6 episodes

Horror series with Iain De Caestecker, Tom Ellis, Lily Loveless, Daniel Kaluuya, Claire Rushbrook, Ruth Gemmell, Joe Dempsie and Natalie Dormer.

A teenager who discovers he can see the souls of the dead gets sucked into an apocalyptic battle in this stylish and clever series. *The Fades* did more world-building in 6 episodes than others do in years. Able to bridge humor and pathos with ease, it's worth a watch just to see Dormer and Kaluuya shine in supporting roles years before they became stars.
🏆 BAFTA for best drama series

The Falcon and the Winter Soldier
TV-14, 2021
Disney+ original, 6 episodes (AD)
Limited series (superhero drama) with Anthony Mackie, Sebastian Stan, Wyatt Russell, Emily VanCamp, Daniel Brühl and Erin Kellyman.

After the events of the *Avengers: Endgame* **movie, a new Avenger is handed the shield of Captain America — and he's a Black man.** Like *Wanda Vision*, *The Falcon and the Winter Soldier* was designed for the 21st-century viewer who expects more socially relevant stories from their Marvel heroes. Sam Wilson (Mackie) and Bucky Barnes (Stan) form an unlikely duo when chaos engulfs the world following the death of Captain America. Besides a radical anti-nationalist insurgency, the two men are confronted with a white man who claims to be the real Captain America. Woven through these compelling storylines is a running discussion of America's treatment of immigrants and people of color.

💬 **From our forums:** "The whole story was set up as a fight over America's soul and seemed to be hard-hitting in the beginning, but in the end it did pull its punches considerably."

Fall River

TV-MA, 2021
Epix original, 4 episodes
Limited series (true crime) directed by
James Buddy Day.

**Fine revisionist docuseries about a
grisly murder spree in the 1970s that
was originally blamed on a Satanic cult.**
Carl Drew was convicted of killing a sex
worker when he was tied to a demonic
group at the height of "Satanic panic." In
this important look-back, we learn how
law enforcement repeatedly ignored the
claims of women that they were pursuing
the wrong men while the real predators
roamed free. It's a story worth telling at
a time when Satanic panic has informed
the QAnon movement — and victims of
sexual violence continue to be ignored.

The Fall

TV-MA, 2013–2016
Acorn TV, 3 seasons, 17 episodes
Crime drama created by Allan Cubitt,
with Gillian Anderson, Jamie Dornan,
Niamh McGrady, John Lynch, Colin
Morgan, Stuart Graham, Valene Kane,
Aisling Franciosi and Bronagh Waugh.

**Gillian Anderson plays a London
detective who travels to Northern
Ireland in pursuit of a serial killer.**
This show is so tense it will make your
skin crawl, and the dread is often even
more effective than the gore. Dornan is
memorably creepy as the killer, not least
because the show refuses to give him a
tidy series of motives or simply write
him off as a psychopathic monster. He
embodies a more mysterious type of
evil that burrows into the imagination.
Anderson, meanwhile, is easy to root for
as an incorrigible detective who refuses to
stop hunting her man.

Family Ties

TV-G, 1982–1989
Paramount+, 7 seasons, 172 episodes

Sitcom with Michael J. Fox, Meredith
Baxter, Michael Gross, Justine Bateman
and Tina Yothers.

**Two hippies settle down to start a family
and end up raising teen Reaganite
Michael J. Fox in this rare '80s sitcom
that still holds up.** If you're of a certain
age, your ears may have perked up while
watching *WandaVision* when it played a
pitch-perfect rendition of the *Family Ties*
theme song. That's just one measure of
the respect that many of us have today for
one of the best network family comedies
of all time. Fox, of course, is the reason,
not just because of the body of work he's
accumulated since *Family Ties* but because
he was given a character with some depth.
Precocious and difficult Alex went from
high school to college with stories that
actually reflect the bumpiness of that
journey. Baxter and Gross had exceptional
chemistry as the parents.

🗩 **From our forums:** "Michael Gross
was so underrated. Like Alan Alda on
M*A*S*H he could do the dramatic stuff
as well as absolutely kill the comedic
moments."

▶▶ A good place to drop the needle is on
the Season 4 opener "The Real Thing,"
where Alex tries dating at college and
winds up meeting Ellen, played by his
future real-life wife Tracy Pollan. Then
take in the two-parter "A, My Name Is
Alex" (S5E23-24), in which Alex takes an
emotional journey through the aftermath
of his friend Greg's death. In lesser hands
it would be one of those regrettable after-
school specials, but this won an Emmy
for the script and is striking for its use of
a spare, theatrical setup for Alex's therapy
session, to which Fox brings genuine soul-
sickness.

🏆 Emmy for best actor in a comedy
(Fox, 3 wins)

For shows sorted by streaming platform, see page 381.

The Family

TV-14, 2019
Netflix, 5 episodes (AD)
Docuseries directed by Jesse Moss, with
Jeff Sharlet, James Cromwell and Larry
Anderson.

**An insider shines a light on the secretive
Christian "fellowship" that has been
influencing D.C. politics for generations.**
The National Prayer Breakfast may seem
like one of those anodyne interfaith
events from the postwar days of religious
unity, but it's actually the creation of "The
Fellowship," a decades-long effort by right-
wing evangelicals to minister Christ to
world leaders. Director Jesse Moss (*Mayor
Pete*) casts a light on this shadowy group
and the questionable alliances it has made
in the name of spreading the gospel.

Fantasy Island (2021)

TV-14, 2021
Hulu, 10 episodes (AD)
Fantasy drama with Roselyn Sanchez
and Kiara Barnes.

**The show that brought magical realism
to the masses gets a welcome refresh
aimed at the ladies.** Veteran showrunners
Liz Craft and Sarah Fain replaced Ricardo
Montalban's smooth, manly, mysterious
Roarke from the 1970s with an equally
suave and mysterious Elena Roarke
(Sanchez). The story arcs are darker and
sexier, as people's fantasies are magically
fulfilled in ways that have both comic and
poignant turns.

🗨 **From our forums:** "Loving the fashion
choices on this show! Lots of great white
outfits. Not really invested in Elena's love
life, but it's good that they want to let
her have a story outside of facilitating
fantasies."

Fargo

TV-MA, 2014
Hulu, 4 seasons, 41 episodes

Anthology series (drama) created by
Noah Hawley, with Billy Bob Thornton,
Martin Freeman, Allison Tolman, Colin
Hanks, Bob Odenkirk, Patrick Wilson, Ted
Danson, Jean Smart, Kirsten Dunst and
Jordan Peele.

**Through creator Noah Hawley's pen
and consummate performances by top
actors, the Coen Brothers' cinematic
world comes alive again.** As it goes
along, each season of *Fargo* seems a bit
less coherent than the one before it, but
it's still maintained an addictive balance
of menace, comedy and what-in-the-
actual-hell surrealism. And *Fargo* remains
one of television's most reliable outlet for
astonishing acting.

🗨 **From our forums:** "The show has done
such a good job of surprising me." "The
'nice' people in this universe tend to end
up screwed no matter what they do."

⏩ *Season 1:* When merciless hitman
Lorne Malvo (Thornton) crosses paths
with milquetoast insurance salesman
Lester Nygaard (Freeman), you know it's
not going to end well. But as with every
season of *Fargo*, the fun is getting to the
bloody conclusion. There's always some
insane structural wrinkle around the
corner, like alien spaceships disrupting a
shootout.

⏩ *Season 2: Fargo* rewinds to 1979 to
explore a killing spree referenced in
Season 1. The beauty of this series is you
don't have to see either the prior season or
the original *Fargo* movie to appreciate the
brilliance on display here.

⏩ Season 3 is set in the 2010s outside
the Twin Cities, starring Ewan McGregor
and Mary Elizabeth Winstead as a couple
caught up in a double murder. For
Season 4, *Fargo* rewinds all the way to
1950 and Kansas City, starring Chris Rock
as an organized crime boss.

🏆 Peabody Award, Emmy for best
limited series

Fast Foodies

TV-14, 2021–present
HBO Max, 10 episodes (AD)
Reality competition with Morgan Evans (host), Kristen Kish, Jeremy Ford and Andrew Morgado.

This quick, light repast is one part unconventional cooking competition, one part affectionate hang-out. Three reality stars (they all appeared on *Top Chef*, though the 2 shows aren't related) welcome a different celebrity guest for each briskly paced half-hour episode that involves some competition, some banter and maybe too much booze. Despite the loose format, this show actually takes convenience food seriously. A cheesy gordita crunch, for example, is broken down into its constituent layers, which the chefs then set about trying to recreate.

Fawlty Towers

TV-PG, 1975–1979
BritBox, 2 seasons, 12 episodes
Classic sitcom created by John Cleese and Connie Booth, with John Cleese, Prunella Scales, Andrew Sachs, Connie Booth and Ballard Berkeley.

John Cleese, at the height of his comedy powers, played incompetent hotelier Basil Fawlty in 12 uproarious episodes that remain a masterwork of British farce 40 years on. Basil, who wants nothing more than to "raise the tone" of his failing hotel, consistently gets in his own way in this classic Britcom. Though just 12 episodes were made of *Fawlty Towers*, they loom large to this day. (Fans never agree which episode was the greatest; your Editor is partial to "The Germans.") As of this writing it's only on streaming through BritBox, which is an apt location for the series that the BBC called "the British sitcom by which all other British sitcoms must be judged."

🏆 2 BAFTA awards for best situation comedy

Fear Street (movie trilogy)

R, 2021
Netflix original, 5 hrs 31 mins (AD)
Anthology series (horror) with Kiana Madeira, Olivia Scott Welch, Benjamin Flores Jr., Julia Rehwald, Sadie Sink, Ashley Zukerman, Emily Rudd, Fred Hechinger and Gillian Jacobs.

Time-traveling films follow a group of teens who discover that an ancient evil may be coming for them. Based on R.L. Stine's horror novels, this is grown-up, sophisticated horror involving a trio of interconnected period films about rival towns, Shadyside and Sunnydale. They have suffered different fates for centuries, but why? This is the mystery that takes us from 1994 in Part One to 1978 in Part Two and all the way back to 1666 for the chilling conclusion. Part One is filled with '90s nostalgia as well as Tarantino-sized buckets of blood. The middle film, set in 1978, references the slasher movies that dominated teen cinema back then. On the whole the characters are well-developed in *Fear Street* and the stories have some depth, e.g., exploring how class wars divided the communities beset by the story's ancient terror.

Fear the Walking Dead

TV-MA, 2015–present
AMC+, Hulu, 6 seasons, 85 episodes
Dystopian drama with Alycia Debnam-Carey, Colman Domingo, Danay Garcia, Rubén Blades, Lennie James, Maggie Grace, Jenna Elfman, Alexa Nisenson, Kim Dickens and Frank Dillane.

At the beginning of the zombie apocalypse chronicled in *The Walking Dead*, a group of Angelenos have to redefine themselves and their society in order to survive. You don't need to watch the original series to enjoy this sister show, which aims to explore how an entire society is reshaped by global cataclysm. The new cast and wider narrative scope gave the zombie franchise a kick in the pants, at least in Season 1; after that fans began to complain about unimaginative, even schlocky storylines.

The Feed
TV-MA, 2019
Prime Video original, 10 episodes (AD)
Sci-fi drama with Guy Burnet, David Thewlis, Shaquille Ali-Yebuah, Michelle Fairley, Osy Ikhile, Jing Lusi, Jeremy Neumark Jones, Chris Reilly and Nina Toussaint-White.

Intriguing alt-future show about a social network you don't need a phone or computer to join — just a chip in your brain. Putting computer software directly into your brain seems like a really bad idea, but science fiction would have us believe it's an inevitability. Should it come to pass, *The Feed* presents a surprisingly plausible depiction of how the technology would change the world and the dangers it would present. The primary pleasures in the show come from witnessing the way it extrapolates how such a technology would affect society.

Feel Good
TV-MA, 2020–2021
Netflix original, 2 seasons, 12 episodes (AD)
British romcom created by Mae Martin and Joe Hampson, with Mae Martin, Charlotte Ritchie, Phil Burgers and Lisa Kudrow.

Standup comic Mae Martin plays a standup comic with an addiction problem who falls for a semi-closeted woman, forcing them both to face their demons in the name of love. Effective use of romcom and sitcom elements help lighten the uncomfortable truths that these 6 episodes explore — such as whether love is like addiction or if it's ever possible in this modern world to be truly happy.

▶▶ Pairs well with *Work in Progress*

Felicity
TV-14, 1998–2002
Hulu, 4 seasons, 84 episodes
Romance drama created by J.J. Abrams and Matt Reeves, with Keri Russell, Scott Speedman, Scott Foley, Tangi Miller, Greg Grunberg, Amanda Foreman, Amy Jo Johnson, Ian Gomez and Janeane Garofalo.

The first television drama to realistically portray the college experience made a star of Keri Russell. As a young, impulsive Stanford-bound freshman who suddenly uproots to New York to follow her high school crush, Russell offered a nuanced performance and mounds of curly hair. It's hard to say which was the greater draw for the young viewers of the WB network, because when she returned for Season 2 with her locks shorn — cue the drama! The show's ratings never recovered their freshman form, though Russell continued to offer weekly proof that she belonged on bigger stages than the WB.

▶▶ In Season 4, *Felicity* took a turn to the supernatural and time travel when the network ordered an additional 5 episodes after what was originally intended to be the series finale. (Co-creator J.J. Abrams would help create *Lost* shortly afterward.)

Firefly
TV-14, 2002–2003
Hulu, 14 episodes
Sci-fi drama created by Joss Whedon, with Nathan Fillion, Gina Torres, Alan Tudyk, Morena Baccarin, Summer Glau, Adam Baldwin, Jewel Staite, Sean Maher and Ron Glass.

This storied sci-fi western starring Nathan Fillion was a victim of low ratings but remains a fan favorite. In the 26th century, a band of mercenaries lives on spaceship *Serenity* at the fringes of civilization, evading the totalitarian alliance that wants them dead or alive. Not just Captain Mal Reynolds (Fillion) but each person on board is distinct and intriguing. The show's spaghetti western soundtrack sets a retro tone, as does an old-fashioned train robbery in the first episode.

📣 **From our forums:** "This show was getting better with every episode. I share in the fans' frustrations that it was canceled so soon. It's nice that Joss wrote a movie to tie things up for the fans."

▶▶ That movie, *Serenity*, which continued the storylines in *Firefly*, is included in the Hulu streaming set for the series, along with 3 episodes that Fox never aired.

Firefly Lane
TV-MA, 2021–present
Netflix original, 10 episodes (AD)
Drama with Katherine Heigl, Sarah Chalke, Ben Lawson, Ali Skovbye, Roan Curtis, Yael Yurman and Jon-Michael Ecker.

Katherine Heigl and Sarah Chalke light up this friendship drama about two women in the 1980s. This multiple-timeline series zig-zags through the decade of big hair and cocaine with a story that's serviceable at best. You watch *Firefly Lane* for its two leads and their chemistry. Heigl, a lightning rod ever since she complained (rightly) about her character on *Grey's Anatomy*, remains a magnetic screen presence. This is the closest that Heigl has played to an Izzy Stevens character since she left *Grey's*, ambitious and headstrong. As Tully, she's the heedless one, while Chalke's Kate is the responsible one. Kate has the seemingly unenviable task of living in Tully's shadow, but she gets to be quirky in her own way.

▶▶ A second season is due to be released in 2022.

First Person
Not Rated, 2000–2001
YouTube, 2 seasons, 17 episodes
Docuseries directed by Errol Morris.

Celebrated documentary maker Errol Morris has curiously strong interviews with intriguing people. In 2020 the Oscar-winning director of *The Thin Blue Line, Fog of War* and other films, posted to his YouTube channel the complete collection of this outstanding but long-forgotten cable series. For many viewers *First Person* was their introduction to the Interrotron, the pre-digital contraption Morris created so he could look his subjects in the eye while they gazed straight into the camera. Subjects included Temple Grandin, the autistic designer of slaughterhouse ramps; a man who had a bizarre turn on *Who Wants to Be a Millionaire*; and a woman who cleans up crime scenes.

Fixer Upper: Welcome Home
TV-G, 2021–present
Discovery+ original, 9 episodes
Reality show with Chip Gaines and Joanna Gaines.

A solid, watchable introduction to the World Wide Waco phenomenon that is Chip and Joanna Gaines. If you don't know your shiplap from a shipwreck, prepare to be immersed in the Gaineses' deceptively ordinary world of home renovation and cocoon-building in the heart of Texas. In this spinoff of their hugely popular *Fixer Upper* series, the Gaineses comport themselves like any other ambitious young couple flipping houses, juggling family and keeping the spark in their marriage. But their style choices are distinct and their chemistry, with each other and their clients, is captivating. After a while you realize why Discovery moved heaven and earth to give Chip and Joanna their own cable channel.

Flack

TV-14, 2019–present
Prime Video original, 2 seasons,
12 episodes (AD)
Dark comedy with Anna Paquin, Sophie
Okonedo, Lydia Wilson, Rebecca Benson,
Genevieve Angelson and Meghan
Treadway.

**Anna Paquin stars as a publicist who
will do anything to protect her client.**
In the rough-and-tumble environment
of London PR, Robyn (Paquin) manages
scandals with aplomb. She has to — her
boss is the ruthless Caroline (Okonedo),
who has no patience for fools. When
it comes to her personal life, though,
Robyn's a complete disaster. *Flack* is risqué
and entertaining and illustrates the price
you can pay when you're good at your job
but forget to take care of yourself.

🎣 **From our forums:** "The perfect balance
between dark and comically absurd. The
dialogue is so sharp and witty at times
that I find myself rewinding to rewatch a
scene."

Flatbush Misdemeanors

TV-MA, 2021–present
Showtime original, 10 episodes
Comedy with Dan Perlman, Kevin Iso,
Kristin Dodson and Hassan Johnson.

**After relocating to Flatbush, Brooklyn,
longtime friends try to overcome their
awkwardness and become a true part of
the neighborhood.** In the vein of loopy
New York series like *Broad City* and *High
Maintenance*, the comedy on this show
is loose and genial. But this allows heavy
topics like racism and gentrification to be
broached with a light touch.

Fleabag

TV-MA, 2016–2019
Prime Video original, 2 seasons,
12 episodes (AD)
British comedy created by Phoebe
Waller-Bridge, with Phoebe Waller-
Bridge, Sian Clifford, Olivia Colman,
Jenny Rainsford, Bill Paterson, Brett
Gelman and Andrew Scott.

**Groundbreaking comedy about a woman
who uses crude humor and serial sex to
escape her guilt about a recent tragedy
is worthy of the honors showered upon
it.** Writer-performer Waller-Bridge makes
numerous appearances in *The Primetimer
Guide*, but this is her *magnum opus* to
date. In just 2 short seasons, she traces
an authentic, unstoppable arc about her
character's journey out of guilt and toward
transcendence. Along the way she keeps
us laughing — and with the arrival of a
charming, flirtatious priest (Scott), she
pushes us to places most shows wouldn't
dare go. Once you finish this, you'll
understand why so many viewers go back
and watch it again.

🏆 Peabody Award, Emmy for best
comedy series, TCA program of the year,
SAG Award for female lead in a comedy
(Waller-Bridge)

The Flight Attendant

TV-MA, 2020–present
HBO Max original, 8 episodes (AD)
Comedy thriller with Kaley Cuoco,
Michiel Huisman, Zosia Mamet, T.R.
Knight, Rosie Perez, Michelle Gomez,
Colin Woodell, Merle Dandridge, Griffin
Matthews and Nolan Gerard Funk.

**Kaley Cuoco delighted viewers as a
stewardess trying to figure out who
killed her lover.** In her first major role
after *The Big Bang Theory*, Cuoco more
than capably sleuths a murder mystery
while avoiding the feds, distracting
suspicious co-workers and facing up
to her substance abuse problems. The
tone of the show veers from suspense to
humor to deep strangeness, with a plot
that is archly complicated. But the dueling
performances of Cuoco and Gomez,
and writing that keeps parceling out

tantalizing plot points, conspire to keep you watching.

🐿 **From our forums:** "More entertaining than *The Undoing*. I liked the humor." "Why can't we get a show that is just episodes of Michelle Gomez throat-punching bad men and rescuing people and maybe one whole episode where she rescues kittens. I would pay to watch that!"

▶▶ A second season was due to arrive in 2022.

Flight of the Conchords
TV-MA, 2007–2009
HBO Max, 2 seasons, 22 episodes
Musical comedy created by Jemaine Clement and Bret McKenzie, with Jemaine Clement, Bret McKenzie, Rhys Darby, Kristen Schaal and Arj Barker.

Deceptively simple and wonderfully sideways comedy follows two mumblecore musicians from New Zealand trying to make it in New York. Jemaine Clement and Bret McKenzie play outsized versions of themselves in this classic HBO comedy featuring amusing ditties composed and performed by the duo. Because the real-life Conchords had no interest in leaving their native country, HBO shut down production on this promising show after just 2 seasons. A concert special, *Flight of the Conchords: Live at the London Apollo*, was produced by HBO in 2018.

Flo and Joan: Alive on Stage
TV-14, 2019
Prime Video original, 1 hr
Comedy special directed by Barbara Wiltshire, with Nicola Dempsey and Rosie Dempsey.

Playing characters named after their real-life grandmothers, the Dempsey sisters use off-the-wall songs to work out their rivalries and tell their anecdotes. This special has become something of an

underground sensation and it'll be a good bet for anyone who enjoys the musical comic stylings of a Tim Minchin or a Bo Burnham.

Floor Is Lava
TV-G, 2020–present
Netflix original, 10 episodes (AD)
Reality competition with Rutledge Wood.

This low-stakes, high-comedy game show, which blows a childhood activity out of all reasonable proportion, was a surprise hit during the pandemic. If you ever played Floor Is Lava as a kid, you know there was only one rule: you couldn't touch the floor, or you were dead. Here, instead of jumping from chair to couch to coffee table in the basement, contestants dash across a room with orange slime on the floor, jumping from one stepping stone to another in an effort to postpone the inevitable. Fun for kids and tweens, but adults may wish it was more action-packed like, say, *Ultimate Tag*.

Flora and Ulysses
PG, 2021
Disney+ original, 1 hr 35 mins (AD)
Movie (family comedy) with Alyson Hannigan, Ben Schwartz, Danny Pudi, Matilda Lawler and Bobby Moynihan.

A young girl is surprised to discover that a squirrel she rescues has superpowers. Very much in the spirit of Kate DiCamillo's novel of the same name, this winning left-field entry in the superhero genre takes a familiar story and reinvigorates it with a cartoon squirrel. The movie's real charm is watching 10-year-old Flora (Lawler) bring life and hope into her unhappy home, with help from her bushy-tailed friend.

For All Mankind
TV-MA, 2019–present
Apple TV+ original, 2 seasons,
20 episodes (AD)
Alternative history with Joel Kinnaman, Sarah Jones, Michael Dorman, Shantel VanSanten, Jodi Balfour, Wrenn Schmidt and Sonya Walger.

Absorbing drama about what might've happened had Russia gotten to the moon first and the space race never ended. What if Walter Cronkite had come on the air one night to show us the first moon landing — and TV viewers saw Soviet cosmonauts? That's the tantalizing premise for this character-driven drama from Ronald D. Moore, who's also reimagined *Battlestar Galactica* and *Star Trek*. Set initially in the weeks following the USSR's triumph, and using characters based on actual *Right Stuff*–era astronauts, the show's exploration of what is inevitable and what isn't is what makes it a fascinating watch. And it challenges us to rethink outer space as it reflects on American identity, both for good and ill.

Forever
TV-MA, 2018
Prime Video original, 8 episodes (AD)
Comedy-drama created by Alan Yang and Matt Hubbard, with Maya Rudolph, Fred Armisen, Catherine Keener and Noah Robbins.

Fred Armisen and Maya Rudolph play a couple whose marriage has gotten in a rut in this tonally complex comedy. Because it quickly wanders onto existential turf, it will remind viewers favorably of *The Good Place*.

🗨 **From our forums:** "This was probably the weirdest show I have ever seen but it was so good. I liked how very little was really explained but you just kind of went with it anyway." "I'm still not sure how I felt about the show as a whole, but I do know that Maya Rudolph was brilliant

throughout."

Fortitude
TV-MA, 2015–2018
Prime Video original, 3 seasons,
25 episodes (AD)
Crime drama with Stanley Tucci, Dennis Quaid, Michael Gambon, Parminder Nagra, Luke Treadaway, Michelle Fairley, Christopher Eccleston, Richard Dormer, Sofie Gråbøl and Björn Hlynur Haraldsson.

In a small island community in the Arctic, a series of bizarre deaths threatens to undo decades of peaceful existence. No matter how familiar the setup might seem, *Fortitude*'s startling turns make it a great ride for Nordic noir fans. The characters are the right kind of strange and there's a palpable menace in every corner of every frame. It's also clear that in one way or another, everyone we meet has some kind of responsibility for the madness that's afoot.

Fosse/Verdon
TV-MA, 2019
Hulu, 8 episodes
Limited series (drama) with Michelle Williams, Sam Rockwell, Margaret Qualley, Norbert Leo Butz, Paul Reiser, Aya Cash, Jake Lacy and Nate Corddry.

Michelle Williams wowed everyone playing dancer-actor Gwen Verdon in this dramatization of Verdon's real-life romance and legendary collaboration with Bob Fosse. An overlooked gem from the heyday of FX, *Fosse/Verdon* tracks the long relationship of Fosse (Rockwell) and his biggest star. Professionally, it was a dance where both partners took the lead, while their love story was likewise unconventional. With Lin-Manuel Miranda producing and Thomas Kail directing, *Fosse/Verdon* has Broadway values and in Williams they have a performance for the ages. She played multiple sides of Verdon's star, from her professional rigor to her myriad career disappointments to the traumas of her youth.

🏆 SAG, Emmy and TCA awards, all for Williams's performance

The Fosters

TV-14, 2013–2018
Hulu, Prime Video, 5 seasons, 104 episodes
Teen drama with Teri Polo, Sherri Saum, Jake T. Austin, Hayden Byerly, David Lambert, Maia Mitchell, Cierra Ramirez, Danny Nucci and Noah Centineo.

Warm-hearted alt-family series follows the biological and foster children raised by two women in San Diego. This teen-oriented drama was never afraid to incorporate headline news into its storylines, yet the main draws were the evolving stories of the children inside Stef (Polo) and Lena's (Saum) expansive house: son Brandon (Lambert), adopted twins Mariana (Ramirez) and Jesus (Centineo) and Jude (Byerly) and Callie (Mitchell), also adopted.

🎙 **From our forums:** "This show helped me be more open-minded; I still consider myself a conservative, but I'm more 'live and let live' than I was before."

▶▶ A spinoff, *Good Trouble* (Hulu), follows several of the younger characters as they leave the house.

Fractured

TV-MA, 2019
Netflix original, 1 hr 39 mins (AD)
Movie (thriller) with Sam Worthington, Lily Rabe, Lucy Capri, Adjoa Andoh and Stephen Tobolowsky.

A couple rushes their daughter to the hospital for an arm injury, then the kid and the wife go missing. This is a knotty mystery that has just enough surprises to keep you hooked.

Framing Britney Spears

TV-PG, 2021
Hulu, 1 hr 14 mins
Movie (documentary) directed by Samantha Stark, with Britney Spears.

This activist documentary brought the plight of the teen pop star, and her years of court-ordered supervision, back into the spotlight. This well-crafted documentary retells how an ostensibly humane court ruling — to place Britney Spears under a conservatorship when it appeared her life was spiraling out of control — had devastating consequences. Along the way it asks whether someone who rocketed into the limelight so rapidly, and was being hounded by paparazzi by the age of 16, ever had a shot at controlling her life. (Appears on Hulu as S1E6 of the documentary series *The New York Times Presents*.)

▶▶ The same team also produced a followup documentary, *Controlling Britney Spears*.

Frank of Ireland

TV-MA, 2021–present
Prime Video original, 6 episodes (AD)
Comedy created by Brian Gleeson, Domhnall Gleeson and Michael Moloney, with Brian Gleeson, Domhnall Gleeson, Pom Boyd, Sarah Greene and Tom Vaughan-Lawlor.

An irreverent and vulgar Irish comedy follows a 32-year-old single man with an advanced case of arrested development. The show's creators — brothers Brian and Domhnall Gleeson — play Frank and Frank's best friend, Doofus. Their chemistry is what elevates the show beyond a simply bawdy comedy about an irresponsible, self-centered jerk. The show has a unique narrative structure that isn't fully revealed until the last episode, so watch to the bitter end for the complete experience.

Frasier

TV-PG, 1993–2004
Paramount+, Hulu, 11 seasons,
263 episodes
Classic sitcom with Kelsey Grammer,
David Hyde Pierce, Jane Leeves, John
Mahoney and Peri Gilpin.

**An uproarious mix of high and low
comedy, *Frasier* proved that a TV show
could be intelligent, even snooty, and
have mass appeal.** *Frasier* was America's
Britcom: a roomful of well-heeled
characters trading highbrow insults and
getting themselves into outlandish capers.
Beautifully written, with a tight, talented
ensemble, a *Frasier* revival is in the works
for Paramount+, with all the leads back
except Mahoney, who died in 2018.

▶▶ New to *Frasier* or considering a
rewatch? Needle-drop at Season 4. This
is the season when Frasier and Lilith's
child had his worst Thanksgiving ever;
when Dad dated Marsha Mason; when
Eddie got the blues; when Megan Mullally
guest-starred on a memorable double-date
episode; and when the gang at KACL put
on a radio play that went deliriously off
the rails.

🏆 Won 37 Emmy Awards, the most for a
scripted show until *Game of Thrones* came
along.

Frayed

TV-MA, 2019–present
HBO Max, 6 episodes
British comedy with Diane Morgan,
Matt Passmore, Doris Younane, Kerry
Armstrong, George Houvardas, Ben
Mingay, Alexandra Jensen and Frazer
Hadfield.

**Under-the-radar Australian dramedy
tracks the unraveling of a London
financier's wife.** Sarah Kendall, the
creator of *Frayed*, has set herself the
daunting task of building her show around
a lying, entitled woman — and playing the
character herself. Amazingly, she pulls it
off. After her hubby's scandalous death,
she relocates with her children to her
native Australia . . . where all the secrets
start spilling out. Kendall's caustic delivery
of killer punchlines (and a lot of poop
jokes) make this overlooked show worth
seeking out.

🗨 **From our forums:** "I love the '80s drag
and the characters are unique. A little bit
of serious, a lot of trashy/vulgar funny and
some awww."

Freaks and Geeks

TV-14, 1999–2000
Paramount+, Hulu, 18 episodes
Comedy-drama created by Paul Feig,
with Linda Cardellini, John Francis Daley,
James Franco, Samm Levine, Seth Rogen,
Jason Segel, Martin Starr, Becky Ann
Baker, Joe Flaherty and Busy Philipps.

**This coming-of-age cult classic launched
the careers of Seth Rogen, James Franco,
Linda Cardellini, Busy Philipps and
more.** Following two fringe groups in a
Michigan high school in the late 1970s,
this funny and sensitive treatment of the
pains of teenagerhood was ahead of its
time. Though poor ratings ended it after
one season, it produced 18 great episodes,
more than most shows these days can
boast.

🏆 Emmy for outstanding casting in a
comedy series

Free Meek

TV-MA, 2019
Prime Video original, 5 episodes (AD)
Limited series (true crime) with Meek
Mill, Jay-Z, Van Jones, Michael Rubin,
Tamika Mallory, Swizz Beatz and Paul
Solotaroff.

**A well-known rapper is tormented by
the criminal-justice system in a shocking
— but one suspects, not uncommon —
abuse of power.** Rihmeek Williams was
19 when he was arrested on trumped-up
charges and entered into the criminal

justice system, where he would make 26 appearances before a sadistic judge. But a funny thing happened along the way: Williams morphed into the hip-hop superstar Meek Mill and eventually acquired the resources to fight back. And as we learn in this ultimately inspiring story, Meek also became an activist, turning his *cause célèbre* into a nationwide movement against wrongful incarceration.

Free Rein

TV-G, 2017–2019
Netflix original, 3 seasons,
32 episodes (AD)
Family comedy-drama with Freddy Carter, Jaylen Barron, Manpreet Bambra, Celine Buckens, Bruce Herbelin-Earle, Kerry Ingram, Carla Woodcock, Navia Robinson and Natalie Gumede.

A different take on the high school drama, set in the equestrian life of England. Two L.A. girls — 15-year-old Zoe Phillips (Barron) and little sister Rosie (Robinson) — are dragged to a picture-perfect island off the English coast by their mum Maggie (Gumede), a native of the island, as she sorts out problems in her marriage. Zoe and Rosie enter the local riding academy, which takes the place of a high school in the teen-drama template. What elevates *Free Rein* above its genre limitations is Zoe's bond with Raven, the stable's most prized and temperamental horse. It's in their relationship that the show finds its true magic.

🏆 Emmy for best children/family series

Fresh Meat

TV-MA, 2011–2016
Prime Video, PlutoTV, Roku Channel, Tubi, 4 seasons, 30 episodes
British comedy with Zawe Ashton, Greg McHugh, Kimberley Nixon, Charlotte Ritchie, Joe Thomas and Jack Whitehall.

This British university sitcom follows six students from their first year through to graduation. If you don't remember how ill-equipped you were for living away from home, the misadventures of these Medlock University students will definitely bring you back. From arguments over who gets what rooms in the house to complicated romantic entanglements, choosing a degree path and figuring out the rest of your life, *Fresh Meat* accurately captured the college experience — its sweetness, absurdities, failings and triumphs.

Friday Night Lights

TV-14, 2006–2011
Peacock, Netflix, Hulu, 5 seasons, 76 episodes (AD)
Drama created by Peter Berg, with Kyle Chandler, Connie Britton, Aimee Teegarden, Brad Leland, Taylor Kitsch, Zach Gilford, Jesse Plemons, Minka Kelly, Adrianne Palicki and Scott Porter.

High school life in football-crazy Texas is memorably captured in this beloved drama noted for strong individual performances. Based on the Buzz Bissinger nonfiction book, *Friday Night Lights* took on a realistic feel with its documentary-style production. Though it struggled in the ratings throughout its run, NBC stuck with the show for prestige reasons. Coach Eric Taylor (Chandler) is a winner who's tough on kids and spouts Lombardi-isms. However, it was Tami (Britton), his loving but no-nonsense wife who was many viewers' favorite. The team-building chant, "Clear eyes, full hearts, can't lose!" became part of the popular culture.

🏆 TCA Program of the Year; Emmys for best actor (Chandler) and writing (Katims) in a drama

Friday Night Tykes

TV-PG, 2014–2017
Peacock, 4 seasons, 41 episodes

Reality show with Morgan Spector (voiceovers).

Compelling yet disturbing show about extreme pee-wee football outlasted its critics, as football does. When it debuted in 2014, this show that followed the Texas Youth Football Association was denounced by a U.S. senator and an NFL spokesman. Viewers were up in arms about scenes showing children, many under the age of 10, suffering through intense practices and game play while coaches and parents screamed at them. Yet *Friday Night Tykes* went on to produce 4 very popular seasons and the show (unlike many older nonfiction series) lives on in streaming. In contrast to exploitative shows like *Toddlers & Tiaras*, this one focuses on adults, not kids, and its straightforward style generates empathy for the children featured on camera.

▶▶ In response to the controversy surrounding *Friday Night Tykes*, the producers announced a special, "Tackling Tykes," hosted by Kevin Frazier, "that delves into important topics and controversies raised in the docuseries" (S1E11).

Friends

TV-PG, 1994–2004
HBO Max, 10 seasons, 235 episodes (AD)
Classic sitcom created by Marta Kauffman and David Crane, with Jennifer Aniston, Courteney Cox, Lisa Kudrow, Matt LeBlanc, Matthew Perry and David Schwimmer.

It still crackles with the energy and hilarity that made it Gen X's signature sitcom. Six friends on madcap adventures in New York City — what a simple formula, and yet NBC tried and failed, again and again, to replicate the magic of *Friends*. That's remarkable enough, but here we are 3 decades on and it is one of the most sought-after properties on Streaming TV. The carefree expression of American silliness that was *Friends* remains the gold standard of TV comedy.

▶▶ If you want to see the gang on a roll in one of the show's classic arcs, drop the needle on "The One With All the Thanksgivings" (S5E8), turn on autoplay and watch the next 6 episodes as Monica (Cox) and Chandler (Perry) try — and fail — to keep their relationship a secret.

🏆 Emmy for best comedy, SAG Award for best ensemble in a comedy

Fringe

TV-14, 2008–2013
IMDb TV, 5 seasons, 100 episodes
Sci-fi drama created by J.J. Abrams, Alex Kurtzman and Roberto Orci, with Anna Torv, Joshua Jackson, Jasika Nicole, John Noble, Lance Reddick, Blair Brown and Leonard Nimoy.

In the Fringe Division of the FBI, three agents investigate a series of paranormal events, many with ties to a parallel universe. The first season is essentially a collection of monster-of-the-week episodes that wanly imitate *The X-Files*, but in Season 2 the show finds itself by introducing the parallel universe concept. The storytelling gets more nuanced and interesting and the cast rises to the challenge. This is especially true of Torv as Agent Olivia Dunham: She's tasked with playing two very different versions of the character in the two different universes, and she nails it. The show also marks the final major role for Nimoy, which gives it an enviable pedigree in the sci-fi canon.

Future Man

TV-MA, 2017–2020
Hulu original, 3 seasons, 34 episodes (AD)
Sci-fi comedy with Josh Hutcherson, Eliza Coupe, Derek Wilson, Haley Joel Osment, Glenne Headly, Ed Begley Jr. and Seth Rogen.

Raunchy humor and sci-fi parody make

an unlikely combination in this well-regarded spoof from the team behind the movie *Sausage Party.* Do you like Seth Rogen humor? Are you fine with parody completely lacking in subtlety, e.g., characters announcing that a certain storyline comes right out of *The Last Starfighter* or *Minority Report*? Then you'll enjoy *Future Man.* After conquering an impossible video game called Bionic Wars, a janitor named Josh (Hutcherson) is recruited by the game's main characters to fight in *actual* bionic wars.

🐷 From our forums: "Going by just the pilot, I expected nothing but gags and raunch with little actual development either in plot or characters, but I was wrong."

Game of Thrones

TV-MA, 2011–2019
HBO Max, 8 seasons, 73 episodes (AD)
Fantasy drama with Peter Dinklage, Lena Headey, Emilia Clarke, Kit Harington, Sophie Turner, Maisie Williams, Nikolaj Coster-Waldau, Iain Glen, John Bradley and Alfie Allen.

One of the defining series of the last decade, this epic fantasy follows the various warriors, monarchs, prophets and thieves that are battling for control of the Seven Kingdoms of Westeros. No matter what you like in your storytelling — action, comedy, magic, massive ensembles, HBO quantities of violence and sex, people riding dragons — there's something for you in this adaptation of George R.R. Martin's novels. The final episodes sparked an insurrection by *GoT* fans, though that likely reflected the fact that people cared so deeply about a show so uncommonly captivating.

▶▶ For suggestions of related shows, see "If You Liked *Game of Thrones*," page 372.

🏆 59 Emmys including best drama series (4 wins)

Gangs of London

TV-MA, 2020–present
AMC+, 9 episodes
Crime drama with Joe Cole, Michelle Fairley, Colm Meaney, Paapa Essiedu and Lucian Msamati.

The violent struggle for power on the mean streets of modern-day London is depicted with compelling characters and lots of blood. After someone kills Finn Wallace (Meaney), the most powerful criminal in modern-day London, his son Sean (Cole) tries to maintain his family's power as a variety of other criminal organizations fight to take the upper hand. It works as both an action series and a comment on how much seethes just below the surface in a city that has stood for civilization for centuries.

Gardeners' World

TV-G, 1968–present
BritBox, Prime Video, 53 seasons, 728 episodes
Docuseries with Monty Don.

As Sir David Attenborough is to wild nature, Monty Don is to cultivated nature — the best-known name in British gardening TV. The BBC's flagship gardening show for decades, it was discovered by many American viewers during the pandemic. The host himself is a study in the healing wonders of gardening, having built a large jewelry business only to lose it all in the 1987 stock market crash. First as a writer, then a broadcaster, Don's gentle, well-informed, encouraging personality is ideally suited to popular horticulture.

▶▶ Each episode is available on BritBox as soon as it finishes airing in the UK.

Gaycation

TV-MA, 2016–2017
AMC+, 2 seasons, 10 episodes
Docuseries with Elliot Page and Ian Daniel.

Ellen (now Elliot) Page and best friend Ian Daniel travel the world talking with people about being LGBTQ. Filmed 2 years after Page came out, this interesting series offers no tips for planning your next gaycation. However, as Page and Daniel strike up casual conversations, they uncover the cultural contradictions of homophobia around the world in a way few shows have done. That they do this while maintaining a friendly, curious tone even with those they strongly disagree with only adds to the show's appeal.

Genius: Einstein

TV-14, 2017
Hulu, 10 episodes
Anthology series (historical drama) with Geoffrey Rush, Johnny Flynn, Samantha Colley, Richard Topol, Michael McElhatton, Emily Watson, Robert Lindsay and Vincent Kartheiser.

The first installment of a new high-concept biopic series explores both the ideas of the man synonymous with "genius" and his dramatic personal side. Adapted from Walter Isaacson's acclaimed biography, *Genius* presents Einstein as a flesh-and-blood human, who seemed to have bedded as many women as championed social causes. This entertaining series, produced by National Geographic, tries to be educational, explaining the physicist's breakthrough theories using analogies to ballroom dancing and bicycle riding.

▶▶ Later seasons of *Genius* gave similar treatments to the art and lives of Pablo Picasso and Aretha Franklin.

Gentefied

TV-MA, 2020–2021
Netflix original, 2 seasons,
18 episodes (AD)
Comedy-drama with Joaquin Cosio, Joseph Julian Soria, Karrie Martin, Carlos Santos, Laura Patalano and Alma Martinez.

Three Mexican-American cousins living in Los Angeles try to make a better life for themselves, even though moving up might mean leaving behind some people and places they love. Less a comedy than a light drama with some funny moments, it has pointed takes on gentrification, one's obligation to community and family, the current immigration mess and more. But what keeps you watching are the characters, who are all heart (not unlike their counterparts on that other Latinx-in-L.A. series, *One Day at a Time*).

Gentleman Jack

TV-MA, 2019–present
HBO Max, 8 episodes (AD)
Historical drama created by Sally Wainwright, with Suranne Jones, Sophie Rundle, Gemma Whelan, Gemma Jones, Timothy West, Rosie Cavaliero, Joe Armstrong, Amelia Bullmore, Peter Davison and Lydia Leonard.

In 19th-century England, a queer woman played by Suranne Jones rejects gender roles by becoming a land owner and wearer of men's suits. This UK hit was based on the journals of the real-life Anne Lister, whose disregard for custom is seen in big ways and small (her habit of exiting the carriage before the footman could scramble to open the door was a recurring gag). Creator Sally Wainwright explores gender roles and the sexual dynamics between Anne and her paramour Ann Walker (Rundle) with smart scripts and stylish production values.

🐾 **From our forums:** "It's refreshing to see a period show that explores another perspective of Georgian life."

Get Duked!

R, 2019
Prime Video original, 1 hr 27 mins (AD)

Movie (comedy-horror) with Lewis Gribben, Rian Gordon, Viraj Juneja, Samuel Bottomley, Jonathan Aris, James Cosmo and Eddie Izzard.

In this gleefully cracked comedy, three doofuses and a nerd think they're competing for an outdoorsman's award, only to discover they're being hunted for sport. Imagine a darker *Naked Gun* set in the Scottish Highlands with hip-hop references. Or *Stand By Me* where the boys are high, on the run and hilariously inept. Better yet, just enjoy this lowbrow farce for what it is.

Get Shorty

TV-MA, 2017–2019
Epix original, 3 seasons, 27 episodes (AD)
Dark comedy with Chris O'Dowd, Ray Romano, Sean Bridgers, Carolyn Dodd, Goya Robles, Lidia Porto, Megan Stevenson, Isaac Keyes, Sarah Stiles and Lucy Walters.

A hit man tries to go legit by becoming a film producer in this TV adaptation of the Elmore Leonard novel. One of those acclaimed small-cable-channel programs that's gotten a wider audience since streaming picked it up.

🐾 From our forums: "Didn't feel like I was watching a retread of anything. The opening scene looks like it's setting up to be some kind of hybrid of *Breaking Bad* and *Fargo*, but then the show goes its own way. Chris O'Dowd and Sean Bridgers are far from the only good things in it."

▶▶ Pairs well with *Barry*

Getting On

TV-MA, 2013–2015
HBO Max, 3 seasons, 18 episodes
Comedy with Laurie Metcalf, Alex Borstein, Niecy Nash, Mel Rodriguez, Ann Morgan Guilbert, Brandon Fobbs, Mark Harelik and Lindsey Kraft.

This quiet, humane series found comedy among health-care professionals caring for people at the end of their lives. *Getting On* threaded a tricky needle, but succeeded thanks to performances from Laurie Metcalf, Niecy Nash and Alex Borstein, who committed fiercely to the concept.

🐾 **From our forums:** "So funny and cringe-worthy and painfully honest. This has to be the best comedy that no one watched, and that is just sad."

▶▶ Pairs well with *The Comeback*

The Gilded Age

TV-MA, 2022
HBO Max, 10 episodes
Historical drama created by Julian Fellowes, with Christine Baranski, Cynthia Nixon, Morgan Spector, Carrie Coon, Louisa Jacobson, Denée Benton, Taissa Farmiga, Blake Ritson, Simon Jones and Harry Richardson.

Christine Baranski and Cynthia Nixon are well matched as high-society sisters in this 1880s drama from the creator of *Downton Abbey*. It's *Downton Abbey* in America, with robber barons. On New York's Upper East Side, a railroad titan and his equally ambitious wife move into their new mansion, across from Old Money sisters Agnes and Ada. Both households employ servants, whose lives we also follow. And in a welcome twist, Fellowes writes a major Black character into the show. Sticking to their screen personas, Baranski and Nixon make a delightful spicy-sweet combo as the sisters. Spector and Coon, each of whom broke out on a previous HBO series, play the New Money power couple, more than holding their own with the ladies across the street.

▶▶ This show's 10-year gestation neatly tracks the transfer of power from network to Streaming TV. NBC ordered *The Gilded Age* in 2012, but with *Downton* a big hit, Fellowes set it aside until 2018. By then his vision had gotten too grandiose for network TV — but the executive who had

Some shows may have moved; see page 183.

greenlighted *The Gilded Age* was by then at WarnerMedia. He picked it up for HBO.

Gilmore Girls

TV-PG, 2000–2007
Netflix, 7 seasons, 154 episodes
Comedy-drama created by Amy Sherman-Palladino, with Lauren Graham, Alexis Bledel, Keiko Agena, Scott Patterson, Yanic Truesdale, Kelly Bishop, Edward Herrmann, Melissa McCarthy, Sean Gunn and Liza Weil.

Amy Sherman-Palladino's series about a chatty and close-knit mother-daughter duo set the template for what's now a crowded field of offbeat dramedies. As helicopter parenting was going mainstream, Palladino stuck the landing with this show that bridged generations and genres. Pairing flighty mom Lorelai (Graham) with wise-beyond-her-years Rory (Bledel), Palladino's voice — as instantly familiar as Aaron Sorkin's — not only delivered reams of pop-culture-filled dialogue every episodes, but explored the ties between two women bonded by birth as no show had before. Lorelai's best friend Sookie (Melissa McCarthy in a career-building role) and stuffy parents added color, as did all the whimsical townsfolk in the Hallmark village of Stars Hollow, where *Gilmore Girls* was set.

▶▶ Palladino and her husband, writer-director Daniel Palladino, didn't take part in Season 7 following a contract dispute, but did reunite with the original stars for *Gilmore Girls: A Year in the Life* (Netflix), 4 well-received episodes that fans consider the show's unofficial eighth season.

🏆 1 Emmy

Ginny & Georgia

TV-14, 2021–present
Netflix original, 10 episodes (AD)
Dark comedy with Brianne Howey, Antonia Gentry, Diesel La Torraca, Jennifer Robertson, Felix Mallard, Sara Waisglass, Scott Porter and Raymond Ablack.

A mother-daughter duo keep secrets from each other and their new small town in this dramatic take on *Gilmore Girls*. Georgia (Howey) and her children, Ginny (Gentry) and Austin (La Torraca), move around a lot. As we learn in flashback, that's owing to some shady dealings in Georgia's past. But Ginny is now 15 — the same age as when Georgia had her — and as the family arrives at their new home in small-town New England, it's clear Ginny is ready for some drama of her own.

💬 **From our forums:** "I went back and forth on Ginny. Sometimes her snark was too much, but I think the show does a good job of suggesting that her internal problems aren't just garden variety teen angst. Her biracial identity is a source of confusion and uneasiness to her."

The Girlfriend Experience

TV-MA, 2016–present
Starz original, 3 seasons, 37 episodes
Anthology series (drama) with Riley Keough, Paul Sparks, Julia Goldani Telles, Mary Lynn Rajskub, Briony Glassco, Carmen Ejogo and Anna Friel.

A new woman every season enters the world of high-class escorting, in the process changing her perspective on herself and the world. Based on the Steven Soderbergh film of the same name, this is a complicated show about a morally ambiguous topic. However, the show's solid writing and excellent production values might upend what you'd expect from a series about prostitution. First-season star Keough made this a breakout role with her steely performance. Though the stories can be titillating, *The Girlfriend Experience* has some things to say about sex, power and ambition that are worth considering.

For a key to terms used in this section, see page 33.

Girls

TV-MA, 2012–2017
HBO Max, 6 seasons, 62 episodes (AD)
Comedy created by Lena Dunham, with Lena Dunham, Allison Williams, Jemima Kirke, Zosia Mamet, Adam Driver, Alex Karpovsky and Andrew Rannells.

Lena Dunham was hailed as the voice of her generation with this millennial take on *Sex and the City*. Given that it aired on HBO and focused on four young single women living in New York City, the comparisons were inevitable, but 25-year-old creator/writer/director/star Dunham made *Girls* her own with her fearless portrayal of a lost and often significantly unlikable 20-something woman trying to find herself in the big city. The core four were backed by a strong supporting cast that includes a post–*Book of Mormon* Rannells and a pre–*Star Wars* Driver.

🏆 Peabody Award, 2 Emmys

Girls5eva

TV-MA, 2021–present
Peacock original, 8 episodes (AD)
Musical comedy with Paula Pell, Sara Bareilles, Busy Philipps, Renée Elise Goldsberry, Ashley Park, Erika Henningsen, Jonathan Hadary, Daniel Breaker, Dean Winters and Andrew Rannells.

A '90s girl group reassembles and tries to recapture fame in a series from the co-creators of *30 Rock* and *Unbreakable Kimmy Schmidt*. Tina Fey and Robert Carlock's signature style — rapid-fire, multi-layered punchlines filled with pop references — is married to a catchy musical format buoyed by four appealing ladies determined to make a comeback on *their* terms. You may be surprised by how well Broadway star Goldsberry can do comedy, or how Philipps holds her own in song.

🎙 From our forums: "I enjoyed the '90s references as much as the puns about

current pop culture. I also liked that the girls looked and acted their age."

Glee

TV-PG, 2009–2015
Netflix, Prime Video, 6 seasons, 121 episodes (AD)
Musical comedy created by Ryan Murphy, Ian Brennan and Brad Falchuk, with Lea Michele, Matthew Morrison, Jane Lynch, Chris Colfer, Kevin McHale, Naya Rivera, Jenna Ushkowitz, Amber Riley, Darren Criss and Cory Monteith.

Ryan Murphy caught lightning in a bottle with his musical comedy about a group of high school outcasts who find comfort in music and each other after they join the school's show choir. With Murphy becoming one of the star producers of Streaming TV, it's worth a rewind to *Glee* to see this early expression of Murphy's quirky, campy, often over-the-top sensibilities. The show lost its thread later on, but the early seasons remain nothing short of a miracle. Operating under network deadlines, the talented cast and crew were able to produce a half-dozen musical numbers in each episode.

▶▶ Tragedy marred *Glee*'s final seasons after series star Cory Monteith died of a drug overdose in 2013. The show paid tribute to his character in S5E3.

🏆 Peabody Award, 6 Emmys, SAG for best ensemble in a comedy

GLOW

TV-MA, 2017–2019
Netflix original, 3 seasons, 30 episodes (AD)
Comedy-drama with Alison Brie, Betty Gilpin, Marc Maron, Sydelle Noel, Kate Nash, Britney Young, Gayle Rankin, Kia Stevens, Jackie Tohn and Britt Baron.

In this winning love letter to the '80s, an out-of-work actor gets cast in a cable TV show called *GLOW*, short for "Gorgeous Ladies of Wrestling." What is there not to love about *GLOW*? The outfits, the female empowerment and all the action! (The show won 2 Emmys for its stuntwork.) Ruth (Brie) is outstanding as the frustrated actress who finds new life as Zoya the Destroya. Debbie (Gilpin) is sublime as a faded soap star with a new baby and a cheating ex. Maron is terrific as the sexist show director, a sardonic role that doesn't actually require much acting.

📢 **From our forums:** "An easy series to binge watch. I love all things '80s so I liked the music, hair and clothes. I've had a little crush on Marc Maron for years so I was glad to see he got a juicy part. Alison Brie with her permed hair, minimum makeup and mom jeans was a nice touch. I will say, though, that I am not that invested in the other women."

The Go-Go's
TV-MA, 2020
Showtime original, 1 hr 38 mins
Movie (documentary) directed by Alison Ellwood, with Belinda Carlisle, Gina Schock, Kathy Valentine, Jane Wiedlin and Charlotte Caffey.

The groundbreaking career of the 1980s all-female rock band is charted in this film that treats their music, feuds and legacy with curiosity and respect. This first-rate rock doc establishes beyond a doubt that, far from being a novelty "girl band," the Go-Go's were a top-tier rock-and-roll ensemble. Buoyed by new interviews with the charming, witty and refreshingly frank band members — who have no problem owning up to their youthful indiscretions — this film celebrates the wildness of youth and the enduring power of sisterhood.

▶▶ Pairs well with *The Bee Gees: How Can You Mend a Broken Heart*

Godless
TV-MA, 2017
Netflix original, 7 episodes (AD)

Limited series (drama) with Jeff Daniels, Michelle Dockery, Merritt Wever, Jack O'Connell, Scoot McNairy, Thomas Brodie-Sangster, Samantha Soule and Sam Waterston.

Jeff Daniels plays an 1880s outlaw who tracks down his ex-partner in a New Mexico town run by tough frontier women. Spectacular cinematography and fine supporting performances from Wever et al. make this a western for the high-def streaming age.

📢 **From our forums:** "*Westworld* aside, it's been a long dry patch for fans of the genre. *Godless* filled that empty space in my fannish heart quite nicely." "A lot of plotlines seem to just end unceremoniously, leading one to wonder why they were introduced in the first place."

🏆 Emmys for best supporting actor and actress in a limited series (Daniels, Wever)

Going Clear
TV-MA, 2015
HBO Max, 2 hrs
Movie (documentary) directed by Alex Gibney.

It's still the most devastating brief against the Church of Scientology. With the subtitle *Scientology and the Prison of Belief,* Alex Gibney's Emmy-winning docuseries put an exclamation mark on Lawrence Wright's outstanding book. *Going Clear* made it common knowledge that Scientology would stop at nothing to silence the "suppressive persons" it considered enemies (including Scientologist Tom Cruise's ex-wife Nicole Kidman, among others). It also vividly exposed the tenets of the L. Ron Hubbard–founded "religion" as a cynically absurd pyramid scheme designed to fleece believers. Come for the weird details about the Sea Org; stay for actor Jason Beghe's disgusted and profane talking-head interviews.

🏆 Emmy for best documentary, Peabody Award

Goliath
TV-MA, 2016–2021
Prime Video original, 4 seasons, 32 episodes (AD)

Drama created by David E. Kelley and Jonathan Shapiro, with Billy Bob Thornton, Nina Arianda, Tania Raymonde, William Hurt, Maria Bello, Olivia Thirlby and Mark Duplass.

Billy Bob Thornton plays a washed-up, guilt-ridden lawyer who is just starting the arduous journey to redemption. Thornton brings all the nuances to the character and David E. Kelley does the rest, surrounding him with a lean and sturdy legal drama that is his *forté*.

📣 **From our forums:** "We've seen his down-at-the-heels LA noirish character many times before but still, Thornton makes him compulsively sympathetic and watchable even when delivering sometimes hacky dialog."

The Good Fight
TV-MA, 2017–present
Paramount+ original, 5 seasons, 50 episodes (AD)

Crime drama created by Michelle King, Robert King and Phil Alden Robinson, with Christine Baranski, Cush Jumbo, Delroy Lindo, Audra McDonald, Rose Leslie, Sarah Steele, Nyambi Nyambi, Michael Boatman and Gary Cole.

Christine Baranski does her thing on the best network TV show that's not on network TV. This sequel to *The Good Wife*, in which Diane Lockhart (Baranski) goes to work at a mostly Black law firm, was one of the first 2 originals on CBS All Access (the other was *Star Trek: Discovery*). Being on streaming has allowed it to take unconventional turns each season — cast shakeups, a Roy Cohn–inspired storyline, musical interstitials — not all of which went down well with fans. But the presence of Baranski in a courtroom reminds them of what drew them to this corner of the streaming world in the first place.

Good Girls
TV-14, 2018–2021
Netflix, Hulu, 4 seasons, 50 episodes (AD)

Dark comedy with Christina Hendricks, Retta, Mae Whitman, Manny Montana, Reno Wilson and Matthew Lillard.

Three Midwestern moms decide to solve their money problems through criminal means. Buckle up! This has one of the more intense, story-loaded pilots you'll see. An armed robbery leads to blackmail of our three heroines. They wind up laundering counterfeit cash because they are over 30 and therefore unmemorable. There are just enough pockets of levity to let viewers breathe. And there's a none-too-subtle undertow to *Good Girls* that what turns three ordinary women into thieves and grifters is an economic system that doesn't allow them the means to achieve financial stability by honest means.

📣 **From our forums:** "Requires a hefty dose of suspension of disbelief and a barrel of moral hand-waving, but as long as I look at it as a guilty pleasure with a great cast, it works for me."

Good Girls Revolt
TV-MA, 2015–2016
Prime Video original, 10 episodes (AD)

Historical drama with Genevieve Angelson, Anna Camp, Erin Darke, Hunter Parrish, Chris Diamantopoulos, Joy Bryant and Jim Belushi.

Acclaimed feminist drama chronicles the 1960s uprising by lady journalists who are tired of menial work and sexist treatment. Controversially canceled by a man who (we're not making this up) later exited Amazon Studios under a sex-harassment cloud, this show puts a deft fictional spin on the true story of the female employees who sued *Newsweek* magazine in 1969. While not quite *Mad Men* quality, *Good Girls Revolt* has a flair for period details and a rich ensemble of characters.

The Good Lord Bird

TV-MA, 2020
Showtime original, 7 episodes
Limited series (historical drama) created by Ethan Hawke and Mark Richard, with Ethan Hawke, Hubert Point-Du Jour, Beau Knapp, Nick Eversman, Joshua Caleb Johnson, Ellar Coltrane, Jack Alcott and Mo Brings Plenty.

Ethan Hawke stars in a wildly entertaining history lesson based on the acclaimed novel about abolitionist John Brown. Hawke, instrumental in getting James McBride's National Book Award winner adapted, plays the man of God turned righteous avenger. After adopting a young escaped slave he mistakes for a girl (Johnson), they embark on rambles through pre–Civil War America, ending in Brown's doomed plan to seize the armory at Harpers Ferry. Mark Richard's lively adaptation and an excellent film score keep things moving. Stay for the haunting final credits, which remind us that race remains America's original, exceptional sin.

Good Omens

TV-MA, 2019–present
Prime Video original, 6 episodes (AD)
Fantasy comedy created by Neil Gaiman and Terry Pratchett, with Michael Sheen, David Tennant, Daniel Mays, Nick Offerman, Sian Brooke, Ned Dennehy, Frances McDormand, Brian Cox and Benedict Cumberbatch.

Neil Gaiman made a lot of fans happy with this adaptation of his novel with Terry Pratchett about an angel and a demon and their unlikely alliance. This metaphysical buddy comedy stars Sheen as the fussy angel Aziraphale and Tennant as the louche demon Crowley, whose colossal mixup has set in motion the countdown to Armageddon. Neither of them want Earth to end — they've been here thousands of years and kinda like the place — so they team up against a host of biblically inspired rivals who actually *do* want the apocalypse. Inspired casting choices add to the fun, like Frances McDormand as the narrator (literally the Voice of God).

▶▶ Sheen and Tennant are set to return for a second season, alongside most of the crew.

The Good Place

TV-14, 2016–2020
Netflix, 4 seasons, 50 episodes (AD)
Sitcom created by Michael Schur, with Kristen Bell, Ted Danson, William Jackson Harper, Jameela Jamil, D'Arcy Carden and Manny Jacinto.

Philosophical-ethical sitcom set in the afterlife has so many twists, turns and brilliant insights the show is already regarded as a classic. Four humans are brought together after death by a gregarious world-builder who's definitely not what he seems. Speaking of world-builders, creator Mike Schur (*Parks & Rec*) managed to take viewers to a place few shows have. Maybe the only sitcom with an ethicist on the payroll, *The Good Place* succeeded not only by being smart and insightful but because these five people are so great together, you don't want their journeys to end.

💬 **From our forums:** "Can't recall the last time I liked a series finale that much. So much to explore on rewatching."

🏆 Peabody Award, TCA Award for outstanding achievement in comedy

The Good Wife

TV-14, 2009–2016
Paramount+, 7 seasons, 156 episodes
Crime drama created by Michelle
King and Robert King, with Julianna
Margulies, Matt Czuchry, Christine
Baranski, Archie Panjabi, Alan Cumming,
Josh Charles and Chris Noth.

**Julianna Margulies headlines one
of the smartest legal dramas of the
millennium.** Thirteen years after leaving
her law firm, Alicia (Margulies) returns by
no choice of her own when her politician
hubby (Noth) is caught with his pants
down and sent to jail. Starting from the
bottom, she fights her way up with help
from allies like Kalinda (Panjabi), an
in-house investigator with a taste for
tequila, men *and* women; Will (Charles),
an old friend and name partner at the
firm; and Diane (Baranski), a crusading
lawyer whose character would be spun off
to *The Good Fight*.

▶▶ If you're looking for a short cut, watch
Season 1 and then skip to Season 5. It
was full of twists that concluded with a
shocking three-episode arc.

🏆 Emmy for lead actress in a drama
(Margulies, twice), Peabody Award

The Goop Lab

TV-MA, 2020–present
Netflix original, 6 episodes (AD)
Celebreality show with Gwyneth Paltrow.

**Better than Gwyneth's detractors
expected it to be, this extension of
her lifestyle brand is an engaging
look at wellness methods currently in
vogue.** Each half-hour show explores
wellness approaches of varying levels of
outlandishness, from the benign (yoga,
vegan diet) to the extreme (psychedelics,
mediums) to some that feel genuinely
dangerous (jumping into ice-cold water).
But Paltrow and her team enter each
experience with a blend of skepticism and
anticipation that feels appropriate to the
endeavor.

▶▶ In 2021 Paltrow returned with a new
series on sex and intimacy titled *Sex, Love
and Goop*.

Gossip Girl (2007)

TV-14, 2007–2012
HBO Max, 6 seasons, 121 episodes (AD)
Teen drama created by Stephanie
Savage and Josh Schwartz, with Blake
Lively, Leighton Meester, Penn Badgley,
Chace Crawford, Ed Westwick, Kelly
Rutherford, Matthew Settle, Taylor
Momsen and Jessica Szohr.

**Who is Gossip Girl, and why is she
blogging such terrible things about the
students at two of New York's toniest
prep schools?** The Internet era's answer
to *Beverly Hills, 90210* was a decidedly
darker coming-of-age drama. Based on
the novels by Cecily von Ziegesar, *Gossip
Girl* chronicled the lives and loves of
the beautiful but troubled offspring of
the ultra-wealthy. Though the storylines
strained credulity (to say the least), *Gossip
Girl* was a magnet for young female
viewers, who tuned in for the fashions
and jewelry worn by the spoiled children
— especially Serena (Lively) and Blair
(Meester) — as much as for the drama.

Gossip Girl (2021)

TV-MA, 2021–present
HBO Max original, 12 episodes (AD)
Teen drama created by Joshua Safran,
with Jordan Alexander, Whitney Peak,
Tavi Gevinson, Eli Brown, Thomas
Doherty, Emily Alyn Lind, Evan Mock,
Johnathan Fernandez, Adam Chanler-
Berat and Zión Moreno.

**Nine years after the original *Gossip
Girl*, this HBO Max reboot is a more
politically correct and raunchier
edition.** Critics, even the ones that liked
the original *Gossip Girl*, panned this
TV-MA reboot. We'll let you decide,

since this quickly became the most-watched HBO Max original series upon its premiere. Set in the same universe as the original, the new series revolves around a diverse new batch of Manhattan private schoolers, albeit with a few nods to the past.

Grace and Frankie
TV-MA, 2015–2022
Netflix original, 7 seasons,
94 episodes (AD)
Comedy created by Marta Kauffman and Howard J. Morris, with Jane Fonda, Lily Tomlin, Sam Waterston, Martin Sheen, Ethan Embry, June Diane Raphael, Baron Vaughn and Brooklyn Decker.

Lily Tomlin and Jane Fonda made old age fun, even sexy, and Netflix viewers couldn't get enough. Grace (Fonda) and Frankie (Tomlin) have never really liked each other, but in late middle age they're forced to become close after their husbands (Waterston and Sheen) announce they're in love with each other. The comparatively long (for Netflix) run of *Grace and Frankie* reflected its success in addressing the challenges and foibles faced by older people, something very few programs have done. It also reflects the fact that Tomlin and Fonda clearly enjoyed the hell out of doing TV together.

💬 **From our forums:** "Lily Tomlin just gets funnier with age. The kids are the absolute worst, but I don't really mind that. Every show needs antagonists and I love seeing Grace and Frankie in solidarity against them."

The Great British Baking Show
TV-PG, 2010–present
Netflix, Hoopla, PBS Passport,
12 seasons, 147 episodes (AD)
Reality competition with Paul Hollywood, Mary Berry, Noel Fielding, Matt Lucas, Sandi Toksvig, Mel Giedroyc, Sue Perkins and Prue Leith.

Many viewers turned to this show during the pandemic for comfort food and comfort TV. Whether it's the kindness and camaraderie of the contestants, the impossible triumph of homey and pastoral location scouting that is The Tent (the show's outdoor venue) or the Pavlovian response to seeing all those baked goods, *GBBS* has an uncanny ability to cast a spell over viewers. What sometimes gets lost in the appreciation of sponge cakes and savory pies is that *GBBS* is also a top-notch reality competition. Even the post–Series 7 shakeup, where judge Berry and original hosts Giedroyc and Perkins were dismissed, couldn't slow the show's momentum.

▸▸ The show is called *The Great British Bake Off* everywhere but in the U.S., where the Pillsbury brand has owned the rights to the word "Bake Off" for decades.

▸▸ Nadiya Hussein translated her Series 6 win into bestselling cookbooks and TV shows like *Nadiya's Time To Eat* (also on Netflix).

▸▸ For suggestions of related shows, see "If You Liked *The Great British Baking Show*," page 373.

🏆 2 BAFTAs

The Great Interior Design Challenge
TV-PG, 2014–2017
Prime Video, 4 seasons, 52 episodes
Reality competition, with Tom Dyckhoff, Daniel Hopwood and Sophie Robinson.

Though not as charmingly twee as *The Great British Bake-Off*, it's a wonderfully evolved version of the design competition show. Unlike other design shows, the work and the people creating it get the focus they deserve. Instead of a deluge of 16 designers who get surface-level introductions, we get to know four amateur designers at a time. One goes home after each episode, with the last one standing advancing to the quarterfinal, after which a new cycle of four hopefuls begins. Judges Hopwood and Robinson are idiosyncratic in their tastes, which makes for surprise outcomes. Host Dyckhoff is excellent when he pops in to offer architectural styles or movements.

Great News

TV-14, 2017–2018
Netflix, 2 seasons, 23 episodes (AD)
Sitcom created by Tracey Wigfield, with Briga Heelan, Andrea Martin, Adam Campbell, Nicole Richie, Horatio Sanz and John Michael Higgins.

30 Rock meets The Office with a mother-daughter twist in this newsroom-centered comedy featuring the great Andrea Martin. Katie (Heelan) is trying to get ahead as a producer at a cable-news station with a Ted Baxter–like anchor (Higgins) when her mom (Martin), taking helicopter parenting to the extreme, gets herself hired as an intern. Rapid-fire comedy from producers Tina Fey and Robert Carlock (30 Rock, Mr. Mayor) is packed with pop-culture references, some of which are already showing their age; others, like the one about Wolf Blitzer's birthday party, are timeless.

From our forums: "Nicole Richie was made for that part, I wonder if they wrote it with her in mind."

The Great Pottery Throw Down

TV-14, 2015–present
HBO Max, 5 seasons, 44 episodes
Reality competition with Siobhan McSweeney, Keith Brymer Jones, Richard Miller, Kate Olivia Malone, Melanie Sykes, Sara Cox and Sue Pryke.

From the Great British Baking Show team, this upbeat competition show makes throwing clay accessible and appealing. The venue is different from the Great British Baking Show, taking place in a crowded shop in the industrial heart of a city. And making is not baking

— just one challenge is involved, taking days to complete. Yet this show's breezy structure turns a multi-day process into entertaining and dramatic television, and its quest for creativity rather than perfection, combined with warm, supportive hosts and contestants with feel-good stories, make this a worthy companion to its culinary counterpart.

The Great

TV-MA, 2020–present
Hulu original, 2 seasons, 20 episodes (AD)
Satirical comedy with Elle Fanning, Nicholas Hoult, Phoebe Fox, Sacha Dhawan, Charity Wakefield, Gwilym Lee, Adam Godley and Belinda Bromilow.

Sexy, violent and gross, this satire of Catherine the Great's reign in 18th-century Russia is part of a wave of historical comedies that are less concerned with factual accuracy than being stylish and fun. Billed as an "occasionally true story" of how Catherine (Fanning) seized the throne from her narcissistic husband Peter (Hoult) was created by Tony McNamara, who parodied British royalty in his 2018 film The Favourite.

From our forums: "A period drama with lavish costumes and sets, great acting, but also dark, over-the-top comedy? Yes please. Nicholas Hoult is absolutely hilarious in this and Elle Fanning is enchanting." "I really like it even if it is not historically accurate. And I like the nod to the horse rumor."

Greek

TV-14, 2007–2011
Hulu, IMDb TV, 4 seasons, 74 episodes
Comedy-drama with Spencer Grammer, Jacob Zachar, Scott Michael Foster, Jake McDorman, Amber Stevens West, Clark Duke, Paul James, Dilshad Vadsaria and Aaron Hill.

Still held in high regard a decade after it signed off, *Greek* is that rare show that captured the transformative drama of the college experience. This modestly seen but deeply beloved show about college kids debuted in the summer of 2007 and (aptly) ran for 4 seasons. Capturing a unique window in young people's lives, when immaturity, ambition and libertinism created a sometimes volatile admixture, *Greek* managed to be both excessive and nuanced about the lives of its characters, not all of whom belonged to fraternities and sororities.

▶▶ Pairs well with *The Sex Lives of College Girls*

Greenleaf

TV-14, 2016–present
Netflix, 5 seasons, 60 episodes (AD)
Drama with Lynn Whitfield, Keith David, Merle Dandridge, Kim Hawthorne, Desiree Ross, Lamman Rucker, Lovie Simone and Deborah Joy Winans.

Solidly acted prime-time soap revolves around a Black family that runs a Memphis megachurch. It's satisfying to see David and Whitfield as the patriarch and matriarch of the Greenleaf clan. These are meaty roles that don't go over-the-top immediately, but develop over several salacious episodes. Like the rest of the cast (including Oprah in a supporting role), they fully commit to the *outre* stakes, which makes it easy to savor the backstabbing, double-crossing, murderous, adulterous fun. Dandridge's more naturalistic performance as a morally conflicted Greenleaf daughter gives the stories some valuable balance.

Grey Gardens

TV-PG, 2009
HBO Max, 1 hr 44 mins
Movie (historical drama) with Jessica Lange, Drew Barrymore, Jeanne

Tripplehorn, Ken Howard, Daniel Baldwin and Malcolm Gets.

Jessica Lange and Drew Barrymore are convincing as two cousins of Jackie Onassis who become recluses living in squalor. Spanning 5 decades of the lives of Big Edie and her daughter Little Edie Beale, this treatment has greater sympathy for the women than the *Grey Gardens* documentary in which the real-life cousins were subjects. Credit two humane performances by Lange and Barrymore as co-dependent eccentrics whose lives slide gently, tragically into decline.

🏆 Emmy and TCA awards for best movie

Grey's Anatomy

TV-14, 2005–present
Netflix, Hulu, 18 seasons, 400 episodes (AD)
Medical drama created by Shonda Rhimes, with Ellen Pompeo, Chandra Wilson, James Pickens Jr., Justin Chambers, Kevin McKidd, Jesse Williams, Patrick Dempsey, Sandra Oh, Sara Ramirez and Jessica Capshaw.

First-rate writing, endlessly inventive drama and a star willing to stay put: they add up to TV's longest-running prime-time soap. *Grey's* has been justly celebrated for its diverse and appealing cast, all those love triangles and the story-twists-we-didn't-see-coming. But what made it a cultural and ratings phenomenon (some 20 million watched each episode, live, in its heyday) was a lot more: crackling dialogue, the blend of serious and silly, the poignant medical dramas and of course, Pompeo's Meredith Grey at the center of one addictive hour of TV after another.

▶▶ The first 5 seasons of *Grey's Anatomy* still hold up, thanks to Meredith's ongoing romance with Dempsey's Dr. Shepherd (aka McDreamy) and great foils in Izzie (Katherine Heigl), Cristina (Oh) and others.

🏆 SAG Award for best ensemble in a drama series

Grimm

TV-14, 2011–2017
Prime Video, 6 seasons,
123 episodes (AD)
Fantasy drama with David Giuntoli, Russell Hornsby, Silas Weir Mitchell, Sasha Roiz, Reggie Lee, Elizabeth Tulloch, Bree Turner and Claire Coffee.

The classic fairy tales are grist for this fantasy procedural about a homicide detective who protects humanity from nefarious mythological beings. Fans immediately loved the cop-show spin on the Brothers Grimm (and other sources), and in time even many critics were on board. The show isn't deep, but it's exciting, tense and frequently pretty funny. Giuntoli is charming as Nick, the detective who learns he is descended from a line of guardians. He has great rapport with his squad-room partner (Hornsby) and there's a loopy throughline with Nick's girlfriend (Tulloch) being forced to endure one magical complication after another.

The Guardian

TV-PG, 2001–2004
Paramount+, Hulu, Prime Video,
3 seasons, 67 episodes
Drama with Simon Baker, Dabney Coleman, Alan Rosenberg, Raphael Sbarge, Charles Malik Whitfield and Wendy Moniz-Grillo.

Overlooked network drama featured Simon Baker in a fine turn as a rakish lawyer turned victim's advocate. Besides his legal troubles and random drug tests, hotshot Nick (Baker) had to deal with a difficult father who happened to be his boss at the law firm (Coleman), as well as competing girlfriends and often volatile clients. But he rises to the occasion, putting his legal skills to use on behalf of the defenseless children he represents. *The Guardian* quietly made Baker a star for CBS, which rewarded him with a higher-profile role on *The Mentalist.*

Guerrilla

TV-MA, 2017
Showtime original, 6 episodes
Limited series (drama) created by John Ridley, with Freida Pinto, Babou Ceesay, Nathaniel Martello-White, Daniel Mays, Denise Gough, Rory Kinnear, Brandon Scott, Zawe Ashton and Idris Elba.

This gem from John Ridley follows a couple in 1970s London whose relationship and ideals are tested when they liberate a political prisoner. With great dialogue that is a Ridley signature, this limited series looks but doesn't feel like a period piece. Through empathetic and serious-minded characters, he explores how far we're willing to go in pursuit of justice as we perceive it.

⏩ Pairs well with *American Crime*

Hacks

TV-MA, 2021–present
HBO Max original, 10 episodes (AD)
Comedy with Jean Smart, Hannah Einbinder, Rose Abdoo, Carl Clemons-Hopkins, Paul W. Downs, Mark Indelicato, Megan Stalter and Christopher McDonald.

Jean Smart stars as a fading comic who's forced to work with a young writer to freshen up her material. If anyone can top Rachel Brosnahan's portrayal of an embattled female comic in *The Marvelous Mrs. Maisel,* it's Jean Smart, who offers a version of Joan Rivers at the end, rather than beginning, of her career. You hear it said that "comedy is hard," but Smart and Einbinder, as her junior partner, really capture the agony of producing jokes that won't land with a thud when delivered.

💬 **From our forums:** "The writers have done a great job portraying how each woman brings out the best in the other — Ava, the young, entitled one, has the opportunity to mature being around a wise older comedian, but even Deborah has grown with Ava's influence."

▶▶ For suggestions of related shows, see "If You Liked *Hacks*," page 373.

🏆 Emmy for best actress in a comedy series (Smart)

Halston

TV-MA, 2021
Netflix original, 5 episodes (AD)
Limited series (historical drama) with Ewan McGregor, Rebecca Dayan, David Pittu, Krysta Rodriguez, Gian Franco Rodriguez, Sietzka Rose and Bill Pullman.

Ewan McGregor is fabulous in this biopic of the iconic American designer. Once so famous that he appeared on *The Love Boat*, Halston is little more than a brand name today. But thanks to a bold performance by McGregor, you learn plenty about the relentless designer who defined mass taste from the 1960s to the '80s.

🏆 Emmy for best actor in a limited series (McGregor)

Halt and Catch Fire

TV-14, 2014–2017
AMC+, 4 seasons, 40 episodes
Historical drama with Lee Pace, Scoot McNairy, Mackenzie Davis, Kerry Bishé and Toby Huss.

Underrated period piece immerses viewers in the high-stakes geekery of the personal-computer era and the subsequent rise of the World Wide Web. Deep in the heart of Texas, a group of Silicon Valley castoffs, nerdy misfits and slick talkers are betting that the PC boom will be their ticket to success and something even more elusive — happiness. Like *Mad Men*, *Halt and Catch Fire* is well-researched and character-driven and offers a nuanced picture of one

of America's major cultural shifts as seen through the eyes of flawed people who want a piece of the action. *Halt and Catch Fire* was an acquired taste for many, which may explain why it made critics' best-of-the-decade lists but was passed over at awards time.

🗨 **From our forums:** "If you go back and rewatch the show, the earlier episodes that seemed so terrible suddenly snap into focus and you realize the showrunners had a better handle on the whole thing than you realized."

Hamilton

PG-13, 2020
Disney+ original, 2 hrs 40 mins (AD)
Movie (staged musical) with Lin-Manuel Miranda, Leslie Odom Jr., Phillipa Soo, Renée Elise Goldsberry, Daveed Diggs, Jonathan Groff, Anthony Ramos, Chris Jackson, Jasmine Cephas Jones and Okieriete Onaodowan.

Filmed on Broadway, while Miranda and the rest of the original *Hamilton* cast were still performing, this is a tight, dynamic production of the iconic musical. If you have a 4K screen and a good sound bar, you'll be immersed in this intimate filmed Broadway production of *Hamilton*. Even on a regular set, characters like Aaron Burr (Odom) feel more present in the movie version than on stage. Some critics were distracted by the audience noise, but that's more than offset by the dynamic hip-hop soundtrack and lively cinematography.

🏆 Emmy for best variety special

The Handmaid's Tale

TV-MA, 2017–present
Hulu original, 4 seasons,
46 episodes (AD)
Dystopian drama with Elisabeth Moss, Joseph Fiennes, Yvonne Strahovski, Alexis Biedel, Madeline Brewer, Ann

Dowd, Max Minghella, Samira Wiley and Bradley Whitford.

It was a new day for streaming TV when Margaret Atwood's patriarchal nightmare dropped on Hulu. One of the best-timed shows in history, *The Handmaid's Tale* debuted 3 months after Donald Trump took the oath of office, sparking Women's Marches across America and adding "handmaid's tale" to the national vocabulary. But was the show a dire warning about the perils of misogyny and the need to smash the patriarchy? M-m-maybe. Probably the real reason it clicked with viewers — for a couple of seasons anyway — was Bruce Miller's tense and skillfully executed adaptation of Atwood's book, powered by outsized performances from Moss, Dowd, Strahovski and Fiennes. Taking the story further than Atwood had, however, proved a challenge, and critics and fans complained that Seasons 3 and 4 dragged.

🐾 **From our forums:** "I wanted to see more of the Gilead world. In a terrorizing regime like that, it's often the tiny little details that are the scariest things. I wish the show had devoted more time to that."

🏆 15 Emmys

Hanna
TV-MA, 2019–2021
Prime Video original, 3 seasons, 22 episodes (AD)
Action with Esme Creed-Miles, Mireille Enos, Joel Kinnaman, Yasmin Monet Prince, Dermot Mulroney and Áine Rose Daly.

A teenage girl has to outrun a CIA assassin after learning she was supposed to become a killer herself. Based on the 2011 film by the same name (and streaming on Peacock), it expands the story in Season 2 when Hanna (Creed-Miles) goes on a journey to find the secret school where girls like her are trained to be assassins.

🐾 **From our forums:** "So many of my criticisms of Season 1 were addressed in Season 2. It was a joy to watch."

Hannah Gadsby: Nanette
TV-MA, 2018
Netflix original, 1 hr 9 mins
Comedy special directed by Jon Olb and Madeleine Parry, with Hannah Gadsby.

The Australian comedian broke through to international stardom with her fierce, unconventional standup special. The hourlong monologue by the *Please Like Me* star begins with light, charming jokes, but then it evolves to look directly at heavier themes and why, indeed, she's had it with standup comedy. This fierce, intense yet often hilarious *tour de force* became an Internet sensation within hours of its release on Netflix.

🏆 Peabody Award, Emmy for writing in a variety special

Hannibal
TV-MA, 2013–2015
Hulu, 3 seasons, 39 episodes (AD)
Crime drama with Hugh Dancy, Mads Mikkelsen, Carolina Dhavernas, Laurence Fishburne, Scott Thompson, Aaron Abrams and Gillian Anderson.

Thoughtful origin story, which portrays Lecter as an FBI profiler years before his unmasking as a cannibalistic murderer, lets you have your brain and eat it, too. Based on the Thomas Harris novels, *Hannibal* depicts Lecter (Mikkelsen) during his years as a forensic psychiatrist investigating serial killers — the anti-*Dexter*, if you will — where he is pitted in a battle of the minds with FBI agent and mortal foe Will Graham (Dancy). The two actors have exceptional chemistry, both attracted to and repelled by each other in a constant quest for the upper hand. Their dynamic gives the show enough charge to power all 3 seasons. Of course, while it explores the psyches of its lead characters, it also features plenty of bloody kills.

Happiest Season
PG-13, 2020
Hulu original, 1 hr 42 mins (AD)
Movie (romantic comedy) directed by Clea DuVall, with Kristen Stewart, Mackenzie Davis, Mary Steenburgen, Dan Levy, Victor Garber, Alison Brie and Aubrey Plaza.

A woman brings her girlfriend home for Christmas with her conservative family, which puts wrinkles in everyone's holiday plans. Refreshingly, this is a classic dysfunctional family holiday film that just happens to focus on LGBTQ characters.

Happy Endings
TV-14, 2011–2013
HBO Max, Netflix, Hulu, 3 seasons, 57 episodes
Sitcom created by David Caspe, with Eliza Coupe, Elisha Cuthbert, Zachary Knighton, Adam Pally, Damon Wayans Jr. and Casey Wilson.

If you liked the goofy relationship elements of *New Girl* and the relentless pace of *30 Rock,* this overlooked sitcom is for you. Set in Chicago, the group of six friends won't remind you of *Friends* at all. The pacing is too manic and these six aren't nearly as likable as Rachel, Ross and the gang. But at just 3 seasons, it's easy to binge.

🎙 **From our forums:** "It's one of the very few sitcoms that I find genuinely funny! It takes me awhile to watch every episode because I keep rewinding to hear all the rapid-fire jokes I'm missing."

Happy Town
TV-14, 2010
ABC, 8 episodes

Thriller with Sam Neill, Amy Acker, M.C. Gainey, Robert Wisdom, Lauren German and Steven Weber.

Sam Neill carries a melodramatic whodunit set in a small Minnesota town where crime doesn't exist, and yet people keep disappearing. There's more than a whiff of Stephen King in the air that wafts through the town of Haplin (get it, "happy town"?), but this network drama, still streaming on the old ABC website, also pays homage to *Twin Peaks*, *Picket Fences* and all those atmospheric dramas of the '00s. Neill, as the mysterious English proprietor of a local relic shop, is the one you can't help but keep your eye on.

Happy Valley
TV-MA, 2014–present
AMC+, Prime Video, 2 seasons, 12 episodes
Crime drama with Sarah Lancashire, Siobhan Finneran, Charlie Murphy, James Norton, George Costigan, Rhys Connah and Shane Zaza.

Taut, darkly amusing thriller follows a detective's obsession with the man who drove her teenage daughter to suicide. After Sergeant Catherine Cawood (Lancashire) learns that the creep is out of jail, she begins an obsessive quest to bring him down, leading to the discovery of another horrific crime. *Happy Valley* is as much a study of Cawood's relationship to her small town and the profession she's served for so long as it is a tense crime story.

▸▸ A third and final season went into production in early 2022.

▸▸ Pairs well with *Mare of Easttown*

🏆 BAFTA for best TV drama (both seasons)

Hard Knocks: Los Angeles
TV-MA, 2020
HBO Max, 5 episodes
Anthology series (documentary).

Featuring both of L.A.'s NFL teams, this is a fine introduction to a critically acclaimed inside-the-locker-room series. From the most honored production unit in professional sports — NFL Films — comes this wonderfully crafted week-by-week reality drama that usually follows one team's travails during one season of play. The gorgeous visuals and high-stakes storylines will be appealing to even non-fans, while other viewers will learn what really happened during key moments in the season that were fodder for sports-talk-show speculation. This season gave viewers both the Rams and Chargers, two teams that hadn't called L.A. home until recently.

Harley Quinn

TV-MA, 2019–present
HBO Max original, 2 seasons, 26 episodes
Animated comedy with Kaley Cuoco, Lake Bell, Alan Tudyk, Ron Funches, Tony Hale, Jason Alexander, Diedrich Bader, Christopher Meloni, J.B. Smoove and Jim Rash.

The Joker's henchwoman from the DC Animated Universe gets her own show and a solid comic voice in Kaley Cuoco. Harley has long been a favorite of DC writers and readers for her irreverence and boundless appetite for mayhem. Here she gets top billing in this fast-paced adult sitcom that, according to a producer, is going for an "animated *Arrested Development* tone." Having broken with the Joker, Harley has forged a tight bond with the charming "eco-terrorist" Poison Ivy (Bell).

🐟 **From our forums:** "I am happy that it has proven to be every bit as funny as I had hoped, but what surprises me is how well thought-out the characters are. Every episode was written with the entire season in mind."

▶▶ A third season is due to arrive in 2022.

Harlots

TV-MA, 2017–2019
Hulu original, 3 seasons,
24 episodes (AD)
Historical drama with Lesley Manville, Kate Fleetwood, Jessica Brown Findlay, Holli Dempsey, Eloise Smyth, Bronwyn James, Pippa Bennett-Warner, Samantha Morton, Danny Sapani and Ellie Heydon.

Bawdy 18th-century brothel drama has interesting notes of *The Wire* and *The Handmaid's Tale*. As many as 50,000 women were in the sex trade in Georgian England and this soapy, witty and entertaining series about competing whorehouses features copious amounts of high-rise cleavage and lowdown screwing. Yet *Harlots*, like *The Handmaid's Tale*, is ultimately a soap about the imbalance of power in society, and what women sometimes had to do with the little power they held over men. Like *The Wire*, the lawbreakers are appealing, often quite funny but ultimately tragic characters.

Hasan Minhaj: Homecoming King

TV-MA, 2017
Netflix original, 1 hr 13 mins
Comedy special directed by Christopher Storer, with Hasan Minhaj.

The *Daily Show* correspondent tells stories from his life as an Indian-American Muslim. Chances are good you didn't have a childhood anything like Hasan Minhaj's. He had a sister he didn't know about until he was 8, his family was targeted after 9/11 and his prom date's family found a white boy for her to go to the dance with instead. As he showed in his gone-too-soon *Patriot Act*, Minhaj has the stage presence to extract maximum emotion from these moments, then pivot to a laugh-out-loud story (like the time his dad tried to return used undies to Costco).

🏆 Peabody Award

The Haunting of Bly Manor

TV-MA, 2020
Netflix original, 9 episodes (AD)
Limited series (horror) created by Mike Flanagan, with Victoria Pedretti, Oliver Jackson-Cohen, Amelia Eve, T'Nia Miller, Rahul Kohli, Henry Thomas, Tahirah Sharif, Amelia Bea Smith, Carla Gugino and Benjamin Evan Ainsworth.

This installment has fewer thrills but more chills than *The Haunting of Hill House*. Flanagan's source for this season are the ghost stories of Henry James, notably his 1898 classic *The Turn of the Screw*. An *au pair* named Dani (Pedretti) is hired by a mysterious man to look after his niece and nephew at his large estate. Soon she begins having troubling visions, which are explained to the viewers through a series of unsettling flashbacks and unexpected reveals.

🐟 **From our forums:** "The gothic nature and love story was quite beautiful and tragic. If anything this is less a story about a haunted house and more a story about haunted people.." "This just didn't hang together with anything approaching the precision of *Hill House*, and it lacked the same jaw-dropping family dynamics and directorial tricks."

The Haunting of Hill House

TV-MA, 2018
Netflix original, 10 episodes (AD)
Limited series (horror) created by Mike Flanagan, with Michiel Huisman, Carla Gugino, Henry Thomas, Elizabeth Reaser, Oliver Jackson-Cohen, Kate Siegel, Victoria Pedretti, Mckenna Grace, Timothy Hutton and Annabeth Gish.

Shirley Jackson's novel is turned into a sweeping tale of family secrets that's no less frightening for its lack of standard horror-genre tropes. Several family members have come to stay at Hill House, convinced that its paranormal powers killed their mom. What they

uncover instead are more mundane but no less creepy family secrets. The debut installment of Mike Flanagan's *Haunting* anthology series, *Hill House* is unusual for the horror genre. It's character-driven, free of special effects.

🐟 **From our forums:** "I am a horror movie/show/story fanatic and this is the first thing I've watched in forever where I had to look through my fingers in anticipation of something scary."

Hear and Now

TV-14, 2007
HBO Max, 1 hr 25 mins
Movie (documentary) directed by Irene Taylor Brodsky.

In their 60s, the director's Deaf parents receive Cochlear implants and then (as in all great unscripted films) things don't go the way you'd think. What happens when two people whose lives have been spent trying *not* to be defined by their disabilities suddenly, in late middle life, lose that disability? That's the focus of Brodsky's very personal look at the ripple effects that a transformative technology has on her subjects.

▶▶ Brodsky's 2019 film *Moonlight Sonata: Deafness in Three Movements* is also streaming on HBO Max.

🏆 Peabody Award

Hearts Beat Loud

PG-13, 2018
Hulu, 1 hr 37 mins
Movie (musical comedy) with Nick Offerman, Kiersey Clemons, Blythe Danner, Toni Collette, Sasha Lane and Ted Danson.

After they write a song together, a father and daughter suddenly become viral music stars. This is a quirky heartwarmer that joins *High Fidelity*, *Rock of Ages* and *Empire Records* in the list of indie movies that brilliantly remind us why music is awesome.

Heaven's Gate: The Cult of Cults

TV-MA, 2021
HBO Max original, 4 episodes
Docuseries created by Clay Tweel, with Bonnie Nettles, Marshall Applewhite, Reza Aslan and Steve Hassan.

Chilling docuseries argues that cults draw their power from stories as much as they do from charismatic leaders. Two decades after 909 members of the U.S.-based People's Temple committed mass suicide in Guyana, 39 members of the Heaven's Gate community took their lives on U.S. soil. This 4-parter, a worthy companion to Stanley Nelson's *Jonestown* documentary (which isn't streamable), attempts to explain how Marshall Applewhite was able to gather a tribe around his bizarre story of a spaceship coming to rescue them and, in the end, persuaded many of them to make the ultimate sacrifice. In the end we're left with the chilling — and extremely relevant — reminder of the power of narrative.

▶▶ Pairs well with *Wild Wild Country*

Helter Skelter: An American Myth

TV-MA, 2020
Epix original, 6 episodes
Limited series (true crime) directed by Lesley Chilcott.

Half a century later, the Tate-LaBianca murders are not forgotten around southern California, as you'll learn from this well-done docuseries about the Manson family and their shocking crime. Though not groundbreaking, the producers make the most out of their access to key figures, including a juror at Manson's trial and two of his followers, Dianne Lake and Catherine Share. Author Jeff Guinn provides insights throughout.

Hemingway

TV-14, 2021
PBS Passport, 3 episodes
Docuseries directed by Ken Burns and Lynn Novick, with Peter Coyote, Jeff Daniels, Patricia Clarkson, Mary-Louise Parker, Keri Russell and Meryl Streep.

Burns and Novick challenge popular myths and misconceptions about author Ernest Hemingway. The veteran collaborators, who have teamed on previous documentaries about Prohibition and the Civil War, keep this surprisingly tight despite its length. None of its 6 parts seems superfluous. The historical overview, the unvarnished treatment of Hemingway the man, the appreciation of his work and assessment of his legacy is consistently engrossing and illuminating.

Heroes

TV-14, 2006–2010
Peacock, IMDb TV, 4 seasons, 78 episodes
Sci-fi drama with Hayden Panettiere, Jack Coleman, Milo Ventimiglia, Masi Oka, Sendhil Ramamurthy, Greg Grunberg, Zachary Quinto and Ali Larter.

A select group of everyday people have extraordinary abilities; one by one they get pulled into a world-shaking battle between good and evil. Before the Marvel or DC universes kicked into gear, this show clicked by serving up complex superhero stories that focused on a vast array of characters. The standouts are arguably Claire (Panettiere), an invincible cheerleader, and Noah (Jack Coleman), her adoptive father and a high-ranking member of a group that studies the "gifted." But because the entire cast does such good work and the writing is so reliably exciting, it's easy to get sucked into multiple arcs at once.

🏆 Emmy for visual effects and a SAG Award for stunt work in a TV series

High Fidelity

TV-MA, 2020
Hulu original, 10 episodes (AD)

For shows sorted by streaming platform, see page 381. **155**

Romantic comedy with Zoë Kravitz, Jake Lacy, Da'Vine Joy Randolph, David H. Holmes, Kingsley Ben-Adir, Rainbow Sun Francks and Nadine Malouf.

Viewers of a certain age will groove to this new adaptation of the Nick Hornby novel starring Zoë Kravitz as a record store owner with encyclopedic musical knowledge and a dense history of failed relationships. Twenty years after the John Cusack-led film moved Hornby's *High Fidelity* from London to Chicago, this version shifts the action to New York and gender-flips its lead. Kravitz plays the part of the romantically torn record shop owner to a tee, and like the film before it, the series has a top-notch soundtrack. Why Hulu canceled the show after one season is as much a mystery as the breakup of the Smiths.

High Maintenance
TV-MA, 2016–2020
HBO Max, 4 seasons, 34 episodes (AD)
Anthology series (comedy) with Ben Sinclair.

Like a fictionalized *Humans of New York*, this is a beautifully shot, well-observed collection of stories about individuals and their unique foibles and minor triumphs. It's one of those shows you'll hear name-dropped by critics who remember it fondly even though most of their readers don't recall a thing about it. But this anthology about all the people connected to a New York City pot dealer is a supremely easy series to dip into, with very little mythology or ongoing narrative arcs as barriers to entry. And it's sweet, a nice counter to much of the antihero fare on HBO.

High School Musical: The Musical - The Series
TV-PG, 2019–present
Disney+ original, 2 seasons,
22 episodes (AD)

Musical comedy with Olivia Rodrigo, Joshua Bassett, Matt Cornett, Larry Saperstein, Julia Lester, Frankie A. Rodriguez, Kate Reinders, Sofia Wylie and Dara Renee.

Moving quickly beyond its wink-wink premise, this meta mockumentary is an entertaining, song-filled look at kids navigating the supersized emotions of high school. Yes, it's a Disney+ show about students at the school where Disney's *High School Musical* was filmed, staging their own version of *High School Musical*. But the musical numbers, many written just for this series, are a joy to watch. And fans of Olivia Rodrigo will want to tune in for the early seasons to see how they paved the way for her blockbuster singing career.

🗫 **From our forums:** "I couldn't help but marvel at one gay kid singing a love song to his boyfriend, accompanied and supported by his straight friend with no drama other than teenage insecurity. *Schitt's Creek* did it first, but not with teenagers!"

High Score
TV-14, 2020
Netflix original, 6 episodes (AD)
Docuseries with Charles Martinet.

It's not quite the epic history of video games that its creators intended but it's an easy binge. Watching *High Score* reminds some of us, anyway, that playing *Space Invaders* at the arcade and Atari games at home and Nintendo's GameBoy on the school bus were things Grandpa did. Video games have evolved at the speed of technology and today's gamers will likely be astounded to learn the industry's origin story in this breezy, cheesy retelling. Their parents — and grandparents — will find *High Score* engaging too.

▶▶ Pairs well with *Halt and Catch Fire*

Hightown

TV-MA, 2020–present
Starz original, 2 seasons, 18 episodes
Crime drama with Monica Raymund, James Badge Dale, Riley Voelkel, Shane Harper, Atkins Estimond, Amaury Nolasco and Dohn Norwood.

Diverse if formulaic crime saga is distinguished by Monica Raymund's performance as an addict drawn into a murder investigation on Cape Cod. Jackie Quinones (Raymund) might work for the National Marine Fisheries Service, and she might have problems with alcohol and drugs, but when she discovers a dead body, she's going to help solve the case whether the police like it or not.

🗨 **From our forums:** "I wasn't hooked right away but it definitely improved by the end, with continuing character growth along with the crime story."

Hillary

TV-MA, 2020
Hulu original, 4 episodes (AD)
Docuseries directed by Nanette Burstein, with Hillary Clinton, Bill Clinton and Chelsea Clinton.

Emotionally powerful retelling of the 2016 campaign and profile of arguably the most remarkable political figure of our time. Director Burstein gets good access to Clinton during her run for the presidency, and the candidate is commendably candid (as well as "on") at all times. Even if you find her tone-deafness exasperating and the replay of the events of 2016 triggering, *Hillary* is worth watching just to see this relentless, charismatic and polarizing public figure during one of the country's strangest political moments.

His Dark Materials

TV-14, 2019–present
HBO Max, 2 seasons, 15 episodes (AD)
Fantasy drama with Ruth Wilson, Dafne Keen, Amir Wilson, Kit Connor, Ariyon Bakare, Will Keen, Cristela Alonzo, Lin-Manuel Miranda and Ruta Gedmintas.

Like *Game of Thrones* and *Watchmen* before it, HBO's latest fantasy series may confound newcomers at first but rewards the patient viewer. In a steampunk version of Victorian England, a young girl is chosen to take on the Magisterium (aka church), which bans people's fondness for magic and their animal spirits. These spirits are known as daemons, and does this mean the show has a lot of scurrying creatures underfoot and birds perched on shoulders? Yes it does. Based on the fantasy trilogy by author Philip Pullman, this universe can feel pretty impenetrable … until it's not. And on the other side of that veil, there's a whole new universe of enjoyment.

▶▶ The series has been renewed for a third and final season, based on *The Amber Spyglass*.

History of Swear Words

TV-MA, 2021
Netflix original, 6 episodes (AD)
Docuseries with Nicolas Cage, Nikki Glaser, London Hughes, Elvis Mitchell, Sarah Silverman, Nick Offerman, Jim Jefferies and Joel Kim Booster.

Nicolas Cage archly presents brief histories of 6 of the most popular curse words of our time. With help from historians, lexicographers and other academics, the series goes surprisingly deep on the origins of profanity. Actors and comedians are dropped in to supply color (and colorful language), making for an easy bleeping binge.

Hoarders

TV-14, 2009–present
Prime Video, Hulu, Netflix, 13 seasons, 149 episodes
Reality show.

Some shows may have moved; see page 183.   **157**

A classic show about addiction to extreme hoarding found new life with super-sized episodes. A&E was never going to run out of hovels to take its cameras and hoarding-disorder psychologists into. But the show's format was tired, and the quick-hit format of early seasons of *Hoarders* had become more voyeuristic than therapeutic. That all changed when the format switched at the end of Season 10. Instead of racing through two different cases, *Cops*-style, in 44 minutes, *Hoarders* explored just a single case in an 85-minute episode. This change allowed the show to dive into the complexity of each case — not only telling more empathic stories about the hoarders and the events of the cleanup, but delving into hoarding as a mental disorder, from denial to codependency, trauma to fear.

🏆 Critics Choice Award for best reality series

Holey Moley
TV-PG, 2019–present
Hulu, 3 seasons, 33 episodes (AD)
Reality competition with Rob Riggle, Joe Tessitore and Stephen Curry.

Rapidly becoming synonymous with summer fun, *Holey Moley* is both completely dumb and a legitimate competition — it's mini-golf if it went pro. This delightfully overbaked casserole of absurdity combines a putt-putt competition with the physical comedy of *Wipeout*, the challenge set design of *Big Brother* and the ridiculous costuming of *American Ninja Warrior*. The mini-golf is narrated with winking, arch sportscaster enthusiasm by Tessitore and Riggle, one of TV's great hosting duos. Season 1 is good but Season 2, which incorporates a number of useful format tweaks, is even funnier and more intense.

Hollywood
TV-MA, 2020
Netflix original, 7 episodes (AD)
Limited series (historical drama) created by Ryan Murphy and Ian Brennan, with Darren Criss, David Corenswet, Laura Harrier, Dylan McDermott, Jake Picking, Joe Mantello, Jeremy Pope, Holland Taylor, Samara Weaving and Jim Parsons.

For once, the creator of *American Horror Story* tries looking on the bright side in this sunny alternate history of La La Land. *Hollywood* plays like two different shows: one a dishy, tawdry tell-all about Hollywood's golden era, the other a bold revisionist history of the movie biz. Murphy creates a production called *Peg* with fictional aspiring actors, writers, directors and producers all trying to break through. The industry's bigotry and predation is explored here, but counters that with stories of earnest strivers fighting adversity.

💬 From our forums: "With more of the cast introduced in Episode 2, I can see where the story is going — and I must be invested because I found myself going over to Wikipedia to check out the stories behind the real characters."

🏆 2 Emmys

Home Before Dark
TV-14, 2020–present
Apple TV+ original, 2 seasons, 20 episodes (AD)
Family comedy with Brooklynn Prince, Jim Sturgess, Abby Miller, Kylie Rogers, Michael Weston, Aziza Scott, Joelle Carter, Louis Herthum and Adrian Hough.

A 9-year-old self-styled investigative journalist uncovers long-buried secrets in town, to the mortification of her dad. Inspired by the true-crime podcast, *Home Before Dark* follows Hilde (Prince), who moves back with her parents and sister after Matt (Sturgess) loses his journalism job. Hilde's character was divisive — some viewers thought she nailed the part, others found her annoying. Though aimed at a younger audience, the show's emotional maturity will appeal to grown-ups, and it's a pretty good mystery Hilde stumbles onto.

🐾 **From our forums:** "I love seeing these free range kids out running around and riding their bikes without supervision."

Homecoming

TV-MA, 2018–2000
Prime Video original, 2 seasons,
17 episodes (AD)
Drama created by Sam Esmail, with Julia Roberts, Stephan James, Alex Karpovsky, Bobby Cannavale, Hong Chau, Janelle Monáe, Shea Whigham, Chris Cooper, Joan Cusack and Sissy Spacek.

Julia Roberts and Janelle Monáe take turns headlining this psychological thriller about a woman who works with soldiers returning from war and slowly recovers their disturbing memories. Based on the scripted podcast of the same name, *Homecoming* is sliced into podcast-sized episodes by director Sam Esmail (*Mr. Robot*).

🐾 **From our forums:** "While I enjoyed the first 5 episodes, I was focused on putting the 'mystery' puzzle together. Each episode the characterization got deeper and the story started to come together."

Homeland

TV-MA, 2011–2020
Showtime original, 8 seasons,
96 episodes
Crime drama with Claire Danes, Mandy Patinkin, Rupert Friend, Damian Lewis, F. Murray Abraham, Maury Sterling and Morena Baccarin.

Claire Danes established herself as one of her generation's great actors in this role as a talented but troubled government agent. From two executive producers of *24*, *Homeland* was *24* for the second decade after 9/11, when America had moved beyond cartoon counter-terrorists like Jack Bauer and craved heroes with more complexity. As Carrie Mathison, a CIA officer with psychological issues, Danes was easy for viewers to root for, even as her judgment wasn't always the best. Lewis as a potentially compromised spy and Patinkin as Carrie's politically ambitious boss also added intrigue. *Homeland* writers and actors routinely met with former CIA agents, military and journalists to discuss national security issues; not surprisingly the show had an enthusiastic following around the D.C. Beltway.

▶▶ *Homeland* has one of the very best fan sites in Hell Yeah Homeland, featuring episode and season recaps, a huge fan forum, still-going podcast and more.

🏆 Emmy for best drama; TCA Award for best new program

The Honourable Woman

TV-14, 2014
Sundance Now original, 8 episodes
Limited series (drama) with Maggie Gyllenhaal, Stephen Rea, Lubna Azabal, Katherine Parkinson, Janet McTeer, Eve Best, Lindsay Duncan, Andrew Buchan and Tobias Menzies.

Maggie Gyllenhaal plays a baroness and keeper of secrets in this underrated spy thriller set in the Israel-Palestine conflict. Gyllenhaal plays Nessa Stein, a powerful and ambitious businesswoman caught up in a web of murder, deceit and shadowy operators. As with *Top of the Lake*, *Big Little Lies* and *Sharp Objects* this overlooked series gave a complicated and bold portrayal of women's autonomy in their professional and personal lives.

🏆 Peabody Award

For shows sorted by streaming platform, see page 381.

Hoop Dreams

PG-13, 1994
HBO Max, Showtime, 2 hrs 50 mins
Movie (documentary) directed by Steve
James, with Arthur Agee and William
Gates.

**A classic of video empathy, *Hoop
Dreams* is a parable about America's
obsession with sports and, more
importantly, people who win at sports.**
Over several years three white filmmakers
tracked the odysseys of Black inner-city
Chicago basketball prodigies Arthur Agee
and William Gates as they attempted
to convert their talents into a ticket to
the American dream. What's striking is
how these promising young men, while
still teenagers, are expected to make
decisions about school, career and life
with little adult guidance. The story is
told with a minimum of narration or
contrivances. Even 3 decades later it
remains a masterpiece of observational
documentary, one that will break your
heart and lift your spirits by the final
credits.

🏆 Peabody Award

House

TV-14, 2004–2012
Prime Video, 8 seasons,
176 episodes (AD)
Medical drama created by David Shore,
with Hugh Laurie, Lisa Edelstein, Robert
Sean Leonard, Omar Epps, Jesse Spencer,
Jennifer Morrison, Peter Jacobson and
Olivia Wilde.

**He avoids consultations, long hours at
the hospital and seeing his patients …
has there ever been a TV doctor like
Greg House?** Hugh Laurie defied all
logic as the sarcastic, Vicodin-popping,
cane-clutching healer in *House*, Fox's first
procedural and still its most successful.
So many tropes developed over the
show's long run: the clashes with hospital
administrator Cuddy (Edelstein) and his

friend and colleague Wilson (Leonard),
the patients forever collapsing in heaps,
House spending half the episode arguing
over the diagnosis before pulling the cure
out of his hat.

▶▶ Needle-drop at Season 2, when the
show was still fresh and having fun with
the simple things like the cold opens and
House's sarcastic *bon mots*.

🏆 5 Emmys

House of Cards

TV-MA, 2013–2018
Netflix original, 6 seasons,
73 episodes (AD)
Drama with Robin Wright, Michael Kelly,
Kevin Spacey, Justin Doescher, Derek
Cecil, Jayne Atkinson, Mahershala Ali
and Neve Campbell.

**In Netflix's first big original hit, Kevin
Spacey and Robin Wright play an amoral
political couple who have no problem
lying, cheating and murdering their
way to the Oval Office.** The show's first
2 seasons were the best kind of high-
quality trash. Spacey, whose character
regularly talks to the camera about his bad
behavior, projects unfettered glee as he
manipulates the political machine, while
Wright's ice-cold performance is the stuff
camp classics are made of. For a while,
anyway, it was great fun to watch these
vipers get everything they want.

🏆 Peabody Award

House of Lies

TV-MA, 2012–2016
Showtime original, 5 seasons,
58 episodes
Comedy-drama with Don Cheadle,
Kristen Bell, Ben Schwartz, Josh Lawson,
Donis Leonard Jr., Glynn Turman and
Dawn Olivieri.

**Don Cheadle fleeces the 1 percent, with
help from Kristen Bell, and has a lot of
fun doing it in this cynical Showtime
comedy.** Management consultant Marty

Kaan (Cheadle) has assembled a team of grifters whose knack for coming up with soak-the-rich schemes gives *House of Lies* its vicarious energy. Like Kevin Spacey on that other *House of* show, Cheadle gets to break the fourth wall and talk to the camera. But this show didn't go 5 seasons without Cheadle getting a lot of help, especially from Bell, whose real-life pregnancy allowed the scriptwriters to go down an avenue they wouldn't have otherwise, to good effect. Like a lot of Showtime fare, *House of Lies* is a bit shaggy and no one will ever confuse it with *Succession*.

▶▶ The series finale was memorable as it was filmed in Havana, making *House of Lies* the first U.S. show made in Cuba since diplomatic relations were restored.

The Housewives of the North Pole
TV-PG, 2021
Peacock original, 1 hr 24 mins
Movie (family comedy) with Betsy Brandt, Kyle Richards, Kyle Selig, Damon Dayoub, Carlos Ponce, Tetona Jackson, Alec Mapa and Jearnest Corchado.
Real Housewives–adjacent made-for-TV holiday movie is everything you expect it to be. Take the Hallmark formula, set it in a small town in Vermont and stir up Trish (*Real Housewives of Beverly Hills* mainstay Richards) and Diana (Brandt), best friends who wind up feuding over nothing and take the rest of the movie to make up. Diana's son Jake (Selig) and Trish's daughter Skye (Corchado) shoulder the romcom roles delightfully.

How I Met Your Father
TV-14, 2022
Hulu original, 10 episodes
Comedy with Hilary Duff, Christopher Lowell, Kim Cattrall, Josh Peck, Suraj Sharma, Daniel Augustin, Francia Raisa, Ashley Reyes, Tien Tran and Tom Ainsley.
A spinoff of *How I Met Your Mother* that flips the premise of the original has Kim Cattrall as the mom reliving her dating years to her son.** It's an update as much as a spinoff. There's no Barney Stinson here with his womanizing and misogynistic language; instead *HIMYF* approaches dating from a sex-positive point of view and it's the show's female characters who openly discuss oral sex. With its more diverse makeup, the gang also offers a much more realistic depiction of actual New Yorkers. Duff's effervescent charm makes her the ideal candidate for the lead role of young Sophie, but it's the strong ensemble that really makes *HIMYF* sing. Raisa, in particular, brings a fantastic energy to her role as Sophie's sex-loving sidekick. Tran and Ainsley have an oddball chemistry that develops nicely, while the more earnest Lowell and Sharma ground the series with their comedic timing.

How I Met Your Mother
TV-14, 2005–2014
Hulu, Prime Video, 9 seasons, 208 episodes
Romantic comedy with Josh Radnor, Jason Segel, Cobie Smulders, Neil Patrick Harris, Alyson Hannigan and Cristin Milioti.
Neil Patrick Harris resuscitated his career in this clever spin on the friends comedy, told as a series of flashbacks about a father's younger days. Though Jennifer Love Hewitt was originally pursued for the role of the young woman who would become the "mother," the show's creators opted for an unknown, Smulders, to play the part and it was a wise choice. Harris, as the wealthy, bon-mot-tossing playboy Barney Stinson, was first among equals in this enjoyable ensemble comedy, which as it settled into its long run on CBS learned to mine the comic possibilities outside its central romantic storyline. The finale sharply divided fans, but by then *HIMYM* had

amassed a track record too great to dismiss.

🏆 10 Emmys

How To Die in Oregon
Not Rated, 2011
Tubi, 1 hr 47 mins
Movie (documentary) directed by Peter Richardson.

Terminally ill patients take part in physician-assisted suicide in one of the few states that allows it. The Death with Dignity Act allows doctors to prescribe life-ending drugs to terminally ill Oregonians. If anyone is opposed to it inside the state, you'd hardly know from this film, which focuses instead on telling the stories of a handful of very sick people who are considering the drastic measure. But the agonized debates that roil their families as these patients plan their own demise offer proof that "death with dignity" is far from the easy way out.

🏆 Grand Jury Prize at the Sundance Film Festival

How To Fix a Drug Scandal
TV-MA, 2020
Netflix original, 4 episodes (AD)
Limited series (true crime) directed by Erin Lee Carr.

An eye-popping look at how tens of thousands of drug convictions were thrown into doubt because of two lab chemists. Another humdinger from Erin Lee Carr (see also *I Love You, Now Die*), this is true-crime catnip involving two Massachusetts lab techs, one a frustrated overachiever in the Stephen Glass mold, the other a junkie. Thousands of lab results were doctored between them, making this one of the biggest scandals in the sordid history of the war on drugs.

How To Get Away with Murder
TV-14, 2014–2020
Netflix, 6 seasons, 90 episodes
Crime drama with Viola Davis, Billy Brown, Jack Falahee, Aja Naomi King, Matt McGorry, Charlie Weber, Liza Weil, Conrad Ricamore, Karla Souza and Alfred Enoch.

Bat-guano-crazy legal thriller stars Viola Davis in an Emmy turn as a law professor trying to cover up the murder of her husband. It's the legal show with no rules. No show (except maybe for sister series *Scandal*) made chaos more compelling in its time. Zanily unpredictable, logic-defying, untethered from the actual criminal justice system, *How To Get Away with Murder* created an alternate reality so convincing that it enlisted viewers in taking seriously the issues that producer Shonda Rhimes and her writers wanted America to think about: systemic racism and sexism, long-term trauma and the corrosive effects of paranoia.

🗣 **From our forums:** "Loved everything about Cicely Tyson." "I don't worship at the altar of Shonda, but she's done a lot more for Black female leads in network dramas than anyone else has in decades."

🏆 Emmy and SAG awards for best actress in a drama (Davis)

How To with John Wilson
TV-MA, 2020–present
HBO Max, 2 seasons, 12 episodes (AD)
Docuseries created by John Wilson, with John Wilson.

Wilson roams NYC ostensibly to learn how to do mundane things, but his real task is to shrewdly and hilariously observe his fellow humans. Don't expect to learn much but prepare to be amused, even touched, by this strange, comic docuseries. The matching of Wilson's voiceovers to his video, mostly shot on the streets of New York, often yields laugh-out-loud results.

▸▸ A standout episode is "How To Appreciate Wine" (S2E2), which seamlessly segues to a mind-blowing story involving Wilson and the NXIVM sex cult.

▸▸ Wilson admired author Susan Orlean so much, he hired her as a writer on Season 2.

Humans
TV-14, 2015–2018
Prime Video, 3 seasons, 24 episodes (AD)
Sci-fi drama with Gemma Chan, Katherine Parkinson, Emily Berrington, Lucy Carless, Colin Morgan, Theo Stevenson, Tom Goodman-Hill, Ivanno Jeremiah, Carrie-Anne Moss and William Hurt.

People rely on lifelike androids to do everything from clean their homes to fulfill their sexual fantasies — and then the synths become self-aware. It's a familiar sci-fi concept, but with a more expansive take. *Humans* explores the emotional, cultural and psychological nuances of humans going just a bit beyond their present-day dependence on digital devices to actual relationships with anthropomorphic synths. Season 3 was more dystopic and not as well-received, and by then the show was overshadowed by *Black Mirror* and *Westworld*.

The Humans
R, 2021
Showtime original, 1 hr 48 mins
Movie (drama) with Richard Jenkins, Amy Schumer, Steven Yeun, Jayne Houdyshell, Beanie Feldstein and June Squibb.

During a Thanksgiving dinner in a run-down New York apartment, a family's ghosts (metaphorical and possibly literal) start making themselves known. This adaptation of the Tony Award–winning play never feels staged, thanks to the creepy apartment where Brigid (Feldstein) and Richard (Yeun) have gathered their family. The place seems alive, restless, ready to attack the guests. But each of the family members are under siege from their inner demons as well. Not a feel-good holiday flick, *The Humans* is effective as a haunted-house movie.

Hunters
TV-MA, 2020–present
Prime Video original, 10 episodes (AD)
Alternative history with Al Pacino, Logan Lerman, Jeannie Berlin, Jerrika Hinton, Greg Austin, Lena Olin, Kate Mulvany, Louis Ozawa, Dylan Baker and Josh Radnor.

In 1970s New York, an eclectic band of vigilantes race to stop an invasion of America by ex-Nazis intent on launching the Fourth Reich. From producer Jordan Peele and creator David Weil, *Hunters* starts out as a violent, comic-book-style revenge fantasy a la *Inglorious Basterds*. Midway through Season 1, however, it becomes something quite different — an indictment of Western hypocrisy toward escaped Nazis after World War II. And then, as if to say "can you top this," it takes a dramatic turn in the finale, setting up an intriguing second season in 2022.

🗨 **From our forums:** "I had to sort of throw logic out the window, since so much of the timeline made little sense and there were quite a few anachronisms. Once I just went along for the ride it was more fun."

I Am a Killer
TV-MA, 2018–2020
Netflix original, 2 seasons, 20 episodes (AD)
True crime created by Franckie Williams and Romaine Chapman.

Don't be turned off by the title — this is an effective look at the many ripples a

killing creates and the spaces it leaves in multiple lives. Each episode is a relatively nuanced 360-degree examination of an inmate on death row — how they got there, what former cellmates and partners think of them, what law enforcement and prison personnel saw in the crime and everything leading up to it, and how their family and the victim's family have managed in the years since the murders, sharing both their grief and weariness.

I Am Not Okay with This
TV-MA, 2020
Netflix original, 7 episodes (AD)
Dark comedy with Sophia Lillis, Wyatt Oleff, Sofia Bryant, Kathleen Rose Perkins, Richard Ellis, Zachary S. Williams, Aidan Wojtak-Hissong and David Theune.

John Hughes meets *Carrie* in a coming-of-age story with a superhero twist. Sydney (Lillis), a jaded teen in the 1980s, is trying to make sense of the ever-changing dynamics of her high school, family and friends while trying to understand and control an emerging superpower she previously did not have. Jonathan Entwistle (*The End of the F***ing World*) adapts Charles Forsman's graphic novel with a quirky visual style to a strong performance by Lillis and an ensemble of promising young actors.

💬 **From our forums:** "I quite enjoyed this series, short and sweet. A head explosion was not even on my radar, but it was spectacular!"

I Am Not Your Negro
R, 2017
Netflix, Hulu, Hoopla, Kanopy, 1 hr 33 mins (AD)
Movie (documentary) directed by Raoul Peck, with James Baldwin and Samuel L. Jackson (narrator).

Thirty years after social critic James Baldwin died, his unfinished manuscript is the basis for this stunningly up-to-date critique of American race relations. "The future of the Negro in this country is precisely as bright or as dark as the future of the country," Baldwin wrote in *Remember This House*, his incomplete civil rights memoir. Director Peck sets the words of the manuscript to a powerful array of images to suggest Baldwin was a prophet about the Black Lives Matter movement — or perhaps to suggest that America still hasn't learned its lesson on race.

▶▶ Peck followed up this film with *Exterminate All the Brutes* (HBO Max).
🏆 BAFTA for best documentary

I Hate Suzie
TV-MA, 2020–present
HBO Max, 8 episodes (AD)
Comedy created by Billie Piper and Lucy Prebble, with Billie Piper, Leila Farzad, Daniel Ings and Matthew Jordan-Caws.

If you like no-holds-barred satire featuring pop-culture "stars" and the ridiculous entertainment culture that supports them, you'll enjoy this. Everything goes haywire for Suzie Pickles (Billie Piper), a former teen pop star and fading actress, when risqué photos are stolen from her phone and leaked to the press. Each episode takes her a step deeper into celebrity hell, e.g., being offered a role in a Monica Lewinsky–themed musical.

▶▶ Pairs well with *The Other Two*

I Know This Much Is True
TV-MA, 2020
HBO Max, 6 episodes (AD)
Limited series (drama) with Mark Ruffalo, John Procaccino, Rob Huebel, Gabe Fazio, Kathryn Hahn, Melissa Leo, Rosie O'Donnell, Archie Panjabi and Michael Greyeyes.

Enthralling, if depressing, adaptation of Wally Lamb's 1998 novel is carried by Mark Ruffalo's performance in dual

roles. Derek Cianfrance, who co-wrote and directed the adaptation, gets the most out of Ruffalo, who plays both the man trying to get his paranoid schizophrenic twin brother released from an asylum and the brother. Their complicated personal history involves mental illness and a mysterious family past and is undeniably a downer. Maybe don't watch this and *Olive Kitteridge* in the same week.

🗨 **From our forums:** "After 5 episodes staying very true to the book, the final episode departed in several ways. I am trying to decide whether it matters. Mark knocked this out of the park."

🏆 Emmy and SAG awards for best actor in a limited series (Ruffalo).

I Love Dick
TV-MA, 2016–2017
Prime Video original, 8 episodes (AD)
Comedy created by Joel Soloway, with Kathryn Hahn, Kevin Bacon, Griffin Dunne, Roberta Colindrez and Bobbi Salvör Menuez.

Another *tour de force* for Kathryn Hahn, she plays a struggling artist lusting after a colleague of her husband (Kevin Bacon). Following her role in *Afternoon Delight* (like this series, created by Soloway seemingly just for her), Hahn showcased her ability to play sexual frustration and the ennui of married life. Even though the show tackles livewire topics like masculinity, femininity and cultural power, there is surprising nuance in Hahn's portrayal of a woman in control of her body and mind.

I Love Lucy
TV-G, 1951–1957
Paramount+, Hulu, 6 seasons, 181 episodes
Classic sitcom with Lucille Ball, Desi Arnaz, Vivian Vance and William Frawley.

All Lucy Ricardo wants is a career in show business like her bandleader husband Ricky — and she's not letting the lack of any discernible talent stop her! Lucille Ball and Desi Arnaz changed the game with their landmark sitcom that still holds up remarkably well. The first TV comedy to film before a live studio audience (that was Desi's idea), *I Love Lucy* presented a female lead with a gift for physical comedy and a daffy personality that made her relatable to millions of housewives. Which was ironic because, as pointed out by Aaron Sorkin's *Being the Ricardos* (see page 62), Ball wielded tremendous power behind the scenes.

▶▶ Among classic episodes, the one with Vitameatavegamin ("Lucy Does a TV Commercial," S1E30) always leads the list, but also try the ones with William Holden ("L.A. at Last," S4E17) and Harpo Marx (S4E28), the one in the chocolate factory ("Job Switching," S2E1) and "Lucy's Italian Movie" (S5E23), aka the grape-stomping episode.

▶▶ If you enjoyed *Being the Ricardos*, the 2 episodes at the heart of that behind-the-scenes movie are worth a rewatch: "Fred and Ethel Fight" (S1E22) and the one that CBS executives swore would never get made, "Lucy Is Enceinte" (S2E10). *Enceinte* is French for pregnant.

🏆 5 Emmys

I Love You, Now Die
TV-MA, 2019
HBO Max, 2 hrs 23 mins
Movie (documentary) directed by Erin Lee Carr.

Insightful true-crime film about Michelle Carter, a teenager charged with involuntary manslaughter after texting her boyfriend to kill himself. Director Carr does an excellent job of probing the human mind and its tortured ways. Whether or not you like Carter (and you probably won't), after this you likely won't judge her as harshly as those on social media did.

I May Destroy You

TV-MA, 2020
HBO Max, 12 episodes (AD)

Drama created by Michaela Coel, with Michaela Coel, Weruche Opia and Paapa Essiedu.

Michaela Coel wrote and stars in this spectacular take on her own sexual assault that happened while writing her breakthrough show *Chewing Gum*. Honest, confrontational and quirky, this is a bracing jolt of a show at times. At other times it moves at a slower, almost frustrating pace. At no time, however, are you unaware that this is the work of *auteur* Michaela Coel, a fresh new voice on the level of Phoebe Waller-Bridge.

🗨 **From our forums:** "I respect Michaela Coel so much for what she was able to do with this series."

🏆 Peabody Award

I Think You Should Leave with Tim Robinson

TV-MA, 2019–present
Netflix original, 2 seasons, 12 episodes (AD)

Sketch comedy created by Tim Robinson and Zach Kanin, with Tim Robinson, Sam Richardson, Vanessa Bayer, Cicely Strong, Will Forte, Andy Samberg, Fred Willard and Tim Heidecker.

Tim Robinson's sketch-comedy series has a lot of standout material for just 12 episodes. This quick binge has far more hits than misses. Robinson is wonderfully obnoxious as an angry game-show host, an elderly passenger on a transatlantic flight and a late-night TV lawyer. But it's a testament to his writing that some of the show's strongest sketches ("Instagram" and "Baby of the Year") don't even feature him.

I, Claudius

Not Rated, 1976
Acorn TV, Hoopla, 13 episodes

Limited series (historical drama) with Derek Jacobi, John Hurt, Siân Phillips, Patrick Stewart, George Baker, Margaret Tyzack and James Faulkner.

Derek Jacobi led a stellar cast in this groundbreaking 1970s series about the heyday of Ancient Rome and the emperor who was much savvier than he let on. The BBC's adaptation of Robert Graves's novels was ratings gold for PBS's *Masterpiece Theatre* and a defining moment in the history of prestige TV. Derek Jacobi's prosthetic job would never pass muster in the high-def era, but the writing is 21st-century gold — cunning and sensual, wryly funny at times — and was brought to life by British acting royalty.

🏆 Named to *Time*'s 100 All-Time TV Shows (2007) and other all-time lists

I'll Be Gone in the Dark

TV-MA, 2020–2021
HBO Max, 7 episodes (AD)

Limited series (true crime) with Patton Oswalt, Amy Ryan, Lauren Orlando, Paul Haynes, Paul Holes, Karen Kilgariff, Billy Jensen, Larry Crompton, Melanie Barbeau and Nancy Miller.

Adaptation of the late author's true-crime bestseller is as much about the stress of the hunt for the Golden State killer as it is about the hunt itself. Sometimes the story of an investigation is as compelling as the investigation itself. That's certainly true of *I'll Be Gone in the Dark*, a book that blogger Michelle McNamara started but which had to be finished by others because McNamara, the wife of comedian Patton Oswalt, died in her sleep at age 46. Veteran docmaker Liz Garbus tells that story as well as of McNamara's dogged attempts to track down the notorious serial killer of the 1970s and '80s.

🗨 **From our forums:** "This was an entertaining extended series. But

Patton's celebrity no doubt helped the posthumous publication of the book and the production of this series. Otherwise it would have been something only for buffs to obsess over."

Icarus
R, 2017
Netflix original, 2 hrs 1 mins (AD)
Movie (documentary) directed by Bryan Fogel, with Bryan Fogel, Don Catlin, Dave Zabriskie, Grigory Rodchenkov, Ben Stone and Dick Pound.

While making his own guerrilla documentary about doping, amateur cyclist Bryan Fogel finds himself in the middle of an epic doping scandal — and Witness A will only talk to him. In the tradition of Morgan Spurlock, Fogel — a good but not great rider — decides to film himself learning how to dope from insiders, then see how his performance improves. What he doesn't know is that he's about to be connected to a charismatic doctor who just happens to run Russia's anti-doping lab. And then it becomes a buddy film, then a cloak-and-dagger film and then … well, you just have to watch to see what happens next.

🏆 Oscar for best documentary feature

Immigration Nation
TV-MA, 2020
Netflix original, 6 episodes (AD)
Docuseries directed by Christina Clusiau and Shaul Schwarz.

Federal agents with ICE heartlessly, even happily, carry out orders to arrest, incarcerate and deport immigrants. The filmmakers, who embedded with ICE for over 2 years early in the Trump Administration, film agents taking thousands of undocumented immigrants into custody; follow refugee families separated at the border; and observed bureaucrats moving undocumented individuals through deportation proceedings with zest. This footage, plus testimony from gutsy lawyers defending the deportees, make a damning case that American immigration enforcement has gone too far.

🏆 Peabody Award

In Treatment
TV-MA, 2008–present
HBO Max, 4 seasons, 130 episodes (AD)
Drama with Gabriel Byrne, Uzo Aduba, Dianne Wiest, Melissa George, Blair Underwood, Hope Davis, John Mahoney, Debra Winger, Anthony Ramos and Joel Kinnaman.

The talking cure is raised to an art form in these mesmerizing dialogues between patients and their psychologist. Seasons 1–3 featured Paul (Byrne), a psychologist whose own personal life is in shambles, and a rotating set of clients (played by some truly tremendous actors). Paul probes each patient for deeper-seated problems, provides some relief for them, then probes deeper, exposing more pain, treating, repeating … and just when it's all getting to be a bit much, in walks Paul's confidante, conscience and counselor, the pleasant Gina (Wiest). Season 4, which was filmed 11 years after the Byrne seasons, marks a complete reboot, with Aduba as Dr. Brooke Lawrence seeing a new set of clients amid the COVID-19 lockdown.

▶▶ In the show's first season, the episodes (which mostly play out in real-time, like an actual therapy session) aired nightly over the course of 2 months, with each patient recurring on the same day each week.

▶▶ Pairs well with *Couples Therapy*

Industry
TV-MA, 2020–present
HBO Max, 8 episodes (AD)
Drama with Myha'la Herrold, Marisa Abela, Harry Lawtey, David Jonsson,

Nabhaan Rizwan, Conor MacNeill, Freya Mavor, Will Tudor and Ken Leung.

Formulaic but fun finance drama about an ambitious young woman doing what it takes to land a permanent position at a London investment bank. Harper Stern (Herrold) may only have a degree from SUNY-Binghamton, but that's not stopping her from vying for a coveted spot at Pierpoint & Co., one of the UK's top banks. Harper coolly shows she belongs here from the opening scene, immediately establishing chemistry with managing director Eric (Leung). She's accepted along with four others, each with their own TV-drama backstories, and in the pressure cooker of high finance — not to mention the steambath of premium cable — sex and drugs are common releases for the young aspirants. But it's Harper who powers this insider soap, which will doubtless earn comparisons to *Succession* although it is less about wielding power than simply accessing it.

🐟 **From our forums:** "I am fascinated with the relationship between Eric and Harper. They have potential to be the Peggy and Don of this series. A mentor/mentee duo that can both be nurturing and extremely toxic."

The Innocence Files
TV-MA, 2020
Netflix original, 9 episodes (AD)
True crime series created by Alex Gibney, Liz Garbus and Roger Ross Williams.

Top documentary filmmakers take on 8 cases of wrongful conviction championed by The Innocence Project. These well-chosen cases of justice long denied benefit from outstanding access to Innocence Project files, defendants, the victims, their families — even embattled prosecutors and expert witnesses. Possibly the series could have delved more deeply into the structural causes of injustice in the system, but enough clues are here for discerning viewers to realize how vast the problem of wrongful incarceration is.

Insecure
TV-MA, 2016–2021
HBO Max, 5 seasons, 44 episodes (AD)
Comedy created by Issa Rae and Larry Wilmore, with Issa Rae, Yvonne Orji, Jay Ellis, Natasha Rothwell, Amanda Seales and Y'lan Noel.

Issa Rae and Yvonne Orji play besties trying to thrive as 20-something Black women in Los Angeles. This character-driven comedy veers between the everyday and the absurd, using fantasy sequences and hip-hop to speak candidly to the unique problems faced by Black people today. Rae, who co-created and co-writes the series, has created not entirely likable characters but this only lends to the show's emotional heft and humanity.

🐟 **From our forums:** "This show reminds me of *Being Mary Jane*, where you see the characters doing dumb shit that you or your friends have done and wanting to scream some sense into them through the TV, lol."

▶▶ For suggestions of related shows, see "If You Liked *Insecure*," page 373.

🏆 Peabody Award

Inside Amy Schumer
TV-14, 2013–2016
HBO Max, Paramount+, 4 seasons, 39 episodes
Sketch comedy created by Amy Schumer and Daniel Powell, with Amy Schumer.

This is the edgy, self-mocking, feminist sketch series that made Schumer a star. Schumer's standup act, which took on issues like body shame and misogyny, was considered too edgy for Letterman. So, like other marginalized comics, she turned to cable TV and sketch comedy, where her unsparing wit and intelligent approach found its voice and an audience.

🏆 Peabody Award, Emmy for best sketch show

Inside Jokes

TV-14, 2018–present
Prime Video original, 10 episodes (AD)
Comedy with Colin Jost, Chelsea Peretti, Gabriel Iglesias, Hannibal Buress, Rosebud Baker, Alonzo Bodden, Daphnique Springs and Kellen Erskine.

Follow 7 talented, charming standup comics as they compete in the New Faces of Comedy showcase in Montreal. This competition has minted some star names (Amy Schumer, Kevin Hart), so a lot is riding on their success in the elimination rounds. In addition to showing us what talent they have onstage, we also get to know them offstage (where, frankly, some of them are funnier). *Inside Jokes* is insightful in showing how much work the comics put into developing their material. We see a comic trying out the same joke multiple times, at different venues, putting great effort into fine-tuning it between performances, making the joke stronger and stronger, and even then it sometimes lands with a thud.

Instant Hotel

TV-MA, 2017–present
Netflix original, 2 seasons,
18 episodes (AD)
Reality competition.

It's the show for anyone who's stayed at a less-than-perfect rental and wishes they could tell their host what they really think. In this hit Australian competitive reality show, five couples try out each other's Airbnbs and then eviscerate them in the reviews. Unlike actual Airbnb, where guests can be way too understanding, the contestants on *Instant Hotel* have no hesitation about dropping a low score on their stay and saying exactly why.

▶▶ Start at Episode 6, where a new cycle begins and the show finds its groove, thanks to three couples who quickly develop mutual contempt. Their comments on each other's rentals are then read aloud in highly entertaining tribal councils.

The Investigation

TV-MA, 2021
HBO Max, 6 episodes
Limited series (crime drama) directed by Tobias Lindholm, with Søren Malling, Pilou Asbæk, Pernilla August, Rolf Lassgård, Laura Christensen, Dulfi Al-Jabouri and Hans Henrik Clemensen.

Absorbing Danish-language docudrama about a grisly murder doesn't make you feel dirty for watching it. Writer-director Lindholm (*Borgen, Mindhunter*) figured out how to subtract the killer almost entirely from this recreation of the investigation into the crime he committed. No moody flashbacks of the crime, no clichéd focus pulls from a suspect sitting smugly in an interrogation room — the killer here is deprived of agency and importance. The shift in stance from "Why'd he do it?" to "How do we prove what he did and punish him?" is disorienting at first, then just feels right.

Invincible

TV-MA, 2021–present
Prime Video original, 8 episodes (AD)
Animated drama with Steven Yeun, Sandra Oh, J.K. Simmons, Zazie Beetz, Grey Griffin, Kevin Michael Richardson, Walton Goggins, Gillian Jacobs, Zachary Quinto and Andrew Rannells.

Robert Kirkman, who created *The Walking Dead*, scores another fresh

take on a shopworn genre, this time
the superhero comic. Ordinary teen
Mark Grayson (Yeun) knows he has
superpowers, because his father Nolan
(Simmons) is from another planet. But
when those superpowers will finally kick
in serves as the fresh take on an origin
story that defines *Invincible*, a show that
is at turns exhilarating, unsettling, fun
and disturbing. The cartoon violence is
remarkably graphic.

The Irishman
R, 2019
Netflix original, 3 hrs 29 mins (AD)

Movie (drama) directed by Martin
Scorsese, with Robert De Niro, Al Pacino,
Joe Pesci, Stephen Graham, Ray Romano,
Harvey Keitel, Bobby Cannavale, Anna
Paquin, Stephanie Kurtzuba and Jesse
Plemons.

**Martin Scorsese reunites his all-stars —
Robert De Niro, Joe Pesci and Harvey
Keitel — with first-time collaborator
Al Pacino for an acclaimed epic told by
an old, broken mob fixer.** Based on the
true story of Frank Sheeran (De Niro),
a truck driver who becomes a fixer for
union leader Jimmy Hoffa (Pacino), *The
Irishman* begins at the end of Frank's
life, when age has made him wiser. Then,
using CGI, the actors are aged down into
their 1950s youth and it's an old-school
Scorsese film, slowly turning into a
historical drama and then a meditation on
the effects of violence on Frank's life in the
tragic, satisfying final act.
🏆 Nominated for 10 Oscars including
best picture, director and supporting actor
(both Pacino and Pesci)

The Irregulars
TV-14, 2021
Netflix original, 8 episodes (AD)
Crime drama with Henry Lloyd-Hughes,
Royce Pierreson, McKell David, Thaddea

Graham, Jojo Macari, Harrison Osterfield,
Darci Shaw and Clarke Peters.

**Adapted from Arthur Conan Doyle's
Sherlock Holmes novels, the series
follows a group of young troublemakers
who help Watson protect London
from various supernatural forces.** A
reimagining of the Baker Street Irregulars,
featured in several of Arthur Conan
Doyle's Sherlock Holmes mysteries, *The
Irregulars* casts an interesting eye on what
are usually background players in the
Conan Doyle *oeuvre*. If you don't need
Holmes to be in the picture, you'll enjoy
this.

It's Always Sunny in Philadelphia
TV-MA, 2005–present
Hulu, 14 seasons, 154 episodes
Sitcom created by Rob McElhenney,
with Charlie Day, Glenn Howerton, Rob
McElhenney, Kaitlin Olson and Danny
DeVito.

**What at first seemed like a slightly
meaner *Seinfeld* set in a Philly bar
got really weird really fast.** The show's
unlikable ensemble specialized in getting
into stupid, often dangerous situations
while tackling (kind of) issues like racism,
abortion, the drug wars and gun control.
Through dips and peaks in quality over
the years, *It's Always Sunny* has remained
remarkably consistent with the same
talented cast and showrunners on board.

▶▶ Beloved is the holiday episode "A Very
Sunny Christmas" (S6E13), featuring an
epic Santa confrontation. Divisive is the
show from DeVito's first season, "Dennis
and Dee Go on Welfare" (S2E3).

It's a Sin
TV-MA, 2021
HBO Max original, 5 episodes
Limited series (drama) created by Russell
T. Davies, with Olly Alexander, Omari
Douglas, Callum Scott Howells, Lydia

West, Nathaniel Curtis, Shaun Dooley and Keeley Hawes.

Devastatingly beautiful and furious history of the AIDS outbreak in Britain. London in the 1980s is the backdrop for this miniseries about devastating loss and a community's defiant response. In light of the pandemic, it's impossible to watch this tragedy without feeling the pang of recognition, seeing a disease that was able to kill for years amid silence, demonization and shame. There's a righteous anger in this five-parter, but series creator Russell T. Davies (*Queer As Folk*) also celebrates the great, loving, exuberant, beautiful, promising human lives who were lost to AIDS.

Jack Ryan

TV-MA, 2018–present
Prime Video original, 2 seasons,
16 episodes (AD)

Action thriller created by Carlton Cuse and Graham Roland, with John Krasinski, Wendell Pierce, John Hoogenakker, Abbie Cornish, Noomi Rapace and Michael Kelly.

John Krasinski is the X factor that makes this big-budget global action series work. The soft-spoken male romantic interest in *The Office* might not seem like action-hero material, but it turns out Krasinski has just about the right intensity to play Jack Ryan, an old-school CIA operative who knows when to step out of the frame. Pierce, as Jack's boss, brings much more personality to the screen. But it's the strong if conventional storyline and high-dollar action scenes, filmed in 11 countries, that make the show entertaining for more than just Clancy completists.

🗨 **From our forums:** "I enjoyed Season 2 more because it reminded me so much of *Clear and Present Danger.*"

Jack Whitehall: Travels with My Father

TV-MA, 2017–2021
Netflix original, 5 seasons,
18 episodes (AD)

British comedy created by Jack Whitehall, with Jack Whitehall and Michael Whitehall.

The British comedian and actor trots around the globe with his reluctant father in this travel show like no other. Michael Whitehall would rather stay home, a fact not lost on the producers of this series. Jack's journeys with his father through Southeast Asia, Eastern Europe, Australia and the U.S. accentuate differences between the two men's personalities and travel styles to comic effect. Some of the show's best moments come when Jack's mum Hilary Whitehall makes a cameo, lending a touch of sweetness to the proceedings. And amidst the grumbling and personality clashes are warm reminders that Michael and Jack are indeed father and son.

Jane

PG, 2017
Disney+ original, 1 hr 30 mins
Movie (documentary) directed by Brett Morgen, with Jane Goodall.

An intimate biographical trek through the life and career of Jane Goodall, the trailblazing primatologist whose story still has the ability to amaze. Director Morgen's access to previously unseen footage allows us to relive those exciting early years when Goodall established herself as the best-known practitioner of a science practiced exclusively by men, ignoring the condescension of peers and pushing on when funding sources fell through. The film also explores how Goodall learned to use her celebrity to advocate for chimpanzees and the globe's dwindling wild places.

For shows sorted by streaming platform, see page 381.

🏆 2 Emmys, Critics Choice Award for best documentary

Jane Eyre
TV-PG, 2007
BritBox, HBO Max, PlutoTV, 4 episodes
Limited series (romance drama) with Ruth Wilson, Toby Stephens, Lorraine Ashbourne, Aidan McArdle, Pam Ferris, Tara Fitzgerald and Arthur Cox.

The BBC's adaptation of the Brontë classic holds up despite not having Judi Dench in the cast. This four-parter, first appearing in 2007 on PBS *Masterpiece*, gives us a pre–*Luther*, pre–*His Dark Materials* Ruth Wilson, and that's pretty good casting, too. She's convincing as grown-up Jane, who has trouble opening her heart after a tough childhood in Gateshead Hall. The longer runtime allows this *Jane Eyre* to hue more closely to Charlotte Brontë's story, as when Jane flees Thornfield Hall and stays with St. John Rivers — a section of the book usually left out of film adaptations. Stephens, whose mother Maggie Smith is well known to lovers of period drama, is solid as the avuncular Mr. Rochester.

🏆 3 Emmys

Jane the Virgin
TV-PG, 2014–2019
Netflix, 5 seasons, 100 episodes
Romantic comedy with Gina Rodriguez, Andrea Navedo, Yael Grobglas, Justin Baldoni, Ivonne Coll, Jaime Camil, Brett Dier and Anthony Mendez.

The beauty of this effervescent, self-aware *telenovela* is that you don't have to know a thing about *telenovelas* to enjoy it. Jane Villanueva (Rodriguez), an ambitious young woman who's "saving herself" for marriage, gets artificially knocked up by a careless ob-gyn. And this sets in motion 5 years of twists, turns and ever-changing relational tangles involving a talented, unsung cast. *Jane the Virgin*

both Americanizes the *telenovela* format and playfully skewers it, thanks to its secret weapon, the Latin Lover Narrator (Mendez), an all-seeing plot expositor and one-man peanut gallery who manages to dominate the show without hijacking it.

▶▶ Needle-drop at S3E15, "Chapter Fifty-Nine." You'll get up to speed quickly and catch the show at its best.

🏆 Peabody Award

Jayde Adams: Serious Black Jumper
TV-MA, 2020
Prime Video original, 1 hr 7 mins (AD)
Comedy special directed by Peter Orton, with Jayde Adams.

The British comedian and host of Netflix's *Crazy Delicious* applies her thoughtful worldview to topics like: What is the very best wardrobe for feminists? Adams has some brilliant takes on the four waves of feminism (the third wave ended with the Spice Girls), the challenges of being a fat person in a business that worships skinny talent and why dressing in black makes people take you more seriously.

Jean-Claude Van Johnson
TV-MA, 2016–2017
Prime Video original, 7 episodes (AD)
Comedy-drama with Jean-Claude Van Damme, Richard Schiff, Moises Arias, Bar Paly, Phylicia Rashād and Kat Foster.

We learn that Jean-Claude Van Damme's entire movie career was a cover for his actual work as a secret agent. Van Damme is game for this goofy good time, which also stars Rashād as his manager-agency boss and Foster as his former hairdresser-handler. It's not a deep show, but it does feature deliciously stupid set-ups like a kung-fu adaptation of *Tom Sawyer* that covers up a secret mission.

Jericho
TV-14, 2006–2008
Paramount+, 2 seasons, 30 episodes
Dystopian drama created by Jon
Turteltaub, Stephen Chbosky and
Jonathan E. Steinberg, with Skeet Ulrich,
Lennie James, Ashley Scott, Kenneth
Mitchell, Brad Beyer, April Parker Jones,
Alicia Coppola and Pamela Reed.

**Small-town Kansas becomes a refuge
following nuclear holocaust in this
standout network drama from the '00s.**
Jericho was a fine example of the post-
apocalyptic drama that caught on years
after CBS canceled this ratings-challenged
show. Ulrich and Scott delivered strong
performances as the couple who try
to keep order in their town. But it was
Lennie James as Mr. Hawkins — a
mysterious newcomer to Jericho and
its only major Black character — who
emerged as the star of the show, presaging
his role on *The Walking Dead*.

🐾 From our forums: "This show did more
world-building than other shows. We got
a taste of the separate nation started in
Texas, of other countries sending aid to
the United States, of other agents involved
and the organization Ravenwood."

Jim Gaffigan: Quality Time
TV-PG, 2019
Prime Video, Tubi, Hoopla,
1 hr 15 mins (AD)
Comedy special directed by Jeannie
Gaffigan, with Jim Gaffigan.

**Aptly named standup special featuring
the funniest clean comic working today,
with not a wasted moment.** This is
Gaffigan at his best, though a close second
is *Noble Ape* (also on both Prime Video
and Tubi). It's nearly as good as this one,
but the edge goes to *Quality Time* for his
stupendous account of avoiding a bear in
Alaska and his epic, multi-voiced riff on
the most improbable of comedic topics:
horses!

Jim: The James Foley Story
TV-MA, 2016
HBO Max, 1 hr 51 mins
Movie (documentary) directed by Brian
Oakes, with James Foley.

**Most Americans only learned about
freelance journalist Foley after ISIS had
killed him; this personal portrait fills in
the blanks.** Learn about the human being
Jim Foley, what made him want to go to
war-torn Syria, where ISIS captured and
beheaded him, and why his friends and
family miss him terribly.

▶▶ Only available for rental is the
acclaimed documentary *The Journalist
and the Jihadi*, about *Wall Street Journal*
reporter Daniel Pearl's kidnapping and
murder at an earlier moment in the war
on terror.

🏆 Emmy for exceptional merit in
documentary film

Jingle Jangle: A Holiday Journey
PG, 2020
Netflix original, 2 hrs 2 mins (AD)
Movie (family comedy) with Forest
Whitaker, Keegan-Michael Key, Anika
Noni Rose, Phylicia Rashād, Hugh
Bonneville, Ricky Martin, Lisa Davina
Phillip and Madalen Mills.

**Keegan-Michael Key highlights a
mostly Black cast in a musical film
about a toymaker who enlists his
granddaughter in the search for his
stolen book of inventions.** This elaborate
production throws a lot of on-screen
bling at the viewer, but the accumulated
effect is undeniably exhilarating (maybe
exhausting).

The Jinx: The Life and Deaths of
Robert Durst
TV-14, 2015
HBO Max, 6 episodes
Limited series (true crime) directed
by Andrew Jarecki, with Robert Durst,

Jeanine Pirro, Gary Jones and Debrah Lee Charatan.

It's the definitive docuseries about the late real-estate heir turned serial killer. In the 1970s and '80s Durst joined the pantheon of Tri-State terrors around New York when he was suspected of having committed 3 murders over time but eluding justice. For *The Jinx*, Durst cooperated with the filmmakers, whose investigation took 7 years and it shows here. Aesthetically the production is flawless, right up to the end of the docuseries, which has one of the great reveals of the true-crime (or any) TV genre.

▶▶ Jarecki's dogged reporting on another notorious Tri-State case resulted in the exceptional film *Capturing the Friedmans* (see page 82).

🏆 Peabody Award; Emmy for best docuseries; TCA Award for best limited series

Joan Didion: The Center Will Not Hold
TV-14, 2017
Netflix original, 1 hr 32 mins (AD)
Movie (documentary) directed by Griffin Dunne, with Joan Didion.

The actor Griffin Dunne makes a personal and probing documentary about his aunt Joan Didion, one of the lions of contemporary American literature. Despite Didion's reputation as a famous memoirist, Dunne's film is a reminder that even self-revealers reveal what they want to. Using carefully assembled footage, he offers some harsh insight into the realities of being Joan Didion, which he tempers with moments that show his aunt's little-known lighter side.

Joe Pera Talks With You
TV-14, 2018–present
HBO Max, 3 seasons, 32 episodes

Comedy created by Joe Pera, with Joe Pera, Jo Firestone, Conner O'Malley, Gene Kelly and Jo Scott.

Pera plays a fictionalized version of himself as a choir teacher on Michigan's Upper Peninsula who likes to talk to his audience about the everyday things that interest him. Pre-pandemic, these performative takes on ordinary life were termed "stoner TV" by more than one critic. Now we know better — this is *soothing* TV at its best. Pera's trippy ruminations on everything from classic rock and rat control, breakfast foods to babysitting will ease the smiles and laughs out of you.

▶▶ Also look for *Relaxing Old Footage with Joe Pera*, a one-off made during the pandemic, on HBO Max.

John Adams
TV-14, 2008
HBO Max, 7 episodes
Limited series (historical drama) with Paul Giamatti, Laura Linney, Tom Wilkinson, David Morse, Stephen Dillane, Sarah Polley, Mamie Gummer, John Dossett, Samuel Barnett and Justin Theroux.

Before *Hamilton*, this miniseries was the cultural event that made American Revolutionary history cool. Like that musical, this breathes life into the Republic's most crucial Founder — and its most maligned. With a great screenplay written off David McCullough's Pulitzer-winning biography, *John Adams* does what television history is supposed to do: it strips the sepia tone off the portraits of epochal events and restores humanity to their actors. Forget about the fancy clothes and British-sounding accents. Here is a man surrendering uneasily to the march of time. There is nothing inexorable about history when you're in the middle of it. It's a star vehicle for Giamatti, who certainly makes Adams seem like the last guy you'd expect to be starting a political dynasty. And he's wonderfully balanced by Linney's kinder, yet no less steely, performance as Abigail Adams.

🏆 13 Emmys, including best miniseries

John Wayne Gacy: Devil in Disguise

TV-14, 2021

Peacock original, 6 episodes (AD)

Limited series (true crime) directed by Rod Blackhurst, with Robert Ressler and John Wayne Gacy.

This new look at one of America's ghastliest killers highlights the opportunities that authorities missed to neutralize him. Important, well-done yet excruciating revisit of the notorious serial-killer case isn't as interested in Gacy as in the question: Why was he able to keep killing for so long? The value of this docuseries comes in highlighting details that have faded over the decades. In particular, the discovery of Gacy's underground chamber of horrors is a chance to ponder how things might have turned out differently. Includes clips from Gacy's 1992 jailhouse interview with profiler Robert Ressler.

Judas and the Black Messiah

R, 2021

HBO Max, 2 hrs 6 mins (AD)

Movie (historical drama) directed by Shaka King, with Daniel Kaluuya, LaKeith Stanfield, Jesse Plemons, Dominique Fishback, Ashton Sanders, Lil Rel Howery and Martin Sheen.

The police killing of a Black Panther Party leader in 1969 is compellingly presented as a tragedy of biblical proportions. Whether you believe that Fred Hampton, the charismatic head of Chicago's Black Panther organization, could have finished the people's revolution that Martin Luther King started, you'll at least be asking the question after this provocative film. Kaluuya, in an Oscar-winning performance, is magnetic as Hampton, brokering a historic gang truce and preaching a socialist message to Black, brown and white Americans fed up with war and discrimination. That puts him in the crosshairs of the FBI, whose leader J. Edgar Hoover (Sheen) finds a "Judas," in the form of William O'Neal (Stanfield), to infiltrate Hampton's inner circle and deliver him to his executioners. The film plays well as a tragedy in which two Black men who could have accomplished much together are instead pitted against each other.

🏆 2 Oscar wins including supporting actor (Kaluuya)

Julie and the Phantoms

TV-G, 2020

Netflix original, 9 episodes (AD)

Musical comedy directed by Kenny Ortega, with Madison Reyes, Charlie Gillespie, Owen Joyner, Jeremy Shada, Jadah Marie, Sacha Carlson, Savannah Lee May, Carlos Ponce, Booboo Stewart and Sonny Bustamante.

High School Musical **meets the afterlife with catchy songs, sparkling choreography, forbidden love — and ghosts.** Three bandmates die in 1995 only to come back as ghosts in 2020. They meet Julie (Reyes) — a quiet, talented high schooler dealing with the death of her mother — one of the few people who can see them. But when all four of them play music together, *more* people can see them. From this charming premise comes an easy-to-binge musical adventure complete with villain, an otherworldly killjoy who wants to break up the band.

🎙 **From our forums:** "All 3 band members are wonderful and make me miss the '90s. The music is catchy and the songs get stuck in my head. And I am loving the choreography."

🏆 3 Emmys

For shows sorted by streaming platform, see page 381.

Justified

TV-MA, 2010–2015
Hulu, 6 seasons, 78 episodes
Crime drama created by Graham Yost, with Timothy Olyphant, Nick Searcy, Joelle Carter, Jacob Pitts, Erica Tazel, Walton Goggins, Jeremy Davies, Jere Burns, Margo Martindale and Mykelti Williamson.

Timothy Olyphant in his most satisfying role as a marshal drawn back to his troubled hometown of Harlan, Kentucky. He plays Raylan Givens, a character originally developed by novelist Elmore Leonard. A coal miner made good, Givens returns to his corner of Appalachia to find an insular community using violence and theft to keep the outside world at bay. For an upright lawman this will never do, but thanks to great performances from Williamson, Martindale, Davies and Goggins as residents of the holler, you understand why they would fight to protect their way of life.

🏆 Peabody Award, Emmy for best supporting actress in a drama (Martindale)

Keep Your Hands Off Eizouken!

TV-14, 2020
HBO Max, 12 episodes
Animated comedy with Sairi Ito, Mutsumi Tamura and Misato Matsuoka.

People who never thought they'd enjoy anime will find this story about a young anime artist irresistible. Based on a popular manga series, this meta-anime series revolves around Asakusa, a high school girl who recruits two friends to help her make it in the anime industry. It's a story about world-building and the harsh realities of show business (the Asian animation industry is no bed of roses). But it's also an enchanting story about that teenage desire to find a place in the world without leaving the cocoon of childhood.

The Keepers

TV-MA, 2017
Netflix original, 7 episodes (AD)
Limited series (true crime) directed by Ryan White.

An often shocking investigation into the death of a nun casts a light on the Catholic Church's coverup of sexual predation. Gemma Hoskins and Abbie Schaub are two women looking into the death of Sister Cathy Cesnik, who taught them in Catholic school. They're charming and inspiring amateur sleuths, persistent and effective, and they carry us along in their dogged pursuit of the truth in a case that the rest of the world has seemingly forgotten. As necessary as the feature film *Spotlight*, *The Keepers* was unfairly overlooked amid the tidal wave of true-crime Netflix docuseries.

💬 **From our forums:** "This is a tough series to watch, I might not be able to binge this one."

Keeping Up With the Kardashians

TV-14, 2006–2021
Hulu, Peacock, 20 seasons, 294 episodes
Celebreality show created by Ryan Seacrest and Eliot Goldberg, with Khloe Kardashian, Kim Kardashian West, Kourtney Kardashian, Kris Jenner, Kendall Jenner, Kylie Jenner, Caitlyn Jenner and Scott Disick.

Who wants to be a billionaire? Various polls have found that a leading goal of young people today is "being famous." The Kardashian sisters, whose wealth initially came from their late father's fortune, built a billion-dollar empire by speaking directly to this demographic. Paris Hilton, who at the peak of her fame hired Kim Kardashian as an assistant, didn't have the staying power of her mentee because she didn't have Kris Jenner as her mom. As ringmaster and chief strategist of *KUWTK* (as the show's long title is rendered), she has done for the Kardashian-Jenner-

West clan what Francis Ford Coppola did for the Corleones — she made them mythic. This is not to say that this show, or its 9 spinoffs, aspire to greatness. But watch an episode (don't worry, your eyes won't fall out) and you'll see that the Kardashians, like the old syndicates, are relentless about the family business. It is in every contrived storyline, every product placement, every image. At its peak *KUTWK* was uncannily tuned into what its audience found fascinating about the Kardashians.

Kevin Can F**k Himself

TV-MA, 2021–present
AMC+, 8 episodes
Dark comedy with Annie Murphy, Eric Petersen, Raymond Lee, Mary Hollis Inboden, Alex Bonifer and Brian Howe.

Annie Murphy (*Schitt's Creek*) plays a woman trapped inside a retro sitcom about a man who is terrible to his wife. In this strange take on the show-within-a-show, Allison (Murphy) is forced to interact brightly during scenes with her sitcom husband Kevin (Petersen). Away from Kevin and his buddies, though, she lives a second existence in a depressing personal hell she longs to escape. The show is carried by Murphy's strong performance as a woman who has gone along to get along for far too long. This is a strong character drama and a savage skewering of a genre we all grew up with.

🗨 **From our forums:** "Something that surprises me is I'm starting to see Allison as the villain of her story more than Kevin."

Kidding

TV-MA, 2018–2020
Showtime original, 2 seasons, 20 episodes
Dark comedy with Jim Carrey, Catherine Keener, Frank Langella, Justin Kirk, Judy Greer, Cole Allen and Juliet Morris.

Jim Carrey is endearing as a Mister Rogers–type TV host who struggles when the cameras are off. Picking up where he left off all too long ago with *The Truman Show* and *Man in the Moon*, Carrey reminds us what he can do as a dramatic actor as he shifts seamlessly between his chipper on-air persona and his grief-stricken private self. The two-season arc of *Kidding* also affords the writers the time to demonstrate in depth how the inherent optimism of doing a kids' program can slowly liberate the people in pain behind the camera.

The Kids Are Alright

TV-PG, 2018–2019
Hulu, 23 episodes
Sitcom created by Tim Doyle, with Mary McCormack, Jack Gore, Sam Straley, Caleb Foote, Sawyer Barth, Christopher Paul Richards, Andy Walken, Santino Barnard, Michael Cudlitz and Tim Doyle.

In this poignant sitcom, blue-collar Catholic parents raise their eight sons during the cultural upheavals of 1970s L.A. A network comedy with a large cast made up mostly of kid actors doesn't sound promising, but *The Kids Are Alright* won critics and viewers over with its funny and warm depictions of family life in the turbulent summer of 1972.

🗨 **From our forums:** "I hadn't watched a network TV comedy in many years, but this show had me hooked." "They developed the characters so well in such a short amount of time."

The Killing (US)

TV-14, 2011–2014
Hulu, IMDb TV, 4 seasons, 44 episodes
Crime drama with Mireille Enos, Joel Kinnaman, Billy Campbell, Liam James, Michelle Forbes, Brent Sexton, Kristin Lehman, Eric Ladin, Jamie Anne Allman and Annie Corley.

Some shows may have moved; see page 183. **177**

Two detectives learn to work together to solve murders in an especially gloomy, rainy Seattle. Based on Danish series *Forbrydelsen*, this cliffhanger-filled drama paired performances from Enos and Kinnaman that critics raved about. Fans of Stieg Larsson thrillers will find the mix of crime and character engaging.

🗨 **From our forums:** "I adore both lead characters and I've found all the cases pretty absorbing." "I watch primarily for the bleak atmosphere and theme music and the interaction between Linden and Holder. The cases themselves leave little or no impression."

▶▶ The original *Forbrydelsen* is available on Topic, a $5.99/month streaming service specializing in Nordic Noir.

Killing Eve
TV-14, 2018–2022
Hulu, AMC+, 4 seasons, 32 episodes (AD)
Action drama with Sandra Oh, Jodie Comer, Fiona Shaw and Kim Bodnia.

Sandra Oh and Jodie Comer play an audacious game of cat-and-mouse in this engrossing thriller. For four seasons, *Killing Eve* tracked the relationship between Eve Polastri (Oh), a spy obsessed with Villanelle (Comer), the female assassin she's trying to apprehend. They are both playful and vicious with each other, giving a gonzo energy to their globe-trotting chase. Phoebe Waller-Bridge *Fleabag* penned the show's magical first season, with a new female head writer taking over each subsequent season.

🏆 Peabody Award; Emmy for best actress in a drama (Comer); SAG Award for best actress in a drama (Oh)

Kim's Convenience
TV-14, 2016–2021
Netflix, 5 seasons, 65 episodes
Sitcom with Paul Sun-Hyung Lee, Jean Yoon, Andrea Bang, Simu Liu, Andrew Phung and Nicole Power.

Culturally astute slice-of-life sitcom revolves around a close-knit Korean-Canadian family that runs a store in Toronto. Three-dimensional characters and small storytelling bring to life the immigrant experience in its many absurd, charming and intimate ways.

🗨 **From our forums:** "I found this show utterly delightful, and some hamminess that bothered me a little at the beginning mellowed as I grew to love the characters."

King of the Hill
TV-PG, 1997–2010
Hulu, 13 seasons, 258 episodes
Animated comedy created by Mike Judge and Greg Daniels, with Mike Judge, Kathy Najimy, Pamela Adlon, Stephen Root, Brittany Murphy and Johnny Hardwick.

Classic cartoon sitcom set in Texas revolved around the deceptively humdrum world of propane salesman Hank Hill, his wife Peggy, son Bobby and their oddball neighbors. Easy to forget because it's no longer in production — and didn't log nearly the mileage of *The Simpsons* or *Family Guy* — *King of the Hill* remains a fan favorite for its easygoing pace, relatable storylines and characters people love to mimic. Indeed, *Beavis and Butt-Head* creator Mike Judge built this world based on his observations while living in Austin. With help from showrunner Daniels (*The Office*), the characters on this show were the most well-rounded of any in the Judge canon.

▶▶ Needle-drop at Season 2, which saw the emergence of trashy Luanne, one of the show's best characters, as well as Hank's stint at the Mega Lo Mart and a cliffhanger that triggered real-life rumors as to whether trumpeter Chuck Mangione had died.

Kingdom

TV-MA, 2019–present
Netflix original, 2 seasons, 13 episodes, dubbed
Thriller with Ju Ji-hoon, Ryu Seung-ryong, Bae Doo-na, Kim Sang-ho, Kim Sung-kyu and Kim Hye-jun.

South Korean zombie series will even appeal to viewers who think they've tired of the genre. Set in medieval Korea, where zombies threaten the ruling dynasty, this drama depicts the undead as a threat not just to the main characters but to the entire country. Both the foreign locations and the time period offer plenty of exotic color for Western viewers and a refreshing change of pace from other recent zombie dramas. The heroes have few guns and must fight the undead with swords, bows, or martial arts. The zombie rules are different from other shows and the short season makes this not the grueling slog that *The Walking Dead* could be.

▶▶ A bonus feature length episode of the series was produced in 2021, titled "Ashin of the North."

Kiri

TV-MA, 2018
Hulu, 4 episodes
Limited series (crime drama) with Sarah Lancashire, Lucian Msamati, Lia Williams, Wunmi Mosaku, Steven Mackintosh and Paapa Essiedu.

The second installment of the UK *National Treasure* **crime anthology explores the kidnapping and killing of a young Black girl and the complicated web of culpability surrounding it.** *Kiri* is not as depressing as its premise suggests, thanks largely to the starring role of Lancashire (*Happy Valley*) as Kiri's no-nonsense social worker, whose normally thankless job takes an awful turn after the child's death. Like the original *National Treasure*, this is a compelling exploration of the ripple effects of crime.

The Kissing Booth

TV-14, 2018
Netflix original, 1 hr 45 mins (AD)
Movie (romantic comedy) with Joey King, Jacob Elordi and Joel Courtney.

Joey King plays a late-blooming teenager whose romance with a bad boy could threaten her long-term friendship with the boy's younger brother. This critic-proof movie was so popular it launched 2 sequels and helped launch the era of streaming romcoms.

Klaus

PG, 2019
Netflix original, 1 hr 36 mins (AD)
Movie (animated comedy) with Jason Schwartzman, J.K. Simmons, Joan Cusack, Norm Macdonald, Will Sasso and Rashida Jones.

Hand-drawn animated film reimagines the Santa Claus origin story as a tale about an indolent postman and a toymaker who lives in the woods. Who hasn't written a letter to Santa, trusting that the mailman will get it to him? That's the premise for this cheerfully wacky fable about a tradition that's, sadly, on the wane in an era of electronic mail. Jesper (Schwartzman), a spoiled adult child, is packed off to a remote village in the Arctic to learn how to deliver the mail — and meets Klaus (Simmons), who will help him find his meaning in life, answering the letters of children.

▶▶ The impressive voice-actor cast is for the English-language version; *Klaus* was originally produced in Spanish and is available in a number of languages.

🏆 BAFTA win and Oscar nomination for best animated feature film

For shows sorted by streaming platform, see page 381.

Knock Down the House
TV-PG, 2019
Netflix original, 1 hr 27 mins (AD)
Movie (documentary) directed by Rachel Lears, with Alexandria Ocasio-Cortez and Cori Bush.

Women motivated by Donald Trump's election run for Congress in 2018, but the odds are stacked against them. An activist group recruited dozens of potential candidates to run in the 2018 elections, including Democratic primary challenges. The star of the show is AOC, a hard-working bartender who lights up the frame and every room she walks into. But just as compelling, if more poignant, are all the women set up in contests they have no chance of winning. Perhaps the big takeaway is that persistence — and publicity — pay off. You'll see a St. Louis nurse and pastor run an unsuccessful primary campaign; thanks in part to *Knock Down the House*, she tried again in 2020 and won.

The L Word
TV-MA, 2004–2009
Showtime original, 6 seasons, 70 episodes
Romance drama created by Ilene Chaiken, Michele Abbot and Kathy Greenberg, with Jennifer Beals, Leisha Hailey, Laurel Holloman, Mia Kirshner, Katherine Moennig and Pam Grier.

There's more queer-friendly TV than ever, yet the shiny, soapy world of *The L Word* remains an escape unlike any other. This pioneering drama about gay and bisexual women in West Hollywood — and their many, many paramours — was nothing special as prime-time soaps go. But it launched in an election year when same-sex marriage had emerged as a wedge issue, which thrust it into the cultural conversation. More significantly, many women saw themselves and their dramas represented in a mainstream TV show for the first time and this gave the show an enthusiastic following. Though Beals was originally touted as the lead, fan interest tended to hover around Kirshner's conniving Jenny Schecter and Moennig's sexy, androgynous Shane.

💬 **From our forums:** "The second time around I enjoy just how far off the deep end Jenny went."

▸▸ After the show's final season in 2009, a companion docuseries launched, *The Real L Word*. Then in 2019 came a spinoff, *The L Word: Generation Q*, featuring several of the original show's characters plus an ensemble of younger, more diverse and politically active queer people.

La Llorona
Not Rated, 2019
AMC+, 1 hr 37 mins
Movie (horror) directed by Jayro Bustamante, with María Mercedes Coroy, Sabrina De La Hoz, Margarita Kenéfic, Julio Diaz, María Telón, Juan Pablo Olyslager and Ayla-Elea Hurtado.

The spirits of native Mayans murdered by a Guatemalan general begin to haunt him and his family. This stylish horror film merges ancient legend and contemporary politics. If you don't remember the Guatemalan civil war of the early 1980s, director Bustamante will sear it into your memory through a chilling tale involving a housekeeper (Coroy) who comes to work for the embattled general charged with war crimes (Diaz), in a film built around the legend of *la Llorona*, the "weeping woman."

🏆 Peabody Award

The Lady and the Dale
TV-14, 2021
HBO Max, 4 episodes (AD)
Docuseries directed by Nick Cammilleri and Zackary Drucker.

The true story of Liz Carmichael and her three-wheeled car is actually

half a dozen stories — and they're all fascinating. Carmichael was the entrepreneur behind the Dale automobile that became a brief marketing sensation in the mid-1970s. Over four smartly-constructed episodes, *Lady and the Dale* chronicles her rise to fame and fall from grace, plus a few crazy twists and turns her life story took. Of note is the crusade by pot-stirrers Dick and Tucker Carlson (yes, that Tucker Carlson) to expose Carmichael — who identified as a man — and "try" her in the court of public opinion.

Lady Dynamite

TV-MA, 2016–2017
Netflix original, 2 seasons,
20 episodes (AD)

Comedy created by Pam Brady and Mitchell Hurwitz, with Maria Bamford, Fred Melamed, Mary Kay Place, Ana Gasteyer, Mo Collins, Ólafur Darri Ólafsson, Lennon Parham and Bridget Everett.

Surreal comedy about a stand-up comic who returns to her hometown after a nervous breakdown, then tries to restart her career. If you're expecting a hard-edged show rife with badass humor, look elsewhere. Based on Bamford's real-life struggles with mental illness, this is a humorous, heartfelt exploration of the mind of a comedian who is trying to succeed on her second attempt at show business, this time with self-care. Maria's pug dog occasionally talks and her manager appears on screen as a sheep, but through these fantasies Maria aims to create a better reality than the one that brought her old life crashing down on her.

🐾 From our forums: "It's even weirder than I expected it to be and I'm occasionally off-put by how crude it is. But I love Maria Bamford and am delighted to see her display her bizarre brilliance in a new medium."

Lake Mungo

R, 2009
AMC+, Prime Video, 1 hr 27 mins
Movie (horror) directed by Joel Anderson, with Rosie Traynor, David Pledger, Martin Sharpe and Talia Zucker.

After a teenage girl disappears, her family makes startling discoveries about her double life. Aptly called an "Oz mockumentary," this is one of those movies, completely overlooked at the time, that has developed a major cult following thanks to streaming services.

▶▶ Prime Video lists the title as *After Dark: Lake Mungo*, but don't worry, it's the same movie.

Landscapers

TV-MA, 2021
HBO Max, 4 episodes (AD)
Limited series (crime drama) with Olivia Colman, David Thewlis, Kate O'Flynn, Dipo Ola, Samuel Anderson, Felicity Montagu, David Hayman and Maanuv Thiara.

In this genre-defying crime series, Olivia Colman and David Thewlis play a mild-mannered English couple who plot to kill her parents and bury them in the back yard. Though it's based on true events, this is an arrestingly strange series. The stylized direction might switch to black and white for a romantic scene between the central couple, or suddenly get bathed in red light during violent moments. Detectives might be played for laughs, bumbling their way through their investigation, before becoming remarkably poignant a few scenes later. This creates the perfect, off-kilter milieu for Thewlis and Colman's characters, who love each other, love their garden, and have absolutely no trouble hiding their crime for over a decade.

Some shows may have moved; see page 183. **181**

The Larkins

TV-14, 2021–present
Prime Video, Roku Channel, Acorn TV,
7 episodes
Family comedy-drama with Bradley
Walsh, Joanna Scanlan, Sabrina Bartlett,
Davina Coleman, Rosie Coleman,
Liam Middleton, Lydia Page and Lola
Shepelev.

**Good-natured series about a randy scrap
dealer, his large, happy family and the
nearby village with the usual assortment
of eccentrics.** This popular British drama,
the latest adaptation of H.E. Yates's
beloved 1958 novel *The Darling Buds of
May*, revolves around the simple pleasures
of life: eating, enjoying the great outdoors
and fooling around.

The Larry Sanders Show

TV-MA, 1992–1998
HBO Max, 6 seasons, 89 episodes
Classic sitcom created by Dennis
Klein and Garry Shandling, with Garry
Shandling, Jeffrey Tambor, Wallace
Langham, Rip Torn, Penny Johnson
Jerald and Janeane Garofalo.

**One of the most influential sitcoms
in history remains one of the best
depictions of show-business culture.**
Would HBO have taken a chance with
The Sopranos if not for *The Larry Sanders
Show*? Would single-camera comedies
have caught on? Was there ever a more
prescient sitcom, with its uncanny read
on the Leno-Letterman late-night wars,
arguably *the* biggest industry story during
the 1990s? Decide for yourself as you
watch Shandling play embattled host
Larry Sanders in an alternate talk-show
universe graced by real-life celebrities
(including, in a memorable scene,
Letterman). Bask in the ego of Larry's
fatuous sidekick Hank (Tambor) and
his pitiless showrunner Arthur (Torn).
The show is adorned with topical jokes
that have lost their sting, but mostly the
comedy holds up.
🏆 3 Emmys (from 56 nominations, a
record at the time for HBO)

The Last Alaskans

TV-14, 2015–present
Discovery+, 4 seasons, 36 episodes
Reality show with Heimo Korth, Edna
Korth, Tyler Selden, Ashley Selden,
Charlie Jagow, Bob Harte, Ray Lewis and
Cindy Lewis.

**Four families living in the Arctic
National Wildlife Refuge face challenges
daily.** Utterly unlike any other reality
show, this is a visually spectacular,
life-affirming show in which reality,
not manufactured drama, is the appeal.
The families are seen living deliberate,
thoughtful, calm lives. Long, extended
takes of the landscape and people are
common on this show, which clearly sees
no need to feed short attention spans.

Last Chance U

TV-MA, 2016–2020
Netflix original, 5 seasons,
40 episodes (AD)
Docuseries created by Greg Whiteley.

**Netflix docuseries found a gold mine
of drama in the junior colleges where
athletes have one last shot at impressing
recruiters at the schools that hand
out scholarships.** The first four seasons
profiled national "juco" powerhouses
stacked with top football talent trying
to make it back to the big schools. These
athletes made the most (or least) of their
last shots to play the game they love as
coaches filled with personality try to get
another ring and keep the kids focused.
▶▶ One knock against *Last Chance U* was
that the coaches played to the cameras
too much. For Season 5, though, the show
relocated to Laney College in inner-city
Oakland, Calif., where students commute
daily, pay their own way and play for a

Some Shows May Have Moved

One of the most frustrating aspects of watching Streaming TV — and of creating this guide — is the fluid movement of shows between streaming platforms. These moves, driven by rights deals, confound the viewer who goes looking for a particular show only to find it missing.

There are four reasons TV shows and movies change streaming platforms:

► **They're streaming hits:** Iconic series like *Seinfeld, The Office, Breaking Bad* and *Mad Men* are the most-watched shows in streaming year after year. Whenever their rights come up, a bidding war ensues and the show often winds up on a new platform.

► **They're needed at home:** Before 2018, most studios signed deals with Netflix or Hulu to stream their shows. Now their parent companies also have streaming platforms, and getting the rights to their own shows is a top priority. WarnerMedia (HBO Max) paid an estimated $1 billion for the streaming rights to *The Big Bang Theory* and *Two and a Half Men,* two shows produced *by* Warner.

► **They're free agents:** Content from independent producers or studios outside the USA tends to be more fluid. As we were putting this book to press, for example, *The Repair Shop,* which is produced in England, quietly hopped from Netflix to Discovery+.

► **They're old:** Legacy content still has value but there's less demand for it, so it gets bundled into bulk streaming deals that seemingly expire at random, as evidenced by those online postings of "what's leaving Netflix and Hulu this month."

Good news: We expect nearly all of the listings in Part II to remain accurate, because *The Primetimer Guide to Streaming TV* is focused on newer content — especially **originals,** shows and movies produced expressly for the platforms where they stream. We also expect this fluidity to settle down in the future somewhat, as more content is produced exclusively for streaming platforms.

In the meantime, if you find yourself typing "where is X streaming" into a search engine because a show isn't where we say it is, our apologies.

head coach who's bred champions for decades and couldn't care less about stardom.

Last Chance U: Basketball
TV-MA, 2021–present
Netflix original, 8 episodes (AD)
Docuseries with John Mosley.

The first Black coach on the popular Netflix docuseries admirably embodies the notion of sports as being more than a game. Coach John Mosley turned around the East Los Angeles College Huskies men's basketball team by recruiting promising athletes with this simple mercenary proposition: Play for me and earn a scholarship to a four-year college. During the 2019–20 season, when Netflix's cameras followed him around, this scrappy coach was blessed with a bumper crop of talent, each of whom will have to overcome some major obstacle to get to the next level. What sets this *Last Chance U* apart is Mosley, whose involvement in his players' lives is total.

▶▶ Pairs well with *We Are: The Brooklyn Saints*

The Last Dance
TV-MA, 2020
Netflix original, 10 episodes (AD)
Docuseries directed by Jason Hehir, with Michael Jordan, Phil Jackson, Scottie Pippen, Steve Kerr and Dennis Rodman.

Even non-basketball fans can easily immerse themselves in this series made from unseen footage of Michael Jordan and other members of the 1990s Chicago Bulls dynasty in their final season. Aware that Bulls management planned to break up the team after the 1997–98 season, the NBA sent a film crew to capture the happenings behind the scenes. Weaving current interviews with Jordan and others into the compelling footage, *The Last Dance* captures a unique organization of talented and unusual individuals

squeezing out one last hurrah before the music stops.

🏆 Emmy for best docuseries

The Last Man on Earth
TV-14, 2015–2018
Hulu, 4 seasons, 66 episodes (AD)
Sitcom created by Will Forte, with Will Forte, Kristen Schaal, January Jones, Mel Rodriguez, Cleopatra Coleman and Mary Steenburgen.

Will Forte plays a survivor of apocalyptic plague who decides that anything goes — until he meets a woman who thinks it's fun to follow the rules. The show's charm is that it gets you to care about Phil Miller (Forte). At the outset he is frankly a huge jerk who plans to play by his own rules and that goes badly, but then he meets Carol (Schaal), who gives him new reason to live and some badly needed structure.

💬 **From our forums:** "I'm a fairly morbid person and have been rewatching this show since the lockdown. Season 2 to mid–season 3 was some really, really enjoyable TV."

Law & Order
TV-14, 1990–2010
Peacock, 20 seasons, 456 episodes
Crime drama created by Dick Wolf, with Jerry Orbach, Sam Waterston, Jesse L. Martin, S. Epatha Merkerson, Steven Hill, Leslie Hendrix, Fred Thompson, Chris Noth and Benjamin Bratt.

Though best watched today with a jaundiced eye, *L&O* in its prime took the police procedural to new heights. The show's unambivalent faith in the criminal justice system makes it the original "copaganda" show, but no writers' room was better at ripping legal and ethical dilemmas from the headlines and turning them into light entertainment. *L&O* creator Wolf insisted that the format was the thing and that stars were interchangeable, a point he seemingly proved when he let several original cast members go and the show's ratings hardly budged. But in Orbach's Lennie Briscoe, who joined in Season 3, *L&O* gained a character who actually bent the format to his crusty personality. Orbach became the heart and soul of the show and when he died after Season 14, it was never was the same.

▶▶ Needle-drop at Season 4, which marked the arrival of Merkerson and Jill Hennessy, the show's most memorable female leads, and the last for Michael Moriarty and Noth. The next four seasons, through its Emmy-winning Season 7, are the high water mark of *L&O*.

🏆 6 Emmys including best drama series (Season 7)

▶▶ As this book went to press, NBC announced plans to revive *Law & Order* for a 21st season in 2022.

Law & Order: SVU

TV-14, 1999–present
Hulu, 22 seasons, 494 episodes (AD)
Crime drama created by Dick Wolf, with Mariska Hargitay, Christopher Meloni, Ice-T, Dann Florek, Richard Belzer, BD Wong, Kelli Giddish and Tamara Tunie.

Not just the most durable *Law & Order* spinoff but the best-executed and most popular of all the *L&O*s, including the original. Long before the #MeToo or streaming eras, it wasn't obvious that a cop procedural focused on sex crimes would be a hit. But as TV got more nichified, the show's intense focus and strong female leads — Hargitay as the fiercely empathetic Benson and Giddish as high-functioning hot mess Rollins — have made *SVU* impossible for many fans to turn off.

🏆 Emmy for best actress in a drama series (Hargitay)

The League

TV-MA, 2009–2015
Hulu, 7 seasons, 84 episodes
Comedy created by Jeff Schaffer and Jackie Marcus Schaffer, with Mark Duplass, Jonathan Lajoie, Nick Kroll, Stephen Rannazzisi, Paul Scheer and Katie Aselton.

Old friends take part in a football fantasy league that brings out their cranky sides — think *Seinfeld* meets *Curb Your Enthusiasm*, only with sports. Husband-wife creators Jeff Schaffer and Jackie Marcus Schaffer created a fresh TV comedy that began as loose outlines and had a spontaneous feel to them. Wonderfully deranged and weirdly specific, *The League* boasted a strong ensemble of annoying characters.

🗨 **From our forums:** "I'll never get tired of 'Taco drafts guys who are no longer in the NFL' jokes. These and other little gags really sell this show as one made by fans of fantasy football."

Leaving Neverland

TV-MA, 2019
HBO Max, 3 hrs 56 mins
Movie (documentary) directed by Dan Reed, with Wade Robson, James Safechuck, Joy Robson, Chantal Robson, Stephanie Safechuck, Laura Primak and Amanda Robson.

Wade Robson and James Safechuck recount how pop superstar Michael Jackson allegedly sexually abused them when they were children, and they discuss how that abuse has continued to affect them as adults. Not unlike *Allen v. Farrow*, this account is told exclusively from the victims' point of view. But it neither extols the accusers nor condemns the accused. It's clearly aimed at the viewer who, like the victims and their families, adored Michael Jackson's music but needs to have this story out in the world.

▶▶ Following its premiere at the 2019

Sundance Film Festival, the four-hour film was split in 2 parts for television.

🏆 Emmy for best documentary

The Leftovers
TV-MA, 2014–2017
HBO Max, 3 seasons, 28 episodes
Fantasy drama created by Damon Lindelof and Tom Perrotta, with Justin Theroux, Carrie Coon, Amy Brenneman, Christopher Eccleston, Chris Zylka, Liv Tyler, Ann Dowd, Jovan Adepo, Margaret Qualley and Regina King.

Emotional, character-driven social experiment asks: What if 2 percent of the world's population mysteriously vanished? Building on themes of loss and otherworldliness that he developed in *Lost*, Damon Lindelof breaks with the conventions of network TV to capture the endless grief and sense of aimlessness that most shows want to wrap up with a bow. Carrie Coon plays a woman who loses her entire family to this Rapture-like event, then travels the world to find her purpose in life. She is the show's emotional center and someone who demands from viewers that they stay uncomfortable with her.

🗨 **From our forums:** "The second half of the first season is much better than the first half. Fans of Carrie Coon will really appreciate Episode 6, 'Guest.' But the second and third seasons are where the show gets its reputation as one of the best shows of the decade."

🏆 TCA Award for individual achievement in drama (Coon)

Legendary
TV-MA, 2020–present
HBO Max original, 2 seasons,
19 episodes (AD)
Reality competition with Jameela Jamil, Law Roach, Leiomy Maldonado, Megan Thee Stallion and Dashaun Wesley.

Lack of prior exposure to competitive queer ballroom is no barrier to understanding and hugely enjoying *Legendary*. Prominent houses from the "ball" scene compete in weekly modeling, performance and dance challenges. They're judged by a panel that includes insiders in the queer-trans ball scene and complete outsiders like Jameela Jamil, who basically needs everything explained to her. *Legendary* knows much of its audience might be as unfamiliar with the world of ballroom as Jamil and is ready and willing to give everyone an education. It's a welcoming show that never feels condescending.

Legion
TV-MA, 2017–2019
Hulu, 3 seasons, 27 episodes
Sci-fi drama created by Noah Hawley, with Dan Stevens, Rachel Keller, Aubrey Plaza, Bill Irwin, Jeremie Harris, Amber Midthunder, Hamish Linklater and Jean Smart.

This TV adaptation of the X-Men comics, from the creator of the *Fargo* series, created its own weirdly distinctive world. In the hands of Noah Hawley, *Legion* blends futuristic technology, retro aesthetics and trippy visuals. Stevens leads the cast with a performance that recalls the comic book character's manic humor while still grounding it in the show's world and story.

🗨 **From our forums:** "Probably the only Marvel-related show to feature a dance-off. I think I'm going to need a few more rewatches but WTF, I loved it." "I liked it more as it went on, but I agree it was a strange trip and often hard to comprehend."

Lenox Hill
TV-MA, 2020–present
Netflix original, 9 episodes (AD)
Docuseries created by Adi Barash and Ruthie Shatz.

You'll love these dedicated health

professionals working in the heart of New York City even before COVID-19 strikes. Two neurosurgeons, an ob-gyn and an ER doctor provide care to a wide range of patients. As they grapple with a dizzying amount of harrowing problems — everything from brain tumors to problem pregnancies to TMJ — we bask in the simple goodness of their competency and care. But it all pales compared to what happens in the concluding episode, filmed during the early weeks of the pandemic, when Lenox Hill Hospital finds itself at Ground Zero of a terrifying outbreak.

Les Misérables

TV-14, 2019
PBS Passport, 6 episodes
Limited series (historical drama) with David Oyelowo, Dominic West, Lily Collins, David Bradley, Olivia Colman, Ellie Bamber and Josh O'Connor.

Here is a fulsome, PBS-worthy take on Hugo's epic tale. This miniseries uses its copious runtime to expand on characters who normally don't get explored in shorter adaptations. In particular Fantine (Collins) and Marius (O'Connor) shine in their newly brightened spotlights.

The Letdown

TV-MA, 2017–present
Netflix, 2 seasons, 13 episodes (AD)
Comedy with Alison Bell, Duncan Fellows, Leon Ford, Sacha Horler, Lucy Durack, Celeste Barber, Leah Vandenberg, Noni Hazlehurst and Xana Tang.

Absorbing Australian comedy about parenting a newborn is full of moments both absurd and tender. Part of a trifecta of catty imports about parenting (*Breeders*, *Workin' Moms*), *The Letdown* follows the amusing and often poignant travails of four very different women whose worlds slowly intertwine through a new mommy group. Somehow Anna (played by co-creator Bell), a disheveled, atheistic feminist, finds common cause with high-powered executive Ester (Horler), stay-at-homer Barb (Barber) and Instagram mommy Sophie (Durack) through the fresh hell they're all going through.

Letterkenny

TV-MA, 2016–present
Hulu original, 10 seasons, 65 episodes (AD)
Comedy created by Jared Keeso, with Jared Keeso, Nathan Dales, Michelle Mylett, Andrew Herr, K. Trevor Wilson, Dylan Playfair, Tyler Johnston and Evan Stern.

Cult Canadian series proved so popular when it dropped on Hulu that Hulu ordered more episodes. Wayne and Daryl are friends who spend their time musing about life in a fictional rural Ontario town — a premise not unlike *Detectorists* and other slow-germinating comedy favorites. They're not the most enlightened fellows (the ladies are forgiven for skipping this one), but the writing is brilliant, with runs of puns, lots of well-placed slang and thought experiments that help explain why *Letterkenny* routinely bested *Schitt's Creek* at Canada's version of the Emmy Awards.

Leverage

TV-PG, 2008–2012
IMDb TV, Hoopla, 5 seasons, 77 episodes
Crime drama with Timothy Hutton, Gina Bellman, Christian Kane, Beth Riesgraf and Aldis Hodge.

Reliable comfort food, this high-gloss caper series follows a group of cons using their extra-legal skills to avenge people being exploited by the wealthy and powerful. Another beauty from *Librarian* mastermind Dean Devlin, *Leverage* is full of Great Recession–era resentments against the rich, yet never takes itself too seriously. Hutton's just perfect as Nate, the world-beaten, seedy avenger.

🗨 **From our forums:** "They caught lightning in a bottle with casting and writing and they never talked down to the fans. I'd rather watch a bad episode of *Leverage* than much of what's on TV."

▶▶ Free streamer IMDb TV smartly revived the series in 2021 as *Leverage: Redemption*.

The Librarians
TV-14, 2014–2018
Hulu, 4 seasons, 42 episodes
Action comedy with Rebecca Romijn, Christian Kane, Lindy Booth, John Harlan Kim, John Larroquette and Noah Wyle.

Building on the *Librarian* TV film franchise, this series introduces new recruits protecting the earth from sinister forces while dashing through history. A gloriously goofy mashup of *National Treasure*, *Indiana Jones* and *The Da Vinci Code*, these action-packed mysteries follow a secret league of guardians over a collection of magical artifacts stored in the bowels of the New York Public Library. Fun-filled and not exactly fact-based.

▶▶ Pairs well with *Leverage*

Life on Mars (UK)
TV-14, 2006–2007
BritBox, 2 seasons, 16 episodes
Crime drama with John Simm, Philip Glenister, Liz White, Dean Andrews, Marshall Lancaster and Noreen Kershaw.

This retro detective series from the UK set the bar high for the time-travel shows that followed. In 2006 Manchester, detective Sam Tyler (Simm) is run over while investigating a murder. The car knocks him back to 1973, apparently, because when Sam wakes up his world and wardrobe have taken on that era's look. Worse, arriving back at the squad room he discovers that DNA profiling has

yet to be invented and he's got a horrid old-school boss. Among BBC One's most popular shows, *Life on Mars* had one of the great all-time endings and led to a sequel with a female cop set in the '80s (*Ashes to Ashes*, also on BritBox).

▶▶ In April 2020, series creator Matthew Graham tweeted that a series revival was in production. As this book went to press it had not yet been released.

Life on the Reef
TV-PG, 2015
PBS Passport, 3 episodes
Docuseries directed by Nick Robinson.

Incredible footage brings you close to the Great Barrier Reef in this three-parter in the same vein as *Planet Earth*. Not from the BBC but the Australian production company Northern Pictures, *Life on the Reef* makes complex marine science understandable, largely through beautiful imagery, from extreme close-ups to epic sweeping shots of the reef. With one episode apiece dedicated to a season of the year (winter, spring and summer), the series emphasizes the affects that climate as well as climate change have on this precious ecosystem.

Line of Duty
TV-14, 2012–2021
Hulu, BritBox, Prime Video, Acorn TV, AMC+, 6 seasons, 36 episodes (AD)
Crime drama with Vicky McClure, Martin Compston, Adrian Dunbar and Craig Parkinson.

Juicy British cop drama about anti-corruption officers who investigate dirty officers in the police force. Wildly popular in its native England, *Line of Duty* is everything that American cop procedurals aren't: morally ambiguous, unpredictable and well-acted. Arnott (Compston), who's transferred to the anti-corruption unit after refusing to cover up misdeeds by his team, gets paired with

Fleming (McClure) to investigate corrupt cops. They're solid, but the real draw for *Line of Duty* are the top-flight guest actors playing the cops under investigation: Lennie James, Keeley Hawes, Thandiwe Newton and Stephen Graham to name a few. Each series is between 5–7 episodes, very bingeable.

▸▸ Seasons 6 and forward are exclusive to BritBox.

Little America
TV-14, 2020–present
Apple TV+ original, 8 episodes (AD)
Anthology series (drama) with Sherilyn Fenn, Zachary Quinto, Jessica Hecht, Harvey Guillén, Mélanie Laurent and Becky Ann Baker.

This understated anthology series tells off-the-beaten-path stories of ordinary people seeking a better life in the United States. Based on true stories, these are immigration tales that don't go as you'd expect. A boy who is left running a motel after his parents are deported. An undocumented girl with a bad attitude who learns to play squash — a white rich person's sport. Great performances and real-life stakes make this series sparkle.

Little Fires Everywhere
TV-MA, 2020
Hulu original, 8 episodes (AD)
Limited series (drama) with Reese Witherspoon, Kerry Washington, Lexi Underwood, Joshua Jackson, Rosemarie DeWitt, Jade Pettyjohn, Megan Stott, Gavin Lewis, Jordan Elsass and Lu Huang.

Reese Witherspoon and Kerry Washington play clashing moms with intertwined families in this soapy treatment of the age just before the Internet took off. Based on Celeste Ng's bestselling novel, the miniseries set in the 1990s explores how preppy, wealthy Elena (Witherspoon) and free-spirited, single

Mia (Washington) get entwined in ways that change their families forever.

🗨 **From our forums:** "Excellent performance by the cast. That there are such strong opinions — mainly against — these characters means everyone from writing to acting did a great job."

▸▸ Pairs well with *Big Little Lies*

Little Monsters
R, 2019
Hulu original, 1 hr 33 mins (AD)
Movie (horror) with Lupita Nyong'o, Alexander England and Josh Gad.

Oscar winner Lupita Nyong'o stars as a kindergarten teacher who has to protect a group of kids from a zombie outbreak at a theme park. The movie has high-quality comedy and high-quality gore, and it's beautifully shot to boot.

Living Single
TV-PG, 1993–1998
Hulu, 5 seasons, 118 episodes
Classic sitcom created by Yvette Lee Bowser, with Queen Latifah, Kim Coles, Erika Alexander, John Henton, Terrence "T.C." Carson and Kim Fields.

A year before *Friends*, Fox debuted this landmark sitcom starring Queen Latifah about six Black 20-somethings sharing a New York City townhouse. Fox's audience embraced it, not only for its humor but for its fully-drawn characters at a time when TV's portrayal of young Black people was often one-note and stereotypical. For instance, while most of the crew on *Friends* was initially underemployed, *Living Single*'s young professionals included an entrepreneur, a lawyer and a stock broker.

Living Undocumented
TV-MA, 2019–present
Netflix original, 6 episodes (AD)

Docuseries directed by Anna Chai and Aaron Saidman.

Heartbreaking, infuriating docuseries captures the human misery being wrought by the United States's aggressive new immigration policies. A woman fleeing her violent community in Mexico finds work, pays taxes, marries a U.S. citizen serving in the military — and is deported anyway. An ICE official shoves an immigration lawyer into a glass door and breaks her foot while cameras for this series are rolling. All in all, just another day in the lives of some of the 11 million undocumented immigrants within our borders and those advocating for them. Not much has changed since *Living Undocumented* aired in 2019, other than who's in the White House, so it's still a vital and depressing watch.

Living with Yourself
TV-MA, 2019
Netflix original, 8 episodes (AD)
Fantasy comedy with Paul Rudd, Aisling Bea, Desmin Borges, Karen Pittman, Zoe Chao and Zach Cherry.

Viewers were divided about this comedy in which Paul Rudd clones his schlubby self and gets a genetically enhanced rival. Unhappy with his life, Miles (Rudd) decides to reboot with a sketchy gene-therapy treatment at a strip mall. *Voilà*, out emerges a more charming, competent, wife-pleasing version of himself. Just one problem: Old Miles, who was supposed to be killed off, has escaped his shallow grave. Critics and viewers were torn over this premise, though everyone agreed that Rudd gave it his all and that Bea was terrific as the trophy wife that the two Mileses fight over.

Locke & Key
TV-14, 2020–present
Netflix original, 2 seasons,
20 episodes (AD)

Horror series with Darby Stanchfield, Connor Jessup, Emilia Jones, Jackson Robert Scott, Asha Bromfield, Aaron Ashmore, Hallea Jones and Brendan Hines.

Producer Carlton Cuse succeeds where others have failed, adapting the spooky comic-book series for the screen. After Rendell Locke is murdered, his family moves across the country into the Locke family home, where the children discover a number of mysterious keys that work in magical ways. Unfortunately, a demonic entity is searching for those keys.

🗨 **From our forums:** "The first few episodes were a compelling sort of Spielberg/Burton mashup. The central episodes were more of a YA/CW plot filtered through Hallmark. The final episodes ramped the story up a bit with an ominous *Stranger Things* feel." "The series did a decent job turning the source material into television. Could have been tighter in places, sure, but the overall spirit was there and it was enjoyable."

Lodge 49
TV-14, 2018–2019
Hulu, 2 seasons, 20 episodes
Comedy with Wyatt Russell, Brent Jennings, Sonya Cassidy, Linda Emond, David Pasquesi, Eric Allan Kramer, Njema Williams, Avis-Marie Barnes, David Ury and Jimmy Gonzales.

Delightfully bizarre show tracks a surfer dude who joins a fraternal order, hoping it will get his life back on track. Dud (Russell) is drifting after the loss of his father, the family business and, thanks to a viper bite, his ability to catch a wave. *Lodge 49* stumbles comically through the existential boneyard, asking this question: Is there another way to live? But really, you don't have to ponder that question too deeply to follow this weird, low-key drama.

🗨 **From our forums:** "It takes a while for

the plot to kick in, but I enjoyed spending time with all the characters, so I wasn't that bothered. I did like how it tied the various components together by the end of the season." "In a strange way, reminds me of the movie *Local Hero.*"

Lois & Clark: The New Adventures of Superman

TV-PG, 1993–1997
HBO Max, 4 seasons, 87 episodes
Superhero drama with Dean Cain, Teri Hatcher, Lane Smith, K Callan and Eddie Jones.

Thanks to the chemistry between Teri Hatcher and Dean Cain, viewers got new insights into the Man of Steel. Was this the show were the reimagining of superheroes as less than heroic started? Cain's Superman was vulnerable, funny and relatable (thanks in part to the presence of Mr. and Mrs. Kent, who are alive in this version). Hatcher's 40-something Lane brought a maturity and world-weariness to the role that it didn't have before. For a couple of seasons *Lois & Clark* was the best romcom on the small or big screen.

From our forums: "No one has done a better job of bringing Lois Lane to life with all her perfect imperfections than Teri Hatcher in *Lois & Clark.* I finally understood why the greatest man on earth fell head over heels."

Loki

TV-14, 2021–present
Disney+ original, 6 episodes (AD)
Superhero drama directed by Kate Herron, with Tom Hiddleston, Gugu Mbatha-Raw, Sophia Di Martino, Owen Wilson and Wunmi Mosaku.

Following the events in *Avengers: Endgame*, Tom Hiddleston's character lands in — of all things — a comic buddy-cop show. In this inspired reset, Loki is now a god stripped of his powers, forced to work for a vast bureaucracy that tries to stop the creation of alternate timelines. His partner is a company man named Mobious (Wilson), and the two quickly develop that familiar cranky chemistry. Adding spice is the mysterious Sylvie (Di Martino), whose true identity kept fans of the Marvel Cinematic Universe guessing all season long.

From our forums: "I thought they nailed it. Loki and Sylvie finished their arcs well, we got a great set–up for what's coming, a great villain and explanation. From a comic book standpoint, I simply thought it was great."

Longmire

TV-14, 2012–2017
Netflix original, 6 seasons, 63 episodes (AD)
Crime drama with Robert Taylor, Katee Sackhoff, Lou Diamond Phillips, Cassidy Freeman, Adam Bartley and Louanne Stephens.

Gorgeously shot Western follows a Wyoming sheriff who uses his salty humor and endless determination to solve crimes in his district. Based on a series of popular novels about Sheriff Walt Longmire, a recent widower who is aware he's an anachronism, an old-school cowboy in the modern world. The pain of his loss seems to drive him harder to solve crimes that come to his corner of the West.

From our forums: "Robert Taylor is perfectly cast. It wasn't until I checked out some of his other work that I realized he is from Australia."

Look Around You

TV-PG, 2002–2005
YouTube, 2 seasons, 15 episodes
Satirical comedy created by Robert Popper and Peter Serafinowicz, with Peter Serafinowicz, Robert Popper, Edgar Wright and Olivia Colman.

For shows sorted by streaming platform, see page 381. **191**

Extremely deadpan parody of children's educational programming. We avoid recommending shows that are only available as YouTube bootlegs, but it seems this is the only way you'll get to appreciate one of the most beloved and finely executed parodies you'll ever see. *Look Around You* is modeled on the dry-as-toast educational shows that generations of British children watched on the BBC, but American viewers of a certain age will recognize the kidvid tropes brilliantly skewered here.

▶▶ Series 2 featured future Oscar and Emmy winner Olivia Colman.

The Looming Tower
TV-MA, 2019
Hulu original, 10 episodes
Limited series (drama) created by Alex Gibney, Dan Futterman and Lawrence Wright, with Jeff Daniels, Tahar Rahim, Michael Stuhlbarg, Wrenn Schmidt, Bill Camp, Louis Cancelmi, Peter Sarsgaard, Virginia Kull, Ella Rae Peck and Sullivan Jones.

Effective dramatization of Lawrence Wright's nonfiction account shows how the 9/11 attacks were planned right under the CIA's and FBI's noses. You can't do better research for a made-for-TV miniseries than a Pulitzer-winning investigation whose author is a co-producer, along with documentary titan Alex Gibney. The role of John O'Neill, the embattled FBI counterterrorism agent who was convinced al Qaeda was prepared to strike on American soil, is pulled off by Daniels in yet another of his stunning turns. Sarsgaard is just as effective as O'Neill's rigid, uncooperative *bête noire* at the CIA, Martin Schmidt. It all adds up to a prestige project that belies the "docudrama" tag that people sometimes attach to such things and underscores the tragedy of the events of September 11, 2001.

Looney Tunes Cartoons
TV-G, 2020–present
HBO Max original, 3 seasons, 51 episodes (AD)
Animated comedy with Eric Bauza, Jeff Bergman, Bob Bergen and Fred Tatasciore.

Pretty much exactly the same Looney Tunes you remember growing up — but new! At least one artifact of our childhoods hasn't been canceled or altered beyond recognition. These brand-new animated shorts faithfully continue the tradition of violent cartoon mayhem that made Tweety and Sylvester, Wile E. Coyote and the Roadrunner, Daffy Duck, Yosemite Sam, Elmer Fudd and Bugs Bunny part of the cultural canon.

Lorena
TV-MA, 2019
Prime Video original, 4 episodes (AD)
Limited series (true crime) directed by Joshua Rofé.

From Oscar-winner Jordan Peele comes a full-bodied retrospective on one of the most scandalous crimes of the 1990s. Howard Stern fans might be the only ones who want to avoid this well-done four-part look at the case of Lorena Bobbitt, who claimed that she severed her husband's penis in order to escape from an abusive marriage. At the time, the event was a goldmine for late-night comedians but especially for Stern, whose obsession with Mrs. Bobbitt now seems especially piggish and gross. Peele's series looks deeper at her claims about being in an abusive marriage, and interviews both Lorena and John Wayne Bobbitt, giving us a fuller picture than the news media did at the time.

Los Espookys
TV-MA, 2019–present
HBO Max, 6 episodes

Fantasy comedy created by Fred Armisen, Julio Torres and Ana Fabrega, with Julio Torres, Ana Fabrega, Bernardo Velasco, Cassandra Ciangherotti, Fred Armisen and José Pablo Minor.

One of those shows that people tell people about, it's almost impossible to describe (in Spanish *or* English). It's a surreal, mostly Spanish-language comedy (with subtitles) about friends in a fictional Latin American country who start a business creating terrifying scenarios for anyone willing to pay. Much like HBO's other very oddball (and very funny) comedy *Flight of the Conchords*, *Los Espookys* has effortlessly charming characters, a sharp comedic wavelength and jokes that never feel like they're pushing too hard for laughs.

Losing Alice

TV-MA, 2021
Apple TV+ original, 8 episodes (AD)
Limited series (romance drama) created by Sigal Avin, with Ayelet Zurer, Lihi Kornowski, Gal Toren, Yossi Marshek, Shai Avivi, Chelli Goldenberg, Hadas Jade Sakori and Sigalit Fuchs.

A 40-something female film director falls for a script (and the woman who wrote it) in this Israeli thriller laden with commentary on age and gender in the entertainment industry. Alice (Zurer), a director married to David (Toren), an actor, is trying to restart her career after taking a break to raise their kids. After crossing paths with a seductive screenwriter named Sophie (Kornowski), Alice thinks she's found the story that will mark her comeback. But she also knows she's making a Faustian bargain that involves a woman half her age, who has eyes for David. The limited series format allows Avin to develop this rich storyline and make her characters more well-rounded than your typical film-noir figures.

▶▶ *Losing Alice* is available in Hebrew with English subtitles; don't forget to turn on Audio Description (which comes in 7 languages!).

Lost

TV-14, 2004–2010
Hulu, IMDb TV, 6 seasons, 119 episodes
Sci-fi drama created by J.J. Abrams, Damon Lindelof and Jeffrey Lieber, with Matthew Fox, Josh Holloway, Evangeline Lilly, Terry O'Quinn, Jorge Garcia, Yunjin Kim, Naveen Andrews, Daniel Dae Kim, Emilie de Ravin and Michael Emerson.

From its wild, disorienting first ten minutes, *Lost* held its audience's attention for 6 seasons and it remains a favorite on streaming. A jet disintegrates at 40,000 feet … and dozens survive, washing up on a mysterious island. A disabled man leaps out of his wheelchair. Someone's dead dad is spotted wandering the island. Not for nothing were millions convinced that *Lost* was some sort of allegory for heaven or purgatory. *Lost* constantly tantalized viewers, revealing detail after detail about its characters and the weird time warp they seem to have landed in. A big, sprawling show, it featured one of TV's most diverse casts at the time. Though still a compelling view, many *Lost* fans say that co-creator Lindelof had a purer expression of his vision when he made *The Leftovers* for HBO.

🏆 Emmy, TCA and SAG awards for best drama series

The Lost Daughter

R, 2021
Netflix original, 2 hrs 1 mins (AD)
Movie (drama) directed by Maggie Gyllenhaal, with Olivia Colman, Jessie Buckley, Dakota Johnson, Ed Harris, Paul Mescal, Peter Sarsgaard and Jack Farthing.

Some shows may have moved; see page 183. **193**

In a top-notch directorial debut, Maggie Gyllenhaal adapts Elena Ferrante's novel about a professor played by Olivia Colman, who's forced to recall her own dark past. As the world around Leda (Colman) starts to reflect her savage inner life, we see her indulge her cruelest instincts with a young mother and her extended family. In flashbacks we see how those instincts were displayed with her own children. But Gyllenhaal's too sophisticated to make Leda a pure villain: She also makes us feel the weight that all mothers have to carry, and she forces us to consider how those expectations and demands could push any woman to feral extremes.

Lost in Space

TV-PG, 2018–2021
Netflix original, 3 seasons,
28 episodes (AD)
Sci-fi drama with Maxwell Jenkins, Molly Parker, Toby Stephens, Taylor Russell, Ignacio Serricchio, Mina Sundwall and Parker Posey.

Netflix's reboot of the classic sci-fi series about space colonists is family-friendly — *modern* family-friendly, that is. The Robinsons are back as the family forced to wander the cosmos after their ship is thrown off course. This edition is better rounded, with John Robinson (Stephens) nicely countered by his wife Maureen (Parker) and brainy Will Robinson countered by two strong sisters. Otherwise this has the original show's DNA, with lots of thrills, fun special effects and a wonderful villain in Dr. Smith (Posey).

🗨 **From our forums:** "I see all the plot holes everyone's mentioned, but I'm enjoying it — it's practically the only thing on TV I can watch with my 13-year-old, who is enjoying it, too."

The Loudest Voice

TV-MA, 2019
Showtime original, 7 episodes
Limited series (drama) created by Tom McCarthy and Gabriel Sherman, with Russell Crowe, Sienna Miller, Seth MacFarlane, Annabelle Wallis, Simon McBurney, Aleksa Palladino, Naomi Watts, Josh Stamberg, Mackenzie Astin and Susan Pourfar.

Russell Crowe embodies the political operative Roger Ailes, who created Fox News Channel and made it No. 1 while dividing the country and creating a toxic work environment. From the Oscar-winning director of *Spotlight* comes this fact-based series about the rise and fall of one of the most influential figures of the early 21st century.

🗨 **From our forums:** "I would recommend this to anyone who cares about media, politics, culture and history. They showed us the disgusting man/monster he truly was. And they gave him his due as a brilliant media and political mind."

Love

TV-MA, 2016–2018
Netflix original, 3 seasons,
34 episodes (AD)
Romantic comedy created by Judd Apatow, Paul Rust and Lesley Arfin, with Gillian Jacobs, Paul Rust, Claudia O'Doherty, Mike Mitchell and Chris Witaske.

Judd Apatow made this very Apatovian romantic comedy for Netflix about two deeply flawed people fumbling their way into an enduring romance. Though elements of this largely overlooked series will be familiar to fans of Apatow's other work — from *Freaks and Geeks* to *The King of Staten Island* — solid casting and acerbic humor make this a delightful car crash of two less-than-likable leads.

The Love Boat (1977)
TV-G, 1977–1987
Paramount+, 10 seasons, 250 episodes
Comedy-drama created by Aaron
Spelling and Wilford Lloyd Baumes,
with Gavin MacLeod, Bernie Kopell, Ted
Lange, Fred Grandy, Lauren Tewes and
Jill Whelan.

**Spend some time on the floating
museum of 1970s popular culture,
made immortal by the hit series from
legendary TV producer Aaron Spelling.**
Come aboard the *Pacific Princess* —
they've been expecting you. *The Love
Boat*'s variety-show formula of light
comedy and campy romance, plus a
steady stream of stars, made it the most
comforting place on the dial.

▶▶ The list of guest stars on *The Love Boat*
is long and impressive, including 32 past
and future Oscar winners, fashion icons
Halston and Gloria Vanderbilt in a special
couture episode (S4E25) and newcomer
Tom Hanks, whose 1980 appearance
marked his TV debut (S4E1).

Love Fraud
TV-MA, 2020
Showtime original, 4 episodes
Limited series (true crime) directed by
Heidi Ewing and Rachel Grady.

**A triumph of true-crime TV, *Love Fraud*
takes a witty and original approach to
its unique subject.** Don't look up the case
at the center of *Love Fraud* before you
watch — it'll spoil your full enjoyment
of this superb docuseries. Ewing and
Grady (*Jesus Camp*) present the case of
Richard Scott Smith, a romantic conman
who bamboozled a ridiculous number
of women. They eventually found each
other, banded together and went after
Smith led by the next great American
documentary character: Carla, a chain-
smoking, F-bomb-dropping bounty
hunter in Kansas City who's determined
to help Smith's exes get better justice than

supervised probation.

Love Is Blind
TV-MA, 2020–present
Netflix original, 2 seasons,
21 episodes (AD)
Reality show with Nick Lachey and
Vanessa Lachey.

**A gorgeous Frankenstein of dating
reality shows — *The Circle* meets
Temptation Island and *Married at First
Sight* — it works because, in an artificial
way, it's true to life.** For 9 episodes, guys
in one house communicate with ladies in
another house … through a speaker. They
never see the person they're talking with.
And yet, by the season finale contestants
are expected to announce whether or not
they'd spend their lives with someone
they'd gotten to know in a couple of days
of chatting. It's so nutty that you may
wonder if *Love Is Blind* is actually a satire
of marriage-focused reality TV. But the
show is refreshingly honest about the
challenges of relationships, especially
those formed on reality shows. *Love Is
Blind* doesn't feel like paint-by-numbers
reality TV.

▶▶ The show's hit first season spawned a
reunion special and three 2021 followup
"After the Altar" specials.

Love Island (UK)
TV-MA, 2015–present
Hulu, 7 seasons, 332 episodes
Reality show with Iain Stirling, Caroline
Flack and Laura Whitmore.

**Ready to make a commitment?
Americans have gladly sat through
50-episode seasons of the British reality
serial.** Not to be confused with the
Americanized version on CBS, the ITV-
produced *Love Island* has been praised
and criticized for its no-rules format that
keeps all the inhabitants on edge (and has
resulted in suicides of two former cast
members and a former host). The format

is familiar enough: Sexy singles spend all summer cavorting in a luxury villa in Mallorca, and eventually one lucky couple wins the big cash prize. Though very pop-British, *Love Island*'s lack of structure and backstage manipulation make for unsettlingly bingeable drama.

🏆 1 BAFTA

Love Life
TV-MA, 2020–present
HBO Max original, 2 seasons,
20 episodes (AD)
Anthology series (romantic comedy) with Anna Kendrick, William Jackson Harper, Zoe Chao, Jessica Williams, Peter Vack, Punkie Johnson, Sasha Compère, Lesley Manville, Steven Boyer and Keith David.

Anna Kendrick and William Jackson Harper's simple likability help sell this relatable anthology series about love in the city. The versatile star of *Pitch Perfect* plays Darby Carter, an aspiring art curator in New York City whose romantic life is full of the stops and starts that most of ours are (or have been). The career stuff, the roommates, the angst — we've seen it all before on a quest for love. Darby's story isn't being sold as remarkable, just relatable, and there is undoubtedly an aspect to Kendrick's vibe that invites you to relate to her, to the way she sparks to certain partners and flirts and banters and alternately pays attention to and ignores her self-preservation instincts. The show's second season features an entirely different narrative arc (which only tangentially intersects with Darby's), this time starring William Jackson Harper (*The Good Place*) as Marcus Watkins, a newly single 30-something who embarks on his own romantic journey.

Love on the Spectrum
TV-14, 2020–present
Netflix original, 2 seasons,
11 episodes (AD)
Reality show directed by Cian O'Clery.

This winner from Down Under follows high-functioning young adults with autism or Asperger's as they inch into the dating scene. O'Clery has found a group of appealing (but quirky) Australians in their 20s who, with help from a dating coach, go out on televised dates. Even their failures are sweet, because they're trying so hard. For their parents, who have struggled all their lives to get their kids into a normal life, this is an emotional journey. You can't help but root for them to find true love.

Love, Death & Robots
TV-MA, 2019–present
Netflix original, 2 seasons,
26 episodes (AD)
Animated sci-fi anthology series created by Tim Miller.

Here's a rare find: a curated set of animated shorts that are as entertaining as they are different. Ranging from comedy to sci-fi to fantasy to horror, these shorts showcase a variety of styles and up-and-coming artists with interesting stories to tell. Viewers must agree, because Netflix plans a third series in 2022.

💬 **From our forums:** "The look was very *Liquid Television* and *Animatrix*, updated for the 21st century. Some were cute, some were wondrous, all were excellently produced."

🏆 9 Creative Arts Emmys

Love, Victor
TV-14, 2020–present
Hulu original, 2 seasons,
20 episodes (AD)
Romantic comedy with Michael Cimino, Bebe Wood, Mason Gooding, George Sear, Ana Ortiz, Isabella Ferreira,

Rachel Hilson, Anthony Turpel, Mateo Fernandez and James Martinez.

Set in the same world as the film *Love, Simon*, from which it was spun off, this charming series follows a high school boy who is coming to terms with his sexuality. This time the closeted teen is Latino with religious parents, but essentially it's *Love, Simon* redux, albeit with an even more appealing lead in Cimino. As he inches his way toward gay romance, he finds comfort in the support of school friends, which offsets the tensions at home. Originally intended for Disney+, this series retains the earnest sweetness of a family show, but its insistence on some mild swearing and scenes with alcohol use and sexual exploration got it kicked to Hulu.

The Lovebirds

R, 2020
Netflix original, 1 hr 26 mins (AD)
Action comedy directed by Michael Showalter, with Issa Rae, Kumail Nanjiani, Paul Sparks and Anna Camp.

While trying to save their relationship with an unforgettable date night, a couple gets caught up in a murder mystery. Showalter (who also directed Nanjiani's Oscar-nominated movie *The Big Sick*) gets strong performances from the two leads.

Lovecraft Country

TV-MA, 2020
HBO Max, 10 episodes (AD)
Sci-fi drama created by Misha Green, with Jonathan Majors, Jurnee Smollett, Aunjanue Ellis, Wunmi Mosaku, Abbey Lee, Jamie Chung, Jada Harris and Michael K. Williams.

Layered, anti-racist take on the writings of horror master HP Lovecraft is set, aptly enough, in the 1950s. Atticus Freeman (Majors) and two others take a road trip to search for his father. The trio encounter not only racist violence but monsters inspired by those in Lovecraft's books. Time shifting is commonplace — Atticus encounters both a slave ancestor and the descendant who will write *Lovecraft Country*, the 2016 novel on which this series is based. Though critically well-received and initially renewed, HBO Max reversed itself and canceled the show.

🗨 **From our forums:** "I thought all the episodes were masterpieces except the last one. It made no sense to me and had none of the artistic touches of the previous episodes."

🏆 Critics Choice Award for best supporting actor in a drama (Williams)

Lovesick

TV-MA, 2014–2018
Netflix original, 3 seasons, 22 episodes (AD)
British romcom with Johnny Flynn, Antonia Thomas, Daniel Ings, Joshua McGuire and Hannah Britland.

Clever storytelling extracts both comedy and romance from an embarrassing premise: A young man has to inform all his former sexual partners that he has chlamydia. Titled *Scrotal Recall* in England, this comedy combines flashbacks of Dylan's (Flynn) randy past with scenes from his sobering present — not just the uncomfortable talks with ex-bedmates but his processing this unpleasant task with his two flatmates, Luke (Ings) and Evie (Thomas) and their college friend Angus (McGuire). Evie is clearly carrying a torch for Luke, so that's the rom in the romcom.

🗨 **From our forums:** "There was just something about this show that made it pleasant to watch even when not much was happening — and it was a lot more subtle than I would have expected for a show called *Scrotal Recall.*"

Lucifer

TV-14, 2016–2021
Netflix original, 6 seasons,
93 episodes (AD)

Crime drama with Tom Ellis, Lauren German, Lesley-Ann Brandt, Kevin Alejandro, D.B. Woodside, Rachael Harris, Scarlett Estevez and Aimee Garcia.

Satan moves to Los Angeles and moonlights with the LAPD solving crimes in this long-running cult favorite. Based on a character in the *Sandman* comic book series, the show's appeal comes from the solid relationship between Lucifer (Ellis) and Detective Chloe Decker (German), its farfetched premise and its oddly decent tone, considering the star of the show is the Lord of Hell.

🗨 **From our forums:** "I never would have thought *Lucifer* would be such a feel-good show. I love the characters, the actors, I laughed out loud a few times — and the second season is even better than the first."

LuLaRich

TV-PG, 2021–present
Prime Video original, 4 episodes (AD)

Docuseries directed by Jenner Furst and Julia Willoughby Nason, with Deanne Stidham, Mark Stidham, Ashleigh Lautaha, Courtney Harwood, LaShae Kimbrough and Roberta Blevins.

The rise and fall of a billion-dollar multi-level-marketing company, is told through the middle-class women who bet their livelihoods on it. Deanne and Mark Stidham, a Mormon couple with a Mormon-sized brood, started LuLaRoe in 2013 to sell comfortable, modest clothing using an army of "fashion consultants," mostly married women selling out of their homes on Instagram. Business expanded rapidly and then imploded, largely owing to the Stidhams' decision to structure their business as a multi-level-marketing scheme or MLM. The Stidhams agreed to a lengthy *sui generis* interview with the filmmakers, but it's the ladies they've recruited to sell their wares that make this docuseries so interesting and heartbreaking. How people can get so deep into an enterprise that they have no ownership stake in, and not only wind up bankrupting themselves but friends and family that get pulled into the scheme as well, is hard to understand. But *LuLaRich* takes a pretty good swing at explaining it.

▶▶ Pairs well with *Love Fraud*

Lupin

TV-MA, 2021–present
Netflix original, 2 seasons, 10 episodes, dubbed (AD)

Crime drama with Omar Sy, Ludivine Sagnier, Hervé Pierre, Soufiane Guerrab, Etan Simon, Shirine Boutella and Vincent Londez.

Surprise French-language Netflix hit follows a thief as he exacts revenge on the man who framed his father in a jewel heist. Combining a heist at the Louvre and a literary theft dating back to 1905, *Lupin* has all the ingredients for a thrilling Parisian ride. Assane Diop (Sy) turns to Maurice Leblanc's gentleman burglar character Arsène Lupin for inspiration to enact his revenge against the wealthy family he holds responsible for his father's death 25 years earlier. And there's a hint of magic, which you'd expect from *Now You See Me* director Louis Leterrier.

🗨 **From our forums:** "Omar Sy is great and makes me forget some of the weaker plot points." "I watched with both the subtitles and the English dubbing, and I prefer the subtitles, it feels more natural."

▶▶ Available in its original French with subtitles.

M*A*S*H

TV-PG, 1972–1983
Hulu, 11 seasons, 251 episodes

Classic sitcom with Alan Alda, Loretta Swit, Jamie Farr, William Christopher,

Harry Morgan, Gary Burghoff, Mike Farrell, Kellye Nakahara, David Ogden Stiers and Wayne Rogers.

With its sublime blend of drama and comedy and courage to take on TV's toughest subject, *M*A*S*H* is truly ageless. From the sad opening chords of theme song "Suicide Is Painless" to its disconcertingly serious finale, *M*A*S*H* never let viewers forget they were watching a war comedy unlike any other. Viewers who grew up on *Sgt. Bilko* and *Hogan's Heroes* were in for a shock as the antics of Hawkeye Pierce (Alda) and Trapper John (Rogers) were offset by deadly serious scenes in which the carnage and futility of foreign wars were all but rubbed in viewers' faces. Some found the messaging heavy-handed, especially over time as lighter characters like Frank Burns (Larry Linville) and Henry Blake (McLean Stevenson) were written out. But the series, on the whole, was a masterclass in storytelling, as our dramedic Streaming TV bears witness. And when it was time to say goodbye to the Korean War — proxy, it was understood, for the more recent Vietnam War — more than 100 million viewers tuned in for the finale, the all-time record for any non-sports TV show.

▸▸ The DVDs of *M*A*S*H* had a setting under the languages menu that allowed users to turn off the canned laughs. Viewers would be well-served if streaming services offered this feature.

🏆 14 Emmys, TCA Heritage Award

Ma Rainey's Black Bottom
R, 2020
Netflix original, 1 hr 34 mins (AD)
Movie (drama) directed by George C. Wolfe, with Viola Davis, Chadwick Boseman, Glynn Turman, Colman Domingo, Michael Potts, Jonny Coyne, Taylour Paige, Dusan Brown and Jeremy Shamos.

Outstanding adaptation of August Wilson's Prohibition-era play stars Viola Davis as a blues queen and Chadwick Boseman as her rival. Set in Chicago, where Ma Rainey (Davis) has gone to make a name for herself, *Ma Rainey's Black Bottom* revolves around a recording session where Rainey and her trumpet player Levee (Boseman) argue over how a song should be played. This escalates into a high-stakes debate over how one remains authentically Black while operating in the white power structure. You can't take your eyes off either one while they're on the screen; for Boseman, this Oscar-nominated role was the last before his death.

🏆 5 nominations including best actor

Mad Men
TV-14, 2007–2015
AMC+, IMDb TV, 7 seasons, 92 episodes (AD)
Historical drama created by Matthew Weiner, with Jon Hamm, Elisabeth Moss, Christina Hendricks, John Slattery, Vincent Kartheiser, January Jones, Kiernan Shipka, Aaron Staton, Rich Sommer and Robert Morse.

One of the pillars of contemporary prestige TV, *Mad Men* took the retro show to new heights and made stars of Jon Hamm, Elisabeth Moss and John Slattery. This pitch-perfect recreation of life on Madison Avenue in the early 1960s beautifully captured not just the clothing and furniture of the late Eisenhower era, but its social mores and cultural conservatism. As the show found its stride, it did something even more remarkable: It dialed down the social commentary and began to develop the stories of its amazing ensemble of characters to a degree rarely seen on a TV drama. Though focused on Don Draper (Hamm), a master at the black art of consumer persuasion and a man whose

For shows sorted by streaming platform, see page 381.

reserves of desire and loneliness run deep, *Mad Men* allocated plenty of time to other characters: his frustrated first wife Betty (Jones); his partner at the firm, Roger Sterling (Slattery), who would evolve from carefree boor to a man with something to prove; Joan Hathaway (Hendricks), the office manager who would be CEO in the non-glass-ceiling age; and Peggy Olson (Moss), whose ascent from Sterling Cooper's secretarial pool to one of its top creatives mirrored Moss's own scintillating rise to top-tier actor.

🏆 Peabody Award, 16 Emmys including best drama series

The Mad Women's Ball

TV-MA, 2021
Prime Video original, 2 hrs 2 mins, dubbed
Movie (drama) directed by Mélanie Laurent , with Mélanie Laurent, Lou de Laâge, Emmanuelle Bercot and Benjamin Voisin.

Mélanie Laurent plays an asylum nurse who agrees to help an unfairly institutionalized woman escape. Laurent (*Inglourious Basterds*) stars, directs and co-writes in this French-language film that is taut, disturbing and totally absorbing.

Made for Love

TV-MA, 2021–present
HBO Max original, 8 episodes (AD)
Sci-fi drama with Cristin Milioti, Billy Magnussen, Ray Romano, Noma Dumezweni, Augusto Aguilera, Shovon Ahmed, Caleb Foote, Dan Bakkedahl and Patti Harrison.

Cristin Milioti plays a woman who is startled to discover her creepy ex-husband has implanted her with a device that tracks her movements and emotions. True to the absurdist novel from which it's adapted, the show's slapstick elements mask a deeper

exploration of control, dependence and our very human need for connection.

💬 **From our forums:** "The show is absurd and not realistic but that's kind of what makes it enjoyable to me." "It did make me sad that it was a *Black Mirror*-style abuse story. I was intrigued by the characters and could never predict what would happen next."

Maid

TV-MA, 2021
Netflix original, 10 episodes
Limited series (drama) with Margaret Qualley, Nick Robinson, Anika Noni Rose, Tracey Vilar, Billy Burke and Andie MacDowell.

One of Netflix's most-watched originals of 2021, *Maid* somehow makes very difficult subjects — abuse, poverty, neglect — highly watchable. Based on Stephanie Land's bestselling memoir, it's carried by a breakthrough role from Qualley, who has viewers rooting for her from the get-go. We quickly surmise the deep hole she is in, trying to escape an abusive relationship, broke and forced to clean filthy bathrooms if she's to keep the state from taking her daughter away. She has no support system. Her mom (played by Qualley's real mom, MacDowell) is barely tethered to reality. Her dad has moved on. Qualley's struggle not to be overwhelmed by her situation and her determination to have a better life puts a face on the realities of American poverty.

▶▶ For suggestions of related shows, see "If You Liked *Maid*," page 374.

Making a Murderer

TV-14, 2015–2018
Netflix original, 2 seasons, 20 episodes (AD)
True crime created by Moira Demos and Laura Ricciardi.

After serving 18 years for a rape he did not commit, Steven Avery is arrested

for a murder he says he didn't commit. This extraordinary series about crime and punishment in a Wisconsin county asks how human beings can make such terrible choices, whether intentionally or accidentally. Ricciardi and Demos have traced a very complicated series of events and woven it into a remarkably coherent narrative about the criminal justice system's failures. About halfway through, the story begins to drag, but that's a feature, not a bug. This is a series about the tedium and occasional horror of process. A second season, filmed 2 years later, updates the story with a number of twists.

🏆 Peabody Award; Emmys for writing, directing and outstanding docuseries

Making It
TV-PG, 2018–present
Peacock, Hulu, 3 seasons, 22 episodes
Reality competition with Amy Poehler and Nick Offerman.

Thanks to Amy Poehler and Nick Offerman, this craftmaking show is lively yet gentle and will charm even viewers who avoid competition shows. Personality is what sets *Making It* apart from almost every other show in the genre. The contestants' work emerges from their life experiences and tells us about them in a way that doesn't simply wedge moments of personal narrative into the competition. And then there are the outsized personalities of Poehler and Offerman. They are reality TV's best hosting duo, able to make each other laugh, poke fun at reality TV (including their own show) and feel genuine lament when someone has to go home at the end of an episode.

▶▶ Pairs well with *The Great British Baking Show*

The Man in the High Castle
TV-MA, 2015–2019
Prime Video original, 4 seasons, 40 episodes (AD)
Alternative history created by Frank Spotnitz, with Alexa Davalos, Joel de la Fuento, Rufus Sewell, Chelah Horsdal, Brennan Brown, DJ Qualls, Stephen Root, Cary-Hiroyuki Tagawa, Rupert Evans and Luke Kleintank.

Nuanced alt-history imagines America after the Nazis and Japanese win World War II. Based on the Philip K. Dick novel, this is an ingenious answer to the question: What happens if the worst-case scenario comes true? Answer: Humans rebound . . . and rebuild. And that premise is what keeps bringing you back to this well-paced, engrossing exercise in world-building.

💬 **From our forums:** "This was a show that grew more interesting as it went along."

🏆 2 Emmys

Manchester by the Sea
R, 2016
Prime Video, 2 hrs 18 mins
Movie (drama) directed by Kenneth Lonergan, with Casey Affleck, Michelle Williams, Kyle Chandler and Gretchen Mol.

Career-best performances from Casey Affleck and Michelle Williams highlight this sober meditation on grief, guilt and forgiveness. Amazon Studios scooped up this affecting character drama from writer/director Kenneth Lonergan at the 2016 Sundance Film Festival and rode it all the way to the Oscars, where it was the first film released by a digital streaming service to be nominated for best picture.

The Mandalorian
TV-14, 2019–present
Disney+ original, 2 seasons, 16 episodes (AD)

Sci-fi drama created by Jon Favreau, with Pedro Pascal, Giancarlo Esposito, Gina Carano and Carl Weathers.

This distinctive action series requires no prior knowledge of *Star Wars* arcana, just a love for spaghetti westerns and quietly powerful characters. The show that launched the new Disney+ streamer into orbit revolves around a mysterious bounty hunter (Pascal) who belongs to an endangered class of warriors called Mandalorians. He talks like Clint Eastwood and flies a barely spaceworthy rustbucket. Season 1 of *The Mandalorian* had a moving-train scene, a Mexican standoff and other western movie tropes. The violence on the show is bloodless, other than some android gore. Mando is old-school, honorable and haunted by a childhood memory. There is, in short, a lot more to this show than just that goofy green Yoda.

🏆 7 Emmys, SAG Award for outstanding stunt ensemble

Manhattan

TV-14, 2014–2015
Hulu, 2 seasons, 23 episodes
Historical drama with Michael Chernus, Christopher Denham, Katja Herbers, John Benjamin Hickey, Harry Lloyd, Olivia Williams, Ashley Zukerman, Daniel Stern and Rachel Brosnahan.

Character-driven historical drama about the race to build the atom bomb, *Manhattan* was the coming-out party for Rachel Brosnahan. Canceled after two low-key (and low-rated) seasons on WGN America, this drama revolved around the rivalry between two teams competing to get the A-bomb built at Los Alamos, a secretive instant town in New Mexico.

▶▶ You can needle-drop at Season 2, which sees the emergence of Brosnahan's character, the bored and bi-curious scientist's wife.

Manhunt: Unabomber

TV-14, 2017
Netflix, 8 episodes (AD)
Limited series (true crime) with Sam Worthington, Paul Bettany, Jeremy Bobb, Keisha Castle-Hughes, Lynn Collins, Chris Noth, Brian F. O'Byrne, Elizabeth Reaser, Ben Weber and Jane Lynch.

An exciting dramatization of the investigation that tracked down one of the most feared and insidious domestic terrorists in history. Even news junkies may have trouble recalling the terror Americans felt each time a bespoke pipe bomb from the Unabomber blew up in its unsuspecting recipient's hands. The hunt to bring him to justice in the 1990s is made into a taut psychological thriller pitting FBI agent Jim Fitzgerald (Worthington) against the elusive whack job Ted Kaczynski (Bettany).

Maniac

TV-MA, 2018
Netflix original, 10 episodes (AD)
Sci-fi drama limited series created by Cary Joji Fukunaga and Patrick Somerville, with Emma Stone, Jonah Hill, Sonoya Mizuno, Justin Theroux, Sally Field, Billy Magnussen, James Monroe Iglehart, Allyce Beasley, Gabriel Byrne and Julia Garner.

Emma Stone and Jonah Hill play two subjects in a pharmaceutical trial that they are promised will solve their problems with no side effects — and no, it doesn't quite work out that way. From the director of the first season of *True Detective* comes a brilliant fable about the near-future where psychoactive drugs promise a happier existence. With terrific assists from Theroux as the mad doctor and Field as his difficult mother, this is a bizarre, comic and occasionally touching look at the eternal puzzle of the human mind.

Manifest

TV-14, 2018–present
Netflix, 3 seasons, 42 episodes
Sci-fi drama created by Jack Rapke,
Jeff Rake and Robert Zemeckis, with
Melissa Roxburgh, Parveen Kaur, Josh
Dallas, Luna Blaise, Athena Karkanis, Jack
Messina, J.R. Ramirez, Matt Long and
Holly Taylor.

**The 4400 meets Lost in this sci-fi thriller
that Netflix gladly rescued after NBC
canceled it.** When Montego Air Flight 828
touches down in New York after a patch of
turbulence, all seems normal until the 191
passengers deplane and learn that more
than 5 years have passed. Like *Lost*, this
show eventually took its large ensemble of
characters through a complex web of time
jumps and introduced a quasi-religious
phenomenon, "callings," that mysteriously
linked the passengers on the flight. But
this wasn't enough to stop the audience
for *Manifest* from shrinking to the point of
cancellation after Season 3. Then Netflix
stepped in, correctly guessing that it
would be a hit with binge watchers. Days
after Season 3 debuted at No. 1 ranking
on Nielsen's streaming chart, *Manifest* was
given a Season 4 renewal.

🐟 **From our forums:** "My husband was
watching this with me for the first time. I
told him I'm not even gonna try to explain
what's happening in this show because
even I'm not really sure."

▶▶ For suggestions of related shows, read
"If You Liked *Manifest*," page 374.

Mank

R, 2020
Netflix original, 2 hrs 11 mins (AD)
Movie (drama) directed by David Fincher,
with Gary Oldman, Amanda Seyfried, Lily
Collins, Tom Pelphrey, Joseph Cross and
Charles Dance.

**Gary Oldman stars in this prestige pic
about screenwriter Herman Mankiewicz
as he's trying to resist his personal
demons long enough to finish the
screenplay for Citizen Kane.** Every inch
of this movie is a meticulous ode to old
Hollywood, from the stellar black-and-
white cinematography to the period
costumes to the slightly heightened
performances that reference acting styles
from the 1930s. The script — by David
Fincher's late father Jack — has all the
satisfying beats of a story about an artist
trying to recover his greatness. And while
Oldman does his customary good work,
it's Seyfried, as actress Marion Davies,
who shows an impressive new part of her
range.

🏆 Oscars for design and cinematography

Mare of Easttown

TV-MA, 2021
HBO Max, 7 episodes (AD)
Limited series (crime drama) with Kate
Winslet, Evan Peters, Jean Smart, Guy
Pearce, Julianne Nicholson, Angourie
Rice, Neal Huff and John Douglas
Thompson.

**Kate Winslet outdoes herself as a
troubled but gutsy detective working
on a murder case that's rocked her
tight-knit community.** How many
shows inspire their own *SNL* parody? But
there's much more to *Mare of Easttown*
than Winslet's gritty performance (and
often-mocked Philly accent). Jean Smart
is stellar as Mare's mom and the script
brims with terrific dialogue, remarkable
storytelling and nifty twists.

🐟 **From our forums:** "Every character was
given a measure of closure and the ability
to take the next step forward in their life,
however painful that would be."

▶▶ For suggestions of related shows, see
"If You Liked *Mare of Easttown*," page
374.

🏆 4 Emmys including best actress
(Winslet), supporting actor (Peters) and
actress (Nicholson)

Maria Bamford: The Special Special Special!

TV-MA, 2012
Netflix, Prime Video, Hoopla, 49 mins

Comedy special directed by Jordan Brady, with Maria Bamford, her parents and her crew.

The comic's comic delivers a solid standup act in her parents' living room. Before *Lady Dynamite* came along, Maria Bamford was like Dave Attell in his standup days, the one whose act other standups loved to watch. This early special gives you the full spectrum of Bamford's talent, from her many voices to going all-in with bizarro concepts — like performing an entire comedy special at home with an audience consisting of her parents and the crew.

Marriage or Mortgage

TV-G, 2021–present
Netflix original, 10 episodes (AD)

Reality show with Sarah Miller and Nichole Holmes.

Wedding shows take a practical turn, as a wedding planner and a real estate agent compete for the savings of an engaged couple. Finally, a TV show that acknowledges the money spent on a typical American wedding *could* fund a down payment on a house. It's an odd conceit for a wedding show to suggest that maybe some couples shouldn't even have a wedding, but planner Sarah Miller and agent Nichole Holmes do their best to convince the couples that one — and only one — of these two dreams is possible with their nest egg.

Marriage Story

R, 2019
Netflix, 2 hrs 17 mins (AD)

Movie (drama) directed by Noah Baumbach, with Scarlett Johansson and Adam Driver.

Scarlett Johansson and Adam Driver give voice to all the conflicting emotions of a divorcing husband and wife in this sharply constructed character drama. Writer-director Baumbach (*The Squid and the Whale*) mines his own divorce from actress Jennifer Jason Leigh for this story, told with compassion, humanity and humor. Johansson and Driver give nuanced performances but for comic relief you can't beat Laura Dern and Alan Alda as their divorce attorneys.

🏆 Oscar for best supporting actress (Dern)

Married at First Sight

TV-14, 2014–present
IMDb TV, Hulu, Prime Video, 13 seasons, 207 episodes

Reality show with Joseph Cilona, Logan Levkoff, Pepper Schwartz, Greg Epstein, Calvin Roberson, Rachel DeAlto, Jessica Griffin and Viviana Coles.

This long-running reality show offers human drama on a scale rarely seen on TV. A panel of experts (including a psychologist, a "sexologist" and a chaplain) match singles who know nothing about each other until they meet at the altar for their legally binding marriages. Three to five couples per season get matched, then are followed by cameras for the next 8 weeks. It's enough time for the newlyweds to go beyond the superficial attraction that animates shows like *The Bachelor* and try to figure out what it takes to make their less-than-ideal relationship work. About 70 percent of the time it doesn't, though for many viewers the worse the mismatch, the better the show.

💬 **From our forums:** "I make myself a cheat sheet every season."

⏩ Needle-drop at Season 11, set in New Orleans. It features two ill-fated pairings of People With Issues that implode spectacularly … *and* two fantastic matchups of adorable people who are perfect for each other.

Marvel's Agent Carter

TV-PG, 2015–2016
Disney+, 2 seasons, 18 episodes
Superhero drama with Hayley Atwell, James D'Arcy, Enver Gjokaj, Chad Michael Murray, Wynn Everett, Reggie Austin, Bridget Regan, Lesley Boone and Dominic Cooper.

Unjustly overlooked product of the Marvel Cinematic Universe featured Peggy Carter from *Captain America: The First Avenger.* Years before *WandaVision*, this gem was quietly dropped into a midseason break for *Agents of S.H.I.E.L.D.* Picking up where the first *Captain America* film left off in the 1940s, Carter (Atwell) is working for the Strategic Scientific Reserve, battling the sexism of her era as she secretly assists Howard Stark (Cooper), wealthy industrialist and future father to Iron Man. An old-timey political/spy thriller with some Avengers connections, it all turns on Atwell's terrifically charismatic lead character. In a more just (and Marvel-run) universe, she'd have multiple Emmys and *Agent Carter* would not have been ended after 2 short seasons.

The Marvelous Mrs. Maisel

TV-MA, 2017–present
Prime Video original, 4 seasons, 34 episodes (AD)
Comedy-drama created by Amy Sherman-Palladino, with Rachel Brosnahan, Alex Borstein, Tony Shalhoub, Marin Hinkle, Michael Zegen, Kevin Pollak, Caroline Aaron and Luke Kirby.

Rachel Brosnahan dazzles as a '50s housewife who discovers she can make crowds laugh, while Alex Borstein shines as her crotchety manager who believes she can make her a star. *Gilmore Girls*

creator Amy Sherman-Palladino finds a new outlet for her trademark snappy dialogue. Watch for memorable turns from Shalhoub and Hinkle as Midge's parents and Kirby as comedy legend Lenny Bruce.

🏆 Peabody Award, 20 Emmys including best comedy series

The Mary Tyler Moore Show

TV-PG, 1970–1977
Hulu, 7 seasons, 168 episodes
Sitcom created by James L. Brooks and Allan Burns, with Mary Tyler Moore, Ed Asner, Gavin MacLeod, Ted Knight, Valerie Harper, Georgia Engel, Betty White and Cloris Leachman.

Forget Archie Bunker — if you want to see the times a-changin' in the 1970s, watch Minneapolis modern Mary Richards and her still-funny sitcom. Mary Tyler Moore was already TV royalty from her years as Laura Petrie on *The Dick Van Dyke Show*, but it was this series from her MTM studio (run by then-husband and later NBC president Grant Tinker) that made her an icon. Mary was an associate TV news producer, so the show posed a triple threat, able to do workplace comedy, poke fun at 1970s mores and make fun of TV itself. Moore was flanked by fabulous castmates, most of whom would go on to hit shows of their own. No less a person than Oprah Winfrey has cited Mary Richards as her inspiration for pursuing a career in television.

▶▶ "Chuckles Bites The Dust" (S6E7) was ranked at #1 on TV Guide's list of "Greatest TV Episodes of All Time" in 1997.

🏆 Peabody Award, 29 Emmys

The Masked Singer

TV-PG, 2019–present
Hulu, 5 seasons, 69 episodes (AD)
Reality competition with Jenny McCarthy, Ken Jeong, Nicole

Scherzinger, Robin Thicke and Nick Cannon.

Wacky global game-show phenomenon had a great couple of seasons in the US before going off the rails. The singing was mostly atrocious, the judging unspeakably useless. And yet, Fox's adaptation of the Japanese format, with celebrities performing from behind elaborate costumes, was irresistible when it debuted. Why? Because viewers wanted to know who the people are behind the masks. Most of the best highlights ended up on social media, so if you're online a lot, watching this may not be as much fun. But for a couple of years, anyway, this objectively bad show was one of the most compelling things on TV.

🔊 From our forums: "Three seasons and this show has run its course. Doesn't help when half the reveals are followed by, 'Who?'"

Master of None
TV-MA, 2015–present
Netflix original, 3 seasons,
25 episodes (AD)
Comedy-drama created by Aziz Ansari and Alan Yang, with Aziz Ansari, Eric Wareheim and Lena Waithe.

Formally daring, *Master of None* uses a variety of cinematic techniques to follow the complex love lives of its central characters. Season 1 has a New York romcom vibe as Ansari's character Dev falls for a manic pixie-dream girl who's more than she seems. Season 2 then pivots to Italy (much of it is spoken in Italian) as Dev finds a new love. In Season 3 Dev steps aside and we get to know Denise (Waithe) and her new wife. The result feels like an anthology, but with characters we can follow and care about across multiple arcs.

🏆 Peabody Award, Emmy for best writing in a comedy (2 wins)

McMillions
TV-14, 2020
HBO Max, 6 episodes (AD)
Docuseries directed by James Lee Hernandez and Brian Lazarte.

The McDonald's Monopoly contest was rigged and no one had a clue until a very chatty FBI agent got involved. *McMillions* is not the most elegantly produced docuseries, but it's got a hell of a story and a central character (a good guy!) to die for. Soon after joining the FBI in 2001, Doug Matthews followed a tip that all of the big prizes in Mickey D's Monopoly game might have been skimmed off by organized crime. And we were off to the races.

🔊 From our forums: "This story is amazing and the documentary makers did such a great job with it. They brought the whole thing full circle with the final episode."

Medical Police
TV-MA, 2020–present
Netflix original, 10 episodes (AD)
Satirical comedy created by David Wain, Rob Corddry, Jonathan Stern and Krister Johnson, with Rob Huebel, Erinn Hayes, Tom Wright, Sarayu Blue, Fred Melamed, Lake Bell, Jason Schwartzman and Randall Park.

The gang behind *Childrens Hospital* reunite for a sequel that parodies both terrorist *and* medical procedurals (no wonder it needed a Netflix budget). Hayes and Huebel's characters find themselves sucked into a sinister plot involving the global outbreak of a deadly virus. Not that such a thing could happen in January 2020, when the show debuted … but the really impressive thing about *Medical Police* is the action sequences. You could mute the thing and swear you were watching a CBS prime-time show, which is probably part of the joke.

▶▶ Because the show's writers never

met a meta-reference they didn't like, Randall Park and David Wain appear in *Medical Police* in the roles they played in a different *Childrens Hospital* spinoff, *Newsreaders*.

The Mentalist

TV-14, 2008–2015
Prime Video, 7 seasons,
151 episodes (AD)
Crime drama with Simon Baker, Robin Tunney, Tim Kang, Owain Yeoman and Amanda Righetti.
Simon Baker sizzled as Patrick Jane, a charming manipulator who mostly uses his people skills for good by outwitting crime suspects. CBS procedurals aren't hard to figure out: charming/mysterious male lead(s) solve stylishly bloody crimes while chasing some bigger, multi-episode target. In Patrick's case it was a serial killer named Red John, who left smiley faces at the scene. Despite the grim story arc, *The Mentalist* had a campy-escapist vibe to it and went down easier than, say, *CSI*.

Mercy Street

TV-14, 2016–2017
PBS Passport, 2 seasons,
12 episodes (AD)
Historical drama with Mary Elizabeth Winstead, AnnaSophia Robb, Gary Cole, Josh Radnor, Tara Summers, Luke Macfarlane, Wade Williams, Norbert Leo Butz, Bryce Pinkham and Patina Miller.
Divided loyalties and perpetual crises vex the workers at a Virginia military hospital during the Civil War. Unjustly cut short after 2 seasons on PBS, *Mercy Street* not only showed a carefully researched portrayal of Civil War medicine, but also how the war created opportunities for white women and free Black people to thrive in a society that usually denied them basic civil rights. Fine performances come from a host of Broadway stars (Butz, Miller, Pinkham)

and as a testy doctor who clashes with his co-workers on everything from medicine to politics, Radnor is a solid lead.

The Mick

TV-14, 2017–2018
Hulu, 2 seasons, 37 episodes (AD)
Sitcom with Kaitlin Olson, Sofia Black-D'Elia, Thomas Barbusca, Carla Jimenez, Jack Stanton and Scott MacArthur.
Kaitlin Olson took a break from *It's Always Sunny in Philadelphia* to play another lovable dirtbag. In this overlooked comedy, Olson is left caring for her monstrously spoiled niece and nephews after her sister skips town to avoid getting arrested for tax fraud. There's great chemistry between Olson, Jimenez as the kids' former housekeeper and Barbusca as the tightly wound middle child. *The Mick* touches on topics like class and gender while avoiding preachiness and feeling smart and humane, despite the deplorable nature of its characters.
🗨 **From our forums:** "It's basically 'Sweet Dee does the babysitting' and for that reason I have no complaints."

Middleditch & Schwartz

TV-MA, 2020–present
Netflix original, 3 episodes (AD)
Comedy special created by Thomas Middleditch and Ben Schwartz, with Thomas Middleditch and Ben Schwartz.
Comic actors update the improvisational TV show with daring feats of spontaneous comedy. Middleditch (*Silicon Valley, B Positive*) and Schwartz (*Parks and Recreation, Space Force*) based each of these 45-minute programs on a single interview with an audience member. They spin out complicated stories that involve multiple characters, locations and running gags — essentially conjuring up one-act plays from suggestions. Improv companies do this kind of exercise all the time, but to see it

on a medium that has known only *Whose Line Is It Anyway?*, it feels thrilling.

The Midnight Gospel

TV-MA, 2020–present
Netflix original, 8 episodes (AD)
Animated comedy with Phil Hendrie and Duncan Trussell.

Surreal animation creates a psychedelic wonderland around audio from the popular *Duncan Trussell Family Hour* podcast (which is not for families). Co-created by Trussell and *Adventure Time*'s Pendleton Ward, *The Midnight Gospel* follows Clancy Gilroy (Trussell), who owns a used "multiverse simulator" (voiced by Hendrie) that allows him to travel to planets in peril and interview people … who happen to be guests from Trussell's podcasts. Ward's trippy picture stories often bear little relationship to the spoken words — yet the effect of combining the two is mesmerizing. At times, like when topics of life and death are discussed, it's even uplifting.

▸▸ The episodes with Anne Lamott (S1E2) and Deneen Fendig, Trussell's late mother (S1E8), are especially powerful.

Midnight Mass

TV-MA, 2021
Netflix original, 7 episodes (AD)
Limited series (horror) created by Mike Flanagan, with Zach Gilford, Kate Siegel, Hamish Linklater, Henry Thomas, Kristin Lehman, Samantha Sloyan, Rahul Kohli and Annabeth Gish.

Spookmaster Mike Flanagan (*The Haunting of Hill House*) returns with a tale about a small town with a charismatic new priest who might be responsible for a series of unfortunate events. Even without this central mystery, this series is alluring for its ingenious use of the supernatural to frame its conversations about faith, forgiveness and healing. As the priest, Linklater

injects dramatic verve into philosophical conversations, and Gilford, as an ex-con struggling to find peace in his hometown, serves admirably as an Everyman who grounds both the creepy and the spiritual aspects of this strange story.

Mildred Pierce

TV-MA, 2011
HBO Max, 5 episodes
Limited series (drama) directed by Todd Haynes, with Kate Winslet, Evan Rachel Wood, Guy Pearce, Mare Winningham, Melissa Leo, Marin Ireland, Brían F. O'Byrne and James Le Gros.

Acclaimed reimagining of the Joan Crawford movie about a wife and mother who rebuilds her life on her own terms after losing everything. Kate Winslet, a different actress than Crawford working in a different era of moviemaking and feminism, is just as convincing in this role as a woman disappointed by the men and the daughter she loves. Some critics said it was more true to James M. Cain's original novel than the earlier film.

▸▸ Pairs well with *Olive Kitteridge*
🏆 Emmy and SAG awards for acting in a miniseries (Winslet)

Mindhunter

TV-MA, 2017–2019
Netflix original, 2 seasons,
19 episodes (AD)
Crime drama with Jonathan Groff, Holt McCallany, Anna Torv, Sonny Valicenti, Stacey Roca, Hannah Gross and Joe Tuttle.

Atmospheric, unsettling series looks into the FBI's efforts in the 1970s to understand the minds of serial killers. David Fincher's moody series about psychopaths and the federal agents willing to poke around in their dark brains isn't what you'd call a feel-good show. It's a show where crimes are investigated but never really thwarted. But it is a satisfying watch if you're a fan of true crime, *Zodiac, Fringe,* Jonathan Groff, historical footnotes or cool song-drops over the end credits.

🐦 **From our forums:** "The actors playing the killers hit it out of the park. They must have been thrilled to get such a showcase." "I thought it started slow and deliberate, which was fine, but it didn't really grab me until around Episode 7. I love Anna Torv."

Minding the Gap
TV-MA, 2018
Hulu, 1 hr 33 mins
Movie (documentary) directed by Bing Liu.

Over 12 years a young skateboarder videotaped the feats of his friends and in the process captured the turbulence of their lives. In rusted-out Rockford, Illinois, Bing Liu has been making skateboard videos since he was a kid. And for a while *Minding the Gap* is a showcase for the skills of his pals, a diverse bunch facing various life challenges. But with guidance from the makers of *Hoop Dreams,* this becomes a much more expansive project about manhood. No amount of wicked moves are going to improve the prospects for Liu's friends in a beaten-down city where role models are scarce.

The Mindy Project
TV-14, 2012–2017
Hulu original, 6 seasons, 117 episodes
Sitcom created by Mindy Kaling, with Mindy Kaling, Ike Barinholtz, Ed Weeks, Chris Messina, Xosha Roquemore, Beth Grant, Adam Pally, Fortune Feimster and Garret Dillahunt.

Mindy Kaling plays a doctor looking for love in this fan favorite that mixed light comedy with romantic stakes. Fresh off *The Office,* Kaling brought her quick wit to Fox (and later Hulu) as the creator and star of this workplace comedy set in a New York obstetrics practice. Though it stumbled before it soared, *The Mindy Project*'s six-year run was consistently strong. The more conservative Danny Castellano (Messina) was the perfect foil to Kaling's free-spirited Mindy and a trio of up-and-coming comedians (Barinholtz, Pally and Feimster) led the supporting cast. Kaling's fellow *Office* star B.J. Novak, Glenn Howerton and the Duplass Brothers were among the comedy all-stars who recurred.

⏩ Canceled by Fox after Season 3, it was picked up by Hulu and produced 3 more seasons.

Miracle Workers
TV-14, 2019–present
HBO Max, 3 seasons, 27 episodes (AD)
Anthology series (comedy) with Daniel Radcliffe, Steve Buscemi, Geraldine Viswanathan, Karan Soni, Jon Bass and Lolly Adefope.

Steve Buscemi plays God and Daniel Radcliffe is one of his angels in this oddball comedy. Created by *SNL* vet and wunderkind writer Simon Rich, a comedy with a boorish, out-of-touch deity (very Buscemi-esque) and his meek angel (Radcliffe) might seem like a one-joke wonder. But *Miracle Workers* adds characters and story as the season goes on. Then in Season 2, it resets in the Middle Ages. Season 3 takes place on the Oregon Trail. Just go with it.

🐦 **From our forums:** "It's not *The Good Place* but it is fun and built to binge watch." "This is the God I could see sending down 7 plagues to Egypt, just to see what happens."

The Missing
TV-MA, 2014–2017
Starz original, 2 seasons, 16 episodes (AD)
Crime drama with Tchéky Karyo, Anastasia Hille, David Morrissey, Keeley Hawes, James Nesbitt and Laura Fraser.

World-weary detective Julien Baptiste tries to solve the disappearance of a child while battling a brain tumor. Seemingly inspired by *Broadchurch*, this assured, propulsive thriller is subtle and ambiguous in ways American dramas about missing children aren't. It goes for the gut often and rarely misses. And it introduces audiences around the world to Julien Baptiste, a detective who more than holds his own in a pantheon of high-concept crime solvers. The show's production adds aesthetic pleasure to the satisfaction of following the case.

▸▸ By popular demand, Karyo reprised his role for the 2020 spinoff *Baptiste* (see page 58).

The Mitchells vs. the Machines
PG, 2021
Netflix original, 1 hr 53 mins (AD)
Animated sci-fi film with Abbi Jacobson, Danny McBride, Maya Rudolph, Eric André, Olivia Colman and Fred Armisen.

A family of four are on a boring road trip when they find themselves in the middle of a robot apocalypse. From director Mike Rianda (*Gravity Falls*) and producers Phil Lord and Chris Miller (*The LEGO Movie*), this sets up as a sort of anti-*Incredibles*, with an average family banding together to find the courage to save themselves and maybe also the world. With an all-star cast, this is a creative, exciting and funny animated adventure.

Mixed-ish
TV-PG, 2019–2021
Hulu, 2 seasons, 36 episodes
Sitcom created by Tracee Ellis Ross, Kenya Barris and Peter Saji, with Mark-Paul Gosselaar, Tika Sumpter, Arica Himmel, Ethan William Childress, Mykal-Michelle Harris, Tracee Ellis Ross, Gary Cole and Christina Anthony.

In 1980s America, a multicultural family adapts to suburban life after leaving their hippie commune. Rapid-fire punchlines meet a Black Lives teach-in on this likable and earnest prequel about the childhood of Bow from *Black-ish*. After cops break up the rural Shangri-La where Bow's hippie parents were raising their kids, they're forced to move into the rental house of Bow's Reaganite grandpa (Cole) and fit in at school and the workplace. The show has a strong '80s vibe, not just the fashion cues but the idea (which *Seinfeld* rebelled against) that sitcoms should impart little lessons. Ross, narrating this show as grown-up Bow, explains police brutality, code-switching, Black hair and more to the viewers. This would get wearisome were it not for the appealing cast and equal-opportunity jabs at lefty PC-ness and rah-rah conservatism.

Modern Family
TV-PG, 2009–2020
Hulu, 11 seasons, 250 episodes (AD)
Sitcom created by Christopher Lloyd and Steven Levitan, with Ed O'Neill, Sofía Vergara, Julie Bowen, Ty Burrell, Jesse Tyler Ferguson, Eric Stonestreet, Rico Rodriguez, Nolan Gould, Sarah Hyland and Ariel Winter.

At its core a brilliantly written and well-cast sitcom that happened to be diverse, *Modern Family* won over viewers of all persuasions. Does popular culture reflect tastes or shape them? You can make a pretty good case that *Modern Family* pushed America in a direction it was already heading … but hadn't quite gotten there yet. It was a top-3 show in both Republican and Democratic homes and both nominees for president in 2012, one of them a conservative Mormon, said it was their favorite show to watch with the whole family. Conceptually, *Modern Family* was a reboot of *Everybody Loves Raymond* — three bickering yet close-knit families related by marriage — only without the studio audience and the 1950s values. In execution it was much more, thanks to great scripts, a free-flowing mockumentary format, Stonestreet and Ferguson's marital foibles and the obvious joy that Burrell brought to the role of hapless Phil.

🏆 Peabody Award, 22 Emmys, SAG Award for best comedy ensemble (4 wins)

Modern Love
TV-MA, 2019–present
Prime Video original, 2 seasons,
16 episodes (AD)
Anthology series (romantic comedy) created by John Carney, with Minnie Driver, Garrett Hedlund, Sofia Boutella, Olivia Cooke, Lucy Boynton, Anne Hathaway, Anna Paquin, Catherine Keener, Cristin Milioti and Dev Patel.

Actors performed dramatized versions of essays that appeared in the *New York Times* "Modern Love" column. Fans of the column and related podcast will enjoy most of these short episodes which typically feature neurotic, self-absorbed New Yorkers looking for love.

▶▶ Season 2 was better than Season 1, in particular "Am I…? Maybe This Quiz Will Tell Me" (S2E5), starring Lulu Wilson as a teen who relies on online quizzes for insight into her sexuality; "A Second Embrace, With Hearts and Eyes Open" (S2E8) starring Tobias Menzies and Sophie Okonedo; and "On a Serpentine Road, With the Top Down" (S2E1), with Minnie Driver as a widow.

The Mole (2001)
TV-14, 2001–2008
Netflix, 5 seasons, 49 episodes
Reality competition with Anderson Cooper.

Thanks to an upcoming reboot, the original Anderson Cooper-hosted version of *The Mole* is back and worth a rewatch by reality lovers. Though at the time it was often compared to *Survivor*, this strategy-based game format imported

from Belgium was more intriguing and action-packed than the island show. (Also, everyone ate well and traveled in style between the four shooting locations in the USA and Europe.) Nine contestants and one "mole" take part in challenges, which the mole is continually sabotaging while trying not to get caught. The players try to hone in on the traitor in their midst, but they're being eliminated one by one. It's a solid format. Netflix has brought back *The Mole* for a 2022 reboot, hence the return of the original's first 2 seasons.

Mom
TV-14, 2013–2021
Paramount+, Hulu, 8 seasons,
170 episodes
Sitcom created by Chuck Lorre, Eddie Gorodetsky and Gemma Baker, with Allison Janney, Anna Faris, Mimi Kennedy, Beth Hall, Jaime Pressly, William Fichtner and Kristen Johnston.

Anna Faris and Allison Janney play a daughter and mother pursuing sobriety together in this late-blooming Chuck Lorre sitcom. Though initially bogged down by the usual sitcom trappings, *Mom* became a long-running hit because it focused on what it's like to be a woman in recovery. Many scenes take place at a females-only AA meeting and explored, with just the right comedic touches, issues related to recovery like making amends, becoming an untroubled social drinker without AA, addicts who refuse help and romance with someone who doesn't have an unhealthy relationship with substances.

▶▶ Standout episodes include "Dropped Soap and a Big Guy on the Throne" (S2E18), first in a 3-parter about painkillers that Bonnie (Janney) is prescribed and enjoys so much that she tries to re-injure her back. Other great needle-drops are "Cornflakes and the Hair of Men" (S3E16), about a wrong number turning into romance; and "One Tiny

Incision and a Coffin Dress" (S7E11) with Johnson, a welcome addition to the cast in later seasons.

🏆 2 more Emmy wins for Janney as best supporting actress, this time in a comedy series

Money Heist (La casa de papel)
TV-MA, 2017–present
Netflix original, 5 seasons, 41 episodes, dubbed (AD)
Crime drama with Úrsula Corberó, Álvaro Morte, Itziar Ituño, Pedro Alonso, Miguel Herrán, Jaime Lorente, Esther Acebo, Enrique Arce, Darko Peric and Alba Flores.

Netflix's first non-English-language breakout hit was this taut, silly, manic crime caper. From its Tarantino-esque rogue's gallery of oddballs to the blaring red jumpsuits to its crazy stunts, Spain's *Money Heist* has a propulsive energy that — as overseas audiences learned long ago about Hollywood action films — transcends language barriers. Morte is dynamite as The Professor, the eccentric mastermind behind the heists.

🎙 **From our forums:** "This was probably one of the most bingeable shows I've watched on Netflix. There were so many riveting aspects and so many cheesy aspects. Like all the sex, including two people with bullet holes getting romantic."

Monk
TV-PG, 2002–2009
Prime Video, 8 seasons, 125 episodes (AD)
Comedy-drama with Tony Shalhoub, Jason Gray-Stanford, Ted Levine and Traylor Howard.

Tony Shalhoub perpetually delights as the brilliant detective who must solve cases without succumbing to OCD, which is hard when you're afraid of so much. Let's give a little credit to Levine, though, who had the thankless task of playing Captain Stottlemeyer, Monk's former boss and the guy tasked with questioning Monk's theories. But as the full trophy case attests, it was Shalhoub's idiosyncratic portrayal of the hand-washing savant that made *Monk*.

🏆 Emmy for best actor in a comedy (Shalhoub, 3 wins), SAG Award for male actor in a comedy (2 wins)

The Morning Show
TV-MA, 2019–present
Apple TV+ original, 2 seasons, 20 episodes (AD)
Drama with Jennifer Aniston, Reese Witherspoon, Billy Crudup, Steve Carell, Gugu Mbatha-Raw, Nestor Carbonell, Bel Powley, Karen Pittman, Desean Terry and Jack Davenport.

Critics panned its slow start, but Apple TV+'s high-visibility debut drama eventually found its footing and ended Season 1 strong. Loosely adapted from Brian Stelter's behind-the-scenes book about the *Today* show, Aniston stars as an anchor on the top-rated morning program whose on-air partner Mitch (Carell) has just been fired for sexual misconduct. Witherspoon co-stars as the upstart reporter who's hastily installed as the show's new co-anchor.

🎙 **From our forums:** "While I think the show had some trouble with pacing (very slow), I loved all the strong female characters, especially Marcia Gay Harden's reporter. I thought Carell did really solid work here. I understood why people would be charmed by him but that tinge of selfish malice you could feel just under the surface, chilling really. On a shallow note, everything Aniston wore screamed money, loved it!"

▶▶ For suggestions of related shows, see "If You Liked *The Morning Show*," page 375.

🏆 Emmy and Critics Choice awards for best supporting actor in a drama (Crudup)

The Mosquito Coast

TV-MA, 2021–present
Apple TV+ original, 7 episodes (AD)
Drama with Justin Theroux, Melissa George, Logan Polish, Gabriel Bateman, Kimberly Elise and James Le Gros.

The TV adaptation of Paul Theroux's novel is full of twists and just enough moments of comic relief. Neil Cross, who created *Luther*, has taken the story that became the 1986 movie with Harrison Ford and has given it a multi-episode arc with the author's nephew, Justin Theroux, in Ford's role as Allie Fox. The biggest shift is that Allie is now a fugitive from justice. His crimes aren't immediately clear, though his anti-government views and connection to a cadre of off-the-grid environmentalists is suspicious. It's clear this is a road trip his wife Margot (George) and their two kids would rather not be taking, but Allie is used to getting his way.

▶▶ Pairs well with *The Americans*

The Most Dangerous Animal of All

TV-14, 2020
Hulu, 4 episodes
Limited series (true crime) directed by Kief Davidson, with Gary L. Stewart, Susan Mustafa and Duffy Jennings.

Convinced his late father was the Zodiac Killer, a man becomes obsessed with proving the link — whether it exists or not. Fascinating and well-built miniseries begins with Stewart, co-author of the bestselling true-crime book of the same name, explaining his 17-year investigation into the man who fathered him and who, he's convinced, was a notorious serial killer. Davidson devotes the first half of the series to respectfully presenting Stewart's claims, and the second half to

unraveling those claims through their own investigation.

The Movies That Made Us

TV-MA, 2019–present
Netflix original, 3 seasons, 14 episodes (AD)
Docuseries directed by Brian Volk-Weiss, with Donald Ian Black and Danny Wallace.

Each episode of this nostalgic series takes a deep dive into the history of a blockbuster film from the 1980s and '90s in breezy detail that will satisfy even hardcore movie fans. From *Pretty Woman* to *Jurassic Park* to *Home Alone*, this show uses jokey narration and visual gags to present the history of a Hollywood classic, from the pitch meeting to the inevitable setbacks to the improbable twists and turns that are almost as compelling as the storyline of the movie itself.

▶▶ This series is a companion to *The Toys That Made Us* and it spawned a two-episode spinoff called *The Holiday Movies That Made Us.*

Mozart in the Jungle

TV-MA, 2014–2018
Prime Video original, 4 seasons, 40 episodes (AD)
Comedy-drama created by Jason Schwartzman, Roman Coppola and Alex Timbers, with Gael García Bernal, Lola Kirke, Saffron Burrows, Bernadette Peters and Malcolm McDowell.

The staid world of classical music is upended lovingly in this fast-paced comedy about an orchestra whose new conductor is a hot mess. This witty behind-the-scenes sitcom at a New York symphony was overshadowed by *Transparent*, another early Amazon original that came out in the same year of 2014. Gael García Bernal is terrific as the charming and chaotic incoming

Some shows may have moved; see page 183. **213**

conductor, but the whole ensemble shines — as befits a top orchestra.

📡 **From our forums:** "Loved all the quirky characters and the politics vs. art in both the orchestra members (seniority, unions) and the endless fundraising that goes into keeping the lights on."

🏆 2 Emmys

Mr. Inbetween
TV-MA, 2018–2021
Hulu, 3 seasons, 26 episodes (AD)
Crime drama created by Scott Ryan, with Scott Ryan, Chika Yasumura, Justin Rosniak and Damon Herriman.

Ray Shoesmith wants to be a good husband, father, brother and friend, but his job as an enforcer keeps complicating things. Hitman shows are practically becoming their own genre, but *Mr. Inbetween* stands out because Australian actor Ryan, who created this role years ago for a film, has the role down cold. He also writes the scripts, which are admirably sophisticated and draw out dimensions of Ray that go far beyond the tortured-antihero template.

Mr. Mayor
TV-PG, 2021–present
Peacock, 10 episodes (AD)
Sitcom created by Tina Fey and Robert Carlock, with Ted Danson, Vella Lovell, Mike Cabellon, Kyla Kenedy, Bobby Moynihan and Holly Hunter.

Ted Danson kills it as L.A.'s new accidental mayor in a sitcom that does for local politics what *30 Rock* did for network TV. Once again Fey and Carlock have assembled a cast of bright young oddballs to surround vets Danson and Hunter (who plays a super-woke councilwoman). But really, it's all about Ted. At times you can almost believe the real Danson got elected mayor and hired the writers of *30 Rock* to follow him around. During a press conference to announce a plastic-straw ban, he is asked how people will drink iced coffee. "Make popsicles!" he says — advice that, like this show, is weirdly brilliant.

Mr. Mercedes
TV-MA, 2017–2019
Peacock, 3 seasons, 30 episodes
Crime drama created by David E. Kelley, with Brendan Gleeson, Harry Treadaway, Holland Taylor, Justine Lupe, Jharrel Jerome, Breeda Wool and Robert Stanton.

One of the best Stephen King adaptations in years. The trilogy follows retired detective Bill Hodges (Gleeson), who is still hunting a criminal that got away. Meanwhile *he* is being hunted by an obsessed and disturbed young man. A fresh take on the serial-killer genre and a fine collaboration between the novelist and super-producer Kelley.

📡 **From our forums:** "So this is supposed to be King's 'straight' detective story, eh? He can't help making it creepy!" "Holland Taylor is a hoot as the thirsty pragmatic neighbor."

Mr. Robot
TV-MA, 2015–2019
Prime Video, 4 seasons, 45 episodes (AD)
Crime drama created by Sam Esmail, with Rami Malek, Christian Slater, Carly Chaikin, Martin Wallström, Portia Doubleday, Michael Cristofer, Grace Gummer and BD Wong.

In the role that made him a star, Rami Malek plays a computer genius who's recruited to join a group of hacktivists planning to upend the capitalist world order. Sam Esmail's paranoia-fueled dissection of corporate power, laced with black comedy, offers a complicated protagonist in Elliot Alderson (Malek), an unreliable narrator whose connection to reality seems tenuous at times but whose hacking skills are perfect for carrying out Mr. Robot's (Slater) scheme to erase all consumer debt. The show embeds the viewer deep in hacker culture, while clever production techniques help us feel Elliot's mental illness as it threatens to overwhelm him at times.

🏆 Peabody Award; Critics Choice Award for best drama series; TCA Award for outstanding new program

Mr. Show with Bob and David

TV-MA, 1995–1998
HBO Max, 4 seasons, 30 episodes
Sketch comedy created by David Cross and Bob Odenkirk, with David Cross and Bob Odenkirk.

Pioneering adult sketch-comedy show still holds up a quarter century later. Imagine if *Monty Python's Flying Circus* had been made for HBO and you're close to the flavor of this absurd and still laugh-out-loud series from deadpan comic Cross and multitalented Odenkirk. Like its British forbear, *Mr. Show* was less a sketch show than a stream of consciousness that seemed to get funnier at each turn.

▶▶ The duo returned to TV sketch comedy in 2015 with the four episode Netflix series *W/ Bob & David*.

Mrs. America

TV-MA, 2020
Hulu, 9 episodes
Limited series (historical drama) with Cate Blanchett, Rose Byrne, Uzo Aduba, Elizabeth Banks, Kayli Carter, Ari Graynor, Melanie Lynskey, Margo Martindale, John Slattery and Jeanne Tripplehorn.

Star-studded dramatization of the rise and fall of the Equal Rights Amendment in the 1970s. Passage of the E.R.A. would be the culminating triumph of second-wave feminism. With bipartisan support, it would usher in equality between the sexes in the workplace, marriage, reproduction and military service — but for Phyllis Schlafly. In a twist that elevates *Mrs. America* to the top tier of historical docudramas, the star isn't an E.R.A. proponent but its staunchest opponent. Blanchett plays the tradition-minded but fiercely ambitious housewife who rallies her own sisterhood to stop the amendment's ratification. Great performances abound with episodes devoted to Gloria Steinem (Byrne), Shirley Chisholm (Aduba), Bella Abzug (Martindale) and other feminist icons. But it's Blanchett's deft performance that helps us understand how there's nothing inevitable about change.

🏆 Emmy and Critics Choice awards for best supporting actress in a limited series (Aduba)

Mrs. Fletcher

TV-MA, 2019
HBO Max, 7 episodes (AD)
Limited series (comedy-drama) with Kathryn Hahn, Jackson White, Owen Teague, Jen Richards, Ifádansi Rashad, Katie Kershaw, Cameron Boyce, Domenick Lombardozzi and Casey Wilson.

Kathryn Hahn carries this sexy comedy as a divorced mom who finds new things to do now that she's an empty nester. Tom Perrotta (*The Leftovers*) adapted his own novel into this steamy character-driven show about Eve Fletcher (Hahn), a woman whose obnoxious jock son Brendan (White) has just gone off to college. After years of catering to other people's needs, she's catering to her own needs (think Internet porn). Meanwhile, entitled Brendan learns a few hard lessons at school. For all the sexy storylines, the show has appeal as a double coming-of-age story for Brendan and his mom, with surprising amounts of empathy for both.

Muhammad Ali

TV-PG, 2021
PBS Passport, 4 episodes

Docuseries directed by Ken Burns, Sarah Burns and David McMahon, with Muhammad Ali, Rasheda Ali, Laila Ali, Belinda Boyd, Salim Muwakkil, Jerry Izenberg, Jonathan Eig, David Remnick, Kareem Abdul-Jabbar and Keith David. **_Tour de force_ biography of the boxer and activist places Ali firmly in his times and gives viewers a deeper appreciation of his achievements.** Written and co-produced by daughter Sarah Burns and son-in-law McMahon, _Muhammad Ali_ goes beyond the biography and engages, in a highly entertaining way, the cultural and political forces around Ali and shows how he, both in and out of the ring, changed that world. This isn't your old-timey Ken Burns film — it has pulse and tempo, with modern graphics and a vibrant score. The fight scenes are thrilling, but so are the scenes of Ali just talking.

Murder on Middle Beach
TV-MA, 2020
HBO Max, 4 episodes (AD)
Limited series (true crime) directed by Madison Hamburg, with Madison Hamburg and Mark E. Safarik.
The director invites the audience to help him untangle his mother's unsolved slaying. Madison Hamburg was only 18 when his mother was killed in March 2010. This four-part docuseries is an attempt to tell her story and light a fire under an investigation that's gone cold in the intervening decade. Like _Strong Island_ and _Dear Zachary_, it's part of a distinct subclass of true crime that bears witness to the violent deaths of loved ones. Hamburg's narrative can be challenging, with theories tossed in at times seemingly at random, or to create episode cliffhangers. But it's effective, and the audience's struggle to fit all the information into a cohesive hypothesis is a potent parallel with Hamburg's struggle to do the same.

Murderball
R, 2005
Tubi, PlutoTV, Peacock, 1 hr 28 mins
Movie (documentary) directed by Henry Alex Rubin and Dana Adam Shapiro.
Quadriplegic rugby players are shown in action, which is compelling enough — but then you get to know them. The guys on Team USA of what's now known as the Wheelchair Rugby Association don't need to be motivated before a match. They've all suffered devastating loss — usually in the prime of life — and they'll go to war at the drop of a ball. Loaded with drama both on and off the court and full of frank talk about quad life (including, yes, descriptions of sex), this is a film about remarkable humans who just happen to play a rough sport.

My Favorite Shapes by Julio Torres
TV-14, 2019
HBO Max, 57 mins
Comedy special with Julio Torres, Lin-Manuel Miranda, Emma Stone and Ryan Gosling.
As a conveyor belt of objects moves in front of him, Torres explains why each object is an example of one of his favorite shapes. The free-associative comedy in this special is also on display in _Los Espookys_, which Torres created.

My Next Guest Needs No Introduction with David Letterman
TV-MA, 2018–present
Netflix original, 3 seasons, 18 episodes (AD)
Talk show with David Letterman.
The TV legend sits down with some of the biggest names in pop culture in this long-form interview series. One

of Netflix's big "gets" from its growth years was Letterman, who brought his lumberjack beard and noticeably mellower personality to Streaming TV for this stripped-down interview show. The once famously ornery host engages in thoughtful extended conversations with the likes of Barack Obama, Malala Yousafzai, Jay-Z and George Clooney. These are usually accompanied by well-done taped pieces in which Letterman visits the guest at home or a place special to them (e.g., the Edmund Pettis Bridge with Rep. John Lewis).

My Octopus Teacher

TV-G, 2020
Netflix, 1 hr 25 mins (AD)
Movie (documentary) directed by Pippa Ehrlich and James Reed, with Craig Foster and Tom Foster.

Oscar-winning account of a marine videographer who forms an unusually intimate bond with an eight-limbed mollusk in an underwater cave. Viewers and award voters were captivated by the video of Craig Foster snorkel-diving, day after day, into the lair of a wild octopus living in the kelp off the coast of South Africa. Over time the creature takes Foster into her confidence and lets him observe her daily routines up-close.

▸▸ Unseen and unacknowledged until the credits, videographer Roger Horrocks captured the interactions between Foster and the octopus.

🏆 Oscar, best documentary feature

My So-Called Life

TV-14, 1994–1995
Hulu, 19 episodes
Teen drama with Claire Danes, Bess Armstrong, A.J. Langer, Wilson Cruz, Devon Gummersall, Devon Odessa, Lisa Wilhoit, Jared Leto and Tom Irwin.

A prodigious 15-year-old Claire Danes gave voice to every teen who's ever tried to reinvent themselves and/or crushed on a dreamy bad boy in this beloved teen drama. A notable victim of the network-era syndrome known as bad scheduling, *My So-Called Life* spent its one low-rated season on ABC competing for eyeballs with NBC's *Friends* and *Mad About You*. Universally praised by critics (who *did* watch the whole series), it marked an important advance in TV's attempts to capture the authentic voice of teenagers. The portrayal of gay teen Rickie Vasquez by Cruz (*Visible: Out on Television*) was equally notable; his fumbling innocence still resonates with many viewers today.

▸▸ Writer-producer Jason Katims (*Friday Night Lights*, *Parenthood*) broke into the business on *My So-Called Life* with three episode credits.

🏆 TCA Award for outstanding drama series

The Mysterious Benedict Society

TV-PG, 2021–present
Disney+ original, 8 episodes (AD)
Family drama with Tony Hale, Kristen Schaal, MaameYaa Boafo, Ryan Hurst, Gia Sandhu, Mystic Inscho, Seth B. Carr, Emmy DeOliveira and Marta Kessler.

Tony Hale (*Veep*) pulls double duty in this charming mystery adventure, playing both Benedict and his evil twin brother Curtain. This adaptation of the children's book by Trenton Lee Stewart, *The Mysterious Benedict Society* follows four gifted orphans recruited by oddball genius Nicolas Benedict to save the world from a mysterious crisis known only as "The Emergency."

The Mystery of D.B. Cooper

TV-14, 2020
HBO Max, 1 hr 25 mins (AD)
Movie (documentary) directed by John Dower.

A new doc on the legendary skyjacking goes way beyond the typical true-crime

TV show treatment of this case. D.B. Cooper hijacked Northwest Orient Flight 305 on Thanksgiving Eve 1971, then parachuted from the aircraft's aft stairs into history as the perpetrator of the only United States skyjacking that remains unsolved. Dower had excellent access to case figures and experts, a solid focus on only the strongest theories instead of chasing endless rabbit holes and, most helpfully, a tone that doesn't take itself too seriously.

Mythic Quest
TV-MA, 2020–present
Apple TV+ original, 2 seasons,
20 episodes (AD)
Comedy created by Rob McElhenney, Charlie Day and Megan Ganz, with Rob McElhenney, F. Murray Abraham, Charlotte Nicdao, Ashly Burch, Jessie Ennis, Imani Hakim, David Hornsby and Danny Pudi.

Believe it or not, the same trio of stars and producers from *It's Always Sunny in Philadelphia* **have created a warm-hearted comedy.** Set at a video game company, *Mythic Quest* is very savvy about gaming culture (being an Apple TV+ show has its benefits) and this allows for scrupulously detailed storytelling. And the character development is surprisingly rich, as these nerds form an affable but competitive community.

🗨 **From our forums:** "The cast has great chemistry. I've seen a few shows do a special quarantine episode but I'm not sure any have done it as well as *Mythic Quest*."

Nadiya Bakes
TV-G, 2020–present
Netflix original, 8 episodes (AD)
Docuseries with Nadiya Hussain.

Nadiya Bakes **is classic instructional cooking TV, like** *Barefoot Contessa* **but for baking, anchored by** *Great British*

Bake-Off **winner Nadiya Hussain.** Hussain's obvious love of her craft comes shining through like the light in her sun-drenched studio where she whips up bread, biscuits (cookies) and other treats. The 30-minute episodes have time for three or four bakes, a profile of another UK pastry chef and Nadiya sharing one of her creations with her crew, a warm hug to the home viewers.

Nail Bomber: Manhunt
TV-MA, 2021
Netflix original, 1 hr 12 mins (AD)
Movie (documentary) directed by Daniel Vernon.

A brisk recount of London's 1999 nail bombings and the race to find the perpetrator. A very capable review of a case many Americans may not know about, the film touches on larger issues like bias in policing, the double-edged sword of facial-recognition technology, and how to know when the Internet boasting of white nationalists is more than empty threats. It's also notable for giving voice to the victims of the attacks.

Nailed It!
TV-PG, 2018–present
Netflix original, 6 seasons,
39 episodes (AD)
Game show with Nicole Byer, Jacques Torres and Weston Bahr.

One of TV's most comforting shows has amateur bakers recreating some of the most ornate, intricate desserts you can imagine — and failing spectacularly. *Nailed It!* (the title comes from an Internet meme for failure) is not actually about baking well, it's about baking less poorly than your competition. The cake disasters on display in any given episode are a jubilant celebration of the joy to be found in failing big. Hosts Nicole Byer and Jacques Torres have maintained the perfect laughing-with-you tone throughout the series's run.

▶▶ Can't get enough *Nailed It!*? Netflix has you covered with a festive spinoff series, *Nailed It! Holiday*, and several international editions including *Nailed It! Mexico, Nailed It! Spain, Nailed It! France* and *Nailed It! Germany*.

Naked and Afraid
TV-14, 2013–present
Discovery+, Hulu, 14 seasons,
159 episodes
Reality competition.

Two hard-core survivalists are stranded for 21 days with no water, food, tools or clothes, and their ordeal is boiled down to a single compelling hour. No, the series doesn't shy away from nudity, at least not when the cast members are filmed from behind. It also breaks the fourth wall to acknowledge that they are being filmed by a small crew that intervenes if necessary, such as for medical emergencies. The narrator is annoying and too intense, but the contestants are obviously facing brutally real challenges, so it's not inaccurate to distill three weeks of survival down to just the most dramatic and interesting moments.

The Nanny
TV-PG, 1993–1999
HBO Max, PlutoTV, 6 seasons,
145 episodes
Classic sitcom created by Fran Drescher and Peter Marc Jacobson, with Fran Drescher, Charles Shaughnessy, Daniel Davis, Lauren Lane, Nicholle Tom, Benjamin Salisbury, Madeline Zima and Renée Taylor.

The lightly regarded 1990s sitcom made a roaring comeback during the pandemic as it reminded viewers of happier times. Fran Drescher's unlikely star vehicle is enjoying an unlikely revival. Partly that's due to its sitcommy aesthetic

— the catchy theme song, the nonstop punchlines, a made-for-TV premise — which gives it nostalgic appeal. But viewers have also noticed that the show gives voice to what film scholar Kathleen Rowe Carlin calls "the unruly woman": someone who uses her laughter, her body and her sexuality to challenge patriarchal power. Whether or not you buy that theory, *The Nanny* is one of a vanishing breed of sitcom that invites audiences to laugh *with* its characters rather than *at* them.

Narcos
TV-MA, 2015–2017
Netflix original, 3 seasons, 30 episodes, dubbed (AD)
Crime drama with Pedro Pascal, Wagner Moura, Boyd Holbrook, Alberto Ammann, Paulina Gaitan and Lizbeth Eden.

Wagner Moura is outstanding as drug kingpin Pablo Escobar in this Spanish-language hit for Netflix. If you're not familiar with Escobar's cocaine cartel and how brutal its reign of terror was inside Colombia, you might find some of the more horrific scenes in Narcos hard to believe. Based on the nonfiction book Finding Pablo, the series details how Escobar and his militia eliminated anyone trying to bring him to justice and destabilized domestic politics. But in the American DEA, led by Agent Javier Pena (Pascal), the psychopath eventually met his match. The global popularity of Narcos led Netflix to keep renewing it, and over time its focus shifted to the DEA's efforts to break up the entire cartel.

🐾 **From our forums:** "This isn't going to go over well with those who can't handle domesticated animal body counts, never mind the substantial human body count or the gang rape."

For shows sorted by streaming platform, see page 381. **219**

Narcos: Mexico

TV-MA, 2018–present
Netflix original, 2 seasons,
20 episodes (AD)

Crime drama with Scoot McNairy, Diego Luna, José María Yazpik , Michael Peña, Matt Letscher, Alejandro Edda and Alfonso Dosal.

Miguel Ángel Félix Gallardo sets up the Mexican illegal drug trade in the 1980s in this companion series to *Narcos.* Faithful to the *Narcos* template, this pits Diego Luna's kingpin against Michael Peña's DEA agent — and once again it's the bad guys who make for the more compelling TV characters. This version is just as intense and well-paced as the original *Narcos*. But it feels more depressing, perhaps because the proximity of Mexico to the U.S. underscores just how long, and how seemingly fruitless, the war on drugs has been.

National Treasure (2016)

TV-MA, 2017
Hulu original, 4 episodes

Limited series (drama) with Robbie Coltrane, Julie Walters, Andrea Riseborough, Babou Ceesay, Mark Lewis Jones, Nadine Marshall, Tim McInnerny and Graeme Hawley.

Robbie Coltrane stars as a beloved UK comedian accused of sexually assaulting multiple women across multiple decades. The British, like the Americans, have been rocked by epic #MeToo scandals (do a search for Jimmy Savile if you have the stomach). This psychological drama from the skilled hand of Jack Thorne (*The Eddy, Harry Potter and the Cursed Child*) explores how the drip, drip, drip of accusations starts to erode the faith of everyone around the accused.

🏆 BAFTA award for best miniseries

NCIS

TV-14, 2003–present
Paramount+, Netflix, 18 seasons,
414 episodes (AD)

Drama created by Donald P. Bellisario, with Mark Harmon, David McCallum, Sean Murray, Pauley Perrette, Brian Dietzen, Michael Weatherly, Rocky Carroll, Cote de Pablo, Emily Wickersham and Lauren Holly.

Network TV's best procedural franchise has just the right measure of character development, patriotism and things that go boom. Being the best network procedural is like making the best pasteurized processed cheese: it's bland but lucrative business. And if you were to add up every NBC *Today* show scandal of the past 25 years, it wouldn't be nearly as costly as the network's decision to cancel the military procedural *JAG* in 1996. CBS scooped up the series and, in 2003, asked its creator for a spinoff. Thus *NCIS* was born. Anchored by a solid ensemble — Harmon's cool hand Gibbs, Weatherly as his right hand, McCallum as the M.E., Perrette and Murray as the juniors — with more character development than the typical cop show of its time, *NCIS* kept growing in popularity. It displaced *CSI* as TV's most-watched scripted show in 2010 and has remained No. 1 in that category ever since.

▸▸ Skip most of the first 2 seasons, which overdid the post-9/11 terrorism storylines, and drop the needle on "SWAK" (S2E22). This episode sets up the third season of *NCIS* that introduces two fan favorites, Ziva (de Pablo) and Shepard (Holly), to the cast, and includes the first — but hardly the last — attempt by Gibbs to quit NCIS.

▸▸ The spinoff has since spun off three other shows: *NCIS: Los Angeles* with LL Cool J and Chris O'Donnell (2009-present), *NCIS: New Orleans* with Scott Bakula (2014-2021) and *NCIS: Hawai'i* with Vanessa Lachey

(2021-present).

Never Have I Ever
TV-14, 2020–present
Netflix original, 2 seasons,
20 episodes (AD)
Romantic comedy created by Mindy
Kaling and Lang Fisher, with Maitreyi
Ramakrishnan, Poorna Jagannathan,
Darren Barnet, Richa Moorjani, John
McEnroe, Ramona Young, Lee Rodriguez,
Jaren Lewison and Benjamin Norris.

**From the mind of Mindy Kaling comes
a romcom built around an ambitious,
goofy teenage girl and her Indian-
American immigrant family.** Devi
Vishwakumar (Ramakrishnan) wants
to be popular in high school. But she
must work around a controlling mother
(Jagannathan) and her perfect cousin
(Moorjani), who moved in after the death
of Devi's dad. Devi isn't just a collection
of first-generation overachiever tropes —
she's also stubborn, spiky and cluelessly
headstrong in a way only teenagers can
be. The show's writers aren't afraid to push
things in unexpected directions because
the characters are so likable; we stick with
them through cringe-worthy humiliations
and some affecting twists and turns.

▶▶ Yes, that *is* tennis legend John
McEnroe's sardonic voice narrating the
show. He was Kaling's idea and he's less
distracting than you might think.

New Girl
TV-14, 2011–2018
Netflix, 7 seasons, 146 episodes (AD)
Sitcom created by Elizabeth Meriwether,
with Zooey Deschanel, Jake Johnson,
Max Greenfield, Lamorne Morris, Hannah
Simone and Damon Wayans Jr.

**Spurned by her boyfriend, bubbly
teacher Jess Day moves in with three
oddball roommates in this quirky
30-something comedy.** Fox PR people
coined the word "adorkable" in marketing

Zooey Deschanel's *New Girl* character.
They weren't wrong — but like most TV
comedies it was the chemistry of the
show's ensemble cast that made it a critical
and popular success.

▶▶ Prince was such a fan of *New Girl* that
he agreed to appear in the show's 2014
post–Super Bowl episode (S3E14), which
drew a whopping 26 million viewers.

The New Pope
TV-MA, 2020
HBO Max, 9 episodes
Limited series (drama) with Jude Law,
John Malkovich, Silvio Orlando, Cécile
de France, Javier Cámara and Ludivine
Sagnier.

**Followup to *The Young Pope* introduces
John Malkovich as a rival to Jude Law's
pontiff, setting off yet another round of
plotting, power-grabbing and head-
spinning dialogue.** As this series begins,
Law's volatile, sexual and controversial
pontiff lies in a coma, leaving room
for Malkovich's cerebral and reserved
character to take over. Just as scheming
and offbeat as its predecessor, the
character to keep your eye on is Voiello
(Orlando), the savvy inside operator who
isn't above getting rid of a pontiff if it will
help the church.

The New Yorker Presents
TV-MA, 2015–2016
Prime Video original, 11 episodes
Docuseries created by Alex Gibney.

**Top doc producer Alex Gibney spares
us the trouble of having to read an
anthology of some of the magazine's
most popular and resonant stories.** Fun
and easy to watch, this series combined
dramatizations, cartoons, poetry readings
and more. A typical episode included a
story about how the FBI and CIA might
have prevented 9/11, a behind-the-scenes
visit to the *New Yorker's* fact-checking
department and a daffy sketch featuring

Paul Giamatti as famously overcaffeinated novelist Honoré de Balzac.

The Newsroom (US)
TV-MA, 2012–2014
HBO Max, 3 seasons, 25 episodes (AD)
Drama created by Aaron Sorkin, with Jeff Daniels, Emily Mortimer, John Gallagher Jr., Alison Pill, Thomas Sadoski, Dev Patel, Olivia Munn and Sam Waterston.

Aaron Sorkin's loquacious, politically-minded drama about a fictional cable news network still hums, even if the topical references are a decade old. Filmed as America's newsrooms were reeling from waves of layoffs and consolidation, *The Newsroom* resonated with its dramas that revolved around journalistic ethics and the spread of information and misinformation. Among the starry ensemble, Daniels is especially good as a high-minded anchorman, and Patel shines in a third-season arc about journalistic integrity. Seasons 2 and 3 are less preachy and add depth to the characters.

🏆 Emmy for best actor in a drama (Daniels)

The Night Manager
TV-14, 2016
Prime Video, 6 episodes
Limited series (crime drama) with Tom Hiddleston, Hugh Laurie, Olivia Colman, Elizabeth Debicki, Alistair Petrie, Douglas Hodge, Tom Hollander and David Harewood.

Tom Hiddleston and Hugh Laurie circle each other in an improbable cat-and-mouse spy game. An adaptation of the novel by John le Carré, the show follows Jonathan Pine (Hiddleston), a night manager at a hotel where he's recruited by a British intelligence agent (Colman) to befriend — and then betray — an arms dealer played to wicked perfection by Laurie.

▶▶ Pairs well with *Killing Eve*

The Night Of
TV-MA, 2016
HBO Max, 8 episodes
Limited series (crime drama) with Riz Ahmed, John Turturro, Bill Camp, Poorna Jagannathan, Payman Maadi, Jeannie Berlin and Michael K. Williams.

Stellar casting and writing set this criminal-justice series apart. After partying all night with a woman he picks up while driving his father's cab, Naz Khan (Ahmed) wakes up to discover her dead. Almost immediately, he's sucked into the tar pit of New York City's biased legal system, where a Pakistani-American like him may never break free. Fortunately, he is matched with Jack Stone (Turturro), a disheveled but dogged lawyer. Richard Price, well known to fans of David Simon dramas, pens a gritty, twist-filled adaptation of the UK series *Criminal Justice*.

▶▶ Jack Stone was originally to be played by James Gandolfini. After his death, the role was offered to Robert De Niro, but a scheduling conflict resulted in Turturro playing Stone. After all that, the Emmy Award for best actor in a limited series went to Riz Ahmed.

▶▶ Pairs well with *The Wire*

Night Stalker: The Hunt for a Serial Killer
TV-MA, 2021
Netflix original, 4 episodes (AD)
Limited series (true crime) directed by James Carroll and Tiller Russell.

An immersive take on the 1985 murder spree that gripped Los Angeles. The terrifying rampage of Richard Ramirez, aka "the Night Stalker," has long been a subject of grim true-crime fascination, but this four-part docuseries from Tiller Russell (*The Last Narc*) is a cut above. He gets excellent access to lead detectives Gil Carrillo and Frank Salerno, offering nuanced beats on the case and reasons why Carrillo, especially, might be so invested in it. The series strikes a good balance between the investigation and survivors' and families' testimony about what happened and what was taken from them.

Nip/Tuck
TV-MA, 2003–2010
Hulu, 6 seasons, 100 episodes
Medical drama created by Ryan Murphy, with Julian McMahon, Dylan Walsh, John Hensley and Joely Richardson.

Ryan Murphy's dramatic debut was this boundary-pushing, sweaty tale of two plastic surgeons in Miami. Murphy would later develop *American Horror Story* and other shows for FX, but *Nip/Tuck* was where he introduced viewers to his particular brand of silly excess, with gory plastic-surgery sequences, a two-season serial killer subplot and Joan Rivers developing a semen-based skincare product.

No Sudden Move
R, 2021
HBO Max original, 1 hr 55 mins (AD)
Movie (thriller) directed by Steven Soderbergh, with Benicio del Toro, Don Cheadle, Jon Hamm, Kieran Culkin, David Harbour and Brendan Fraser.

A gang of criminals think they're coming together for a simple job until things start spinning out of control. Director Soderbergh brings his usual flair to this stylish riff on the crime thriller.

Noelle
G, 2019
Disney+ original, 1 hr 40 mins (AD)
Movie (family comedy) with Anna Kendrick, Bill Hader, Shirley MacLaine,

Kingsley Ben-Adir, Julie Hagerty, Billy Eichner, Michael Gross and Ron Funches.

Few family-friendly Christmas movies in recent years have checked as many boxes as well as this one. After the newly installed Santa (Hader) gets cold feet and flees the North Pole for Arizona, it falls to Kendrick — aka Noelle — to save Christmas. And already you want to watch! Aided by an impressively game Shirley MacLaine as a grandmother elf, the likable cast and clever writing make this Disney+ original holiday film rewatchable fun for everyone.

Nomadland
R, 2020
Hulu, 1 hr 48 mins (AD)
Movie (drama) directed by Chloé Zhao, with Frances McDormand, David Strathairn, Linda May, Swankie, Gay DeForest, Patricia Grier and Angela Reyes.

The Hulu-funded Best Picture winner is a spare, open-eyed celebration of everyday people getting by in the New Economy. Director Zhao (*The Rider*) loves mixing the spontaneity and authenticity of documentaries with the narrative structure of a feature, and in *Nomadland* — based on the nonfiction bestseller about Americans who work seasonal jobs while moving around the country in campers — she found a big story to tell. McDormand won her third Academy Award playing a widow and novice nomad who learns the ropes from veterans (some of the actors are nomads in real life). Strathairn is his usual strong vulnerable self as a widowed nomad who takes a shine to her.
🏆 3 Oscars including best director

The Normal Heart
TV-MA, 2014
HBO Max, 2 hrs 12 mins
Movie (historical drama) directed by Ryan Murphy, with Mark Ruffalo, Julia

For shows sorted by streaming platform, see page 381.

Roberts, Matt Bomer, Alfred Molina, Joe Mantello, Jim Parsons, Jonathan Groff, BD Wong and Taylor Kitsch.

Mark Ruffalo stars in this essential film version of Larry Kramer's autobiographical play about the early days of AIDS activism. Ruffalo is compelling as Ned Weeks, an activist who is fighting to make both gay men and New York City politicians take AIDS seriously. Ryan Murphy, the king of excessive TV, is the perfect producer to take on this adaptation, which thrums with the explosive emotions and furious poetry of human beings in crisis.

🏆 Emmy for best TV movie; SAG Award (Ruffalo)

Normal People
TV-MA, 2020
Hulu original, 12 episodes (AD)
Limited series (romance drama) with Daisy Edgar-Jones and Paul Mescal.

Sally Rooney pulled off a spare, thoughtful adaptation of her 2018 novel about two Irish teenagers in an on-again, off-again affair. Rooney's novel was a literary sensation when it was published, but it was also filled with internal dialogue that's hard to put on screen. Yet this version — neatly chopped up into a dozen short episodes — succeeds in large part because the two leads are empathy magnets. You *want* them to succeed. And though there are moments of drama, and lots of sex, the most affecting parts of *Normal People* are the normal ones, the daily encounters where these two young people manage to communicate strong emotions with just a look or a brief pause.

The North Water
TV-MA, 2021
AMC+ original, 5 episodes
Limited series (drama) with Jack O'Connell and Colin Farrell.

Dark 1850s maritime drama about survival aboard an ill-starred fishing boat. It's telling that this show is directed by Andrew Haigh, who also helmed the crumbling marriage drama *45 Years* and created HBO's gay-men-growing-up series *Looking*. Like those titles, this one is equally adept at showing us the landmines hiding in silences, glances and small gestures. But this time, instead of poignant interpersonal conflicts, all that deft character building explodes into malice and murder. As an almost operatically evil seaman, Colin Farrell arrives at key moments to give this story a snarling wildness that's hard to shake.

Nuclear Family
TV-MA, 2021
HBO Max, 3 episodes (AD)
Docuseries directed by Ry Russo-Young.

The woman at the center of a historic custody battle between gay parents in the '80s revisits the ordeal and the toll it took. When two women looking to have a child called on a prominent gay activist to be their sperm donor, no one could have imagined the drama ahead. This docuseries benefits from copious access to home movies and living subjects on both sides of the court case.

The OA
TV-MA, 2016–2019
Netflix original, 2 seasons, 16 episodes (AD)
Sci-fi drama with Brit Marling, Emory Cohen, Patrick Gibson, Jason Isaacs and Phyllis Smith.

Stranger than *Stranger Things*, this engrossing sci-fi series is a challenge to watch but builds to an emotionally satisfying coda. Marling co-developed this line-blurring series and stars in it as Prairie, a woman convinced she's the OA, or original angel. Revealing her supernatural agenda to a band of young allies, they set off across America to save unfortunates from peril. Nothing if not innovative, this labor of love from Marling and Zal Batmanglij, who spent years developing it, divided critics in its early run. But many were won over by the end of the first season, when its bold and uncompromising vision of beauty delivered an emotional wallop in the finale.

From our forums: "It does drag in episodes 4–6, like it was originally a movie script that's been stretched to fit 8 episodes of a Netflix order. But the satisfying ending is worth it."

Oakland Trilogy: The Waiting Room, The Force, Homeroom
Not Rated, 2012–2021
Hulu original, 3 episodes
Docuseries directed by Peter Nicks.

Director Pete Nicks captures a major American city through these caring portraits of its most vital public institutions. From the opening minutes of *The Waiting Room*, the first of his films about Oakland, Calif., released over a 9-year span, it's clear Nicks has an eye and ear for meaningful moments. We eavesdrop on intimate conversations between people waiting their turn at a noisy, crowded emergency room. In *The Force*, we see the impact of protests and scandal on the Oakland Police Department through a lens that resists the easy narratives of *Cops* and the defund movements. And in *Homeroom* Nicks takes us beyond the urban-school documentary tropes to explore student governance and how the once-protective wall between school and the outside world is gone.

The Odd Couple (1970)
TV-G, 1970–1975
Hulu, 5 seasons, 114 episodes

Classic sitcom created by Jerry Belson and Garry Marshall, with Tony Randall, Jack Klugman, Al Molinaro, Penny Marshall and Brett Somers.

As finicky Felix and schlubby Oscar, Tony Randall and Jack Klugman were a comedy duo second only to Gleason and Carney. Before he created *Happy Days* (and *Laverne & Shirley* and *Mork & Mindy*), Garry Marshall helped adapt Neil Simon's play and movie for TV. The premise, in the form of a question asked at the top of each episode: "Can two divorced men share an apartment without driving each other crazy?" Randall embodied Felix, the neatnik, as did Klugman as sportswriter Oscar, the slob, and they did it so well that their personas followed them the rest of their careers. The show had some of the best comedy writing of the 1970s, but was at its best when the two sparring partners showed us their emotionally wounded sides.

▶▶ Skip the first season, which was filmed single-camera with a canned laugh track, and start with Season 2, when it began life as a multi-camera sitcom shot before a live studio audience. Our favorites are "A Night to Dismember" (S2E21), with Blanche (Somers) and Oscar recalling the party that led to their splitting up; the great "Password" episode with Betty White (S3E11); and "The Odd Father (S3E12), where Oscar helps Felix communicate with his daughter.

🏆 3 Emmys

The Office (UK)
TV-MA, 2001–2003
Prime Video, 3 seasons, 14 episodes
British comedy created by Ricky Gervais and Stephen Merchant, with Ricky Gervais, Martin Freeman, Mackenzie Crook, Lucy Davis and Ewen MacIntosh.

It's almost nothing like the American version, which is a blessing for lovers of British humour. It's raunchier, very

British — and they made 186 fewer episodes of it than the Yanks did of theirs. There's no point comparing Ricky Gervais's David Brent with Steve Carell's Michael Scott, because each one is true to a comic version of a typical blowhard middle manager in his respective country. Also, the collaborator you don't see on screen — Gervais's comedy partner Stephen Merchant — has a more wicked sensibility than Greg Daniels and Mike Schur of the U.S. *Office*. In short, you should enjoy one of the classics of UK comedy on its own terms. (But turn on the subtitles first.)

🏆 Peabody Award

The Office (US)
TV-14, 2005–2013
Peacock, 9 seasons, 201 episodes
Sitcom created by Ricky Gervais, Stephen Merchant and Greg Daniels, with Steve Carell, Rainn Wilson, John Krasinski, Jenna Fischer, Leslie David Baker, Brian Baumgartner, Angela Kinsey, Kate Flannery, Phyllis Smith and Creed Bratton.

People can't stop watching *The Office* for the same reason they haven't stopped watching *Cheers*, *M*A*S*H* or *Andy Griffith* — it's comfort TV well done. Once a show enters reruns you learn its true staying power. Andy, Barney and Aunt Bea endeared themselves to viewers from the '60s through the '80s. After that it was Hawkeye and B.J., then Sam and Diane, then Jerry and Kramer. Fans of those shows may not understand the appeal of *The Office* to its current generation of viewers, with its mockumentary style and less-than-lovable characters like Dwight Schrute (Wilson) and Michael Scott (Carell). But time has shown that Daniels and Schur, in adapting the UK *Office* for an American audience, put together a comedic cast for the ages. The show's love-hate relationship with the

workplace makes it the perfect comedy for the post-COVID age. Might as well get to like it, because it's not going anywhere.

▶▶ Peacock offers "superfan" cuts of classic episodes from Seasons 1 through 4 with deleted scenes, bloopers, featurettes and interviews.

▶▶ The two-part Season 7 finale that marked Carell's exit has an ingenious crossover appearance from his UK counterpart Ricky Gervais, creator of *The Office*.

🏆 Emmys for outstanding comedy series and writing

The Old Guard
R, 2020
Netflix original, 2 hrs 5 mins (AD)
Movie (action) directed by Gina Prince-Blythewood, with Charlize Theron, Chiwetel Ejiofor, KiKi Layne, Matthias Schoenaerts, Marwan Kenzari and Luca Marinelli.

Charlize Theron is in her element as the leader of a band of immortal mercenaries who discover a new member of their group just as they realize they're being hunted by someone who wants to destroy them. This comic book adaptation broke well beyond its core geek audience, which is one reason a sequel is on the way.

Olive Kitteridge
TV-14, 2014
HBO Max, 4 episodes
Limited series (drama) with Frances McDormand, Richard Jenkins, Ann Dowd, John Gallagher Jr., Peter Mullan, Rosemarie DeWitt, Zoe Kazan, Jesse Plemons, Martha Wainwright and Bill Murray.

Frances McDormand is the reason to stick with this depressing adaptation of the Pulitzer Prize–winning novel about a misanthropic math teacher in small-town Maine. With a stubborn spirit and sardonic humor, Olive (McDormand) is determined to press on even as her world falls apart around her. Despite the title, *Olive Kitteridge* is more than the story of a single person; it also delves into the lives of Olive's neighbors, whose stories intertwine with hers and are represented by a typically strong HBO ensemble.

🏆 8 Emmys including best limited series; SAG Award (McDormand)

On Becoming a God in Central Florida

TV-MA, 2019
Showtime original, 10 episodes
Dark comedy with Kirsten Dunst, Théodore Pellerin, Mel Rodriguez, Beth Ditto, Ted Levine, Usman Ally, Julie Benz and Alexander Skarsgård.

Kirsten Dunst plays a new mom who plots a very unusual revenge against the multi-level marketing company that ruins her family. Set in the 1990s, the show is not an examination of the psychology that pulls people into MLM schemes (see *LuLaRich* instead). Rather, it's just a rollicking vehicle for Dunst as she rides to the rescue of her husband (Skarsgard) who's hopelessly tied up in the company's cult of personality.

🎞 **From our forums:** "The first 6 episodes were good, then 7–9 felt rough to get through but the finale tied it up well."

On My Block

TV-14, 2018–2021
Netflix original, 4 seasons,
38 episodes (AD)
Comedy-drama with Sierra Capri, Jason Genao, Brett Gray, Diego Tinoco, Jessica Marie Garcia, Julio Macias and Peggy Blow.

Refreshingly mellow coming-of-age series follows a racially diverse bunch of high school friends in South Central Los Angeles. There's never been a teen show like *On My Block*, one that Latinx,

Black and urban kids could truly call their own. The "core four" — Monse, Cesar, Jamal and Ruby — are growing up in a neighborhood loaded with dangers like drugs and gangs and the ubiquitous gunshots (guessing the caliber of the gun from the sound is their version of identifying bird calls). Yet this charming show allows them to be goofy adolescents who learn to become comfortable in their skin, assert themselves in the world and impress (or try not to be shunned by) their peers.

▶▶ Netflix is developing a spinoff series called *Freeridge*.

▶▶ For suggestions of related shows, see "If You Liked *On My Block*," page 375.

On the Record

TV-MA, 2020
HBO Max original, 1 hr 35 mins (AD)
Movie (documentary) directed by Kirby Dick and Amy Ziering.

Two established documentarians take on hip-hop mogul Russell Simmons, accumulating a hefty dossier of sex abuse and harassment charges that point to a wider problem the industry has with women. Though not a bombshell of investigation and revelation like *Surviving R. Kelly*, this mustering of facts on the public record into a damning narrative makes it worth the watch.

▶▶ Not to be confused with the 2001 Bob Costas-hosted HBO series of the same name, or its 2021 followup *Back on the Record With Bob Costas*.

On the Rocks

R, 2020
Apple TV+ original, 1 hr 36 mins (AD)
Movie (comedy) directed by Sofia Coppola, with Bill Murray, Rashida Jones, Marlon Wayans and Jenny Slate.

After her marriage falls apart, a woman finds unexpected solace by going on a variety of adventures with her aging

playboy of a father. Coppola reunites with Murray and the result is nearly as delightful as what they made with *Lost in Translation*.

Once Upon a Time
TV-PG, 2011–2018
Disney+, 7 seasons, 156 episodes
Fantasy drama with Jennifer Morrison, Ginnifer Goodwin, Lana Parrilla, Robert Carlyle, Josh Dallas, Jared Gilmore, Colin O'Donoghue and Emilie de Ravin.

Lighthearted fantasy series about a small town in Maine where most of the residents are actually fairy tale characters who have slipped into our world. The show's ingenious conceit is that it not only shows characters like Snow White and Rumpelstiltskin living in everyday America, but also flashes back to their time in the fairy tale kingdom. That provides added depth and lets the actors have fun with two very different tones. Plus, there are always new characters popping up to bring another classic story into the mix.

▶▶ A time jump in the final season focused on a grown-up Henry.

One Child Nation
R, 2019
Prime Video original, 1 hr 23 mins (AD)
Movie (documentary) directed by Nanfu Wang and Jialing Zhang.

A filmmaker returns to her rural Chinese home to give the most personal account the West has ever seen of China's disturbing one-child-per-family policy. From 1979 to 2015 the Chinese government's one-child policy led to rampant abortions, a distorted birth rate that favored boys over girls and other social harms. Nanfu, who grew up poor in rural China, confronts family members and others in the village where she lived over their role in upholding this horror of social engineering.

🏆 Sundance Film Festival Grand Jury Prize

One Day at a Time (2017)
TV-PG, 2017–2020
Netflix original, 4 seasons,
46 episodes (AD)
Sitcom with Justina Machado, Todd Grinnell, Isabella Gomez, Marcel Ruiz, Stephen Tobolowsky and Rita Moreno.

This Latinx reboot of Norman Lear's 1970s sitcom has a distinct and entertaining voice all its own. The Bonnie Franklin original wasn't much more than a penciled-in canvas for this version of *One Day*. Machado's character was modeled on Franklin's: a single mom raising kids in a crowded apartment in L.A. And there was a building super who made himself a member of the family. Otherwise, the show found its own characters and stories in the Latino experience. Led by Machado and Moreno, the appealing cast took on seemingly every hot-button topic and somehow made LOL comedy from it: substance abuse, PTSD, ageism, 9/11, same-sex teen dating, immigration, self-love, private Instagram accounts, open relationships and more.

▶▶ Season 4 was the show's best. It was highlighted by a whip-smart "Politics Episode," which was animated owing to pandemic shutdown of the set. Unfortunately, it's not on streaming right now, but Paramount+ has the rights to carry it.

🏆 2 Emmys

One Mississippi
TV-MA, 2015–2017
Prime Video original, 2 seasons,
12 episodes (AD)
Dark comedy created by Diablo Cody and Tig Notaro, with Tig Notaro, Rya Kihlstedt, John Rothman, Noah Harpster and Stephanie Allynne.

Tig Notaro plays a comic named Tig in a show a lot like herself — whimsical but with a dark side. After Tig's mom becomes seriously ill, she decides to return to her Mississippi hometown. While there she has to cope with more than her mother's decline; she's recovering from a double mastectomy (like the real Tig) and must sort out past and present problems in her personal life. Co-created with Diablo Cody (*United States of Tara*), who's no stranger to dark, autobiographical comedy, *One Mississippi* shows Notaro at her most painfully candid, and you do feel at times like you're watching her work out her troubles through the medium of dark comedy.

🐾 **From our forums:** "So far, I like everybody. The scenery is gorgeous, and the show is not depending on cynicism or mockery for its punch."

One Night in Miami...

R, 2020
Prime Video original, 1 hr 54 mins (AD)
Movie (historical drama) directed by Regina King, with Kingsley Ben-Adir, Eli Goree, Aldis Hodge, Leslie Odom Jr., Michael Imperioli and Beau Bridges.

Four iconic Black men share unique perspectives on racial progress in an imagined gathering on the night of the 1964 Clay-Liston fight. Regina King directed this sparkling adaptation of the Kemp Powers play, set at a Negroes-only motel in Miami in the aftermath of the shocking KO of Sonny Liston by Cassius Clay, soon to be Muhammad Ali (Goree). Celebrating are his spiritual guide Malcolm X (Ben-Adir), singer Sam Cooke (Odom) and NFL great Jim Brown (Hodge). But the four men are soon in lively debate over what Black men should be doing in the decade ahead, one that holds much promise for African-Americans.

One of Us Is Lying

TV-MA, 2021–present
Peacock original, 8 episodes (AD)
Crime drama with Annalisa Cochrane, Chibuikem Uche, Marianly Tejada, Cooper van Grootel, Barrett Carnahan, Jessica McLeod, Mark McKenna, Melissa Collazo and Sara Thompson.

It's a breezy, bonkers twist on *The Breakfast Club*: Someone dies in high school detention and one of the other students in the room probably killed him. Based on a No. 1 bestselling YA mystery, this binge watch has enough twists to keep you guessing and suitable intrigue among the fresh-faced cast members with their friendships, affairs and backstabbing schemes. As a druggie on probation, van Grootel is the find of the cast, bringing daffy charm to the show's dark premise.

One Strange Rock

TV-PG, 2018–present
Disney+, 10 episodes
Docuseries with Will Smith.

If *Planet Earth* was thrown into a blender with *Gravity* and *The Fifth Element*, an electronic dance party and the musings of Neil deGrasse Tyson, the colorful smoothie that resulted would be this unscripted series. Hosted by Will Smith, *One Strange Rock* uses the smallest details to illustrate the interconnectedness of everything on earth. It has a sublime soundtrack and staggeringly weird visuals that all weave together in surprising and smart ways.

Only Murders in the Building

TV-MA, 2021–present
Hulu original, 10 episodes (AD)
Comedy thriller created by Steve Martin and John Hoffman, with Steve Martin, Martin Short, Selena Gomez, Amy Ryan and Aaron Dominguez.

Steve Martin, Martin Short and Selena Gomez are true-crime podcast aficionados turned local gumshoes in this satisfying murder mystery with millennial twists. It's the *Murder, She Wrote* reboot we didn't know we needed. Martin and Martin bring their comedy act to this sweet, silly, witty 10-part mystery set in a New York apartment building. Along with Gomez, they form an unlikely trio after a resident dies suspiciously. Not only are they keen to solve the case, they want to make a true-crime podcast and sell it to their favorite host (Fey, in a classic Fey turn).

▶▶ For suggestions of related shows, see "If You Liked *If Only Murders in the Building*," page 375.

Operation Varsity Blues
R, 2021
Netflix original, 1 hr 40 mins (AD)
Movie (documentary) with Matthew Modine, Roger Rignack, Jillian Peterson and Wallace Langham.

The notorious admission scam that allowed wealthy people to buy their kids' way into prestigious universities gets a strong hybrid treatment. Using the actual wiretap transcripts of corrupt admissions counsel Rick Singer, who agreed to wear a wire when federal agents got wind of his scam, Matthew Modine effectively reenacts the backroom dealings of Singer (although often he's in a very fancy room, chatting on a cell phone), playing him with a brutish charisma that makes it easy to understand how he controlled his network of powerful parents. Modine's reenactment scenes pair well with the rest of the film, a documentary that offers fresh insights into these crimes and a reminder that they caused real damage and ruined more than a few celebrity reputations.

Orange Is the New Black
TV-MA, 2013–2019
Netflix original, 7 seasons,
91 episodes (AD)
Dark comedy created by Jenji Kohan, with Taylor Schilling, Kate Mulgrew, Uzo Aduba, Danielle Brooks, Dascha Polanco, Selenis Leyva, Nick Sandow, Yael Stone, Adrienne C. Moore, Taryn Manning and Laura Prepon.

A revelation when it came out, *OITNB* sustained its momentum for years to become one of Streaming TV's first binge-worthy series. When privileged artisan soapmaker Piper (Schilling) is unexpectedly packed off to federal prison, she has to adjust real fast. Just as quickly, creator Kohan pivoted to other characters in her show's diverse cast to tell stories about the disenfranchised and underrepresented women around Piper. The fabulous Taystee (Brooks) and Cindy (Moore), among others, used humor as armor, making *OITNB* one of the early genre-busting streaming shows, winning for best comedy series at the Emmys. As the show progressed, it explored larger themes like prisons-for-profit, immigration and being queer behind bars.
🏆 Peabody Award, 4 Emmys and SAG Awards for best comedy ensemble

Orphan Black
TV-MA, 2013–2017
AMC+, Prime Video, 5 seasons,
50 episodes
Sci-fi drama with Tatiana Maslany, Jordan Gavaris, Maria Doyle Kennedy, Kristian Bruun, Kevin Hanchard, Skyler Wexler, Josh Vokey, Ari Millen, Evelyne Brochu and Dylan Bruce.

Tatiana Maslany dazzles as a character with many clones who are all being pursued by shadowy forces. Shortly after she gets mistaken for a cop who looks exactly like her, petty criminal Sarah Manning learns that she's only one of many identical sisters. Along with Sarah, Maslany plays all the other clones, often appearing as multiple characters in a single scene, yet they are all different!

🐟 **From our forums:** "She reminds me of Buffy. She's scrappy, she doesn't give up, she's resourceful, and she has good instincts/reflexes."

🏆 Peabody Award, Emmy for best actress in a drama

The Other Two

TV-MA, 2019–present
HBO Max original, 2 seasons,
20 episodes (AD)
Comedy with Drew Tarver, Heléne York, Case Walker, Molly Shannon and Ken Marino.

A rollicking satire of Internet fame that also offers a poignant look at social media's impact on our relationships. After their prepubescent brother rides a viral video called "Marry U at Recess" to worldwide fame, 30-somethings Cary (Tarver) and Brooke (Yorke) are forced to take stock of their own wayward lives. From two former *SNL* writers, *The Other Two* has a POV unlike any other sitcom — young adults who are bewildered by the alternate reality of Instagram and TikTok but aren't exactly lighting the real world on fire, either. Though jam-packed with jokes and musical numbers, this show has a less frantic tone than similar sitcoms, thanks in part to Shannon's low-key performance as the siblings' mom.

Our Boys

TV-MA, 2019
HBO Max, 10 episodes
Limited series (drama) with Shlomi Elkabetz, Johnny Arbid, Adam Gabay, Ruba Blal, Yaacov Cohen, Or Ben-Melech, Eyal Shikratzi, Lior Ashkenazi, Michael Aloni and Shmil Ben Ari.

Absorbing slow-TV import turns the Israeli-Palestinian conflict into a **crime procedural.** In 2014 a 15-year-old Arab boy was murdered in retaliation for the kidnap-murder of three Israeli teenagers by Hamas loyalists. The Israelis are the "our boys" of the show title, but this series is, in fact, about the hunt for those who committed the revenge killing. In this carefully (some might say ploddingly) paced detective series, we follow domestic-terrorism agent Simon (Elkabetz) as he slowly hones in on his persons of interest. They include a tender ultra-Orthodox teen named Avishai (Gabay), whose role in the murder captures so much of what's gone haywire in a world where political leaders, whose words should be urging calm and understanding, instead use them to incite hatred and violence.

Our Planet

TV-G, 2019
Netflix original, 8 episodes (AD)
Docuseries with David Attenborough.

Nature extravaganza is infused with dire warnings that all this natural beauty could vanish if humans don't change their ways. The beloved television explainer of nature has turned his attention to the threat of climate change in recent years. Attenborough doesn't have to haul in any climate scientists to tell viewers that coral reefs are under assault — he just calls upon the immense authority he's earned with viewers and details how global warming ruins natural habitats using words and pictures.

🏆 Emmys for outstanding narrator and docuseries

Outcry

TV-MA, 2020
Showtime original, 5 episodes
Limited series (true crime) directed by Pat Kondelis.

The story of a Texas high school football star's quest to overturn his conviction

on child molestation charges is so absorbing and twisty, you won't want to Google it. Director Pat Kondelis (*Disgraced*) uses his access with the accused, Greg Kelley, his family and legal team and interrogation videos, to tell a chilling story of justice denied— for years on end, as attorneys hide behind privilege and judges punt decisions to higher courts.

▶▶ Pairs well with *Last Chance U*

Outer Banks

TV-MA, 2020–present
Netflix original, 2 seasons,
20 episodes (AD)

Teen drama with Chase Stokes, Madelyn Cline, Madison Bailey, Jonathan Daviss, Rudy Pankow, Austin North, Charles Esten, Drew Starkey, Cullen Moss and Adina Porter.

Escapist soap pits a group of working-class teens against their wealthier peers in a seaside town where a newly found treasure map contains explosive secrets. If you like watching shirtless young men strolling the beaches of coastal Carolina, scavenger hunts and fun storylines that make no sense, kick off your shoes and settle in.

🐟 **From our forums:** "It's kind of like *Bloodline* but teens." "I binged this in 2 days, which I never do. What a wild ride. I just wish the episodes weren't so long."

Outlander

TV-MA, 2014–present
Starz original, 6 seasons, 75 episodes
Romance drama created by Ronald D. Moore, with Caitriona Balfe, Sam Heughan, Duncan Lacroix, Sophie Skelton, Richard Rankin, Tobias Menzies, César Domboy, Lauren Lyle, John Bell and Graham McTavish.

If the only thing you like more than a time-travel romance is three or four of them rolled into one, then this is your show. From the protean mind of Ronald D. Moore (*Battlestar Galactica*, *Star Trek*) comes a fantasy set in 1740s Europe … and 1940s Boston … and 1770s North Carolina … and a few more stops along the way. This time-traveling romantic adventure includes flashbacks to the American Revolution, Jacobite Rebellion and the big-hair 1960s. Wearing all the period costumes is Claire (Balfe), whom we first meet as a post–World War II British nurse.

🐟 **From our forums:** "Grown-up, sensual, tender, emotional and sexy . . . so much better than anything on *Game of Thrones*."

▶▶ Diana Gabaldon's Outlander novels, on which the series is based, were in turn inspired by the author watching the 1969 *Doctor Who* serial that introduced — what else? — the Time Lords.

The Outsider

TV-MA, 2020
HBO Max, 10 episodes (AD)
Limited series (crime drama) with Ben Mendelsohn, Bill Camp, Jeremy Bobb, Mare Winningham, Paddy Considine, Yul Vazquez, Cynthia Erivo and Jason Bateman.

A small Georgia town unravels following the gruesome murder of a young boy in this creepy adaptation of a Stephen King book. Besides correcting the oft-unbearable whiteness of its source material with a more diverse staff, the TV version adds and subtracts characters in ways that move the story along and add emotional heft to what is a very uncomfortable premise: an outsider whose mere presence in a community can bring out the worst in people.

🐟 **From our forums:** "I could watch those actors endlessly, especially Mendelsohn and Winningham. I enjoyed the finale and the series. Sure, it could have been compressed into fewer episodes but that didn't detract from the show for me."

Having read a ton of King's novels, I am well aware of the letdown endings. I've accepted that most of his tales are about the journey and not the destination."

Oz

TV-MA, 1997–2003
HBO Max, 6 seasons, 56 episodes
Crime drama with Ernie Hudson, J.K. Simmons, Lee Tergesen, Dean Winters, George Morfogen, Terry Kinney, Rita Moreno, Harold Perrineau, Eamonn Walker and Lance Reddick.

HBO's intense but ingratiating prison drama centered on life in the experimental wing of a maximum-security pen. Fontana and Levinson followed their triumph with *Homicide: Life on the Street* with this fan favorite about life behind bars. It was a great showcase for emerging talent that would distinguish themselves on other shows, including Reddick, Simmons and Edie Falco. And at a time when network shows rarely gave actors of color the spotlight, *Oz* was the most diverse drama on TV.

Ozark

TV-MA, 2017–2022
Netflix original, 4 seasons,
44 episodes (AD)
Crime drama with Jason Bateman, Laura Linney, Julia Garner, Lisa Emery, Sofia Hublitz, Skylar Gaertner, Charlie Tahan, Janet McTeer, Peter Mullan and Jason Butler Harner.

Jason Bateman and Laura Linney light up this super-dark drama, which takes one of TV's oldest forms and makes it exciting and unpredictable — and extremely violent. After a money laundering scheme goes awry, corrupt financial adviser Marty Byrde (Bateman) tries to make amends — and protect his family — by agreeing to launch an even bigger illegal scheme in the Ozarks. Once there, he and wife Wendy (Linney) are sucked into a lakeside morass of drug dealing and blackmail. With local villains like Ruth (Garner) and Darlene (Emery) adding interest, *Ozark* avoids the fate of many crime serials and actually builds momentum and complexity with each new season.

▶▶ At press time the second half of the show's fourth and final season was set for release later in 2022.

▶▶ For suggestions of related shows, see "If You Liked *Ozark*," page 376.

🏆 Emmys for best supporting actress in a drama (Garner, twice) and directing; SAG Award for best actor in a drama (Bateman, twice)

P-Valley

TV-MA, 2020–present
Starz original, 8 episodes
Drama with Brandee Evans, Nicco Annan, Shannon Thornton, Elarica Johnson, Skyler Joy, J. Alphonse Nicholson, Parker Sawyers, Harriett D. Foy, Tyler Lepley and Isaiah Washington.

Cinematic, complex treatment of a Black woman's reinvention at — of all places — a strip club in the South. A woman named Autumn Night (Johnson) begins dancing at a strip club in the Mississippi Delta called The Pynk. We don't know much about her except she's survived a flood. The club's boss, Uncle Clifford (Annan), taps the club's senior dancer Mercedes (Evans) to help her (and us) understand what it means to be a sex worker. Over time *P-Valley* delves deeply into their lives and those of the fine cast members surrounding them.

Paddleton

TV-MA, 2019
Netflix original, 1 hr 29 mins (AD)
Movie (dark comedy) with Mark Duplass, Ray Romano and Christine Woods.
Two nerdy, somewhat reclusive neighbors deepen their friendship after

one of them is diagnosed with cancer. Duplass (*Togetherness*) specializes in this kind of sad-funny storytelling, and Romano is a perfect foil as his co-star.

Painting with John
TV-MA, 2021–present
HBO Max, 6 episodes (AD)
Reality show created by John Lurie, with John Lurie, Nesrin Wolf and Ann Mary Gludd James.

The artist and raconteur's return to TV features a quirky and absorbing set of meditations on painting and life, all shot on the island home where he lives. Lurie, the irascible, multitalented performer and artist, created a cult classic in the 1990s with a cable-TV parody of travel shows called *Fishing with John*. This show is quite different. For one thing, it's mostly him, telling stories about his life as he paints with watercolors at his faraway tropical villa. Occasionally he wanders outside to take in the scenery or chitchat with the women who work for him. It's all very soothing, right down to the original music Lurie composed for the show.

▶▶ Fun fact: Lurie co-wrote the boisterous theme song for *Late Night With Conan O'Brien*.

Palm Springs
R, 2020
Hulu original, 1 hr 30 mins (AD)
Movie (fantasy comedy) with Andy Samberg, Cristin Milioti, J.K. Simmons, Peter Gallagher, June Squibb, Meredith Hagner, Camila Mendes and Tyler Hoechlin.

Andy Samberg and Cristin Milioti are wedding guests stuck in a time loop in a sharp, funny and ultimately moving romcom. It took nearly 30 years but someone finally came up with a worthy successor to *Groundhog Day*. To be clear, *Palm Springs* is its own hilarious and raunchy self. Both he and she come to realize they're caught up in the time-loop continuum and, eventually, that they are destined to forge their future together — if they ever get there, anyway.

▶▶ For those who miss DVD commentary tracks, Samberg and Milioti recorded a great commentary video for *Palm Springs*, with writer Andy Siari popping up at times. Look for it on the Extras tab.

Palmer
R, 2021
Apple TV+ original, 1 hr 50 mins (AD)
Movie (drama) directed by Fisher Stevens, with Justin Timberlake, Juno Temple, Alisha Wainwright, June Squibb and Ryder Allen.

Shortly after he gets out of prison, an ex-con strikes up an unlikely friendship with a troubled young boy. Timberlake got some of the best reviews of his acting career for this performance, and the script lets the characters be thorny without judging them for it.

Panic
TV-14, 2021
Prime Video original, 10 episodes (AD)
Crime drama with Olivia Scott Welch, Mike Faist, Jessica Sula, Ray Nicholson, Camron Jones, Enrique Murciano, Todd Williams, Lee Eddy, David W. Thompson and Leslie Ann Leal.

This addictive YA drama is based on Lauren Oliver's bestseller. Set in the sultry Texas summer, *Panic* follows a group of recent high school graduates as they compete for a $50,000 cash prize and an opportunity to escape their small town. Over the course of the competition, the players are asked to face their deepest fears, and each must decide how much they're willing to risk in order to win. At first Oliver, who adapted her own novel, relies solely on this intriguing premise — but in Episode 4 a steamy romance

For a key to terms used in this section, see page 33.

emerges and this YA romp finds its groove.

🗨 **From our forums:** "Who knew dramatic *Fear Factor* would be this entertaining?" "Nothing profound, just an entertaining if sometimes confusing mystery. I was reminded of *Friday Night Lights* because of the all the beer and booze those teens had ready access to."

Parenthood

TV-PG, 2010–2015
Hulu, Peacock, 6 seasons, 103 episodes
Family drama created by Jason Katims, with Peter Krause, Lauren Graham, Dax Shepard, Monica Potter, Erika Christensen, Sam Jaeger, Joy Bryant, Mae Whitman, Miles Heizer and Craig T. Nelson.

In Berkeley, California, three generations of the Braverman family navigate the ups and downs of daily life. Inspired by the 1980s movie but tonally very different, *Parenthood* was like *Brothers & Sisters* before it and *This Is Us* after it — that sprawling, messy yet idealized family drama that network TV always seems to have one of. (An even earlier show of the type, *Friday Night Lights*, was also created by Katims.) Over 6 seasons the show's deep ensemble were always easy to relate to and care about, though by the time it signed off in 2015 it was clear that audiences wanted a change; along came *This Is Us*.

🗨 **From our forums:** "What a forum *Parenthood* had for sharing so much valuable information about autism. What a waste."

Parks and Recreation

TV-14, 2009–2015
Peacock, 7 seasons, 124 episodes (AD)
Workplace comedy created by Greg Daniels and Michael Schur, with Amy Poehler, Nick Offerman, Aubrey Plaza, Aziz Ansari, Jim O'Heir, Retta, Chris Pratt, Rashida Jones, Adam Scott and Rob Lowe.

The series brought quirky comedy into the mainstream — but only after Amy Poehler's character got a makeover during Season 1. Shot mockumentary-style, this comedy from the makers of NBC's *The Office* was set in the equally low-stakes arena of local government, where Leslie Knope (Poehler) played an endlessly cheerful can-do bureaucrat dealing with various minor challenges. For critics and viewers, though, *Parks and Rec* was a little too much like *The Office* — Knope reminded people of Michael Scott, and not in a good way. Gradually her character began filling out, supporting characters like Ann Perkins (Jones) and Ron Swanson (Offerman) stepped up, and the show's tone became sweeter and, yes, quirkier.

▶▶ During the COVID-19 lockdown, the cast and writers of the show reunited remotely in 2020 to make *A Parks And Recreation Special*, shot mostly on iPhones.

🏆 TCA Award for outstanding comedy series

Party Down

TV-14, 2009–present
Starz original, 2 seasons, 20 episodes
Comedy with Adam Scott, Ken Marino, Ryan Hansen, Martin Starr, Lizzy Caplan, Megan Mullally and Jane Lynch.

Tack-sharp comedy follows a group of cater-waiters in Los Angeles. Every low-rated show from the '00s is coming back; it's just a matter of time. Look at *Party Down*, a great show that virtually defined "cult following" during its quiet run on Starz. Now it's back with an announced 2022 revival, 12 years after it was canceled. In hindsight it's easy to recognized the Mt. Rushmore of comic talent in the cast, who were well-served by the writers. Their wiseass, rapid-fire jokes hold up, with

Party of Five (2020)

timeless observations about the weirdness of work crushes and the indignity of serving crudité to entitled jerks. With only 20 half-hour episodes in the original batch, you can devour the entire thing in the time it takes to empty a tray of shrimp cocktails.

Party of Five (2020)
TV-14, 2020
Hulu, 10 episodes
Teen drama with Brandon Larracuente, Niko Guardado, Emily Tosta and Elle Paris Legaspi.

Remake of the 1990s coming-of-age favorite imagines that the five Acosta children are immigrants and separated from their parents by ICE. The original *Party of Five* took on tough issues that Gen Xers were dealing with, like drug addiction and HIV, while showing the daily drama of five young siblings raising themselves after their parents die in a car crash. This reboot from the original show's creators is tonally similar, but raises the emotional stakes when the Acostas' parents are deported. They're still there, reachable by smartphone, but they're not *really* there. So the Acosta children do the best with the hand that's dealt them. They don't always make good choices, but they have grit and heart and so does this drama which was canceled too soon.

▶▶ Pairs well with *Living Undocumented*

Passing
PG-13, 2021
Netflix original, 1 hr 38 mins (AD)
Movie (drama) directed by Rebecca Hall, with Tessa Thompson, Ruth Negga, André Holland, Bill Camp and Alexander Skarsgård.

In her directing and screenwriting debut, British actor Rebecca Hall tells a gripping story about a Black woman in 1920s Harlem who discovers her childhood friend is now passing for white. This movie refuses to be pinned down: Sometimes it's a tender portrait of two friends learning to support each other; other times it's a tense thriller about a secret that could have violent consequences. But the pieces cohere to make us care about the characters, who are all struggling to define what makes a satisfying life. As Clare, the friend who's passing, Ruth Negga gives a career-making performance. She's enigmatic and alluring, full of the life and energy and barely concealed sadness of someone who loves her good fortune and can't forget what it cost her.

The Path
TV-MA, 2016–2018
Hulu original, 3 seasons, 36 episodes
Drama with Aaron Paul, Michelle Monaghan, Hugh Dancy, Emma Greenwell, Kyle Allen, Deirdre O'Connell, Aimee Laurence, Ali Ahn, Patch Darragh and Rockmond Dunbar.

Aaron Paul in his first major role post–*Breaking Bad* plays a member of a religious order called The Path, who discovers the group's dark side when he has a crisis of faith. Paul is convincing as Eddie and Dancy is chilling as the cult's charismatic leader, but it's Monaghan as Eddie's wife Sarah who stands out. Sarah was raised in the community and is battling doubts herself, but she's torn between her love for Eddie and for a community that has defined her whole life. *The Path*'s non-linear narrative style may be a turn-off to some. Viewers were divided on the show's weirdly supernatural turn toward the end of Season 1.

Patrick Melrose
TV-MA, 2018
Showtime original, 5 episodes
Limited series (comedy-drama) with Benedict Cumberbatch, Jennifer Jason

236   For descriptions of streaming platforms in this guide, see page 19.

Leigh, Hugo Weaving, Sebastian Maltz and Jessica Raine.

Widely acknowledged as Benedict Cumberbatch's finest performance, it's also a downer: He plays the abused, drug-addicted scion of an upper-class English monster. This five-part adaptation of the *Patrick Melrose* novels by Edward St. Aubyn follows Patrick as he struggles to get off the junk while coping with the painful memories of the cruelty his father David (Weaving) dealt out to him over the years. Critics have noted that the novels have more of a satirical edge than the adaptation.

🐿 **From our forums:** "Brilliant! The story had more impact because it wasn't pushed on the viewer. The focus was on the character of Patrick and the story unfolded."

Patriot
TV-MA, 2017–2018
Prime Video original, 2 seasons,
18 episodes (AD)
Drama with Michael Dorman, Kurtwood Smith, Michael Chernus, Kathleen Monroe, Aliette Opheim, Chris Conrad, Terry O'Quinn and Debra Winger.

Entertaining, category-defying show follows an off-the-books hit man who undertakes dangerous spy missions and then writes folk songs about them. This show works because of the star. Dorman sells the bizarre concept of a credible spook working for his dad (O'Quinn, also great) while depressed and addled with PTSD *and* capable of penning and singing doleful songs about his sad life. Don't judge, just watch.

🐿 **From our forums:** "So artfully filmed and darkly comic. Every single episode I have a couple of 'OMG, how the heck is he gonna get out of *this* one?' moments."

Peacemaker
TV-MA, 2022
HBO Max original, 8 episodes
Drama created by James Gunn, with John Cena, Danielle Brooks, Jennifer Holland, Freddie Stroma, Robert Patrick, Steve Agee, Chukwudi Iwuji, Nhut Le and Christopher Heyerdahl.

John Cena continues to elevate his career, owning the title of world's most malevolent superhero in this DC spinoff of 2021's *The Suicide Squad* movie. Besides being his usual charming self and displaying some of his character's unhinged humor, Cena gets to flex dramatically as he grapples with his role in the universe. Is he really keeping the peace, or does his enthusiasm for the kill make a mockery of that? Brooks is a find in the role of Adebayo, new to Peacemaker's pack. Intense action scenes add to the appreciation of *Peacemaker* as a superhero/antihero show that hits all the genre's sweet spots.

🐿 **From our forums:** "As a huge fan of Cena back in the day, I've been more mixed on his acting career, but he was perfection as Peacemaker in *The Suicide Squad*. I like that he still is the douchebag he always was, just one who will hopefully go after the worst people!"

Peaky Blinders
TV-MA, 2014–present
Netflix original, 5 seasons,
30 episodes (AD)
Crime drama with Cillian Murphy, Helen McCrory, Paul Anderson, Sophie Rundle, Finn Cole, Ian Peck, Natasha O'Keeffe, Sam Neill, Anya Taylor-Joy and Tom Hardy.

If you're willing to make the commitment, this epic family drama set in post–World War I England just gets better with each passing season. In 1919, Tommy Shelby (Murphy in a career role) leads a clan that runs their part of

Birmingham with bookmaking and other illegal rackets. He'd like to go legit and is talented enough to do so, but blood ties are too powerful. This sounds like other family crime dramas, but what elevates *Peaky Blinders* are its unbridled energy and the show's outsized characters. It's also a fabulous period piece — the grimy, factory-laden outdoor sets are spectacular and the war flashbacks chilling.

🔊 **From our forums:** "*Downton Abbey* pales in comparison to this gem."

PEN15

TV-MA, 2019–2021
Hulu original, 2 seasons,
25 episodes (AD)
Comedy created by Maya Erskine, Anna Konkle and Sam Zvibleman, with Maya Erskine and Anna Konkle.

In an amazing sleight of hand, Anna Konkle and Maya Erskine play themselves as 7th-graders and it's utterly compelling. The best and truest-to-life of an excellent batch of school-set shows that include *Big Mouth*, *Sex Education* and *American Vandal*, PEN15 is a kind of memory trap, where everything that happened to Erskine and Konkle when they were 13 gets reflected back here at twice the intensity. The illusion works because the 30-something leads surround themselves with great tween acting talent, like the almost preternaturally mean gaggle of girls playing Anna and Maya's friends.

▶▶ Production on Season 2 was interrupted by COVID-19, resulting in an animated special titled "Jacuzzi" (S2E18), which takes full advantage of the medium to address the battlefield of adolescence that the girls face.

Penguin Town

TV-G, 2021–present
Netflix original, 8 episodes (AD)
Docuseries with Patton Oswalt.

Penguins take over a town, with Patton Oswalt calling the play-by-play — and yes, it's as adorably amusing as it sounds. A group of penguins descend upon a small South African community, where the rules of polite society go out the window. The penguins can be seen hooking up (repeatedly), fighting and trekking through human environments in search of food and shelter. Oswalt's voice-overs, introducing the penguins as couples, *Real Housewives*–style, adds just the right level of absurdity. Netflix has taken everything it's learned from years of creative experimentation in reality TV and put it into *Penguin Town*, a nature doc unlike anything that's come before it.

Penny Dreadful

TV-MA, 2014–2016
Showtime original, 3 seasons,
27 episodes
Horror series with Timothy Dalton, Rory Kinnear, Eva Green, Reeve Carney, Billie Piper, Harry Treadaway and Josh Hartnett.

Dark, romantic and violent spookfest based on a hodgepodge of legends is artful horror done right. This mashup on the legends of Dracula, the Wolfman, Frankenstein and Dorian Gray is sexy, bloody and completely over-the-top. But thanks to performances from the likes of Eva Green, Rory Kinnear, Timothy Dalton and Patti LuPone (not to mention Josh Hartnett and Reeve Carney going to town on each other), along with delicious production design, it rarely fails to deliver.

🔊 **From our forums:** "There's something lush and unsettling about it, and the sound design is fantastic — all sorts of weird sounds and moans, whispers and sighs that are just as unsettling as the visual shadows and mold and blood."

Penny Dreadful: City of Angels
TV-MA, 2020
Showtime original, 10 episodes
Crime drama with Natalie Dormer, Nathan Lane, Kerry Bishé, Adriana Barraza, Jessica Garza, Michael Gladis, Rory Kinnear and Johnathan Nieves.

Two cops battle demons and Nazis in 1930s Hollywood in a well-made spinoff that requires no foreknowledge of the original *Penny Dreadful* series. A shapeshifting demon helps unleash Nazism and general mayhem on the city. Two LAPD detectives — played effectively by Daniel Zovatto and Nathan Lane — battle both supernatural evil and the racism of their fellow cops.

🗨 **From our forums:** "I think it was good enough to stand on its own without Penny Dreadful tacked onto its name." "Was great up until the very end, when it got just a tad too didactic."

People of Earth
TV-MA, 2016–2017
Hulu, 2 seasons, 20 episodes
Sci-fi comedy with Wyatt Cenac, Luka Jones, Alice Wetterlund, Michael Cassidy, Tracee Chimo Pallero, Brian Huskey, Nancy Lenehan, Da'Vine Joy Randolph and Ana Gasteyer.

Wyatt Cenac (*The Daily Show*) plays a journalist investigating a support group for people who claim they were abducted by aliens — and starts to wonder if he was once abducted himself. Don't be fooled by the far-out premise: This is a smart, off-kilter sitcom perfectly attuned to Cenac's deadpan comic affect.

🗨 **From our forums:** "Witty and delivers the funny as well. I love that the resolutions at the end of each episode are not too pat."

▶▶ Pairs well with *Los Espookys*

A Perfect Planet
TV-PG, 2021
Discovery+, 5 episodes
Docuseries with David Attenborough.

Attenborough's growing sense of urgency about climate change informs, but doesn't overwhelm, this signature entertainment that emphasizes Earth's unique capacities. "There is only one universe on the planet, so far as we know, that supports life," intones Sir David at the beginning of this standout series. Filmed over four years in 31 countries, *A Perfect Planet* is classic Attenborough, calling attention to natural forces that have always been with us, yet without which the cycle of life that sustains us would not be possible. And though inevitably he turns to the existential threat that humans pose, he tries to strike a more constructive tone than in his previous series.

Perpetual Grace, LTD
TV-MA, 2019
Epix original, 10 episodes
Crime drama with Ben Kingsley, Jimmi Simpson, Luis Guzmán, Jacki Weaver, Damon Herriman, Chris Conrad and Terry O'Quinn.

A drifter gets sucked into a scheme to kidnap a pastor and his wife, only to realize they're much more menacing than they seem. Largely overlooked because it aired on a small premium cable network, this playful series throws together chunks of noir thriller and ridiculous con game, delivers pitch-perfect lines from characters played by the likes of Kingsley and *Lost*'s O'Quinn and the result is a tonally perfect caper … that Epix canceled after one season.

▶▶ At press time there still weren't details on a "limited run followup," promised in 2020, that would tie up the strands left over from Episode 10's cliffhanger.

For shows sorted by streaming platform, see page 381. **239**

Perry Mason (2020)
TV-MA, 2020–present
HBO Max, 8 episodes (AD)

Crime drama with Matthew Rhys, Juliet Rylance, Chris Chalk, Shea Whigham, Tatiana Maslany, John Lithgow, Gayle Rankin, Andrew Howard, Lili Taylor and Stephen Root.

Perry's a private dick in this stylish, engaging reimagining in noirish Los Angeles. Raymond Burr's Mason defended clients who were victims of sloppy or biased police work, but Matthew Rhys's Mason is a gumshoe who gets hired by clients because nobody — *nobody* — trusts the LAPD. As Perry and his team get to the bottom of a kidnapping case, this show ambitiously touches on a range of subjects — the 1932 Olympics, union-busting, the nascent aviation industry and Sister Alice McKeegan (Mislay), a charismatic preacher who's a barely fictionalized version of Aimee Semple McPherson. Highly watchable if darkly cynical anti-copaganda.

The Pharmacist
TV-MA, 2020
Netflix original, 4 episodes (AD)

Limited series (true crime) directed by Jenner Furst and Julia Willoughby Nason, with Dan Schneider.

Obsessed with avenging his son's death, a Louisiana pharmacist pursues an opioid pill mill in his community. In 1999, when Dan Schneider's son was murdered in a drug deal, cops were too overwhelmed with such crimes to solve it. So Schneider made it his personal crusade — and in the process he led the feds to one of the most notorious prescribers of OxyContin in the country. Based on journalist Jed Lipinski's reporting, this is a gripping tale.

Philip K. Dick's Electric Dreams
TV-MA, 2018
Prime Video original, 10 episodes (AD)

Sci-fi drama anthology series with Steve Buscemi, Geraldine Chaplin, Bryan Cranston, Terrence Howard, Richard Madden, Timothy Spall, Greg Kinnear, Mel Rodriguez and Juno Temple.

Ten standalone stories from one of the O.G.'s of genre writing are backed by a top-tier cast. This anthology revels in the possibilities that Streaming TV offers talented TV creators to tell expansive stories with name talent. *Battlestar Galactica*'s Ronald D. Moore is a co-producer on this adaptation of the celebrated sci-fi author's work.

🗨 **From our forums:** "The Anna Paquin one was the most classic sci-fi. The one with the Amazon factory was good because I didn't see the twist coming. One thing that helps this series is that it is based on established Dick stories. Most series suffer because they are written to cater to a cast of actors and the story gets lower priority."

Philly D.A.
TV-PG, 2021
PBS Passport, 8 episodes

Docuseries directed by Ted Passon and Yoni Brook, with Larry Krasner.

Real-life drama unfolds behind the scenes as a reformer enacts sweeping changes to the way criminal justice is dispensed in Philadelphia. After longtime public defender Larry Krasner took on Philly's power establishment and won election as the city's district attorney, he and his team allowed cameras inside their offices as they try to make good on their promise to shake up the criminal justice system. The powerful police union and city bureaucracy seem determined to resist the D.A. every inch of the way. The nation is watching and the stakes couldn't be higher. Each episode is a riveting, self-contained hour — almost an anti-procedural — featuring a clash between the old guard and Krasner's office.

Physical

TV-MA, 2021–present
Apple TV+ original, 10 episodes (AD)
Comedy-drama with Rose Byrne, Rory Scovel, Dierdre Friel, Paul Sparks, Della Saba, Lou Taylor Pucci, Geoffrey Arend and Ian Gomez.

Rose Byrne kills it as a deeply unhappy woman who finds salvation — and a lot of money — riding the personal-fitness wave of the 1980s. Rarely does a TV show zero in so acutely on the psychology of self-hatred as *Physical*, which expresses that self-hatred through voice-overs in which Sheila (Byrne) tells us how awful, worthless, fat and pathetic she is. How this works hand-in-hand with her eating disorder is pretty traumatic, so be warned. This show also has a lot to say about the Reagan era and the craze for fitness back then, but it only works because Byrne is able to nail such a complicated, dark, nasty-but-sympathetic character.

Plan B

TV-MA, 2021
Hulu original, 1 hr 47 mins (AD)
Movie (comedy) directed by Natalie Morales, with Kuhoo Verma, Victoria Moroles, Michael Provost, Mason Cook, Edi Patterson and Rachel Dratch.

Two high school friends have to track down a morning-after pill in America's heartland. After acting in high-quality sitcoms like *Girls* and *Parks and Recreation*, Morales proves that she knows how to direct a story with an equal amount of humor and heart.

Planet Earth II

TV-G, 2017
Discovery+, 6 episodes
Docuseries with David Attenborough.

Sir David Attenborough, our greatest explainer of the wild spaces, raises his game even higher in this sequel to *Planet Earth*. Shot over three years in 40 different countries, *Planet Earth II* is divided into episodes on islands, mountains, jungles, deserts, grasslands and cities. Two things set this apart from its predecessor. First, the cinematography, which was already pretty spectacular, is raised to an even higher art here, with more stunning close-ups and "how did they get *that* shot" scenes to count. Second, although Attenborough's narration is as informative and wry as ever, he now makes a point of explaining the impact of climate change on the wonders of nature he observes and, he fears, are soon fading away forever.

▸▸ *Planet Earth II* was ranked #1 on IMDb's all-time list of television series.

🏆 Emmys for outstanding cinematography and docuseries

Please Like Me

TV-MA, 2013–2016
Hulu, 4 seasons, 32 episodes
Dark comedy created by Josh Thomas, with Josh Thomas, Thomas Ward, David Roberts, Debra Lawrance, Hannah Gadsby, Renee Lim, Keegan Joyce and Caitlin Stasey.

Unflinching Australian comedy-drama about 20-something slacker Josh (Josh Thomas) who learns to embrace his homosexuality while helping his mother navigate her depression. This much-admired forerunner to today's wave of queer-positive TV deftly managed the tricky balance between teenage depths (suicide is a major theme) and deadpan comedy. During its 4-season run, characters evolved organically though not always sympathetically.

The Plot Against America

TV-MA, 2020
HBO Max, 6 episodes (AD)

Some shows may have moved; see page 183.

Limited series (alternative history) created by David Simon and Ed Burns, with Winona Ryder, Zoe Kazan, Morgan Spector, Anthony Boyle, Michael Kostroff, David Krumholtz, Azhy Robertson, Caleb Malis, Jacob Laval and John Turturro.

The creator of *The Wire* makes Philip Roth's alternate history of World War II suddenly urgent. Philip Roth's 2004 novel — which imagines his Jewish family enduring the election of Charles Lindbergh in 1940 and the anti-Semitic wave of terror that follows — obviously resonates today. David Simon's adaptation takes a while to get there as he world-builds, but when he drops the hammer, it's memorable. Aided by performances by Spector as Philip's dad and Kazan as his mom, Simon powerfully argues (as he did with *The Wire* and *Show Me a Hero*) that civil society is more fragile than we think.

Plus One

Not Rated, 2019
Hulu, 1 hr 38 mins
Movie (romantic comedy) with Maya Erskine, Jack Quaid and Ed Begley Jr.

Two friends agree to be each other's +1 to every wedding they've been invited to that summer. Fans of *PEN15* will enjoy Erskine in a more straightforward comic role. This movie was barely released in theaters, which means streaming is the only way to discover its charms.

The Politician

TV-14, 2019–present
Netflix original, 2 seasons,
15 episodes (AD)
Dark comedy created by Ryan Murphy, Ian Brennan and Brad Falchuk, with Ben Platt, Zoey Deutch, Lucy Boynton, Julia Schlaepfer, Laura Dreyfuss, Theo Germaine, Rahne Jones, David Corenswet, Gwyneth Paltrow and Judith Light.

Ryan Murphy's first Netflix series was widely panned upon its premiere, but it does get better. After signing the creator of *Glee* and *American Horror Story* to one of TV's biggest deals ever, Netflix executives must have winced when the reviews for *The Politician* came in: "tediously cynical," "aggressively kitschy," and so on. The idea was to track the political career of Payton Hobart (Platt) with a new campaign each season, starting with student body president and ending at the White House. Murphy has pressed pause on *The Politician* but plans to bring it back when its young star is older.

▸▸ The 27-minute episode "The Voter" (S1E5) follows an undecided voter named Elliott through the entirety of Election Day. It's a brilliant little film that doesn't oblige you to watch the rest of the series.

Portlandia

TV-14, 2011–2018
AMC+, 8 seasons, 79 episodes
Sketch comedy created by Fred Armisen, Jonathan Krisel and Carrie Brownstein, with Fred Armisen and Carrie Brownstein.

No show embodied the whimsy of the Obama years like *Portlandia*, whose bite-sized sketches go down easy even now. Armisen and Brownstein created this show and the myriad *Portlandia* characters who inhabited it — a menagerie of wide-eyed, crunchy, hippie and hipster types, whether they were cab drivers, store owners, podcasters, or just folks about town. (In fairness to the City of Roses, these twee types exist everywhere.) Sketches like "Put a Bird on It" established the duo's writing chops and proved influential to later comedies like *You're the Worst*.

🏆 Peabody Award, 4 Emmys

Portrait Artist of the Year

TV-G, 2013–present
Prime Video, 8 seasons, 77 episodes
Reality competition with Stephen Mangan, Frank Skinner, Kate Bryan, Tai Shan Schierenberg, Kathleen Soriano and Joan Bakewell.

Much more exciting than watching paint dry is this competition among British portraiture artists painting celebrities and politicians. This long-running British series has recently been added to Prime Video along with its counterpart, *Landscape Artist of the Year*. The competition has real-world stakes, as the finalists have their works displayed at the National Portrait Gallery in London and the winner is awarded a British Library commission.

🗩 **From our forums:** "I loved the guy who said he'd been doing four-hour portraits to prepare for the show. That's the kind of preparation I totally approve of!"

Pose

TV-MA, 2018–2021
Netflix, 3 seasons, 26 episodes
Drama created by Ryan Murphy, Brad Falchuk and Steven Canals, with Billy Porter, MJ Rodriguez, Dominique Jackson, Indya Moore, Angel Bismark Curiel, Hailie Sahar, Angelica Ross, Evan Peters, Sandra Bernhard and Charlayne Woodard.

Soulful, fun-to-watch drama about the Harlem ball culture of the late '80s and early '90s features trans and queer people banding together against AIDS, discrimination and bad fashion. Notably inclusive even for a Ryan Murphy production, *Pose* places multiple trans women — played *by* trans women — at the center of the story, charting the rise of drag houses in 1980s New York. To make the narrative complete, it surrounds those women with a galaxy of LGBT folk, people of color, ciswomen and James Van Der

Beek. The house ball scenes alone deserve repeat viewings, if only because they give Porter a chance to showcase why he's been a theater icon for so long. The family scenes are uniquely nourishing. To see characters loving one another, knowing mainstream society doesn't love them at all, is good for the soul.

🏆 Peabody Award, Emmy for best actor in a drama series (Porter)

The Power of the Dog

R, 2021
Netflix original, 2 hrs 6 mins (AD)
Movie (drama) directed by Jane Campion, with Benedict Cumberbatch, Kirsten Dunst, Jesse Plemons and Kodi Smit-McPhee.

After a 12-year drought, Jane Campion returned to feature filmmaking with this sharp-edged Western about a rancher who tries to psychologically control his brother and his brother's new wife. This movie burrows under the skin. Everything from the sparse dialogue to the beautifully filmed landscapes reflects on the mental and emotional battles among the central characters. We know these people so well — perhaps better than they know themselves — that we feel every ripple from the consequences of their actions.

The Practice

TV-14, 1997–2004
Hulu, 8 seasons, 167 episodes
Crime drama created by David E. Kelley, with Dylan McDermott, Steve Harris, Camryn Manheim, Michael Badalucco, LisaGay Hamilton, Kelli Williams, Lara Flynn Boyle, Marla Sokoloff and Holland Taylor.

The Practice was the standard by which other TV dramas were judged; it even scored an Emmy upset over *The Sopranos*. If *Ally McBeal* was the sexy, quirky side of Kelley's late-'90s creative output, *The Practice* was its hard-nosed

For shows sorted by streaming platform, see page 381. **243**

cousin. Focusing on a small but ferocious band of Boston lawyers who took whatever cases were available to them and did whatever it took to win, *The Practice* worked some incredible drama, thanks to a fantastic central ensemble led by McDermott, Harris, Williams, Badalucco, Manheim and Hamilton. The show couldn't maintain peak quality for all 8 seasons, but for a while no one did it better.

🏆 Peabody Award, Emmy Awards for best drama series (2 wins) and best supporting actress (Manheim, Taylor)

Pretend It's a City
TV-14, 2021
Netflix original, 7 episodes (AD)
Docuseries directed by Martin Scorsese, with Fran Lebowitz, Martin Scorsese, Alec Baldwin and Spike Lee.

Author-raconteur Fran Lebowitz at her observational and idiosyncratic best. At first, 7 episodes seem a lot for someone who's only published 2 books and plays a fairly two-dimensional New Yorker. But you'll likely be clamoring for more Lebowitz after gobbling down these fast-paced, entertaining half-hours, each framed around a particular passion or annoyance of the author. Clips from earlier specials are seamlessly woven into new material.

Pretty Little Liars
TV-14, 2010–2017
HBO Max, 7 seasons, 160 episodes
Teen drama created by I. Marlene King, with Troian Bellisario, Ashley Benson, ', Shay Mitchell, Sasha Pieterse, Ian Harding, Laura Leighton, Tyler Blackburn, Keegan Allen and Holly Marie Combs.

Long before *Cruel Summer*, this teen sensation redefined young adult drama. Crazy, creepy and twisted, *Pretty Little Liars* stood out for its racial and sexual diversity at a time when teen dramas

were just a bit too privileged for their own good. Thanks to its summer airdates, it was deeply beloved by its small but dedicated fan base of high school- and college-age viewers.

▶▶ Spawned 2 spinoffs — *Ravenswood* (2013) and *Pretty Little Liars: the Perfectionists* (2019) — both canceled after one season. A reboot titled *Pretty Little Liars: Original Sin* is set for release on HBO Max in 2022.

Pride
TV-MA, 2021
Hulu, 6 episodes
Docuseries.

Six renowned queer directors take on 6 decades of LGBTQ+ activism, and the result is a warts-and-all compendium of a movement. More tightly focused than other recent queer-history efforts like *Equal*, these 6 films center the history of gay activism in the queer experience. Each director brings their own style — some like reenactments, others prefer news footage and talking heads — but the overall effect is to shift away from the historical emphasis on white, cisgender gay men in queer media and present a history inclusive of transgender people and queer people of color.

Pride and Prejudice
TV-PG, 1995
Hulu, HBO Max, BritBox, 6 episodes
Limited series (romance drama) with Colin Firth, Jennifer Ehle, Susannah Harker, Julia Sawalha, Alison Steadman, Benjamin Whitrow, Crispin Bonham-Carter, Polly Maberly, Lucy Briers and Anna Chancellor.

This gold standard of Austen adaptations follows the romantic and social travails of Elizabeth Bennet and her sisters in 19th-century England. The costumes and sets on this version from master adapter Andrew Davies created the template for every British countryside drama that came after. By now Firth has become the uber-Darcy; his portrayal of Elizabeth's suitor is so emotionally rich yet also so fiercely alive. The rest of the cast is equally adept.

▶▶ This was a co-production of the BBC and, believe it or not, A&E back when the A and E actually stood for something.

▶▶ Pairs well with *Jane Eyre*

🏆 Emmy for best costume design in a miniseries

The Princess Switch
TV-PG, 2018
Netflix original, 1 hr 41 mins (AD)
Movie (romantic comedy) with Vanessa Hudgens, Sam Palladio and Nick Sagar.

While traveling abroad for a baking competition, a Chicago woman swaps identities with her doppelgänger, who happens to be the fiancee of a prince. There are now three movies in this frothy-but-pleasant series.

The Profit
TV-14, 2013–2021
Peacock, 8 seasons, 107 episodes
Reality show with Marcus Lemonis.

Investor Marcus Lemonis steps in with money and expertise to fix failing businesses — that is, if the owners will let him. Though similar to *Shark Tank*, *The Profit* is shot over time on site, imbuing it with an authenticity you can't get in a TV studio. Lemonis, a real-life corporate CEO, bets on businesses with broken processes, bad owner dynamics, all kinds of woes. Mostly he's invests in people, betting that they'll wake up and change the way they do business.

🎙 **From our forums:** "I enjoyed Marcus. His 'People, Product, Process' strategy is a sound one that I've applied to my own real estate practice." "I felt like he's been phoning it in lately. The businesses they

showed were more for the trainwreck factor rather than solid businesses that needed help. I'm glad it's ending."

▶▶ The ancillary series *The Profit: An Inside Look* — where Lemonis and executive producer Amber Mazzola watch past episodes and comment — is also entertaining.

Project Greenlight
TV-MA, 2001–present
HBO Max original, 4 seasons, 44 episodes
Reality competition with Ben Affleck and Matt Damon.

Great news — one of the best reality competitions of the pre-streaming era is making a comeback. Here's the concept: Give two budding directors with vastly different filmmaking styles the same story idea and budget, then see who delivers the better movie. Over the course of four seasons, *Project Greenlight* was dependably entertaining as ego-driven *auteurs* struggled to turn their vision into a bankable product. Apparently, though, the concept appealed only to film geeks and TV critics, because the show hopped from HBO to Bravo after Season 2, back to HBO after Season 3 and then was canceled after Season 4. But with Issa Rae signed to deliver a new season of *Greenlight* in 2022, it's time to acquaint yourself with this engaging sausage-making competition.

Project Runway
TV-PG, 2004–present
Peacock, 19 seasons, 273 episodes
Reality competition with Heidi Klum, Tim Gunn, Karlie Kloss, Christian Siriano, Brandon Maxwell, Nina Garcia, Elaine Welteroth and Michael Kors.

Now that the show has moved back to Bravo/Peacock and moved on from Heidi Klum and Tim Gunn, it's better than ever. *Project Runway* is a double competition: fashion designers are eliminated each week toward a final

For shows sorted by streaming platform, see page 381. **245**

winner, and so are runway models. But the focus, rightly, is on the designers, whose ability to make something enchanting out of a few bits of fabric and a meager budget have proven to be the show's secret sauce (and an inspiration to later competition shows like *Top Chef*). Like many long-running reality series, *Project Runway* has gone in for alterations every now and then to keep its look fresh.

▶▶ Season 2 was the show's coming-out party, full of attitude and glamor and, above all, personalities like Santino Rice, Chloe Rao and Daniel Franco. Season 17, its first after moving back to Bravo and saying goodbye to longtime hosts Gunn and Klum, was a revelation: an entire episode filmed in the woods, a much-needed increase in racial diversity and arguably the deepest bench of creatives ever in competition.

▶▶ Unlike many long-running reality hits, *Project Runway* was not a ratings success at first. But Bravo chief Lauren Zalaznick was passionate about the show and relentlessly aired it in repeats until it found an audience. Eventually the format was franchised to 30 countries.

🏆 Peabody Award,; 2 Emmys

Psych

TV-PG, 2006–2014
Prime Video, 8 seasons,
120 episodes (AD)
Comedy-drama with James Roday Rodriguez, Dulé Hill, Timothy Omundson, Maggie Lawson, Corbin Bernsen and Kirsten Nelson.

After he convinces the police he has psychic abilities, an especially talented amateur sleuth gets assigned to high profile cases, and he gets his uptight best friend to help him solve them. Part of USA Network's early-10s line-up of character-driven comic dramas (see also: *Suits*, *White Collar*, etc.), this one has become an apparently immortal hit,

with reunion movies popping up every few years. That's partly because of the goofy good humor and the agreeably interesting cases, but it's mostly because Rodriguez and Hill are so magnetic as the best friends at the center of the show. We believe in them as guys who have cared about (and exasperated) each other for years, and it's always fun to spend time with them.

Pure (2017)

TV-MA, 2017–2019
Hulu, 2 seasons, 12 episodes
Drama created by Michael Amo, with Jessica Clement, Dylan Everett, Victor Gomez, Alex Paxton-Beesley, A.J. Buckley, Rosie Perez, Alyson Hannigan and Zoie Palmer.

Reclusive, isolated Mennonites are forced into laboring for a Colombian drug cartel. This Canadian thriller offers an authentic look inside a tightly-knit subculture. You can probably enjoy it without prior knowledge of Mennonites — they're like the Amish, only different — but part of the show's intrigue is how the community copes with the violent threat to their existence, and it's probably not how you'd react.

💬 **From our forums:** "Sad that this show doesn't generate a larger audience — it has a strong premise and a strong female cast that got stronger in the second season. Plus all the fangirling that should be going on now that Alyson Hannigan has joined the cast with Zoie Palmer."

▶▶ Pairs well with *The Handmaid's Tale*

Pure (2019)

TV-MA, 2019
HBO Max original, 6 episodes
Limited series (comedy-drama) with Charly Clive, Joe Cole, Kiran Sonia Sawar, Niamh Algar and Anthony Welsh.

A young woman in London sees unwanted (and very graphic) sexual

images every single, day in this complex comedy about mental illness. Since she was 14, Marnie (Clive) has had graphic, sexual thoughts almost nonstop, but after she moves to London, gets a diagnosis for her condition and develops a network of new friends, she begins taking control of her life. Instead of huge breakthroughs conveniently timed to the end of each episode, *Pure* lets Marnie evolve, slowly, out of the disconcerting condition that overwhelms her mind.

The Pursuit of Love
TV-MA, 2021
Prime Video original, 3 episodes (AD)
Limited series (historical drama) directed by Emily Mortimer, with Lily James, Emily Beecham, Dominic West, Emily Mortimer, Dolly Wells, Andrew Scott, Freddie Fox, James Frecheville and Assaad Bouab.

Lily James and Dominic West never cease to entertain in this comic romp based on Nancy Mitford's 1945 novel about her nutty upper-class English family. James and Beecham play British cousins of marrying age between world wars. *The Pursuit of Love* succeeds more as a character drama than period piece, thanks to great casting. Mortimer, who stars, also wrote and directed this adaptation and her guiding hand resists traditional costume drama at every turn, injecting a modern soundtrack that includes New Order and Sleater-Kinney and a refreshing lack of stuffiness.

Pushing Daisies
TV-PG, 2007–2009
HBO Max, 2 seasons, 22 episodes
Comedy-drama created by Bryan Fuller, with Lee Pace, Anna Friel, Chi McBride, Jim Dale, Ellen Greene, Swoosie Kurtz and Kristin Chenoweth.

A private eye and a pie-maker team up to solve murder cases in one of the most underappreciated shows of the 2000s. Whimsical? Check: Ned (Pace) is the proprietor of the Pie Hole, but he also has the magical ability to raise the dead long enough for his partner Emerson Cod (McBride) to find out who killed them. Fanciful? Check: The set looked like an idealized small town painted in Easter-egg coloring. Sentimental? Check: Who doesn't have a food memory from their past that involves delicious pie? This quirky show about life, death and sweet treats checked all the comfort-TV boxes, but in those days before streaming ABC had no idea what to do with it.
🏆 7 Emmys

Q: Into the Storm
TV-MA, 2021
HBO Max, 6 episodes (AD)
Docuseries directed by Cullen Hoback.

Get uncomfortably close to people involved in the QAnon conspiracy cult in this expertly guided tour into the heart of paranoia. While some critics accused director Hoback of throwing too much material against the wall, the dizzyingly long list of points he wants to make keep you watching his longish docuseries. And to his credit, *Q: Into the Storm* decisively knocks down the myths surrounding the rise of the movement behind the January 6 attack on the U.S. Capitol.

Queen Sugar
TV-14, 2016–present
Hulu, 6 seasons, 75 episodes
Drama created by Ava DuVernay, with Rutina Wesley, Dawn-Lyen Gardner, Kofi Siriboe, Omar J. Dorsey, Nicholas L. Ashe, Tina Lifford, Ethan Hutchison and Bianca Lawson.

Quietly powerful drama about Black siblings in rural Louisiana weaves the region's troubled history into storylines. "Lived-in" is a fine compliment to this show, which has an unforced quality to

Some shows may have moved; see page 183. **247**

everything about it. The camerawork and performances allow us to linger over details of the Southern, class-based society where the story unfolds. As creator and frequent writer on the series, DuVernay brings her customary eye for the complexities of Black American experience, not to mention the realities of various rungs on the economic ladder. The characters feel rich and textured.

🗨 **From our forums:** "Family dramas and adult sibling relationships are my jam so I'm loving this."

The Queen's Gambit
TV-MA, 2020
Netflix original, 7 episodes (AD)
Limited series (historical drama) with Anya Taylor-Joy, Moses Ingram, Thomas Brodie-Sangster, Marielle Heller, Harry Melling and Bill Camp.

The grandmaster of retro dramas, this Netflix adaptation of the Walter Tevis novel sold a ton of chess sets and introduced millions to the pleasures of Anya Taylor-Joy. When Beth (Taylor-Joy) is sent to an orphanage at age 9, she develops an uncanny knack for chess. Coming of age in the 1960s, Beth soars to the top of USA grandmaster ranks and a Cold War chess showdown with Russia's best. But will her addiction to little green pills bring Beth down? Taylor-Jay has justly won accolades as the fierce, brooding lead, but a strong supporting cast includes Beth's adoptive mother (Heller), her one true friend Jolene (Ingram) and fellow grandmaster and frenemy Benny (Brodie-Sangster). Despite the subcurrent of drug abuse, *The Queen's Gambit* ultimately tells its audience that dreams, not nightmares, come true.

🏆 9 Emmys, including outstanding limited series and acting (Taylor-Joy)

Queer as Folk (US)
TV-MA, 2000–2005
Showtime original, 5 seasons, 83 episodes
Romance drama with Michelle Clunie, Thea Gill, Gale Harold, Randy Harrison, Scott Lowell, Peter Paige, Hal Sparks and Sharon Gless.

Developed from the British series, the Canadian-American version's long run allowed viewers to enmesh in the characters' lives more deeply. What would've happened to the original *Queer as Folk* characters if the UK version had gone beyond 10 episodes? This series explored that idea using characters who were counterparts of the original show's cast.

🗨 **From our forums:** "This show introduced me to a lot of new bands and/or songs that are now my favorites. I was disappointed to hear that when the show recently went up on Netflix, most of the music had been replaced."

Queer Eye
TV-14, 2018–present
Netflix original, 6 seasons, 52 episodes (AD)
Reality show with Bobby Berk, Karamo Brown, Tan France, Antoni Porowski and Jonathan Van Ness.

Bravo's early signature series gets an essential reboot, with uplifting stories of personal transformation that are more than skin deep. Bravo's *Queer Eye for the Straight Guy* was a sensation at the time, arguably the highest-profile TV show with an all-gay cast. But its superficiality and penchant for cheap jokes wore thin. In the Netflix version, the superficial problems of its subjects serve as windows to deeper emotional chaos and self-inflicted damage that can't be remedied with a celebrity house call. The show's Fab Five do everything with kindness and empathy, effectively delivering on the show's promise: "More than a Makeover."

🏆 Emmy winner for best structured reality show four years running (2018–21)

Quiz
TV-14, 2020
AMC+, 3 episodes
Docuseries directed by Stephen Frears, with Matthew Macfadyen, Sian Clifford, Mark Bonnar, Aisling Bea, Helen McCrory and Michael Sheen.

Britain's *Who Wants To Be a Millionaire* scandal is entertainingly revisited. *Millionaire* actually began as a quiz show on England's ITV, which is where some the show's most passionate early fans figured out how to crack the game code. The elaborate conspiracy was eventually uncovered, leading to a spectacular criminal trial and a documentary that everyone from the Crown on down watched. This superb drama, airing 17 years after that infamous broadcast, calls into question seemingly everything uncovered in the first investigation. British citizenship is not required to enjoy *Quiz*.

Race to the Center of the Earth
TV-14, 2021–present
Disney+, 7 episodes (AD)
Reality competition with Chris Payne Gilbert.

From the creators of *The Amazing Race* comes another global treasure hunt with *TAR*'s worst features eliminated. The teammates know each other, and the challenges come from interpersonal dynamics as much as the natural environment, so that's familiar territory for *TAR* views. But this *Race* has no overbearing host, just a narrator; the teams are racing against the clock rather than each other (they start in different places); and best of all, no frenetic manufactured energy or pointless eliminations. All this makes for a slower, more scenic and more character-driven race.

Ragdoll
TV-MA, 2021–present
AMC+ original, 6 episodes
Thriller with Henry Lloyd-Hughes, Thalissa Teixeira, Lucy Hale and Ali Cook.

Agreeable if gory series follows a downtrodden British detective who's being taunted by a serial killer. Yes, there are gruesome murders to solve (the title refers to how the killer sews body parts of his various victims together), but this series stands out in the British crime drama pack because of the sharp banter and warm relationships between the central characters. It's a crime show for people with a taste for talky dramas.

💬 **From our forums:** "I like it when the audience knows a killer's identity and watches him stay one step ahead of the investigators. This also has something interesting to say about cops and accountability; it doesn't glorify breaking the rules."

Raised by Wolves
TV-MA, 2020–present
HBO Max original, 2 seasons, 20 episodes (AD)
Sci-fi drama created by Aaron Guzikowski, with Amanda Collin, Abubakar Salim, Winta McGrath, Travis Fimmel, Niamh Algar and Jordan Loughran.

Dazzling new take on a classic sci-fi premise finds two androids in charge of keeping humanity going on a new planet after Earth is destroyed. The opening episodes (directed by Ridley Scott in a style reminiscent of his earliest work) treat viewers to a technically stunning visage of life in the 22nd century. As deeply strange as much of the imagery is, the show's central tension is positively medieval — a violent battle between atheism and religion over the future course of humanity. The relationship between androids Mother (Collin) and Father (Salim) and their mortal charges is weirdly fascinating. The world of *Raised by Wolves* is unlike any other on TV.

🐟 **From our forums:** "The costuming makes all of the humans look like they stopped off to do a little colonizing on their way to a ski weekend with a pseudo-religious dress code."

Raising Dion

TV-G, 2019–present
Netflix original, 2 seasons,
17 episodes (AD)
Sci-fi drama with Alisha Wainwright, Ja'Siah Young, Ali Ahn, Gavin Munn, Sammi Haney, Jason Ritter and Michael B. Jordan.

A newly widowed mother is startled to realize her young son has supernatural abilities. This action-filled G-rated series has some real character development and unexpected story beats, so it's appealing to youngsters and grownups alike. The kiddie superhero's discovery of his extraordinary abilities comes with important lessons about empathy and love.

🐟 **From our forums:** "It's a unique look at the superhero-origin story, like if Superman was told from Martha Kent's point of view."

Ramy

TV-MA, 2019–present
Hulu original, 2 seasons,
20 episodes (AD)
Comedy created by Ramy Youssef, Ari Katcher and Ryan Welch, with Ramy Youssef, Amr Waked, Mohammed Amer, Hiam Abbass, Dave Merheje, Laith Nakli, May Calamawy, Steve Way and Mahershala Ali.

Triumphant, funny, occasionally raunchy *tour de force* follows a first-generation American Muslim trying to navigate his culture, family and faith. Though at first it seems like another everybro comedy about one's twenties, the show's distinctive voice soon emerges. Ramy lives at home with his Egyptian-American parents, puts up with his uncle's anti-Semitism to maintain a paycheck and tries to apply a Muslim moral compass to all the bad advice he gets from his buddies.

▶▶ After you've gotten to know Ramy's family, check out these outstanding episodes told from their perspectives: "They" (S2E6); "3riana Grande" (S2E5) "Frank in the Future" (S2E8) and "Uncle Naseem" (S2E9).

🏆 Peabody Award

The Ranch

TV-MA, 2016–2020
Netflix original, 4 seasons,
80 episodes (AD)
Sitcom with Ashton Kutcher, Sam Elliott, Danny Masterson, Elisha Cuthbert, Debra Winger and Megyn Price.

A ridiculously talented cast adds spice to this laid-back sitcom about a ranching family in Colorado. One of Netflix's under-the-radar hits, *The Ranch* featured no less an actress than Winger as a pot-smoking mom who's left her husband and lives in a trailer behind the bar she owns. Elliott (*1883*) plays her ex, and their chemistry transforms what could've been two-dimensional characters into full-fledged folks that we care about, giving the show its tart-sweetness.

Random Acts of Flyness

TV-MA, 2018–present
HBO Max, 6 episodes
Sketch comedy created by Terence Nance, with Terence Nance, Anthony Chisholm, Dominique Fishback, Kelley Robins and Tonya Pinkins.

Absorbing and drily funny vignettes about contemporary Black life are told

in singular fashion. Creator Nance has been credited with doing for the late-night sketch show what *Atlanta* did for the sitcom. Creating a dreamlike sequence of amusing bits, music and brutally honest interviews on subjects like police brutality, *Random Acts of Flyness* seems engineered for its white audience to awake from its viewing, well, *woke*. Nance's provocations on race and Blackness (e.g., the politics of hair) have been well received by African-American viewers as well.

🏆 Peabody Award

Ray Donovan
TV-MA, 2013–2020
Showtime original, 7 seasons,
82 episodes
Crime drama with Liev Schreiber, Eddie Marsan, Dash Mihok, Pooch Hall, Kerris Dorsey and Jon Voight.

Liev Schreiber stars as a professional fixer, making powerful people's problems disappear while trying to manage the constant crises in his own family. As Ray's troublemaking father Mickey, Voight does career-reviving work and his scenes with Schreiber make up for the awkwardly over-the-top moments that sneak into the plot. Alan Alda as Ray's psychiatrist in later seasons is a welcome addition who won't remind you of Dr. Melfi.

🗨 **From our forums:** "Ray is a serial killer and a sociopath, but Liev Schreiber makes him in some way likable. It's a miracle how TV f*cks with our heads."

▶▶ Fans loved this show so much that after it was abruptly canceled, they successfully lobbied Showtime to make a finale movie that premiered in early 2022.

The Real Housewives of Atlanta
TV-14, 2008–present
Hulu, Peacock, 13 seasons, 285 episodes
Reality show.

The most stable (if that's the right word) of the *Housewives* shows features a cast of mostly Black women who are easy to love. A study in how the best reality shows are continuously improving, *Atlanta* took several seasons to develop into the viewing pleasure it is today. Music mogul Kandi Burruss joined in Season 2 and several ladies were added over the next three seasons, including "supporting cast" members left off the PR photos but who added to the show's appeal.

▶▶ Season 5 is the highlight, led by queen bee Nene Leakes. The *Atlanta* women read each other for filth constantly and won't hesitate to drag one another if they deem it necessary. But the way they can bounce back from drama and become close again speaks to what a well-built cast this is.

The Real Housewives of Beverly Hills
TV-14, 2010–present
Hulu, Peacock, 11 seasons, 244 episodes
Reality show.

The notorious *RHOBH* generates more off-screen drama than any other *Housewives*, and it's all grist for the mill. Lisa Vanderpump and her doggie adoption gone south. Denise Richards, caught (allegedly!) sleeping with another Housewife. Erika Jayne's legal woes … what is it with these ladies? For intrigue that most closely mirrors the Tinseltown just a short limo ride away, nothing tops *RHOBH*.

▶▶ Season 1 is the highlight. Kyle Richards (Denise's sister) and Vanderpump establish their signature roles alongside former Housewives Camille Grammer and Taylor Armstrong, and the revelations of alcoholism and spousal abuse put the "real" into *Real Housewives* for once.

🏆 Critics Choice Award for best reality series

The Real Housewives of Dallas
TV-14, 2016–present
Peacock, 5 seasons, 78 episodes
Reality show.

Like the 1980s soap, *Dallas* is as dramatic as a *Housewives* franchise gets, yet it never sacrifices plot for comedy. Accusations of affairs, screaming matches between former best friends and … pink dog food? It's all in a day's work at *Real Housewives of Dallas*, though it took a ragged first season to get there.

▶▶ Season 2 is the highlight. Viewers were introduced to LeeAnne Locken, who quickly became the star of the show. This former carny and forever "true Texan" is the stuff reality TV casting dreams are made of. Joining her are Stephanie Hollman, Brandi Redmond, D'Andra Simmons, Kameron Westcott, Cary Deuber — a lineup whose various combinations of drama kept viewers entertained for 2 seasons.

The Real Housewives of New Jersey
TV-14, 2009–present
Hulu, Peacock, 12 seasons, 206 episodes
Reality show.

If you like family drama, *Real Housewives of New Jersey* is a drama machine unlike any other. Deep-seated family rivalries drove this franchise for its first 7 seasons, and it was all there from the start.

▶▶ The storied table-flip episode happened in Season 1, but needle-drop at Season 3 to enjoy a cast completely loaded with toxic couples. Future jailbird Teresa Guidice and her husband were joined by Melissa, buttinsky supreme Kathy Walkile and two others who would fall out spectacularly with Teresa, giving the show its most sustained stretch of potent drama.

The Real Housewives of New York City
TV-14, 2008–present
Hulu, Peacock, 13 seasons, 262 episodes
Reality show.

If you like a little less drama and more slapstick, *RHONY* is the *Housewives* for you. Whether it's Countess Luann de Lesseps falling into the rose bushes drunk on tequila or the wacky misadventures of Ramona Singer and Sonja Morgan, *RHONY* is the purest sitcom of the *Housewives* shows. Note, however, that this mostly applies to Seasons 7 and beyond.

▶▶ Season 3 is a highlight, though what you'll see is arguably more of a horror show than a comedy. That season included the must-see Bethenny Frankel and her ally-turned-enemy Jill, Alex and her off-putting husband, LuAnn and her Miss Manners routine that somehow morphed into a vanity music career, and others who all went on an excursion to "Scary Island," still among the best *Housewives* episodes of all time.

The Real Housewives of Orange County
TV-14, 2006–present
Hulu, Peacock, 16 seasons, 279 episodes
Reality show.

The OC is the O.G. of *Real Housewives* shows. Though they may grate on the nerves, Vicki Gunvalson and Tamra Judge are the backbone of *RHOC*.

▶▶ Season 10 — with Vicki, Tamra, Heather Dubrow, Shannon Storms Beador and Meghan King Edmonds — refreshed the series after years of malaise thanks to Shannon, who formed an alliance for the ages with Vicki and Tamra, aka the Tres Amigas. Keep your eye on Meghan, an underrated cast member who exposed Vicki's then-boyfriend Brooks Ayers as having faked cancer.

The Real Housewives of Potomac

TV-14, 2016–present
Hulu, Peacock, 6 seasons, 114 episodes
Reality show.

***Potomac* is your choice if you like a little bit of everything in your reality show.** Though it's only been on for a short time, *Potomac* has quickly established itself as being as shady as *Atlanta*, as fun as *RHONY* and often as dramatic as *Dallas*. Gizelle Bryant and Karen Huger alone are worth the price of admission. Candiance Dillard's drag-out drama is also a hoot.

▶▶ Season 3 is a highlight. The show added intergenerational drama that year, pitting the older generation against three younger girls. It's reflective of how *Potomac,* more than any other *Real Housewives* franchise, features women of all ages coming together.

The Real World Homecoming

TV-MA, 2021–present
Paramount+ original, 2 seasons,
14 episodes (AD)
Reality show.

Things get real — like, *really* real — when former reality TV roommates move back in with each other nearly three decades later and share what life has taught them. This meta-reality series is not only worthwhile on its own merits but also as a fascinating looking-glass into *The Real World*'s legacy and the profound effect that reality's pioneering series had on those who took part. There are shades of Michael Apted's *Up* series as the roommates reveal the various paths their lives have taken them in the years since we last saw them, and the bond they share for having lived their lives on camera together.

The Real World

TV-14, 1992–2019
Paramount+, Hoopla, Prime Video,
33 seasons, 654 episodes

Anthology series (reality show).

MTV's pathbreaking series not only introduced reality TV to the masses, but in many ways showed viewers what reality TV was capable of and helped chart its future. Inspired by the 1972 PBS series *An American Family*, Mary-Ellis Bunim and Jonathan Murray pitched MTV on a social experiment: Have a casting call, pick a group of total strangers, put them together and make them interact while cameras rolled 24/7. Though they resembled scripted TV in their reliance on casting directors and story editors, *The Real World* looked and felt unlike anything on TV. Cheap to produce, it defined a brand-new genre — reality TV — and spawned hundreds (thousands?) of imitators.

▶▶ Season 3, set in San Francisco, has been consistently rated one of the best all-time seasons of a reality show. One cast member died of AIDS, another was evicted and later went to prison. It's a still-watchable time capsule of *Real World* in its messy, unpredictable adolescence.

Recount

TV-MA, 2008
HBO Max, 1 hr 56 mins
Movie (drama) directed by Jay Roach, with Laura Dern, Bob Balaban, Ed Begley Jr., John Hurt, Denis Leary, Tom Wilkinson, Jayne Atkinson and Kevin Spacey.

Get completely embroiled, again, in the escalating drama that made Florida the epicenter of the disputed 2000 presidential election. With the pacing of a thriller and performances well above your ordinary docudrama, the Emmy-winning *Recount* captures the chaotic, emotional fight for control of the Electoral College as it played out in the poorly designed election system of the Sunshine State. Dern is the standout as Katherine

Harris, the Florida Secretary of State and the most polarizing figure of the recount.

Rectify

TV-14, 2013–2016
Sundance Now original, 4 seasons, 30 episodes
Drama with Aden Young, Abigail Spencer, J. Smith-Cameron, Adelaide Clemens, Clayne Crawford, Luke Kirby and Jake Austin Walker.

Aden Young's quiet performance stood out in this 2013 drama about an ex-prisoner's bewildering first weeks of freedom after leaving death row. Short on dialogue and long on empathy, *Rectify* marked the zenith of "slow TV," with a tempo that rewarded patient viewers. Creator Ray McKinnon was digging deep, trying to get viewers to look at crime and punishment a whole different way, through the readjustment of Daniel Holden (Young), finally released after 19 years but still eyed suspiciously by many in his Georgia community. Holden struggles to find meaning in this world, a real challenge for anyone emerging from long incarceration and a storyline rarely explored by a medium that's much more interested in the rush to judgment.

🏆 Peabody Award

Red Notice

PG-13, 2021
Netflix original, 1 hr 58 mins (AD)
Action comedy with Dwayne Johnson, Ryan Reynolds and Gal Gadot.

As they all hunt for ancient and priceless artworks, an FBI agent and pair of art thieves snare each other in a variety of cons and schemes. Critics were divided on this big-budget action comedy but audiences ate it up, probably because Wonder Woman, The Rock and Deadpool are so watchable. They have exactly the right chemistry to make this movie a fizzy treat.

Red Oaks

TV-MA, 2014–2017
Prime Video original, 3 seasons, 26 episodes (AD)
Comedy-drama with Craig Roberts, Ennis Esmer, Oliver Cooper, Richard Kind, Paul Reiser, Alexandra Turshen, Jennifer Grey, Alexandra Socha, Josh Meyers and Gina Gershon.

Funny, heartfelt nostalgia series set in the 1980s at a country club may give you *Caddyshack* vibes. This charming dramedy, which Amazon killed off after just 26 episodes, revolves around NYU student David (Roberts), who spends his summers teaching tennis, romancing a girl (Socha) whose dad (Reiser) runs the country club — and dealing with his own parents' expectations for his future.

💬 From our forums: "David is such a good guy, how can you not root for him? I love that it's set in the '80s but not about the '80s like *The Goldbergs*." "I totally relate to it, having been the age of these young adults back at that time."

Reno 911!

TV-14, 2003–2020
HBO Max, Paramount+, 7 seasons, 113 episodes
Satirical comedy created by Thomas Lennon, Ben Garant and Kerri Kenney-Silver, with Thomas Lennon, Cedric Yarbrough, Robert Ben Garant, Kerri Kenney, Niecy Nash, Wendi McLendon-Covey, Carlos Alazraqui, Mary Birdsong, Ian Roberts and Joe Lo Truglio.

Before *The Office* or *Parks and Rec*, this *Cops* parody was the great American mockumentary. Pioneering MTV comedy sketch troupe The State specialized in spoofing TV's cherished formulas, never more successfully than with this long-running series purported to show the "real" cops of the (nonexistent) "Reno Sheriff's Department," whose pettiness and personal foibles always got in the way of apprehending suspects. Not for the easily offended, the show has a fair amount of dated humor that might not pass muster today, but its cheerful embrace of political incorrectness is something we could use more of these days.

▶▶ A seventh season consisting of 25 mini-episodes produced for the now-defunct Quibi service is available on the Roku Channel. The series also spawned the 2007 film *Reno 911!: Miami* and the 2021 Paramount+ special *Reno 911! The Hunt for QAnon*.

The Repair Shop
TV-PG, 2017–present
Discovery+, 8 seasons, 160 episodes
Reality show with Jay Blades, Will Kirk, Steve Fletcher and Kirsten Ramsay.

Skilled and caring restorationists help people make their busted family heirlooms whole again. It's *Antiques Roadshow* for the rest of us — a roomful of experts who, instead of appraising things in your attic, will "resurrect, revive and rejuvenate" them. The repairs are explained in almost loving detail on *The Repair Shop*, but cost or monetary value never is. Clearly, though, the emotional value to the shop's grateful customers is incalculable. This old British favorite is soothing TV at its best.

Rescue Me
TV-MA, 2004–2011
Hulu, Starz, 7 seasons, 95 episodes
Comedy-drama created by Denis Leary and Peter Tolan, with Denis Leary, John Scurti, Daniel Sunjata, Michael Lombardi, Steven Pasquale, Andrea Roth, Callie Thorne and Tatum O'Neal.

Denis Leary's tragicomedy about a FDNY firefighter, his shambles of a family life and the post-9/11 chaos raging inside his own head was a revelation. Leary, a career comedian, responded to the sense of trauma, loss and responsibility of first responders and their loved ones with this decidedly dramatic turn. He played Tommy Gavin, who was haunted by the loss of his buddies in the World Trade Center attacks. Gavin depended on his job saving lives and the insular, insult-driven culture of work to keep him sane, barely. As an old school sexist with a big mouth, Gavin had a way of getting himself into some first-rate misadventures. *Rescue Me* took its characters through issues like depression, trauma, alcoholism and homophobia, allowing Leary to show members of the Bravest in all their humanity.

▶▶ After watching Season 1, needle-drop at Season 5 for an interesting reexamination of 9/11 through the character of Franco, a firefighter fully immersed in the conspiracy theories surrounding the attack.

Reservation Dogs
TV-MA, 2021–present
Hulu, 8 episodes (AD)
Comedy created by Taika Waititi and Sterlin Harjo, with D'Pharaoh Woon-A-Tai, Devery Jacobs, Lane Factor, Paulina Alexis, Elva Guerra and Amanda Pearce.

Four Indigenous teenagers in Oklahoma run various grifts and cons in order to pay their way to the promised land of California. Both highly specific and broadly relatable, *Reservation Dogs* — TV's first show in which every writer, director and series regular is Indigenous — unsparingly presents Indian life in its many varieties and foibles. The comedy works best during slice-of-life scenes that expand the unique world of the show (the second episode takes place in the packed waiting room of the Indian Health Service clinic).

▶▶ Pairs well with *Derry Girls*

Resident Alien
TV-14, 2021–present
Peacock, 2 seasons, 20 episodes
Sci-fi comedy with Alan Tudyk,
Sara Tomko, Corey Reynolds, Alice
Wetterlund, Levi Fiehler, Meredith
Garretson and Elizabeth Bowen.

A small-town doctor is actually a crash-landed alien in disguise in this mostly lighthearted mystery. Tudyk, whose pipes are well known from his voiceover work (notably as K-2SO in *Rogue One: A Star Wars Story*), stars in this adaptation of the Dark Horse comic series. The opening storyline gets off to full gallop, as Dr. Harry van Der Spiegel (Tudyk) gets called into a murder investigation in the small town of Patience, Colorado, which is ironic since he's an interplanetary killer here to take out humans. The show has some legacy callbacks: Dr. Harry's alien oddball is reminiscent of Dick Solomon from *3rd Rock from the Sun* and Patience has a Cicely, Alaska, feel to it. But with viewers still flocking to funky old cable shows like *Leverage* and *Psych*, *Resident Alien* actually blends right in.

Rich Hill
TV-MA, 2014
PlutoTV, Roku Channel, Tubi,
1 hr 31 mins
Movie (documentary) directed by
Andrew Droz Palermo and Tracy Droz
Tragos.

Sensitive portrayal of poor white kids in rural Missouri helps us understand why it's so hard to get ahead. Tracy Droz Tragos, who won an Emmy for *Be Good, Smile Pretty*, a film about her father — a Vietnam soldier killed on the Mekong Delta — returns to her hometown of Rich Hill, Mo., and befriends three charming adolescent boys and their families. Their stories are heartbreaking but their resolve and willingness to do what it takes to get by is admirable. If you don't live in a place like Rich Hill and want to understand places like this better, start here.
🏆 Sundance Film Festival Grand Jury Prize

The Riches
TV-MA, 2007–2008
Hulu, 2 seasons, 20 episodes
Comedy-drama with Eddie Izzard,
Minnie Driver, Shannon Woodward, Noel
Fisher, Margo Martindale, Aidan Mitchell,
Todd Stashwick and Gregg Henry.

Minnie Driver and Eddie Izzard were terrific as married grifters who assume the identity of a wealthy couple. In the mid-2000s, a basic cable formula involved an actress currently being ill-served by Hollywood's feature films paired with a dysfunctional family and given one complication (like Laura Linney's cancer in *The Big C*). Here it was Driver and Izzard as Irish-American "travelers," running cons with their children, scamming their way into the mansion and lives of two rich people who perished in a car accident. The capers they pull are great fun but the real show was Driver's performance as a tough, bruised woman fighting hard for the life she thinks her family deserves.

Rick and Morty
TV-MA, 2013–present
HBO Max, Hulu, 5 seasons,
51 episodes (AD)
Animated comedy with Justin Roiland,
Chris Parnell, Spencer Grammer and
Sarah Chalke.

TV's unlikeliest cartoon classic follows the wildly strange adventures of a drunken maniac who takes his grandson on interplanetary travels to show him the chaotic and pointless nature of the universe. Dark matter indeed, but Rick's cynical outbursts are nicely countered by Morty's earnestness and surprising insights. This show was developed for

Adult Swim, the late-night cable block that introduced a generation of viewers to a fast-paced, dissonant style of humor that was once considered alternative but has gone mainstream thanks to shows like *Rick and Morty*.

🏆 Emmy for best animated program (2 wins)

The Right Stuff
TV-14, 2020
Disney+ original, 8 episodes (AD)
Historical drama with Patrick J. Adams, Patrick Fischler, Eric Ladin, James Lafferty, Jack McDorman, Shannon Lucio and Colin O'Donoghue.

Disney+ winningly adapts Tom Wolfe's bestselling account of the Mercury space program for a new generation. The miniseries, which comes to Disney+ under the National Geographic banner, is well made, with the expected attention given to period detail. Oddly, the most nostalgic element is the portrayal of a functional government agency, operating with the general support of the public, to realize a national project with the potential to change the course of human events.

The Righteous Gemstones
TV-MA, 2019–present
HBO Max, 2 seasons, 18 episodes
Dark comedy created by Danny McBride, with Danny McBride, Walton Goggins, John Goodman, Adam Devine, Edi Patterson, Tony Cavalero, Cassidy Freeman, Skyler Gisondo, Jennifer Nettles and Dermot Mulroney.

Superstars of the megachurch world, the Gemstones hide their backstabbing, power-mad, increasingly criminal behavior behind a facade of religious propriety. Dr. Eli Gemstone (Goodman), the widowed patriarch of the Salvation Center, and his three adult children live splendidly off the tithes of others.

McBride, the show's creator — who also was behind *Eastbound and Down* and *Vice Principals* on HBO — plays son Jesse, whose debauched lifestyle leaves him vulnerable to a blackmail plot. Goggins is outstanding as Eli's brother-in-law, who's called to lead a prayer center at a shopping mall.

💬 **From our forums:** "I know that all the characters are terrible and that's the point, but I liked that there was some heart and kindness to multiple story lines."

▶▶ Pairs well with *Greenleaf*

Riverdale
TV-14, 2017–present
Netflix, 6 seasons, 100 episodes (AD)
Teen drama created by Roberto Aguirre-Sacasa, with K.J. Apa, Lili Reinhart, Camila Mendes, Cole Sprouse, Madelaine Petsch, Casey Cott, Mädchen Amick, Mark Consuelos, Vanessa Morgan and Skeet Ulrich.

Considered one of the most unpredictable series on TV today, this Archie-Comics-in-name-only adaptation follows the gang on a series of campy, sexy and bloody mysteries. Series creator Aguirre-Sacasa (*The Chilling Adventures of Sabrina*) has a knack for turning teenybopper comics into black drama. *Riverdale*'s mix of bitchy humor, sex and format shifts — plus its smart self-understanding of its own outré sensibility — make it an irresistible mess. Adding to the gorgeous cast are former teen stars Skeet Ulrich and Luke Perry (whose death was somberly incorporated into the S4 premiere).

Rob Delaney: Jackie
TV-MA, 2020
Prime Video original, 1 hr 2 mins (AD)
Comedy special directed by Barbara Wiltshire, with Rob Delaney.

Like a real-life version of his series *Catastrophe*, Delaney uses this standup

set to talk about his chaotic time living in London. The high-energy comic sweats his way through a set that will delight progressives (although anti-Trump material, as a rule, doesn't age well). Viewers may be put off by the laugh track, a concession to doing comedy in a pandemic.

Roma
R, 2018
Netflix, 2 hrs 15 mins (AD)
Movie (drama) directed by Alfonso Cuarón, with Yalitza Aparicio, Marina de Tavira, Marco Graf and Daniela Demesa.

Alfonso Cuarón's semi-autobiographical drama about an upper-middle-class family living in 1970s Mexico City is regarded as a modern masterwork. Mexican-born Cuarón wrote and directed this film as a tribute to the nanny who raised him (and still lives with his family). Told from the point of view of the nanny, Cleo (Aparicio), an indigenous Mixtec woman, *Roma* is able to go big — capturing the political turbulence in Mexico at that time — and get astonishingly small, capturing intimate moments between the boy Pepe (Graf) and Cleo in splendid black-and-white scenes filmed by the director himself.
🏆 3 Oscars including best director and best foreign film

The Romanoffs
TV-MA, 2018
Prime Video original, 8 episodes (AD)
Anthology series (drama) created by Matthew Weiner, with Diane Lane, JJ Feild, Aaron Eckhart, John Slattery, Kathryn Hahn, Christina Hendricks, Amanda Peet, Hugh Skinner, Corey Stoll and Andrew Rannells.

For his first post-*Mad Men* TV project, Matthew Weiner produced this unusual anthology series about people around the world who believe they're descendants of the Russian royal family. Historical drama is something Weiner obviously relishes doing, though like other TV anthologies the 8 self-contained episodes of this lavishly produced and starry project are hit-or-miss. *Mad Men* completists will want to see the 2 episodes starring show alumni Hendricks ("House of Special Purpose") and Slattery ("Expectation").
▶▶ The show's best episode, "End of the Line" features Kathryn Hahn and Jay R. Ferguson (another *Mad Men* star) as an American couple suffering from infertility who travel to Russia to adopt a baby.

Ronny Chieng: Asian Comedian Destroys America!
TV-MA, 2019
Netflix original, 1 hr 3 mins (AD)
Comedy special with Ronny Chieng.

The *Daily Show* correspondent riffs on modern life from his distinct perspective of a Chinese-Malaysian American. Chieng's material and hyperactive delivery certainly live up to the title. His well-observed, energetically delivered bit on New York subway warriors is the standout on this standup special, which tees off on how the Internet is making us dumber, Japanese toilets and having to travel across the globe to get married.

Room 104
TV-MA, 2017–2020
HBO Max, 4 seasons, 48 episodes (AD)
Anthology series (dark comedy) created by Mark and Jay Duplass, with Michael Shannon, Mae Whitman, Dave Bautista, Cobie Smulders, Jay Duplass, Mahershala Ali, Judy Greer, Keir Gilchrist, Melissa Fumero and Mark Duplass.

Unpredictable anthology series about guests staying in the same hotel features stories that run the gamut from tragic to laugh-out-loud to terrifying. It's just a small, dingy room in a motel, but you truly don't know what you'll find inside each time you check in. Sometimes you'll find regular people facing a relatable crisis; other times the room seems like its own dimension of time. Short, unconnected episodes make for an easy binge.

🐟 **From our forums:** "I liked it, but then, I like Duplass Brothers productions. I like weird, *Twilight Zone*-y stuff." "This show makes me feel like I've taken bad drugs."

Rose Matafeo: Horndog
TV-MA, 2020
HBO Max original, 55 mins (AD)
Comedy special directed by Barbara Wiltshire, with Rose Matafeo.

The New Zealand native assures viewers that she's the perfect person to discuss sex in the modern world, since she has kissed almost 10 boys. This is the filmed version of a show that won a major award at the Edinburgh Fringe Festival.

Rotten
TV-MA, 2018–2019
Netflix original, 2 seasons,
12 episodes (AD)
Docuseries with Latif Nasser.

From avocados to bottled water to edibles, this series digs into the hidden costs of the supply chains that bring us our food. The title is oversell: There's nothing in this lively, largely informative series that stinks, and the eye-opening video will not turn you away from your delicious Hass avocados or plastic bottles filled with clean water. But if you believe that you are what you eat (or drink), you'll appreciate *Rotten* for its unfiltered view of the global consequences of some of our favorite consumables.

▶▶ Netflix has made a cottage industry out of these exposé-ish docuseries — besides *Rotten*, there's *(Un)Well* about the wellness industry, *Cowspiracy* about Big Ag and *Seaspiracy* about Big Fishing.

Run
PG-13, 2020
Hulu original, 1 hr 30 mins (AD)
Movie (thriller) with Sarah Paulson and Kiera Allen.

Sarah Paulson plays a mother with a disabled teenage daughter and some disturbing secrets. Kiera Allen, who is paralyzed, plays the homebound child who slowly gets clued into the weirdness happening under their roof. This movie has some serious nail-biting moments, and Paulson is sensational as the possibly unhinged matriarch.

Run the World
TV-MA, 2021–present
Starz original, 8 episodes
Comedy-drama with Amber Stevens West, Bresha Webb, Corbin Reid and Andrea Bordeaux.

Another winner from the creator of *Dear White People* follows four Black women who are ambitious best friends living in Harlem. The women in this show feel like actual residents of the 21st century, facing daily dramas and long-term life questions that almost anyone will recognize. The writing also pays attention to being a Black woman in particular, which roots the characters in specific circumstances. They're all flawed and easy to love, and their friendship is a delight to behold.

RuPaul's Drag Race
TV-14, 2009–present
Paramount+, Hulu, 14 seasons,
180 episodes
Reality competition created by RuPaul, with RuPaul and many, many aspiring queens.

Empire-launching reality competition turns the stage over to drag queens who think they have the stuff of legend. It's pretty hard to avoid *RuPaul's Drag Race* these days — reruns appear on cable,

Paramount+ and Hulu and PlutoTV occasionally devotes a 24/7 channel to it. But when *Drag Race* premiered back in 2009, many critics couldn't be bothered to cover it. Besides having an irresistible on-air presence, RuPaul had a keen intuition and saw, before most us, the increasingly performative, Instagram-driven nature of mediated life; the celebration of fat, queer and fierce archetypes in the popular culture; and the global demand for drag queens, which would lead to a slew of spinoffs. Blessed with a stable format and savvy production team, *Drag Race* is arguably the most comforting competition show this side of *Jeopardy!* and a worldwide influencer in fashion and slang.

▸▸ If you haven't experienced the show's unique mixture of campy comedy, queer empowerment and astonishing outfits, jump in at Season 4, by which time the format is well-established.

🏆 11 Emmy awards for best reality competition and best host, making RuPaul the most-honored Black artist in Television Academy history

Russian Doll
TV-MA, 2019–present
Netflix original, 8 episodes (AD)
Dark comedy created by Natasha Lyonne, Amy Poehler and Leslye Headland, with Natasha Lyonne, Greta Lee, Yul Vazquez, Charlie Barnett and Elizabeth Ashley.

Natasha Lyonne creates a vehicle for her singular talents in this time-warp comedy full of surprising twists and knowing observations about life and death. After she dies at her 36th birthday party, Nadia (Lyonne) finds herself in a loop, constantly returning to the party and trying to figure out what's going on before she dies again. But it's not *Groundhog Day* — it's more intricate (like the toy in the title) with a stronger supporting cast and its own comic sensibility.

🎬 **From our forums:** "Brilliant mashup of *Run Lola Run, Sliding Doors, Groundhog Day, Eternal Sunshine of the Spotless Mind, Hang the DJ, The Butterfly Effect* and perhaps a dash of *Memento*? Will rewatch, I'm that intrigued and obsessed."

🏆 3 Emmys

Rutherford Falls
TV-14, 2021–present
Peacock original, 10 episodes (AD)
Sitcom created by Ed Helms, Michael Schur and Sierra Teller Ornelas, with Ed Helms, Michael Greyeyes, Jana Schmieding, Jesse Leigh and Dustin Milligan.

Indigenous and white historical narratives clash in a small-town comedy that's sweet and philosophical. From *Parks and Recreation* and *Good Place* creator Mike Schur among others, *Rutherford Falls* is the first show to mine the battle over history — which version we believe, whose statue gets to sit in the town square — for laughs. Nathan Rutherford (Helms) works tirelessly preserving the town's history and educating people about his family through his well-funded museum. His friend Reagan (Schmieding) is a Minishonka woman who runs the barebones cultural center inside the tribe's massive casino. When someone proposes moving the statue of Nathan's forbear, "Big Larry" Rutherford, from its traffic-stopping location, tensions flare, podcasters fire up their recorders and the small-town eccentrics come spilling out. The show's Indigenous showrunner, writers and star are notable, but the comedy sells it.

🎬 **From our forums:** "It started a little slow and I was worried that I would always see Ed Helms as Andy Bernard, but by the fourth episode the characters dig in and the show gains momentum."

▶▶ Pairs well with *Parks and Recreation*

Safety
PG, 2020
Disney+ original, 2 hrs 2 mins (AD)
Movie (drama) with Jay Reeves, Corinne Foxx, James Badge Dale and Matthew Glave.

This feel-good sports film is based on the true story of Ray-Ray McElrathbey, who secretly raised his little brother on the Clemson campus after his home life became too volatile. Striving to be a bit more than a serviceable inspirational biopic, *Safety* explores the mental and emotional strain Ray-Ray (wonderfully played by Reeves) is putting on himself to protect his brother and keep up with the demands of football and school, and how in the end, the team lifts them up.

Salt Fat Acid Heat
TV-PG, 2018
Netflix original, 4 episodes (AD)
Docuseries with Samin Nosrat.

Lively adaptation of Samin Nosrat's bestselling book surveys the four essentials to flavorful cooking. Nosrat, a celebrity culinary writer (she makes an appearance in Michael Pollan's *Cooked* as his teacher), explores a different culture in each episode of this series, which is as much a satisfying travelogue as it is a primer on cooking. Exploring oils in Italy, salts in Japan, lively acids in Mexico and hot things in California, Nosrat is able to give each ingredient — and episode — its own personality.

Santa Clarita Diet
TV-MA, 2017–2019
Netflix original, 3 seasons, 30 episodes (AD)
Comedy-horror series with Drew Barrymore, Timothy Olyphant, Liv Hewson and Skyler Gisondo.

Drew Barrymore plays Sheila, a real estate agent with a craving for human flesh, in a comedy that turns out to be as delightful as Drew is. In this blood-soaked absurdist romp, Sheila and husband Joel (Olyphant) are raising a daughter and trying to go about their normal lives while (a) harvesting their fellow humans to keep Sheila going and (b) trying to find a cure for what's eating at Sheila … er, what's keeping Sheila eating at … well, you get the point.

🗨 **From our forums:** "Timothy Olyphant continues to be a comedy revelation." "I did the same damn thing I did with last season, which I swore I wouldn't. I binged the whole thing in one day. Totally worth it."

▶▶ The show was canceled without proper closure, leaving viewers with a *major* cliffhanger.

Saturday Night Live
TV-14, 1975–present
Peacock, Hulu, 47 seasons, 925 episodes
Sketch comedy created by Lorne Michaels, with Kenan Thompson, Seth Meyers, Fred Armisen, Bobby Moynihan, Kate McKinnon, Tim Meadows, Aidy Bryant, Cecily Strong, Jason Sudeikis and many, many more.

SNL's ability to right its ship every few years and steam back into the forefront of popular culture is never more apparent than now, as it approaches half a century on TV. After the last of the Not Ready for Prime Time players departed in 1980, *SNL* nearly fell over and expired. Two years after winning the Emmy in 1993, critics declared it dead. And so it's gone for decades. America's premier satirical show has wobbled at times, but thanks to an endlessly renewable resource of young comedy talent — drawn into *SNL*'s lair with the incentive of one day scoring a TV or movie franchise inside Lorne Michaels's vast entertainment empire — there now seems little doubt that the show will be poking fun at politicians and celebs well into the next half century.

🏆 92 Emmys, more than any entertainment show in history, including best variety show in 1976, 1993 and 2017–2021

Saved by the Bell (2020)
TV-14, 2020–present
Peacock original, 2 seasons,
20 episodes (AD)

Sitcom created by Tracey Wigfield, with Haskiri Velazquez, Mitchell Hoog, Josie Totah, Alycia Pascual-Pena, Belmont Cameli, Dexter Darden, John Michael Higgins, Elizabeth Berkley, Mario Lopez and Mark-Paul Gosselaar.

The beloved '90s teen series gets a sharp reboot, with Jessie and Slater from the original *Saved by the Bell* now working at Bayside High. Creator Tracey Wigfield's reimagining features some callbacks to the old show (Mario Lopez and Elizabeth Berkley reprise their roles). But this is *Saved by the Bell* for a new generation, more self-aware and serious than the original but calibrated not to alienate the earlier show's fans who tuned in for the amusing high school hijinks and nostalgic callbacks.

📣 **From our forums:** "You can tell this show came from a *30 Rock* alum." "One thing I did appreciate was how it addressed stuff that was okay in the old show but is not okay now."

Scandal
TV-14, 2012–2018
Hulu, 7 seasons, 124 episodes

Drama created by Shonda Rhimes, with Kerry Washington, Darby Stanchfield, Katie Lowes, Joshua Malina, Bellamy Young, Tony Goldwyn and Scott Foley.

Kerry Washington excels as a crisis manager whose firm is constantly pulled into political plots, sexual escapades and other shady dealings. Thanks to its wild weekly twists, this was one of the first shows that got people live-tweeting while they watched. The nonstop escalating drama (which involved international murder plots by the end of the run) is addictive. And Washington has the right balance of empathy and moxie push it forward.

🏆 Peabody Award, 2 Emmys

Scenes from a Marriage
TV-MA, 2021
HBO Max, 5 episodes (AD)

Limited series (drama) created by Hagai Levi, with Jessica Chastain and Oscar Isaac.

The 1973 Ingmar Bergman TV series is hauntingly reimagined as a 21st-century psychodrama between two people whose solid bond disintegrates. The tale of a modern, well-educated couple who, as Bergman put it, "can't handle the simplest of emotional ABCs" has influenced filmmakers for half a century. Now, thanks to emotionally savvy tweaks made by Levi (who created the Israeli *In Treatment*), it resonates again. Mira (Chastain), as a driven tech executive who lets infidelity creep into her marriage, and Jonathan (Isaac), the sensitive if passive-aggressive prof, have outstanding chemistry even as they play lovers drifting apart.

▶▶ Try not to be thrown off by the episodes' verité-style openings, showing the actors arriving on set in masks — a concession to the weirdness of shooting in a pandemic.

Schitt's Creek
TV-14, 2015–2020
Netflix, IMDb TV, 6 seasons, 80 episodes

Sitcom created by Eugene Levy and Dan Levy, with Eugene Levy, Catherine O'Hara, Dan Levy, Annie Murphy, Chris Elliott, Emily Hampshire, Jennifer

Robertson, Sarah Levy, Dustin Milligan and Noah Reid.

One of the great slow-burn success stories in TV, this sitcom began as an under-the-radar oddity and ended as a beloved and much-honored juggernaut. The Rose family suddenly lose all their money and have to move into a crumbling motel in the backwater town of Schitt's Creek. The show's magic is that nobody is particularly *likable,* yet the humanity of these characters slowly drips out like water from the motel's leaky ceiling. O'Hara is especially winning as dramatic onetime soap star Moira Rose. She never fully accepts her diminished role but gradually adapts to small-town life while remaining as hilariously over-the-top as ever.

▶▶ Eugene Levy co-created the show with son Dan Levy, then persuaded O'Hara, his former *SCTV* and movie castmate, to join the show. O'Hara turned down the role initially, citing "laziness."

▶▶ For suggestions of related shows, see "If You Liked *Schitt's Creek,*" page 376.

🏆 In its final season *Schitt's Creek* not only took the Emmy for best comedy series but, in an Emmy first, all four acting prizes (Eugene Levy, O'Hara, Dan Levy, Murphy)

Schmigadoon!

TV-14, 2021–present
Apple TV+ original, 6 episodes (AD)
Musical comedy with Keegan-Michael Key, Cecily Strong, Fred Armisen, Dove Cameron, Jaime Camil, Kristin Chenoweth, Alan Cumming, Jane Krakowski, Martin Short and Aaron Tveit.

Cecily Strong and Keegan-Michael Key star in a pitch-perfect satire as travelers who stumble into an enchanted town where everyone is a performer in a 1940s musical. The show's concept should be familiar to anyone who's seen *Brigadoon*: a couple on a backpacking excursion come upon a hidden, magical town called Schmigadoon, which exists within the milieu of Golden Age stage and screen musicals. Our couple, whose relationship is on the rocks, try to leave this melodic quagmire but find they can't — not until they find true love. From *Despicable Me* screenwriters Cinco Paul and Ken Daurio, the supporting cast is a veritable buffet of musical talent.

Search Party

TV-MA, 2016–2022
HBO Max original, 5 seasons, 50 episodes (AD)
Dark comedy created by Sarah Violet-Bliss and Charles Rogers, with Alia Shawkat, John Reynolds, John Early and Meredith Hagner.

Audacious dark comedy follows a group of college friends whose lives are upended after they start investigating a classmate's disappearance. This is worth a watch all the way through. So well crafted that it's easy to follow these characters on their rather unhinged path; by the end of Season 5, you'll marvel at where they all end up. Shawkat, playing the stubborn and charismatic ringleader, is spectacular, able to pull laughs out of throwaway moments while carefully shading her character's growth. Show creators Violet-Bliss and Rogers write and direct nearly every episode, giving *Search Party* a uniquely unified vision throughout its run.

🗨 **From our forums:** "I really enjoyed it. The characters were terrible but I couldn't bring myself to hate them."

▶▶ Seasons 1–2 originally aired on TBS before the series hopped to HBO Max in 2020.

Seinfeld

TV-PG, 1989–1998
Netflix, 9 seasons, 173 episodes (AD)
Classic sitcom created by Jerry Seinfeld and Larry David, with Jerry Seinfeld,

Jason Alexander, Michael Richards and Julia Louis-Dreyfus.

Netflix reportedly forked over $500 million for the rights to *Seinfeld*; we know a few reasons why. More than 30 years after Jerry Seinfeld appeared in a little-hyped summer schedule-filler — just another standup comedian who made a sitcom pilot — *Seinfeld* remains one of the most popular and quoted shows of all time. Seinfeld and David insisted their creation was a "show about nothing," but the show's genius was its ability to turn nothingburgers into high-stakes comedy that held up through multiple rewatches.

▶▶ Several classic episodes involved only-in-New-York escalations: "The Parking Space" (S3E6), "The Chinese Restaurant" (S2E11), "The Soup Nazi" (S7E6). Others involved odd dating partners, notably "The Opposite" (S5E22) and "The Yada Yada" (S8E19), though it's hard to think of a less dateable trio than George, Kramer and Elaine.

▶▶ Season 4 was the show's high water mark, with classic episodes like "The Junior Mint" (S4E20), "The Implant" (S4E8) and "The Contest" (S4E11), the latter 2 episodes involving touchy subjects for prime-time comedy. That's also the season with our favorite *Seinfeld* arc, in which Jerry and George pitch NBC on — and cast the pilot for — their very own show about nothing.

▶▶ Don't hold your breath that the *Seinfeld* gang will get back together for a Streaming TV revival. They already did that during a Season 7 arc of *Curb Your Enthusiasm*, including new scenes shot on the show's original set.

🏆 Peabody Award, 10 Emmys, 6 SAG Awards, TCA Heritage Award

Self Made: Inspired by the Life of Madam C.J. Walker

TV-MA, 2020
Netflix original, 4 episodes (AD)

Limited series (historical drama) with Octavia Spencer, Tiffany Haddish, Carmen Ejogo, Kevin Carroll, Blair Underwood and Garrett Morris.

Octavia Spencer brings to life the forgotten trailblazing Black hair care entrepreneur known as Madam C.J. Walker. Spencer plays Sarah Breedlove, whose early years in post–Civil War America were marked by poverty, early marriage and enough stress to make her hair fall out — the inspiration that an empire was built upon. As the film's subtitle suggests, liberties are taken with Breedlove's story, but the struggle was real. *Self Made* shows what she had to overcome to succeed, not only personal struggles and inner demons but the general low regard with which society held Black women in the early 1900s.

The Sentence

TV-PG, 2018
HBO Max, 1 hr 25 mins
Movie (documentary) directed by Rudy Valdez.

A mandatory-sentencing law sent the director's sister to prison — and wreaked extraordinary havoc on her family. The directing debut of cameraman Rudy Valdez, *The Sentence* started as a personal project after his sister was sentenced to 15 years in prison for what seems like a petty offense. Valdez found himself documenting the carnage and creating a compelling narrative about how the institution of the family can be undermined by an ever-expanding criminal justice system.

🏆 Emmy for merit in documentary filmmaking

A Series of Unfortunate Events

TV-PG, 2017–2019
Netflix original, 3 seasons, 25 episodes (AD)

Dark comedy created by Barry Sonnenfeld and Daniel Handler, with Neil Patrick Harris, Patrick Warburton, Malina Weissman, Louis Hynes, K. Todd Freeman, Presley Smith and Usman Ally.

Neil Patrick Harris headlines this macabre comic adaptation of the middle-grade novels. Harris is wonderfully wicked as Count Olaf, pursuing the Baudelaire children and trying to lay his hands on their inheritance. But it's Warburton — breaking the fourth wall as narrator Lemony Snicket — who steals the show.

🐟 **From our forums:** "As someone who grew up with the books and is a huge fan, I really enjoyed this. The tone was spot on, that perfect mix of whimsy and heartbreaking reality." "My 11-year-old is a dedicated reader of the series, so we watched Episode 1 tonight and it earned my kid's seal of approval. I love the Tim Burton/Wes Anderson mashup feel of the design."

🏆 Peabody Award

Servant

TV-MA, 2019–present
Apple TV+ original, 3 seasons, 30 episodes (AD)
Horror created by Tony Basgallop, with Lauren Ambrose, Toby Kebbell, Nell Tiger Free and Rupert Grint.

This M. Night Shyamalan-produced thriller might be better enjoyed as a (creepy) domestic comedy. When a TV reporter (Ambrose) becomes catatonic following the death of her infant child, she's given a therapy doll that can help her transition — except she becomes so enamored of the doll that she treats it as real and persuades her husband (Kebbell) to get a *nanny* for the doll so she can go back to work. *Servant* is on-brand for Shyamalan, spooky and magical and weird with some effective reveals. But

the endless bizarro turns and long, slow stretches may be too much for some.

🐟 **From our forums:** "I hated these people; the show trafficked in social criticism of the shallow rich, which deprived the characters of any reality. That's a problem when creepy stuff starts to happen, because you don't give a rat's ass what happens to these people. *The Outsider*, by contrast, has characters with enough specificity that I want to them to be OK."

Seven Seconds

TV-MA, 2018
Netflix original, 10 episodes (AD)
Limited series (drama) with Regina King, Clare-Hope Ashitey, Beau Knapp, Michael Mosley, David Lyons, Russell Hornsby, Raúl Castillo, Patrick Murney, Zackary Momoh and Michelle Veintimilla.

Regina King powers this suspenseful tale of a New Jersey community upended after a white cop kills her child in a hit-and-run. Don't expect a lot of woke exposition about social issues here. This is a good old-fashioned thriller from the creator of *The Killing* in which systemic racism is mostly brought in as a useful plot lubricant. As the cop, Knapp effectively embodies the torment of a man who knows he's made two horrible mistakes — the crime *and* the cover-up.

🐟 **From our forums:** "King was excellent. She was mired in grief and it felt exhausting because grief is exhausting."

🏆 Emmy for best actress in a limited series (King)

Sex and the City

TV-MA, 1998–2004
HBO Max, 6 seasons, 94 episodes (AD)
Romantic comedy created by Darren Star, with Sarah Jessica Parker, Kim Cattrall, Kristin Davis and Cynthia Nixon.

The storylines may not have aged that well, but this is still a comedy ensemble

for the ages. Despite all the now-obvious shortcomings with *Sex and the City* — notably its lack of racial, sexual or income diversity — the show remains watchable for two reasons. First, as a useful snapshot of sex and commitment among certain New Yorkers, the kind who eagerly consumed Candace Bushnell's *New York Observer* columns on which this show is based. Second, as a model for sophisticated female-centered comedy. The four women at the heart of *SATC* have rarely, if ever, been matched for their chemistry and camaraderie.

▶▶ The *SATC* saga continued in followup feature films and the revival series *And Just Like That...* (see page 51).

🏆 Emmys for best comedy series and best actress (Parker) and supporting actress (Nixon)

Sex Education
TV-MA, 2019–present
Netflix original, 3 seasons,
24 episodes (AD)
Comedy-drama with Asa Butterfield, Gillian Anderson, Emma Mackey, Ncuti Gatwa, Aimee Lou Wood, Connor Swindells, Kedar Williams-Stirling and Alistair Petrie.

Two British teenagers set up an underground sex therapy clinic at their school in this clever and tender mashup of *Big Mouth*, Hal Hartley films and Dr Ruth. Thanks to his delightfully frank-talking sex therapist mother (Anderson), Otis (Butterfield) thinks he knows a lot about sex. So he teams up with his troubled classmate Maeve (Mackey) to dispense advice to classmates, even though they're hardly pros at intimacy. There's more here than explicit sex talk and an occasional gross-out scene. *Sex Education* explores the complexities and complications of what the Brits call shagging in a way few comedies have attempted.

💬 **From our forums:** "I was watching for Gillian but it wound up being a really good show. Does Gillian have a clause in her contract that she always has to be put in the most awful wigs possible? Because it keeps happening."

The Sex Lives of College Girls
TV-MA, 2021–present
HBO Max original, 10 episodes (AD)
Romantic comedy created by Mindy Kaling and Justin Noble, with Pauline Chalamet, Amrit Kaur, Reneé Rapp and Alyah Chanelle Scott.

This good-natured and sexually frank comedy follows four college freshmen dealing with their sudden freedom to do almost anything (and anyone) they want. Like Kaling's other shows, this one lets female characters be the center of familiar stories about sex, dating and figuring yourself out. It also taps the comic gold mine of an 18-year-old kid who is let loose on campus. The four leads are carefully designed to represent a variety of economic, sexual and racial perspectives, and the fact that they all get along as roommates points to the optimism beneath the antics.

Shameless (US)
TV-MA, 2011–2021
Showtime original, 11 seasons,
134 episodes
Dark comedy with William H. Macy, Emmy Rossum, Ethan Cutkosky, Jeremy Allen White, Shanola Hampton, Steve Howey, Emma Kenney and Cameron Monaghan.

Adaptation of the UK show about a ne'er-do-well dad is as good as the original. This dark comedy about a large working-class Chicago family, headed by hopeless alcoholic and junkie Frank Gallagher (Macy), is based on the critically acclaimed series from England's Channel 4. Though Frank was a lovable scoundrel and patriarch who somehow managed to survive to middle age despite poor life choices, *Shameless* was carried by his kids, notably oldest daughter Fiona (Rossum). They had more appealing personalities and, needless to say, more aspirational storylines than their old man. With plenty of screwing, swearing and bad behavior, this show was even more over-the-top than the UK original, but fit perfectly into Showtime's adult lineup.

🏆 4 Emmys, SAG Award for acting in a comedy (Macy, 3 wins)

Shark Tank
TV-PG, 2009–present
Hulu, 12 seasons, 273 episodes (AD)
Reality competition with Mark Cuban, Kevin O'Leary, Robert Herjavec, Lori Greiner and Barbara Corcoran.

The show that introduced Ring doorbells and Bombas footwear to millions of Americans remains one of the most authentic and watchable reality shows on TV. If someone had pitched us *Shark Tank* — a show where entrepreneurs try to convince a panel ofventure capitalists to invest in their product — we'd have said "sold!" Thanks to periodic refreshes of its set and format (like showing backstage moments as the entrepreneurs prepare to pitch), this show involving real money and high stakes pulls a rare double feat, as good TV with positive impacts off-camera.

🏆 Emmy for best structured reality show (4 wins)

Sharp Objects
TV-MA, 2018
HBO Max, 8 episodes
Limited series (crime drama) created by Marti Noxon, with Amy Adams, Patricia Clarkson, Chris Messina, Eliza Scanlen, Matt Craven, Henry Czerny, Elizabeth Perkins, Sophia Lillis, Miguel Sandoval and Lulu Wilson.

Amy Adams is impressive as the broken, self-destructive crime reporter at the center of Gillian Flynn's murder mystery. This dark and moody thriller — ostensibly about Camille (Adams) returning to her hometown to investigate the killing of two girls — doubles as a study of a hollow mother-daughter relationship. Clarkson, as Camille's mother Adora, keeps up appearances in the community, but her cruelty is evidenced behind closed doors and from the razor scars that Camille keeps covered up.

🎯 **From our forums:** "In spite of the terrific actors, I am disappointed; too many boring moments and not enough coherent exposition." "People are going to complain about the slow slow burn and sudden ending, but I really liked it."

The Shield
TV-MA, 2002–2008
Hulu, 7 seasons, 89 episodes
Drama created by Shawn Ryan, with Michael Chiklis, Michael Jace, Jay Karnes, CCH Pounder, Walton Goggins, Benito Martinez, Catherine Dent, Cathy Cahlin Ryan and David Rees Snell.

Groundbreaking series rewrote the rules for cop shows — in part by lionizing police corruption. Brutal, funny, ingenious, with a *Fugitive*-like story arc that spanned its entire 7-season run on FX, *The Shield* set the tone for that network's decade of redefining dramas. While Tony Soprano got there first, Chiklis's Vic Mackey cemented the 2000s as the Age of the Antihero. Ryan's ambitious, character-intensive writing set the standard that all other basic cable dramas would be measured by, and gave memorable roles to Chiklis's castmates Jace, Martinez, Karnes, Goggins and Pounder.

🏆 Emmy for best actor in a drama, a first for basic cable (Chiklis); Peabody Award

Show Me a Hero
TV-MA, 2015
HBO Max, 6 episodes
Limited series (historical drama) created by David Simon, with Oscar Isaac, Winona Ryder, Dominique Fishback, Bob Balaban, Catherine Keener, Alfred Molina, LaTanya Richardson Jackson, Peter Riegert, Carla Quevedo and Ilfenesh Hadera.

The Wire creator David Simon turned the story of a housing desegregation crisis into an enthralling miniseries. Instead of watching *The Wire* again, try this sprawling story of a public housing community in Yonkers, New York, and the grinding attempts by the city's mayor Nick Wasicsko (Isaac) in the 1980s and '90s at integration. With a particular eye on the political machinations that both advanced and stalled the cause, the show feels like a bit of a miracle — a steady slow burn that actually informs viewers about a critical issue without being in the slightest bit tedious. *Show Me a Hero* is one of the decade's most underrated gems.

Shrill
TV-MA, 2019–2021
Hulu original, 3 seasons,
22 episodes (AD)
Comedy-drama with Aidy Bryant, John Cameron Mitchell, Lolly Adefope, Luka Jones, Ian Owens, Julia Sweeney and Daniel Stern.

Aidy Bryant plays a self-proclaimed fat advocate learning to live her life loud and proud — and does it with a light touch. This adaptation of Lindy West's memoir stars the *SNL* mainstay as Annie Easton, a writer for a Portland alt-weekly who's learning to have more fun, more sex and more self-confidence.

🗨 **From our forums:** "Not laugh-out-loud funny but there was a lot of heart and nuance to Aidy's performance. I was glad to have a show where I genuinely liked the main character." " I especially appreciate how well they did the abortion storyline in the first episode. I haven't seen many shows that don't f—- that up."

Shtisel
TV-14, 2013–present
Netflix original, 3 seasons, 33 episodes
Drama with Doval'e Glickman, Michael Aloni, Neta Riskin, Shira Haas and Zohar Strauss.

Blockbuster Israeli series that follows life in an ultra-Orthodox Jewish community in Jerusalem. This show is so packed with detail — in food, in costuming, in furniture, in Yiddish and Hebrew slang — that it might make you feel nostalgic for a place you've never visited or a family you've never had. The stories mix big incidents (a man abandons his family) and small dramas (a teenager sneaks a forbidden novel into the house) and the cumulative impact feels as much like world building as anything seen on a fantasy series. Because so many international viewers eventually devoured the first 2 seasons, a third was made in 2020, after a four-year break.

▸▸ Hebrew and Yiddish spoken, English subtitles available.

Silicon Valley
TV-MA, 2014–2019
HBO Max, 6 seasons, 53 episodes (AD)
Workplace comedy created by Mike Judge, Alec Berg, John Altschuler and Dave Krinsky, with Thomas Middleditch, Martin Starr, Kumail Nanjiani, Amanda Crew, Zach Woods, Josh Brener, Matt Ross, Jimmy O. Yang, Suzanne Cryer and T.J. Miller.

Hilarious sendup of the tech life that felt true to insiders, right down to Thomas Middleditch's lackluster, uncompelling lead character. *Silicon Valley* had great bones: *Office Space* writer/director Mike Judge and Alec Berg (*Curb Your*

Enthusiasm) created Richard Hendricks (Middleditch), a bland nerd cut from the same cloth as Mark Zuckerberg. Big Tech culture offers an almost bottomless trove of things to mock — its self-absorption, its assurances that it will "make a better world," its mindless consumerism and petty demands of its nouveau riche workforce — and *Silicon Valley* mocked with abandon. As Big Tech's reputation has darkened in recent years, the show's later seasons tried to adjust while keeping it funny.

🏆 2 Emmys

The Simpsons

TV-PG, 1989–present
Disney+, 33 seasons, 727 episodes (AD)
Animated comedy created by Matt Groening, with Dan Castellaneta, Nancy Cartwright, Harry Shearer, Julie Kavner, Yeardley Smith, Hank Azaria, Pamela Hayden and Tress MacNeille.

The beauty of streaming is that you don't have to watch all the lame *Simpsons* episodes! Complaining that *The Simpsons* has lost its edge is perhaps the Internet's oldest pastime. But why does it even matter anymore? With on-demand access to every episode on Disney+, why not just get a list of the greatest *Simpsons*, pull up a Duff and a donut and enjoy?

▶▶ It's been said *The Simpsons* declined after Season 9, which if true would still be a remarkable run for any show. Yet there were inarguably standout episodes in each of the first 20 seasons of *The Simpsons*. If you like to needle-drop, here is one from each: "Simpsons Roasting on an Open Fire" (S1E1), the first "Treehouse of Horror" (S2E3), "When Flanders Failed" (S3E3), "Marge versus the Monorail" (S4E12), "Cape Feare" (S5E2), "Who Shot Mr. Burns? Part One" (S6E25), "King Size Homer" (S7E7), "Homer's Enemy" (S8E23), "The City of New York versus Homer Simpson" (S9E1), "Mayored to

the Mob" (S10E9), "Behind the Laughter" (S11E22), "HOMR" (S12E9), "Weekend at Burnsie's" (S13E16), "Moe Baby Blues" (S14E22), "Treehouse of Horror XIV" (S15E1), "Don't Fear the Roofer" (S16E16), "The Seemingly Never-Ending Story" (S17E13), documentary parody "Springfield Up" (S18E13), "Eternal Moonshine of the Simpson Mind" (S19E9) and "Coming to Homerica" (S20E21).

🏆 Peabody Award, 35 Emmys

Sinatra: All Or Nothing at All

TV-14, 2015
Netflix, 4 hrs 4 mins
Movie (documentary) directed by Alex Gibney.

Alex Gibney's film is a candid and highly watchable portrait of Frank Sinatra and his immense impact on music, culture and politics. Built around several songs that Sinatra hand-selected for his "farewell concert" (he would go on to perform for another three decades), this documentary eschews talking heads to make use of its abundant trove of archival footage and keep our ears trained on the sound that defined an era. Though authorized by the Sinatra estate, it doesn't shy away from discussing Frank's infidelity, mob buddies and rage issues. Yet Gibney is also very good at getting at why Sinatra touched millions of his generation so deeply.

The Sinner

TV-MA, 2017–present
Netflix, 3 seasons, 24 episodes (AD)
Anthology series (crime drama) with Bill Pullman, Jessica Biel, Christopher Abbott, Carrie Coon, Matt Bomer, Chris Messina, Jessica Hecht and Tracy Letts.

Intriguing "why-dunnit" stars Bill Pullman as a detective investigating a different case each season to uncover people's hidden motivations and secrets. The series begins with a murder in broad daylight and a clear suspect: a troubled

For shows sorted by streaming platform, see page 381. **269**

woman played by Jessica Biel. The job of Harry Ambrose (Pullman), in this and each subsequent season of *The Sinner,* is to probe behind a bizarre crime with more questions than answers. Far from a dry, intellectual pursuit, though, Harry's investigations pull him into the lives of the suspects, often taking enormous personal risks en route to each season's emotionally wrenching finale.

🗨 **From our forums:** "What is it with this new trend of loose-ends ambiguous endings? We have to make up our own because the writers can't seem to get there?" "I really liked the show. I don't need everything wrapped up in a nice red bow."

The Sit-In: Harry Belafonte Hosts the Tonight Show
TV-14, 2020
Peacock original, 1 hr 15 mins (AD)
Movie (documentary) with Harry Belafonte.

Harry Belafonte guest hosted Johnny Carson's show for one remarkable week in 1968, just before all hell broke loose. Succinct and thought provoking, this documentary succeeds even though most of the footage from Belafonte's hosting stint has been lost. Present-day interviews with Belafonte and some of the many artists he inspired help draw intriguing parallels between the 60s and today.

Six Feet Under
TV-MA, 2001–2005
HBO Max, 5 seasons, 63 episodes
Comedy-drama with Peter Krause, Michael C. Hall, Frances Conroy, Lauren Ambrose, Freddy Rodriguez, Mathew St. Patrick, Rachel Griffiths, Justina Machado and Jeremy Sisto.

Is it now more beloved than *The Sopranos*? Time has been kind to the Fishers and their dramatic lives that center on the family funeral home.

Overshadowed for most of its run on HBO, *Six Feet Under* seems to be having the last laugh. Its finale is now considered one of the most satisfying in television history (*The Sopranos*'s finale is regarded as one of the most baffling). Though the storylines aren't especially memorable, the show's leitmotif about life and death in a mortuary remains uniquely funny, surprising and even heartbreaking.

▶▶ Creator Alan Ball knew how to begin and end strong: Seasons 1 and 5 are the best.

🏆 Peabody Award; 9 Emmys; SAG Award for best TV drama

Skin Wars
TV-14, 2014–2016
PlutoTV, Hulu, 3 seasons, 29 episodes
Reality competition with Rebecca Romijn (host), RuPaul, Craig Tracy and Robin Slonina.

Over-the-top, campy body-painting contest defies you to dislike it. The ridiculousness level on *Skin Wars* is high, but painting naked bodies is a niche-bordering-on-novelty craft, and let's face it, painting a midget wrestler makes for way more entertaining TV than painting a normal body. The producers' relentless amping-up of drama wouldn't work on *The Great Pottery Throwdown*, but *Skin Wars* contestants seem happy to roll with it. Even the show's goodbye phrase, "Please wash off your canvas," is perfect precisely because the loser *doesn't* wash up. RuPaul, as usual, gets to play the grownup on the judging panel.

Slings and Arrows
TV-MA, 2003–2006
AMC+, Acorn TV, 3 seasons, 18 episodes
Comedy-drama with Paul Gross, Martha Burns, Stephen Ouimette, Susan Coyne, Don McKellar and Mark McKinney.

Ten years before *Schitt's Creek*, Canada graced us with another comedy classic,

this one set in a small theater company that performs a Shakespeare play each year. Rarely has television woven high culture, gut-busting gags, nimble dialogue and grown-up situations together so successfully as in the three seasons of *Slings and Arrows*. After the artistic director of the New Burbage theater company suddenly dies, Geoffrey Tennant (Gross) is called in — even though this is the place, and the play, where he suffered a breakdown 7 years prior. He survives the backstage drama and puts on the play, returning in Season 2 to do *Macbeth* and then in Season 3, *King Lear*. The show is witty and farcical enough to enjoy without catching all of the Shakespeare references.

▶▶ Pairs well with *Mozart in the Jungle*

Small Axe
TV-MA, 2020
Apple TV+ original, 5 episodes (AD)
Limited series (historical drama) created by Steve McQueen, with John Boyega, Letitia Wright, Antonia Thomas, Kedar Williams-Stirling, Jack Lowden, Naomi Ackie and Malachi Kirby.

British Black history in 5 movements, ambitiously told by the Oscar-winning director of *12 Years a Slave*. McQueen, raised in London by West Indian parents, has already won cinema's biggest prize for his story about American slavery, but he's not letting up just because the stories of his people seem minor by comparison. These 5 film-length stories, four of them based on real events, do more than provide representation to British-Caribbeans. Stylistically diverse and assuredly told, they offer dynamic proof that structural racism is a thing, that it is global and that, with imagination and heart, it can be overcome.

🏆 Critics Choice Award for best actor in a limited series (Boyega)

Small Fortune
TV-PG, 2021–present
Peacock, 5 episodes
Reality competition with Lil Rel Howery (host).

Don't let the micro-sized game boards and silly tone fool you — this is a legitimately challenging competition. A game that takes place on a moon set and asks a blindfolded contestant to plant a tiny American flag in a small circle is called "One Small Step," and is introduced thusly: "Buzz Smalldrin and Neil Fingerstrong just landed on this miniature moon…" But the nonsense is confined to the writing. This American take on the UK reality hit pays considerable attention to detail, resulting in some awfully difficult games that involve manipulating tiny objects with speed or precision and even some actual strategy. Lil Rel asks good questions, keeping the players focused and the game moving.

▶▶ Pairs well with *Holey Moley*

Small Town News: KPVM Pahrump
TV-14, 2021
HBO Max, 6 episodes (AD)
Docuseries.

Delightful fly-on-the-wall look at one of America's tiniest TV stations honors the people who keep it on the air. KPVM, created in 1997 by Vern Van Winkle in Pahrump, Nevada, just west of Las Vegas, is run by a handful of people who are kind and just naturally have fun with each other. They are absolutely committed to their work, wearing multiple hats while broadcasting the kind of content that is often mocked by Hollywood and late-night TV hosts. Some may watch *Small Town News* with derision, but more generous-minded viewers will see the station's role in connecting members of the community with each other, an act becoming increasingly rare as local news operations have been decimated.

▶▶ Pairs well with *Sunderland 'Til I Die*

SMILF
TV-MA, 2017–2019
Showtime original, 2 seasons,
18 episodes
Comedy created by Frankie Shaw, with
Frankie Shaw, Rosie O'Donnell, Miguel
Gomez, Samara Weaving, Connie Britton
and Sherie Renee Scott.

**Frankie Shaw wrote, directed and
starred in this appealing comedy about
a single mom in South Boston with a lot
of stuff and issues and oh yeah, a toddler
she's trying to raise herself.** Shaw also
made a film that made it to Sundance,
a fact that's helpful when approaching
SMILF. Like many indie films, it takes a
couple of episodes to warm to our heroine,
who's a bit unhinged and has so many
issues you're not sure whether to embrace
her or run away. But with support from
O'Donnell as her tough-love mom, the
show is able to take on topics like mental
illness, eating disorders and terrible first
dates in an authentic way.

▶▶ It might be interesting to watch
SMILF and compare Shaw to her semi-
autobiographical character, knowing
that she was fired and the show abruptly
canceled after complaints of improper
sexual conduct by her on the set.

Sneaky Pete
TV-MA, 2015–2019
Prime Video original, 3 seasons,
30 episodes (AD)
Crime drama created by Bryan Cranston
and David Shore, with Giovanni Ribisi,
Marin Ireland, Margo Martindale,
Peter Gerety, Shane McRae, Libe Barer,
Alison Wright, Ethan Embry and Bryan
Cranston.

**After assuming the identity of his
former cellmate, a con man convinces
the dead man's clan that he's their
long-lost relative.** *Breaking Bad* star
Cranston obviously picked up a few
ideas about building a show around an
antihero. Marius (Ribisi) has more than
met his match in the Murphys, who have
shady secrets of their own and are led by
the redoubtable Martindale, once again
effortlessly inhabiting the role of the
intimidating matriarch.

🗨 **From our forums:** "A wild ride. There
were points I was confused about, but
I'll forgive them because the acting was
spectacular." "I found the third season
easier to follow than the second, and
overall I liked it better, but it wasn't
without its issues."

Snowfall
TV-MA, 2017–present
Hulu, 4 seasons, 41 episodes (AD)
Crime drama created by John Singleton,
Eric Amadio and Dave Andron, with
Damson Idris, Carter Hudson, Isaiah
John, Sergio Peris-Mencheta, Amin
Joseph, Angela Lewis, Michael Hyatt and
Kevin Carroll.

**A sprawling Los Angeles drama
imagines how the crack epidemic
took off in the early '80s.** There's scant
evidence to the belief that the CIA was
responsible for getting crack cocaine
into America's inner cities, any more
than the idea that Russians posing as
D.C. suburbanites somehow infiltrated
the government. But we watch *The
Americans*, don't we? *Snowfall* isn't high
drama or good history like *Narcos* is,
but it developed a loyal following for its
assemblage of fascinating characters and
intertwined storylines. It offers a distinct
if controversial take on the Reagan years,
when it seemed like the feds would
go to almost any lengths to beat the
Communists in Central America.

🗨 **From our forums:** "This show never
lived up to its massive premise, imo, but
it did create a compelling world and a few
excellent characters."

The Social Dilemma
PG-13, 2020
Netflix original, 1 hr 34 mins (AD)
Movie (documentary) directed by Jeff Orlowski, with Tristan Harris, Jeff Seibert, Tim Kendall, Skyler Gisondo, Kara Hayward, Sophia Hammons and Vincent Kartheiser.

The people who helped create today's online universe go on camera to warn that social media is causing far more harm than good. What could be more innocuous than the Facebook "Like" button? And yet, the co-creator of that symbol of social connectedness says in *The Social Dilemma* that "likes" are being used to push polarization and hate, all in the name of corporate profits. You've heard these charges leveled elsewhere, but there's nothing like a Netflix documentary to serve up some steak with lots of sizzle, courtesy of director Orlowski (*Chasing Coral*), who gets great quotage from the former president of Pinterest (who was once the "director of monetization" for Facebook) and Harris of the Center for Humane Technology.

🏆 2 Emmys for nonfiction writing and editing

The Society
TV-MA, 2019
Netflix original, 10 episodes (AD)
Teen drama with Kathryn Newton, Gideon Adlon, Sean Berdy, Natasha Liu Bordizzo, Jacques Colimon, Olivia DeJonge, Alex Fitzalan, Kristine Froseth, José Julián and Salena Qureshi.

After everyone in their town disappears, a group of teenagers is forced to create a new society. Sounds like another take on Netflix's post-apocalyptic YA series *Between* — but that would be selling short this thoughtful and entertaining series from *Party of Five* co-creator Christopher Keyser. *The Society* explores what it would mean to recreate a world without adult guidance (besides lots of partying and uninhibited sex). It's an intriguing blend of teen entertainment and social analysis.

🐾 **From our forums:** "These types of shows typically turn into war and the strong hoarding of everything pretty fast. This seems more realistic."

▶▶ *The Society* was initially renewed for a second season, but Netflix later canceled the show, citing the pandemic.

Solar Opposites
TV-MA, 2020–present
Hulu original, 2 seasons, 16 episodes (AD)
Animated comedy created by Justin Roiland and Mike McMahan, with Justin Roiland, Thomas Middleditch, Sean Giambrone and Mary Mack.

From the creators of *Rick and Morty*, a sendup of sitcoms involving a group of aliens who hide out in middle America after their home planet is destroyed. A fresh take on sitcom tropes, *Solar Opposites* is every bit as bizarre and joke-packed as *Rick and Morty*, but fans of that show will be surprised at the fond regard that members of the alien family have for each other. It's still weird: An ongoing Season 1 storyline involves a wall that one of the aliens builds out of humans who make him angry — he shrinks them to the size of bricks.

🐾 **From our forums:** "I think I would find a spinoff about the wall more interesting than this show. I like the show overall, but the wall is where it's at."

Somebody Somewhere
TV-MA, 2022–present
HBO Max, 7 episodes
Comedy created by Hannah Bos and Paul Thureen, with Bridget Everett, Jeff Hiller, Jane Brody, Jon Hudson Odom, Danny McCarthy and Murray Hill.

Bridget Everett is a revelation as a lonely 40-something woman who returns to

For shows sorted by streaming platform, see page 381.

her Kansas hometown and finds new purpose in life belting out songs to her fellow misfits. The title is a rebuttal: When we first meet Sam (Everett), she feels like a nobody living in the middle of nowhere, even though Manhattan, Kansas, is her home and her family still lives there. But thanks to a goofy coworker named Joel (Hiller), Sam is introduced to "choir practice," a kind of alt-church where nonconformist types can sing, drink and let go. Besides the show's loose, improvisatory energy and big-hearted writing, *Somebody Somewhere* offers an authentic, warts-and-all celebration of flyover America. The unusual people here aren't trying to escape small-town life, they're figuring out how to thrive in it. For anyone who only knows Everett from her bawdy cameos on *Inside Amy Schumer*, her gentle performance in this series — loosely based on her own Kansas upbringing — will be an impressive surprise.

Song Exploder
TV-MA, 2020–present
Netflix original, 2 seasons,
8 episodes (AD)
Docuseries with Hrishikesh Hirway.

You'll never hear your favorite song the same way after it gets the *Song Exploder* deep dive. Hrishikesh Hirway interviews artists in-depth about the creation of a single song in this adaptation of his popular podcast. *Song Exploder* reveals dimensions of pop hits that will appeal to casual listeners and music geeks alike. Hirway knows his material, yet he still has questions, lots of questions. The result is a series that's all hits and no misses.

Sons of Anarchy
TV-MA, 2008–2014
Hulu, 7 seasons, 92 episodes
Drama created by Kurt Sutter, with Charlie Hunnam, Katey Sagal, Mark

Boone Junior, Kim Coates, Tommy Flanagan, Theo Rossi, Dayton Callie, Maggie Siff and Ron Perlman.

At its peak, the high drama of the Sons of Anarchy Motorcycle Club (Redwood Original) made for incredibly addictive television. Churning out more than the usual amount of basic-cable TV mayhem, this Hamlet-in-a-biker-gang drama was set in a quiet Northern California town that SAMCRO had treated as its small-town fiefdom for decades. Kurt Sutter's burly, violent ode to brotherhood became more oriented around its "old ladies" over time — especially Sagal's complex Lady Macbeth character, Gemma.

▶▶ Needle-drop at Season 2, when a mall developer (played by smooth-talking Alan Arkin) figures out how to drive a wedge between SAMCRO leaders Clay (Perlman) and Jax (Hunnam).

The Sons of Sam: A Descent into Darkness
TV-MA, 2021
Netflix original, 4 episodes (AD)
Limited series (true crime) directed by Joshua Zeman, with Paul Giamatti.

Terrific meta-series about David Berkowitz, crackpot theories and how true-crime stories become obsessions. Veteran genre director Zeman revisits the 1977 summer spree by the self-proclaimed Son of Sam and the subsequent attempts by journalist Maury Terry to tie Berkowitz into a globe-spanning web of satanic cults and snuff films. Zeman has access to case figures, to footage and pics we haven't already seen a thousand times, and particularly to Terry's notes and files, read for you by Giamatti, who brings just the right obsessive tone to the proceedings without going totally over the top.

Sophie: A Murder in West Cork
TV-14, 2021
Netflix original, 3 episodes (AD)

Limited series (true crime) directed by John Dower.

Sophie Toscan du Plantier, a French television producer, was killed outside her vacation house in Ireland in 1996. This series untangles the bizarre and heartbreaking truth of what happened. One of the benefits of a longer true-crime docuseries is that it gives the director time to humanize the person whose story, and death, is at the heart of the program. This is beautifully accomplished in *Sophie*, which was made with the cooperation of Toscan du Plantier's family.

The Sopranos
TV-MA, 1999–2007
HBO Max, 6 seasons, 86 episodes (AD)
Drama created by David Chase, with James Gandolfini, Edie Falco, Michael Imperioli, Steven Van Zandt, Robert Iler, Tony Sirico, Jamie-Lynn Sigler, Lorraine Bracco, Dominic Chianese and Steve Schirripa.

This remains one of HBO's most popular series, and it's not hard to see why. Besides inventing the modern TV antihero, *The Sopranos* remains a hoot 20 years on. David Chase's idea about "a mobster with mother issues" started out as a movie pitch. But Chase, a veteran of the TV business, wound up doing it for HBO — and changed the medium forever. Gandolfini made Tony Soprano one of the most memorable characters ever on TV, but lots of characters on *The Sopranos* got ample screen time to develop and even turn over new leaves (though these *are* mobsters and their enablers we're talking about).

▶▶ Prequel movie *The Many Saints of Newark* (2021) stars James Gandolfini's son Michael Gandolfini as a young Tony Soprano.

▶▶ Seasons 1–2, both Peabody Award winners, showed *The Sopranos* at its crackling best, with Tony's mother Livia (Nancy Marchand) trying to reverse-Oedipus her son out of the syndicate and replace him with her brother-in-law, the unforgettable Uncle Junior (Chianese), whom Livia played like a Stradivarius. Unfortunately, Marchand's death in 2000 put an all-too-premature end to this storyline.

🏆 2 Peabody Awards; 21 Emmys including outstanding drama series (2 wins)

Sorry for Your Loss
TV-14, 2018–2019
Facebook Watch original, 2 seasons, 20 episodes
Drama with Elizabeth Olsen, Kelly Marie Tran, Jovan Adepo, Mamoudou Athie and Janet McTeer.

A woman tries to move on after the death of her husband. Hailed by critics, *Sorry for Your Loss* flew under most viewers' radar even though it's on the most widely distributed streaming channel on the planet — Facebook. Yes, the social network has produced a handful of scripted TV shows, and this one's the best of the bunch. Elizabeth Olsen, best known as the Scarlet Witch in Marvel's Avengers films, plays Leigh, a young woman who moves back home three months after the death of her husband. She takes a job and tries to work through her grief and family issues. Backed by strong performances from McTeer as Leigh's mother, Tran as her sister Jules and Athie as her late husband Matt, *Sorry for Your Loss* is a meditation on loss and a beautiful love story, albeit one told in reverse.

Soul
PG, 2020
Disney+ original, 1 hr 41 mins (AD)
Movie (animated comedy) directed by Kemp Powers and Pete Docter, with Jamie Foxx, Tina Fey, Phylicia Rashād, Graham Norton, Rachel House, Ahmir-

Khalib Thompson, Alice Braga and Richard Ayoade.

The Oscar winner for best animated film of 2020 is an absolute delight and one of very few things we'll remember warmly about being stuck at home during the pandemic. As with *Hamilton*, this big-budget theatrical release from Pixar got rerouted to Disney+ when COVID-19 emptied out the cineplexes. It's a masterwork of jazz fusion, combining an imaginative take on the afterlife with a relatable story about finding meaning in our everyday lives. Enveloped by Jon Batiste's syncopated score, dazzled by the wondrous animation of Pixar and tickled by the partnership of frustrated musician Joe (Foxx) and his soulmate in the great beyond, 22 (Fey), you'll be enthralled by this surprisingly deep yet sufficiently silly and uplifting family feature.

Sound of Metal

R, 2020
Prime Video original, 2 hrs 1 mins
Movie (drama) directed by Darius Marder, with Riz Ahmed, Olivia Cooke, Paul Raci and Lauren Ridloff.

Riz Ahmed plays a heavy metal drummer who experiences sudden but permanent hearing loss and struggles to accept his new condition. This sensitive film is carried by the powerhouse performance of Ahmed and by Raci, who plays the head of a Deaf community that takes Ahmed's character in.

🏆 2 Oscars for best sound and best film editing

South Park

TV-MA, 1997–present
HBO Max, 25 seasons, 311 episodes
Animated comedy created by Trey Parker and Matt Stone, with Trey Parker, Matt Stone, Mona Marshall, April Stewart and Isaac Hayes.

From the poop emoji to its pandemic special, *South Park* has been spoofing popular culture while also contributing to it for a quarter century. Tom Cruise. Anti-vaxxers. Pokémon. Catholic Church sex abuse. School shootings. China. Canada. UFO and 9/11 truthers. *South Park* has vented its sardonic spleen at these targets and many, many others over the years. As critics have pointed out, the outrageous behavior that *South Park* lampoons these days is not very different from the obnoxiousness that got *South Park* noticed back in the pre-Internet era, when fans passed around the VHS tape of the "Spirit of Christmas" pilot. And it's true, the show has been around long enough to change its tune on climate change (though not yet on transgender people). But criticizing hot takes from old *South Park* episodes is like mocking old Rolling Stones lyrics now that Mick is 80. *South Park* remains one of Streaming TV's most watched shows because for the most part, it's aged well. Cartman, Stan, Wendy, Chef, Kenny, Randy, Butters and the rest of the gang are timeless idiots we want to keep laughing at.

▶▶ The show is renewed through Season 30 in 2026.

🏆 Peabody Award, Emmy for best animated program (5 wins from 2005 to 2013)

Southern Comfort

TV-MA, 2001
Tubi, 1 hr 30 mins
Movie (documentary) directed by Kate Davis, with Robert Eads and Lola Cola.

Director Kate Davis followed Robert Eads as he desperately sought a doctor who would treat his ovarian cancer in this classic transgender film. Eads mothered two children before becoming a man and settling down in a rural community in Georgia where, one might suspect, transgender people weren't that welcome. There's no artificial drama or pumped-up conflict in this HBO documentary, which humanely shows Eads struggling to overcome cultural barriers to the medical care that is his right.

🏆 Sundance Film Festival's Grand Jury Prize

Space Force

TV-MA, 2020–present
Netflix original, 2 seasons,
17 episodes (AD)

Workplace comedy created by Steve Carell and Greg Daniels, with Steve Carell, John Malkovich, Ben Schwartz, Diana Silvers, Tawny Newsome, Jimmy O. Yang, Dan Bakkedahl, Lisa Kudrow, Noah Emmerich and Fred Willard.

Imagine *The Office* set in a military compound in the middle of nowhere, and Steve Carell's job is to get an army into space. Don't be fooled by the general's uniform Carell wears, or the title of the show which echoes the newly created sixth branch of the military. This is a workplace comedy from the creators of *The Office*, who have cast John Malkovich as a zany scientist and Lisa Kudrow as Carell's wife. The first episode is a hoot; after that you'll have to decide if the show's uneven tone and hit-or-miss story ideas are worth sitting through.

📣 **From our forums:** "The second half of Season 1 was better. I actually got a few laughs from some of the episodes."

The Spoils of Babylon

TV-14, 2014
AMC+, 6 episodes

Satirical comedy with Kristen Wiig, Tobey Maguire, Will Ferrell, Cal Bartlett, Tim Robbins, Jessica Alba, Haley Joel Osment and Val Kilmer.

Kristen Wiig, Tobey Maguire and Will Ferrell deliver marvelously on the premise of spoofing the epic miniseries that were such a big deal in the 1980s.

Wiig and Maguire play adopted siblings who leave their humble Texas roots behind to set out on a quest for power and influence — not to mention a forbidden romance with one another. In a meta-twist, Ferrell plays Eric Jonrosh, the creator of this fictional show, who is being interviewed about how it was made. Nobody will confuse this goofy lark with high art, but it may lead viewers of a certain age to question the viewing choices they made in the '80s.

The SpongeBob Movie: Sponge on the Run

PG, 2020
Paramount+, 1 hr 31 mins (AD)

Movie (family comedy) with Clancy Brown, Bill Fagerbakke, Rodger Bumpass, Mr. Lawrence, Carolyn Lawrence, Tom Kenny, Awkwafina and Keanu Reeves.

After his pet snail goes missing, SpongeBob embarks on a harrowing adventure to bring him home. Clever deployment of guest stars like Reeves — and a general sense of good-natured mayhem — make this a solid, streaming-only addition to the franchise.

Spy City

TV-MA, 2020
AMC+, 6 episodes

Limited series (thriller) created by William Boyd, with Dominic Cooper, Leonie Benesch, Romane Portail, Tonio Arango, Johanna Wokalek, Ben Münchow and Seumas F. Sargent.

Cold War–era Berlin is the setting for this stylish paranoid thriller about a British agent who tries to root out a mole and winds up stepping on a hornet's nest of spies. Set in 1961, just before the wall went up, the German metropolis is crawling with spooks from the four countries in charge of Berlin. It's the perfect setup for layers of intrigue that can unfold with head-spinning rapidity,

For shows sorted by streaming platform, see page 381.

or slow down to the pace of a meticulous investigation. Cooper is superb as the bewildered spy trying to figure it all out.

The Spy

TV-MA, 2019
Netflix original, 6 episodes (AD)
Limited series (historical drama) with Sacha Baron Cohen, Hadar Ratzon Rotem, Yael Eitan, Noah Emmerich, Nassim Lyes, Moni Moshonov, Alona Tal and Mourad Zaoui.

Sacha Baron Cohen brings intensity to this role as Eli Cohen, a real-life Mossad agent who infiltrated Israel's enemies in the 1960s. When we first meet Eli, an emigrant from Egypt, he is toiling in a department store back office — an unlikely place to find a spook. But his Arab features and burning ambition to serve his adopted land make him the perfect spy. His devoted wife Nadia (Rotem) and caring handler Dan (Emmerich, who had a similar role on *The Americans*) add emotional hues to this miniseries. A tense, fact-based drama about an epic yet little-known intelligence caper.

Squid Game

TV-MA, 2021–present
Netflix original, 9 episodes, dubbed (AD)
Dystopian drama created by Hwang Dong-hyuk, with Lee Jung-jae, Park Hae-soo, Jung Ho-yeon, Wi Ha-jun, Oh Yeong-su, Heo Sung-tae, Kim Joo-ryoung, Anupam Tripathi and Lee You-mi.

Whatever its other merits (or demerits), no movie or TV show captured the bleakness and depravity of its time like this global megahit out of Korea. Netflix's most-watched show of all time is a brilliant update of Stephen King's 1982 novel-turned-film *The Running Man*, with colorful uniforms, heartbreaking twists, senseless violence, stunning cinematography and English dubbing that isn't distracting (though people on the Internet will quarrel over that). But would *Squid Game* have mattered as much to a world not trapped in their homes by a mutant virus, with nothing better to do than binge Netflix?

🗨 **From our forums:** "The situation was kind of ridiculous and surreal, but it was filmed and acted in such a way that you had to take it seriously. I felt like I was right there with them in all of their horrible challenges, staring across the field at people who were going to die. I thought the social commentary was also really sharp."

▶▶ For suggestions of related shows, see "If You Liked *Squid Game*," page 376.

Staged

TV-14, 2020–present
Hulu, 2 seasons, 14 episodes
Comedy-drama with Michael Sheen, David Tennant, Georgia Tennant, Anna Lundberg and Lucy Eaton.

One of the keepers from a year of pandemic-related TV is this self-parody from David Tennant and Michael Sheen, playing insufferable actors trying to rehearse a play via Zoom. This silly, quick binge features two well-known British comic actors in what was clearly meant as a breezy escape from the slog of lockdown. Fans loved it so much that BBC One ordered a second series.

🗨 **From our forums:** "IMO you should have an affinity for both Tennant and Sheen and know a bit about their friendship to truly get the show. But I honestly can't remember a comedy that was so funny all the way through. My jaws hurt!"

▶▶ Season 2 follows the successful aftermath of Season 1, including attempts to make an American version of the show.

The Staircase
TV-MA, 2004–2018
Netflix original, 13 episodes (AD)
Limited series (true crime) directed by
Jean-Xavier de Lestrade.

The first great true-crime docuseries followed American novelist Michael Peterson, who was accused of killing his wife in 2001 and making it look like an accident. Viewing the case through the eyes of the defense, French filmmakers Jean-Xavier de Lestrade and Denis Poncet show a morally upright legal team undercutting the prosecution's case at every turn, exposing its flimsy construction and, thus, calling into question the motives of the DA's office. At the same time, *The Staircase*'s unblinking eye shows the defense's case slowly coming apart. Peterson is revealed as an unsavory fellow with dark secrets in his past, each revelation more damning than the one before. By refusing to take sides, *The Staircase* produces a relentless tug of war that engages viewers from start to end, leaving many of us unsure if the jury has reached the right verdict. When Netflix picked up *The Staircase* in 2018, three new episodes were added, updating viewers of the Peterson saga.

🏆 Peabody Award

Star Trek: Discovery
TV-14, 2017–present
Paramount+ original, 4 seasons,
55 episodes (AD)
Sci-fi drama with Sonequa Martin-Green, Doug Jones, Anthony Rapp, Mary Wiseman, Emily Coutts, Oyin Oladejo, Patrick Kwok-Choon, Wilson Cruz, Michelle Yeoh and Jason Isaacs.

The first new *Trek* franchise in over a decade is a complex saga that begins 10 years before the events of the original series. This show has brought many welcome additions to the *Star Trek* universe, especially Martin-Green as the controversial Captain Burnham. Her maverick ways get her initially demoted to ensign, but her intelligence, grit and rogue spirit eventually make her indispensable as the *Discovery* lurches from one perilous adventure to the next — and eventually, 10 centuries forward in time. Other crew members are solid additions to the Trekverse, including chief engineer Stamets (Rapp) and medical officer Culber (Cruz), *Star Trek*'s first openly gay couple; Lorca (Isaacs) as the fill-in captain, who's got some dark secrets; and Yeoh as the Chinese-born captain of another ship (who will be heading to yet another *Trek* spinoff soon).

🎙 **From our forums:** "This show is simultaneously boring on a plot level and watchable on a character level."

Star Trek: Lower Decks
TV-MA, 2020–present
Paramount+ original, 2 seasons,
20 episodes (AD)
Animated sci-fi created by Mike McMahan, with Tawny Newsome, Jack Quaid, Noël Wells, Eugene Cordero, Dawnn Lewis, Jerry O'Connell, Gillian Vigman and Paul Scheer.

***Star Trek*'s branded adult animated comedy has found a distinct and beloved niche in the Trekverse.** Unlike other *Star Trek* offshoots that try to elevate Gene Roddenberry's idea to prestige drama, *Star Trek: Lower Decks* boldly goes for broad comedy, and is more like *Futurama* than *Discovery*. Set on board a battered warhorse called the USS *Cerritos* in the year 2380, the show (as the title suggests) is focused on the least important crew members of one of Starfleet's least important ships. At first *Lower Decks* is a copious name-dropper, referencing other ships, characters and storylines from the Trekverse. By Season 2, however, it establishes its own identity with relatable characters and a galaxy of interesting subplots.

🔊 **From our forums:** "This show evolved from something that I found amusing to something that I truly loved."

Star Trek: Picard
TV-MA, 2020–present
Paramount+ original, 10 episodes (AD)
Sci-fi drama with Patrick Stewart, Alison Pill, Isa Briones, Michelle Hurd, Santiago Cabrera and Harry Treadaway.

Two decades after he last appeared in the role, Patrick Stewart's character boldly goes where no *Star Trek* **character has gone before.** We won't spoil the intriguing transformation that allowed Picard to return to series TV without seeming like a 20th-century retread. That said, Sir Patrick's gravitas and avuncular wit does make him a great ambassador for the *Trek* values we could use more of these days.

Star Wars: The Clone Wars
TV-PG, 2008–2020
Disney+, 7 seasons, 133 episodes (AD)
Animated drama created by George Lucas, with Tom Kane, Dee Bradley Baker, Matt Lanter, James Arnold Taylor, Ashley Eckstein, Matthew Wood and Corey Burton.

Prior *Star Wars* **fandom isn't required to enjoy this on-brand Disney+ animated series with your kids or grandkids.** The idea here is that Obi-Wan Kenobi and Luke Skywalker's dad (the future Darth Vader) were buddies before they were mortal enemies, co-combatants in the massive intergalactic barfight known as the Clone Wars. The show benefits from tight, well-executed stories and a manageable set of characters who don't banter like your usual cartoon figures.
▶▶ The original version, called *Star Wars: Clone Wars* without the "the," was created for Cartoon Network in 2003 by the legendary animator Genndy Tartakovsky (reportedly it took him about two weeks).

George Lucas is said to have hated it, but that did lead to this more successful version.

Stargirl
PG, 2020
Disney+ original, 1 hr 47 mins (AD)
Movie (family comedy) with Grace VanderWaal, Graham Verchere and Giancarlo Esposito.

In this sweet-natured romance, a shy boy finds himself falling for a quirky girl who pushes him out of his comfort zone. Teenage singer-songwriter VanderWaal (who won Season 11 of *America's Got Talent*) charms in this Disney+ original. The movie gets an extra kick — and bonus points with older viewers who might be watching — by organically weaving in performances of classic songs like "We Got the Beat" and "Just What I Needed."
▶▶ Not to be confused with the CW series *DC's Stargirl*.

Starstruck
TV-MA, 2021–present
HBO Max original, 6 episodes (AD)
British romcom created by Rose Matafeo, with Rose Matafeo, Nikesh Patel and Emma Sidi.

Notes of *Notting Hill* **flavor this easygoing binge about a woman whose one-night stand takes an unexpected turn when she realizes her partner is a movie star.** This female-centric romcom has great banter and a story that is guaranteed to keep fans of the genre flying through the episodes.

🔊 **From our forums:** "Absolutely bloody delightful. The kind of scenario I hate in chick-lit books, but Rose Matafeo makes it work in this series. It's the best romcom type piece of art I've seen in years." "The contrivances to keep them apart is exhausting, but I will keep watching because the leads have fantastic chemistry."

StartupU

TV-14, 2015
Apple TV+, 10 episodes
Reality show.

Draper University of Heroes, a sort of Hogwarts for would-be tech entrepreneurs is the subject of this entertaining docuseries. Yes, that is its real name and yes, it does seem like it was made for reality television. But the school, founded by eccentric billionaire Tim Draper, has existed since 2013. As we learn in this mashup of *The Real World* and *Shark Tank*, the students are in competition for millions of dollars in investment for their companies. With cameras present to watch them learn to develop their ideas into winning pitches, *StartupU* does have more of the air of a reality show than a docuseries, but whatever you call it, it's high-stakes competition and it's compelling.

Stateless

TV-MA, 2020
Netflix original, 6 episodes (AD)
Limited series (drama) created by Cate Blanchett, Tony Ayres and Elise McCredie, with Yvonne Strahovski, Jai Courtney, Asher Keddie, Fayssal Bazzi, Dominic West, Marta Dusseldorp and Cate Blanchett.

Cate Blanchett produced and has a small role in this fact-based psychological drama about a refugee internment camp where everyone slowly loses their mind. Set in the early 2000s, when Australia was warehousing asylum seekers in remote compounds, *Stateless* does a slow build toward a confrontation between the guards and the internees. One subplot involves Sofie (Strahovski), an Australian whose mental illness accidentally lands her in the camp, where she has a front-row seat to the chaos that breaks out.

🎙 **From our forums:** "While I don't think Sofie's story overshadowed the others, Strahovski's performance was head and shoulders above her cast mates. *Stateless* is something everyone should see. That said, I don't think I have the mental or emotional fortitude to watch this again in the near future."

Station Eleven

TV-MA, 2021–present
HBO Max original, 10 episodes (AD)
Limited series (dystopian drama) with Mackenzie Davis, Joe Pingue, Danielle Deadwyler, Himesh Patel, Nabhaan Rizwan, Dylan Taylor, David Wilmot, Matilda Lawler, Caitlin FitzGerald and Gael García Bernal.

Twenty years after a pandemic decimates civilization, a group of performers travels the country, trying to survive. The show nails the humanist hopefulness in Emily St. John Mandel's original novel, and it does so with flourishes that are designed for the specific possibilities of the screen. From depicting an apparently mystical creature who observes the characters to making everyday objects seem startlingly beautiful, it imagines the apocalypse as an opportunity to rediscover the mystery of being alive.

Stay Here

TV-PG, 2018
Netflix original, 8 episodes (AD)
Reality show with Genevieve Gorder and Peter Lorimer.

In this appealing makeover show, designer Genevieve Gorder and real estate expert Peter Lorimer help homeowners turn their short-term rentals into spectacular stays. Though it covers similar ground as *Instant Hotel*, the tone of *Stay Here* is very different. No one yells at anyone; no one is suddenly turned into a villain; last-minute problems don't arise just to add drama. Everyone is good-natured, and even when property owners are skeptical about Gen's proposed changes to their rentals, they roll with it — and are usually overjoyed at the results. Prospective rental operators will learn a few things from this show.

Steven Universe
TV-PG, 2013–2020
HBO Max, Hulu, 6 seasons, 175 episodes
Animated comedy with Zach Callison, Deedee Magno, Michaela Dietz, Estelle and Tom Scharpling.

Loving, beautiful, poignant cartoon about a young boy who lives with extraterrestrials, *Steven Universe* busts every stereotype you had about cartoons. Steven's friends, a nuanced and lively community of aliens called the Crystal Gems, protect humanity from a variety of monsters. In terms that are accessible to children but emotionally resonant for adults, this show explores everything from body dysmorphia to gender identity to racism, and it does so without resorting to the snark one might expect from an adult-friendly cartoon.

🏆 Peabody Award, Emmy for outstanding achievement in animation

Stop Making Sense
G, 1984
Prime Video, Tubi, PlutoTV, 1 hr 28 mins
Movie (musical) directed by Jonathan Demme, with David Byrne, Jerry Harrison, Tina Weymouth and Chris Frantz.

This stylish snapshot of the pop darlings at their 1980s peak is arguably the greatest concert film made. Director Demme visually rearranged the landscape of your typical stadium concert, turning David Byrne, Weymouth and the other musicians into opera stars, creating a cinematic feast for both the eyes and ears.

▶▶ Pairs well with *David Byrne's American Utopia*

Stranger Things
TV-14, 2016–present
Netflix original, 3 seasons, 25 episodes (AD)
Sci-fi drama with Winona Ryder, David Harbour, Finn Wolfhard, Millie Bobby Brown, Gaten Matarazzo, Caleb McLaughlin, Natalia Dyer, Charlie Heaton, Joe Keery and Noah Schnapp.

It's not hard to see why this became one of Netflix's biggest hits and possibly its first "classic" show. Streaming TV's superpower is its ability to fuse unlikely genres into new hybrids that don't require a large viewership to justify their existence. But *Stranger Things* wound up attracting a huge audience, thanks to its enchanting combination of creepy sci-fi, teenage mystery and (for the grownups) an endless parade of 1980s cultural references.

💬 **From our forums:** "As someone who graduated from high school in the late 1980s, I really enjoyed the '80s feel to everything. Even though I complained about plot holes and some pretty cheesy situations, overall the series was entertaining."

▶▶ For suggestions of related shows, see "If You Liked *Stranger Things*," page 377.
🏆 Peabody Award, 7 Emmys and a SAG Award for outstanding ensemble in a drama

The Stranger
TV-MA, 2020
Netflix original, 8 episodes (AD)
Limited series (drama) created by Harlan Coben, with Richard Armitage, Jennifer Saunders, Anthony Head, Stephen Rea, Shaun Dooley, Siobhan Finneran, Jacob Dudman, Ella-Rae Smith, Kadiff Kirwan and Hannah John-Kamen.

Richard Armitage plays a man whose life is upended when a woman he's never seen before tells him a devastating secret that involves his wife. And that's just the first of many surprises to unfold in this crackling thriller, based on the novel by Harlan Coben, that may prove impossible *not* to binge. Turns out the stranger (John-Kamen) enjoys walking up to people in this town in Northern England and ruining their lives, and with each person pulled into her web, the mysteries get more interconnected and intriguing. A murderers' row of British TV favorites (Head, Saunders, Rea) add even more appeal.

🗨 **From our forums:** "That was a hard show to binge and now I'm so tired, but it was worth it. It had the perfect balance of intrigue and intensity without the gratuitous nudity that many shows depend on."

Succession

TV-MA, 2018–present
HBO Max, 3 seasons, 30 episodes (AD)

Dark comedy with Brian Cox, Jeremy Strong, Kieran Culkin, Sarah Snook, Nicholas Braun, Matthew Macfadyen, Alan Ruck, J. Smith-Cameron, Peter Friedman and Hiam Abbass.

HBO's latest "it" show crackles with the sick burns and power moves among the family members viciously battling for control of their media empire.

Do you like to watch deplorable people mocking, cajoling and outright torturing each other like it's their favorite sport — and you've already watched every episode of *Veep*? Then *Succession* is for you. Originally pitched as a movie based on the toxic relationships in the family of Fox News founder Rupert Murdoch, this satire of the new aristocracy is like a mashup of *Billions* and an Ibsen play.

▶▶ For suggestions of related shows, see "If You Liked *Succession*," page 377.

🏆 9 Emmy Awards including best drama and lead actor (Strong), Peabody Award

Summer of Soul

PG-13, 2021
Hulu original, 1 hr 58 mins

Movie (documentary) directed by Ahmir "Questlove" Thompson, with Gladys Knight, Stevie Wonder, Marilyn McCoo and Billy Davis Jr., Charlayne Hunter-Gault, Hugh Masekela, The Chambers Brothers, Mahalia Jackson, Greg Tate, Al Sharpton and Tony Lawrence.

What a find — hours of eye-popping, soul-stirring footage from the 1969 Harlem Culture Festival, uncovered and lovingly edited. The music, the acts, the wild fashions … they're all here in living color, shot by Hal Tulchin during a multi-week celebration of Black music and culture at Mount Morris Park. It was also the summer of Woodstock, and maybe for that reason or others, Tulchin could never get a producer interested in his video. Then producer Joseph Patel learned about the existence of these 40 hours of two-inch videotape, got the tape digitized and landed Questlove, who tells this story with just the right mix of history and music and an eye for the joyful moments. Highlights include the recollections of attendees Dorinda Drake and Barbara Bland-Acosta, the Edwin Hawkins Singers' lime-green outfits, Sly and the Family Stone's exuberant takeover of the festival stage and Nina Simone's show-stopping rendition of "Are You Ready Black People."

Sunderland 'Til I Die

TV-MA, 2018–2020
Netflix original, 2 seasons,
14 episodes (AD)

Docuseries with Nick Barnes, George Honeyman and Aiden McGeady.

Follow the trials and tribulations of an English football team as it deals with relegation from the Premier League. If you've been following *Ted Lasso*, this is the real thing. In the northern working-class town of Sunderland, where football is closer to life, being at the bottom of the "table" (aka standings) feels like your whole town is on life support. With superb behind-the-scenes access and great characters from the town, this is a lovely slice of life that even Americans who think football involves pigskin will appreciate.

Superintelligence
PG, 2020
HBO Max original, 1 hr 46 mins (AD)
Sci-fi comedy film directed by Ben Falcone, with Melissa McCarthy, Bobby Cannavale, Brian Tyree Henry, Jean Smart, James Corden, Ben Falcone and Sam Richardson.

Melissa McCarthy is great in a PG thriller as she tries to convince a supercomputer not to destroy the human race. This is a silly movie with a charming performance from McCarthy, making it the rare action movie that kids and grownups can enjoy together.

Superman & Lois
TV-14, 2021–present
HBO Max, 15 episodes
Superhero drama created by Greg Berlanti and Todd Helbing, with Tyler Hoechlin, Elizabeth Tulloch, Jordan Elsass, Alex Garfin, Erik Valdez, Inde Navarrette, Wolé Parks, Adam Rayner, Dylan Walsh and Emmanuelle Chriqui.

Lois Lane and Clark Kent are married with kids, in this female-forward reimagining from the creator of *Everwood* and a writer for *The Flash*. *Superman & Lois* was created for the CW, and it certainly seems like an arranged marriage of that network's DC Comics and family-drama sides. After Clark's newspaper is bought out, he and Lois move back to Smallville with their two teen sons, where Lana Lang (also married) lives. But trouble soon follows them, and his name is Luthor.

💬 From our forums: "The Clark/Lois

relationship is delightful. Their chemistry is lovely. I liked the nods to modern small-town America, with everyone leaving and all the abandoned storefronts and the meth problem. A bit darker than what I would expect from a Superman show, but good." "I fall more in love with Tyler Hoechlin's Superman/Clark every time. There's a lot of layers to the character and he reminds me of my childhood fave Dean Cain."

Superstore
TV-14, 2015–2021
Peacock, Hulu, 6 seasons, 113 episodes
Sitcom with America Ferrera, Ben Feldman, Lauren Ash, Colton Dunn, Nico Santos, Mark McKinney, Nichole Sakura, Kaliko Kauahi, Kelly Schumann and Jon Barinholtz.

America Ferrera leads a retail workplace ensemble in a sparkling show that targets hot-button issues without missing a comedic beat. This sitcom unfolds in Cloud 9, a big box store in St. Louis where the employees are trying to balance their personal dreams with the daily realities of corporate retail. Other comedies have explored this territory, but *Superstore*'s truly bizarre storylines stand out, as does its cast of characters, which offer a remarkable variety of ethnicity, ability, class and religion, making it one of the more socially impactful series on TV.

▶▶ After watching the pilot, skip ahead to Season 3, where the show really starts to come together.

Surviving Jeffrey Epstein
TV-14, 2020
Hoopla, 4 episodes
Docuseries directed by Ricki Stern and Anne Sundberg.

Survivors of the wealthy sex trafficker are given a place to speak out. Other documentaries on Jeffrey Epstein's crimes focus too much on him. Analyzing sociopaths doesn't go anywhere and just gives them more attention. *Surviving Jeffrey Epstein* does not lay out a linear account of his predatory sexual behavior across decades and state lines, nor explain that behavior and its motivations to us. The point of this series is to bear witness, and explain to the audience, via the victims, attorneys and psychologists on-camera, how a serial sexual predator operates — and why victim-blaming isn't appropriate.

Surviving R. Kelly
TV-MA, 2019
Netflix, 6 episodes
Docuseries.

This game-changing exposé of the R&B superstar's decades-long abuse of girls and women resulted in new criminal charges and a conviction. For decades rumors had swirled around R. Kelly, yet the reporting of Chicago music writer Jim DeRogatis and testimony of the few who would speak out against Kelly were unable to sway public opinion. But that all changed after this series for the Lifetime channel aired in January 2019. Producers Jesse Daniels and Tamara Simmons interviewed an extensive list of survivors who documented the abuse and the "cult" he had kept them in, away from their families. One month after the broadcast, Kelly was formally charged with 10 counts of aggravated criminal sexual abuse. The second season, subtitled "The Reckoning," details the case against him.

▶▶ Two followup specials, *Surviving R. Kelly: Survivors Speak Out, Part 2* and *Surviving R. Kelly: The Impact,* are on Netflix.

🏆 Peabody Award

Survivor
TV-PG, 2000–present
Paramount+, Hulu, Prime Video, Netflix, 41 seasons, 605 episodes (AD)

Reality competition with Jeff Probst.

America's ultimate reality competition pits 18 to 20 scantily-clad *Survivor* fans against each other in an ever-surprising chess match where the winner takes home $1 million. While it has had weak seasons and some unfortunate turns (like when CBS failed to rein in a male contestant who was touching female contestants inappropriately), *Survivor* on the whole is a wonder of modern television production. The game manages to stay fresh and addicting with minor rule tweaks (at least when compared with the NFL).

▶▶ Watch Season 1 (*Borneo*) to enjoy a show that didn't quite know what it wanted to be yet and made some fantastic, never-to-be-matched casting choices. Season 20 (*Heroes vs. Villains*) brought back some of the show's most memorable contestants for an all-star season that capitalized on some of its most memorable long-game narratives, with some fun twists.

🏆 Emmy for best nonfiction program

Sweet Magnolias
TV-14, 2020–present
Netflix original, 2 seasons,
20 episodes (AD)
Drama with JoAnna Garcia Swisher, Brooke Elliott, Heather Headley, Anneliese Judge, Carson Rowland, Jamie Lynn Spears, Justin Breuning, Chris Klein, Dion Johnstone and Brandon Quinn.

The Hallmark-Lifetime vibes are strong in this romance drama about a trio of Southern women who help each other navigate love, work and family. Based on the popular series of books by Sherryl Woods, *Sweet Magnolias* is set against the charming small-town backdrop of Serenity, South Carolina. The show also ramps up the drama with cliffhanger plots about car crashes and babies with mysterious parentage. The whole thing is

For shows sorted by streaming platform, see page 381.

held together by the chemistry among the three leads, including Elliott, who rose to fame in the similarly femme-focused Lifetime series *Drop Dead Diva*. Spears plays a new Serenity resident in her first role since *Zoey 101*.

🐟 **From our forums:** "This show really is the TV equivalent of sweet tea: not particularly healthy and can be a bit much, but when you're in the right mood it goes down easy."

Sweet Tooth
TV-14, 2021–present
Netflix original, 8 episodes (AD)
Dystopian drama with Christian Convery, Nonso Anozie, Stefania LaVie Owen, Dania Ramirez, Adeel Akhtar, Aliza Vellani and James Brolin.

Strangely warm and cuddly drama imagines a dystopian future where babies suddenly start birthing as half-human, half-animal hybrids. Based on a DC comic, the show centers on Gus (Convery), a deer-boy, and Jeppard (Anozie), a human, as they travel through what's left of a plague-ravaged America, trying to understand how the world changed and what it has become. Some scenes may trigger unpleasant memories of the pandemic at its worst, but the show also has heart, a touch of whimsy and an unexpected cute factor from those baby hybrids.

🐟 **From our forums:** "I love fantasy but not so much that centered on kids, yet I thought this was excellent. The kid who plays Gus is very winsome and a decent actor."

Sylvie's Love
PG-13, 2020
Prime Video original, 1 hr 54 mins (AD)
Movie (romance drama) directed by Eugene Ashe, with Tessa Thompson, Nnamdi Asomugha , Aja Naomi King, Regé-Jean Page , Ryan Michelle Bathe,

Eva Longoria, Jemima Kirke and Tone Bell.

Tessa Thompson plays an ambitious woman in 1950s Harlem whose life changes forever when a trumpeter played by Nnamdi Asomugha walks through the door of her father's record shop. Somewhat overlooked because it didn't have Oscar buzz surrounding it, this beautifully filmed and scored romance is another winner in a year of Black period dramas. It's not just that Thompson and Asomugha have great chemistry. It's that they allows us to look back at the 1950s with new eyes and see a non-white couple experiencing their own Hollywood-style love story.

The Tale
TV-MA, 2018
HBO Max, 1 hr 54 mins
Movie (drama) with Laura Dern, Jason Ritter, Common, Elizabeth Debicki, Ellen Burstyn, John Heard and Isabelle Nélisse.

Laura Dern in a bravura performance plays a filmmaker whose work sends her tumbling into her past. Based on the actual experiences of writer-director Jennifer Fox, this formally daring film follows Jennifer (Dern), a documentarian forced to reexamine her adolescent relationship with two adults she once admired.

Tales from the Loop
TV-MA, 2020–present
Prime Video original, 8 episodes (AD)
Sci-fi drama with Rebecca Hall, Jonathan Pryce, Ato Essandoh, Jane Alexander, Lauren Weedman, Daniel Zolghadri, Paul Schneider, Robert Nahum Allen, Duncan Joiner and Nicole Law.

Intriguing character-based anthology tells stories about the residents of a small town who are affected by The Loop, a machine that can cause seemingly impossible things to happen. Despite the wide-open premise of a mystery machine housed in an experimental underground lab, *Tales from the Loop* is a quiet, almost mystical show about a group of humans living in rural Ohio who make powerful discoveries about themselves when they interact with The Loop.

🗨 **From our forums:** "It had a *Black Mirror* feel to it, but unlike that show, this didn't have as solid a premise. Seems like it was designed chiefly to tug at the heartstrings but with a sci-fi premise."

▶▶ Pairs well with *Little America*

Tales of the City
TV-MA, 2019
Netflix original, 10 episodes (AD)

Limited series (drama) with Laura Linney, Elliot Page, Paul Gross, Murray Bartlett, Charlie Barnett, Olympia Dukakis, Victor Garber, Ashley Park and Zosia Mamet.

Armistead Maupin's novels about 1970s queer San Francisco were first adapted by PBS, then Showtime and most recently, Netflix. *Tales of the City* holds a place of cherished honor in gay pop culture. The tales center on a boarding house at 28 Barbary Lane, overseen by the eccentric Anna Madrigal (Dukakis). Linney played Mary Ann Singleton, whose sheltered eyes were opened by the San Francisco scene before AIDS. Over the course of the original miniseries and its 2 later seasons on Showtime, *Tales of the City* presented a frank and celebratory queerness that didn't exist on television. In 2019 Netflix produced new episodes with Linney and Dukakis reprising their old roles, joined by Bartlett, Page and others.

Taste the Nation with Padma Lakshmi
TV-14, 2020–present
Hulu original, 2 seasons,
20 episodes (AD)

Docuseries with Padma Lakshmi.

Charismatic *Top Chef* host travels America exploring its food cultures with an emphasis on the immigrant experience. "What exactly is American food?" Lakshmi asks at the start of every episode of this engaging travel series. The answer is usually "immigrant food," brought here by refugees or enslaved people. Each episode is a different mix of history lesson, biography, travelogue and culinary investigation. *Taste the Nation* is a food show that doesn't minimize the exploitation and racism that the people making that food have experienced. This could be a recipe for a leaden viewing experience, but Lakshmi's curiosity and generosity bring this series to life.

Ted Lasso
TV-MA, 2020–present
Apple TV+ original, 2 seasons,
22 episodes (AD)

Comedy-drama created by Jason Sudeikis, Brendan Hunt, Bill Lawrence and Joe Kelly, with Jason Sudeikis, Hannah Waddingham, Jeremy Swift , Phil Dunster, Brett Goldstein, Brendan Hunt, Nick Mohammed and Juno Temple.

It's the sports comedy America didn't know it needed: Jason Sudeikis plays a Kansas football coach thrown into the shark tank of English soccer. Sudeikis's character — hatched, strangely enough, during a 2013 campaign to promote soccer on NBC — knows nothing about English football, has a well-honed cornpone routine and actually seems to believe the inspirational bromides he doles out on an hourly basis. Yet Lasso's philosophy slowly pays dividends in the show's charming first season. If anything, the second season is even more uplifting and sweetly funny. Comedy aficionados will also recognize the name of producer Lawrence, whose previous efforts (*Scrubs*, *Cougar Town*) deserved but never got this kind of reception.

▶▶ For suggestions of related shows, see

"If You Liked *Ted Lasso*," page 377.

🏆 An Emmy sweep in 2021: best comedy series, best actor (Sudeikis), supporting actress (Waddingham) and supporting actor (Goldstein); Peabody Award

Teenage Bounty Hunters

TV-MA, 2020
Netflix original, 10 episodes (AD)

Comedy with Maddie Phillips, Anjelica Bette Fellini, Kadeem Hardison, Virginia Williams, Mackenzie Astin and Shirley Rumierk.

After they damage their father's pickup truck, two fraternal twin sisters secretly take up bounty hunting in order to cover the cost of repairs. Set in well-off Christian suburbia, the show rises above standard high school comedies by exploring and parodying social issues while staying as light as a feather.

🗨 **From our forums:** "The other characters — and the writing — are funny enough, but Blair is hilarious and steals every scene."

Temple Grandin

TV-PG, 2010
HBO Max, 1 hr 47 mins

Movie (drama) with Claire Danes, Julia Ormond, Catherine O'Hara and David Strathairn.

Claire Danes stars in this biopic as the autistic scientist whose innovative devices pioneered the practice of humanely handling livestock. The story of Temple Grandin is one of continuous improvement and, frankly, lucky breaks. A non-communicative child who could have easily wound up in an institution — if not for her persistent mother (Ormond), supportive aunt (O'Hara) and a teacher who fired her interest in science (Strathairn) — Grandin became one of the most innovative minds in agribusiness, applying what she experienced as a child to such inventions as the "squeeze machine," which holds and calms livestock as they're being inoculated. Danes, always underrated as an actor, brings Grandin's memoir to life, showing how this evolution happened, step by arduous step.

🏆 Peabody Award, 7 Emmys including best movie and actress (Danes)

Temptation Island (2019)

TV-14, 2019–present
Peacock, 3 seasons, 36 episodes (AD)

Reality show with Mark L. Walberg.

In this surprisingly well-done reality reboot, couples agree to date other people and then discuss the results with each other on camera. For those who remember the racy ads for the original *Temptation Island* in the early '00s, this version is a revelation. It's just people dating other people, to see how that helps them with their significant other. There's very little reality TV artifice other than the bonfire, where they watch some clips of their dates and then talk over their feelings, and even that has plenty of raw unscripted drama to it. The result is an intriguing window into what lovers value in their relationships.

Terrace House

TV-14, 2015–2016
Netflix original, 46 episodes, dubbed

Reality show.

In Japan, when six strangers agree to live in a house and keep it real, they do it like normal people, which is weirdly calming. All those *Real World* moments are here, but they take place in a culture where politeness and formality is cherished, even during strong disagreements. If there are issues, the housemates talk it over, rather than shout and get into others' faces. It's rare that such a simple format provides such intriguing insights into human beings. *Terrace House* also offers some interesting peeks at Japanese culture.

Terriers
TV-MA, 2010
Hulu, 13 episodes
Crime drama created by Shawn Ryan, with Donal Logue, Michael Raymond-James, Laura Allen, Kimberly Quinn, Jamie Denbo and Rockmond Dunbar.

The creator of *The Shield* offered up this smart if short-lived procedural about two private detectives whose shoddy personal lives dovetailed with the ransoms, blackmails and kidnappings they solved. Set in the laid-back, idyllic Ocean Beach community in San Diego, *Terriers* starred Logue and Raymond-James as investigators with checkered pasts. They doggedly pursue cases that prove to be part of an escalating series of interconnected crimes involving some really bad dudes. *Terriers* was more of an exploration of the two lead characters than a *Burn Notice* knockoff. Viewers avoided it and FX canceled the show after one season.

The Terror
TV-14, 2018–2019
Hulu, 2 seasons, 20 episodes
Anthology series (horror) with Jared Harris, Derek Mio, Tobias Menzies, Kiki Sukezane, Paul Ready, Cristina Rodlo, Adam Nagaitis, Shingo Usami, Ian Hart and Naoko Mori.

Slow-building horror, based on historical events, seasoned with monsters, adds up to maximum fear. A 10-episode season is a very slow drip, but it's one that this psychological terror anthology series leans into, to good effect. Each series takes a well-known tragedy, frames it as a horror story then builds slowly to its awful conclusion.

From our forums: "Wow, that was intense. I can usually take all kinds of gore, but what was with the guy hooking the watch chains into his face?"

▶▶ *Season 1*: Come aboard two state-of-the-art ships (including *HMS Terror*) as they set off for the Arctic in 1846 to find the Northwest Passage. As ice closes in and prospects worsen, order breaks down, madness creeps in and, if that weren't enough, an Inuit spirit called Tuunbaq is stalking them.

▶▶ *Season 2*: George Takei stars in "The Terror: Infamy," set inside a World War II Japanese internment camp. This, too, had a haunting spirit, one that critics felt distracted viewers from the real-life horror of the prison camps.

The Third Day
TV-MA, 2020
HBO Max, 6 episodes (AD)
Limited series (thriller) with Jude Law, Naomie Harris, Katherine Waterston, Paddy Considine, Emily Watson, John Dagleish, Mark Lewis Jones and Freya Allan.

Jude Law wanders onto a mysterious island whose inhabitants are fiercely protective of their traditional lifestyle. You'll be yelling "Don't go there!" during this bloody, nerve-jangling series — and not just at Law's character but his wife (Harris) when *she* goes to the island searching for him. An unsettling thriller full of twists, surprises, fake-outs and jump scares.

From our forums: "I am a sucker for these 'creepy little town with a dark secret' stories, and this one is very *Wicker Man*-ish, right down to the guy getting dragged into this weird town out of concern for a girl who may be in danger. The cinematography is really nice, so even when I inevitably get confused by the plot I will have something pretty to look at."

This Close
TV-MA, 2018–present
Sundance Now original, 2 seasons, 14 episodes

Drama with Shoshannah Stern, Joshua Feldman, Colt Prattes, Zach Gilford, Cheryl Hines, Marlee Matlin and Nyle DiMarco.

Deaf BFFs rely on each other in this groundbreaking — but not unfamiliar — dramedy about love and life in L.A. Stern and Feldman, who are besties in real life, co-wrote the series and are Deaf. They play best friends Kate and Michael, whose experiences as Deaf people are embedded into every scene — and even inject some unexpected drama, as when Michael gets his wrist strapped to a hospital gurney and is unable to sign. The other nice thing about *This Close* is that the characters (including Matlin as Michael's mom) are relatable and ordinary. Their problems emerge slowly, not with the melodramatic speed of a nighttime soap, and aren't tidily resolved in an episode's 30 minutes.

This Is a Robbery: The World's Greatest Art Heist

TV-MA, 2021
Netflix original, 4 episodes (AD)
Limited series (true crime) directed by Colin Barnicle.

How in the world did thieves steal hundreds of millions of dollars' worth of art from a museum in Boston — and get away with it? In 1990, a perfectly executed armed robbery cost the Isabella Stewart Gardner Museum some of its greatest masterworks. This engaging docuseries burrows into what happened, who might have done it, and how the crime still lingers in the cultural imagination. With its twisty storyline and probing look into the dark underworld of fine-art theft, it's a perfect fit for Netflix's documentary template.

This Is Us

TV-14, 2016–present
Hulu, Peacock, 5 seasons,
88 episodes (AD)

Family drama created by Dan Fogelman, with Mandy Moore, Milo Ventimiglia, Sterling K. Brown, Justin Hartley, Chrissy Metz, Susan Kelechi Watson, Chris Sullivan, Jon Huertas, Caitlin Thompson and Ron Cephas Jones.

Three siblings live their lives across decades in one of TV's most popular shows of the late 2010s. Even though it's a network drama, with all that that entails, *This Is Us* is essential viewing if one is to understand the wave of representational and fractured-timeline series that have overtaken streaming TV. Besides, the stories keep you watching.

🗨 **From our forums:** "Wait . . . what just happened???!!" "I can safely say I did not see that coming."

⏩ For suggestions of related shows, see "If You Liked *This Is Us*," page 378.

🏆 Emmys for lead actor in a drama (Brown) and guest actor (Jones, twice); TCA Award, best new show

This Way Up

TV-MA, 2019–present
Hulu original, 2 seasons,
12 episodes (AD)

Dark comedy created by Aisling Bea, with Aisling Bea, Sharon Horgan, Aasif Mandvi, Kadiff Kirwan, Indira Varma and Tobias Menzies.

Thoughtful comedy follows a woman recovering from a nervous breakdown with her sister's help. Irish comedian Aisling Bea, who's also a writer on the series, won a BAFTA for her role as Aine, whose journey back from the brink is aided by her frustrated sister Shona (Horgan) and her job tutoring a young boy. Though much of the appeal of this show is the sisters' loving, unfiltered relationship, fans of Menzies from *The Crown* will enjoy him here as Richard, the man who comes into Aine's life.

The Tick
TV-MA, 2016–2019
Prime Video original, 2 seasons,
22 episodes (AD)
Action comedy created by Ben Edlund, with Peter Serafinowicz, Griffin Newman, Valorie Curry, Brendan Hines, Yara Martinez, Scott Speiser and Alan Tudyk.

The newest incarnation of the offbeat amnesiac superhero is every bit as silly and enjoyable as the classic version. Hard to believe the original and beloved live-action *Tick* — starring Patrick Warburton as the hulk in a blue suit, with no memory of his past — produced only 9 episodes. (Perhaps because Comedy Central ran them for years; it was the channel's *Fawlty Towers*.) But this is a fine successor, thanks not only to the oddly likable personalities of Serafinowicz's Tick and Newman's Arthur but the world that formed around them, including Arthur's sister Dot (Curry) and an AI-equipped boat voiced by Tudyk that, in Season 2, developed a crush on Arthur.

🔊 **From our forums:** "Bummer it's already been canceled. It's got such a weird charm about it. They added unexpected depth to Dot and other characters. And I loved all the Superman parodies."

Tick, Tick ... Boom!
PG-13, 2021
Netflix original, 1 hr 55 mins (AD)
Movie (musical) directed by Lin-Manuel Miranda, with Andrew Garfield, Alexandra Shipp, Robin de Jesus, Vanessa Hudgens, Judith Light, Bradley Whitford and Laura Benanti.

Effervescent production highlights the life of a composer who died young, shortly after creating Broadway's signature Gen X musical. *Tick, Tick ... Boom!* began its life in 1990 as a solo production by playwright and composer Jonathan Larson, who a few years later would write *Rent*. Larson tragically passed away on the eve of its off-Broadway premiere, and this semi-autobiographical play became a cult favorite among musical theater fans for years. Thanks to a deservedly upbeat filmed version (directed by Lin-Manuel Miranda, no less), the world can now enjoy this story of bringing a dream to life.

Tidying Up with Marie Kondo
TV-PG, 2019
Netflix original, 8 episodes (AD)
Reality show with Marie Kondo.

The organizational expert helps families declutter in a show that feels like *Hoarders* without the deep-rooted familial discord. In each episode Kondo, bestselling author of *The Life-Changing Magic of Tidying Up*, enters a messy home whose occupants have agreed to let her try her KonMari method on their place. We get to know the families (a little), raising the emotional stakes of the makeover they're about to get. There's no sensationalism, no *Trading Spaces*–esque potential for disaster. Kondo brings compassion to her makeovers. Though a very appealing showcase for her holistic philosophy, Netflix halted production after one season and launched another series, *Sparking Joy*, that featured Kondo in a more central role.

Tiger King
TV-MA, 2020–2021
Netflix original, 3 seasons,
16 episodes (AD)
Limited series (true crime) with Joe Exotic, Carole Baskin, Rick Kirkham, John Finlay, Kelci Saffery and John Reinke.

If you've managed to avoid the Netflix sensation so far, it may be time you took a bite. The first season of this relentlessly over-the-top docuseries investigates how zookeeper Joe Exotic came to be convicted of both violating the Endangered Species Act and placing a hit on Carole Baskin, the owner of a big cat rescue organization. Perhaps you avoid such lurid reality fare, but another argument for watching *Tiger King* is the uncanny way that the battle between Joe and Carole — and their armies of supporters — resembles the larger culture war going on across America.

▸▸ Following the unprecedented success of the show's first season, Netflix produced a followup hosted by Joel McHale titled *The Tiger King and I* and ordered far less well-received second and third seasons that primarily focused on the original show's more peripheral players.

Tigertail
PG, 2020
Netflix original, 1 hr 31 mins, dubbed (AD)
Movie (drama) directed by Alan Yang, with Joan Chen, James Saito, Tzi Ma, Christine Ko, Hong-Chi Lee and Queenie Yu-Hsin Fang.

This film recounts decades in the life of a Taiwanese man who leaves a love and family behind to emigrate to the U.S. Inspired by the story of the director's father — he's the narrator — this earnest film with dialogue in Mandarin, Taiwanese and English is a modern take on the Asian-American immigration story. However, critics wished Yang had fleshed out the characters better.

▸▸ This is the feature directorial debut for Yang, who won an Emmy for his work on *Master of None*.

Timeless
TV-14, 2016–2018
Hulu, 2 seasons, 28 episodes
Sci-fi drama created by Eric Kripke and Shawn Ryan, with Abigail Spencer, Matt Lanter, Malcolm Barrett, Paterson Joseph, Sakina Jaffrey, Claudia Doumit and Goran Visnjic.

After a mysterious thief steals a time machine with plans to rewrite history, a history professor, an engineer and a soldier join forces to stop him. Burdened by a weak pilot episode, *Timeless* proved to be a slow-build adventure series that could have lasted several seasons on streaming. As it was, the show's devoted fan base managed to convince NBC to extend the series for a second season and a movie-length finale that offered a proper ending.

Timmy Failure: Mistakes Were Made
PG, 2020
Disney+ original, 1 hr 39 mins (AD)
Movie (family comedy) directed by Tom McCarthy, with Winslow Fegley, Ophelia Lovibond, Craig Robinson and Wallace Shawn.

Adaptation of the children's book follows an 11-year-old boy who runs a detective agency with the help of his imaginary friend, a giant polar bear. Directed and co-written by Oscar-winner McCarthy (*Spotlight*), this is the kind of family movie that treats kids like they're smart.

Tin Star
TV-MA, 2017–2020
Prime Video original, 3 seasons, 25 episodes (AD)
Crime drama with Tim Roth, Genevieve O'Reilly, Abigail Lawrie, Oliver Coopersmith and Christina Hendricks.

When his family is threatened by figures from his past, the police chief of a small mountain town has to resurrect the violent alter ego he thought he could leave behind. *Ozark* it is not, but this slow-paced, bloody drama — carried, for the most part, by Roth, the hero with a dark side — endeared itself to fans who loved the showdowns between small-town good guys and corporate evildoers. If you stick it out to the end, *Tin Star* rewards you with a satisfying conclusion.

To All the Boys I've Loved Before (movie trilogy)
TV-14, 2018–2021
Netflix original, 3 episodes (AD)
Teen drama with Lana Condor, Noah Centineo, Janel Parrish, Anna Cathcart, Madeleine Arthur, Emilija Baranac, Israel Broussard, John Corbett, Holland Taylor and Ross Butler.

Netflix's popular adaptation of Jenny Han's YA trilogy has appeal beyond its teenage-girl core audience. Sixteen-year-old Lara Jean Song Covey (Condor) has never had a boyfriend, but she's written love letters to five of her crushes. Then her younger sister Kitty (Cathcart) mails off the letters, and complications ensue. Older viewers will appreciate the films' modern and diverse take on boy-meets-girl, as well as the casting of Corbett as the girls' widowed dad.

Too Close
TV-14, 2021
AMC+, 3 episodes
Limited series (thriller) with Emily Watson, Denise Gough, Thalissa Teixeria, Karl Johnson, Jamie Sives, Risteard Cooper, Eileen Davies, Chizzy Akudolu and Nina Wadia.

When a shrink is brought in to evaluate a young woman's competency to stand trial, the two become trapped in a tense, sexually charged psychodrama. Watson (*Chernobyl*) plays Emma, a forensic psychiatrist assigned to work with Connie (Gough), whose horrible crime is shown in the opening scene. Dubbed the Yummy Mummy Monster by the British tabloids, Connie will either be jailed, committed for life or given a chance at rehab and release. While assessing her patient, Emma becomes, well, *too close* to her, and in the ensuing entanglement it's hard to tell who's analyzing whom.

▸▸ Pairs well with *Cheat*

Too Funny to Fail
R, 2017
Hulu original, 1 hr 35 mins (AD)
Movie (documentary) with Dana Carvey, Steve Carell, Stephen Colbert, Robert Smigel, Bill Chott and Heather Morgan.

A fond look back at what was surely the funniest show to be canceled after 7 episodes, and the outsized influence it had. *The Dana Carvey Show* was the popular impressionist's first effort after leaving *SNL* and it's amazing how wrong everyone was about it. Critics panned it, sponsors objected to the show's edgy content and ABC quickly dropped it from its schedule. But the show would help launch the careers of its writers and stars, including Stephen Colbert, Robert Smigel and Steve Carell. And while some of the sketches are dated (like "The Ambiguously Gay Duo"), others hold up amazingly well.

▸▸ Original episodes of *The Dana Carvey Show* are hard to find, but at press time they were available through the web streaming services Crackle and Plex.

Too Hot to Handle
TV-MA, 2020–present
Netflix original, 3 seasons, 19 episodes (AD)
Reality competition with Desiree Burch (narrator), Jeff Dye (host, Season 2) and Dariany Santana (host, Season 3).

It's the *Seinfeld* "Contest" episode, but dumber and hotter: A group of singles occupy a TV house and whoever can hold off their natural urges the longest wins a cash prize. Ten hotties arrive at a gorgeous estate on Turks and Caicos thinking they're taking part in a very *different* kind of reality show, only to be informed (by a talking lava lamp, no less) that the $100,000 purse will be drawn down every time one of the spy cams catches anyone kissing, fornicating or, yes,

For shows sorted by streaming platform, see page 381.

self-pleasuring. Tawdry and occasionally tender, *Too Hot to Handle* is sustained by Burch's snarky voiceovers and the occasional moments where two of the hotties sit next to each other and just … talk.

▶▶ And don't miss the inevitable spinoffs, *Too Hot to Handle: Brazil* and *Too Hot to Handle: Latino* (Mexico).

Top Chef

TV-14, 2006–present
Hulu, Peacock, 18 seasons, 279 episodes
Reality competition with Padma Lakshmi, Tom Colicchio and Gail Simmons.

The gold standard of American reality TV talent competitions, *Top Chef* **keeps improving its recipe every season.** The casting, the challenge design, the locations—everything is better on *Top Chef*. That even extends to the "Last Chance Kitchen," which began life as a blatant ripoff of Survivor's "Redemption Island," where eliminated contestants battle for the right to reenter the game. Yet this gimmick quickly became a vital part of the competition, offering not only second chances but cheeky opportunities for redemption. The show has evolved; once unable to seriously discuss the racial pain involved in America's food history (the Charleston series), diversity and respect for cultural pathways is baked into every season.

▶▶ Start with *Top Chef All-Stars L.A.*, filmed during the pandemic. It has inspiring storylines galore and ends with a fist-pumping triumph. Then sample *Top Chef: Portland*, with food from the African diaspora, a very funny "drive-in challenge" (because pandemic) and some first-rate play action.

🏆 Emmy for outstanding reality competition program

Top of the Lake

TV-MA, 2013–2017
Hulu, 2 seasons, 13 episodes
Crime drama created by Jane Campion and Gerard Lee, with Elisabeth Moss, David Wenham, Peter Mullan, Gwendoline Christie, Holly Hunter and Nicole Kidman.

Elisabeth Moss brings real depth to a stock role. Rocking a Kiwi accent, Moss plays Robin Griffin, an Australia-based detective investigating sex crimes. Campion, who co-wrote the show, invests heavily in linking Robin's emotional baggage to the cases she takes on. This being a Sundance TV production, there's the requisite quirky B story, which involves a women's commune run by Hunter. The second season features a new story and guest stars, including Kidman.

💬 From our forums: "Season 2 is not as good as Season 1. Moss is still great but Kidman is pretty much wasted and I sometimes forgot she was in it."

Transhood

TV-14, 2020
HBO Max, 1 hr 36 mins (AD)
Movie (documentary) directed by Sharon Liese.

Unflinching documentary captures the struggles faced by transgender kids and their families. Shot over 5 years in the heart of America, Liese (*High School Confidential*) follows children ages 4 to 15 who self-identify as other than their given gender. *Transhood* is less of an advocacy film than it is a raw, unflinching look at the emotional toll that is taken not just on transgender children, but the families they've come out to.

Transparent

TV-MA, 2014–2019
Prime Video original, 4 seasons, 42 episodes (AD)

Comedy-drama created by Joey Soloway, with Jeffrey Tambor, Judith Light, Gaby Hoffmann, Amy Landecker, Jay Duplass, Rob Huebel, Kathryn Hahn, Alexandra Billings, Bradley Whitford and Cherry Jones.

Jeffrey Tambor plays a woman whose transgender decision forces her entire family to evolve into a more outspoken, honest and overtly flawed tribe. The whole conversation on gays and transgender people in America changed when families started talking. That's the idea behind this acclaimed series, which explores gender identity issues through the lives of the Pfefferman family, each of whom have to reckon with their own myopia and selfishness once Mort (Tambor) announces he is now Maura. Despite widespread accolades for its lead character's performance, by Season 2 this show is a masterpiece by committee.

▶▶ The two-hour musical series finale was missing its star; Tambor had exited after harassment allegations from two transgender actors on the show.

🏆 Peabody Award; 8 Emmys including best actor in a comedy (Tambor, twice)

Treme
TV-MA, 2010–2013
HBO Max, 4 seasons, 36 episodes
Drama created by Eric Overmyer and David Simon, with Khandi Alexander, Rob Brown, Kim Dickens, Melissa Leo, Lucia Micarelli, Clarke Peters, Wendell Pierce, Steve Zahn, Michiel Huisman and David Morse.

The creator of *The Wire* explored a different kind of urban devastation in this richly textured account of life in New Orleans in the aftermath of Hurricane Katrina. Many critics consider this their second-favorite David Simon series after *The Wire*. It's easy to see why: a second-line parade of great performances led by Pierce as a down-on-his-luck

trombonist, Alexander as a bar owner with a missing brother and Peters as a survivor with seemingly nothing left after Katrina but his pride. And the music. Simon loves creating worlds and it's clear he enjoyed creating the world of *Treme* more than any other show.

Trial 4
TV-MA, 2020
Netflix original, 8 episodes (AD)
Limited series (true crime) directed by Rémy Burkel and Jean-Xavier de Lestrade, with Sean Ellis, William C. Dwyer, Toni Locy and Rosemary Scapicchio.

Why do Boston prosecutors insist on trying the same man over and over for a crime he plainly didn't commit? Sean Ellis was a 19-year-old man in 1993 when he was charged in the execution-style murder of an off-duty cop. The killing was so sensational that Ellis's name became a household word — so he had to be guilty, right? In this typically engrossing effort from the French directors of *The Staircase*, discover how a culture of ineptitude and CYA dragged out Ellis's case through four court trials, while the real people who needed to be held accountable weren't.

The Trial of Christine Keeler
TV-MA, 2019–2020
HBO Max, 6 episodes
Limited series (historical drama) with Sophie Cookson, James Norton, Ellie Bamber, Emilia Fox, Ben Miles, Michael Maloney, Sam Troughton, Anthony Welsh, Jack Greenlees and Chloe Harris.

In-depth dramatization revisits the British sex scandal that caused an international crisis in 1963 and brought down a government. "The Profumo affair," shorthand for the tabloid story that brought down John Profumo — Harold Macmillan's Secretary of State for War, and ultimately the Macmillan government itself — was covered briefly in Season 2 of *The Crown*. This narrative, starring the very effective Cookson as the sex worker at the heart of the affair and Norton as Profumo, delves far deeper than Keeler's showgirl and model status, revealing the gender and class divide that still plays a role in the damaging British tabloid machine nearly 60 years later.

The Trial of the Chicago 7
R, 2020
Netflix original, 2 hrs 9 mins (AD)
Movie (historical drama) directed by Aaron Sorkin, with Eddie Redmayne, Alex Sharp, Sacha Baron Cohen, Jeremy Strong, John Carroll Lynch, Yahya Abdul-Mateen II, Mark Rylance, Joseph Gordon-Levitt, Frank Langella and Michael Keaton.

From Aaron Sorkin's script, an all-star cast reenacts a show trial from 1969. Despite the outsized Left personalities featured here and the speechifying common to Sorkin's work, it's the narrative that powers this film: Chicago's cops staged a police riot at the 1968 Democratic Convention and the victims were the only ones held responsible. The standouts are Cohen as the motor-mouthed rebel Abbie Hoffman and Langella as Julius Hoffman (no relation), whose bias and incompetence as the trial judge are the only reasons we remember this case.
🏆 SAG Award for outstanding performance by a cast in a movie

The Trials of Gabriel Fernandez
TV-MA, 2020
Netflix original, 6 episodes (AD)
Limited series (true crime) directed by Brian Knappenberger.

Disturbing series about the death of an 8-year-old boy raises important questions about how child welfare is handled in this country. It's hard to recommend a series that meticulously walks us through the prolonged abuse and killing of a child. What's more, this series casts a harsh light on the child welfare system, which responded to young Gabriel's plight with bureaucratic negligence that was itself criminal. But it's a well-sourced docuseries thanks to the cooperation of family members.

Trouble the Water
Not Rated, 2008
AMC+, Kanopy, 1 hr 33 mins
Movie (documentary) directed by Carl Deal and Tia Lessin.

Harrowing first-person account of surviving Hurricane Katrina will leave you moved by the resiliency of those who had little to lose — and lost it all. Kimberly Roberts was in her attic with her family, riding out the fury unleashed by Hurricane Katrina in New Orleans's Lower Ninth, when she picked up the used camcorder she'd recently bought on a street corner and took the incredible storm video that is the centerpiece of *Trouble the Water*. Afterward we follow Kim and family on their odyssey out of New Orleans, but not before encountering roadblocks, insults and setbacks. Despite shoddy treatment from their own government, their unbreakable spirit will move you.
🏆 Sundance Film Festival's Grand Jury Prize

True Blood
TV-MA, 2008–2014
HBO Max, 7 seasons, 80 episodes (AD)
Fantasy drama created by Alan Ball, with Anna Paquin, Stephen Moyer, Sam Trammell, Ryan Kwanten, Chris Bauer, Nelsan Ellis, Carrie Preston, Rutina Wesley and Alexander Skarsgård.

Life in a Louisiana town is changed forever after the local vampires decide to "come out of the coffin" and live openly among their neighbors. Gory, sexy, homoerotic, funny and trashy: The first few seasons of this supernatural soap opera are fantastic. Creator Alan Ball shows the same knack for character development he honed with *Six Feet Under* and adds a layer of mischievous fun as the show investigates the day-to-day details of vamp-human co-habitation. And don't forget the other creatures: Paquin stars as Sookie Stackhouse, a sassy, self-confident waitress with psychic abilities, and soon enough, we meet shape shifters, were-panthers and faeries. They add to the sense that anything can happen at any time. The less said about the final 2 seasons the better, but at its best *True Blood* is top-notch pulp.

🏆 TCA Award for outstanding new program

True Detective

TV-MA, 2014–2019
HBO Max, 3 seasons, 24 episodes
Anthology series (crime drama) with Matthew McConaughey, Woody Harrelson, Michelle Monaghan, Michael Potts, Tory Kittles, Alexandra Daddario, Kevin Dunn, Clarke Peters and Jay O. Sanders.

Matthew McConaughey and Woody Harrelson are stellar as detectives revisiting a murder case they first investigated 20 years earlier. Nic Pizzolatto's metaphysically minded crime anthology never got the kind of attention in its later seasons that it got in Season 1. Using strange dialogue, endless timeline jumps and ambitious production values, McConaughey and Harrelson's characters delight the audience every step of the way through what is, at its core, a classic whodunit.

🏆 5 Emmys

Truth Be Told

TV-MA, 2019–present
Apple TV+ original, 2 seasons,
18 episodes (AD)
Crime drama with Octavia Spencer, Aaron Paul, Kate Hudson, Michael Beach, Mekhi Phifer, Tracie Thoms, Ron Cephas Jones, Haneefah Wood, Katherine LaNasa, Lizzy Caplan and Elizabeth Perkins.

Octavia Spencer and Aaron Paul are reason enough to watch this wrongful conviction drama. Investigative reporter Poppy Parnell (Spencer) revisits a murder case she worked 20 years ago after getting a tip that she helped put away the wrong man (Paul). Racial animosity, class aspirations, gender and religion all add to the dramatic tension. The Apple product placement is distracting, and Poppy's attempt to document her journey via real-time podcast is absurd. But strong performances, including Caplan in a dual role as twins, and some surprising racial dynamics should carry you through that noise.

Tuca & Bertie

TV-MA, 2019–present
Netflix original, 2 seasons,
20 episodes (AD)
Animated comedy created by Lisa Hanawalt, with Tiffany Haddish, Ali Wong, Steven Yeun and Nicole Byer.

Tiffany Haddish and Ali Wong are the fast-talking voices of two bird-women who are besties living their big-city lives together. Animation is dominated by guys and it seems whenever women try to break in they scarcely get a chance (*Bless the Harts* comes to mind). This lightly bizarro show, built around the strong bond between free-spirited Tuca (Haddish) and neurotic Bertie (Wong), won over critics but apparently not enough viewers for Netflix's tastes. (Adult Swim picked up the show after the first season.) Similar to *BoJack Horseman* (on which creator Hanawalt worked) in its treatment of issues like addiction and sexual assault.

▸▸ Only Season 1 is available for streaming on Netflix.

▸▸ Pairs well with *Broad City*

Turn: Washington's Spies
TV-14, 2014–2017
Netflix, 4 seasons, 40 episodes
Historical drama with Jamie Bell, Seth Numrich, Daniel Henshall, Meegan Warner, Heather Lind, Kevin McNally, Samuel Roukin, Burn Gorman, Ian Kahn and Angus Macfadyen.

Historically sound drama introduces us to the Culper Ring, which played a crucial but little known role in the Revolutionary War. During the years that the British Army occupied New York City, a hardy band of patriots ferried critical intelligence about the enemy to General George Washington. Based on Alexander Rose's nonfiction book, *Turn* brims with fascinating storylines and larger-than-life characters, notably Abraham Woodhull (Bell), Benjamin Tallmadge (Numrich) and Anna Strong (Lind).

🎣 **From our forums:** "I truly loved this show and was sorry to see it end, but the finale had too much cutting and pasting, trying to match the fictional narratives with the factual outcomes."

▸▸ Pairs well with *The Spy*

Turning Point: 9/11 and the War on Terror
TV-MA, 2021
Netflix original, 5 episodes
Docuseries directed by Brian Knappenberger.

With the perspective of 20 years, this searing docuseries relives the Sept. 11 attacks and retraces their tragic aftermath. The story of the 9/11 attacks has been told so often that it seems hardly possible to see it with fresh eyes. Yet *Turning Point* does just that. Its five expertly compressed episodes move briskly yet with care, choosing the moments and memories that have maximum impact. Knappenberger and an Afghan crew conducted 88 interviews with survivors, journalists, experts and insiders. And from start to finish it takes the full measure of the consequences of America's response to the 9/11 attacks, including an ill-advised invasion of Iraq and a poorly defined agenda for fighting terrorism (or rather, "terror").

The Twelve
TV-MA, 2019–2020
Netflix original, 10 episodes
Limited series (thriller) with Maaike Cafmeyer, Charlotte De Bruyne, Tom Vermeir and Maaike Neuville.

Belgian courtroom drama revolves around a jury as it is affected by testimony in a grim murder trial. A woman is accused of murdering her daughter and best friend. Each day the jurors must listen to the horrible details. The weight of the case affects their personal lives. Finally, the jurors' baggage begins to sway the trial in unexpected ways. Totally absorbing whether you follow the subtitles or the English dubbing (though the subtitles are better).

The Twilight Zone (1959)
TV-PG, 1959–1964
Paramount+, Hulu, 5 seasons, 156 episodes
Classic sci-fi anthology created by Rod Serling, with Rod Serling (host).

The finest collection of one-act plays ever produced for television. *The Twilight Zone* is included as a "genre classic" in our list, "If You Liked *Stranger Things*," page 377.

▶▶ Future big-name stars who appeared in *Twilight Zone* episodes include Ron Howard in "Walking Distance" (S1E5), Charles Bronson in "Two" (S3E1), Peter Falk wearing full Fidel Castro drag in "The Mirror" (S3E6), Leonard Nimoy in "A Quality of Mercy" (S3E15), an impossibly boyish Robert Redford in "Nothing in the Dark" (S3E16), Carol Burnett in the rare comedic episode "Cavender Is Coming" (S3E36), Dennis Hopper as a neo-Nazi in "He's Alive" (S4E4), Burt Reynolds in "The Bard" (S4E18) and, last but not least, one of the all-time classic *Twilight Zone*s, "Nightmare at 20,000 Feet" (S5E3), with William Shatner as an airline passenger who swears there's a monster sitting on the wing.

🏆 3 Emmys

Two and a Half Men

TV-14, 2003–2015
Peacock, 12 seasons, 262 episodes
Sitcom created by Chuck Lorre and Lee Aronsohn, with Charlie Sheen, Jon Cryer, Ashton Kutcher, Angus T. Jones, Conchata Ferrell, Holland Taylor and Marin Hinkle.

Though overshadowed by the offstage antics of Charlie Sheen, this was first-rate TV comedy thanks to Jon Cryer's and Conchata Ferrell's chemistry with Sheen. A wealthy, oversexed jingle writer (Sheen) has to take in his brother (Cryer) and young son (Jones) after his wife kicks him out. Although Sheen's character hasn't aged well, in its best seasons there was no better comedy on TV, thanks to three perfectly cast stars: Sheen, Cryer and Ferrell, who played Charlie's sarcastic housekeeper.

▶▶ Needle-drop at Season 5, where the writers are in fine fettle, churning out one great episode after the next, like "City of Great Racks" (S5E4) and the wonderfully childish "Is There a Mrs. Waffles?" (S5E8). Cryer wins his first Emmy for Season 6

and Season 7 has the hilarious "Gorp, Fnark, Schmegle" episode where Charlie tries to double his pleasure (S7E8). Sheen's offstage crackup necessitated his replacement by Kutcher in Season 9; by then the show was just playing out the string.

🏆 2 Emmys for Cryer, one for best supporting actor in a comedy and then, after Sheen left, for best *lead* actor

The Two Popes

R, 2019
Netflix original, 2 hr 5 min
Movie (drama) created by Anthony McCarten, with Anthony Hopkins and Jonathan Pryce.

Anthony Hopkins and Jonathan Pryce play two top Catholics having an argument about toleration in this engaging, Oscar-nominated film from the writer of *The Theory of Everything*. McCarten (who also gave us the Freddie Mercury biopic *Bohemian Rhapsody*) imagines what then-pope Benedict (Hopkins) and then-archbishop Bergoglio (Pryce) might have talked about in the years leading up to Benedict's abdication. It's a fascinating idea for a dialogue — the strict theologian Benedict butting heads with the future "who am I to judge?" Pope Francis — and the points they touch on go beyond Catholicism to the larger question of accepting others with heterodox views. Director Meirelles fills the screen with lovely touches, like when Benedict sits at the piano and serenades Bergoglio.

The Umbrella Academy

TV-14, 2019–present
Netflix original, 3 seasons,
30 episodes (AD)
Superhero drama with Elliot Page, Tom Hopper, David Castañeda, Emmy Raver-Lampman, Robert Sheehan, Aidan Gallagher, Justin H. Min, Colm Feore and Mary J. Blige.

Some shows may have moved; see page 183.

Perhaps the pinnacle of offbeat superhero shows, *The Umbrella Academy* combined bad family dynamics and apocalyptic stakes in a franchise that (eventually) became irresistible. Based on Gerard Way and Gabriel Ba's comic of the same name, the adventures of 7 siblings of varying super-abilities, raised by an abusive billionaire, took some time to find its creative stride. No matter: the show trailed only *Stranger Things* as Netflix's most-watched series of 2019. Likely that's because *The Umbrella Academy* is a great big shiny box of streaming-TV bonbons: appealing young leads (led by Ellen, now Elliot, Page's Number Seven), a convolution of storylines in which personal and global crises intermix, time travel and so much more.

From our forums: "Having read the comics after watching this, the TV show elevates the source material greatly, not unlike S1 and 2 of *The Walking Dead*." "I loved this show so hard. It was like someone at Netflix decided to make a show specifically for me."

Unbelievable
TV-MA, 2019
Netflix original, 8 episodes (AD)
Limited series (drama) with Toni Collette, Merritt Wever and Kaitlyn Dever.

One of 2019's most acclaimed dramas, this fact-based drama about an elusive rapist is elevated by its three female leads. *Unbelievable* stands out as a female-oriented cop drama centered on a sexual assault that we never see committed on screen. Dever, Wever and Collette play three-dimensional characters and this limited series has time to explore their moods and thoughts without losing the thread. It brings emotional heft to this powerful indictment of a system that allows sexual predators to evade justice.

Peabody Award

Unbreakable Kimmy Schmidt
TV-14, 2015–2019
Netflix original, 4 seasons, 51 episodes (AD)
Sitcom created by Tina Fey and Robert Carlock, with Ellie Kemper, Tituss Burgess, Jane Krakowski, Carol Kane and Jon Hamm.

After being held captive in a bunker for 15 years, Kimmy Schmidt hurls herself into life in NYC, where her relentless cheer and guileless nature land her in various fixes but also win over unlikely allies. The high-energy zing of Tina Fey and Robert Carlock's writing plus Kemper's boundless enthusiasm made for a winning combination even as this show veered into surreal territory. In lesser hands this sitcom about a woman who's endured horrible abuse (including rape) would be just icky, but the backstory only makes Kimmy's can-do attitude that much more endearing.

Uncle Frank
R, 2020
Prime Video original, 1 hr 35 mins (AD)
Movie (drama) directed by Alan Ball, with Paul Bettany, Sophia Lillis, Peter Macdissi, Steve Zahn, Judy Greer, Margo Martindale, Stephen Root and Lois Smith.

In 1973 a young woman and her favorite uncle, who's gay, take a road trip to the hometown that he's been avoiding for years. And they're not alone — Frank's lover, Walid (Macdissi), himself an outcast from his Muslim family, is along for this road trip. It's another gem from writer-director Alan Ball (*Six Feet Under*, *American Beauty*), exploring a queer past he would've been just old enough to experience himself.

Undercover Billionaire
TV-PG, 2019–present
Discovery+, 2 seasons, 22 episodes

Reality show with Glenn Stearns, Grant Cardone, Monique Idlett-Mosley and Elaine Culotti.

Entrepreneurs are given $100 and embedded in cities where no one knows them in a social experiment about nature, nurture and making money. In Season 1 wealthy businessman Stearns was dropped into a rust belt town with one Franklin, one wiped cell phone and one old pickup. Forbidden to call associates or otherwise leverage his past, he was given 90 days to help total strangers build a million-dollar business. In Season 2 three entrepreneurs repeated the experiment. There's a big idea here: that generational wealth (or white male privilege, in Season 2) isn't required to be financially successful. But it's the reality-show idea — *will they pull this off?* — that makes this worth watching.

▶▶ Pairs well with *The Profit*

The Underground Railroad

TV-MA, 2021
Prime Video original, 10 episodes (AD)
Limited series (dystopian drama) created by Barry Jenkins, with Thuso Mbedu, Chase Dillon, Aaron Pierre, Joel Edgerton, Sheila Atim, Peter Mullan and William Jackson Harper.

An adaptation as surreal and button-pushing as the Pulitzer Prize–winning book on which it's based. Jenkins (*Moonlight*) directs and co-adapted Colson Whitehead's alt-history novel about Cora (Mbedu), a slave who escapes the South on a literal underground railroad, complete with conductors, tracks and train cars. Mbedu is mesmerizing in every scene and the series is true to the author's goal of showing the generational damage caused by slavery.

🗨 **From our forums:** "I couldn't finish even the first episode. Too horrifying. And I read the book."

Underwater

PG-13, 2020
HBO Max, 1 hr 35 mins
Sci-fi drama with Kristen Stewart, Vincent Cassel, Mamoudou Athie, T.J. Miller, John Gallagher Jr. and Jessica Henwick.

Deep sea researchers have to get above water fast after an earthquake rattles their research facility in the Mariana Trench. There's a creepy twist that has helped this movie become a slow-burn hit on streaming.

The Undoing

TV-MA, 2020
HBO Max, 6 episodes (AD)
Limited series (drama) created by David E. Kelley, with Nicole Kidman, Hugh Grant, Edgar Ramírez, Noah Jupe, Lily Rabe and Donald Sutherland.

Nicole Kidman and Hugh Grant play a power couple who are rocked by the revelation of a well-concealed secret and a murder investigation in this messy mini that ends with a bang. Throughout its six-week run on HBO, viewers complained that this latest product from the David E. Kelley hitmaking factory paled next to *Big Little Lies*, Kelley's earlier series about rich people behaving badly. Fair point. But if you're less interested in character development and story coherence and just want a thriller that go-go-goes, you'll take a shine to *The Undoing*. And you'll be talking about the finale — and Donald Sutherland's ridiculously posh apartment — with everyone else who watched it.

Undone

TV-MA, 2019–present
Prime Video original, 8 episodes (AD)
Animated drama with Rosa Salazar, Angelique Cabral, Constance Marie, Siddharth Dhananjay, Daveed Diggs, Bob Odenkirk and Jeanne Tripplehorn.

Dreamlike animated drama about loss and memory will make you feel like you're watching a very imaginative live-action show. After a car accident, Alma (Salazar) awakens with the ability to slip around in time. She decides to go back to her father's death and unravel its mystery. But does Alma actually have a new power or is she suffering from mental illness? This is tricky, *Life of Pi* territory, but *Undone* navigates it deftly using rotoscope, in which human forms are traced over and animated. It's this mesmerizing technique that makes the show's tonal shifts possible, allowing us to ponder both the possibility that Alma is living in a dream world and that she actually can reel in the years.

United States of Tara
TV-MA, 2009–2011
Showtime original, 3 seasons,
36 episodes
Dark comedy created by Diablo Cody, with Toni Collette, John Corbett, Rosemarie DeWitt, Keir Gilchrist, Brie Larson and Patton Oswalt.

Toni Collette's first leading role in television was a complete triumph, playing a woman with multiple personalities trying to live a normal suburban life. Based on an idea by Steven Spielberg, *United States of Tara* was an early attempt at dark comedy before it took off in the streaming era. Collette brilliantly brought to life Tara's several personalities, or "alters," including a Stepfordian *hausfrau*, a horny, thong-sporting teenager and an aggressively foul-mouthed man. The show explored how these varying sides of Tara are actually expressions of childhood trauma, which she's processing with the support of her roll-with-it family and liberal doses of mordant humor.
🏆 Emmy for best actress in a comedy series (Collette)

The United States vs. Billie Holiday
R, 2021
Hulu original, 2 hrs 6 mins (AD)
Movie (historical drama) directed by Lee Daniels, with Andra Day, Trevante Rhodes, Garrett Hedlund, Natasha Lyonne and Leslie Jordan.

Singer Andra Day makes a remarkable film debut in this biopic of Billie Holiday that paints her as a victim of a federal witch hunt. Director Daniels also created the series *Empire*, and as in that show he uses the ups and downs of the music industry as the backdrop for this melodramatic fever dream. Ghosts of Holiday's past move freely through the present day, although given the disorienting intensity of her battles with racism, addiction and no-good men, these surreal touches are emotionally justified. Day, in an Oscar-nominated turn, is sensational — rippling with feeling and more than capable of selling the musical moments.

Unorthodox
TV-MA, 2020
Netflix original, 4 episodes (AD)
Limited series (drama) directed by Maria Schrader, with Shira Haas, Amit Rahav, Jeff Wilbusch, Alex Reid, Ronit Asheri, Delia Mayer, Dina Doron, David Mandelbaum, Gera Sandler and Eli Rosen.

A young woman tries to flee her suffocating ultra-Orthodox sect in this fine coming-of-age drama. Based loosely on Deborah Feldman's memoir, *Unorthodox* feels at times like an immersive documentary about the price of individual freedom when one's life has been defined by community.
▶▶ Pairs well with *Shtisel*

Unpregnant
PG-13, 2020
HBO Max original, 1 hr 43 mins (AD)

Movie (comedy) directed by Rachel Lee Goldenberg, with Haley Lu Richardson, Barbie Ferreira, Alex MacNicoll, Breckin Meyer, Giancarlo Esposito and Mary McCormack.

A high schooler convinces her ex-pal to take a road trip to New Mexico for her abortion. Marrying the story line of *Juno* to a goofy road-trip comedy is certainly one way to wade into the waters of a heavy, controversial topic, but *Unpregnant* pulls it off. Indeed, the movie works because of the friendship that's repaired over the course of this rollicking trip to a faraway abortion clinic.

UnREAL

TV-MA, 2015–2018
Hulu, 4 seasons, 38 episodes
Drama created by Sarah Gertrude Shapiro, with Shiri Appleby, Constance Zimmer, Craig Bierko, Jeffrey Bowyer-Chapman, Brennan Elliott, Genevieve Buechner, Josh Kelly and Donavon Stinson.

This scripted series about the making of a reality dating show has far more truth and reality to it than *The Bachelor* ever did. This is no mere *Bachelor* parody. It's trenchant drama that casts a light on how some reality shows are created. Shapiro, a producer on 9 cycles of *The Bachelor*, sets *UnREAL* at an imagined dating show called *Everlasting*, but many of the appalling decisions we see made by the producers ring true. The backstage drama is led by producers Quinn (Zimmer), a *House of Cards*-level villain who will stop at nothing to get what she wants on the air; and Rachel (Appleby), who's much more conflicted about her job. The media is usefully co-indicted for ignoring the manipulations that go into scenes that are presented as "real" on the show.

🏆 Peabody Award

Unsolved Mysteries

TV-MA, 2020–present
Netflix original, 2 seasons, 12 episodes (AD)
Docuseries.

Smart choices went into the reboot of this TV classic that helped invent the true-crime genre. Dating back to the 1980s, revived for cable TV twice, hosted by Robert Stack, then Dennis Farina, this long-running series about anything mysterious — whether supernatural encounters, unexplained disappearances or just plain unsolved crimes — was brought back by the show's original creators for Netflix. Teaming with the producers of *Stranger Things*, they chose not to replace the actors (now both deceased) with a new narrator, but let the talking heads move the story along. And the show now focuses on just one case per episode. But the same suspenseful storytelling is there and the refreshed version of the original, iconic theme song will be instantly recognizable.

The Up Series

TV-14, 1964–present
BritBox, 9 episodes
Docuseries directed by Michael Apted.
Roger Ebert called Michael Apted's decades-spanning documentary series "the noblest project in cinema history" — but it's actually a TV show. On assignment for Granada Television in 1964, Apted helped profile a group of 7-year-olds whose contrasting backgrounds showed the realities of Britain's class system. Having made that point and the special *7 Up*, Apted returned every 7 years for check-ins, titled *14 Up*, *21 Up* and so on. The series has only improved with age. Those who agreed to continue taking part (some didn't) added the twists and turns of their own seemingly ordinary stories to what, in the aggregate, formed an epic narrative that

Some shows may have moved; see page 183.

was more spellbinding as it went on. By the time of the latest installment *63 Up*, the *Up* series had come to be as much about the relationships the subjects had developed with the audience and Apted as their own lives, making it the first modern reality TV show. Apted's death in 2021 leaves the franchise's future in doubt, but with longtime producer Claire Lewis still in touch with many of the subjects, why can't the show go on?

Upload

TV-MA, 2020–present
Prime Video original, 10 episodes (AD)
Sci-fi comedy created by Greg Daniels, with Robbie Amell, Andy Allo, Allegra Edwards, Zainab Johnson, Kevin Bigley, Owen Daniels, Andrea Rosen, Chris Williams and Jessica Tuck.

Greg Daniels's Amazon comedy is a worthy successor to shows like *The Good Place* and *Forever*. Oh no, another comedy about the afterlife. But it's in good hands with Daniels, who developed the Steve Carell version of *The Office*. Nathan (Amell), a programmer who meets an untimely death, is able to access a luxurious afterlife thanks to his wealthy girlfriend, Ingrid (Edwards). Now add Nora (Allo), a human being who works for the tech company in charge of the afterlife and who communicates with Nathan through virtual reality. It makes for a strange but appealing love triangle across the unbridgeable chasm of life and death. *Upload* is funnier than *Forever* but also is effective at keeping up the techno-corporate mystery surrounding Nathan's death.

Utopia

TV-MA, 2020
Prime Video original, 8 episodes (AD)
Limited series (dystopian drama) created by Gillian Flynn, with John Cusack, Sasha Lane, Ashleigh LaThrop, Dan Byrd,

Desmin Borges, Christopher Denham, Farrah Mackenzie, Cory Michael Smith, Jeanine Serralles and Rainn Wilson.

After pooling their money to buy an extremely rare comic book, a group of fans discover that it contains dangerous secrets about a global conspiracy. Showrunner Gillian Flynn wrote the novels *Gone Girl* and *Sharp Objects*, and she's right at home in this densely plotted, staggeringly violent tale about the threat of communal panic. Viewers were mixed about how well the narrative played out over the course of 8 episodes. What's beyond dispute is that a drama in 2020 involving the release of engineered diseases was the entertainment that pandemic paranoia deserved.

Vacation Friends

R, 2021
Hulu original, 1 hr 43 mins (AD)
Movie (comedy) with Lil Rel Howery, Yvonne Orji, John Cena and Meredith Hagner.

Hijinks ensue when a couple's wedding gets crashed by the friends they made during a drunken vacation. Streaming TV favorites Howery and Orji play the straitlaced couple who meet a pair of serious partiers (Cena and Hagner) while vacationing in Mexico and let it all hang out — a decision they will regret months later. A sequel is already in the works.

The Vampire Diaries

TV-14, 2009–2017
Netflix, 8 seasons, 171 episodes
Fantasy drama created by Kevin Williamson and Julie Plec, with Paul Wesley, Ian Somerhalder, Nina Dobrev, Kat Graham, Candice King, Zach Roerig, Michael Trevino, Steven R. McQueen and Matthew Davis.

A teenage girl from small-town Virginia gets pulled into a love triangle with a pair of vampire brothers. Kevin

Williamson shows the same flair for family drama and heated adolescent emotion that he brought to *Dawson's Creek*, so it's no wonder fans went wild for the undead Salvatore brothers and Elena, the girl they both love. Eventually, the show's sprawling network of supporting characters became so rich and entertaining that a group of them got their own spinoff, *The Originals*.

Vanity Fair
TV-14, 2018
Prime Video original, 7 episodes (AD)
Limited series (historical drama) with Olivia Cooke, Tom Bateman, Claudia Jessie, Johnny Flynn, Charlie Rowe, Martin Clunes, David Fynn, Ellie Kendrick, Frances de la Tour and Michael Palin.

Thackeray's 19th-century satirical novel gets a lavish adaptation headlined by Olivia Cooke's turn as enterprising schemer Becky Sharp. After failing to climb the ranks of high-society London, Becky must resort to becoming a governess in the countryside, where in Sir Pitt Crawley's (Clunes) employ, she finds opportunities for advancement, finding favor with Sir Pitt's wealthy sister Matilda (de la Tour) and his son Rawdon (Bateman).

📡 **From our forums:** "Becky is actually quite a difficult character to get right. She is coming across as self-interested but not mean-spirited. You can see why people want her to do well." "I read the novel years ago and know most of what is coming up, but the wonderful performances have me hooked."

Veep
TV-MA, 2012–2019
HBO Max, 7 seasons, 65 episodes
Sitcom created by Armando Iannucci, with Julia Louis-Dreyfus, Anna Chlumsky, Tony Hale, Reid Scott, Timothy Simons, Matt Walsh, Sufe Bradshaw, Kevin Dunn, Gary Cole and Hugh Laurie.

Julia Louis-Dreyfus won 6 Emmys for her all-in portrayal of a grasping, amoral vice president from the Party of Awesomely Sick Burns. A gleefully foul-mouthed political satire and uproarious workplace comedy rolled into one, *Veep* follows Selina Meyer (Louis-Dreyfus), a calculating opportunist who wanted to be president but settled for the East Wing instead. There she and her aides haplessly attempt to, as they say, make a difference in Washington. Accompanying their madcap antics and failed schemes are some of the sharpest and most savage portrayals of Washington political culture anywhere.

📡 **From our forums:** "OMG, this show brings me so much joy. Oh, these people are so horrible." "This show makes me tired. So many press conferences, doctor visits, staff meetings, personnel updates. No wonder Selina is a hot mess."

🏆 17 Emmys including best comedy series (3 wins), Peabody Award

The Velvet Underground
R, 2021
Apple TV+ original, 2 hrs 1 mins (AD)
Movie (documentary) directed by Todd Haynes.

Todd Haynes's documentary viscerally recreates the 1960s New York art scene that birthed a legendary band. Using archival footage and the recollections of the people who were there, Haynes plants us inside Andy Warhol's Factory, a haven of creative freedom where the Velvet Underground had room to create a sound that would inspire generations. Frontman Lou Reed died in 2013, but John Cale, Reed's musical counterpart in the band, proves to be a phenomenal storyteller with a mellifluous Welsh voice. Haynes's fractured visual presentation, where the screen might at any moment be showing three multiple images at a time, conveys how so many disparate elements merged into one cultural moment.

Veneno
TV-MA, 2020
HBO Max original, 8 episodes (AD)

Limited series (drama) with Lola Rodríguez, Isabel Torres, Paca la Piraña and Daniela Santiago.

Upbeat, absorbing biopic of Spain's beloved transgender icon offers a complicated but ultimately positive portrayal of a trans woman who battled her way to public recognition. Known as La Veneno, Cristina Ortiz Rodríguez was a singer, TV star and transgender icon in her native Spain, and her life is recounted in this Spanish-language series. Played by three transgender actresses at different stages of her life, Cristina (Santiago in her La Veneno years) recounts her life to journalist Valeria Vegas (Rodríguez), who herself will come out as a trans woman. Some reenactments border on the surreal, but those are offset by the true-to-life performances of these transgender women supporting each other as they reinvent themselves.

Veronica Mars
TV-14, 2004–2019
Hulu, 4 seasons, 72 episodes (AD)

Crime drama with Kristen Bell, Jason Dohring, Enrico Colantoni, Percy Daggs III, Francis Capra, Ryan Hansen and Tina Majorino.

One of the more remarkable survival acts in television, this lovable noir drama about a student moonlighting as a PI was kept afloat by devoted fans and eventually earned a reboot. Even now, the mysteries are still juicy, the characters are still lovable and Bell's performance as the indomitable lead remains one for the ages. *Veronica Mars* was that all-too-rare show that makes being smart and basically

decent look incredibly cool. This show may have history's most effective fans, considering their Kickstarter donations funded a followup movie and their ongoing loyalty led to a revival season 12 years after the original.

A Very English Scandal
TV-14, 2018
Prime Video original, 3 episodes (AD)

Limited series (historical drama) directed by Stephen Frears, with Hugh Grant, Ben Whishaw, Alex Jennings, Patricia Hodge and Paul Bettany.

Hugh Grant digs into this role as a British politician who wants an ex-lover rubbed out before he exposes their relationship. Based on the true story of Jeremy Thorpe — a Liberal MP whose closeted affair with young Norman Scott in the 1960s was kept hidden for years — this adaptation by Russell T. Davies opts for a cheery, buoyant tone that makes a mockery of English manners, as it becomes clear that Thorpe will do just about anything to keep this explosive scandal pushed down at all costs. The fact that Grant seems to be relishing every scene, including the attempt to execute the dirty deed that goes terribly awry, only adds to the fun.

Victoria
TV-PG, 2016–2019
Prime Video, PBS Passport, 3 seasons, 25 episodes (AD)

Historical drama with Jenna Coleman, Tom Hughes, Rufus Sewell, Diana Rigg, Alex Jennings, David Oakes, Nell Hudson, Anna Wilson-Jones, Nigel Lindsay and Tommy Knight.

A fresh and lively look at England's 19th-century queen in the early years of her reign. To understand Queen Victoria's hold over the British imagination, this series argues, is to understand her not as a dowdy matriarch but as a youthful, exuberant, canny leader embodying her empire's industrial-age ambitions. Also, she loved her Albert dearly. This is PBS drama at its best.

Vida
TV-MA, 2018–2020
Starz original, 3 seasons, 22 episodes
Drama with Melissa Barrera, Mishel Prada, Ser Anzoategui, Chelsea Rendon, Carlos Miranda and Roberta Colindrez.

A single-camera adult comedy written, produced by and starring Latinx talent is so rare in American TV that it's reason enough to check out *Vida*, but the show has many other things to commend it. Two sisters return to their home in East L.A. after their mother dies, only to learn a secret their mom had been keeping from them. The women revisit old loves and make new lovers, all in the very specific context of Mexican-American life and culture, as seen from the perspectives of two very different sisters whose acclimation to the white world comes into sharp focus now that they're back home.

🐾 **From our forums:** "I love that fact that both sisters own their sexuality and are unapologetic about it. Love the Spanglish — reminds me of home."

The Vietnam War
TV-MA, 2017
PBS Passport, Hoopla, 10 episodes (AD)
Docuseries directed by Ken Burns and Lynn Novick, with Peter Coyote.

A characteristically stellar, if uncharacteristically controversial, visual and oral history of America's most contentious foreign war from Ken Burns and Lynn Novick. This ambitious "film" (outside Burns World, it's a limited series) is a tapestry of stories that seek to personalize the Vietnam War much as Burns did the Civil War — with perspectives from both sides of the conflict. Persons who directed, covered and fought the Vietnam War are all included. What's not included, as some commentators pointed out, is any suggestion that U.S. involvement in Vietnam, Cambodia and Laos had any merit or was anything other than a tragic adventure. Assuming you agree with this viewpoint, you'll find the interviewees appealing and the series compelling.

Vikings
TV-MA, 2013–2020
Prime Video original, 6 seasons, 89 episodes (AD)
Historical drama created by Michael Hirst, with Katheryn Winnick, Gustaf Skarsgård, Alexander Ludwig, Georgia Hirst, Alex Høgh Andersen, Jordan Patrick Smith, Marco Ilsø, Peter Franzén, Travis Fimmel and Clive Standen.

Inspired by the life of Norse hero Ragnar Lothbrok, this rollicking fan favorite follows Ragnar and his family as they upend kings and lords across North America and Europe. Though Travis Fimmel is swashbucklingly (and knee-bucklingly) great as Ragnar, *Vikings* isn't an in-depth character study into what drove a simple peasant to become a voyager and warrior-king. And despite the fact it aired in the U.S. on the History channel, there's a lot historically wrong with *Vikings*. No matter; this is an energetic portrayal of a movement that rose up unexpectedly to reset the balance of Western power in the ninth century.

🐾 **From our forums:** "Thank you, *Vikings*. You made me much more curious about how the Vikings lived, their journeys and their traditions. You went out on a relatively high note and respected your audience."

▶▶ Netflix is set to unveil the spinoff *Vikings: Valhalla*, also created by Hirst, in 2022.

Virgin River
TV-14, 2019–present
Netflix original, 3 seasons,
30 episodes (AD)
Romance drama with Alexandra Breckenridge, Martin Henderson, Colin Lawrence, Jenny Cooper, Lauren Hammersley, Tim Matheson, Grayson Maxwell Gurnsey, Sarah Dugdale, Benjamin Hollingsworth and Annette O'Toole.

Quirky, romantic and scenic, *Virgin River* will appeal to romcom and *Northern Exposure* fans alike. Nurse/midwife Mel (Breckinridge) shows up in a small Northern California town (it's shot in Vancouver) to take over for aging Doc (Otter from *Animal House*) at the behest of his ex-wife Hope (Lana Lang in *Superman III*). Mel has left L.A. under mysterious circumstances and is looking for a fresh start. Naturally she ends up in the only bar in town which happens to be owned by Kurt Russell lookalike Jack (Henderson) and there's instant chemistry. Mel struggles to win Doc over and fit into the idyllic looking hamlet as we discover the quirks of the locals and the secrets they're hiding. Based on the series by novelist Robyn Carr.

Visible: Out on Television
TV-MA, 2020
Apple TV+ original, 5 episodes (AD)
Docuseries created by David Bender and Wilson Cruz, with Wilson Cruz, Wanda Sykes, Margaret Cho, Anderson Cooper, Ilana Glazer, Abbi Jacobson, Carson Kressley, Janet Mock and Billy Porter.

More than a docuseries about gays on TV, *Visible* expands and improves the history of American television. This lovingly crafted 5-part docuseries shows how every step of America's evolution to LGBTQ acceptance was televised. Cruz and Bender spent 7 years piecing together interviews and footage of news

and entertainment programs dating back to the early 1950s to tell its story from both sides of the screen — the people making TV, as well as those consuming it. The result is a thoroughly convincing revisionist history that shows how the journey of gay people from pariahs to pathbreakers wasn't obvious and required both ingenuity and courage.

Voir
TV-MA, 2021–present
Netflix original, 6 episodes (AD)
Docuseries created by David Fincher and David Prior.

David Fincher's ode to cinema explores the relationship between film and the audiences that interpret it. With this docuseries Netflix adds to its movie appreciation micro-genre (*The Movies That Made Us*). Fincher — who directed cinema classics *Se7en* and *Fight Club* before moving to Netflix with *Mindhunter* and *Mank* — calls on six filmmakers and critics to compose paeans to films that changed their lives. Walter Chaw's episode on *48 Hours*, with its racial deconstruction of Walter Hill's buddy film, is a standout, showing how Hill and star Eddie Murphy were working on a higher level than many of the film's fans even realize.

The Vow
TV-MA, 2020
HBO Max, 9 episodes (AD)
Limited series (true crime) with Mark Vicente, Sarah Edmondson, Bonnie Piesse, Catherine Oxenberg and Anthony Ames.

The most complete documentary account of NXIVM, the multi-level marketing organization and sex cult. Two former high-ranking officials, Sarah Edmondson and Mark Vicente, take us deep inside NXIVM. Vicente shot hours of video footage, allowing us to see for ourselves how NXIVM leaders Keith

Raniere and Nancy Salzman used their followers' desire to improve themselves to manipulate them into shocking depths of self-abasement. Beyond the accusations of sexual humiliation and branding, what makes *The Vow* worth the multi-episode build is that it lays bare the process by which intelligent, well-intentioned people get sucked into cults.

▶▶ A planned followup, *The Vow: Part 2*, is expected in 2022.

▶▶ For suggestions of related shows, see "If You Liked *The Vow*," page 378.

Waiting for "Superman"
PG, 2010
Netflix, 1 hr 51 mins
Movie (documentary) directed by Davis Guggenheim, with Geoffrey Canada, Michelle Rhee and Randi Weingarten.

The director of *An Inconvenient Truth* made a passionate plea for charter schools that proved just as divisive as his climate-change film. Davis Guggenheim made this documentary to show how at-risk children are better served when they win the lottery that allows them to bypass ordinary public schools and attend charters instead. His film was condemned by teachers' unions on its release in 2010 and the charter movement has since stalled, but Guggenheim's argument for shaking up inner-city education remains strong.

▶▶ Guggenheim also has an impressive record in series TV that includes directing the pilot of *Deadwood*.

The Walking Dead
TV-14, 2010–present
AMC+, Netflix, PlutoTV, 11 seasons, 177 episodes
Dystopian drama created by Frank Darabont, with Andrew Lincoln, Norman Reedus, Melissa McBride, Lauren Cohan, Josh McDermitt, Christian Serratos, Danai Gurira, Seth Gilliam and Jeffrey Dean Morgan.

What does a zombie apocalypse do to the survivors? That's the core question that animates this powerhouse franchise. With undead "walkers" roaming the countryside looking for victims, humans must do more than survive. They must find meaning in the new normal, forming communities of resistance — even if that means resisting other communities who view the same existential threat in starkly different ways. Though *Jericho* gave a taste of what that grim feudalistic future might look like, *The Walking Dead* explored it in greater scope and depth. Plus, zombies! For 8 seasons much of the drama went through Rick Grimes (Lincoln), a sheriff's deputy and leader of a group of survivors defending themselves not only against zombies but other anti-zombie militias, all the while trying to find love and meaning in the new normal. Rick's place was later taken by Daryl (Reedus), a fan favorite who will be part of a planned *Walking Dead* spinoff series in 2023.

▶▶ Many TV critics were not sold on this adaptation of the popular comic book series, especially not on AMC, the prestige home of *Mad Men*. But viewers flocked to *The Walking Dead*, breaking all records for a cable drama series.

WandaVision
TV-PG, 2021
Disney+ original, 9 episodes (AD)
Limited series (superhero drama), with Elizabeth Olsen, Paul Bettany, Kathryn Hahn, Teyonah Parris, Randall Park, Kat Dennings, Debra Jo Rupp, Asif Ali and Evan Peters.

Marvel's first TV series from its Cinematic Universe won over a lot of non-comic-book fans, thanks to its nifty premise and an appealing storyline. After the events of *Avengers: Endgame*, superheroes Wanda (Olsen) and The

Vision (Bettany) take up the black-and-white life in suburbia. It's a wonderful sendup of early sitcoms, with a strong *Pleasantville* vibe; there's even a wacky neighbor (Hahn) always popping in to say hi. But then things take off in weird new directions; illusions are shattered; and the inner emotional life of a superhero — something Marvel films never were much interested in — becomes the focus of this remarkable epic and takes its appeal far beyond the comic universe.

💬 **From our forums:** "This show is the best, most ambitious and most emotionally resonant thing the Marvel Cinematic Universe has made."

🏆 3 Emmys

Wanderlust
TV-MA, 2018
Netflix original, 6 episodes (AD)
Comedy-drama created by Nick Payne, with Toni Collette, Steven Mackintosh, Joe Hurst, Emma D'Arcy, Zawe Ashton, Celeste Dring, Isis Hainsworth, Royce Pierreson, Kate O'Flynn and Paul Kaye.

The always-watchable Toni Collette boosts this British series about a couple entering into an open marriage. No offense to Payne, who does a fine job adapting his stage play (that has nothing to do with the 2012 film of the same name), but the exploration of polyamory in *Wanderlust* is less interesting than watching Collette explore middle age. Once Joy (Collette) and hubby Paul (Mackintosh) decide to put a little spice in their marriage — and how they get there, as they say, is complicated — the story then becomes one about longing and regret, and this is where Collette shines.

Watch the Sound with Mark Ronson
TV-MA, 2021
Apple TV+ original, 6 episodes (AD)
Docuseries with Mark Ronson.

A Grammy-winning producer takes you inside the recording studio for immersive lessons about the technology that shapes today's popular music. In four right-sized episodes, Ronson combines interviews with top recording artists and music engineers, plus his own wealth of producing experience, to vastly expand viewers' understanding of Auto-Tune, sampling and other technologies that go into today's popular music. The experience is enlightening and a lot of fun, regardless of how you feel about the songs themselves.

⏩ Pairs well with *Song Exploder*

Watchmen
TV-MA, 2019
HBO Max, 9 episodes (AD)
Limited series (drama) created by Damon Lindelof, with Regina King, Yahya Abdul-Mateen II, Jeremy Irons, Louis Gossett Jr., Jean Smart, Tim Blake Nelson, Hong Chau, Don Johnson, Jovan Adepo and James Wolk.

Who'd have guessed that this wildly expansive superhero story would teach so many viewers about the 1921 Tulsa race riot? Set in an alternate history, *Watchmen* is based on an iconic graphic novel story about masked heroes who have been outlawed for their perceived threat to society. In modern-day Tulsa, Oklahoma, in 2019, Detective Angela Abar (King) combats racially motivated violence in her community, resisting white supremacy as both an officer and — secretly — a hero with surprising ties to other outcast vigilantes. There are many tonal shifts through the 9 episodes, with stylistic flourishes and forays into everything from noir cinema to parody. But it will largely be remembered for its opening scene, a recreation of the bloody Tulsa massacre in which whites firebombed an entire Black neighborhood, killing hundreds.

▶▶ For suggestions of related shows, see "If You Liked *Watchmen*," page 378.

🏆 Peabody Award; 11 Emmys; TCA Award for best new program

The Water Man
PG, 2020
Netflix, Hoopla, 1 hr 31 mins (AD)
Movie (family comedy) directed by David Oyelowo, with David Oyelowo, Rosario Dawson, Alfred Molina, Lonnie Chavis and Maria Bello.

After his mother gets sick, a boy embarks on a quest to find a man he's heard has magical healing powers. Oyelowo also directs this moving and beautifully made film.

The Way Down
TV-MA, 2021–2022
HBO Max original, 5 episodes (AD)
Docuseries directed by Marina Zenovich.

Weight loss meets Jesus in this spellbinding profile of a 21st-century guru whose ministry drew thousands before going off the rails. The subtitle is "God, Greed and the Cult of Gwen Shamblin" and while the word "cult" gets tossed around too casually these days —one person's cult is another person's tight-knit community — there's little doubt that Gwen Shamblin Lara created a powerful tribe around the idea of dropping pounds for the Lord. But as she transitioned her extremely loyal following to a megachurch, Shamblin developed an unhealthy appetite for cash and used her undeniable charisma on her followers to feed her need.

▶▶ Zenovich (whose *Roman Polanski: Wanted and Desired*, not streamable, is the definitive work on the disgraced director and explores similar themes of attraction and manipulation) was putting the finishing touches on this docuseries when Shamblin was killed in a plane crash. As a result *The Way Down* will add 2 episodes

in 2022.

We Are Lady Parts
TV-MA, 2021–present
Peacock original, 6 episodes (AD)
British comedy with Anjana Vasan, Sarah Kameela Impey, Faith Omole, Lucie Shorthouse, Aiysha Hart and Juliette Motamed.

A dorky PhD student is recruited to play lead guitar for a Muslim female punk band called Lady Parts and unleashes a hidden side of herself, as well as some wicked licks. Part of a welcome wave of female ensemble comedies, this creation from writer-director Nida Manzoor subverts stereotypes about Muslim women by portraying the bond between five ladies in traditional garb who just want to rock.

🗨 **From our forums:** "The cast is great — love that the parents are actually more secular than the younger generation — the songs are hilarious but good at the same time." "When marginalized people are allowed to tell their stories without being whitewashed or viewed from a white gaze, you get full, rich stories and great shows."

We Are the Champions
TV-MA, 2020–present
Netflix original, 6 episodes (AD)
Docuseries with Rainn Wilson.

Unabashedly feel-good look at humans who strive to be the very best at obscure competitions. Each episode takes a half-hour deep dive into an obscure or idiosyncratic competition. Wilson's serene narration lends the proceedings gravitas, even when the contest in question is inherently ridiculous (frog jumping) or disgusting (eating hot chili peppers); the Wes Anderson–manqué titles and art direction contribute to a sense of timelessness.

We Are Who We Are

TV-MA, 2020
HBO Max, 8 episodes (AD)
Drama directed by Luca Guadagnino, with Jack Dylan Grazer, Jordan Kristine Seamón, Kid Cudi, Francesca Scorsese, Spence Moore II, Faith Alabi and Chloë Sevigny.

European director offers a fresh take on the coming-of-age genre that captures the drift and delight of teenagerdom. Fraser (Grazer)'s family — he has two moms, one of whom is a colonel (Sevigny) — has just moved from New York City to an Italian military base. He soon connects with his next-door neighbor Caitlin (Seamón), who's the same age, and as they get closer, rather than lose themselves in each other, they become more articulate about themselves. Their pointed conversations, plus seaside cinematography and stylish music, carry this unorthodox show along.

🐟 **From our forums:** "What a weird show with weird people. Yet I will keep watching — it seems like a cross between *Euphoria* and *My Brilliant Friend*."

We Are: The Brooklyn Saints

TV-14, 2021–present
Netflix original, 4 episodes (AD)
Docuseries directed by Rudy Valdez.

Kids in a hardscrabble part of NYC are molded into one of the nation's premier pee-wee football teams by a group of hard-working Black men. At first director Valdez seems to be making a feel-good docuseries about boys and football. But soon it's clear his real subject is the men who coach them — working-class New Yorkers who see it as their mission to mold the next generation of men, through football and the camaraderie that comes from building a team. You do wonder, though, if there are better ways to build social capital than having small boys running into each other.

We're Here

TV-MA, 2020–present
HBO Max, 2 seasons, 14 episodes (AD)
Reality show with Shangela, Bob the Drag Queen and Eureka O'Hara.

Feel-good show about superstar drag queens who win over rural America one small town at a time. In each episode Shangela, Eureka and Bob the Drag Queen roll into a small American town in full makeup-and-gown regalia. After selecting local residents to adopt as "drag daughters," they go through several days of makeovers, rehearsals and intimate conversations, culminating in the baby queens' very first drag performance for friends and neighbors. The show's upbeat tone tends to gloss over whatever pushback the queens might be getting from the townsfolk, emphasizing instead that open-hearted people live everywhere.

The Wedding Coach

TV-MA, 2021–present
Netflix original, 6 episodes (AD)
Reality show with Jamie Lee.

Comedian Jamie Lee solves couples' wedding-related conundrums in a refreshing reality show that actually tries to *lower* the drama. As Lee says at the outset, "Wedding perfection is unattainable … but wedding stress is real." Whether setting up centerpieces or helping couples navigate family squabbles, *The Wedding Coach* seems less concerned with turning personal drama into entertainment than it is with ending the episode with cathartic hugs and the relief of having dodged another bridezilla moment. (Whether or not the wedding itself went off without a hitch seems almost immaterial.) Cameos from comedians like Fortune Feimster help lighten the load and keep things in perspective.

Weiner

R, 2016
AMC+, 1 hr 36 mins
Movie (documentary) directed by Josh Kriegman and Elyse Steinberg.

Fly-on-the-wall account of congressional leader Anthony Weiner's career as it unravels is a sad reminder that one will go far in politics these days by being a dick (just don't show it off). Never one to say "turn off the camera," the onetime rising star in liberal politics allowed a film crew to document his self-immolation, as women came forward with inappropriate texts he sent them in between appearances on MSNBC and the House floor. Appearing in theaters the same year that Donald Trump was on the ticket, *Weiner* served as a reminder that celebrity — whether in business, entertainment, religion or politics — is a largely amoral force.

🏆 Sundance Film Festival's Grand Jury Prize

Welcome to Chechnya

TV-MA, 2020
HBO Max, 1 hr 47 mins (AD)
Movie (documentary) directed by David France.

A grim account of how queer people are being hunted down, tortured and killed in the breakaway republic — and the effort by activists to stop it. Another important film from director David France (*How to Survive a Plague*), these profiles in courage are enhanced thanks to the use of digital alteration, (which Martin Scorsese used in *The Irishman)*. This conceals the identity of its subjects while allowing us to see their emotions.

The West Wing

TV-14, 1999–2006
HBO Max, 7 seasons, 155 episodes
Drama created by Aaron Sorkin, with Allison Janney, John Spencer, Bradley

Whitford, Martin Sheen, Janel Moloney, Richard Schiff, Dulé Hill, Joshua Malina, Stockard Channing and Rob Lowe.

Call Aaron Sorkin's White House drama liberal, call it utopian, but as long as he was writing it, you could never call it dull. At the time it was an antidote for the moral mess that was the Clinton presidency, set in an alternate America where speeches still had the power to sway voters off the fence, and political leaders said what they believed and did what they said, most of the time. Sheen lent the show *gravitas* but the show was loaded with talent.

▶▶ Seasons 1–4 were notable for long scenes of dialogue between people tracked by a camera as they fast-walked through twisting corridors. And the dialogue had more laughs than most sitcoms of the age. Then Sorkin left.

🏆 26 Emmys including four wins for outstanding drama series and four for Janney as lead actress in a drama; 2 Peabody Awards

WeWork: Or the Making and Breaking of a $47 Billion Unicorn

TV-MA, 2021
Hulu original, 1 hr 44 mins (AD)
Movie (documentary) directed by Jed Rothstein.

The inside story of how a co-working startup rapidly transformed into a darling of Wall Street and how its founder's cult of personality ultimately undid the company. American business lore is replete with the stories of those who tried to game the system, from the directors of Enron to Bernie Madoff to Elizabeth Holmes. WeWork, led by a charismatic Israeli named Adam Neumann, convinced a large Japanese bank to fund its massive expansion into commercial real estate for its plan to dominate co-working office space. Despite gushing billions in red ink, Neumann convinced the market that it had a sound plan for the future. What's different about WeWork is that no crimes were committed; eventually investors dug into the company's financials and figuring out there was no there there. How that unfolded is the story here, told with a sure hand by Oscar nominee Jed Rothstein.

What Happened, Miss Simone?
TV-14, 2015
Netflix original, 1 hr 42 mins (AD)
Movie (documentary) directed by Liz Garbus, with Nina Simone and Lisa Simone Kelly.

This candid and stylish film explains why the aspiring jazz pianist, who became a leading protest voice in the 1960s, vanished from the public eye. From master documentarian Garbus comes the unvarnished truth behind the mysterious disappearance of Simone, done with the participation of Simone's daughter Kelly and other friends of the late singer. Almost as interesting is the story of how a classically trained pianist, whose first album was a sparkling revue of jazz standards, became the singer-songwriter of bracing civil-rights-era songs like "Mississippi Goddam."

🏆 Peabody Award, Emmy for best documentary

What the Health
TV-PG, 2017
Netflix, 1 hr 37 mins
Movie (documentary) directed by Kip Andersen and Keegan Kuhn.

Netflix's provocative salvo across the bow of Big Food is worth a watch even if you don't buy its pro-vegan agenda. As in his other films, *Cowspiracy* and *Seaspiracy*, director-narrator Andersen has two points he hammers home relentlessly: One, there are extreme environmental and nutritional costs to eating meat, dairy or fish — harms to our bodies, our oceans and our climate. Two, the medical and scientific groups that should be publicizing these harms have little incentive to do so because they rely heavily on support from multinational food companies. One doesn't have to accept this conspiracy theory, though, to be unsettled by the evidence Andersen presents of the downsides of the Western diet.

What We Do in the Shadows
TV-MA, 2019–present
Hulu, 3 seasons, 30 episodes (AD)
Sitcom created by Jemaine Clement, with Matt Berry, Kayvan Novak, Natasia Demetriou, Harvey Guillén and Mark Proksch.

Sublime mockumentary about roommates living in a *Real Housewives*-meets-vampire world. This small-screen take on Jemaine Clement and Taika Waititi's cult-hit 2014 film — with episodes written and directed by the original duo — keeps the best elements from the original concept and adds an appealing cast.

💬 **From our forums:** "The sheer absurdity of this show — that vampires have chore lists, live on Staten Island and go to Super Bowl parties, that the name Jackie Daytona is a thing — that's why I love this show."

The Wheel of Time
TV-14, 2021–present
Prime Video original, 8 episodes (AD)
Fantasy drama with Rosamund Pike, Daniel Henney, Madeleine Madden, Zoë Robins, Josha Stradowski, Marcus Rutherford, Barney Harris and Kate Fleetwood.

Rosamund Pike plays a woman of magic who must lead a group of five young people on a treacherous journey in the hopes that one of them is the chosen one. Based on the acclaimed fantasy novels by Robert Jordan, this big-budget blockbuster from Prime Video features the usual assortment of magic, mystical prophecies and monsters (including porcine ones). But maybe the best part of this epic adventure is that women are leading it.

🗨 **From our forums:** "Episode 4 was the best episode so far, good balance between exposition and action." "Sophie Okonedo exceeded my hopes for Siuan. She was everything."

When They See Us
TV-MA, 2019
Netflix original, 4 episodes (AD)

Limited series (drama) created by Ava DuVernay, with Jharrel Jerome, Asante Blackk, Caleel Harris, Marsha Stephanie Blake, Michael K. Williams, John Leguizamo, Aunjanue Ellis, Niecy Nash, Felicity Huffman and Vera Farmiga.

A dramatized version of the Central Park Five case offers painful lessons about how easy it is to succumb to mass hysteria over a sensational news story amplified by race. Director and co-writer Ava DuVernay has returned to the case of five teenagers falsely imprisoned for the rape and assault of a jogger in New York's Central Park in the 1980s. Though already the subject of an excellent documentary (*The Central Park Five*), viewers may be more deeply affected by this scripted treatment, which goes beyond the outrageous details of the case to show how years of imprisonment — inside a system built by mass incarceration, the subject of DuVernay's *13TH* documentary (see page 35) — stole precious years from the Black and Latino boys who were convicted.

🏆 Peabody Award, Critics Choice Award for best limited series

When We First Met
TV-14, 2018
Netflix original, 1 hr 37 mins (AD)

Movie (romantic comedy) with Adam Devine, Alexandra Daddario, Shelley Hennig, Andrew Bachelor and Robbie Amell.

Devine plays a guy who keeps going back in time to the moment he met the woman of his dreams, hoping he can make her fall for him. The *Groundhog Day* premise gets a sweet-natured update, and Devine's salty comic style gets to shine.

▶▶ Pairs well with *Palm Springs*

White Collar
TV-PG, 2009–2014
IMDb TV, Hulu, 6 seasons, 81 episodes

Comedy-drama with Matt Bomer, Tim DeKay, Willie Garson, Tiffani Thiessen and Sharif Atkins.

One of USA Network's enduring comic dramas starred Matt Bomer as a con artist who works off his prison sentence by helping an FBI agent capture white collar criminals. Bomer is a charm machine as Neal, and he has great chemistry with Dekay as the rumpled FBI agent. As with sidecar shows *Burn Notice* and *Psych*, well-written repartee is the main ingredient, but the cinematography and just-complex-enough criminal capers add flavor.

The White Lotus
TV-MA, 2021–present
HBO Max, 6 episodes (AD)

Anthology series (dark comedy) created by Mike White, with Connie Britton, Jennifer Coolidge, Alexandra Daddario, Jake Lacy, Steve Zahn, Murray Bartlett, Fred Hechinger, Brittany O'Grady, Natasha Rothwell and Sydney Sweeney.

Wicked sendup of white privilege revolves around guests at a Hawaiian resort who spend their time in Paradise

tearing each other to shreds. From the creator of the vastly underrated *Enlightened*, Mike White, comes this dark comedy about a handful of well-off white people who have checked in for a week of wellness at the White Lotus hotel. Their pampered, cloistered existence is what makes their interactions with each other and the staff so funny. Coolidge gives the performance of her life as, essentially, Sonja Morgan from *The Real Housewives of NYC*. Yet along with contemptible weakness, White never fails to find deep reserves of humanity in the unlikely characters and situations he creates.

Whitmer Thomas: The Golden One

TV-MA, 2020
HBO Max, 1 hr 3 mins
Comedy special directed by Whitmer Thomas and Clay Tatum, with Whitmer Thomas and Clay Tatum.

With original songs and storytelling, the Alabama native tries to make peace with being an "aging emo kid." This special earned glowing reviews because Thomas digs with depth and wit into his strange and occasionally tragic life.

Who Killed Malcolm X?

TV-MA, 2020
Netflix original, 6 episodes
Docuseries with Abdur-Rahman Muhammad, David Garrow, Jelani Cobb and Muhammad A. Aziz.

A remarkable story of perseverance and truth-telling about one of the 20th century's highest-profile killings. *Who Killed Malcolm X?* is that rarest of true-crime docs — a reexamination that leads to the exoneration of the wrongly convicted. For decades a respected independent scholar has been slowly chipping away at what actually happened on the morning of Feb. 21, 1965, when Malcolm X was assassinated while addressing a rally in Harlem. This riveting series exposes failures by law enforcement to seek justice in Malcolm's murder and makes the persuasive case that two innocent men went to prison (their convictions were overturned in 2021 after this series streamed on Netflix). We're also given a powerful summary of Malcolm's impact on Black America and what was lost on that day.

Wild Wild Country

TV-MA, 2018
Netflix original, 6 episodes (AD)
Limited series (true crime) directed by Chapman Way and Maclain Way.

A 1980s Oregon cult is at the center of one of the most jaw-dropping docuseries on Netflix — and that's saying something. Thousands of intentional communities, many of them religious, have formed on the uniquely fertile soil of the U.S. What powers them, and what usually causes them to unravel, are questions *Wild Wild Country* brings unusual insight to. This tautly assembled narrative of news footage and current interviews pieces together the strange story of the Bhagwan Shree Rajneesh, an Indian guru who relocated his ashram to rural Oregon in 1981. When the commune — in particular the guru's secretary, the power behind the power — starts asserting itself as a local power, the locals react poorly. Part social doc, part true-crime series, *Wild Wild Country* taps into everything we fear about cults.

🏆 Emmy for outstanding docuseries

The Wilds

TV-14, 2020–present
Prime Video original, 10 episodes (AD)
Teen drama with Sophia Ali, Shannon Berry, Jenna Clause, Reign Edwards, Mia Healey, Helena Howard, Erana James, Sarah Pidgeon, David Sullivan and Rachel Griffiths.

For a key to terms used in this section, see page 33.

This plane-crash-on-a-desert-island thriller has an ingenious twist: All the survivors are girls. The premise is familiar but almost nothing else feels that way, because this is that rare Hollywood drama made by young women for young women *about* young women. Though it's got the obligatory *Lost*-style intrigues (e.g., what invisible forces might be haunting the island), *The Wilds* is at its best when exploring the lives of the survivors and how this adventure will change them.

Will & Grace
TV-14, 1998–2020
Hulu, 11 seasons, 246 episodes
Classic sitcom with Eric McCormack, Debra Messing, Megan Mullally and Sean Hayes.

Don't bother with the 2016 reboot, but the earlier version of this sitcom, widely credited with bringing gay culture mainstream, still has its moments. Think of Messing and McCormack as a modern-day Lucy and Ricky, if Ricky were a gay lawyer and Lucy his straight interior decorator best friend and roommate. Rounding out the show's rapid-fire comedy troupe were Hayes as Will and Grace's flamboyantly gay actor neighbor and Mullally as Grace's alcoholic socialite boss. Some have criticized the show for reinforcing stereotypes, but in its heyday from 1998 to 2006, *Will & Grace* turned a lot of heads and paved the way for more nuanced gay portrayals in mainstream culture.

🏆 18 Emmys including best comedy series and individual acting awards for all four leads (2 wins for Mullally); 7 GLAAD media awards

The Wire
TV-MA, 2002–2008
HBO Max, 5 seasons, 60 episodes
Drama created by David Simon, with Dominic West, John Doman, Idris Elba, Wood Harris, Deirdre Lovejoy, Wendell Pierce, Lance Reddick, Aidan Gillen, Sonja Sohn, Seth Gilliam, Domenick Lombardozzi, Clarke Peters and Michael K. Williams.

A panoramic view of one broken American city at the dawn of the millennium, *The Wire* is the *Blonde on Blonde* of television drama: an instant classic that has only grown in stature over time. It's the sheer ambition of the show that makes it worth watching over and over. Superlative character drama meets multi-layered narrative, all with a novelist's ear for dialogue and a documentarian's eye into how institutions work and how they might fail. The list of memorable *Wire* characters is long and includes McNulty (West), whose preoccupation with busting Baltimore's drug gangs overrules any imperative to clean up his wretched personal life; gang leader Avon Barksdale (Harris), whose marginalization shows the futility of putting away kingpins so long as the pipeline stays open; Stringer Bell, a hustler-businessman played by Elba, who showed here the qualities that would establish him as a bankable star; the wild card, Omar Little (Williams), a freelance thug beholden to no one; Carcetti (Gillen), the reformer politician who swears everything is going to change when he's in charge … and the parade of characters went gloriously on and on for 5 seasons.
▶▶ *The Wire* topped BBC Culture's 2021 critics poll of the greatest TV series of the 21st century.

🏆 Peabody Award, TCA Heritage Award

Wit
PG-13, 2001
HBO Max, 1 hr 39 mins
Movie (drama) directed by Mike Nichols, with Emma Thompson, Audra McDonald, Christopher Lloyd, Eileen Atkins, Harold Pinter and Jonathan M. Woodward.

For shows sorted by streaming platform, see page 381.

Emma Thompson plays a woman with terminal cancer in this acclaimed performance of the Pulitzer-winning play. Thompson plays Vivian Bearing, a brilliant, funny and determined-not-to-be-terrified woman who often speaks directly to the camera as she confronts her experience with cancer.

🏆 Peabody Award; 3 Emmys, including outstanding made for television movie and outstanding directing for a miniseries, movie or special (Nichols)

The Witcher
TV-MA, 2019–present
Netflix original, 2 seasons,
16 episodes (AD)
Fantasy drama with Henry Cavill, Anna Shaffer, Freya Allan, Simon Callow, Graham McTavish, Liz Carr, Chris Fulton, Kevin Doyle, Cassie Clare and Adjoa Andoh.

Henry Cavill alone is worth the price of admission in this fun, multi-layered fantasy world with notes of *Xena* and *Outlander*. Based on the Polish book series by Andrzej Sapkowski (which inspired a popular video game series), *The Witcher* introduces viewers to a mythological world where Cavill's character — a hunky bounty hunter who kills very interesting monsters — is surrounded by enchanting ladies whose backstories take up much of the action-packed, if messy, Season 1.

💬 **From our forums:** "Surprised over how humorous this show could be. One character even made a meta reference by pointing out how he was just basically there to do exposition."

▶▶ Pairs well with *Outlander*

Without Remorse
R, 2021
Prime Video original, 1 hr 49 mins (AD)
Movie (thriller) with Michael B. Jordan, Jodie Turner-Smith, Jamie Bell, Guy Pearce, Cam Gigandet, Brett Gelman and Colman Domingo.

While he's trying to avenge his wife's murder, a Navy SEAL gets sucked into a deadly conspiracy. Adapted from Tom Clancy's blockbuster novel, it hits the familiar thriller beats in a satisfying way.

Woke
TV-MA, 2020–present
Hulu original, 8 episodes (AD)
Comedy with Lamorne Morris, Blake Anderson, Sasheer Zamata, T. Murph, Rose McIver, J.B. Smoove, Eddie Griffin, Nicole Byer, Jack McBrayer and Keith David.

The hero of this tonally deft comedy-drama struggles to define himself as an artist and Black man while putting up with well-meaning white people. Based on cartoonist Keith Knight's life and work, *Woke* stars Morris as Keef, whose innocuous comic strips never touch on hot-button topics like race. When Keef has an encounter with the police, though, his cartoons start talking to him as some kind of post-traumatic response. Some of the voices are wokey, some are jokey (most are voiced by comedians like Smoove and Byer). Keef tries to sort it out in disarming conversations with his buds Clovis and Gunther (Murph and Anderson). *Woke* explores the awakening of a social conscience while trying not to take itself too seriously.

Wolf Hall
TV-14, 2015
PBS Passport, Hoopla, 6 episodes
Limited series (historical drama) with Mark Rylance, Damian Lewis, Claire Foy, Thomas Brodie-Sangster, Joss Porter, Bernard Hill, Hannah Steele, Jessica Raine, Jonathan Pryce and Anton Lesser.

Hilary Mantel's first 2 books about Thomas Cromwell are adapted into this sumptuous miniseries, which focuses on

his time as a trusted adviser to Henry VIII. Six hours feels like not enough time with Rylance's Cromwell, especially in his interactions with Lewis as Henry, Pryce as Wolsey and especially Lesser as Sir Thomas More.

🗨 **From our forums:** "This was the most frightening portrayal of Anne Boleyn's fall that I have seen. Claire Foy was just superb — the wide-eyed fear growing exponentially, while she struggled to maintain some dignity. This was great television, and Rylance in his stillness was commanding."

🏆 Peabody Award, 2 BAFTAs including best drama series

Wolf Like Me
TV-MA, 2022
Peacock original, 6 episodes
Drama-comedy created by Abe Forsythe, with Isla Fisher, Josh Gad, Ariel Donoghue and Emma Lung.

Josh Gad plays a depressed single dad and Isla Fisher the woman he meets by accident in this genre-defying sci-fi dramedy. Combining romance with dark comedy and elements of supernatural science fiction, *Wolf Like Me* pairs actors known more for their musical and comedic work in something more dramatic and spooky than they're used to. All this is to say that creator Forsythe (*Little Monsters*) struggles a bit to find a singular tone for this series. But it's a quick binge that sets up nicely for Season 2 should that occur, and Fisher and Gad have a natural chemistry that never leaves viewers wondering why these two damaged characters would be attracted to one another.

The Wolfpack
R, 2015
HBO Max, YouTube, Kanopy, 1 hr 30 mins
Movie (documentary) directed by Crystal Moselle.

A paranoid father kept his wife and their 13 children locked in their apartment for years — and then one of the boys escaped. Harrowing and hard-to-believe, this story of captivity and liberation is a case of headlines being ripped from a documentary instead of the other way around. Filmmaker Moselle had noticed some unusual-looking boys on the street, approached them and their incredible story came tumbling out.

▶▶ Pairs well with *Hear and Now*
🏆 Sundance Film Festival's Grand Jury Prize

Wolfwalkers
PG, 2020
Apple TV+ original, 1 hr 43 mins (AD)
Animated sci-fi film with Sean Bean, Maria Doyle Kennedy, Simon McBurney and Honor Kneafsey.

In this beautifully animated fable, an Irish girl who has promised to help destroy a pack of wolves meets a child who may very well turn into a wolf at night. One of those highly esteemed films that get overlooked because it doesn't air on Netflix or Disney+, the gorgeously animated *Wolfwalkers* is actually the third part of an Irish folklore trilogy from Cartoon Saloon. Sadly, Apple TV+ did not acquire the rights to the first 2 films, also Oscar–nominated, and only one is available for streaming, *The Secret of Kells* (Hoopla, Kanopy).

The Wonder Years (2021)
TV-PG, 2020–present
Hulu, 22 episodes (AD)
Family comedy with Elisha Williams, Dulé Hill, Saycon Sengbloh, Laura Kariuki, Amari O'Neil, Julian Lerner, Milan Ray and Don Cheadle.

Totally engaging remake of a show about the 1960s as seen through the eyes of a 12-year-old suburban boy … this time, he and his family are Black. What a difference 30 years makes. Television has a much more nuanced way of looking back in time than when Fred Savage starred in the original *Wonder Years*. With rich voiceovers by Cheadle and a real star in Williams (who no doubt benefited from Savage directing the pilot), this show draws you and takes you back to a perspective on a turbulent era you've never seen before.

Work in Progress
TV-MA, 2019–present
Showtime original, 2 seasons, 18 episodes
Comedy with Abby McEnany, Karin Anglin, Celeste Pechous and Theo Germaine.

Self-described "fat, queer dyke" Abby McEnany drives a truckload of personality through this semi-autobiographical comedy with a strong indie vibe. Abby's sitcom adventures bring her to the edge of either romantic breakthrough or depressive breakdown, depending on the day. Chris (Germaine), a trans man and Abby's love interest, complements her wonderfully. And McEnany isn't afraid to go meta: In the first 2 seasons she got Julia Sweeney and musician "Weird" Al Yankovic to play themselves so that Abby could confront them about their earlier portrayals of gender-fluid and fat people.

Workin' Moms
TV-MA, 2017–present
Netflix, 5 seasons, 57 episodes (AD)
Comedy created by Catherine Reitman, with Catherine Reitman, Jessalyn Wanlim, Dani Kind and Juno Rinaldi.

The not-so-life-affirming aspects of parenting are explored in this comedy with moments of poignant drama in between lactation gags. This Canadian series revolves around four women in a mommy support group who are struggling with postpartum psychosis, the financial challenges of raising a child and other relatable themes rarely explored on TV — like Reitman's character's guilt at actually enjoying her job while away from the kiddos. Tonally similar but with fewer episodes is *The Letdown*.

World on Fire
TV-14, 2019–present
PBS Passport, 7 episodes
Drama with Jonah Hauer-King, Helen Hunt, Sean Bean, Leslie Manville, Julia Brown, Zofia Wichlacz, Brian J. Smith, Parker Sawyers and Blake Harrison.

A group of loosely connected characters scattered across Europe navigate their personal secrets and the perils of living through the first year of World War II. It'd be easy to let the show's massive cast and tangle of storylines go undeveloped or fall into tropes, but *World on Fire* navigates its density with both narrative and moral clarity. The characters here are forced to make hard choices under the worst possible conditions, and the outcomes are oddly comforting in a classic PBS drama kind of way.

Wormwood
TV-14, 2017
Netflix original, 6 episodes (AD)
Limited series (drama) directed by Errol Morris, with Peter Sarsgaard, Christian Camargo, Molly Parker, Scott Shepherd, Tim Blake Nelson, Bob Balaban and Eric Olson.

Errol Morris explores the sketchy 1953 suicide of a Cold War scientist in an inventive miniseries. Frank Olson, who was doing biowarfare research for the CIA, fell to his death at New York's Statler Hotel. The press and his widow weren't told the truth about what happened, but the family pressed for 20 years until a White House aide named Dick Cheney told them a new story — which was also not true. In this artful blend of docudrama, featuring Sarsgaard as Frank, and interviews with Eric Olson, who believes his dad was murdered, Morris tries to piece together what really happened. His take is rather conspiratorial and regards the Cold War too lightly, but is fascinating to watch unfold.

The Worst Cooks in America
TV-G, 2010–present
Discovery+, Hulu, 22 seasons, 158 episodes
Reality competition with Anne Burrell, Beau MacMillan, Robert Irvine, Bobby Flay, Tyler Florence, Rachael Ray and Michael Symon.

Years before *Nailed It!* was this contest to see who could burn dinner the least. The difference is that the all-star chefs on this show perform cooking interventions in the hopes of improving what these Calamity Janes and Johns create in the kitchen. And the tone's sharper on *Worst Cooks*; the pros aren't afraid to dunk on the creations of the amateurs.

Wynonna Earp
TV-14, 2016–2021
Netflix, 4 seasons, 49 episodes
Fantasy drama created by Emily Andras, with Melanie Scrofano, Tim Rozon, Dominique Provost-Chalkley, Katherine Barrell, Varun Saranga and Greg Lawson.

Cult favorite based on the comic series about Wyatt Earp's great-granddaughter gives off 21st-century *Buffy* vibes. Set in the town of Purgatory, this supernatural Western had lots of genre potential and creator Andras delivered, filling the show's world with richly layered characters led by Wynonna (Scrofano), one the most well-drawn female leads the fantasy genre has seen. Two other notable female characters, Waverly (Provost-Chalkley) and Nicole (Barrell), show how to tell queer love

stories without resorting to tired screen clichés.

▶▶ Though never large, *Wynonna Earp*'s audience was passionate and had a close bond with the creator; Andras was known to assure nervous fans publicly that a favorite character wasn't being killed off. An epic fan campaign helped bring *Wynonna Earp* back for a fourth season and a satisfying finale.

Years And Years
TV-MA, 2019
HBO Max, 6 episodes (AD)
Limited series (drama) created by Russell T. Davies, with Emma Thompson, Rory Kinnear, T'Nia Miller, Russell Tovey, Jessica Hynes, Lydia West, Ruth Madeley and Anne Reid.

Emma Thompson plays a Donald Trump–esque prime minister in a dark if genre-busting serial that feels like an amalgam of *Black Mirror* and *This Is Us*. Russell T. Davies (creator of *Queer as Folk* among other shows) does an all-too-convincing job of projecting the world in 2019 forward to 2034, as a hundred simmering crises of our present day eventually grow into massive tire fires that politicians are helpless to combat but can still capitalize upon. This grim, dystopian vision of Western society is told through the lives of the intergenerational Lyons family, led by aspiring politician Vivian Rook (Thompson), who fancies herself the second coming of Trump or Nigel Farage or name-your-populist. Thompson is only the most famous name in a talented ensemble whose individual sagas, wound together in a typically bracing Davies narrative, make for an absorbing, if not exactly uplifting, watch.

Yellowjackets
TV-MA, 2021–present
Showtime original, 10 episodes

For shows sorted by streaming platform, see page 381. **321**

Thriller with Melanie Lynskey, Tawny Cypress, Christina Ricci and Juliette Lewis.

After a plane crash a girls soccer team survives for over 18 months in the wilderness and then decades later, as grown women, they come to terms with what they did to stay alive. If *The Wilds* was pieced together through a series of chilling flashbacks, it would be *Yellowjackets*. You'll likely find the story from the island more compelling than the years-later scenes involving the girls as adults.

Yellowstone

TV-MA, 2018–present
Peacock, 4 seasons, 37 episodes
Drama created by John Linson and Taylor Sheridan, with Kevin Costner, Kelly Reilly, Luke Grimes, Wes Bentley and Cole Hauser.

The show that critics were mild about, fans have been wild about. Costner plays Jack Dutton, widower and patriarch of the Dutton Ranch which, as we learn in the prequel *1883* (see page 38), has been in the family for generations. Jack will protect his family's assets and culture no matter what. He runs his own militia and tells state officials what to do, not the other way around. *Yellowstone's* many pleasures include its diverse cast, which includes politically connected Indians and the Duttons' salty ranch hands; its cinematic look, which restores our understanding of the West as both beautiful and forbidding; and the human interactions that bring both aggression and tenderness to almost every scene. Sheridan, who writes most episodes, has shown he can maintain a season-long story arc and finish strong.

▸▸ For suggestions of related shows, see "If You Liked *Yellowstone*," page 379.

Yes, Minister

TV-PG, 1980–1988
BritBox, 5 seasons, 39 episodes
British comedy with Paul Eddington, Nigel Hawthorne and Derek Fowlds.

The creator of *Veep* has cited as one of his inspirations this 1980s classic about a British Cabinet member with a habit of embarrassing himself. Eddington is a splendid doofus as Jim Hacker, who despite being handed a portfolio that's considered a political graveyard, manages to fail upward all the way to 10 Downing Street (the series title was updated to *Yes, Prime Minister* after that). You certainly don't have to understand UK politics or culture to get a kick out of this Britcom.

▸▸ *Yes, Minister* counted then-prime minister Margaret Thatcher among its fans. "Its clearly-observed portrayal of what goes on in the corridors of power has given me hours of pure joy," the Iron Lady declared.

🏆 7 BAFTAs

You

TV-MA, 2018–present
Netflix original, 3 seasons, 30 episodes (AD)
Crime drama created by Greg Berlanti and Sera Gamble, with Penn Badgley, Victoria Pedretti, Elizabeth Lail, Ambyr Childers, James Scully, Saffron Burrows, Travis Van Winkle, Kathryn Gallagher and Scott Speedman.

A man looking for true love finds his penchant for obsessive stalking getting in the way. Though it started on cable's Lifetime, this addictive thriller found its footing on Netflix, where fans could binge full seasons and zealously follow all of the romantic twists and lurid turns. And it's only getting better with age. In Season 2, lead character Joe Goldberg (Badgley) meets Love Quinn (Pedretti), who matches his batso intensity. Their chemistry, plus their move to the … *suburbs?* … pushes the story in exhilarating directions.

▶▶ For suggestions of related shows, see "If You Liked *You*," page 379.

You're the Worst

TV-MA, 2014–2019
Hulu, 5 seasons, 62 episodes
Dark comedy created by Stephen Falk, with Chris Geere, Aya Cash, Desmin Borges, Kether Donohue, Allan McLeod, Todd Robert Anderson, Janet Varney and Brandon Mychal Smith.

A British novelist and a Hollywood publicist are two reprehensible people who fall for each other, despite their best efforts. Replete with poor behavior, withering dialogue and aggressive sex, *You're the Worst* is able to satirize romantic comedies while also being, despite the protestations of its leads, a romance itself. It's also a wise study of contemporary depression, delivering unsentimental compassion beneath its onslaught of barbarous wit.

The Young Pope

TV-MA, 2017
HBO Max, 10 episodes
Limited series (dark comedy) created by Paolo Sorrentino, with Jude Law, Diane Keaton, James Cromwell, Scott Shepherd, Silvio Orlando, Javier Cámara, Cécile de France, Ludivine Sagnier, Toni Bertorelli and Ignazio Oliva.

Jude Law plays the first American Pope in this polarizing, big-budget series about scandal, intrigue and duplicity inside the Vatican. Using surreal visuals and deadpan humor, Italian filmmaker Sorrentino (*The Great Beauty*) delivers the story of Pius XIII, aka Lenny, a pope with issues who immediately sets about to upend hallowed traditions and recent political changes in the church. He's assisted by his right hand, Sister Mary (Keaton), who raised him in an orphanage

and plays a pretty mean game of hardball herself.

🐿 **From our forums:** "Very interesting and puzzling. It's a rare show that has the same impact as some new type of literature that you're not sure you like at first but soon you cannot put it down. At first I liked parts of it — the acting, filming, visuals — without being sure if I liked the whole of it or not. As I got more involved in the story and characters, it all sort of made sense."

▶▶ A followup series was produced, *The New Pope*, also in this guide.

Young Rock

TV-14, 2020–present
Peacock, Hulu, 11 episodes (AD)
Sitcom created by Nahnatchka Khan and Jeff Chiang, with Dwayne Johnson, Joseph Lee Anderson, Stacey Leilua, Ana Tuisila, Adrian Groulx, Bradley Constant and Uli Latukefu.

Appealing sitcom is based on the childhood of wrestler-actor Dwayne "The Rock" Johnson. Besides being a popular character both on and off the screen, Johnson has entertained the notion of running for public office someday. *Young Rock* uses a hypothetical future Rock candidacy as the framing device for a comedic memoir about his life growing up in a wrestling family in Hawaii. Co-creator Nahnatchka Khan (*Fresh Off the Boat*) covers Johnson's life in three distinct timelines. As a 10-year-old (Groulx) obsessed with pro wrestling, the show is its funniest and most nostalgic. The timelines that show young Rock as a high schooler (Constant) and college football player (Latukefu) are less knee-slapping, more documentary-like. The real-life Johnson makes appearances.

🐿 **From our forums:** "While it didn't break any comedic barriers, I thought it was very charming on a lot of levels. Loved all the wrestling."

Younger
TV-14, 2015–2021
Hulu, Paramount+, 7 seasons,
84 episodes (AD)
Romantic comedy created by Darren Star, with Sutton Foster, Hilary Duff, Debi Mazar, Nico Tortorella, Miriam Shor, Peter Hermann and Molly Bernard.

In yet another overlooked TV triumph for Sutton Foster, she plays a 40-something mom passing as 20-something in order to reinvent herself. As her fans know, Foster has the verve necessary to sell her character's youthful ruse, as she chases a job in the cutthroat (and ageist) publishing industry. Creator Darren Star (*Sex and the City*, *Emily in Paris*) brings his trademark fizzy charm, but the show's real secret may be its ability to sympathize with both Gen X-ers who feel outmoded and millennials who struggle to make a place for themselves. Almost everyone who watches can feel seen.

Your Honor
TV-MA, 2020–present
Showtime original, 10 episodes
Crime drama with Bryan Cranston, Hunter Doohan, Hope Davis, Michael Stuhlbarg, Tony Curran, Lilli Kay, Carmen Ejogo, Isiah Whitlock Jr., Benjamin Flores Jr. and Amy Landecker.

Bryan Cranston returns to antihero mode as a judge who tries to cover up his teenager's hit-and-run killing of a mafia kingpin's son. Though not as sophisticated as *Breaking Bad*, the story is compelling and the New Orleans setting is easier on the eyes than dusty New Mexico. And who doesn't want to see Cranston reprise his role as an essentially moral man whose desire to protect his family pulls him deeper into danger?

▶▶ Originally billed as a limited series, a second season is set to air in 2022.

Yvonne Orji: Momma, I Made It!
TV-MA, 2020
HBO Max, 1 hr 2 mins (AD)
Comedy special with Yvonne Orji.

Star of *Insecure* riffs on her life as a Nigerian living in America in this standup special interpolated with footage of Orji in Africa visiting family. For those who've enjoyed her role as Issa Rae's friend and alter ego, this is Orji's chance to shine. The family video brings subtlety and warmth to her standup act, which is long on *Bob Hearts Abishola*-level jokes about Nigerians.

ZeroZeroZero
TV-MA, 2020
Prime Video original, 8 episodes (AD)
Limited series (drama) with Dane DeHaan, Andrea Riseborough, Giuseppe De Domenico, Harold Torres, Francesco Colella, Diego Cataño and Gabriel Byrne.

Rich, expansive crime drama about people in three countries whose lives are impacted by a massive shipment of cocaine. Filmed in Mexico, Italy and Louisiana, *ZeroZeroZero* is a different kind of globalization tale. We get to know the parties involved — the seller, buyer and broker — in a complex drug deal and how, despite their justifications for being in an illicit trade, it's not just business as usual. Though it will appeal to fans of crime thrillers, especially with its international flavor (there's dialogue in 6 languages), this is a human story about the corrupting influence of ill-gotten gains.

Ziwe
TV-MA, 2021–present
Showtime original, 6 episodes (AD)
Comedy with Ziwe Fumudoh.

Hybrid talk/sketch show gets its biggest laughs from provoking racial discomfort. Former *Desus & Mero* writer Ziwe Fumudoh has brought the confrontational style that helped her become an Instagram star to a quasi–talk show format that combines interviews, comedy sketches and parody music videos. When Ziwe asks professional grump Fran Lebowitz what bothers her more — slow walkers or racism — Lebowitz's response makes clear she's in on the joke. (The same can't be said of the panel of middle-aged white women named Karen who take issue with their name being used to describe entitled middle-aged white women.)

Zoey's Extraordinary Playlist
TV-14, 2020–2021
Peacock, Hulu, Roku Channel, 2 seasons, 25 episodes
Musical comedy created by Austin Winsberg, with Jane Levy, Skylar Astin, Alex Newell, Peter Gallagher, Mary Steenburgen and Lauren Graham.

Glee meets _Crazy Ex-Girlfriend_ when Zoey (Jane Levy) can hear her co-workers' thoughts expressed as fully choreographed musical numbers set to familiar pop tunes. Fans of _Grey's Anatomy_ may recognize this magical-realist premise as the "Callie in a coma" musical episode from that show's Season 7. Levy is charming as Zoey, and Steenburgen and Gallagher bring an emotionally potent storyline as Zoey's parents.

🗩 **From our forums:** "I'm a fan of shows where nice people develop strange abilities and start helping people — _Early Edition_, _Kevin Probably Saves the World_ — so this is right up my alley." "This show is so good at the emotional whiplash. I went from screaming and cheering to crying."

▶▶ Canceled by NBC after Season 2, _Zoey's Extraordinary Playlist_ produced a holiday movie for the Roku Channel in late 2021, which could lead to more episodes down the line.

Part III

–

What Will You Watch Next?
A Finding Aid

Curated Lists

We've sorted many of our recommended shows from Part II into lists that will spark your interest and help you quickly find something worthwhile.

DRAMA & LIMITED SERIES

Our Favorite Drama Series

The Americans [Prime Video]
Sleek alt-history set in the Reagan years, starring Keri Russell and Matthew Rhys as Russian spies who embed in America as ordinary suburbanites.

Better Call Saul [Netflix]
Bob Odenkirk kills it as low-rent lawyer Jimmy McGill, who evolves (if that is the right word) into *Breaking Bad*'s flashy but morally compromised Saul Goodman.

Big Little Lies [HBO Max]
Reese Witherspoon and Nicole Kidman headline this high-gloss whodunit that spawned a raft of imitators.

Black Mirror [Netflix]
The stories in this acclaimed futuristic drama explore our fixation with technology and how it has the potential to undermine society as we know it.

Breaking Bad [Netflix]
Bryan Cranston created one of TV's most indelible characters in Walter White, a milquetoast chemistry teacher who evolves into a ruthless drug kingpin.

The Crown [Netflix]
Eight decades of British royal history, from Elizabeth II's childhood as queen-in-waiting to the present, reimagined by Peter Morgan and a prestige cast.

The Deuce [HBO Max]
The creator of *The Wire* digs deep into another gritty subculture, exploring how porn and prostitution shaped Times Square in the 1970s and '80s.

Downton Abbey [PBS Passport, BritBox]
The upheaval of British society in the early 20th century is pleasingly told through secret romances and untidy kitchens.

Evil [Paramount+, Netflix]
Creepily good Catholic-themed network procedural got even better when it moved to streaming.

Game of Thrones [HBO Max]
If you thought *Game of Thrones* was definitely not for you, read our review.

Homeland [Showtime, Hulu]
Claire Danes established herself as one of her generation's great actors in this role as a talented but troubled government agent.

Justified [Hulu]
Timothy Olyphant in his most satisfying role as a marshal drawn back to his hometown of Harlan, Kentucky.

The Leftovers [HBO Max]
Emotional, character-driven social experiment asks: What if 2 percent of the world's population mysteriously vanished?

Mad Men [AMC+, IMDb TV]
A pillar of contemporary prestige TV, *Mad Men* took the retro show to new heights, as well as the careers of Jon Hamm, Elisabeth Moss and John Slattery.

Ozark [Netflix]
Jason Bateman and Laura Linney light up this super-dark drama, making it exciting, unpredictable — and extremely violent.

Peaky Blinders [Netflix]
This epic family drama set in post-World War I England gets better with each passing season.

The Shield [Hulu]
Groundbreaking series rewrote the rules for cop shows — in part by lionizing police corruption.

Six Feet Under [HBO Max]
Is it now more beloved than *The Sopranos*? Time has been kind to the Fishers and their dramatic lives at the funeral home.

The Sopranos [HBO Max]
Besides expanding our sense of what was possible with television, it remains one of HBO's most popular series, rightly so.

Succession [HBO Max]
The newest addition to the HBO pantheon crackles with sick burns as family members battle over their media empire.

The Wire [HBO Max]
The Wire is the *Blonde on Blonde* of TV drama, an instant classic that has only grown in stature over time.

Drama Unlimited: Our Favorite Limited Series

The Act [Hulu]
Patricia Arquette is eerily effective as a mom who forces her child to feign mental illness in this drama based on real life.

Alias Grace [Netflix]
Enjoyably chilling adaptation of Margaret Atwood's historical novel, based on a brutal frontier murder in 1840s Canada.

American Crime Story (Season 1): The People v. O.J. Simpson [Netflix]
Ryan Murphy's true-crime anthology launched with this bold take on a well-known media story.

American Crime Story (Season 2): The Assassination of Gianni Versace [Netflix]
Murphy then followed with a well-told account of the 1997 crime spree that ended in the fashion designer's murder.

American Horror Story (Season 3): Coven [Prime Video, Netflix, Hulu]
High-concept camp at its best, this installment of the horror anthology is also its most female-centric.

Band of Brothers [HBO Max]
The Steven Spielberg series remains the best screen dramatization of the bonds that men form under the duress of war.

Chernobyl [HBO Max]
This unflinching dramatization of the 1986 nuclear disaster in Ukraine generated critical buzz for months.

Fargo (Season 1) [Hulu]
Through creator Noah Hawley's pen and a consummate performance by Billy Bob Thornton, the Coen Brothers' cinematic world comes alive again.

Fosse/Verdon [Hulu]
Michelle Williams wowed everyone in this dramatization of dancer-actor Verdon's real-life romance and legendary collaboration with Bob Fosse.

Godless [Netflix]
Jeff Daniels plays an 1880s outlaw who tracks down his ex-partner in a town run by tough frontier women.

330

The Good Lord Bird [Showtime]
Ethan Hawke stars in a wildly entertaining history lesson based on the acclaimed novel about abolitionist John Brown.

Halston [Netflix]
Ewan McGregor is faaaabulous in this biopic of the iconic American designer.

The Honourable Woman [HBO Max]
Maggie Gyllenhaal plays a baroness and keeper of secrets in this underrated spy thriller set in the Israel-Palestine conflict.

Little Fires Everywhere [Hulu]
Reese Witherspoon and Kerry Washington play clashing moms with intertwined families in this soapy treatment of life in the Nineties.

Maid [Netflix]
One of the most-viewed series of 2021, *Maid* makes very difficult subjects both watchable and relatable.

Mare of Easttown [HBO Max]
Kate Winslet outdoes herself as a troubled but gutsy detective working on a case that's rocked her tight-knit community.

Mildred Pierce [HBO Max]
Acclaimed reimagining of the Joan Crawford movie about a wife and mother who rebuilds her life on her own terms after losing everything.

Normal People [Hulu]
The sex is sexy, the emotions are raw … for such a quiet show it packs a wallop.

Our Boys [HBO Max]
Absorbing slow-TV import turns the Israeli-Palestinian conflict into a crime procedural.

Patrick Melrose [Showtime]
Widely acknowledged as Benedict Cumberbatch's finest performance, it's also a downer: He plays the drug-addicted scion of an upper-class English monster.

The Queen's Gambit [Netflix]
The grandmaster of retro dramas, this adaptation of the Walter Tevis novel sold a ton of chess sets and introduced millions to the pleasures of Anya Taylor-Joy.

Seven Seconds [Netflix]
Regina King powers this suspenseful tale of a community upended after a white cop kills her child in a hit-and-run.

Sharp Objects [HBO Max]
Amy Adams is impressive as the broken, self-destructive crime reporter at the center of Gillian Flynn's murder mystery.

Too Close [AMC+]
When a shrink is brought in to evaluate a young woman's competency to stand trial, the two become trapped in a tense, sexually charged psychodrama.

Unbelievable [Netflix]
Fact-based drama about an elusive rapist is elevated by its three female leads.

Watchmen [HBO Max]
Who'd have guessed this wildly expansive superhero story would teach so many viewers about the 1921 Tulsa race riot?

When They See Us [Netflix]
Dramatized version of *The Central Park Five* has painful lessons about how easy it is to succumb to mass hysteria amplified by race.

Landmark Performances in Drama

Bloodline [Netflix]
Ben Mendelsohn won an Emmy for his role in this thriller about a family being torn apart by secrets.

Counterpart [Prime Video]
Starring J.K. Simmons … and J.K. Simmons.

Goliath [Prime Video]
Billy Bob Thornton plays a washed-up, guilt-ridden lawyer who is just starting the arduous journey to redemption.

The Good Fight [Paramount+]
Christine Baranski does her thing on the best network show not on network TV.

I May Destroy You [HBO Max]
Michaela Coel wrote and stars in this
spectacular take on her sexual assault.

Longmire [Netflix]
Gorgeously shot Western follows a
Wyoming sheriff who uses his salty humor
and endless determination to solve crimes
in his district.

Orphan Black [AMC+, Prime Video]
Tatiana Maslany dazzles as a character
with many clones who are all being
pursued by shadowy forces.

Rectify [AMC+]
Aden Young's quiet performance stood out
in this 2013 drama about an ex-prisoner's
bewildering first weeks of freedom after
leaving death row.

The Tale [HBO Max]
Laura Dern in a bravura performance
plays a filmmaker whose work sends her
tumbling into her past.

Very British Drama

Baptiste [PBS Passport]
Pure catnip for fans of mysteries and
crime dramas, this spinoff of British
drama *The Missing* marks the return of
Tchéky Karyo as detective Julien Baptiste.

The Beast Must Die [AMC+]
Better-than-average British prestige
detective series stars Cush Jumbo as a
mother out for revenge against the man
she believes killed her son.

Broadchurch [Netflix]
David Tennant and Olivia Colman are
paired up as detectives who are haunted
by the death of an 11-year-old boy.

The Capture [Peacock]
Intelligent, up-to-date thriller will
heighten your paranoia about deepfake
video technology.

Cheat [Hoopla]
Perfectly paced psychological thriller
centers on two brainy women trying to get
in the other's head — and a man getting
murdered in the process.

Deadwater Fell [AMC+, Acorn TV]
Another gritty British crime drama with
David Tennant, this time as the sole
survivor of a suspicious house fire.

The Drowning [AMC+, Acorn TV]
Years after a woman is told her boy has
drowned, she thinks she sees him in a
crowd, and is determined to bond with
him again.

Happy Valley [AMC+, Prime Video]
Taut, darkly amusing thriller follows a
detective's obsession with the man who
drove her teenage daughter to suicide.

Kiri [Hulu]
The second installment of the UK
National Treasure crime anthology
explores the kidnapping and killing of a
young Black girl and the complicated web
of culpability surrounding it.

The Missing [Prime Video, Starz,
Acorn TV]
World-weary detective Julien Baptiste tries
to solve the disappearance of a child while
battling a brain tumor.

National Treasure (2016) [Hulu]
Robbie Coltrane stars as a beloved UK
comedian accused of sexually assaulting
multiple women across multiple decades.

Ragdoll [AMC+]
Agreeably quirky, gory series about a
downtrodden British detective who's being
taunted by a serial killer.

The Stranger [Netflix]
Richard Armitage plays a man whose life
is upended when a woman he's never seen
before tells him a devastating secret that
involves his wife.

A Very English Scandal [Prime Video]
Hugh Grant digs into this role as a British
politician who wants an ex-lover rubbed
out before he exposes their relationship.

Beyond Britain: Global Dramas Americans Are Importing

Babylon Berlin [Netflix]
Lavish period drama brings to life Weimar Germany, where messy democracy rules the day and anything-goes libertinism fuels the night.

Deutschland 83/Deutschland 86/ Deutschland 89 [Hulu]
Likable spy thriller follows an East German double agent in West Germany.

The Investigation [HBO Max]
Absorbing Danish-language docudrama about a grisly murder that doesn't make you feel dirty for watching it.

Money Heist [Netflix]
Netflix's first non-English-language breakout hit was this manic crime caper.

Narcos [Netflix]
Wagner Moura is outstanding in this Spanish-language hit as pathological Colombian drug kingpin Pablo Escobar.

The Twelve [Netflix]
Belgian courtroom drama revolves around a jury as it is affected by testimony in a grim murder trial.

Unorthodox [Netflix]
A young woman tries to flee her suffocating ultra-Orthodox sect in this fine coming-of-age drama.

ZeroZeroZero [Prime Video]
Expansive crime drama about people in three countries whose lives are impacted by a massive shipment of cocaine.

Political And Social Dramas

The Chi [Showtime]
On Chicago's South Side, teens and adults strive for a better life while looking danger and occasionally death in the eye.

Hightown [Starz]
Diverse if formulaic crime saga is distinguished by Monica Raymund's performance as an addict drawn into a murder investigation.

Judas and the Black Messiah [HBO Max]
The police killing of a Black Panther Party leader in 1969 is compellingly presented as a tragedy of biblical proportions.

The Loudest Voice [Showtime]
Russell Crowe eerily resembles Roger Ailes, who created Fox News Channel and made it No. 1 while creating a toxic work environment.

Mrs. America [Hulu]
Cate Blanchett, Rose Byrne and Uzo Aduba play leading figures in this reenactment of the battle over the Equal Rights Amendment in the 1970s.

One Night in Miami [Prime Video]
Four iconic Black men share unique perspectives on racial progress in an imagined gathering on the night of the 1964 Clay-Liston fight.

The Plot Against America [HBO Max]
The creator of *The Wire* makes Philip Roth's alternate history of World War II suddenly urgent.

Seven Seconds [Netflix]
Regina King powers this suspenseful tale of a New Jersey community upended after a white cop kills her child.

Show Me a Hero [HBO Max]
The Wire creator David Simon turned the story of a housing desegregation crisis into an enthralling miniseries.

Stateless [Netflix]
Cate Blanchett produced and has a role in this fact-based psychological drama about a refugee internment camp.

Treme [HBO Max]

The creator of *The Wire* explored a different kind of urban devastation in this richly textured account of life in post-Katrina New Orleans.

The Trial of the Chicago 7 [Netflix]

An all-star cast entertainingly re-enacts the show trial that followed the riots at the 1968 Democratic Convention in Chicago.

The West Wing [HBO Max]

Call Aaron Sorkin's White House drama liberal, call it utopian, but as long as he was writing it, you could never call it dull.

When They See Us [Netflix]

A dramatized version of the Central Park Five case offers painful lessons about how easy it is to succumb to mass hysteria.

Modern Black Drama

All American [Netflix]

Taye Diggs and Daniel Ezra light up the screen in this richly drawn teen drama inspired by the life of NFL player Spencer Paysinger.

Blindspotting [Starz]

Charming and occasionally surreal spinoff to the 2018 film.

David Makes Man [HBO Max]

Character-driven coming-of-age drama about a 14-year-old Black boy in Miami who dreams of a better life.

The Eddy [Netflix]

Rich ensemble drama is centered on a struggling jazz club and the rundown Paris neighborhood where it's located.

I May Destroy You [HBO Max]

Michaela Coel wrote and stars in this spectacular take on her own sexual assault that happened while writing her breakthrough show *Chewing Gum*.

Little Fires Everywhere [Hulu]

Reese Witherspoon and Kerry Washington play clashing moms with intertwined families in this soapy treatment of the age just before the Internet took off.

P-Valley [Starz]

Cinematic, complex treatment of a Black woman's reinvention at — of all places — a strip club in the South.

Queen Sugar [Hulu]

Quiet drama about Black siblings in rural Louisiana ingeniously weaves the region's troubled history into storylines.

This Is Us [Hulu, Peacock]

Sterling K. Brown's character arguably forms the beating heart of this hit network drama about three very unlike siblings.

Treme [HBO Max]

Wendell Pierce and the creator of *The Wire* reunite in this richly textured account of life in New Orleans post-Katrina.

The Underground Railroad [Prime Video]

An adaptation as surreal and button-pushing as the Pulitzer Prize–winning book on which it's based.

Watchmen [HBO Max]

Regina King won all the awards for her portrayal of a detective fighting racially-motivated violence while doubling as a superhero in this tonally complex, historically bold limited series.

LGBTQ+ Drama

Angels in America [HBO Max]
Emma Thompson and Al Pacino dazzled in this adaptation of the acclaimed play about AIDS in 1980s New York City.

Behind the Candelabra [HBO Max]
Michael Douglas is Liberace and Matt Damon is the boy toy he adopts — do we really need to say more?

Fear Street (movie trilogy) [Netflix]
Time-traveling films follow a group of teens who discover that an ancient evil may be coming for them.

Gentleman Jack [HBO Max]
In 19th-century England, a queer woman played by Suranne Jones rejects gender roles by becoming a land owner.

It's a Sin [HBO Max]
Devastating and furious history of the AIDS outbreak in Britain.

The Normal Heart [HBO Max]
Mark Ruffalo stars in the film version of Larry Kramer's autobiographical play about the early days of AIDS activism.

Pose [Netflix]
Soulful, fun-to-watch drama about the Harlem ball culture of the late '80s and early '90s.

Uncle Frank [Prime Video]
In 1973, a young woman and her gay uncle take a road trip to the hometown that he's been avoiding for years.

Veneno [HBO Max]
Upbeat, absorbing biopic of Spain's beloved transgender icon.

A Very English Scandal [Prime Video]
Hugh Grant digs into this role as a British politician who wants an ex-lover rubbed out before he exposes their relationship.

World on Fire [PBS Passport]
Loosely connected characters scattered across Europe navigate their personal secrets and the perils of living through the first year of World War II.

Counterfactual: Great Moments in Alt-History

The Americans [Prime Video]
Attractive couple hangs out in the D.C. suburbs for years, secretly spying for the Commies.

For All Mankind [Apple TV+]
Absorbing drama about what might've happened had Russia gotten to the moon first and the space race never ended.

Hollywood [Netflix]
For once, the creator of *American Horror Story* tries looking on the bright side in this sunny alternate history of La La Land.

Hunters [Prime Video]
In 1970s New York, an eclectic band of vigilantes race to stop an invasion of America by ex-Nazis.

The Man in the High Castle [Prime Video]
Nuanced alt-history, based on the Philip K. Dick novel, imagines America after the Nazis and Japanese win WWII.

The Plot Against America [HBO Max]
The creator of *The Wire* makes Philip Roth's alternate history of World War II suddenly urgent.

Inventive Spy Shows

Alex Rider [Prime Video, IMDb TV]
A teenager recruited to be a British secret agent makes for an appealing take on the spy genre.

Alias [Prime Video]
In the series that made her a star, Jennifer Garner plays Sidney Bristow, who's recruited out of college to spy for a shadowy syndicate.

Hanna [Prime Video]
A teenage girl has to outrun a CIA assassin after learning she was supposed to become a killer herself.

Killing Eve [Hulu, AMC+]
Sandra Oh played a spy obsessed with the female target she's trying to bring in, and viewers loved it — for a season, anyway.

The Night Manager [Prime Video]
Tom Hiddleston and Hugh Laurie circle each other in an improbable cat-and-mouse spy game.

Patriot [Prime Video]
Entertaining, category-defying show about an off-the-books hit man who undertakes dangerous spy missions and then writes folk songs about them.

Spy City [AMC+]
Cold War–era Berlin is the setting for this stylish paranoid thriller about a British agent who steps on a hornet's nest of spies.

Turn: Washington's Spies [Netflix]
Historically sound drama about the Culper Ring, which played a key but little known role in the Revolutionary War.

Detectives with Emotional Baggage

The Fall [Prime Video, AMC+, Peacock]
Gillian Anderson plays a London detective who's in Northern Ireland to find a killer.

Happy Valley [AMC+, Prime Video]
Sarah Lancashire is terrific as a detective with a longstanding relationship with the village she serves.

Mare of Easttown [HBO Max]
Kate Winslet outdoes herself as a troubled but gutsy detective on a murder case that's rocked her tight-knit community.

Perry Mason [HBO Max]
Perry's a troubled private dick in this stylish, engaging reimagining in noirish Los Angeles.

The Sinner [Netflix]
Intriguing why-dunnit stars Bill Pullman as a detective investigating people's hidden motivations and secrets.

Top of the Lake [Hulu]
Elisabeth Moss brings real depth to a stock role.

Structurally Audacious Storytelling

Dark [Netflix]
German-language thriller has the most complex, time-bending narrative you may ever see.

Euphoria [HBO Max]
A group of high-school students navigate sex, drugs, love, friendship and identity with a variety of intense results.

Kevin Can F**k Himself [AMC+]
Annie Murphy (*Schitt's Creek*) plays a woman trapped inside a retro sitcom about a man who is terrible to his wife.

The Leftovers [HBO Max]
Emotional, character-driven social experiment asks: What if 2 percent of the world's population mysteriously vanished?

Lodge 49 [Hulu]
Chill, delightfully bizarre show tracks a surfer dude who joins a fraternal order, hoping it will get his life back on track.

Love, Death & Robots [Netflix]
Here's a rare find: a curated set of animated shorts that are as entertaining as they are different.

The Midnight Gospel [Netflix]
Surreal animation creates a psychedelic wonderland from interviews on Duncan Trussell's popular podcast.

Random Acts of Flyness [HBO Max]
Absorbing, occasionally hilarious expression of contemporary Black life told in a series of vignettes.

Tales from the Loop [Prime Video]
This anthology followes residents of a small town where a machine makes seemingly impossible things happen.

Undone [Prime Video, IMDb TV]
Dreamlike animated drama about loss and memory that's like watching a very imaginative live-action show.

We Used To Call Them Docudramas

American Crime Story [Netflix]
Season 1's re-enactment of the O.J. Simpson trial is as good as the Oscar-winning documentary.

Behind the Candelabra [HBO Max]
Michael Douglas is Liberace and Matt Damon is the boy toy he adopts — do we really need to say more?

The Comey Rule [Showtime, Netflix]
Lightly fictionalized adaptation of the former FBI director's memoir about dealing with Donald Trump.

Confirmation [HBO Max]
Kerry Washington stars in an A-list dramatization of the 1991 nomination hearings for Clarence Thomas.

Dirty John: The Betty Broderick Story [Netflix]
One of the most lurid and well-known true-crime cases in recent memory gets a powerful refresh thanks to Amanda Peet's portrayal of the scorned Betty.

Dopesick [Hulu]
Michael Keaton plays a doctor whose community is decimated by OxyContin in this adaptation of the nonfiction bestseller.

The Looming Tower [Hulu]
Effective dramatization of Lawrence Wright's nonfiction account of how the 9/11 attacks happened right under the CIA's and FBI's noses.

The Loudest Voice [Showtime]
Russell Crowe is chilling as Roger Ailes, who created Fox News and made it No. 1 while dividing the country and creating a toxic work environment.

Recount [HBO Max]
Get completely embroiled, again, in the drama that made Florida the epicenter of the disputed 2000 presidential election.

Drama Series from Before 2000 That Still Hold Up

Buffy [Hulu, Prime Video]
This Gen X blend of romance, mystery and the undead marked an important cultural shift in TV storytelling.

Freaks and Geeks [Paramount+, Hulu]
This coming-of-age cult classic launched the careers of Seth Rogen, James Franco, Linda Cardellini, Busy Philipps and more.

Law & Order: SVU [Hulu]
Not just the most durable *Law & Order* spinoff but the best-executed of the *L&Os*, including the original.

My So-Called Life [Hulu]
The show that convinced many of us Claire Danes would be a big star someday.

Outer Limits, The (1963) [PlutoTV]
Do not adjust your television set — this remains, along with *The Twilight Zone*, one of TV's finest anthology shows.

Oz [HBO Max]
Intense but ingratiating drama centered on the experimental wing of a max prison.

Party of Five (1994) [PlutoTV, Tubi]
The breakthrough show about an orphaned family was saved from cancellation by passionate Gen Ys.

The Practice [Hulu]
The Practice was the standard by which network dramas in the '00s were judged.

The Prisoner [IMDb TV, AMC+, PlutoTV]
Patrick McGoohan created, wrote and starred in this 1967 classic about an ex-spy banished to a very strange island exile.

The Twilight Zone [Paramount+, Hulu]
Perhaps the finest collection of one-act plays ever produced for television.

Twin Peaks [Paramount+, Hulu]
The sequel was pretty good, too.

The West Wing [HBO Max]
Call Aaron Sorkin's White House drama liberal, call it utopian, but as long as he was writing it, you could never call it dull.

Drama Series from 2000 to 2010 That Still Hold Up

24 [Hulu, IMDb TV]
One of the best thrillers ever made for television, *24* made Kiefer Sutherland's Jack Bauer an enduring action hero.

Big Love [HBO Max]
The show that made polyamory respectable, this Mormon-themed drama also took faith and (yes) fidelity seriously.

Bones [Hulu, Prime Video]
Sparks fly between an FBI agent and a forensic anthropologist in this breezy crime procedural.

Boston Legal [Hulu, IMDb TV]
The interplay between James Spader and William Shatner may never again be matched in lawyer shows.

Burn Notice [Hulu, Prime Video]
Maybe the best of USA Network's light, fun procedurals from the '00s.

Damages [Hulu, Starz]
Glenn Close and Rose Byrne chewed every bit of scenery in an unpredictable legal thriller that's been rarely matched.

Desperate Housewives [Hulu, IMDb TV]
Season 1 was absolutely magical. Season 2 is worth a rewatch as well.

Firefly [Hulu]
The Nathan Fillion sci-fi western was a victim of low ratings but got a lot of love.

Friday Night Lights [Peacock, Netflix]
High school life in football-crazy Texas was beautifully captured in a series noted for strong individual performances.

Fringe [Prime Video]
J.J. Abrams and Alex Kurtzman teamed well on this network thriller about FBI agents investigating paranormal events.

The Good Wife [Paramount+]
Julianna Margulies headlines one of the smartest legal dramas of the millennium.

Jericho [Paramount+]
Small-town Kansas becomes a refuge following nuclear holocaust in this unusual network drama from the '00s.

Leverage [IMDb TV, Hoopla]
This slice of caper comfort TV follows a group of cons using their skills to help those being exploited by the powerful.

Life on Mars (UK) [BritBox]
This retro detective series set the bar high for the time-travel shows that followed.

Lost [Hulu, IMDb TV]
From its wild, disorienting debut, *Lost* held its audience's attention for 6 seasons.

The Mentalist [Prime Video]
Simon Baker sizzled as a charming manipulator who outwits crime suspects.

NCIS [Paramount+, Netflix]
Network TV's best procedural franchise has just the right measure of character development, patriotism and action.

Nip/Tuck [Hulu]
Ryan Murphy's dramatic debut was this boundary-pushing sweaty tale of two plastic surgeons in Miami.

Once Upon a Time [Disney+]
In a small town in Maine, most of the residents are actually fairy tale characters who have slipped into our world.

Oz [HBO Max]
HBO's intense but ingratiating prison drama made J.K. Simmons a star.

Parenthood [Hulu, Peacock]
You couldn't have *This Is Us* without *Parenthood*.

Queer as Folk (US) [Showtime, Prime Video]
This well-timed adaptation arrived as gay commitment was a political wedge issue.

Rescue Me [Hulu, Starz]
Denis Leary's tragicomedy about FDNY firefighters and the post-9/11 chaos raging through their lives was a blast.

The Riches [Hulu]
Minnie Driver and Eddie Izzard were terrific as married grifters who assume the identity of a wealthy couple.

Sons of Anarchy [Hulu]
At its peak, the high drama of the Redwood Original motorcycle club made for incredibly addictive TV.

True Blood [HBO Max]
Life in a Louisiana town is changed after local vampires "come out of the coffin" and live openly among their neighbors.

Soapy Good Times

Dynasty (2017) [Netflix]
The remake of the 1980s hit has the DNA of the original but is smartly updated to our own age of excess.

Grey's Anatomy [Netflix, Hulu]
First-rate writing, endlessly inventive drama and a star willing to stay put add up to TV's longest-running nighttime soap.

The L Word [Showtime, Hulu]
There's more queer-friendly TV than ever, yet the shiny, soapy world of *The L Word* remains an escape unlike any other.

The New Pope [HBO Max]
Follow-up to *The Young Pope*, introduces John Malkovich as a rival to Jude Law's pontiff.

Outer Banks [Netflix]
A group of working-class teens are pitted against wealthier peers in a seaside town where they've just found a treasure map.

Outlander [Starz, Netflix]
If the only thing you like more than a time-travel romance is three or four of them rolled into one, this is your show.

The Great Book Adaptations

Doctor Thorne [Prime Video]
Downton Abbey's creator adapts Anthony Trollope's novel about a penniless young woman coming of age among high society.

Hamilton [Disney+]
Ron Chernow's masterful bio is set even more masterfully to music — and then captured on film.

The Haunting of Bly Manor [Netflix]
Henry James's *Turning of the Screw* is
given a 21st-century treatment.

The Haunting of Hill House [Netflix]
Shirley Jackson's novel is turned into a
sweeping tale of family secrets that avoids
standard horror-genre tropes.

John Adams [HBO Max]
Before *Hamilton*, this miniseries was
the cultural event that made American
Revolutionary history cool.

The Mosquito Coast [Apple TV+]
The TV adaptation of Paul Theroux's novel
is full of twists and just enough moments
of comic relief — stressful yet riveting.

Normal People [Hulu]
Sally Rooney pulled off a spare, thoughtful
adaptation of her 2018 novel about Irish
teenagers in an on-again, off-again affair.

Olive Kitteridge [HBO Max]
Frances McDormand is the reason to stick
with this depressing adaptation of the
Pulitzer Prize–winning novel.

The Plot Against America [HBO Max]
The creator of *The Wire* makes Philip
Roth's alternate history of World War II
feel urgent.

Pride and Prejudice [Hulu, HBO Max,
BritBox]
The 1995 BBC series with Jennifer Ehle
and Colin Firth remains the gold standard
of Austen adaptations.

The Pursuit of Love [Prime Video]
Lily James and Dominic West never cease
to entertain in this comic romp based on
Nancy Mitford's 1945 novel.

The Right Stuff [Disney+]
Tom Wolfe's bestselling account of the
Mercury space program is winningly
reimagined for a new generation.

Sharp Objects [HBO Max]
Amy Adams is impressive as the broken,
self-destructive crime reporter at the
center of Gillian Flynn's murder mystery.

Teen and YA Dramas Are Forever

13 Reasons Why [Netflix]
Dark, controversial series about a teen
who kills herself and leaves 13 audio
cassettes behind.

Beverly Hills 90210 [Paramount+, Hulu]
Before *Sex And the City*, Darren Star
helped reinvent teen TV with this soapy
treatment of upper-crust high school.

Bunheads [Hulu]
Way too short-lived dance-themed series
from the creators of *Gilmore Girls*, starring
Broadway great Sutton Foster.

Cruel Summer [Hulu]
Hooky cable hit about two teen girls and
the crime that ties them together.

Dawson's Creek [Hulu, Netflix]
They didn't speak like any Gen Y's we
knew, but these high school mates set the
tone for a new breed of teen soaps.

Degrassi [HBO Max, PlutoTV, Tubi]
This pioneering Canadian teen soap has
always taken on the tough topics.

Fresh Meat [Prime Video, PlutoTV, Tubi]
This British university sitcom followed five
students from their first year through to
graduation.

Greek [Hulu, IMDb TV]
Still held in high regard for capturing the
transformative drama of college.

The O.C. [HBO Max]
Welcome to the millennium, bitch.

Panic [Prime Video]
Addictive YA drama is based on Lauren
Oliver's bestseller.

Pretty Little Liars [HBO Max]
Crazy, creepy *Pretty Little Liars* stood
out for its diversity at a time when teen
dramas were very straight and white.

When Antiheroes Were the New Heroes

Barry [HBO Max]
Bill Hader showed us something when he played a hit man whose life changes when he walks into an acting class.

Billions [Showtime, Prime Video]
It's an over-the-top, unrealistic portrait of misdeeds on Wall Street, but it's got Damian Lewis facing off against Paul Giamatti — what more do you need?

Get Shorty [Prime Video, Epix]
A hit man tries to go legit by becoming a film producer in this TV adaptation of the Elmore Leonard novel.

Mr. Inbetween [Hulu]
Ray Shoesmith wants to be a good husband, brother and friend but his job as an enforcer keeps complicating things.

Ray Donovan [Showtime]
Liev Schreiber stars as a professional fixer, making powerful people's problems disappear while trying to manage the constant crises in his own family.

The Shield [Hulu]
Groundbreaking series rewrote the rules for cop shows — in part by lionizing police corruption.

COMEDY & DRAMEDY

Our Favorite Comedy Series

Archer [Hulu]
Long-running sendup of the spy genre is always changing things up, making each new season a distinct delight.

Atlanta [Hulu]
Glover stars, writes and directs this comic drama about being young, Black, ambitious and poor in America.

Baskets [Hulu]
Zach Galifianakis plays Chip — an unsuccessful clown who returns home to star in the family rodeo — and his twin brother Dale.

The Big Bang Theory [HBO Max, Paramount+]
The Big Bang Theory remained true to itself yet fresh and entertaining as ever, season after season.

Bob's Burgers [Paramount+, Prime Video, Hulu]
Burger Bob and family are as much a part of the popular culture as *The Simpsons*.

BoJack Horseman [Netflix]
Alternately hilarious and sad, this complex Hollywood satire about a former animal star is already a cartoon classic.

The Good Place [Netflix]
Philosophical-ethical sitcom set in the afterlife has so many twists, turns and brilliant insights the show is already regarded as a classic.

It's Always Sunny in Philadelphia [Hulu]
What at first seemed like a slightly meaner *Seinfeld* ensemble comedy set in a Philly bar got really weird really fast.

The Marvelous Mrs. Maisel [Prime Video]
Rachel Brosnahan dazzles as a '50s housewife who makes crowds laugh, while Alex Borstein crackles as her manager.

Mom [Paramount+, Hulu]
Anna Faris and Allison Janney hilariously play a daughter and mother pursuing sobriety together.

341

The Office (US) [Peacock]
People can't stop watching it for the same reason they haven't stopped watching *Cheers*, *M*A*S*H* or *Andy Griffith* — it's comfort TV well done.

Orange Is the New Black [Netflix]
A revelation when it came out, *OITNB* sustained its momentum for years to become one of streaming TV's first binge-worthy series.

Rick and Morty [HBO Max, Hulu]
Wildly strange adventures of a maniac who takes his grandson on interplanetary travels to show him the chaotic, pointless nature of the universe.

Schitt's Creek [Netflix, IMDb TV]
Hard to believe Catherine O'Hara almost turned down this role.

The Simpsons [Disney+]
The beauty of streaming is that you don't have to watch all the lame *Simpsons* episodes!

Ted Lasso [Apple TV+]
It's the sports comedy America didn't know it needed: Jason Sudeikis aa a Kansas motivator coaching English soccer.

Veep [HBO Max]
Julia Louis-Dreyfus won six Emmys for her all-in portrayal of an amoral vice president from the Party of Sick Burns.

Landmark Performances: Comedy Edition

Better Things [Hulu]
Pamela Adlon co-created and stars in this groundbreaking show about a single mom with three daughters and a lot of issues.

Brockmire [Hulu]
Hank Azaria hit an inside-the-park home run as minor-league sportscaster Jim Brockmire.

The Comeback [HBO Max]
Lisa Kudrow's daring turn as a washed-up sitcom star may have been the most impressive turn by a *Friends* cast member.

Comedians in Cars Getting Coffee [Netflix]
Jerry Seinfeld struck comedy gold yet again, filming spirited conversations between himself and a funny guest.

Curb Your Enthusiasm [HBO Max]
Larry David cast himself at the center of TV's defining cringe comedy.

Fleabag [Prime Video]
Groundbreaking comedy about a woman who uses crude humor and serial sex to escape her guilt about a recent tragedy is worthy of the honors showered upon it.

The Flight Attendant [HBO Max]
Kaley Cuoco delighted viewers as a stewardess trying to figure out who killed her lover.

Hacks [HBO Max]
Jean Smart stars as a fading comic who's forced to work with a young writer to freshen up her material.

Kidding [Showtime]
Jim Carrey is endearing as a Mister Rogers–type TV host who struggles when the cameras are off.

Russian Doll [Netflix]
Natasha Lyonne creates a vehicle for her singular talents in this time-warp comedy full of twists and knowing observations.

United States of Tara [Showtime, Hulu]
Toni Collette's first leading role in television was a complete triumph, playing a woman with multiple personalities trying to live a suburban life.

Vida [Starz]
A single-camera adult comedy written, produced by and starring Latinx talent has many things to commend it.

Best of the Satires

American Vandal [Netflix]
Teenagers steal the show in this intelligent, snarky, hilarious, trope-packed sendup of the true-crime TV genre.

Angie Tribeca [Hulu]
Steve and Nancy Carell created this gloriously dumb spoof of police procedurals.

Burning Love [PlutoTV]
Everything you would expect from a *Bachelor-Bachelorette* parody — plus a giant panda outfit.

Childrens Hospital [Hulu]
Often-hysterical sendup of medical dramas offers bite-sized parodies of a well-worn genre.

Comrade Detective [Prime Video]
Weirdly subversive miniseries parodied '80s buddy-cop films, Communist propaganda and anti-Americanism.

Documentary Now! [Netflix]
You don't have to love docs to enjoy this high-concept anthology series.

Eagleheart [HBO Max]
Alt-comedy legend Chris Elliott plays marshal Chris Monsanto in this spot-on *Walker, Texas Ranger* spoof.

Future Man [Hulu]
Raunchy humor and sci-fi parody make an unlikely combination in this spoof from the team that made *Sausage Party*.

I Hate Suzie [HBO Max]
No-holds-barred satire lampoons pop-culture stars and the ridiculous entertainment culture that supports them.

Medical Police [Netflix]
The gang behind *Childrens Hospital* reunite for a sequel that parodies both terrorist *and* medical procedurals.

Reno 911! [HBO Max, Paramount+]
Before *The Office* or *Parks and Rec*, this *Cops* parody was the great American mockumentary.

The Spoils of Babylon [AMC+]
Kristen Wiig, Tobey Maguire and Will Ferrell deliver marvelously on the premise of spoofing the epic miniseries that were such a big deal in the 1980s.

Dramedies: Hard To Categorize, Easy To Like

Atypical [Netflix]
Well-above-average sitcom about a teenager on the spectrum who seeks a more independent life.

Back to Life [Showtime]
Daisy Haggard co-wrote and shines in the starring role as a woman returning to her insular hometown after 18 years in prison.

Dead to Me [Netflix]
Christina Applegate and Linda Cardellini kill it as women in a grief support group.

Everything's Gonna Be Okay [Hulu]
Creator-star Josh Thomas (*Please Like Me*) takes on autism, grieving and puberty with an off-kilter perspective.

Ginny & Georgia [Netflix]
A mother-daughter duo keep secrets from each other and their new small town in this dramatic take on *Gilmore Girls*.

GLOW [Netflix]
In this winning love letter to the '80s, an out-of-work actor gets cast in the cable TV show *Gorgeous Ladies Of Wrestling*.

Only Murders in the Building [Hulu]
Steve Martin, Martin Short and Selena
Gomez are true-crime aficionados turned
gumshoes in a satisfying murder mystery.

Pushing Daisies [HBO Max]
A private eye and a pie-maker team up
to solve murder cases in one of the most
underappreciated shows of the '00s.

Psych [Prime Video]
Another one of those fun USA Network
dramedies (*Burn Notice, Monk*).

This Close [AMC+]
Deaf BFFs rely on each other in this
dramedy about love and life in L.A.

Dark Comedy Is the New Comedy …

After Life [Netflix]
Ricky Gervais stars in this deep, dark
yet remarkably nuanced and tender
examination of death and the hereafter.

The End of the F*ing World** [Netflix]
Maybe the unlikeliest teen romance ever,
James plans to kills Alyssa but instead
bonds with her on a road trip.

Flack [Prime Video]
Anna Paquin stars as a publicist who will
do anything to protect her client.

Get Shorty [Prime Video, Epix]
A hit man tries to go legit by becoming a
producer; from Elmore Leonard.

Good Omens [Prime Video]
Adaptation of the Neil Gaiman-Terry
Pratchett novel about an unlikely alliance
between an angel and a demon.

The Great [Hulu]
Catherine the Great's reign is relived with
little concern to factual accuracy and more
with being gross, violent and fun.

Kevin Can Fk Himself** [AMC+]
Annie Murphy (*Schitt's Creek*) plays a
woman trapped inside a retro sitcom
about a man who is terrible to his wife.

Mrs. Fletcher [HBO Max]
Kathryn Hahn carries this sexy comedy as
a divorced mom who finds new things to
do now that she's an empty nester.

**On Becoming a God in Central
Florida** [Showtime]
Kirsten Dunst plays a new mom who plots
unusual revenge against the multi-level
marketing company that ruins her family.

One Mississippi [Prime Video]
Tig Notaro plays a comic named Tig in a
show that's whimsical with a dark side.

Please Like Me [Hulu]
Unflinching comedy-drama stars Josh
Thomas as a young slacker helping his
mother navigate her depression.

Pure [HBO Max]
A young woman in London sees unwanted
(and very graphic) sexual images daily in
this complex comedy about mental illness.

The Righteous Gemstones [HBO Max]
Superstars of the megachurch world
hide their power-mad criminal behavior
behind a facade of religious propriety.

Search Party [HBO Max]
A group of self-absorbed young adults
learn that an old classmate has gone
missing.

**A Series of Unfortunate
Events** [Netflix]
Neil Patrick Harris headlines this macabre
comic adaptation of the middle-grade
novels.

Shameless (US) [Showtime, Netflix]
Adaptation of the UK show about a ne'er-
do-well dad is as good as the original.

This Way Up [Hulu]
Delightful, thoughtful comedy about
a woman recovering from a nervous
breakdown with her sister's help.

You're the Worst [Hulu]
Two reprehensible people fall for each
other, despite their best efforts not to.

... But We Still Love These Trad Sitcoms

A.P. Bio [Peacock]
Glenn Howerton plays a failed professor now teaching high school in this sitcom where the humiliations of teenagerdom and teaching converge.

Black-ish [Hulu]
Sitcom about a Black family in an affluent and white neighborhood is both edgy and familiar, and never not funny.

Bob (Hearts) Abishola [Paramount+]
Slow-build romance between an African national and a regular guy from Detroit is loaded with laughs and touching moments.

Brooklyn Nine-Nine [Peacock, Hulu]
Basically it's *Barney Miller* on Adderall. But funnier.

The Conners [Hulu]
A handful of sitcoms have survived the departure of their leads, but none did it as well as *The Conners*, which is actually better without Roseanne.

Doogie Kamealoha, M.D. [Disney+]
Delightful re-imagining of *Doogie Howser* with a teenage girl practicing medicine in sunny Hawaii.

Grace and Frankie [Netflix]
Lily Tomlin and Jane Fonda made old age fun — sexy, even — and viewers couldn't get enough of them.

Happy Endings [Hulu, HBO Max, Netflix]
If you liked the goofy relationships of *New Girl* and the relentless pace of *30 Rock*, this overlooked sitcom is for you.

Ramy [Hulu]
Triumphant, funny, sometimes raunchy sitcom about a first-gen American Muslim navigating his culture, family and faith.

Saved by the Bell (2020) [Peacock]
The '90s teen series gets a sharp reboot, with Jessie and Slater from the original series now working at Bayside High.

Superstore [Peacock, Hulu]
America Ferrera leads a retail workplace ensemble in a sparkling show that targets hot-button issues without missing a comedic beat.

We Are Lady Parts [Peacock]
A dorky PhD student is recruited to play lead guitar for a Muslim female punk band and unleashes a hidden side of herself, as well as some wicked licks.

Wonder Years, The (2021) [Hulu]
Engaging remake of a show about the Sixties as seen through the eyes of a 12-year-old suburban boy; this time, he and his family are Black.

SNL Alums Starring in Excellent Shows

30 Rock [Peacock, Netflix]
Tina Fey's pioneering comedy brought the rapid-fire pace of a cartoon to a workplace sitcom filled with appealingly quirky characters.

Barry [HBO Max]
Bill Hader showed us something when he played a hit man whose life changes when he walks into an acting class.

Forever [Prime Video]
Fred Armisen and Maya Rudolph play a couple whose marriage has gotten in a rut in a tonally complex comedy.

The Last Man on Earth [Hulu]
Will Forte plays a survivor of apocalyptic plague who decides that anything goes — that is, until he meets a woman who thinks it's fun to follow the rules.

Los Espookys [HBO Max]
One of those shows that people tell people about, even though it's almost impossible to describe (in Spanish *or* English).

Parks and Recreation [Peacock]
The series brought quirky comedy into the mainstream — but only after Amy Poehler's character got a makeover during Season 1.

Portlandia [AMC+]
No show better embodied the rise of whimsy; its bite-sized sketches go down easy even now.

Schmigadoon! [Apple TV+]
Cecily Strong and Keegan-Michael Key star in a spot-on satire as travelers who happen on an enchanted town that's basically a 1940s musical.

Shrill [Hulu]
Aidy Bryant plays a self-proclaimed fat advocate learning to live her life loud and proud — and does it with a light touch.

The Spoils of Babylon [AMC+]
Kristen Wiig, Tobey Maguire and Will Ferrell deliver marvelously on the premise of spoofing the epic miniseries that were such a big deal in the 1980s.

Ted Lasso [Apple TV+]
Maybe you've heard Jason Sudeikis has a show on Apple TV+?

Veep [HBO Max]
Julia Louis-Dreyfus won six Emmys for her all-in portrayal of a grasping, amoral vice president from the Party of Awesomely Sick Burns.

Sketch Comedy That Isn't Sketchy

The Amber Ruffin Show [Peacock]
Her critically acclaimed comedy show is the first late-night hit of the streaming-TV era.

Astronomy Club [Netflix]
Binge this blend of social satire and pure silliness, then ask yourself why Netflix stopped at one season.

Baroness Von Sketch Show [AMC+]
Another fine under-the-radar Canadian comedy in the tradition of *Schitt's Creek*.

A Black Lady Sketch Show [HBO Max]
Robin Thede's humor explores the lives of Black women with gags on everything from church to parenting to office culture.

I Think You Should Leave with Tim Robinson [Netflix]
Tim Robinson's sketch-comedy series has a lot of standout material for just 12 episodes.

Inside Amy Schumer [HBO Max, Paramount+]
This is the edgy, self-mocking, feminist sketch series that made Schumer a star.

The Kids in the Hall [AMC+]
Once a hard-to-find Canadian import, now streaming near you.

Mr. Show with Bob and David [HBO Max]
Pioneering adult sketch-comedy show still holds up a quarter century later.

Portlandia [AMC+]
It's more than a city — it's a state of being.

Random Acts of Flyness [HBO Max]
Moody, wry takes on blackness in the modern world.

Saturday Night Live [Peacock]
SNL's ability to storm back into the forefront of popular culture is never more apparent than now.

Excellent Use of Musical Numbers

Bo Burnham: Inside [Netflix]
Burnham wrote and performed solo in this unusual special while in lockdown.

Central Park [Apple TV+]
Ambitious cartoon from the creator of *Bob's Burgers* has a song in its heart.

Crazy Ex-Girlfriend [Netflix]
Rachel Bloom's groundbreaking series made musical numbers hip again.

Dave [Hulu]
White YouTube rapping sensation gets his own sitcom that has been aptly described as *Curb Your Enthusiasm* meets *Atlanta*.

Flight of the Conchords [HBO Max]
Wonderfully sideways comedy about two musicians from New Zealand in NYC.

Girls5eva [Peacock]
A '90s girl group reassembles and tries to recapture fame in a series from the co-creators of *Unbreakable Kimmy Schmidt*.

Glee [Netflix, Prime Video]
Ryan Murphy caught lightning in a bottle with this comedy about high school outcasts who bond in show choir.

Mozart in the Jungle [Prime Video]
The staid world of classical is upended lovingly in this comedy about an orchestra whose new conductor is a hot mess.

The Other Two [HBO Max]
A rollicking satire of Internet fame that also offers a poignant look at social media's impact on our relationships.

Patriot [Prime Video]
Entertaining, category-defying show about an off-the-books hit man who undertakes dangerous spy missions and then writes folk songs about them.

Somebody Somewhere [HBO Max]
Bridget Everett plays a 40-something woman who returns to her Kansas hometown and finds new purpose in life belting out songs to her fellow misfits.

Zoey's Extraordinary Playlist [Peacock, Hulu, Roku Channel]
Glee meets *Crazy Ex-Girlfriend* when Zoey (Jane Levy) can hear her co-workers' thoughts expressed as fully choreographed musical numbers set to familiar pop tunes.

Work Can Be Funny

Betas [Prime Video]
Raunchy millennial comedy follows a group of tech wannabes trying to make a fortune with their online dating app.

Corporate [Paramount+]
Two junior execs grapple with their soul-sucking work at a corporation that makes everything from snack foods to weapons of mass destruction.

Detroiters [Paramount+]
Sam Richardson and Tim Robinson are touchingly great as best friends and hopeful idiots who make local TV ads.

Enlightened [HBO Max]
Laura Dern's portrayal of a woman who goes on a holistic wellness retreat after a nervous breakdown at work has only grown in stature since it first aired.

Kim's Convenience [Netflix]
Culturally astute slice-of-life sitcom about a close-knit Korean-Canadian family that runs a store in Toronto.

Silicon Valley [HBO Max]
Hilarious sendup of the tech life that felt true to insiders, right down to Thomas Middleditch's lackluster lead character.

LGBTQ+ Comedy

One Mississippi [Prime Video]
Tig Notaro plays a comic named Tig in a
show a lot like herself — whimsical but
with a dark side.

Orange Is the New Black [Netflix]
In later seasons, this early genre-busting
streaming show explored larger themes
like prisons-for-profit, immigration and
being queer behind bars.

Please Like Me [Hulu]
Unflinching comedy-drama stars Josh
Thomas as a young gay man learning to
embrace homosexuality while helping his
mother navigate her depression.

Transparent [Prime Video]
Jeffrey Tambor plays a woman whose
transgender decision forces her entire
family to evolve into a more outspoken,
honest and overtly flawed tribe.

Will & Grace [Hulu]
Don't bother with the 2016 reboot, but the
original, mainstream-influencing version
still has its moments.

Work in Progress [Showtime]
Self-described fat, queer dyke Abby
McEnany drives a truckload of personality
through this semi-autobiographical
comedy with a strong indie vibe.

British Humour

Are You Being Served? [BritBox]
Of all the classic Britcoms, this one,
—set at venerable but fading London
department store — has had the most
staying power.

Back [AMC+]
After their father dies, estranged foster
brothers struggle for control over the
family pub in a small British town.

Breeders [Hulu]
British couple with young children
alternate between the joys of parenting
and the despair of having to parent.

Crashing [Netflix]
A group of 20-somethings in London
share a run-down decommissioned
hospital they agree to watch over in
exchange for cheap rent.

Detectorists [Acorn TV, IMDb TV]
Classic comedy about men devoted to
hobbies and the women who love them
despite that.

The Duchess [Netflix]
Britcom about an unapologetic single
mom trying to have another kid is
raunchy and occasionally heartwarming.

Fawlty Towers [BritBox]
John Cleese, at the height of his comedy
powers, played incompetent hotelier Basil
Fawlty in 12 uproarious episodes that
remain a masterwork of British farce 40
years on.

Lovesick [Netflix]
Clever storytelling extracts both comedy
and romance from an mortifying premise,
when a young man has to inform former
sexual partners that he has chlamydia.

The Office (UK) [Prime Video]
It's almost nothing like the American
version, which is a blessing for lovers of
British humour.

Yes, Minister [BritBox]
The creator of *Veep* has cited as one of
his inspirations this 1980s classic about a
British Cabinet member with a habit of
embarassing himself.

Female-Driven Slice-of-Life Comedies

Awkwafina Is Nora from Queens [HBO Max]
The rapper-actress plays a fictionalized version of herself, growing up in NYC and trying to live a more exciting life.

Betty [HBO Max]
An all-girls skateboarding collective in NYC crashes the sport's aggressively male subculture in this fast-moving show.

Broad City [Hulu]
Two funny New York women enjoy their adventures together more than being with men, doing drugs or holding bizarre jobs.

Dollface [Hulu]
Slightly trippy comedy about a woman seeking to restore her long-neglected female friendships after getting dumped.

Feel Good [Netflix]
Mae Martin plays a standup comic with an addiction problem who falls for a semi-closeted woman, forcing them both to face their demons in the name of love.

I Love Dick [Prime Video]
Another *tour de force* for Kathryn Hahn, who plays a struggling artist lusting after a colleague of her husband (Kevin Bacon).

Insecure [HBO Max]
Issa Rae and Yvonne Orji play besties trying to thrive as twentysomething Black women in Los Angeles.

Somebody Somewhere [HBO Max]
Bridget Everett is a revelation in this semi-autobiographical comedy as a 40-something woman who returns to her Kansas hometown and takes a few new swings at life.

Coming-of-Age Never Gets Old

Derry Girls [Netflix]
Biting, raunchy comedy about working-class Catholic schoolkids in 1990s Northern Ireland.

Dickinson [Apple TV+]
Period piece fancifully imagines how poet Emily Dickinson spent her teenage years, like getting high with Wiz Khalifa.

I Am Not Okay With This
John Hughes meets *Carrie* in a coming-of-age story with a superhero twist.

Love, Victor [Hulu]
Charming *Love, Simon* spinoff follows a high school boy coming to terms with his sexuality.

Never Have I Ever [Netflix]
From the mind of Mindy Kaling comes a satisfying sitcom about an ambitious teenager and her immigrant family.

On My Block [Netflix]
Refreshingly mellow coming-of-age series about a racially diverse bunch of high-school friends in South Central L.A.

PEN15 [Hulu]
Like *Freaks and Geeks*, only set in the year 2000 with grownups playing teenagers.

Red Oaks [Prime Video]
Funny, heartfelt nostalgia series set in the 1980s at a country club that may give you *Caddyshack* vibes.

Reservation Dogs [Hulu]
Four Indigenous teenagers in Oklahoma run various grifts and cons in order to pay their way to the promised land of California.

What We Do in the Shadows [Hulu]
Sublime mockumentary about roommates living in a *Real Housewives*-meets-vampire world.

Wonder Years, The (2021) [Hulu]
Totally engaging remake of a show about the Sixties as seen through the eyes of a 12-year-old suburban boy … this time, he and his family are Black.

Young Rock [Peacock, Hulu]
Sitcom based on the childhood of wrestler-actor Dwayne "The Rock" Johnson.

Shows That Lightly Compel Us To Contemplate Our Mortality

After Life [Netflix]
Ricky Gervais stars in this deep, dark yet remarkably nuanced and tender examination of death and the hereafter.

Forever [Prime Video]
Fred Armisen and Maya Rudolph play a couple whose marriage has gotten in a rut in a tonally complex comedy.

The Good Place [Netflix]
Philosophical-ethical sitcom set in the afterlife has so many twists, turns and brilliant insights the show is already regarded as a classic.

Miracle Workers [HBO Max]
Steve Buscemi plays God and Daniel Radcliffe is one of his angels in this oddball comedy.

Russian Doll [Netflix]
Natasha Lyonne creates a vehicle for her singular talents in this time-warp comedy full of surprising twists and knowing observations about life and death.

Upload [Prime Video]
Greg Daniels's Amazon comedy is a worthy successor to shows like *The Good Place* and *Forever*.

Comedy Series from Before 2000 That Still Hold Up

3rd Rock from the Sun [Peacock, Hoopla, PlutoTV, IMDb TV]
John Lithgow farce about aliens studying and mimicking the ways of humans tapped a bottomless font of hilarity.

Ally McBeal [Hulu]
A sensation when it debuted in 1997, David E. Kelley's sexy lawyer show makes for a deeply fascinating rewatch.

The Bob Newhart Show [Hulu]
Of all the Bobs played by Newhart over the decades, it was Chicago psychologist Bob Hartley who was the most enduring. See page 73 for recommended episodes.

Cheers [Paramount+, Peacock]
After Norman Lear and *M*A*S*H* but before *Seinfeld* and *Friends*, this was TV's favorite gathering place. See page 87 for recommended episodes.

Daria [Paramount+]
The *Beavis And Butt-Head* spinoff was nothing like the original — or anything else on TV at the time, either.

Doogie Howser, M.D. [Hulu]
Sweet, unlikely collaboration between three future TV heavyweights.

Family Ties [Paramount+]
Michael J. Fox but also Michael Gross are great. See page 125 for recommended episodes.

Frasier [Paramount+, Hulu]
The uproarious mix of high and low proved that a comedy could be intelligent, snooty even, and have mass appeal. See page 134 for recommended episodes.

I Love Lucy [Paramount+, Hulu]
All Lucy Ricardo wants is a career in show business — and she's not letting the lack of any discernible talent stop her! See page 165 for recommended episodes.

The Larry Sanders Show [HBO Max]
Garry Shandling was the force behind one of TV's most influential sitcoms that's still a trenchant take on showbiz culture.

M*A*S*H [Hulu]
With its sublime blend of drama and comedy and courage to take on TV's toughest subject, *M*A*S*H* is ageless. See page 198 for recommended episodes.

The Mary Tyler Moore Show [Hulu]
Forget Archie Bunker — if you want to see times a-changin' in the 1970s, watch Mary Richards and her still-funny sitcom.

The Odd Couple [Hulu]
As finicky Felix and schlubby Oscar, Tony Randall and Jack Klugman were one of TV's all-time comedy duos. See page 225 for recommended episodes.

Reno 911! [HBO Max, Paramount+]
Before *The Office*, this *Cops* spoof was the great American mockumentary.

Roseanne (1988) [Peacock, Hoopla]
There's a reason they revived the original show with the original cast.

Seinfeld [Netflix]
Turn to our *Seinfeld* entry in Part II and re-acquaint yourself with some of the show's greatest episodes. See page 263 for recommended episodes

Sex and the City [HBO Max]
You may look at the four leading ladies in a different light these days.

The Simpsons [Disney+]
The beauty of streaming is that you don't have to watch all the lame episodes. See page 269 for recommended episodes.

Comedy Series from 2000 to 2010 That Still Hold Up

Cougar Town [Hulu, Prime Video]
Writer-producer Bill Lawrence (*Ted Lasso*) cooked up a delightfully loony show about the lives of 40-something women.

Dead Set [Netflix]
Isolated in their sequestered house, the cast of UK *Big Brother* fail to realize the zombie apocalypse is happening outside.

Flight of the Conchords [HBO Max]
Simple and wonderfully sideways comedy about mumblecore musicians from New Zealand trying to make it in New York.

How I Met Your Mother [Hulu, Prime Video]
Neil Patrick Harris resuscitated his career in this clever spin on the friends comedy, told as flashbacks to Dad's younger days.

The League [Hulu]
Cranky friends take part in a football fantasy league — think *Seinfeld* meets *Curb Your Enthusiasm*, only with sports.

Monk [Prime Video]
Tony Shalhoub perpetually delights as the brilliant detective who must solve cases without succumbing to OCD.

Parks & Recreation [Peacock]
Quirky comedy entered the mainstream in large part through this show, starring Amy Poehler as an Indiana do-gooder.

Two and a Half Men [Peacock]
Though overshadowed by the antics of Charlie Sheen, this was first-rate farce thanks to Jon Cryer and Conchata Ferrell.

SCIENCE FICTION, FANTASY & HORROR

Our Favorite Horror and Thrillers

American Horror Story (Season 3): Coven [Prime Video, Netflix, Hulu]
High-concept camp at its best, this installment of Ryan Murphy's anthology series is also its most female-centric.

Black Mirror [Netflix]
The stories in this acclaimed futuristic drama explore our fixation with technology and how it has the potential to undermine society as we know it.

Black Summer [Netflix]
Fast-paced and loaded with political and cultural references, this isn't your everyday zombie apocalypse show.

Dead Set [Netflix]
Sequestered inside, the cast of a British season of *Big Brother* fail to realize a zombie apocalypse is happening outside.

Fear Street (movie trilogy) [Netflix]
Time-traveling films follow a group of teens who discover that an ancient evil may be coming for them.

Hanna [Prime Video]
A teenage girl has to outrun a CIA assassin after learning she was supposed to become a killer herself.

The Haunting of Bly Manor [Netflix]
This installment features fewer thrills and more chills than *Haunting of Hill House*.

The Haunting of Hill House [Netflix]
Shirley Jackson's novel is turned into a sweeping tale of family secrets that's no less frightening for its lack of standard horror-genre tropes.

Homecoming [Prime Video]
Julia Roberts and Janelle Monae take turns headlining this psychological thriller about a woman who works with soldiers returning from war and slowly recovers their disturbing memories.

La Llorona [AMC+]
The spirits of native Mayans murdered by a Guatemalan general begin to haunt him and his family.

Love, Death & Robots [Netflix]
Here's a rare find: a curated set of animated shorts that are as entertaining as they are different.

The Walking Dead [AMC+, Netflix, PlutoTV]
What does a zombie apocalypse do to the survivors? That's the core question that animates this powerhouse franchise.

The Wilds [Prime Video]
This plane-crash-on-a-desert-island thriller has an ingenious twist: All the survivors are girls.

Sci-Fi Worth Your Wi-Fi

Castlevania [Netflix]
Nifty and very adult adaptation of the classic Konami/Nintendo video game that gets more expansive with each season.

Devs [Hulu]
In this near-future thriller, Nick Offerman leads a strong cast that brings our worst fears about Big Tech to life.

The Expanse [Prime Video]
Ambitious space opera got better after it was rescued by Amazon (reportedly at the behest of Jeff Bezos).

The Feed [Prime Video]
Intriguing alt-future show about a social network you don't need a device to join, just a chip in your brain.

Made for Love [HBO Max]
Cristin Milioti plays a woman whose ex-husband has implanted her with a device that tracks her movements and emotions.

Philip K. Dick's Electric Dreams [Prime Video]
Standalone stories from one of the OGs of genre writing, backed by a top-tier cast.

Raised by Wolves [HBO Max]
Two androids are in charge of keeping humanity going on a new planet in this dazzling take on a classic premise.

Tales From the Loop [Prime Video]
Intriguing character-driven anthology set in a small town with a machine that makes seemingly impossible things happen.

It's Not Dystopia — They're Just Remixing Humanity

The 100 [Netflix]
Decades after nuclear war, 100 juvenile delinquents are sent back to Earth to see if it's habitable again.

Altered Carbon [Netflix]
Stylish alt-future allegory imagines that the rich can avoid death by having their thoughts transferred to another body.

The Handmaid's Tale [Hulu]
It was a new day for streaming TV when Margaret Atwood's patriarchal nightmare dropped on Hulu.

Humans [Prime Video]
People rely on lifelike androids to do everything from clean their homes to fulfill their sexual fantasies — and then the synths become self-aware.

The Society [Netflix]
After everyone in their town disappears, a group of teenagers is forced to create a new society.

The Third Day [HBO Max]
Jude Law wanders onto a mysterious island whose inhabitants are fiercely protective of their traditional lifestyle.

Watchmen [HBO Max]
Who'd have guessed that this wildly expansive superhero story would teach so many viewers about the 1921 Tulsa race riot?

The Wilds [Prime Video]
This plane-crash-on-a-desert-island thriller has an ingenious twist: All the survivors are girls.

Nothing Cartoonish About These Superheroes

The Boys [Prime Video]
Superheroes turn out to be horrible people working for a mega-corporation bent on world domination — enter The Boys!

Doom Patrol [HBO Max]
Well-received adaptation of the DC Comics title about outcasts who earn their superpowers through traumatic events.

The Falcon and the Winter Soldier [Disney+]
A new Avenger is handed the shield of Captain America — and he's a Black man.

Heroes [Peacock, IMDb TV]
Save the cheerleader, save the world! Everyday people with superpowers are pulled into a battle between good and evil.

Invincible [Prime Video]
Robert Kirkman (*The Walking Dead*) pens another fresh take on a shopworn genre, this time the superhero comic.

Marvel's Agent Carter [Disney+]
Unjustly overlooked series featured Peggy Carter from *Captain America: The First Avenger*.

Peacemaker [HBO Max]
John Cena reprises his role as the world's most malevolent superhero in this DC spinoff of 2021's *The Suicide Squad* movie.

Raising Dion [Netflix]
A newly widowed mother is startled to realize her young son has supernatural abilities.

The Umbrella Academy [Netflix]
Maybe the pinnacle of offbeat superhero shows, where terrible family dynamics meet apocalyptic stakes.

WandaVision [Disney+]
This Marvel series won over a lot of non-superhero fans, thanks to its 1950s-sitcom premise and appealing storyline.

Stephen King Adaptations That Worked

11.22.63 [Hulu]
James Franco plays an English teacher who travels back in time to stop the Kennedy assassination.

1922 [Netflix]
A farmer wants to kill his wife and convinces his son to help, but there are brutal, unintended consequences.

Black Summer [Netflix]
Fast-paced and loaded with political and cultural references, this isn't your everyday zombie apocalypse show.

Castle Rock [Hulu]
Well-known King characters (plus a couple of newbies) are deployed in macabre stories set in the fictional town of Castle Rock, Maine.

Mr. Mercedes [Peacock]
One of the best Stephen King adaptations in years, about a detective on the hunt for a killer; the detective is being hunted, too.

The Outsider [HBO Max]
A small Georgia town unravels following the gruesome murder of a young boy.

Horror That Leaves You Unsure Whether To Laugh Or Gasp

Ash vs. Evil Dead [Starz, Netflix]
Bruce Campbell returns as Ash Williams, who has to give up his mundane existence working at a convenience store to once again fight off an army of the undead.

Get Duked! [Prime Video]
In this gleefully cracked comedy, four dudes think they're competing for an outdoorsman's award, only to discover they're being hunted for sport.

Los Espookys [HBO Max]
One of those shows that people tell people about, even though it's almost impossible to describe (in Spanish *or* English).

Santa Clarita Diet [Netflix]
Drew Barrymore plays Sheila, a real estate agent with a craving for human flesh, in a comedy that turns out to be as delightful as Drew is.

Vintage Thrills: Horror in History

The Alienist [HBO Max]
Caleb Carr's blockbuster novels about 19th-century detectives become a well-acted period police procedural.

Kingdom [Netflix]
Zombies in medieval Korea threaten the ruling dynasty in this martial-arts-themed take on a shopworn genre.

Lovecraft Country [HBO Max]
Layered, anti-racist take on the writings of horror master HP Lovecraft is set, aptly enough, in the 1950s.

Penny Dreadful [Showtime, Netflix]
Dark, romantic and violent spookfest based on a hodgepodge of legends is artful horror done right.

Reality, True Crime & Documentary

Our Favorite Reality Shows

Couples Therapy [Showtime]
The best TV therapy show, hands down.

Dating Around [Netflix]
A remarkably effective gimmick whisks the viewer through five first dates.

Deadliest Catch [Discovery+]
Crab fisherman is one of the most dangerous jobs in the world, and you'll understand why in this perennial favorite.

Hoarders [Prime Video, Hulu, Netflix]
It's a simple concept, but the varieties of hoarding and the people who do it are seemingly infinite.

Legendary [HBO Max]
Lack of prior exposure to competitive queer ballroom is no barrier to hugely enjoying this show.

Making It [Peacock, Hulu]
Amy Poehler and Nick Offerman make this crafts-oriented show charming even to viewers who avoid competition shows.

Married at First Sight [IMDb TV, Hulu, Prime Video]
This long-running reality show offers drama on a scale rarely seen on TV.

The Mole [Netflix]
Thanks to an upcoming reboot, the original Anderson Cooper-hosted version is back and worth a rewatch.

The Profit [Peacock]
Investor Marcus Lemonis steps in with money and expertise to fix failing businesses — if the owners will let him.

Project Greenlight [HBO Max]
Great news: One of the best reality competitions of the pre-streaming era is making a comeback.

Queer Eye [Netflix]
This uplifting reboot of the Bravo series goes more than skin deep.

The Real World: Homecoming [Paramount+]
Things get *really* real when former *Real World* roommates move back in together after three decades and share what life has taught them.

Top Chef [Hulu, Peacock]
The gold standard of American reality TV talent competitions, *Top Chef* keeps improving its recipe every season.

Play-Hard Reality Competitions

America's Got Talent [Peacock, Hulu]
Years of tweaking with the format, host and judges has produced the ultimate short-attention-span show.

American Idol [Hulu]
One of the earliest competition shows, its meteoric success destroyed the idols that music and TV industry executives had built to their ideas of success.

The Bachelor/Bachelorette [Hulu, HBO Max]
Arguably the most phenomenal of all prime-time reality phenomena, well-suited to the era of social media outrage.

Big Brother [Paramount+]
It is formulaic, occasionally awesome, and one of the most successful American reality franchises ever.

355

The Circle [Netflix]
Viewers can't believe how easily they got hooked on a show where dating prospects send texts to each other.

Design Star: Next Gen [Discovery+]
The spinoff is better than the original because it's pure design, no reality drama.

Floor is Lava [Netflix]
Low-stakes game show that blows a childhood activity out of all reasonable proportion was a hit during the pandemic.

Love Is Blind [Netflix]
Gorgeous Frankenstein of dating reality shows is authentic in a very artificial way.

Love Island (UK) [Hulu]
Ready to make a commitment? Americans have gladly sat through 50-episode seasons of the British reality serial.

Naked and Afraid [Discovery+, Hulu]
Hard-core survivalists are stranded for 21 days without water, food, tools or clothes.

Portrait Artist of the Year [Prime Video]
Much more exciting than watching paint dry is this British competition among painters of celebrities and politicians.

Project Runway [Peacock]
Now that the show has moved back to Bravo/Peacock and moved on from Heidi Klum and Tim Gunn, it's better than ever.

Race to the Center of the Earth [Disney+]
From the creators of *The Amazing Race* comes another global treasure hunt with *Race*'s worst features eliminated.

RuPaul's Drag Race [Paramount+, Hulu, PlutoTV]
It's RuPaul's world now, so don't eff it up.

Survivor [Paramount+]
America's ultimate competition pits 18 to 20 scantily-clad *Survivor* fans against each other in an ever-surprising chess match.

Celebreality and Reality Celebs

American Pickers [Hulu, Prime Video]
Antique hunters roam the backroads of America looking for undiscovered treasures in shops, barns and homes.

Amy Schumer Learns to Cook [Discovery+]
During the pandemic the comic decided to spend more time in the kitchen, even though her husband is a chef.

Cardi Tries [Facebook Watch]
Hip-hop superstar Cardi B delights as she tries something new in each episode.

Cheer [Netflix]
First it was a feel-good show about college cheerleading; then it became a stomach-turning drama after a *Cheer* star's arrest.

Clarkson's Farm [Prime Video]
Longtime *Top Gear UK* host bought a farm in 2008; now he's running it.

DeMarcus Family Rules [Netflix]
A nice throwback to the early days of celebrity couple reality shows, featuring the Rascal Flatts bassist and his wife.

Duck Dynasty [Tubi, PlutoTV]
The Robertsons used to make their living selling products to duck hunters; now they've become a pop-culture brand.

Fixer Upper: Welcome Home [Discovery+]
A solid, watchable introduction to the phenomenon of Chip and Joanna Gaines.

The Goop Lab [Netflix]
This extension of Gwyneth Paltrow's lifestyle brand is better than detractors expected it to be.

Keeping Up with the Kardashians [Hulu, Peacock]
Who wants to be a billionaire?

Play-Nice Reality Competitions

The American Barbecue Showdown [Netflix]
Hyper-focused cooking competition where contestants grill and smoke meats is a fitting all-American response to *The Great British Baking Show*.

Blown Away [Netflix]
A glassblowing competition proves to be soothing entertainment as artists immerse you in the highly particular craft of turning sand into art.

The Great British Baking Show [Netflix, Hoopla, PBS Passport]
Many viewers turned to this show during the pandemic as comfort TV.

Holey Moley [Hulu]
Amusing competition imagines mini-golf if it went pro.

Nailed It! [Netflix]
Amateur bakers recreating some of the most ornate, intricate desserts you can imagine, and usually fail spectacularly.

Small Fortune [Peacock]
Don't let the micro-sized game boards and silly tone fool you — this is a legitimately challenging competition.

The Worst Cooks in America [Discovery+, Hulu]
Years before *Nailed It!* was this contest to see who could burn dinner the least.

Quirky But Soothing

Casketeers [Netflix]
Unexpectedly uplifting docuseries about a Maori-run mortuary business in Auckland, New Zealand.

Gardeners' World [BritBox, Prime Video]
As Sir David Attenborough is to wild nature, Monty Don is to cultivated nature, the best-known name in gardening TV.

How to with John Wilson [HBO Max]
Wilson roams NYC ostensibly to learn how to do mundane things, but really to shrewdly observe his fellow humans.

Joe Pera Talks With You [HBO Max]
Pera plays a fictionalized version of himself as a calm-talking Michigander.

Love on the Spectrum [Netflix]
High-functioning autistic young adults cautiously enter the dating scene.

Painting with John [HBO Max]
The artist and raconteur's return to TV features a quirky and absorbing set of meditations on painting and life, all shot on the island home where he lives.

The Repair Shop [Netflix]
Skilled and caring restorationists help people make their busted family heirlooms whole again.

Terrace House [Netflix]
Japanese *Real World*–type show where young people converse without drama.

True-Crime WTF

Crime Scene [Netflix]
A new take on the true-crime genre is this compelling "wheredunnit" from a veteran documentary filmmaker.

Don't F**k With Cats: Hunting an Internet Killer [Netflix]
They always say that psycho killers start by torturing animals; this guy did it online.

I Love You, Now Die [HBO Max]
Insightful film about a teenager charged with involuntary manslaughter after texting her boyfriend to kill himself.

Tiger King [Netflix]
You've managed to avoid the Netflix sensation so far — isn't it time you took a bite?

Injustice Is Served: When Courts and Cops Go Bad

The Confession Tapes [Netflix]
Videotaped confessions are broken down, raising troubling questions about how they were procured.

Crime + Punishment [Hulu]
Damning investigation into abusive policing at the NYPD has lessons for every city and town in America.

Framing Britney Spears [Hulu]
Activist documentary brought the plight of the teen pop star, under court-ordered supervision for years, into public view.

Free Meek [Prime Video]
Well-known rapper is tormented by the criminal-justice system in a shocking abuse of power.

How to Fix a Drug Scandal [Netflix]
Tens of thousands of drug convictions were thrown into doubt, thanks to two lab chemists.

Making a Murderer [Netflix]
After serving 18 years for a rape he didn't commit, Steven Avery is arrested for a murder he says he didn't commit.

Philly D.A. [PBS Passport]
Real-life drama unfolds behind the scenes as a reformer enacts sweeping changes to the legal system in Philadelphia.

Surviving R. Kelly [Netflix]
This game-changing exposé of the R&B superstar's decades-long abuse of girls and women resulted in new criminal charges.

Trial 4 [Netflix]
Why do Boston prosecutors insist on trying the same man over and over for a crime he plainly didn't commit?

Unbelievable [Netflix]
Top-notch dramatization of the Pulitzer Prize investigation into a serial rapist who avoided detection for years.

New Looks at Old Serial Killers

Conversations with a Killer: The Ted Bundy Tapes [Netflix]
For those who never get tired of going down this rabbit hole, a new angle on a defining story in American crime.

Crazy, Not Insane [HBO Max]
The findings of a forensic psychiatrist who has dedicated her career to the study of murderers and their motives.

I'll Be Gone in the Dark [HBO Max]
Adaptation of the true-crime bestseller is as much about the stress of hunting for the Golden State killer as it is the hunt itself.

The Jinx: The Life and Deaths of Robert Durst [HBO Max]
The definitive docuseries about the real-estate heir turned serial killer.

John Wayne Gacy: Devil in Disguise [Peacock]
Authorities missed many chances to neutralize America's ghastliest killer.

The Most Dangerous Animal of All [Hulu]
Convinced his late father was the Zodiac Killer, a man becomes obsessed with proving the link, whether it exists or not.

Sex Crimes

Allen v. Farrow [HBO Max]
No one's been charged in the alleged assault of Dylan Farrow, and this docuseries asks why.

The Keepers [Netflix]
A shocking and exceptional investigation into the death of a nun and the Catholic hierarchy's coverup of sexual predation.

Leaving Neverland [HBO Max]
Two adults recount how pop superstar Michael Jackson allegedly sexually abused them when they were children.

On the Record [HBO Max]
Two documentarians take on charges against hip-hop mogul Russell Simmons.

Surviving Jeffrey Epstein [Hoopla]
Survivors of the wealthy sex trafficker are given a place to speak out.

Surviving R. Kelly [Netflix]
The victims finally had their say in a blockbuster series that led to new charges and a conviction against the musician.

The Vow [HBO Max]
The most complete documentary account of NXIVM, the multi-level marketing organization and sex cult.

Captivating Capers, Certified Killer-Free

The Lady and the Dale [HBO Max]
The fascinating true story of the three-wheeled car and its enigmatic inventor.

McMillions [HBO Max]
The McDonald's Monopoly contest was rigged and no one had a clue until a very chatty FBI agent got involved.

The Mystery of D.B. Cooper [HBO Max]
New doc on the 1971 skyjacking goes way beyond the typical true-crime treatment.

Quiz [AMC+]
Britain's *Who Wants To Be a Millionaire* scandal is entertainingly revisited.

This Is a Robbery: The World's Greatest Art Heist [Netflix]
How in the world did thieves take hundreds of millions of dollars' worth of art from a tiny museum little known outside of Boston — and get away with it?

Our Favorite Docuseries

Challenger: The Final Flight [Netflix]
Relive that terrible month when America's space program lost its innocence.

Deaf U [Netflix]
Illuminating real-life drama follows 7 students at Gallaudet University, the nation's only all-deaf school of higher learning.

The Dog House: UK [HBO Max]
Intimate look at the adoption process inside a British dog shelter.

History of Swear Words [Netflix]
Nicolas Cage archly presents brief histories of popular curse words.

The Last Dance [Netflix]
Even non-basketball fans will get caught up in the final season of the Michael Jordan-led 1990s Chicago Bulls dynasty, told with previously unseen footage.

Lenox Hill [Netflix]
You'll love these dedicated health professionals working in the heart of New York City even before COVID-19 strikes.

LuLaRich [Prime Video]
The rise and fall of a billion-dollar multi-level-marketing company, as told through the women who bet their livelihoods on it.

Pretend It's a City [Netflix]
Author-raconteur Fran Lebowitz at her hilarious and idiosyncratic best in an artfully themed easy binge.

Small Town News [HBO Max]
Delightful fly-on-the-wall look at one of America's tiniest TV stations honors the people who keep it on the air.

The "Up" Series [BritBox]
Michael Apted's decades-spanning series has been called "the noblest project in cinema history"— but it's a TV show.

Social Issues Docuseries

16 And Recovering [Paramount+]
Students battling addiction to alcohol and opioids attend a special high school where they can be themselves and get better.

Amend: The Fight for America [Netflix]
A compelling, multi-part look at the most important constitutional amendment you've never heard of.

America to Me [Starz]
A moving and troubling look into life at a public high school where Black and white students have very different experiences.

Asian Americans [PBS Passport]
Timely, eye-opening look at the group that experienced the largest increase in racially motivated attacks in the past decade.

The Black Church [PBS Passport]
Henry Louis Gates Jr. takes us on a lively tour of American history as seen through the lens of the Black churches.

Black Love [Hulu]
Notable Black couples interestingly discuss why their relationships work.

Bobby Kennedy for President [Netflix]
Striking footage offers a fresh look at RFK's ascent from JFK's enforcer to singular voice in American politics.

The Circus [Showtime]
Real-time weekly political docuseries feels more substantial than what's on the news.

City So Real [Hulu]
In 2019 Chicago chose a new mayor, and after watching this tough-minded series you may wonder who would want the job.

Dirty Money [Netflix]
If *American Greed* and *Frontline* had a child that was allowed to use curse words, it would be *Dirty Money*.

Exterminate All the Brutes [HBO Max]
From the director of *I Am Not Your Negro* comes a heavy-handed, messy take on white history that's hard to stop watching.

The Family [Netflix]
An inside tour of the secretive Christian "fellowship" that has been influencing D.C. politics for generations.

First Person [YouTube]
Celebrated documentary maker Errol Morris has curiously intense interviews with intriguing people.

Gaycation [AMC+]
Ellen (now Elliot) Page and best friend Ian Daniel travel the world talking with people about being LGBTQ.

Hillary [Hulu]
Emotionally powerful retelling of the 2016 campaign and profile of arguably the most remarkable political figure of our time.

Living Undocumented [Netflix]
Heartbreaking, infuriating docuseries captures the human misery being wrought by aggressive new immigration policies.

Nuclear Family [HBO Max]
The woman at the center of a historic custody battle between gay parents in the '80s revisits the ordeal and the toll it took.

Oakland Trilogy: The Waiting Room, The Force, Homeroom [Hulu]
A major American city as seen through these caring portraits of its most vital public institutions.

Pride [Hulu]
Six renowned queer directors take on six decades of LGBTQ+ activism, and the result is a warts-and-all compendium of a movement.

Q: Into the Storm [HBO Max]
Get uncomfortably close to people involved in QAnon with this expertly guided tour into the heart of paranoia.

Who Killed Malcolm X? [Netflix]
A remarkable story of perseverance and truth-telling about one of the 20th century's highest-profile killings.

Sports Docuseries

100 Foot Wave [HBO Max]
A surfing legend finds a terrifying ride ever off the coast of Portugal.

All or Nothing: Manchester City [Prime Video]
Go behind the scenes with the greatest coach in the world's biggest sport as his club pursues another title.

Behind the Mask [Hulu]
Team mascots are revealed in this highly entertaining docuseries.

Cheer [Netflix]
Between seasons, scandal rocked this hit reality show about an elite junior-college cheerleading squad.

Dallas Cowboys Cheerleaders: Making the Team [Paramount+]
The most amazing long-running reality show you probably have never heard of.

Hard Knocks: Los Angeles [HBO Max]
Featuring both of L.A.'s NFL teams, this season is a fine introduction to acclaimed inside-the-locker-room series.

Last Chance U [Netflix]
Docuseries found a gold mine of drama at junior colleges where athletes have one last shot at impressing recruiters.

Last Chance U: Basketball [Netflix]
The first Black coach on the popular Netflix docuseries beautifully embodies the notion of sports as more than a game.

We Are: The Brooklyn Saints [Netflix]
Kids are molded into one of the nation's premier pee-wee football teams by a group of hard-working Black men.

We Are the Champions [Netflix]
Feel-good look at humans who strive to be the very best at obscure competitions.

Pop Culture Docuseries

1971: The Year Music Changed Everything [Apple TV+]
Music legends help Americans pivot from the devastating aftermath of the 1960s.

The Beatles: Get Back [Disney+]
Director Peter Jackson's awe-inspiring distillation of previously unseen footage uses AI to get us this close to the Beatles as they create the album *Let It Be*.

The Comedy Store [Showtime]
America's most influential comedy club is recalled by those who worked there.

High Score [Netflix]
Learn how video games have evolved at the speed of technology in this easy binge.

The Movies That Made Us [Netflix]
Take a deep dive into the history of several blockbuster films from the 1980s and '90s that will satisfy even hardcore movie fans.

Song Exploder [Netflix]
You'll never hear your favorite song the same way after it gets the *Song Exploder* deep dive.

Watch the Sound with Mark Ronson [Apple TV+]
A top producer offers immersive lessons about the technology that shapes today's popular music.

The Doctor of Docuseries: Ken Burns's Greatest Hits

Baseball [PBS Passport]
Widely regarded as Burns' best work after his masterpiece on the Civil War.

The Central Park Five [PBS Passport]
The exposé of a 1980s travesty of justice led to the miniseries *When They See Us*.

The Civil War [PBS Passport]
Time hasn't tarnished Burns's magnum opus on the suffering, romance and moral necessity of America's greatest conflict.

Country Music [PBS Passport]
An eye-opening, ear-pleasing series about country's multiracial roots and impact.

Muhammad Ali [PBS Passport]
Tour de force biography of the boxer and activist plants Ali firmly in his times.

The Vietnam War [PBS Passport, Hoopla]
America's tragic adventure in Southeast Asia is told by the people who directed it, covered it and fought it — on both sides.

Humans, Non-Humans and Nature

Chasing Coral [Netflix]
Coral reefs around the world are turning pale; as this spectacular underwater doc explains, that's a very bad thing.

Continent 7: Antarctica [Disney+]
Antarctica's first reality show will flip your idea of it upside down.

The Last Alaskans [Discovery+]
Four families living in the Arctic National Wildlife Refuge face challenges daily.

One Strange Rock [Disney+]
If *Planet Earth* was thrown into a blender with *Gravity* and *The Fifth Element*, an electronic dance party and the musings of Neil deGrasse Tyson, you might get this.

Penguin Town [Netflix]
Penguins take over a town, with Patton Oswalt calling the play-by-play — and it's as adorably hilarious as it sounds.

Food Obsessions

The Chef Show [Netflix]
Writer-director Jon Favreau is joined by chef Roy Choi and famous guests in a cooking show as cozy as a warm kitchen.

Chef's Table [Netflix]
The show that gets back to basics — just great cooks with a passion for their work.

Nadiya Bakes [Netflix]
Classic instructional cooking TV like *Barefoot Contessa*, anchored by *Great British Bake-Off* winner Nadiya Hussain.

Salt Fat Acid Heat [Netflix]
No, it's not another Netflix exposé of unhealthy diets, but a celebration of what makes food irresistible.

Taco Chronicles [Netflix]
You'll be hungry when you finish this Spanish-language docuseries.

Taste the Nation with Padma Lakshmi [Hulu]
Charismatic *Top Chef* host travels America exploring its food cultures with an emphasis on the immigrant experience.

Planet Man: The Best of Sir David Attenborough

Blue Planet [Discovery+]
Two decades later, it remains a marvel of cinematography, revealing marine marvels that had previously escaped human notice.

Blue Planet II [Discovery+]
Attenborough takes us on a breathtaking look at the world's oceans, with a focus on the impact of Earth's rising temperatures.

Dynasties [Discovery+]
Embedding with just one group of animals per episode, this is a nice change of pace from Attenborough's usual format.

Our Planet [Netflix]
A visual extravaganza infused with dire warnings that all this natural beauty could vanish if humans don't change their ways.

A Perfect Planet [Discovery+]
Attenborough's urgency about climate change informs, but doesn't overwhelm, this series about Earth's unique capacities.

Planet Earth II [Discovery+]
Sir David raises his game even higher in this sequel to Planet Earth.

One Night Only: Films and Specials

When you don't want to binge, here are more than 200 movies and specials you can start and finish tonight.

Oscar Winners & Nominees

13TH [Netflix]
Essential documentary about a historic but fraught constitutional amendment.

American Factory [Netflix]
Vital Obama-produced doc about the Chinese takeover of an Ohio auto plant.

Borat Subsequent Moviefilm [Prime Video]
Famous Kazakhstani return with glorious video of maga-uncomfortable scenes.

Crip Camp [Netflix]
Rollicking, inspiring account of a 1970s summer camp that launched a movement.

Dick Johnson Is Dead [Netflix]
A man gamely reenacts his own death in this wildly imaginative documentary.

I Am Not Your Negro [Prime Video]
James Baldwin's manuscript drives this visceral critique of race in America.

Icarus [Netflix]
While making this documentary, the director stumbles into an epic scandal.

The Irishman [Netflix]
Martin Scorsese uses CGI and his all-stars to powerful effect in this acclaimed epic.

Judas and the Black Messiah [HBO Max]
The 1969 killing of a Black Panther leader is compellingly presented as a tragedy.

Ma Rainey's Black Bottom [Netflix]
August Wilson's Prohibition-era play sparkles with Viola Davis as a blues queen.

Manchester by the Sea [Prime Video]
Casey Affleck and Michelle Williams in a meditation on grief, guilt and forgiveness.

Mank [Netflix]
Gary Oldman is Herman Mankiewicz, battling demons as he writes *Citizen Kane*.

Marriage Story [Netflix]
Scarlett Johansson and Adam Driver in a sharply constructed character drama.

Minding the Gap [Hulu]
A skateboarder videotapes his friends and captures the turbulence of their lives.

My Octopus Teacher [Netflix]
Marine videographer chronicles his unusually intimate bond with a mollusk.

Nomadland [Hulu]
Spare, beautiful celebration of everyday people getting by in the New Economy.

One Night in Miami... [Prime Video]
Four iconic Black men have an imagined dialogue after the Clay-Liston fight.

Roma [Netflix]
Alfonso Cuarón's semi-autobiographical drama is a modern masterwork.

Soul [Disney+]
The Oscar winner for best animated film of 2020 is an absolute delight.

Sound of Metal [Prime Video]
Riz Ahmed plays a drummer struggling with sudden hearing loss.

The Trial of Chicago 7 [Netflix]
From Aaron Sorkin's script, an all-star cast re-enacts a show trial from 1969.

The Two Popes [Netflix]
Anthony Hopkins and Jonathan Pryce argue grandly about faith and toleration.

The United States vs. Billie Holiday [Hulu]
Singer Andra Day makes a remarkable film debut in this biopic.

Wolfwalkers [Apple TV+]
Gorgeously animated fable about an Irish girl who meets a child who may be a wolf.

Family Movies

Clifford the Big Red Dog [Paramount+]
Parents (if not critics) loved the adaptation
of the children's book about the plus-sized
pooch and the girl who loves him.

Flora and Ulysses [Disney+]
A young girl is surprised to discover that a
squirrel she rescues has superpowers.

**The Mitchells vs. The
Machines** [Netflix]
A family's boring road trip gets a jolt when
they suddenly wind up in the middle of a
robot apocalypse.

The SpongeBob Movie [Paramount+]
After his pet snail goes missing,
SpongeBob embarks on a harrowing
adventure to bring him home.

Soul [Disney+]
Pixar enchantment is an imaginative take
on the afterlife with a relatable story and
Jon Batiste's syncopated score.

**Timmy Failure: Mistakes Were
Made** [Disney+]
Smart adaptation of the book about an
11-year-old boy who runs a detective
agency with an imaginary polar bear.

The Water Man [Netflix, Hoopla]
After his mother gets sick, a boy embarks
on a quest to find a man he's heard has
magical healing powers.

Wolfwalkers [Apple TV+]
Beautifully animated fable about an Irish
girl who is hunting a pack of wolves when
she encounters a child who may be a wolf.

Thoughtful Drama Films

Charm City Kings [HBO Max]
A 14-year-old in Baltimore wants to be
part of a group of motorbike riders.

CODA [Apple TV+]
A hearing girl leaves her deaf parents to
attend music school.

The Humans [Showtime]
During a family Thanksgiving gathering,
external and internal ghosts haunt them.

Palmer [Apple TV+]
An ex-con forms an unlikely friendship
with a troubled young boy.

Safety [Disney+]
Feel-good film is based on the true story
of Ray-Ray McElrathbey, who secretly
raised his little brother at college after
home life became too volatile.

Tigertail [Netflix]
This film follows decades in the life of
a Taiwanese man who leaves a love and
family behind to emigrate to the U.S.

Uncle Frank [Prime Video]
In 1973, a young woman and her gay
uncle take a road trip to the hometown
that he's been avoiding for years.

Horror Films

The Babysitter [Netflix]
A boy has a crush on his babysitter until
he discovers she's in a satanic cult that
holds meetings in his family's living room.

Calibre [Netflix]
Two friends on a hunting trip try to cover
up a horrifying accident, but the residents
of a nearby town suspect them anyway.

Fear Street Trilogy [Netflix]
Time-traveling films follow a group of
teens who discover that an ancient evil
may be coming for them.

Lake Mungo [AMC+, Prime Video]
After a teenage girl disappears, her family
makes startling discoveries about her.

La Llorona [AMC+]
The spirits of native Mayans murdered by a Guatemalan general begin to haunt him and his family.

Little Monsters [Hulu]
Lupita Nyong'o stars as a kindergarten teacher who has to protect a group of kids from a zombie outbreak at a theme park.

Romcoms

Always Be My Maybe [Netflix]
Randall Park and Ali Wong play childhood friends who discover they might have feelings for each other.

Plus One [Hulu]
Two friends agree to be each other's "plus one" to every wedding they've been invited to that summer.

Happiest Season [Hulu]
A woman brings her girlfriend home for Christmas with her conservative family, putting a wrinkle in everyone's plans.

Stargirl [Disney+]
In this sweet-natured romance, a shy boy finds himself falling for a quirky girl who pushes him out of his comfort zone.

The Kissing Booth [Netflix]
This critic-proof hit revolves around the romance of a late-blooming teenager and her best friend's brother.

To All the Boys I've Loved Before [Netflix]
Jenny Han's YA trilogy has appeal beyond its teenage-girl core audience.

The Princess Switch [Netflix]
A Chicago woman swaps identities with her *doppelgänger*, who happens to be the fiancee of a prince.

When We First Met [Netflix]
Noah Devine goes back in time to the moment he met the woman of his dreams, hoping he can make her fall for him.

Action Flicks

Boss Level [Hulu]
Special forces agent has to escape a time loop that keeps resulting in his murder.

The Old Guard [Netflix]
Charlize Theron is in her element as leader of a band of immortal mercenaries.

Cut Throat City [Netflix, Hoopla]
Hip-hop superstar RZA directs this story about friends who reluctantly agree to a heist in post-Katrina New Orleans.

Red Notice [Netflix]
Critics were divided on this big-budget action comedy but audiences ate it up, probably because Wonder Woman, The Rock and Deadpool are so watchable.

Da 5 Bloods [Netflix]
A Spike Lee career highlight, this Oscar nominee follows four veterans with PTSD as they return to Vietnam to dig up a treasure they buried there.

Superintelligence [HBO Max]
Melissa McCarthy is great in a PG thriller trying to convince a supercomputer to not destroy the human race.

Enola Holmes [Netflix]
Stranger Things star adds to the enjoyment of this family-friendly film about Sherlock Holmes's little sister.

Underwater [HBO Max]
Deep sea researchers have to get above water fast after an earthquake rattles their research facility in the Mariana Trench.

Thriller Films

Bird Box [Netflix]
Sandra Bullock riveted millions as a mom trying to save her children from a mysterious suicidal force.

Fractured [Netflix]
A couple rushes their daughter to the hospital for an arm injury, then the kid and the wife go missing.

The Mad Women's Ball [Prime Video]
Mélanie Laurent plays an asylum nurse who agrees to help an unfairly institutionalized woman escape.

No Sudden Move [HBO Max]
A gang of criminals think they're coming together for a simple job until things start spinning out of control.

Run [Hulu]
Sarah Paulson plays a mother with a disabled teenage daughter and some disturbing secrets.

Without Remorse [Prime Video]
While he's trying to avenge his wife's murder, a Navy SEAL gets sucked into a deadly conspiracy in this Tom Clancy tale.

Top Comics at Work

Ali Wong: Baby Cobra [Netflix]
Wong broke into the mainstream with this hilarious set that she filmed while pregnant.

Amy Schumer: Live at the Apollo [HBO Max]
With a sweet smile and hilarious daggers, Schumer eviscerates double standards about sex, sexuality and pleasure.

Bo Burnham: Inside [Netflix]
Burnham wrote and performed this solo special while in pandemic lockdown.

Dave Chappelle: Sticks & Stones [Netflix]
Almost as controversial as his 2021 special *The Closer*, but with better material.

Ellen Degeneres: Here and Now [HBO Max]
Filmed before her talk show started, this now-classic special proved that Ellen had the chops to be an all-time great.

Rob Delaney: Jackie [Prime Video]
Like a real-life version of his *Catastrophe*, Delaney uses this stand-up set to talk about his chaotic time living in London.

Jim Gaffigan: Quality Time [Tubi, Hoopla, Prime Video]
There's not a wasted minute with the funniest clean comic working today.

Hannah Gadsby: Nanette [Netflix]
The Australian comedian broke through with this bravura performance.

Standup Comedy's Up-And-Comers

Jayde Adams: Serious Black Jumper [Prime Video]
The British comedian applies her skewed and goofy worldview to topics like the very best wardrobe for true feminists.

Flo and Joan: Alive On Stage [Prime Video]
The Dempsey sisters use off-the-wall songs to work out their rivalries and tell their anecdotes.

Hasan Minhaj: Homecoming King [Netflix]
Daily Show correspondent tells stories from his Indian-American Muslim life.

My Favorite Shapes by Julio Torres [HBO Max]
Torres picks objects of various shapes off a conveyor belt and riffs on them.

Ronny Chieng: Asian Comedian Destroys America! [Netflix]
Daily Show correspondent tells stories about modern life from a Chinese-Malaysian-American POV.

Rose Matafeo: Horndog [HBO Max]
Kiwi comic says she's the perfect person to discuss sex in the modern world, since she has kissed almost 10 boys.

Whitmer Thomas: The Golden One [HBO Max]
With original songs, Thomas tries to make peace with being an "aging emo kid."

Yvonne Orji: Momma, I Made It! [HBO Max]
Insecure co-star on her life as a Nigerian living in America, with home movies.

Comedy Films for Adults

An American Pickle [HBO Max]
An immigrant worker in a pickle factory is preserved in brine for 100 years and wakes up in contemporary Brooklyn.

Bad Education [HBO Max]
Hugh Jackman and Allison Janney headline this based-on-true-events film about a beloved school superintendent who bilks his district out of millions.

Bad Trip [Netflix]
Two buddies try to get out of a rut by going on a road trip to NYC.

Barb and Star Go to Vista Del Mar [Hulu]
Two gal pals take a vacation to a Florida resort only to become embroiled in a nefarious plot to destroy everyone there.

Borat Subsequent Moviefilm [Prime Video]
The Kazakhstani returns to America in a series of hilariously uncomfortable scenes.

Don't Look Up [Netflix]
In this A-lister satire, two astronomers try to convince the world to care that a comet is hurtling toward Earth.

Eurovision Song Contest: The Story of Fire Saga [Netflix]
Will Farrell kills it as one half of an Icelandic duo who represent their country in the Eurovision Song Contest.

The Lovebirds [Netflix]
While trying to save their relationship with an unforgettable date night, a couple gets caught up in a murder mystery.

Paddleton [Netflix]
Two nerdy, somewhat reclusive neighbors deepen their friendship after one of them is diagnosed with cancer.

Vacation Friends [Hulu]
Hijinks ensue when a couple's wedding gets crashed by the friends they made during a drunken vacation.

Quirky Comedy Films

Big Time Adolescence [Hulu]
A high school student comes of age under the dubious tutelage of the 20-something burnout who used to date his sister.

Dolemite Is My Name [Netflix]
Eddie Murphy's acclaimed passion project explains how Rudy Ray Moore became a Blaxploitation icon.

Get Duked! [Prime Video]
In this gleefully cracked Scottish comedy, three doofuses and a nerd discover they're being hunted for sport.

Hearts Beat Loud [Hulu]
After they write a song together, a father and daughter suddenly become viral music stars.

On the Rocks [Apple TV+]
A woman (Rashida Jones) finds solace for her failed marriage going on adventures with her aging playboy dad (Bill Murray).

Paddleton [Netflix]
Two nerdy, somewhat reclusive neighbors deepen their friendship after one of them is diagnosed with cancer.

Palm Springs [Hulu]
Andy Samberg and Cristin Milioti are stuck in a time loop in this sharp, funny and ultimately moving romcom.

Plan B [Hulu]
A slacker and a nerd have to track down a morning-after pill in America's heartland.

Holiday Movies

8-Bit Christmas [HBO Max]
In the late 80s, a kid goes on an epic quest to acquire a Nintendo Entertainment System for Christmas.

A Boy Called Christmas [Netflix]
Star-studded cast assembles to tell a beautifully rendered origin story of Santa Claus.

Dolly Parton's Christmas on the Square [Netflix]
A rich woman plans to sell the small town she owns and ruin the residents' lives — and then an angel arrives …

Happiest Season [Hulu]
A woman brings her girlfriend home for Christmas with her conservative family, upending everyone's holiday plans.

Housewives of the North Pole [Peacock]
Real Housewives-adjacent holiday movie is everything you expect it to be.

Jingle Jangle [Netflix]
In this musical film, a toymaker with magical gifts may be on the brink of ruin, unless he and his granddaughter can recover his stolen book of inventions.

Klaus [Netflix]
Hand-drawn animated film replaces the traditional Santa story beats with a tale of a disaffected postman and a toymaker.

Noelle [Disney+]
Few family-friendly Christmas movies in recent years have checked as many boxes and done it so well.

They Lined Up for These Docs at Sundance

Blood Brother [Tubi, Kanopy]
An aimless young American finds his purpose in life in caring for HIV/AIDS kids in India.

Born into Brothels [Tubi, Hoopla]
Insightful and even inspiring film about children whose mothers are prostitutes in Calcutta's red-light district.

Capturing the Friedmans [HBO Max]
Director Andrew Jarecki revisits a screaming-headlines case from the 1980s and finds a massive injustice was done.

Chasing Coral [Netflix]
Coral reefs around the world are turning a ghastly shade of pale and as this spectacular underwater doc explains, that's a very bad thing.

Crime + Punishment [Hulu]
Damning investigation into abusive policing at the NYPD has lessons for every city and town in America.

Crip Camp [Netflix]
A rollicking and inspiring account of a 1970s summer camp that launched a movement.

Hear and Now [HBO Max]
In their 60s, the director's deaf parents receive cochlear implants and things don't turn out the way you'd expect.

Hoop Dreams [HBO Max, Showtime]
A classic of video empathy, *Hoop Dreams* is a parable about America's obsession with sports and, more importantly, people who win at sports.

How to Die in Oregon [Tubi]
Terminally ill patients take part in physician-assisted suicide in one of the few states that allows it.

I Am Not Your Negro [Netflix, Hulu, Hoopla, Kanopy]
Thirty years after social critic James Baldwin died, his unfinished manuscript is the basis for this stunningly up-to-date critique of American race relations.

Jim: The James Foley Story [HBO Max]
Most Americans only learned about the freelance journalist after ISIS had killed him; this portrait fills in the blanks.

Murderball [Tubi, PlutoTV, Peacock]
Quadriplegic rugby players are shown in action, which is compelling enough — but then you get to know them.

One Child Nation [Prime Video]
A filmmaker returns to her rural Chinese home to give a personal account of China's disturbing one-child-per-family policy.

Rich Hill [PlutoTV]
Sensitive portrayal of the challenges facing poor white kids in rural Missouri.

The Sentence [HBO Max]
A mandatory-sentencing law sent the director's sister to prison — and wreaked extraordinary havoc on her family.

Southern Comfort [Tubi]
Director Kate Davis followed Robert Eads as he desperately sought a doctor who would treat his ovarian cancer in this classic transgender film.

Trouble the Water [AMC+, Kanopy]
Harrowing first-person account of surviving Hurricane Katrina will leave you moved by the resiliency of those who had little to lose — and lost it all.

The Wolfpack [HBO Max, YouTube, Kanopy]
A paranoid father kept his wife and their 13 children locked in their apartment for years — and then one of the boys escaped.

Political Documentaries

13TH [Netflix]
Essential documentary about a historic but fraught constitutional amendment.

Agents of Chaos [HBO Max]
Alex Gibney's fast-paced and slickly produced rewind of the 2016 presidential campaign offers a paranoid scenario that Russian agents helped elect Trump.

American Factory [Netflix]
Vital documentary about the Chinese takeover of an American auto plant won an Academy Award for the Obamas.

Boys State [Apple TV+]
Spend an exhilarating week with 1, 100 teenagers in a yearly civics exercise to learn why our politics are broken.

Icarus [Netflix]
While making a guerrilla documentary about doping, Bryan Fogel finds himself in the middle of an epic doping scandal.

Knock Down the House [Netflix]
Women motivated by Donald Trump's election run for Congress in 2018, but the odds are stacked against them.

Waiting for "Superman" [Netflix]
Director of *An Inconvenient Truth* makes a controversial plea for charter schools.

Weiner [AMC+]
Fly-on-the-wall account of Anthony Weiner's political career as it unravels is a sad reminder that one will go far in politics these days by being a dick.

Music Documentaries

The Bee Gees: How Can You Mend a Broken Heart [HBO Max]
Fabulous retrospective about the brother act who were pop's greatest chameleons.

The Go-Go's [Showtime]
The groundbreaking 1980s all-female rock band — their music, feuds and legacy — are recalled with curiosity and respect.

Sinatra: All Or Nothing at All [Netflix]
Alex Gibney presents a highly watchable portrait of Sinatra and his immense impact on music, culture and politics.

Stop Making Sense [Prime Video, Tubi]
This snapshot of the pop darlings at their

1980s peak is arguably the greatest concert film made.

Summer of Soul [Hulu]
What a find — hours of exciting historic footage from the 1969 Harlem Culture Festival, lovingly restored.

The Velvet Underground [Apple TV+]
Todd Haynes's documentary viscerally recreates the 1960s New York art scene that birthed a legendary band.

What Happened, Miss Simone? [Netflix]
This candid film explains why the onetime jazz pianist, who became a leading protest voice in the 1960s, dropped out of sight.

IF YOU LIKED THAT … YOU'LL LIKE THIS

No algorithms here — these were hand-curated by Primetimer editors.

If you liked *The Blacklist* …

How to Get Away With Murder [Netflix]
Bat-guano-crazy legal thriller stars Viola Davis as a law professor trying to cover up the murder of her husband.

Lucifer [Netflix]
Satan moves to Los Angeles and moonlights with the LAPD solving crimes in this long-running cult classic.

Money Heist [Netflix]
Netflix's first non-English-language breakout hit was this manic crime caper.

Outer Banks [Netflix]
Escapist soap pits working-class teens against wealthier peers in a seaside town where they've just uncovered a treasure map.

Pretty Little Liars [HBO Max]
Years before *Cruel Summer*, this twisted teen sensation redefined young adult drama.

Sneaky Pete [Prime Video]
A con man convinces a dead man's clan that he's their long-lost relative.

Genre classic: *Alias* • Boundary pusher: *Escape at Dannemora*

If you liked *Bridgerton* …

Dash and Lily [Netflix]
Super-cute adaptation of YA novel about two teens getting to know each other through a notebook left around NYC.

Doctor Thorne [Prime Video]
Downton Abbey's creator adapts Anthony Trollope's novel about a penniless woman and her high society benefactors.

Emily in Paris [Netflix]
Sex and the City meets *Younger* in this story of an American millennial unapologetically reveling in Paris.

Gentleman Jack [HBO Max]
In 19th-century England, a queer woman rejects gender roles by becoming a land owner and wearer of men's suits.

Vanity Fair [Prime Video]
Thackeray's satirical novel gets a lavish adaptation headlined by Olivia Cooke's turn as enterprising schemer Becky Sharp.

The Young Pope [HBO Max]
Jude Law plays the first American Pope in this big-budget series about scandal and intrigue inside the Vatican.

Genre classic: *I, Claudius* • Boundary pusher: *Pushing Daisies*

If you liked *The Circle* …

Are You the One? [Paramount+, Hulu, Netflix]
The fascinating 8th season of this hookup show was devoted to bisexual, trans and non-binary people looking for love.

Dating Around [Netflix]
Seamless editing whisks the viewer through five first dates, demonstrating what a blur it is for all involved.

Love Is Blind [Netflix]
This gorgeous Frankenstein of dating reality shows works because it's honest about what's going on.

Love Island (UK) [Hulu]
Ready to make a commitment? Americans have gladly sat through 50-episode seasons of the British reality serial.

Temptation Island (2019) [Peacock]
Couples date other people on TV, then discuss the results, offering a window into what people truly value in relationships.

Terrace House [Netflix]
In Japan, when six strangers agree to live in a house and keep it real, they do it like normal people, which is weirdly calming.

Genre classic: *Married at First Sight* • Boundary pusher: *The Wedding Coach*

If you liked *The Crown* …

Chernobyl [HBO Max]
Unflinching dramatization of the 1986 nuclear disaster in present-day Ukraine.

Manhattan [Hulu]
Character-driven historical drama about the race to build the atom bomb, featuring Rachel Brosnahan.

Mrs. America [Hulu]
Star-studded dramatization of the rise and fall of the Equal Rights Amendment in the 1970s.

Self-Made [Netflix]
Octavia Spencer brings to life the trailblazing Black hair care entrepreneur known as Madam C.J. Walker.

Victoria [Prime Video, PBS Passport]
Fresh, appealing look at England's 19th-century queen in early years.

World on Fire [PBS Passport]
Loosely connected characters across Europe navigate their personal secrets and the first year of World War II.

Genre classic: *Wolf Hall* • Boundary pusher: *The Great*

If you liked *Game of Thrones* …

Black Sails [Starz, Hulu]
The lives of pirates, as thrillingly portrayed by a talented ensemble of non-American actors.

Outlander [Starz, Netflix]
If the only thing you like more than a time-travel romance is three or four of them rolled into one, this is your show.

Penny Dreadful [Showtime, Netflix]
Dark, romantic and violent spookfest based on a hodgepodge of legends is artful horror done right.

Raised By Wolves [HBO Max]
Dazzling take on a classic sci-fi premise finds two androids in charge of keeping humanity going on a new planet.

Vikings [Prime Video, Hulu]
Norse hero Ragnar Lothbrok and family barge across North America and Europe, upending kings and lords.

The Witcher [Netflix]
Henry Cavill headlines this multi-layered fantasy romp with notes of *Xena: Warrior Princess* and *Outlander*.

Genre classic: *Grimm* • Boundary pusher: *Castlevania*

If you liked *The Great British Baking Show* …

The American Barbecue Showdown [Netflix]
Hyper-focused competition on grilling and smoking meats is our country's fitting response to *The Great British Baking Show.*

Blown Away [Netflix]
A glassblowing competition proves to be crackerjack entertainment.

The Great Pottery Throwdown [HBO Max]
The Great British Baking Show producers make throwing clay appealing in this upbeat, accessible competition.

Making It [Peacock, Hulu]
Thanks to Amy Poehler and Nick Offerman, this craftmaking show is lively yet gentle and will charm even viewers who avoid competition shows.

Portrait Artist of the Year [Prime Video]
Way more exciting than watching paint dry is this competition among British artists who paint the notables.

The Repair Shop [Discovery+]
Skilled and caring restorationists help people make their busted family heirlooms whole again.

Genre classic: *Top Chef* • Boundary pusher: *Skin Wars*

If you liked *Hacks* …

Bunheads [Hulu]
Sutton Foster plays a Vegas showgirl-turned-small town dance instructor, leading a cast of young dancers.

The Other Two [HBO Max]
A rollicking satire of Internet fame that also offers a poignant look at social media's impact on our relationships.

Shrill [Hulu]
Aidy Bryant plays a self-proclaimed fat advocate learning to live her life loud and proud — but with a light touch.

Workin' Moms [Netflix]
The not-so-life-affirming aspects of parenting are explored through poignant drama and lactation gags.

Genre classic: *The Larry Sanders Show* • Boundary pusher: *Broad City*

If you liked *Insecure* …

A Black Lady Sketch Show [HBO Max]
Robin Thede's humor explores everything from church to parenting to office culture.

Chewing Gum [HBO Max]
Michaela Coel plays an ultra-religious virgin who decides it's time to have sex.

The Mindy Project [Hulu]
Mindy Kaling plays a doctor looking for love in this fan fave that mixed light comedy with romantic stakes.

Never Have I Ever [Netflix]
Highly satisfying sitcom about a goofy teenager and her immigrant family.

One Day at a Time [Paramount+, Netflix]
Latino reboot of the 1970s sitcom has a distinct and entertaining voice all its own.

Run the World [Starz]
Another winner from the creator of *Dear White People* about four ambitious Black women living in Harlem.

Genre classic: *Living Single* • Boundary pusher: *Tuca and Bertie*

If you liked *Maid* …

Little Fires Everywhere [Hulu]
Reese Witherspoon and Kerry
Washington and their families are
intertwined in this 1990s-era soap.

The Tale [HBO Max]
Laura Dern in a bravura performance
plays a filmmaker whose work sends her
tumbling into her past.

Unbelievable [Netflix]
Acclaimed fact-based miniseries about an
elusive rapist is carried by its female leads.

Unorthodox [Netflix]
A young woman tries to flee her
suffocating ultra-Orthodox sect in this
fine coming-of-age drama.

Unpregnant [HBO Max]
High schooler convinces her ex-pal to join
her on a road trip for an abortion.

Veneno [HBO Max]
Upbeat biopic of Spain's beloved
transgender icon, a complicated woman
who battled her way to public recognition.

Genre classic: *Confirmation* • Boundary pusher: *Undone*

If you liked *Manifest* …

Babylon Berlin [Netflix]
Lavish period drama brings to life Weimar
Germany, where messy democracy rules
the day and libertinism fuels the night.

Homecoming [Prime Video]
Fact-based thriller about a woman who
helps soldiers recover memories of war.

People of Earth [Hulu]
Wyatt Cenac plays a journalist who joins
a support group for people claiming
abduction by aliens.

Timeless [Hulu]
An unlikely trio are in hot pursuit of a
criminal who's stolen a time machine.

Upload [Prime Video]
This comedy is a worthy successor to *The
Good Place* and *Forever*.

The Wilds [Prime Video]
In this plane-crash-on-a-desert-island
thriller, all the survivors are girls.

Yellowjackets [Showtime]
Imagine *The Wilds* pieced together
through a series of chilling flashbacks.

Genre classic: *Lost* • Boundary pusher: *Forever*

If you liked *Mare of Easttown* …

Bloodlands [Acorn TV]
Grim, unpredictable thriller wraps a
detective's and Northern Ireland's troubled
histories around a kidnapping case.

Happy Town [ABC.com]
Melodramatic, enjoyable murder mystery
is set in a small Minnesota town where no
crime has been committed in years.

Hightown [Starz]
Diverse crime saga is elevated by Monica
Raymund's turn as an addict.

Terriers [Hulu]
Short-lived, delightful procedural about
detectives whose shoddy personal lives
dovetailed with the crimes they solved.

Top of the Lake [Hulu]
Elisabeth Moss brings real depth to a
stock role.

The Twelve [Netflix]
Belgian drama revolves around a jury as it
is affected by testimony in a murder trial.

Genre classic: *Broadchurch* • Boundary pusher: *Alias Grace*

If you liked *The Morning Show* …

Black Monday [Showtime]
Farcical period piece about financial titans behaving badly in the Reagan era.

Gentefied [Netflix]
Mexican-American cousins in L.A. make a better life for themselves even as they leave behind people and places they love.

Good Girls Revolt [Prime Video]
Acclaimed feminist drama about a 1960s uprising by lady journalists suffered a most ironic ending.

Halt and Catch Fire [AMC+]
This underrated period piece immerses viewers in the high-stakes geekery of the PC and early Internet eras.

Harlots [Hulu]
Bawdy 18th-century brothel drama has interesting notes of *The Wire* and *The Handmaids Tale*.

The White Lotus [HBO Max]
Wicked sendup of white privilege revolves around guests at a Hawaiian resort who tear each other to shreds.

Genre classic: *Mad Men* • Boundary pusher: *The Comeback*

If you liked *On My Block* …

Betty [HBO Max]
An all-girls skateboarding group in NYC crashes the sport's aggressively male subculture in this fast-moving show.

Everything Sucks! [Netflix]
At a high school in 1990s Oregon, teen misfits from the AV club and drama club band together to make a movie.

Ginny & Georgia [Netflix]
A mother and daughter keep secrets from their new small town (and each other) in this twist on *Gilmore Girls*.

Reservation Dogs [Hulu]
Four Indigenous teenagers in Oklahoma run grifts and cons to pay their way to the promised land of California.

Vida [Starz]
Latinx sisters return to East L.A. after their mother dies, only to learn a secret she'd been keeping from them.

We Are Who We Are [HBO Max]
European director offers a fresh take on the coming-of-age genre that captures the drift and delight of teenagerdom.

Genre classic: *My So-Called Life* • Boundary pusher: *I Am Not Okay With This*

If you liked *Only Murders in the Building* …

Barry [HBO Max]
Bill Hader and Henry Winkler won Emmys for their delightfully dark turns as a hit man and his acting coach.

Blindspotting [Starz]
Charming and occasionally surreal spinoff to the 2018 film.

The Righteous Gemstones [HBO Max]
Superstars of the megachurch world hide their increasingly criminal behavior.

Search Party [HBO Max]
Self-absorbed young adults find themselves covering up a murder.

Teenage Bounty Hunters [Netflix]
Ribald comedy set in Christian suburbia follows two sisters who need cash fast.

Woke [Hulu]
A Black comic-book artist struggles with identity issues while putting up with well-meaning white people.

Genre classic: *Catastrophe* • Boundary pusher: *Random Acts of Flyness*

If you liked *Ozark* …

Defending Jacob [Apple TV+]
Effective adaptation of the bestselling crime novel about a teenager whose parents will do anything to clear his name.

The Night Manager [Prime Video]
Tom Hiddleston and Hugh Laurie circle each other in an improbable cat-and-mouse spy game.

The Night Of [HBO Max]
Stellar casting and writing set apart this multiple-Emmy-winning series about criminal justice.

Your Honor [Showtime]
Bryan Cranston plays a judge covering up a crime by his son in one of Showtime's biggest hits in years.

Genre classic: *Breaking Bad* • Boundary pusher: *McMillions*

If you liked *Schitt's Creek* …

Better Things [Hulu]
Groundbreaking show about a single mom with daughters and a lot of issues.

Everything's Gonna Be Okay [Hulu]
Josh Thomas created and stars in this dramedy with an off-kilter take on autism, grieving and puberty.

The Other Two [HBO Max]
A rollicking satire of Internet fame and a poignant look at social media's impact on our relationships.

Please Like Me [Hulu]
Josh Thomas in an unflinching show about a gay man helping his mother navigate depression.

Rutherford Falls [Peacock]
Indigenous and white cultures clash in a small-town comedy that's surprisingly sweet and philosophical.

This Close [AMC+]
Deaf BFFs rely on each other in this dramedy about love and life in L.A.

Genre classic: *Family Ties* • Boundary pusher: *Solar Opposites*

If you liked *Squid Game* …

Altered Carbon [Netflix]
Stylish alt-future allegory where the rich avoid death by having their thoughts and memories transferred to another body.

Jericho [Paramount+]
A small town in Kansas becomes a refuge post-nuclear holocaust in this underrated CBS drama from the '00s.

Panic [Prime Video]
Addictive YA drama based on Lauren Oliver's bestseller.

The Society [Netflix]
Everyone in town disappears, so a group of teenagers must create society anew.

The Third Day [HBO Max]
Jude Law wanders onto a mysterious island whose inhabitants are fiercely protective of their way of life.

Yellowjackets [Showtime]
Decades after surviving a plane crash as girls, a group of women come to terms with what they did to stay alive.

Genre classic: *Mr. Robot* • Boundary pusher: *Sweet Tooth*

If you liked *Stranger Things* …

Counterpart [Prime Video]
J.K. Simmons stars in a tantalizing dual role as characters in parallel universes.

The OA [Netflix]
Engrossing sci-fi series is a challenge to watch but builds to an emotionally satisfying coda.

Room 104 [HBO Max]
Unpredictable anthology series about guests staying in the same hotel.

Servant [Apple TV+]
M. Night Shyamalan's thriller might be better enjoyed as a creepy comedy.

Tales From the Loop [Prime Video]
Character-driven anthology set in a small town where a machine makes seemingly impossible things happen.

The Terror [AMC+]
Slow-building horror, based on historical events, seasoned with monsters, adds up to maximum fear.

Genre classic: *The Twilight Zone* • Boundary pusher: *Resident Alien*

If you liked *Succession* …

Billions [Showtime, Prime Video]
It's over-the-top and unrealistic, but it's got Damian Lewis facing off against Paul Giamatti; what more do you need?

The Deuce [HBO Max]
The Wire's creator digs into the gritty subculture of porn in Times Square in the 1970s and '80s.

Greenleaf [Netflix]
Solidly acted prime-time soap about a Black family that runs a Memphis megachurch.

Industry [HBO Max]
Formulaic but fun finance drama about a young woman doing what it takes to succeed at a London investment bank.

Peaky Blinders [Netflix]
This epic family drama set in post–World War I England gets better with each season.

Ray Donovan [Showtime]
Liev Schreiber is brilliant as a professional fixer who's less successful managing the constant crises in his own family.

Genre classic: *Dynasty* • Boundary pusher: *House of Lies*

If you liked *Ted Lasso* …

All Creatures Great and Small [PBS Passport]
Remake of the 1978 James Herriot series about an English country vet updates the story but remains sweet and humane.

Brooklyn Nine-Nine [Peacock, Hulu]
Mike Schur reimagines *Barney Miller* with his usual subtlety, heart and inside jokes.

GLOW [Netflix]
Follow the Gorgeous Ladies of Wrestling in this winning love letter to the '80s.

Slings and Arrows [AMC+, Acorn TV]
Ten years before *Schitt's Creek*, Canada graced us with another comedy classic.

Sunderland 'Til I Die [Netflix]
Follow an English football team and its fans as they deal with relegation from the Premier League.

We Are Lady Parts [Peacock]
Dorky PhD student is recruited to play guitar for a Muslim female punk band in this unusual comedy.

Genre classic: *Parks and Recreation* • Boundary pusher: *We Are the Champions*

If you liked *This Is Us* …

The Fosters [Hulu, Prime Video]
Warm-hearted alt-family series follows
the biological and foster children raised by
two women in San Diego.

Queen Sugar [Hulu]
Quietly powerful drama about Black
siblings in rural Louisiana weaves the
region's troubled history into storylines.

Sorry for Your Loss [Facebook Watch]
A woman tries to move on after the death
of her husband.

Virgin River [Netflix]
Quirky, scenic romcom meets *Northern
Exposure*.

Wanderlust [Netflix]
The always watchable Toni Collette boosts
this British series about a couple entering
into an open marriage.

Younger [Hulu, Paramount+]
An overlooked TV triumph for Sutton
Foster as a 40-something mom passing as
20-something in order to reinvent her life.

Genre classic: *Parenthood* • Boundary pusher: *This Way Up*

If you liked *The Vow* …

Going Clear [HBO Max]
Still the most devastating brief against the
Church of Scientology.

Heaven's Gate [HBO Max]
Cults don't have power, this chilling
docuseries argues; cults draw their power
from stories and storytellers.

LuLaRich [Prime Video]
The rise and fall of a billion-dollar scheme,
as told by the middle-class women who
bet their livelihoods on it.

The Way Down [HBO Max]
Weight loss meets Jesus in this
spellbinding profile of a 21st-century guru
whose ministry went off the rails.

WeWork [Hulu]
How a $47 billion startup turned into a
disastrous cult of personality.

Wild Wild Country [Netflix]
A 1980s Oregon sect is the topic of one of
the jaw-droppingest docuseries on Netflix,
which is saying something.

Genre classic: *Jonestown* • Boundary pusher: *Baby God*

If you liked *Watchmen* …

11.22.63 [Hulu]
An English teacher travels back in time to
stop the JFK assassination in this affecting
adaptation of Stephen King's novel.

The Boys [Prime Video]
Superheroes turn out to be horrible people
working for a mega-corporation bent on
world domination — enter The Boys!

Humans [Prime Video]
People rely on lifelike androids to do all
kinds of human tasks. One day, the synths
become self-aware.

The Man in the High Castle [Prime Video]
Nuanced alt-history, based on the Philip
K. Dick novel, imagines America after the
Nazis and Japanese win World War II.

Orphan Black [AMC+, Prime Video]
Tatiana Maslany dazzles as a character
with many clones who are all being
pursued by shadowy forces.

WandaVision [Disney+]
This Marvel series won over a lot of non-
superhero fans, thanks to its 1950s-sitcom
premise and appealing storyline.

Genre classic: *Battlestar Galactica* • Boundary pusher: *The Leftovers*

If you liked *Yellowstone* and *1883* ...

Big Sky [Hulu]
Better-than-average network thriller has two female private detectives taking on a kidnapping ring in Montana.

Godless [Netflix]
Jeff Daniels plays an 1880s outlaw in a New Mexico town run by tough women.

The Good Lord Bird [Showtime]
Ethan Hawke stars in a wildly entertaining romp through history, based on the acclaimed novel about abolitionist John Brown.

Longmire [Netflix]
Gorgeously shot Western follows a sheriff who uses salty humor and endless determination to solve crimes.

The North Water [AMC+]
Dark, absorbing 1850s maritime drama about survival aboard an ill-starred fishing boat.

Perpetual Grace, LTD [Epix]
A drifter is sucked into a scheme to kidnap a pastor and his wife, who are more menacing than they seem.

Genre classic: *Deadwood* • Boundary pusher: *Wynonna Earp*

If you liked *You* ...

The Beast Must Die [AMC+, BritBox]
Cush Jumbo plays a mom out for revenge against a man she believes killed her son.

Cruel Summer [Hulu]
Hooky cable hit about two teen girls and the crime that ties them together.

Damages [Hulu, Starz]
Glenn Close and Rose Byrne chewed every bit of scenery in an unpredictable legal thriller that's been rarely matched.

Landscapers [HBO Max]
Olivia Colman and David Thewlis play an English couple who plot to kill her parents and bury them in the back yard.

Losing Alice [Apple TV+]
Older female film director falls for a script and the young woman who wrote it.

The Stranger [Netflix]
A man's life is upended when a stranger tells him a secret involving his wife.

Genre classic: *Gossip Girl* • Boundary pusher: *Kevin Can F**k Himself*

Shows So Nice, They Made Them Twice

It's not a matter of *if* but *when* Streaming TV reboots your favorite show.

Battlestar Galactica
1970s version: Lorne Greene in a *Star Wars* imitation. '00s version: Smart, feminized allegory for a post-9/11 world.

Beverly Hills 90210
Nineties version: High school idealized for Gen Y. 2008 version: New cast, new characters, new energy. 2019 version: The original cast returns, only to find the world has moved on.

Charmed
'00s version: Three sisters discover they're the world's most powerful good witches. New version: The sisters are Latinx and they're still a force for good.

Doogie Howser, MD
1980s version: "Doogie Howser is too young to be practicing medicine!" New version: "Hey, this teenage doctor reminds me of Doogie Howser!"

Dynasty
1980s version: Joan Collins makes being an entitled rich lady fun to watch. New version: Awful rich people suffering consequences is fun to watch.

The Equalizer
Nineties version: Middle-aged Brit can get you out of a fix. New version: Let Queen Latifah be your mama bear.

Fantasy Island
1970s version: Island version of *The Love Boat*. New version: Female-forward magical realism.

Gossip Girl
'00s version: Bitchy soap about NYC prep schoolers. New version: Sexier, not as catty or self-important as the original.

How I Met your Mother
'00s version: "Your mom and I met on a sitcom with these hilarious friends." New version: "Your dad and I met on a sitcom that the critics didn't like."

iCarly
'00s version: Goofy kids make a hit web series. New version: Everyone's older, nobody's changed — and they're still making a show on the web.

One Day at a Time
1970s version: Innocuous sitcom gets bogged down by co-star's off-camera issues. New version: The cast is Latinx and issues happen *on* camera.

Party of Five
Nineties version: Five children are orphaned when their parents die. New version: Parents are deported.

Perry Mason
Classic version: Perry is the squeaky clean, no-nonsense defender who has your back. New version: Perry is a private dick in an R-rated noir film.

Saved By the Bell
1980s version: Jessie and Slater are students at Bayside High. New version: Jessie and Slater *work* at Bayside High.

Veronica Mars
'00s version: Lovable noir drama about a student moonlighting as a P.I. New version: Same show, fan service edition.

The Wonder Years
1980s version: A man looks back on growing up in white suburbia during the 1960s. New version: A Black man looks back on growing up in white suburbia during the 1960s.

380

Recommended Shows Sorted by Premium Streamer

Note: Many of these titles are also available on ad-supported streaming channels. For more information, consult the show's listing in Part II.

Acorn TV
Bloodlands   *Crime drama*
Deadwater Fell   *Limited series (crime drama)*
Detectorists   *British comedy*
The Drowning   *Limited series (thriller)*
I, Claudius   *Limited series (historical drama)*
The Larkins   *Family comedy-drama*
Line of Duty   *Crime drama*
The Missing   *Crime drama*
Slings and Arrows   *Comedy-drama*

AMC+
Back   *Dark comedy*
Baroness Von Sketch Show   *Sketch comedy*
The Beast Must Die   *Anthology series (thriller)*
Deadwater Fell   *Limited series (crime drama)*
Dispatches from Elsewhere   *Drama*
The Drowning   *Limited series (thriller)*
The Fall   *Crime drama*
Fear the Walking Dead   *Dystopian drama*
Gangs of London   *Crime drama*
Gaycation   *Docuseries*
Halt and Catch Fire   *Historical drama*
Happy Valley   *Crime drama*
Kevin Can F**k Himself   *Dark comedy*
Killing Eve   *Action drama*
La Llorona   *Movie (horror)*
Lake Mungo   *Movie (horror)*
Mad Men   *Historical drama*
The North Water   *Limited series (drama)*
Orphan Black   *Sci-fi drama*
Portlandia   *Sketch comedy*
Quiz   *Docuseries*
Ragdoll   *Thriller*
Rectify   *Drama*
Slings and Arrows   *Comedy-drama*
The Spoils of Babylon   *Satirical comedy*
Spy City   *Limited series (thriller)*

This Close   *Drama*
Too Close   *Limited series (thriller)*
Trouble the Water   *Movie (documentary)*
The Walking Dead   *Dystopian drama*
Weiner   *Movie (documentary)*

Apple TV+
1971: The Year That Music Changed
   Everything   *Docuseries*
Acapulco   *Comedy*
Boys State   *Movie (documentary)*
Central Park   *Animated comedy*
CODA   *Movie (drama)*
Defending Jacob   *Limited series (crime drama)*
Dickinson   *Comedy-drama*
For All Mankind   *Alternative history*
Home Before Dark   *Family comedy*
Little America   *Anthology series (drama)*
Losing Alice   *Limited series (romance drama)*
The Morning Show   *Drama*
The Mosquito Coast   *Drama*
Mythic Quest   *Comedy*
On the Rocks   *Movie (comedy)*
Palmer   *Movie (drama)*
Physical   *Comedy-drama*
Schmigadoon!   *Musical comedy*
Servant   *Horror*
StartupU   *Reality*
Ted Lasso   *Comedy-drama*
Truth Be Told   *Crime drama*
The Velvet Underground   *Movie (documentary)*
Visible: Out on Television   *Docuseries*
Watch the Sound with Mark Ronson
   Docuseries
Wolfwalkers   *Animated sci-fi film*

BritBox
Are You Being Served?   *British comedy*

The Beast Must Die *Anthology series (thriller)*
Doctor Who *Sci-fi drama*
Downton Abbey *Historical drama*
The Fall *Crime drama*
Fawlty Towers *Classic sitcom*
Gardeners' World *Docuseries*
Jane Eyre *Limited series (romance drama)*
Life on Mars (UK) *Crime drama*
Line of Duty *Crime drama*
Pride and Prejudice *Limited series (romance drama)*
The Up Series *Docuseries*
Yes, Minister *British comedy*

Discovery+

Accused: Guilty or Innocent *True crime*
Amy Schumer Learns to Cook *CelebReality*
The Bachelor/Bachelorette *Reality competition*
BattleBots *Reality competition*
Blue Planet *Docuseries*
Blue Planet II *Docuseries*
Chasing the Thunder *Movie (documentary)*
Deadliest Catch *Reality*
Design Star: Next Gen *Reality competition*
Dynasties *Docuseries*
Fixer Upper: Welcome Home *Reality*
The Last Alaskans *Reality*
Naked and Afraid *Reality competition*
A Perfect Planet *Docuseries*
Planet Earth II *Docuseries*
The Repair Shop *Reality*
Undercover Billionaire *Reality*
The Worst Cooks in America *Reality competition*

Disney+

The Beatles: Get Back *Docuseries*
Becoming Cousteau *Movie (documentary)*
Big Shot *Family comedy-drama*
The Book of Boba Fett *Drama*
Continent 7: Antarctica *Docuseries*
Doogie Kamealoha, M.D. *Family comedy*
Encore! *Musical*
The Falcon and the Winter Soldier *Limited series (superhero drama)*
Flora and Ulysses *Movie (family comedy)*
Hamilton *Movie (staged musical)*
High School Musical: The Musical - The Series *Musical comedy*
Jane *Movie (documentary)*
Loki *Superhero drama*
The Mandalorian *Sci-fi drama*
Marvel's Agent Carter *Superhero drama*
The Mysterious Benedict Society *Family drama*
Noelle *Movie (family comedy)*
Once Upon a Time *Fantasy drama*
One Strange Rock *Docuseries*
Race to the Center of the Earth *Reality competition*

The Right Stuff *Historical drama*
Safety *Movie (drama)*
The Simpsons *Animated comedy*
Soul *Movie (animated comedy)*
Star Wars: The Clone Wars *Animated drama*
Stargirl *Movie (family comedy)*
Timmy Failure: Mistakes Were Made *Movie (family comedy)*
WandaVision *Superhero drama limited series,Marvel,lim*

Epix

Fall River *Limited series (true crime)*
Get Shorty *Dark comedy*
Helter Skelter: An American Myth *Limited series (true crime)*
Perpetual Grace, LTD *Crime drama*

HBO Max

100 Foot Wave *Docuseries*
8-Bit Christmas *Movie (family comedy)*
Adventure Time *Animated comedy*
Agents of Chaos *Movie (documentary)*
The Alienist *Crime drama*
Allen v. Farrow *Docuseries*
An American Pickle *Movie (comedy)*
American Splendor *Movie (documentary)*
Amy Schumer: Live at the Apollo *Comedy special*
And Just Like That… *Comedy-drama*
Angels in America *Limited series (drama)*
At Home with Amy Sedaris *Sketch comedy*
Awkwafina Is Nora from Queens *Comedy*
Baby God *Movie (documentary)*
The Bachelor/Bachelorette *Reality competition*
Bad Education *Movie (dark comedy)*
Band of Brothers *Limited series (historical drama)*
Barry *Dark comedy*
Batwoman *Superhero drama*
Beanie Mania *Movie (documentary)*
The Bee Gees: How Can You Mend a Broken Heart *Movie (documentary)*
Behind the Candelabra *Movie (drama)*
Bessie *Movie (drama)*
Betty *Comedy-drama*
The Big Bang Theory *Sitcom*
Big Little Lies *Drama*
Big Love *Drama*
Billy on the Street *Comedy,Reality*
A Black Lady Sketch Show *Sketch comedy*
Boardwalk Empire *Drama*
Bored to Death *Comedy*
Capturing the Friedmans *Movie (documentary)*
Charm City Kings *Movie (drama)*
Chernobyl *Limited series (historical drama)*
Chewing Gum *British comedy*
Class Action Park *Movie (documentary)*

The Comeback *Comedy*
Confirmation *Movie (drama)*
Crazy, Not Insane *Movie (true crime)*
The Crime of the Century *Limited series (true crime)*
Curb Your Enthusiasm *Comedy*
David Byrne's American Utopia *Musical special*
David Makes Man *Drama*
Deadwood *Historical drama*
Degrassi: The Next Generation *Teen drama*
The Deuce *Historical drama*
Divorce *Comedy-drama*
Doctor Who *Sci-fi drama*
The Dog House: UK *Docuseries*
Doom Patrol *Fantasy comedy*
Eagleheart *Satirical comedy*
Ellen Degeneres: Here and Now *Comedy special*
Enlightened *Comedy-drama*
Euphoria *Teen drama*
Exterminate All the Brutes *Docuseries*
The Fades *Horror*
Fast Foodies *Reality competition*
The Flight Attendant *Comedy thriller*
Flight of the Conchords *Musical comedy*
Frayed *British comedy*
Friends *Classic sitcom*
Game of Thrones *Fantasy drama*
Gentleman Jack *Historical drama*
Getting On *Comedy*
The Gilded Age *Historical drama*
Girls *Comedy*
Going Clear *Movie (documentary)*
Gossip Girl (2007) *Teen drama*
Gossip Girl (2021) *Teen drama*
The Great Pottery Throw Down *Reality competition*
Grey Gardens *Movie (historical drama)*
Hacks *Comedy*
Happy Endings *Sitcom*
Hard Knocks: Los Angeles *Anthology series (documentary)*
Harley Quinn *Animated comedy*
Hear and Now *Movie (documentary)*
Heaven's Gate: The Cult of Cults *Docuseries*
High Maintenance *Anthology series (comedy)*
His Dark Materials *Fantasy drama*
The Honourable Woman *Limited series (drama)*
Hoop Dreams *Movie (documentary)*
How To with John Wilson *Docuseries*
I Hate Suzie *Comedy*
I Know This Much Is True *Limited series (drama)*
I Love You, Now Die *Movie (documentary)*
I May Destroy You *Drama*
I'll Be Gone in the Dark *Limited series (true crime)*
In Treatment *Drama*
Industry *Drama*
Insecure *Comedy*
The Investigation *Limited series (crime drama)*
It's a Sin *Limited series (drama)*

Jane Eyre *Limited series (romance drama)*
Jim: The James Foley Story *Movie (documentary)*
The Jinx: The Life and Deaths of Robert Durst *Limited series (true crime)*
Joe Pera Talks With You *Comedy*
John Adams *Limited series (historical drama)*
Judas and the Black Messiah *Movie (historical drama)*
Keep Your Hands Off Eizouken! *Animated comedy*
The Lady and the Dale *Docuseries*
Landscapers *Limited series (crime drama)*
The Larry Sanders Show *Classic sitcom*
Leaving Neverland *Movie (documentary)*
The Leftovers *Fantasy drama*
Legendary *Reality competition*
Lois & Clark: The New Adventures of Superman *Superhero drama*
Looney Tunes Cartoons *Animated comedy*
Los Espookys *Fantasy comedy*
Love Life *Anthology series (romantic comedy)*
Lovecraft Country *Sci-fi drama*
Made for Love *Sci-fi drama*
Mare of Easttown *Limited series (crime drama)*
McMillions *Docuseries*
Mildred Pierce *Limited series (drama)*
Miracle Workers *Anthology series (comedy)*
Mr. Show with Bob and David *Sketch comedy*
Mrs. Fletcher *Comedy-drama limited series*
Murder on Middle Beach *Limited series (true crime)*
My Favorite Shapes by Julio Torres *Comedy special*
The Mystery of D.B. Cooper *Movie (documentary)*
The Nanny *Classic sitcom*
The New Pope *Limited series (drama)*
The Newsroom (US) *Drama*
The Night Of *Limited series (crime drama)*
No Sudden Move *Movie (thriller)*
The Normal Heart *Movie (historical drama)*
Nuclear Family *Docuseries*
Olive Kitteridge *Limited series (drama)*
On the Record *Movie (documentary)*
The Other Two *Comedy*
Our Boys *Limited series (drama)*
The Outsider *Limited series (crime drama)*
Oz *Crime drama*
Painting with John *Reality*
Peacemaker *Drama*
Perry Mason (2020) *Crime drama*
The Plot Against America *Limited series (alternative history)*
Pretty Little Liars *Teen drama*
Pride and Prejudice *Limited series (romance drama)*
Project Greenlight *Reality competition*
Pure (2019) *Comedy-drama limited series*
Pushing Daisies *Comedy-drama*
Q: Into the Storm *Docuseries*

Raised by Wolves   *Sci-fi drama*
Random Acts of Flyness   *Sketch comedy*
Recount   *Movie (drama)*
Reno 911!   *Satirical comedy*
Reno 911!   *Satirical comedy*
Rick and Morty   *Animated comedy*
The Righteous Gemstones   *Dark comedy*
Room 104   *Anthology series (dark comedy)*
Rose Matafeo: Horndog   *Comedy special*
Scenes from a Marriage   *Limited series (drama)*
Search Party   *Dark comedy*
The Sentence   *Movie (documentary)*
Sex and the City   *Romantic comedy*
The Sex Lives of College Girls   *Romantic comedy*
Sharp Objects   *Limited series (crime drama)*
Show Me a Hero   *Limited series (historical drama)*
Silicon Valley   *Workplace comedy*
Six Feet Under   *Comedy-drama*
Small Town News: KPVM Pahrump   *Docuseries*
Somebody Somewhere   *Comedy*
The Sopranos   *Drama*
South Park   *Animated comedy*
Starstruck   *British romcom*
Station Eleven   *Limited series (dystopian drama)*
Steven Universe   *Animated comedy*
Succession   *Dark comedy*
Superintelligence   *Sci-fi comedy film*
Superman & Lois   *Superhero drama*
The Tale   *Movie (drama)*
Temple Grandin   *Movie (drama)*
The Third Day   *Limited series (thriller)*
Transhood   *Movie (documentary)*
Treme   *Drama*
The Trial of Christine Keeler   *Limited series
   (historical drama)*
True Blood   *Fantasy drama*
True Detective   *Anthology series (crime drama)*
Underwater   *Sci-fi drama*
The Undoing   *Limited series (drama)*
Unpregnant   *Movie (comedy)*
Veep   *Sitcom*
Veneno   *Limited series (drama)*
The Vow   *Limited series (true crime)*
Watchmen   *Limited series (drama)*
The Way Down   *Docuseries*
We Are Who We Are   *Drama*
We're Here   *Reality*
Welcome to Chechnya   *Movie (documentary)*
The West Wing   *Drama*
The White Lotus   *Anthology series (dark comedy)*
Whitmer Thomas: The Golden One   *Comedy
   special*
The Wire   *Drama*
Wit   *Movie (drama)*
The Wolfpack   *Movie (documentary)*
Years And Years   *Limited series (drama)*
The Young Pope   *Limited series (dark comedy)*
Yvonne Orji: Momma, I Made It!   *Comedy special*

384

Hulu

24   *Action thriller*
11.22.63   *Limited series (historical drama)*
9-1-1   *Medical drama*
9-1-1: Lone Star   *Medical drama*
Abbott Elementary   *Sitcom*
Accused: Guilty or Innocent   *True crime*
The Act   *Limited series (drama)*
Adventure Time   *Animated comedy*
Ally McBeal   *Comedy-drama*
America's Got Talent   *Reality competition*
America's Next Top Model   *Reality competition*
American Crime   *Drama anthology series*
American Horror Story   *Anthology series (horror)*
American Idol   *Reality competition*
American Pickers   *Reality*
Angie Tribeca   *Satirical comedy*
Archer   *Animated comedy*
Are You The One?   *Reality competition*
Arrested Development   *Sitcom*
Atlanta   *Comedy*
The Bachelor/Bachelorette   *Reality competition*
Baghdad Central   *Historical drama*
Barb and Star Go to Vista Del Mar   *Movie
   (comedy)*
Baskets   *Dark comedy*
Behind the Mask   *Docuseries*
Better Things   *Comedy*
Beverly Hills 90210   *Teen drama*
Big Sky   *Drama*
Big Time Adolescence   *Movie (comedy)*
Black Love   *Docuseries*
Black Sails   *Fantasy drama*
Black-ish   *Sitcom*
Bless the Harts   *Animated comedy*
The Bob Newhart Show   *Classic sitcom*
Bob's Burgers   *Animated comedy*
Bones   *Drama*
Boss Level   *Movie (action)*
Boston Legal   *Drama*
Breeders   *British comedy*
Broad City   *Comedy*
Brockmire   *Comedy*
Brooklyn Nine-Nine   *Sitcom*
Buffy the Vampire Slayer   *Fantasy drama*
Bunheads   *Comedy-drama*
Burn Notice   *Crime drama*
Castle Rock   *Horror*
Casual   *Comedy-drama*
Cheers   *Sitcom*
Childrens Hospital   *Satirical comedy*
City So Real   *Docuseries*
Community   *Sitcom*
The Conners   *Sitcom*
Cougar Town   *Sitcom*
Crime + Punishment   *Movie (documentary)*
Cruel Summer   *Teen drama*
Damages   *Drama*
Dave   *Comedy*
Dawson's Creek   *Teen drama*

Deutschland 83/Deutschland 86/Deutschland 89   *Historical drama*
Devs   *Sci-fi drama*
Dollface   *Comedy*
Doogie Howser, M.D.   *Family comedy*
Dopesick   *Limited series (drama)*
Elementary   *Crime drama*
Everything's Gonna Be Okay   *Comedy*
The Fades   *Horror*
Fantasy Island (2021)   *Fantasy drama*
Fargo   *Anthology series (drama)*
Fear the Walking Dead   *Dystopian drama*
Felicity   *Romance drama*
Firefly   *Sci-fi drama*
Fosse/Verdon   *Limited series (drama)*
The Fosters   *Teen drama*
Framing Britney Spears   *Movie (documentary)*
Frasier   *Classic sitcom*
Freaks and Geeks   *Comedy-drama*
Friday Night Lights   *Drama*
Future Man   *Sci-fi comedy*
Genius: Einstein   *Anthology series (historical drama)*
Good Girls   *Dark comedy*
The Great   *Satirical comedy*
Greek   *Comedy-drama*
Grey's Anatomy   *Medical drama*
The Guardian   *Drama*
The Handmaid's Tale   *Dystopian drama*
Hannibal   *Crime drama*
Happiest Season   *Movie (romantic comedy)*
Happy Endings   *Sitcom*
Harlots   *Historical drama*
Hearts Beat Loud   *Movie (musical comedy)*
High Fidelity   *Romantic comedy*
Hillary   *Docuseries*
Hoarders   *Reality*
Holey Moley   *Reality competition*
Homeland   *Crime drama*
How I Met Your Father   *Comedy*
How I Met Your Mother   *Romantic comedy*
I Love Lucy   *Classic sitcom*
It's Always Sunny in Philadelphia   *Sitcom*
Justified   *Crime drama*
Keeping Up With the Kardashians   *CelebReality*
The Kids Are Alright   *Sitcom*
The Killing (US)   *Crime drama*
Killing Eve   *Action drama*
King of the Hill   *Animated comedy*
Kiri   *Limited series (crime drama)*
The L Word   *Romance drama*
The Last Man on Earth   *Sitcom*
Law & Order: SVU   *Crime drama*
The League   *Comedy*
Legion   *Sci-fi drama*
Letterkenny   *Comedy*
The Librarians   *Action comedy*
Line of Duty   *Crime drama*
Little Fires Everywhere   *Limited series (drama)*
Little Monsters   *Movie (horror)*

Living Single   *Classic sitcom*
Lodge 49   *Comedy*
The Looming Tower   *Limited series (drama)*
Lost   *Sci-fi drama*
Love Island (UK)   *Reality*
Love, Victor   *Romantic comedy*
M*A*S*H   *Classic sitcom*
Making It   *Reality competition*
Manhattan   *Historical drama*
Married at First Sight   *Reality*
The Mary Tyler Moore Show   *Sitcom*
The Masked Singer   *Reality competition*
The Mick   *Sitcom*
Minding the Gap   *Movie (documentary)*
The Mindy Project   *Sitcom*
Mixed-ish   *Sitcom*
Modern Family   *Sitcom*
Mom   *Sitcom*
The Most Dangerous Animal of All   *Limited series (true crime)*
Mr. Inbetween   *Crime drama*
Mrs. America   *Limited series (historical drama)*
My So-Called Life   *Teen drama*
Naked and Afraid   *Reality competition*
National Treasure (2016)   *Limited series (drama)*
Nip/Tuck   *Medical drama*
Nomadland   *Movie (drama)*
Normal People   *Limited series (romance drama)*
Oakland Trilogy: The Waiting Room, The Force, Homeroom   *Docuseries*
The Odd Couple (1970)   *Classic sitcom*
Only Murders in the Building   *Comedy thriller*
Palm Springs   *Movie (fantasy comedy)*
Parenthood   *Family drama*
Party Down   *Comedy*
Party of Five (2020)   *Teen drama*
The Path   *Drama*
PEN15   *Comedy*
People of Earth   *Sci-fi comedy*
Plan B   *Movie (comedy)*
Please Like Me   *Dark comedy*
Plus One   *Movie (romantic comedy)*
The Practice   *Crime drama*
Pride   *Docuseries*
Pride and Prejudice   *Limited series (romance drama)*
Pure (2017)   *Drama*
Queen Sugar   *Drama*
Ramy   *Comedy*
The Real Housewives of Atlanta   *Reality*
The Real Housewives of Beverly Hills   *Reality*
The Real Housewives of New Jersey   *Reality*
The Real Housewives of New York City   *Reality*
The Real Housewives of Orange County   *Reality*
The Real Housewives of Potomac   *Reality*
Rescue Me   *Comedy-drama*
Reservation Dogs   *Comedy*
The Riches   *Comedy-drama*
Rick and Morty   *Animated comedy*

Run *Movie (thriller)*
RuPaul's Drag Race *Reality competition*
Saturday Night Live *Sketch comedy*
Scandal *Drama*
Shark Tank *Reality competition*
The Shield *Drama*
Shrill *Comedy-drama*
Skin Wars *Reality competition*
Snowfall *Crime drama*
Solar Opposites *Animated comedy*
Sons of Anarchy *Drama*
Staged *Comedy-drama*
Steven Universe *Animated comedy*
Summer of Soul *Movie (documentary)*
Superstore *Sitcom*
Survivor *Reality competition*
Taste the Nation with Padma Lakshmi
    Docuseries
Terriers *Crime drama*
The Terror *Anthology series (horror)*
This Is Us *Family drama*
This Way Up *Dark comedy*
Timeless *Historical drama*
Too Funny to Fail *Movie (documentary)*
Top Chef *Reality competition*
Top of the Lake *Crime drama*
The Twilight Zone (1959) *Classic sci-fi anthology*
United States of Tara *Dark comedy*
The United States vs. Billie Holiday *Movie*
    (historical drama)
UnREAL *Drama*
Vacation Friends *Movie (comedy)*
Veronica Mars *Crime drama*
Vikings *Historical drama*
WeWork: Or the Making and Breaking of a $47
    Billion Unicorn *Movie (documentary)*
What We Do in the Shadows *Sitcom*
White Collar *Comedy-drama*
Will & Grace *Classic sitcom*
Woke *Comedy*
The Wonder Years (2021) *Family comedy*
The Worst Cooks in America *Reality competition*
You're the Worst *Dark comedy*
Young Rock *Sitcom*
Younger *Romantic comedy*
Zoey's Extraordinary Playlist *Musical comedy*

Netflix

1922 *Movie (horror)*
The 100 *Sci-fi drama*
13 Reasons Why *Teen drama*
13TH *Movie (documentary)*
30 Rock *Workplace comedy*
After Life *Dark comedy*
Ali Wong: Baby Cobra *Comedy special*
Alias Grace *Limited series (historical drama)*
All American *Drama*
Altered Carbon *Sci-fi drama*
Always Be My Maybe *Movie (romantic comedy)*

Amend: The Fight for America *Docuseries*
America's Next Top Model *Reality competition*
The American Barbecue Showdown *Reality*
    competition
American Crime Story *Limited series (drama)*
American Factory *Movie (documentary)*
American Horror Story *Anthology series (horror)*
American Murder: The Family Next Door *Movie*
    (true crime)
American Vandal *Satirical comedy*
Amy Schumer: Growing *Comedy special*
Anne with an E *Family drama*
Are You The One? *Reality competition*
Arrested Development *Sitcom*
Arrow *Superhero drama*
Ash vs. Evil Dead *Comedy-horror show*
Astronomy Club *Sketch comedy*
Atypical *Comedy-drama*
Away *Drama*
The Baby-Sitters Club *Family comedy*
Babylon Berlin *Historical drama*
The Babysitter *Movie (horror)*
Bad Trip *Movie (comedy)*
Best Leftovers Ever! *Reality competition*
Better Call Saul *Drama*
Big Mouth *Animated comedy*
Bird Box *Movie (thriller)*
Black Mirror *Anthology series (dystopian drama)*
Black Summer *Horror*
The Blacklist *Drama*
Bling Empire *Reality*
Bloodline *Drama*
Blown Away *Reality competition*
Bo Burnham: Inside *Comedy special*
Bobby Kennedy for President *Docuseries*
BoJack Horseman *Animated comedy*
Bonding *Comedy-drama*
A Boy Called Christmas *Movie (family comedy)*
Breaking Bad *Drama*
Bridgerton *Historical drama*
Broadchurch *Crime drama*
Calibre *Movie (thriller)*
Call the Midwife *Historical drama*
The Casketeers *Docuseries*
Castlevania *Animated drama*
The Chair *Comedy-drama*
Challenger: The Final Flight *Docuseries*
Charmed (2018) *Fantasy drama*
Chasing Coral *Movie (documentary)*
Cheer *Docuseries*
The Chef Show *Docuseries*
Chef's Table *Docuseries*
Chilling Adventures of Sabrina *Fantasy drama*
The Circle *Reality competition*
Cobra Kai *Comedy-drama*
Cocaine Cowboys: The Kings of Miami *Limited*
    series (crime drama)
Colin in Black & White *Limited series (drama)*
Comedians in Cars Getting Coffee *Talk show*
The Comey Rule *Limited series (historical drama)*

Community *Sitcom*
The Confession Tapes *Limited series (true crime)*
Conversations with a Killer: The Ted Bundy Tapes *True crime*
Crashing (British series) *Limited series (British comedy)*
Crazy Delicious *Reality competition*
Crazy Ex-Girlfriend *Musical comedy*
Crime Scene *True crime*
Crip Camp *Movie (documentary)*
The Crown *Historical drama*
Cut Throat City *Movie (action)*
Da 5 Bloods *Action,Drama*
Dark *Thriller*
The Dark Crystal: Age of Resistance *Fantasy drama*
Dash & Lily *Romantic comedy*
Dating Around *Reality*
Dave Chappelle: Sticks & Stones *Comedy special*
Dawson's Creek *Teen drama*
Dead Set *Comedy-horrorshow limited series*
Dead to Me *Dark comedy*
Deaf U *Docuseries*
Dear White People *Comedy-drama*
DeMarcus Family Rules *CelebReality*
Derry Girls *British comedy*
Dick Johnson Is Dead *Movie (documentary)*
Dirty John: The Betty Broderick Story *Anthology series (drama)*
Dirty Money *Docuseries*
Disenchantment *Animated comedy*
Documentary Now! *Comedy*
Dolemite Is My Name *Movie (comedy)*
Dolly Parton's Christmas on the Square *Movie (family comedy)*
Dolly Parton's Heartstrings *Musical,Drama anthology series*
Don't F**k With Cats: Hunting an Internet Killer *Limited series (true crime)*
Don't Look Up *Sci-fi comedy*
The Duchess *Comedy-drama*
Dynasty (2017) *Drama*
Easy (2016) *Anthology series (comedy)*
The Eddy *Limited series (drama)*
Emily in Paris *Romantic comedy*
The End of the F***ing World *Dark comedy*
The English Game *Limited series (British drama)*
Enola Holmes *Movie (action)*
Episodes *Comedy*
Eurovision Song Contest: The Story of Fire Saga *Movie (musical comedy)*
Everything Sucks! *Limited series (comedy)*
Evil *Drama*
F Is For Family *Animated comedy*
The Family *Docuseries*
Fear Street (movie trilogy) *Anthology series (horror)*
Feel Good *British romcom*
Firefly Lane *Drama*

Floor Is Lava *Reality competition*
Fractured *Movie (thriller)*
Free Rein *Family comedy-drama*
Friday Night Lights *Drama*
Gentefied *Comedy-drama*
Gilmore Girls *Comedy-drama*
Ginny & Georgia *Dark comedy*
Glee *Musical comedy*
GLOW *Comedy-drama*
Godless *Limited series (drama)*
Good Girls *Dark comedy*
The Good Place *Sitcom*
The Goop Lab *CelebReality*
Grace and Frankie *Comedy*
The Great British Baking Show *Reality competition*
Great News *Sitcom*
Greenleaf *Drama*
Grey's Anatomy *Medical drama*
Halston *Limited series (historical drama)*
Hannah Gadsby: Nanette *Comedy special*
Happy Endings *Sitcom*
Hasan Minhaj: Homecoming King *Comedy special*
The Haunting of Bly Manor *Limited series (horror)*
The Haunting of Hill House *Limited series (horror)*
High Score *Docuseries*
History of Swear Words *Docuseries*
Hoarders *Reality*
Hollywood *Limited series (historical drama)*
House of Cards *Drama*
How To Fix a Drug Scandal *Limited series (true crime)*
How To Get Away with Murder *Crime drama*
I Am a Killer *True crime*
I Am Not Okay with This *Dark comedy*
I Am Not Your Negro *Movie (documentary)*
I Think You Should Leave with Tim Robinson *Sketch comedy*
Icarus *Movie (documentary)*
Immigration Nation *Docuseries*
The Innocence Files *True crime*
Instant Hotel *Reality competition*
The Irishman *Movie (drama)*
The Irregulars *Crime drama*
Jack Whitehall: Travels with My Father *British comedy*
Jane the Virgin *Romantic comedy*
Jingle Jangle: A Holiday Journey *Movie (family comedy)*
Joan Didion: The Center Will Not Hold *Movie (documentary)*
Julie and the Phantoms *Musical comedy*
The Keepers *Limited series (true crime)*
Kim's Convenience *Sitcom*
Kingdom *Thriller*
The Kissing Booth *Movie (romantic comedy)*
Klaus *Movie (animated comedy)*

Knock Down the House *Movie (documentary)*
Lady Dynamite *Comedy*
Last Chance U *Docuseries*
Last Chance U: Basketball *Docuseries*
The Last Dance *Docuseries*
Lenox Hill *Docuseries*
The Letdown *Comedy*
Living Undocumented *Docuseries*
Living with Yourself *Fantasy comedy*
Locke & Key *Horror*
Longmire *Crime drama*
The Lost Daughter *Movie (drama)*
Lost in Space *Sci-fi drama*
Love *Romantic comedy*
Love Is Blind *Reality*
Love on the Spectrum *Reality*
Love, Death & Robots *Animated sci-fi anthology series*
The Lovebirds *Action comedy*
Lovesick *British romcom*
Lucifer *Crime drama*
Lupin *Crime drama*
Ma Rainey's Black Bottom
Maid *Limited series (drama)*
Making a Murderer *True crime*
Manhunt: Unabomber *Limited series (true crime)*
Maniac *Sci-fi drama limited series*
Mank *Movie (drama)*
Maria Bamford: The Special Special Special! *Comedy special*
Marriage or Mortgage *Reality*
Marriage Story *Movie (drama)*
Master of None *Comedy-drama*
Medical Police *Satirical comedy*
Middleditch & Schwartz *Comedy special*
The Midnight Gospel *Animated comedy*
Midnight Mass *Limited series (horror)*
Mindhunter *Crime drama*
The Mitchells vs. the Machines *Animated sci-fi film*
The Mole (2001) *Reality competition*
Money Heist (La casa de papel) *Crime drama*
The Movies That Made Us *Docuseries*
My Next Guest Needs No Introduction with David Letterman *Talk show*
My Octopus Teacher *Movie (documentary)*
Nadiya Bakes *Docuseries*
Nail Bomber: Manhunt *Movie (documentary)*
Nailed It! *Game show*
Narcos *Crime drama*
Narcos: Mexico *Crime drama*
NCIS *Drama*
Never Have I Ever *Romantic comedy*
New Girl *Sitcom*
Night Stalker: The Hunt for a Serial Killer *Limited series (true crime)*
The OA *Sci-fi drama*
The Old Guard *Movie (action)*
On My Block *Comedy-drama*
Operation Varsity Blues *Movie (documentary)*

Orange Is the New Black *Dark comedy*
Our Planet *Docuseries*
Outer Banks *Teen drama*
Outlander *Romance drama*
Ozark *Crime drama*
Paddleton *Movie (dark comedy)*
Passing *Movie (drama)*
Peaky Blinders *Crime drama*
Penguin Town *Docuseries*
Penny Dreadful *Horror*
The Pharmacist *Limited series (true crime)*
The Politician *Dark comedy*
Pose *Drama*
The Power of the Dog *Movie (drama)*
Pretend It's a City *Docuseries*
The Princess Switch *Movie (romantic comedy)*
The Queen's Gambit *Limited series (historical drama)*
Queer Eye *Reality*
Raising Dion *Sci-fi drama*
The Ranch *Sitcom*
Red Notice *Action comedy*
The Ritual *Movie (thriller)*
Riverdale *Teen drama*
Roma *Movie (drama)*
Ronny Chieng: Asian Comedian Destroys America! *Comedy special*
Rotten *Docuseries*
Russian Doll *Dark comedy*
Salt Fat Acid Heat *Docuseries*
Santa Clarita Diet *Comedy-horrorshow*
Schitt's Creek *Sitcom*
Seinfeld *Classic sitcom*
Self Made: Inspired by the Life of Madam C.J. Walker *Limited series (historical drama)*
A Series of Unfortunate Events *Dark comedy*
Seven Seconds *Limited series (drama)*
Sex Education *Comedy-drama*
Shameless (US) *Dark comedy*
Shtisel *Drama*
Sinatra: All Or Nothing at All *Movie (documentary)*
The Sinner *Anthology series (crime drama)*
The Social Dilemma *Movie (documentary)*
The Society *Teen drama*
Song Exploder *Docuseries*
Sons of Sam, The: A Descent into Darkness *Limited series (true crime)*
Sophie: A Murder in West Cork *Limited series (true crime)*
Space Force *Workplace comedy*
The Spy *Limited series (historical drama)*
Squid Game *Dystopian drama*
The Staircase *Limited series (true crime)*
Stateless *Limited series (drama)*
Stay Here *Reality*
Stranger Things *Sci-fi drama*
The Stranger *Limited series (drama)*
Sunderland 'Til I Die *Docuseries*
Surviving R. Kelly *Docuseries*

Survivor   *Reality competition*
Sweet Magnolias   *Drama*
Sweet Tooth   *Dystopian drama*
Tales of the City   *Limited series (drama)*
Teenage Bounty Hunters   *Comedy*
Terrace House   *Reality*
This Is a Robbery: The World's Greatest Art
   Heist   *Limited series (true crime)*
Tick, Tick … Boom!   *Movie (musical)*
Tidying Up with Marie Kondo   *Reality*
Tiger King   *Limited series (true crime)*
Tigertail   *Movie (drama)*
To All the Boys I've Loved Before (movie
   trilogy)   *Teen drama*
Too Hot to Handle   *Reality competition*
Trial 4   *Limited series (true crime)*
The Trial of the Chicago 7   *Movie (historical
   drama)*
The Trials of Gabriel Fernandez   *Limited series
   (true crime)*
Tuca & Bertie   *Animated comedy*
Turn: Washington's Spies   *Historical drama*
The Twelve   *Limited series (thriller)*
The Two Popes   *Movie (drama)*
The Umbrella Academy   *Superhero drama*
Unbelievable   *Limited series (drama)*
Unbreakable Kimmy Schmidt   *Sitcom*
Unorthodox   *Limited series (drama)*
Unsolved Mysteries   *Docuseries*
The Vampire Diaries   *Fantasy drama*
Virgin River   *Romance drama*
Voir   *Docuseries*
Waiting for "Superman"   *Movie (documentary)*
The Walking Dead   *Dystopian drama*
Wanderlust   *Comedy-drama*
The Water Man   *Movie (family comedy)*
We Are the Champions   *Docuseries*
We Are: The Brooklyn Saints   *Docuseries*
The Wedding Coach   *Reality*
What Happened, Miss Simone?   *Movie
   (documentary)*
What the Health   *Movie (documentary)*
When They See Us   *Limited series (drama)*
When We First Met   *Movie (romantic comedy)*
Who Killed Malcolm X?   *Docuseries*
Wild Wild Country   *Limited series (true crime)*
The Witcher   *Fantasy drama*
Workin' Moms   *Comedy*
Wormwood   *Limited series (drama)*
Wynonna Earp   *Fantasy drama*
You   *Crime drama*

Paramount+

1883   *Historical drama*
16 And Recovering   *Docuseries*
76 Days   *Movie (documentary)*
Are You The One?   *Reality competition*
Beverly Hills 90210   *Teen drama*
The Big Bang Theory   *Sitcom*

Big Brother   *Reality competition*
Bob (Hearts) Abishola   *Sitcom*
Bob's Burgers   *Animated comedy*
Cheers   *Sitcom*
Clarice   *Crime drama*
Clifford the Big Red Dog   *Movie (family comedy)*
Corporate   *Comedy*
CSI: Vegas   *Crime drama*
Dallas Cowboys Cheerleaders: Making the
   Team   *Reality competition*
Daria   *Animated comedy*
Detroiters   *Comedy*
Elementary   *Crime drama*
The Equalizer (2021)   *Crime drama*
Evil   *Crime drama*
Family Ties   *Sitcom*
Frasier   *Classic sitcom*
Freaks and Geeks   *Comedy-drama*
The Good Fight   *Crime drama*
The Good Wife   *Crime drama*
The Guardian   *Drama*
I Love Lucy   *Classic sitcom*
Inside Amy Schumer   *Sketch comedy*
Inside Amy Schumer   *Sketch comedy*
Jericho   *Dystopian drama*
The Love Boat (1977)   *Comedy-drama*
Mom   *Sitcom*
NCIS   *Drama*
One Day at a Time (2017)   *Sitcom*
One Day at a Time (2017)   *Sitcom*
The Real World Homecoming   *Reality*
The Real World   *Anthology series (Reality)*
RuPaul's Drag Race   *Reality competition*
The SpongeBob Movie: Sponge on the Run
   Movie (family comedy)
Star Trek: Discovery   *Sci-fi drama*
Star Trek: Lower Decks   *Animated sci-fi*
Star Trek: Picard   *Sci-fi drama*
Survivor   *Reality competition*
The Twilight Zone (1959)   *Classic sci-fi anthology*
Younger   *Romantic comedy*

PBS Passport

Abacus: Small Enough to Jail   *Movie
   (documentary)*
All Creatures Great and Small   *Historical drama*
American Experience: The Voice of Freedom
   Movie (documentary)
Asian Americans   *Docuseries*
Baptiste   *Drama*
Baseball   *Docuseries*
The Black Church   *Movie (documentary)*
Call the Midwife   *Historical drama*
The Central Park Five   *Movie (documentary)*
The Civil War   *Docuseries*
Country Music: A Film by Ken Burns   *Docuseries*
Downton Abbey   *Historical drama*
The Great British Baking Show   *Reality
   competition*

Hemingway *Docuseries*
Les Misérables *Limited series (historical drama)*
Life on the Reef *Docuseries*
Mercy Street *Historical drama*
Muhammad Ali *Docuseries*
Philly D.A. *Docuseries*
Victoria *Historical drama*
The Vietnam War *Docuseries*
Wolf Hall *Limited series (historical drama)*
World on Fire *Drama*

Peacock
30 Rock *Workplace comedy*
3rd Rock from the Sun *Classic sitcom*
A.P. Bio *Comedy*
The Amber Ruffin Show *Sketch comedy*
America's Got Talent *Reality competition*
Battlestar Galactica (2004) *Sci-fi drama*
Brooklyn Nine-Nine *Sitcom*
The Capture *British drama*
Cheers *Sitcom*
Chicago Fire *Drama*
Departure *Drama*
Dr. Death *Limited series (crime drama)*
The Fall *Crime drama*
Friday Night Lights *Drama*
Friday Night Tykes *Reality*
Girls5eva *Musical comedy*
Heroes *Sci-fi drama*
The Housewives of the North Pole *Movie (family comedy)*
John Wayne Gacy: Devil in Disguise *Limited series (true crime)*
Keeping Up With the Kardashians *CelebReality*
Law & Order *Crime drama*
Making It *Reality competition*
Manifest *Sci-fi drama*
Mr. Mayor *Sitcom*
Mr. Mercedes *Crime drama*
Murderball *Movie (documentary)*
The Office (US) *Sitcom*
One of Us Is Lying *Crime drama*
Parenthood *Family drama*
Parks and Recreation *Workplace comedy*
The Profit *Reality*
Project Runway *Reality competition*
The Real Housewives of Atlanta *Reality*
The Real Housewives of Beverly Hills *Reality*
The Real Housewives of Dallas *Reality*
The Real Housewives of New Jersey *Reality*
The Real Housewives of New York City *Reality*
The Real Housewives of Orange County *Reality*
The Real Housewives of Potomac *Reality*
Resident Alien *Sci-fi comedy*
Rutherford Falls *Sitcom*
Saturday Night Live *Sketch comedy*
Saved by the Bell (2020) *Sitcom*
Sit-In, The: Harry Belafonte Hosts the Tonight Show *Movie (documentary)*

Small Fortune *Reality competition*
Superstore *Sitcom*
Temptation Island (2019) *Reality*
This Is Us *Family drama*
Top Chef *Reality competition*
Two and a Half Men *Sitcom*
We Are Lady Parts *British comedy*
Wolf Like Me *Drama-comedy*
Yellowstone *Drama*
Young Rock *Sitcom*
Zoey's Extraordinary Playlist *Musical comedy*

Prime Video
The A Word *Drama*
Alex Rider *Action drama*
Alias *Action drama*
All or Nothing: Manchester City *Docuseries*
Alpha House *Satirical comedy*
America's Next Top Model *Reality competition*
American Horror Story *Anthology series (horror)*
American Pickers *Reality*
The Americans *Drama*
Being the Ricardos *Historical drama*
Betas *Comedy*
Between Two Ferns with Zach Galifianakis *Comedy, Talk show*
Billions *Drama*
Bob's Burgers *Animated comedy*
Bones *Drama*
Borat Subsequent Moviefilm *Movie (comedy)*
Bosch *Crime drama*
The Boys *Superhero drama*
Buffy the Vampire Slayer *Fantasy drama*
Burn Notice *Crime drama*
Catastrophe *Comedy*
City on a Hill *Crime drama*
Clarkson's Farm *CelebReality*
Community *Sitcom*
Comrade Detective *Satirical comedy*
Cougar Town *Sitcom*
Counterpart *Sci-fi drama*
Doctor Thorne *Limited series (historical drama)*
Downton Abbey *Historical drama*
Escape at Dannemora *Limited series (crime drama)*
The Expanse *Sci-fi drama*
The Fades *Horror*
The Fall *Crime drama*
The Feed *Sci-fi drama*
Flack *Dark comedy*
Fleabag *British comedy*
Flo and Joan: Alive on Stage *Comedy special*
Forever *Comedy-drama*
Fortitude *Crime drama*
The Fosters *Teen drama*
Frank of Ireland *Comedy*
Free Meek *Limited series (true crime)*
Fresh Meat *British comedy*
Fresh Meat *British comedy*
Gardeners' World *Docuseries*

Get Duked! *Comedy-horrorshow film*
Get Shorty *Dark comedy*
Glee *Musical comedy*
Goliath *Drama*
Good Girls Revolt *Historical drama*
Good Omens *Fantasy comedy*
The Great Interior Design Challenge *Reality competition*
Grimm *Fantasy drama*
The Guardian *Drama*
Hanna *Action*
Happy Valley *Crime drama*
Hoarders *Reality*
Homecoming *Drama*
House *Medical drama*
How I Met Your Mother *Romantic comedy*
Humans *Sci-fi drama*
Hunters *Alternative history*
I Love Dick *Comedy*
Inside Jokes *Comedy*
Invincible *Animated drama*
Jack Ryan *Action thriller*
Jayde Adams: Serious Black Jumper *Comedy special*
Jean-Claude Van Johnson *Comedy-drama*
Jim Gaffigan: Quality Time *Comedy special*
Lake Mungo *Movie (horror)*
The Larkins *Family comedy-drama*
Line of Duty *Crime drama*
Lorena *Limited series (true crime)*
LuLaRich *Docuseries*
The Mad Women's Ball *Movie (drama)*
The Man in the High Castle *Alternative history*
Manchester by the Sea *Movie (drama)*
Maria Bamford: The Special Special Special! *Comedy special*
Married at First Sight *Reality*
The Marvelous Mrs. Maisel *Comedy-drama*
The Mentalist *Crime drama*
The Missing *Crime drama*
Modern Love *Anthology series (romantic comedy)*
Monk *Comedy-drama*
Mozart in the Jungle *Comedy-drama*
Mr. Robot *Crime drama*
The New Yorker Presents *Docuseries*
The Night Manager *Limited series (crime drama)*
The Office (UK) *British comedy*
One Child Nation *Movie (documentary)*
One Mississippi *Dark comedy*
One Night in Miami... *Movie (historical drama)*
Orphan Black *Sci-fi drama*
Panic *Crime drama*
Patrick Melrose *Comedy-drama limited series*
Patriot *Drama*
Philip K. Dick's Electric Dreams *Sci-fi drama anthology series*
Portrait Artist of the Year *Reality competition*
Psych *Comedy-drama*
The Pursuit of Love *Limited series (historical drama)*

Queer as Folk (US) *Romance drama*
The Real World *Anthology series (Reality)*
Red Oaks *Comedy-drama*
Rob Delaney: Jackie *Comedy special*
The Romanoffs *Anthology series (drama)*
Small Axe *Limited series (historical drama)*
Sneaky Pete *Crime drama*
Sound of Metal *Movie (drama)*
Stop Making Sense *Movie (musical)*
Survivor *Reality competition*
Sylvie's Love *Movie (romance drama)*
Tales from the Loop *Sci-fi drama*
The Tick *Action comedy*
Tin Star *Crime drama*
Transparent *Comedy-drama*
Uncle Frank *Movie (drama)*
The Underground Railroad *Limited series (dystopian drama)*
Undone *Animated drama*
Upload *Sci-fi comedy*
Utopia *Limited series (dystopian drama)*
Vanity Fair *Limited series (historical drama)*
A Very English Scandal *Limited series (historical drama)*
Victoria *Historical drama*
Vikings *Historical drama*
The Wheel of Time *Fantasy drama*
The Wilds *Teen drama*
Without Remorse *Movie (thriller)*
ZeroZeroZero *Limited series (drama)*

Showtime

Back to Life *Comedy-drama*
Belushi *Movie (documentary)*
Billions *Drama*
Black Monday *Comedy*
Californication *Comedy-drama*
The Chi *Drama*
Cinema Toast *Comedy-drama anthology series*
The Circus *Docuseries*
City on a Hill *Crime drama*
The Comedy Store *Docuseries*
The Comey Rule *Limited series (historical drama)*
Couples Therapy *Reality*
Dexter *Crime drama*
Dexter: New Blood *Limited series (crime drama)*
Episodes *Comedy*
Escape at Dannemora *Limited series (crime drama)*
Flatbush Misdemeanors *Comedy*
The Go-Go's *Movie (documentary)*
The Good Lord Bird *Limited series (historical drama)*
Guerrilla *Limited series (drama)*
Homeland *Crime drama*
House of Lies *Comedy-drama*
The Humans *Movie (drama)*
Kidding *Dark comedy*
The L Word *Romance drama*
The Loudest Voice *Limited series (drama)*

Love Fraud   *Limited series (true crime)*
On Becoming a God in Central Florida   *Dark comedy*
Outcry   *Limited series (true crime)*
Penny Dreadful   *Horror*
Penny Dreadful: City of Angels   *Crime drama*
Queer as Folk (US)   *Romance drama*
Ray Donovan   *Crime drama*
Shameless (US)   *Dark comedy*
SMILF   *Comedy*
United States of Tara   *Dark comedy*
Work in Progress   *Comedy*
Yellowjackets   *Thriller*
Your Honor   *Crime drama*
Ziwe   *Comedy*

Starz

America to Me   *Docuseries*
American Gods   *Fantasy drama*
Ash vs. Evil Dead
Black Sails   *Fantasy drama*
Blindspotting   *Comedy-drama*
Damages   *Drama*
The Girlfriend Experience   *Anthology series (drama)*
Hightown   *Crime drama*
The Missing   *Crime drama*
Outlander   *Romance drama*
P-Valley   *Crime drama*
Party Down   *Comedy*
Rescue Me   *Comedy-drama*
Run the World   *Comedy-drama*
Vida   *Drama*

Index of Names

Index of Names

Index of Names

About the Editor
and Primetimer

Aaron Barnhart is senior editor of Primetimer and the editor of *The Primetimer Guide to Streaming TV*. He has written about television over three decades for the *Kansas City Star, New York Times, Village Voice* and other publications. He broke into the world of TV criticism with a weekly newsletter, *Late Show News,* that he wrote from 1994 to 1999.

Primetimer is one of the most trusted and widely-read sites covering the Streaming TV revolution. Its contributors founded the classic websites Television Without Pity, Jump the Shark, TV Barn and TV Tattle. It is online at primetimer.com.